TRAVELER'S TOOL KIT

How to Travel Absolutely Anywhere

ROBERT
POWELL
SANGSTER

Menasha
Ridge
Press
1996

All photographs by Rob Sangster except the following:
back cover, Sheila Macdonald; page 6, Sally Sears;
page 157, Scott Sangster; page 284, Tom Gettlefinger;
page 381, Rutledge Forney; page 396 and 406, Ritchie
Smith; and page 439, Jack Kenner.

Web page at http://www.travelers-tool-kit.com,
designed by Scott Sangster

Manufactured in the United States of America
Design by Barbara E. Williams

Published by
Menasha Ridge Press
P.O. Box 43059
Birmingham, AL 35243

Library of Congress
Cataloging-in-Publication Data:
The traveler's tool kit : how
to travel absolutely anywhere /
by Rob Sangster. — 1st ed.
p.   cm.
Includes bibliographical
references (p. –)
and index.
ISBN 0-89732-201-0
1. Travel   I. Title.
G151.S185   1996
S10'.2'02—dc20
95-39406
CIP

I loved writing *Traveler's Tool Kit* and hope it enables many people to board their personal magic carpet.

I am deeply grateful to all those who provided continuing personal and professional support while I was writing this book. My warmest thanks to Lisa C. Turner, gifted writer and traveler of the mind who gave me loving inspiration. As travel partners, I've had three of the finest: Dr. V. Rutledge Forney, who said, "That's a great idea" one late afternoon at a campsite in Botswana's Okavango Delta and stuck with the project from there on; Sally J. Sears, an intrepid adventurer who kept an eye on the breaking news from Ladakh to the Australian Gold Coast; and my son and best friend, Scott Sangster, explorer of the present and future. Jo Frances Powell Sangster and Robert Francis Sangster, my parents, showed me that experiencing the whole world should be a priority, and Kathy Lowry, my sister, made everything easier through her friendship.

ACKNOWLEDGMENTS

The manuscript of *Traveler's Tool Kit* benefited greatly from the generous attention of: Dr. Allison Apple, pharmacist; Betty Goff Cartwright, septuagenarian traveler of the century; Nancy and Ray Feldman, hardy travelers who live the good life; Dr. Ann Livingstone, international political scientist, born and gowned abroad; Dr. Emily McClure, tropical medical consultant; Robert McMurry, computer consultant; Dr. Patricia Murrell, cognitive consultant; Peter Pilafian, high climber, outdoor photographer, and adventurer; Ms. Ellen Rolfes, generous advisor; Dr. Michael G. Threlkeld, travel medicine expert, Ted Wood, photography consultant, and Bob Sehlinger, for his continuing enthusiasm and counsel.

And finally, I salute all the kindred spirits with whom I've shared the wonders of the road.

CONTENTS

Introduction   1

Chapter 1: The Most Powerful Reasons to Travel   9

PART ONE: Planning Your Trip ("On Your Mark . . .")

Chapter 2: How to Choose Where to Go   19

Choosing where *you* really want to go   19
Deciding how much time to take   27
How much do you want to spend?   28
The changing world   30
Drafting an itinerary   31
Resources (travel agents, guidebooks, Internet, and more)   33

Chapter 3: How to Decide Whether to Travel Solo—or With
a Partner   57

Why travel alone?   57
Why travel with a partner?   58
Characteristics of the ideal travel partner   60
How to find your travel partner   63
How to avoid losing your travel partner   64

Chapter 4: The Organized Tour   67

Reasons to travel with a tour operator   68
Reasons *not* to travel with a tour operator   70
Tours—high cost to low cost   73
How to choose the best tour operator   76
Ecological responsibility   79
Eight very unusual tour opportunities   80

PART TWO: Getting Ready ("Get Set . . .")

Chapter 5: Going Into Action   93

Documents you will need   93

More before you go (rail passes, airline tickets, insurance, and hotel reservations)   105

CHECKLIST: What needs to be done when   117

Chapter 6: Money   119

How to save money (air fare, lodging, adventures, and more)   120

How to prepare a reliable budget   146

CHECKLIST: Budget   149

How to manage money successfully (travelers checks, credit cards, exchanging money, and more)   150

Chapter 7: Travel Gear   175

Choosing luggage   176

How to pack   184

Choosing clothing   185

CHECKLIST: Clothing   188

CHECKLIST: Toiletries   192

CHECKLIST: Miscellaneous Gear   193

CHECKLIST: Documents to Take Along   196

CHECKLIST: Optional Equipment   197

CHECKLIST: What Not to Take   200

Chapter 8: Keeping Healthy   203

Thirteen practical tips   207

Minor health problems—and what to do about them   211

Major health problems—and what to do about them   229

Travel medicine kit   251

CHECKLIST: Shots to Get Before You Go   253

Chapter 9: When It's Time to Go   255

CHECKLIST: Last-Minute Tasks   256

CHECKLIST: Guardian Angel   258

PART THREE: On the Road ("Go!")

Chapter 10: The Day You Get There   263

Chapter 11: Lodging   267

How to find great places to spend the night   268

How to choose lodging that's best for you   270

Other innovative choices   278

Chapter 12: Eating and Drinking   283

How to find food you really like   283

How to eat healthy   286
How to drink healthy   289

Chapter 13: Safety and Security   297

Which countries to skip   299
How to protect yourself with a magic cloak   301
Where trouble comes from—and how to avoid it   306
Losing your valuables   325

Chapter 14: Woman on Her Own   329

How to travel safely   330

Chapter 15: Language   335

How to overcome a language barrier   336
Where to get information and assistance   338
When speaking English   340
How to ask questions   340

Chapter 16: Transportation   343

Traveling by bus   344
Traveling by train   350
Traveling by air   362
Local transport   369
Car rental   374
Traveling by water   385
Hitchhiking   390

Chapter 17: Etiquette   393

Customs   394
Begging   400
Tipping   402
Bribes   403
Doing favors   404

Chapter 18: Meeting People   405

Meeting local folks   405
Meeting other travelers   407
Romance on the road   409

Chapter 19: How to Get the Most Out of Your Trip   411

State of mind   411
Give yourself a treat   415

Chapter 20: How to Stay in Touch With Home Base   417

    Telephones   417
    Mail   420
    Fax machines and electronic mail   421

Chapter 21: To Buy or Not to Buy: That Is the Question   423

    How to prepare yourself before buying   424
    How to tell if it's the real thing   425
    How to get what you bought   426
    How to get it home   427
    Vat/gst refunds   427
    Customs   428
    Importing   431

Chapter 22: Remembering   437

    Keeping a journal   437
    Taking fine photographs   439
    Remembering people and places   453

Part Four: The Finish Line ("And the Winner Is . . . !")

Chapter 23: Home Again, Home Again   457

Chapter 24: Rare Destinations   461

    Appendix   473
    Bibliography   481
    Index   500

Introduction

Whatever you can do, or dream you can, begin it.
Boldness has genius and magic in it.
— Johann Wolfgang von Goethe

The sun was high as we glided into Picton Harbor aboard the *Arahua*, a white-hulled ferry that sails between the north and south islands of New Zealand. Gulls hung suspended against the wind, casting dark shadows on the teak decks. The moment the lines were fast, I bounded down the gangway. No one held up a chalkboard with my name written on it; no tour bus waited for me at the end of the wharf. Backpack over my shoulder, I was on my own. Time and direction were mine to command. I was free!

During the next few weeks, I strolled through tranquil rain forests, puffed across alpine passes, jammed spiked crampons into the flank of a glacier, and hung on with all my strength in a jet boat as it careened along the flinty wall of a river canyon. After skiing at Coronet Peak, I drifted into Queenstown beneath a parasail rainbow. Along the way, I read some wonderful books and listened to rugby boasts in local pubs. For better or worse, each one of those choices was my own.

In other words, I was a traveler. And the fact is that every one of us is already a traveler—in a big way. After all, we're passengers aboard a giant rock speeding through space at more than sixty-six thousand miles per hour. As long as we're exploring the universe, doesn't it make sense to get to know our home planet better?

Traveler's Tool Kit is a practical "how to" book that will help you break free from ruts and visit the places of your dreams. There's an abundance of beauty in this world and you can bring much more of it into your life.

The information in this book prepares you for travel experiences that far surpass those of a mere vacation. Too many vacations consist of lying down,

Water seller.
Marrakesh, Morocco.

dressing up, and paying someone else a lot of money; too many vacations are limited to seeing in "life" what you've already seen dozens of times in travel posters and school books. On too many vacations sights are collected as trophies to be displayed during dinner party conversations by collectors who never know how much they missed.

Rather than offering opinions about where to eat in Paris, Traveler's Tool Kit shows you how to find delicious, affordable meals anywhere in the world. Instead of rating the world's "best" hotels (usually meaning the most expensive), this book shows you how to locate comfortable, affordable lodging anywhere in the world. You'll learn how to travel happily by train throughout Europe, negotiate successfully with cab drivers in New Delhi, and dramatically cut the costs of travel to any destination. You will be convinced you can afford to travel—and that you can't afford not to.

Hundreds of books recount daring adventures at altitudes or depths most of us will never reach. While I couldn't resist describing some remarkable places and including a few adventure stories, the goal of this book is to help you discover where *you* really want to go and show you how to plan your own adventures.

This book is for you if

- you are *curious about the rest of the world*;
- you are contemplating your *first foreign travel*;
- you want to *travel farther and more independently*;
- you choose to *travel on a budget*;
- you are a *business traveler*;
- you feel *inhibited by the unknowns of international travel*;
- you are interested in *personal safety and avoiding illness*;
- you have the *time and desire to travel*;
- you know that *life offers more than a two-week vacation once a year.*

Planning a trip is like running a whitewater rapid—preparation determines success. Scout the rapid carefully, evaluate alternative routes, then plot your course. As you begin your run through the whitewater, you will know what to expect and will be in the right state of mind. After that, it's mostly a matter of hanging on for an exciting ride. If, on the other hand, you enter a rapid without a good plan, you may get a chilly surprise. In the same way, planning a trip to a foreign destination can seem mystifying initially, but learning a simple process will enable you to avoid costly, frustrating, and possibly dangerous mistakes.

Assuming that money is an issue for you, as it is for most of us, *Traveler's Tool Kit* shows you dozens of ways to SAVE MONEY without detracting from the quality of your trip. Here's a quick example. A friend wanted to visit Moldavia, one of the republics of the former Soviet Union. When her travel agent quoted a round-trip ticket price of $1,850, she decided she couldn't afford to go. Using a telephone number I gave her, one of many in this book, she purchased the same ticket for only $875. That savings convinced her to make the trip—and to stay an extra week!

With respect to money, I hope to persuade you that sometimes spending less gets you more. By avoiding high-priced tourist circuits, you meet more local people and learn about their hopes and values. You get the *feel* of a place; you experience the essence of travel.

You'll learn how to connect with a network of travelers who will help you find the most enjoyable things to do and provide guidance on how much to pay for them. You'll even learn how to earn money from your travels after returning home.

Common sense tells you a lot about what kind of travel clothing and equipment you'll need—but not everything. You can learn the rest the hard way, on the road, or the easy way, right here in *Traveler's Tool Kit*. Take the wrong kind of mosquito protection to Africa and you'll see what I mean.

Travel provides an opportunity to think of beginnings and endings.

Travel provides an opportunity to think of beginnings and endings, to spend time alone, to challenge fears and inhibitions, to experience freedom and joy. The traveler becomes a treasure-house filled with images of the Sistine Chapel, of a cheetah bounding behind a terrified wildebeest, the Li River flowing like liquid jade between black karst peaks, and the lights of Hong Kong harbor sparkling like stars in never-never land.

I know international travel may seem overwhelming to someone who's never tried it. Before traveling abroad, most people have little reason to know the difference between a passport and a visa. Add issues of language, currency, customs, transportation, food and lodging, and there's a lot to think about. Even a short trip to Mexico may be intimidating, never mind a trek in Nepal.

Nobody says you have to fling yourself into the water as if you're an Olympic swimmer. If you're more comfortable testing the water with a toe, do it that way. Start slowly. Build confidence by limiting challenges, keeping the number of unknowns manageable.

For example, a trip from the United States to Canada or vice versa will introduce you to crossing a border, and possibly changing currency, but won't require a passport or dealing with a foreign language. As confidence builds, catch a spur-of-the-moment package deal to Acapulco. Get the feel of being in a place where English isn't the mother tongue and experience unfamiliar food and standards of sanitation somewhat different from those to which you're accustomed. You might also engage gently in the virtually worldwide practice of bargaining. At the same time, you'll be in a culture used to dealing with travelers beginning their careers in international travel. In short, no big surprises. With a taste of Canada and Mexico as a warm-up, you're ready to range farther afield.

What about testing your wings next in London? Rely on a travel agent's helping hand, sign up for one of the many tour packages available, or plan your own itinerary. The local language is surprisingly recognizable, the streets are safe, and the people are friendly. Like many of the great cities of the world, London has an extensive, efficient mass transit system. The assurance you develop from mastering the London "tube" enables you to look forward with confidence to using mass transit in Budapest, Moscow, Paris, Rome, Tokyo—anywhere you like.

By this point, you'll notice that it's not so difficult to travel in foreign countries and the so-called language barrier is really made of papier-mâché. Having experienced crossing borders, exchanging currency, and hopping aboard public transport, you're ready for independent travel wherever you choose.

Organizing a trip is one of the ways to take charge of your life. Shakespeare's Caesar said it well: "Men at some time are masters of their fates. The fault, dear Brutus, is not with our stars, but in ourselves, that we are underlings." On the same subject, Tom Robbins said, in *Jitterbug Perfume*, "If you insist on leaving your fate to the gods, the gods will repay your weakness by having a grin or two at your expense." If you believe, as I do, that travel is essential to a fulfilling life, it's up to you to make it happen. The starting bell rang for each of us at birth and there's all too little time to get through the gate and down the track.

Carpe Diem!

Above all else, you must make the decision to overcome inertia. Here's a parable to illustrate what I mean. Two couples, the Browns and the Greens, were Midwestern neighbors in their youth. The Greens moved away, but stayed in touch. One day, Mrs. Green called Mrs. Brown to say the Greens were planning a trip to Europe and to invite the Browns to come along. Well, Mr. Brown said he was just too busy, couldn't get away from his job right then. That evening he told his wife he didn't much like the idea of going someplace where people didn't speak English. The Greens made that trip and invited the Browns on a couple of others, but the answer was always about the same. After all, said Mr. Brown, "We'll have plenty of time to travel after I retire." The Greens kept traveling and the Browns couldn't figure out how the Greens could afford it, much less where they got the courage to go to such exotic places. After Mrs. Green started an importing business and Mr. Green joined the board of directors of the World Wildlife Fund, the couples fell out of touch.

Mr. Brown finally did retire, but by then he didn't feel much like traveling; in fact, those foreign places seemed more and more intimidating. Before long, Mr. Brown died—and Mrs. Brown just didn't have the energy to go anywhere.

One sunny afternoon, years later, Mrs. Green thought, "I wonder whatever happened to the Browns?" Glancing up, she waved at her husband as he jogged toward her on the beach in Bora Bora.

ABOUT THE AUTHOR

You'll receive the greatest benefit from the following pages if you feel you can rely on what I say. I hope my words will establish that trust as we go along. Still, when I'm reading a book, especially one offering advice, I want to know a little about the author. In case you're like me, here's a sketch of the person behind these words.

As I grew up in Boston, my parents often used nice weekends to visit New England's nooks and crannies such as the Old North Church in Boston and the stone fences of Lexington from behind which farmers struck blows for independence. We vacationed in New Hampshire's apple orchards and the deep, cool woods of Maine. Later, living in Houston, the family traveled from the eerie bayous of Louisiana to the bone-dry canyons of Big Bend National Park. In other words, travel, even of limited scope, was established as a value in my mind.

Author (far right) with travel partners. Ladakh, India.

Since the Navy paid most of the costs of my college education, at graduation I received a formal invitation to board an aircraft carrier for a three-year guided and catered tour (conducted by the biggest tour operator of them all). Fortunately, the tour took place during a period when no one was shooting at anyone, so I had the opportunity to read books I'd missed along the way and, as recruiting posters promise, "see the world"—well, at least the part of the world visited by the Seventh Fleet. But it kept the travel bug well-nourished.

After the Navy, I went to Stanford Law School to prepare for what could have been a fairly conventional life. As it turned out though, after practicing corporate law for a few years, I switched to the public sector for jobs in finance and housing policy in Washington, DC. Then I returned to the private sector as a real estate developer with some interesting entrepreneurial adventures thrown in (including a natural foods restaurant, an importing company, and a foundation which donates to Third World villages equipment that disinfects contaminated water).

For a number of those years I did a little domestic travel, such as river trips, skiing, and hiking, but limited myself to the standard one or two week vacation. Then I had an unexpected opportunity to join a group running 277 miles of Colorado River whitewater in the Grand Canyon in fourteen-foot wooden dories. As it happened, the chance to take the three week trip came at a time when I thought I was too busy to get away. Wrestling my left brain to the ground, I went anyway.

The length of the trip gave me enough time to separate myself from home and business and to synchronize myself completely with where I was; time to appreciate the geological evidence of more than a billion years of earth cycles, the tales of the ancient Anasazi recorded in their artifacts, and the profound night-silence. Above all, I learned how important it is to be on the road long enough at a stretch for a magic "click" to occur in my psyche. That was my first glimmer of the potential rewards of travel and it was a turning point.

When I returned from that trip, everything was under control. My office was only days away from issuing $80 million in bonds but everyone had done his or her job beautifully. The day I gave up the fantasy of being indispensable, I was emancipated. I was also a sitting duck for an article in *National Geographic* a few months later that described New Zealand's Milford Track as "the finest walk in the world." I realized I was ready to see the rest of the world— and bought an airline ticket the next day.

Living fully is infinitely more important to me than earning the last possible dollar. Besides, learning about people and experiencing the physical majesty of our planet are like money in the bank. I think of the priest who reportedly said, "In all my years, I've never once heard a man on his deathbed say, 'My only regret in life is that I didn't spend more time in the office.'" I'll never say that either.

At the time I write this, I've traveled in India, China, other Asian and Southeast Asian countries, Central America, about half of the countries in Africa and South America, a fair number of the Pacific islands, most of Western and Eastern Europe, the former Soviet Union, Australia, New Zealand, Antarctica—and throughout the United States. I've visited favorite places more than once. India and New Zealand are at the top of the list, but then there's Peru, Botswana, Namibia, Egypt, Chile, and . . . We'll talk more about special places as we go along.

Literary Housekeeping

This is a good place for a little literary housekeeping. I place an asterisk (*) or one of a series of symbols after a place name that may be unfamiliar, then describe its location and say a few words about it in a footnote. I've included many such place names because, as they enter your vocabulary, they become keys to the rest of the world. From the first time you see the name of some exotic place, you begin to make it yours. Perhaps my brief mention will strike a spark, igniting a desire to take a look for yourself.

It is difficult to find pronouns that automatically include both genders and it is tedious to use the phrase "he and she" repeatedly. Grammar and common usage in our language haven't caught up with social consciousness. I have, as appropriate, alternated male and female references. My heart is in the right place even if my pen is grammar-tied on occasion.

Finally, a comment about the term "Third World." I use it reluctantly because it's often used carelessly as a catchall for countries characterized by poverty and political instability. Through such usage, the term has gained an undertone of disapproval or condescension. Historically, the phrase gained popularity at the 1955 Conference of Non-Aligned Nations in Bandung, Indonesia. Participants described NATO countries as the First World and the Warsaw Pact countries as the Second World. Choosing non-alignment with either, conference participants referred to themselves as the Third World. I suppose the demise of the Warsaw Pact technically took the Second World out of the lineup. I wonder if that means the Third World is moving up a step?

Plowshares Institute substitutes the term "Two-Thirds World" as a reminder that we're referring to countries that include more than two-thirds of the people, resources, and land mass of this planet, not-inconsiderable factors in our future. I could refer to the "rest of the world," but that's a little confusing. In *Africa: Dispatches from a Fragile Continent*, Blaine Harden called Africa the "Nth World" to convey the sense of conditions far inferior even to the rest of the Third World. His term reminds us that Third World countries exist across a very broad spectrum. Standards of living in Hong Kong and Singapore have little in common with those in Bolivia, Madagascar, and Zaire.

Countries constituting the Third World can be described as diversified, fascinating, intriguing, and spellbinding but, since none of those words carries enough recognition, we're left with "Third World." When I use the term, it is as a shorthand geographical description and I intend no negative connotation.

Both the Index and the Bibliography are extensive and I urge you to take advantage of them. The Index is a road map to help direct you to all references in the book on a particular topic or place. The Bibliography is a fine collection and I've annotated it to make it easier for you to make selections.

1

The Most Powerful Reasons to Travel

> The world is a book, and those who
> do not travel read only a page.
> — St. Augustine

Penny Hardaway slashes to the hoop for a reverse lay-up. Five seconds left in the game, Orlando Magic up by two. Rodman brings the ball in by firing a long pass to Michael Jordan. Jordan spins at the three-point line and goes up to shoot his trademark jumper. . . . Sure, it's exciting, but whichever team you root for you're still only a spectator, not a participant—and life is meant to be lived, not watched. It takes more effort to travel than it does to sit in front of the tube. So what makes it worthwhile? Most people say they take a vacation to relax, perhaps fish, play golf or tennis, or lie on the beach. Given the amount of stress in daily life, it's no surprise that relaxation is the first thing that comes to mind. However, the rewards of travel are many. Here are some that seem most compelling:

Perspective. Freed from the cocoon of familiar places, the traveler learns how people elsewhere live and what they care about. Perspective expands. After you've been there, you own a bit of London, you know something of the people of Bangkok, and you begin to understand the emotions in Jerusalem. When expressions of artists in a dozen cultures have enriched your mind, you develop true appreciation for the immense breadth of human creativity. A small article reporting that an earthquake has devastated a village high in the Peruvian Andes will escape the scanning eye of most readers, but if you've met those villagers and listened to their music, that article leaps off the page. Having been to India, you no longer skim past an article describing a violent clash between Hindus and Muslims; you read it and your heart aches.

Travelers develop a deeper understanding of the strivings of billions of humans, of lives filled with achievement as well as lives filled from dawn to dusk with hard work, disease, and hopelessness. Learning about the religions, politics, customs, and attitudes of very different cultures helps us understand our own culture better. We come to realize that much of what we accept as true reflects the values of the country, even the neighborhood, in which each of us grew up.

Do you remember the fable of the blind men and the elephant? One blind man puts his arms around the elephant's sturdy front leg and says the animal resembles a tree. Another grasps the trunk and insists the elephant is like a snake. A third runs his hand along the great flank and declares that an elephant is very like a wall. None got it right. In other words, it's hard to have an accurate perspective on humankind when your experience is limited to a single culture.

Beauty. The greatest beauty devised by humans and nature awaits you: music, landscapes, and sunsets; the architectural brilliance of cathedrals and palaces; the breathtaking majesty of the Himalayas and the redwood forests. Beauty surrounds you when gliding silently in a dugout through the papyrus-bordered waterways of the Okavango Delta, strolling in the south of France, or listening to the roar of the lion or the roar of the sea.

Special Places. You may be compelled to travel by the lure of a specific place, a vision with a mysterious resonance. It may be Kathmandu, a cavern, or a carnival; any image reinforced until it becomes a command. It may be a yearning, ingrained by childhood tales, to return to the "old country" to see how your ancestors lived.

Special Interests. Sail to Madagascar to seek rare orchids, trek along Peru's Tambopata River in search of nearly extinct birds, or dive among exotic tropical fish at the Great Barrier Reef. Whether it's art, wine, food, architecture, Siberian tigers, or just better weather, travel can gratify your special interests.

Personal Growth. A person would have to be almost brain-dead to wander about the world for weeks or months without growing from the experience. On the road, there's no phone ringing and no lawn to be mowed. Instead, there's plenty of time for contemplation, even solitude. Personal growth may take years to be recognized, or it may become evident with dramatic suddenness.

Personal Challenges. Trekking, diving, and climbing stretch physical capabilities and awaken what someone called the "adrenaline angel." Other activities challenge the mind. Surely, some of the finest moments of our lives are those when we're stretched the most.

Self-Esteem. Planning a complicated trip, say to a half-dozen Asian countries, is no easy task. When you return, having successfully solved every problem that came up along the way, your feelings of competence and confidence are strengthened. For example, after riding a bicycle solo from Ireland to India, the writer Dervla Murphy probably felt little need to conform to the conventional Irish view of a "woman's role."

New Priorities. Travel provides the opportunity to set new priorities and decide how to reallocate your time. If you write down your insights as you travel, they won't be swept away by the familiar routines of home.

Renewed Energy. After the exercise, daily mental stimulation, constant variety, and excitement of travel, you return home full of plans, eager to re-energize your life and get into action.

Escape. Some people travel not to get to some place as much as to get away from some place. From beaches to bar stools, people talk about travel as an escape—from a weak economy, a lost job, an unhappy relationship, or the daily treadmill. Some travelers are recent graduates, perhaps waiting for a new job to start. Others, looking ahead to careers and family, feel it might be now or never for travel. Some, dissatisfied, tired of responsibility, or newly retired, hope that travel will stimulate changes in their lives.

Curiosity. Travel satiates, at least in part, our curiosity about the other side of the mountain. It enables us to see beyond the horizon, to learn about people in far away places. In the big picture, the earth is no more than a tiny mass, not really the center of anything. At the very least, we should satisfy our curiosity about it as well as we can.

Business Expertise. Knowledge of the world can be a major asset in business. Western nations continue to increase their trade with the three billion people who live in the less-developed world. When you've traveled in a country and understand its politics and business practices, and have a sense of the place not revealed by statistics, you're a valuable resource when decisions are made about doing business in that country. On a résumé, visits to less-traveled places imply independence, confidence, energy, and intellectual curiosity.

> "Most of us abandoned the idea of a life full of adventure and travel sometime between puberty and our first job. Our dreams die under the dark weight of responsibility. Occasionally the old urge surfaces, and we label it with names that suggest psychological aberrations: the big chill, a mid-life crisis."
> —Tim Cahill, *Jaguars Ripped My Flesh*, 1987

Awakened Emotions. Travel evokes not only positive emotions such as excitement and awe, but other emotions as well. You'll sometimes be in the midst of people whose living conditions are *wretched*. Not quaint, or merely lower than those of Western societies, but wretched. In some countries, many people can't afford education or even nutritious food. They're chronically ill with diseases that could easily be prevented or cured in the developed world.

They can't earn a living because there's no longer a market for the products of their labor. After seeing people as individual human beings rather than electronic images on a screen, you may find yourself emotionally kidnapped, compelled by compassion to do something to improve their conditions. It doesn't happen to all travelers, but it could happen to you.

Memories. Can it be better said than Hemingway said it? "If you are lucky enough to have lived in Paris as a young man, then wherever you go for the rest of your life, it stays with you, for Paris is a moveable feast." Memories of travel experiences are a treasure.

> Memories of travel experiences are a treasure.

Friendship. For the fortunate traveler, memories of people last the longest. As we travel, we luxuriate in trading life stories, speaking our minds, breaking free from our familiar roles. Friendships made on the road, with local people as well as other travelers, are one of life's deepest pleasures.

Romance. More than a few people hit the road with romance on their minds. They hear about the allure of men or women in foreign lands and decide to see for themselves. Some relationships pass with the sunset, some remain vivid for years, and a few last a lifetime.

First-Hand Information. Traveling frees you from having to rely on what's reported on television or in newspapers. You become able to interpret and respond to international events on your own. Relations among nations are affected by how well people in different cultures know one another as individuals rather than as stereotypes.

Reward. Many people finally figure out that they deserve a treat. They've worked hard and want to reward themselves. Travel is that reward.

Freedom. In the end, travel is freedom. Freedom from the weight of possessions and from ruts, freedom to be the person you think of yourself as being.

Evan Connell said something to the effect that "Some people do not travel the way most of us travel. Not only do they sometimes choose odd vehicles, they take dangerous and unusual trips for incomprehensible reasons." If you understand the reasons for your desire to travel, that's good. If not, "incomprehensible reasons" do fine. Someone suggested, perhaps with tongue in cheek, that the desire to travel may be genetically programmed into some people. If so, I have that gene. I can't *not* travel.

HOW WE TALK OURSELVES OUT OF TRAVELING

Since the reasons to travel are so compelling, why do people stay at home? I put that question to quite a few people and came up with the answers I've summarized below. Most people said travel was a high priority—even though they weren't doing it. However, as you'll see, the reasons given for not traveling can all be overcome by knowledge and motivation. That's what this book provides.

Lack of Knowledge. Jean thought about traveling, but she had no idea how to choose a destination. She hadn't seen a geography book since fourth grade and had dropped out of her only world history course. Where should she go? What should she take? Would she find decent places to stay? Would the bathrooms be clean? Until she knows what to expect, Jean will never leave home.

Money. The prices listed in tour brochures persuaded Vicki she couldn't afford to travel abroad. The photographs were beautiful and the hotels appealing, but the prices were stratospheric. The Kenya safari she liked best cost over $300 a day and that didn't even include airfare from home (she couldn't believe what the travel agent told her that would cost). When her neighbor said a glass of orange juice cost $5 in Rome, Vicki concluded that foreign destinations were for jet-setters only.

Vicki has no idea that the actual costs of travel are far lower than she believes them to be. She tossed the safari brochure away without realizing she could contact a local safari operator directly and cut the cost by 75 percent. She didn't know she could cut 30 percent off the quoted air fare and she would have scoffed at the idea that good food and lodging are available in most of the world for one-fourth of what she routinely pays at home. Of course, her attitude about money needs adjustment; if she changes her spending habits at home, she can easily free more money for travel.

Actual costs of travel are far lower than you think.

Lack of time. William said, "I just can't get away." He feels harried—not just one day, but every day. He thinks he's indispensable at work and doesn't want to hear otherwise. The idea that he could organize his life so that everything would carry on successfully in his absence has never occurred to him. Secretly, he feels best when his nose is jammed to the grindstone. He can't conceive of taking a two-month sabbatical. He'll die sooner than he should—or maybe he'll read this book!

Barbara, on the other hand, said, "*They* won't let me get away." Her employer's manual says she's entitled to only one week of paid vacation a year—and she's never questioned it. She doesn't realize how many options she has that could free more of her time for living a full life.

"And don't let the feeble excuse of work keep you back; remember the Haitian proverb: If work is such a good thing, how come the rich haven't grabbed it all for themselves."
—John Hatt, *The Tropical Traveler,* 1982

Traditional-style Thai house. Bangkok, Thailand.

Language. The only foreign words Jeannine knows came from menus in Mexican restaurants. That never bothered her until she began thinking about taking a trip overseas. As far as she knows, English is spoken in only England and Australia and she's not about to go any place where "they" don't speak English. She has no idea that the English language has spread throughout large parts of the world and she could communicate easily even where no English is spoken.

Inertia. For Harold, the primary obstacle is plain old inertia; the beer-and-TV barrier. His homebound rut is too comfortable. When he considers forcing himself out of the house for a vacation, he doesn't see any reason not to return to the same old places. To him, "remote" means the instrument he uses to flick from channel to channel. Although he uses television primarily to fall asleep, he sometimes stumbles onto an exciting National Geographic program. Someone else might see the same program and start planning—but not Harold. Why make the effort to go to Athens when he can bring a pale electronic image of it into his home with his index finger?

Control. Dupont sees himself as being in control of his little world and that's the way he likes it. When he thinks of traveling abroad, he feels uneasy. Even in France, let alone someplace like China, he's afraid he wouldn't know what was going on and couldn't possibly be in charge. Besides, at home everyone knows who he is; over there, he'd be just another guy. He doesn't like the feel of that at all.

Safety. Jo Ann heard of a woman who went to Costa del Sol in Spain and had her purse stolen "right there on the beach the very first night." So Jo Ann decided to stay put. She'll never find out how mistaken she is about safety abroad and how easily she could protect herself.

Health. Michael figured that if people get sick in Mexico, he'd be crazy to go someplace like India. He has never bothered to learn anything about the actual likelihood of health problems or how to prevent or cure anything he might encounter. He doesn't know that it's easy to keep yourself healthy on the road if you know how.

Most of these reasons for staying at home are understandable. Travel can be expensive if you don't learn how to spend money wisely. Health and safety can be at risk unless you understand the risks and guard against them. You have to know what to expect and have the knowledge to make the right choices. By the time you reach the end of *Traveler's Tool Kit*, you'll find that every reason not to travel was written on the wind.

PART ONE

Planning
Your Trip
("On Your
Mark")

2

How to Choose Where to Go

All journeys have secret destinations of which
the traveler is unaware.
— Martin Buber

Where do you most want to go in this fascinating world? Since identifying your favorite destinations is essential to a fulfilling trip, look first inside, not out. Before starting to name possible destinations, forget about self-imposed limitations and answer two questions: What kinds of experiences do you want, and what do you want to gain from the trip?

What would you be doing? Would the days be peaceful, or would they be full of activities? Would you be alone or meeting lots of other people? Do you lust for fine food, sensuous beaches, wildlife, spectacular landscapes, physical challenges—or do you seek insights and internal change, perhaps a new direction for your life? Choosing a purpose for your trip and writing it down helps you get in touch with your feelings and gives you something to review when you get back. Your answers enable you to think about where to go without being influenced by the popularity of a destination or a desire to impress people.

The moment you've made up your mind to go somewhere, the most difficult part of the trip is behind you. You've overcome inertia and the risk of doing nothing.

CHOOSING WHERE *YOU* REALLY WANT TO GO

Many people choose destinations on the basis of beautiful scenery, climate, and available activities. Or they've been to a place before and liked it, or they have a friend or spouse who wants to go there. They're concerned about affordability, health, and personal safety and want to avoid unsanitary hotels, attempts by "locals" to rip them off, bad weather, extreme poverty, high costs, and tourist traps. No surprises there.

These are reasonable criteria—but I urge you not to settle for some destination just because it meets them. Make your choice of destination more personal. Close your eyes and conjure up the names of places that make your heart beat fast. Brainstorm. Think of cultures that appeal to you, parts of the world with a history that fascinates you, less-traveled places that have beckoned since childhood.

Think of cultures that appeal to you.

What places offer the adventures, weather, or scenery you most enjoy? Whose art and music do you love? List every one of these places without worrying about practicality.

> "Not bound to swear allegiance to any master, wherever the wind takes me I travel as a visitor."
> —Horace, Roman poet

Next, prompt your memory with a world map. Continent by continent, country by country, add new places to your list. Read travel books to stimulate your imagination. Skim back copies of *National Geographic, Outside, International Travel News,* and *Condé Nast Traveler*. Attend local travelogues. Watch the Travel Channel, the Discovery Channel, and "National Geographic Explorer." Seek out travel tales from friends and travel agents.

Make a list of destinations, then group your choices by continent or geographic region. Post this list on the refrigerator or bathroom mirror, anywhere that will keep it in your consciousness. After you've lived with this list for a while, cut it to a dozen or so magic places. With your original objectives clearly in mind, rank them and let the following factors influence your decision.

Factors to Consider

At this point, practical considerations should begin to affect your choice of destinations: Would you prefer to survey many countries or to focus on a single country or region? Are political conditions a problem at any of the destinations on your list? Would a certain destination present more of a mental or physical challenge than you want? Would local language seem to be a deterrent?

One Country—or Many?

The differences between a survey trip through many countries and a trip that focuses on a single country or region are substantial. If you have just a week or two, a tightly focused trip, dealing with only one language, one transportation system, and one culture, may be ideal. In general, your daily costs of transportation, lodging, and food are lower when you spend more time in one place. On the other hand, a multi-country trip is like a buffet table loaded with rich and varied dishes, many of which will be new to your palate. It requires more effort and a faster pace to sample everything on the table.

A tightly focused choice might be a trip to London with side trips to Cambridge and the Cotswolds, or a trip to Cuzco that includes hiking the Inca Trail and wandering in the sacred valley of the Urubamba.* A multi-country trip might take you cross-country from Amsterdam to Athens, or overland from London to Lagos,† or maybe from Kathmandu to Kalimantan.§

Either type of trip can be rewarding but, to make an informed choice, understand that they differ.

Political Conditions

Research the political situation at destinations you're considering. It was risky to visit Chile during the decades in which the Pinochet military dictatorship governed. However, Chile had its second modern democratic election in 1994 and is again one of the world's most rewarding—and safe—destinations. While conditions in Kashmir, Colombia, and Mozambique may not be as dangerous for travelers as media reports suggest, it's better to defer trips to places like these until things quiet down. Sri Lanka is wonderful, but I'm not going back until the Tamils and the Sinhalese decide they want to live in harmony. Even the excitement of visiting mountain gorillas in Rwanda isn't worth being caught in a fire fight between Hutus and Tutsis. When the welcome mat has blood on it, think twice about crossing the threshold.

Mental and Physical Fitness

There are times on the road when you won't know exactly what's happening, or why, or what will happen next. Ask yourself how much input you can handle from cultures very different from your own, and for how long. If your tolerance for ambiguity is low, you may prefer traveling in Western-style cultures until you're a more seasoned traveler.

Physical fitness should also affect your decisions. Don't underestimate the rigors of walking the halls of art museums and galleries in Paris for a week, let alone visiting dozens of Egyptian temples and tombs. Where heat, altitude, or exertion will be factors, be honest with yourself about the physical condition

---

* *Sacred valley of the Urubamba.* This lovely valley near Cuzco in southern Peru is the site of several towns built on and out of Inca stones. Don't miss Ollantaytambo and Machu Picchu.

† *Lagos.* The capital of Nigeria, this city is located on the southern border on the Bight of Benin. Think of noise, pollution, dense traffic, greed, corruption, and incredibly high prices, and you'll appreciate Lagos's reputation as a "hell hole."

§ *Kalimantan.* The name of the Indonesian part of the Island of Borneo (the northern part is Malaysian). Straight south of Hong Kong, it is the third largest island in the world.

required. If you're considering trekking in the Zanskar Valley* or to the summit of Kilimanjaro,† don't think in terms of how fit you were when you were eighteen, or how fit you could be if you worked out for three months. Think of how fit you actually will be when you board the plane.

Decide how much exertion you want to handle. For some, making a strenuous effort is part of the reward; achieving a goal and the ensuing fitness are worth a little pain. Others prefer a more languorous trip. At the beginning of your international travel life, err on the side of caution and stay well within your capacity. After a trip or two, you'll know much more about what you can, and choose to, handle. At that point, you may want to test yourself a bit.

As departure date approaches, step up your physical conditioning a notch or two. Unless you're already fit, consider walking a brisk three miles a day three times a week for six or eight weeks before you go. It's like preparing for the ski season; it's mostly a matter of building up your legs and stamina. No need to let sore muscles take you out of action.

To the extent it's connected to fitness, age is a consideration but need not be a deterrent. I've met many travelers well beyond their mid-sixties. Aboard a bus in steamy Tamil Nadu,§ I leaned across the aisle and struck up a conversation with a sturdy, white-haired woman who looked to be about sixty-five years old. As we got off the bus, I swung my backpack down from the overhead rack and asked if I might help with hers. She thanked me and suggested we have tea.

Age need not be a deterrent to travel.

I wasn't surprised when she said she'd been a British civil servant for more than forty years, but I was amazed when she told me the rest of her story. She'd just completed a solo bicycle ride the entire length of India and, several years earlier, had ridden more or less around the world. She exemplifies the point that age need not be a disqualification when the flame is burning brightly. Ben Franklin said that "Travel is one way of lengthening life," and few activities keep a person feeling as young as does independent travel.

The more remote reaches of the world are not very accommodating to persons with physical handicaps. Nevertheless, I've met people traveling suc-

---

* *Zanskar Valley.* This remote valley in the far north of India was opened only recently to hardy trekkers.

† *Kilimanjaro.* Over nineteen thousand feet, this snowcapped volcano on the Kenya/Tanzania border is a popular five- or six-day trek. Because of fees and mandatory guides, it's a somewhat expensive trip.

§ *Tamil Nadu.* Located in the southeast corner of the Indian subcontinent, this state is sometimes called the most Indian part of India. It's a Hindu showplace in terms of architecture (particularly ornate temples), dance, and food. It also offers wildlife preserves, hundreds of miles of beaches, and comparatively cool hill stations.

cessfully with what seem to be fairly severe physical handicaps. It can be done; it's just more of a hassle. In the Bibliography I've listed several publications that provide information on traveling with various disabilities.

Local Languages

Since we humans use more than fifty-eight hundred different languages and dialects, some prospective travelers may worry about inability to communicate. They needn't. First, English is rapidly becoming a global language. Second, where English is not spoken there's plenty of help available in the form of pocket-size dictionaries and phrase books with functional sections containing words for shopping, asking directions, ordering meals, and changing money. Third, language training courses on cassettes and accelerated language classes in community colleges can bring you up to speed quickly. Fourth, even when you have absolutely no language in common, it's amazing how much can be communicated nonverbally. Sure, it's sometimes more difficult than talking across the back fence, but lack of familiarity with a foreign language should not deter you from going somewhere you really want to go.

If you take a cross-country trek out of Iquitos, Peru, with several Aymara Indians, your inability to speak Spanish or Quechua won't matter much though you will miss out on stories told around the campfire. In more populated areas, say Portugal or Germany, lack of knowledge of the local language can make handling daily details a bit difficult, but a few phrases and a couple of dozen words will get you by anywhere. You need not avoid non-English-speaking destinations.

We'll talk more about language in Chapter 14. I mention it here only to signal that it is a factor to consider as you choose destinations.

A few final thoughts about destinations. If your interests are in less-developed countries, expect to invest more effort than if you travel to places such as England, France, or Sweden. Rather than staring passively at marble sculptures and cracked paintings, your trip is likely to be more active, focusing on wild animals, magnificent landscapes, and the people of unique cultures.

Also, be aware that some places on your list may bear little relationship today to the romantic images established in literature from an earlier age. For me, such places include Buenos Aires, Cairo, Casablanca, Papeete, Singapore, and Timbuktu. Ladakh (in northern India), Nepal, Sri Lanka, and Thailand are still jewels, but they've lost a little of their luster in recent decades as they've become more widely known. Up-to-date information will help you make better choices.

Lastly, if this is your first overseas experience, the turmoil of India or the travails of Zaire may be a bit much. Or maybe not. Just be clear about how big a bite you want to take the first time out. If you feel uncertain, take an easier trial run. After all, you have a lifetime of trips coming up.

Timing

If you feel locked into taking a trip during a specified period—by an employer, kids, school, or whatever—the following factors may also influence your choice of destinations. If you've already chosen a destination, they'll help you know what to expect. If you have flexibility as to when you go, these factors should definitely affect where you go.

Weather. On a world where climatic temperatures range from above 130 degrees to below minus 130 degrees Fahrenheit, and monsoons and drought are common, weather always matters to some degree. It may determine your timing, especially for activities such as skiing, trekking, and hanging out on a beach. If it's not possible to go someplace when the weather there is ideal, at least avoid extremes in temperature and rainfall. If you can travel only at a certain time of year, find out what weather to expect so you'll be prepared.

Does continuous rain get you down? A rousing thunderstorm may be exciting, but dark skies day after day dampen most spirits. In many countries, heavy rains close the roads and transform trails into slick, muddy chutes.

Altitude affects local weather. As you slowly melt into a puddle in the steamy Kenyan port of Mombasa,* people are cool in nearby Nairobi on its high plateau. Even in tropical countries, temperatures can be very cold at high altitudes.

Continents tend not to have a single, predictable climate. For example, Europe has three distinct climate zones, north to south. In Africa, dry deserts in the north and south flank hot, wet tropics in between. On high plateaus, where nature preserves such as Masai Mara are located, temperatures are moderate, even during summer, because of the altitude. Also keep in mind that seasons in the Southern Hemisphere are the reverse of those in the Northern Hemisphere.

Asia ranges from a severely cold, dry arctic climate in the far north to excruciatingly hot summers in the southwest and monsoons in India. If generalizations hold, expect greater extremes of temperature inland and more rainfall on coastal areas. November to March is a relatively cooler period in Southeast Asia, while the rest of the year is likely to be rainy and humid. Monsoons are more common in June and July. Find out when they occur at your destination and avoid them.

In South America, the summer season comes during winter in the Northern Hemisphere. Summer in the lowlands is extremely hot and humid but destinations at high altitudes, such as much of Peru, almost never experience extreme heat.

---

* Mombasa. This Kenyan port, the largest on Africa's east coast, was formerly an Arab trading post, and retains much of that aura today. Of the six hundred thousand inhabitants, 30 percent are Asian.

A hard-core traveler with a passion for a certain place will
opportunity arises, even if that may mean hell *and* high water; aft
living there get through it. But why suffer if you have a choice? T
renowned for friendly people, unique dance performances, and
temples, but why visit in May when heat and humidity will
brain? Go to countries on the Mediterranean Sea in May when weather there
is at its best. Why walk the beautiful trails in Nepal in March when pouring
rain quenches your spirit and mists conceal the great peaks? Go in September
when it rains least and visibility is best.

In the wet season, when they can find drinking water anywhere, wild
animals scatter all over the African landscape. That means you can spend
hours searching for them. In the dry season, animals must go to the few
remaining waterholes—where you await them with your camera.

Since the timing of wet and dry seasons, as well as the temperature, differs
region by region, you need specific information. The following are useful
resources:

- The U.S. Department of Commerce *Climates of the World* booklet,
  available from the Government Printing Office (GPO), reports
  average precipitation by month in cities around the world. However, average temperature and rainfall reports are not as helpful as
  they should be. What you need are highs and lows.
- The GPO also publishes National Weather Service reports on
  international climates.
- Some guidebooks have good information on weather.
- Good travel agents and tour operators are familiar with international weather.
- The Current Conditions section in the back of *Condé Nast Traveler*
  magazine provides information on the climate (temperature highs
  and lows, humidity, rain, and so on) in different destinations.
- Call The Weather Channel Connection at (900) WEATHER (932-
  8437). The cost is ninety-five cents a minute.
- Local newspapers give daily high and low temperatures for fifty or
  so cities around the world.
- Call American Express at (800) 554-2639 for worldwide weather
  reports and forecasts.
- National tourist offices can be good sources but, because they
  promote tourism, it's wise to be a little skeptical of their reports.
  For example, the tourist office in Panama denies the existence of a
  rainy season. It admits only to a "Green Season." Oh, sure.

Tourist Seasons. Because crowds of tourists rank with monsoons as things to
avoid, know when the tourist high season begins and ends at a potential
destination. In general, it's June through September in the Northern Hemi-

.ere, including Europe, and November through February in the Southern .4emisphere, but there are exceptions. The tourist high season may not always coincide with the best weather. Instead, it may reflect the time of year when most people are free to travel.

Crowds change every travel experience—almost always for the worse. Limited facilities become crowded in high season and local people become noticeably less congenial. Prices go up, sometimes tripling. Avoiding tourist high season should be a major factor in planning.

When your ferry ties up to the wharf in Lamu,* Kenya, in May, a swarm of young men compete to guide you to a fine hotel room overlooking the water or take you out in their sailing dhows. Prices are rock bottom. If you arrive in December, you'll find the tiny hotels packed and you'll have to pay whatever is demanded. Now, I ask you . . . ?

If you can't avoid high season, keep your sanity by visiting popular tourist sights very early in the morning or as late as permitted in the evening. Take a leisurely stroll while tourists are still wolfing down heavy breakfasts, then hole up in a museum during the heat of the day. Shoulder seasons, on either side of high and low, are often the best times to visit.

Local Holidays, School Recesses, and Special Events. Local holidays and school recesses create their own high season, with the majority of travelers being local people. The moment school is out, young people and families hit the road. Since local people know those dates, they book transportation and accommodations far in advance.

If you're committed to participating in the running of the bulls or watching the World Cup, make preparations well in advance. Watch for major events like these so you can incorporate them into your planning, one way or the other. Find out about special events through tour brochures, guide books, national tourist offices, travel agents, and Culturegrams (discussed later in this chapter).

The first time I tried to get to the Island of Zanzibar from Tanzania, I forgot that religious restrictions of the Islamic period of Ramadan were ending and joyful celebrations beginning. The few planes and cross-channel boats were packed with people seeking pleasure after an ascetic month. I never did get to Zanzibar, but I could have if I'd left a couple of days earlier.

---

* *Lamu.* This tiny island off the coast of Kenya was nicknamed the "Kathmandu of Africa" as it became a haven for travelers. Its cool, narrow streets are traveled by Abyssinian asses (and only one motor car). The traditional Arab architecture and intricate carvings are unchanged from centuries past. It's a perfect place to take a break: lie on Shela Beach, sail a dhow out to the reef to snorkel, and enjoy the camaraderie and a cool Tusker at Petley's Inn in the evening.

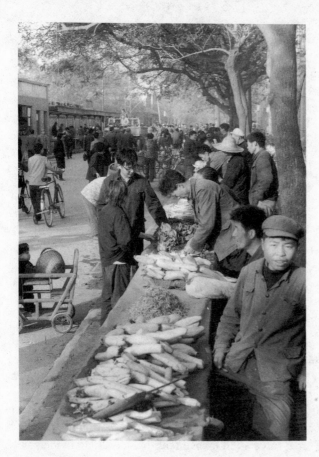

Street food in one
of the free markets.
Xi'an, China.

DECIDING HOW MUCH TIME TO TAKE

The typical vacation is usually not long enough to fully disengage from work, friends, and habits and become fully immersed in where you are. And a trip of short duration means other limitations. The countdown to return begins almost as soon as you walk out the door. You may wind up spending most of your time in big cities and seeing only the most well-known sites. You travel at a hectic pace, always on the move, struggling to absorb what's around you. When you're rushed, it's hard to be flexible, to change your route with your mood or fall in with other travelers for a side trip.

As you think about allotting time for your trip, don't accept the idea of a two-week vacation as natural or inevitable. Would it surprise you that working people in most other developed countries routinely take more than two weeks away from their jobs? Swedes get up to eight weeks a year; Germans, the French, and Finns get six weeks. Other Europeans expect no less than five weeks. On average, a European takes three times as much time away from work as an American does. As Europeans put it: *we work to live while Americans live to work.* European employers believe, and there is evidence to back them, that time off improves efficiency and productivity and is undoubtedly related to morale.

Try negotiating with your employer. Can you get more time off if part of it is unpaid? Can you trade some overtime work for time off? Or can you take an unpaid leave of absence? Life is too short to limit ourselves to two-week bursts of interaction with the rest of the world. Do everything you can, including loosening restrictions you place on yourself, to take long trips—the ultimate trip being open-ended.

Having said all that, if time or money or other constraints mean that you can absolutely get away for only fourteen days, or ten, or five—do it! Every bit of the world you see will motivate you to experience more next time. Draw as much juice from those days as you can. Just don't accept two weeks quietly if you can have more.

HOW MUCH DO YOU WANT TO SPEND?

There are at two ways to go about deciding how much you want to spend:

1. Review your resources and competing priorities and *choose an amount of money you're comfortable spending on a trip*. In other words, set a maximum and then select destinations. When choosing the amount, don't forget to consider all the money you won't be spending at home for food, entertainment, utilities, and so on. If this is your approach, and it's a rational one, I'll wager that you'll increasingly raise the figure as you come to recognize that travel is an investment that pays rich dividends.

   Obviously, the amount you set influences your choice of destinations. If a destination is far away and the cost-of-living there is high, you won't be able to stay very long. Suppose you choose $2,500. Subtract from $2,500 the approximate costs of getting to a potential destination and back. Let's say that leaves a balance of $1,700. Use the Checklist in Chapter 6 to estimate local daily costs of traveling. Dividing that daily cost into $1,700 reveals how long—or short—your trip can be. If it's too short, and you want to stay within your maximum, you may have to go somewhere else.

2. *Choose your favorite destination,* and make it your highest priority. Then figure out how many days it will take to experience everything you want to. Next, use the Checklist in Chapter 6 to calculate how much that many days will cost. Now all you have to do is persuade yourself to spend that amount. If you absolutely can't make the case, or the cupboard is too bare for the grandest scheme, cut back on the level of accommodations, class of tickets, or even time, until you have a match. The main point is: don't persuade yourself that you can't afford to do

what you really want to do. *Traveler's Tool Kit* will help empower you to go wherever you want.

Obviously, choice of destinations greatly affects the cost of the trip. Tokyo (more than twice as expensive as New York City), Moscow, Paris, Oslo, Copenhagen, Geneva, Frankfurt, and Brussels are among the most expensive cities. Notice a pattern? Most are European and all are Northern Hemisphere. The nine least expensive cities are Belgrade, Bogotá, Colombo, Johannesburg, Karachi, Lima, Lusaka, New Delhi, and Tunis. Notice a pattern?

Traveling in South America, Africa, India, and Southeast Asia can be moderately expensive if you stay in international hotel chains, eat at tourist restaurants, and hire private transportation. But for savvy travelers, these places can be *very inexpensive*. You can travel comfortably in Peru or Indonesia for six months on what you would spend in Norway or Japan in a month or two.

> Expect higher costs in tourist areas.

However, be wary about making generalizations about an entire continent. For example, in sub-Saharan Africa, Kenya is inexpensive, neighboring Rwanda is moderate, and South Africa is comparatively expensive. In Southeast Asia, Thailand and Indonesia are inexpensive but costs are sharply higher in neighboring Cambodia and Myanmar (that's the historic name; Burma was a more recent name used by the British). Nepal is cheap, but in nearby Bhutan you're likely to have to spend at least $250 per day. Expect high travel costs wherever governments channel tourists through expensive hotels, restaurants, and transportation.

By the way, if someone says that the cost-of-living in a certain place is inexpensive, be certain you and that person agree on what inexpensive means—and the information is current. When I say inexpensive, I'm thinking of a private room with two beds, and sometimes a private bath, for $8 to $15 a night.

The cost of travel in a given country also depends in part on the strength of your currency in relation to that country's. Years ago, when the U.S. dollar was strong and European currencies were weak, *Europe on $5 a Day* was the book carried by students and it was possible to travel for that. How world economics have changed. Today, the cost of buying a Coca-Cola in Holland may not seem extraordinary to someone paying with marks, francs, or guilders, but if you're using U.S. currency, that Coke could cost you three or four dollars. Imagine what you'd spend for a night on the town. A haircut that costs $4 in Caracas costs $43 in Tokyo. For a fast food meal that costs $2.50 in Hong Kong, you'd pay $6.75 in Paris. These things add up fast on a long trip.

In some countries, costs to travelers are artificially high because the government doesn't permit its currency to 'float.' That is, it doesn't allow world market forces to establish the true value of its currency. Instead, the government simply announces what their currency is worth as you convert yours to theirs. The former Soviet Union was an example. As the ruble is now slowly being allowed to float, it is valued at far less than the government always asserted it was worth. Theoretically, that should give your currency much more buying power in the new Confederation of Independent States. Ah, if only life were that simple. Sometimes when a government devalues its currency, prices for goods and services are increased at the same time, offsetting your advantage.

The existence of a black market (euphemistically referred to by economists as a "parallel" or "alternative" market) and the extent to which you participate in it also influence the cost of travel. Exchanging your money for local currency on the black market can lower costs by 15 to 50 percent in some countries. We'll discuss black markets in Chapter 6.

THE CHANGING WORLD

I want to comment on one other factor that I hope will influence your decisions concerning destinations and timing: the relentless rate at which the world is changing.

In Keoladeo National Park outside Bharatpur, India, I sat motionless, resting my hands on palm-worn oars, watching majestic Siberian cranes sweep into sight like a flight of snow-white arrows. They dropped gracefully from fifteen thousand feet to nest at the end of a three thousand–mile migration. Hovering on seven-foot wings above the marsh, they settled as softly as giant snowflakes, seeming to radiate rather than reflect light from their breasts. That sight will always remain in my memory. In 1980, more than two hundred Siberian cranes made the annual migration to India that their ancestors have flown for millennia. In 1992, only five cranes arrived.

Wildness is disappearing from our world; distinct cultures are blending together into a shapeless mass. Diversity is sacrificed to unimaginable increases in population. Where millions of people must plant crops and burn forests to survive, elephants, lemurs, and gorillas are inevitably condemned to extinction. Where multinational greed rapes forests, turns mountains inside out, and spews toxic chemicals across the earth, can any species survive in the long run?

It's too late for us to share with Stanley and Livingstone, or Burton and Speke, the experience of forging trails across an Africa never before traversed. In fact, it wouldn't surprise me today to find a new Pizza Hut at one of their old campsites. We can no longer follow Thesiger across harsh Arabian deserts and encounter the nomadic cultures about which he wrote with such respect and affection. Those same deserts are now, only a few decades later, crisscrossed by oily black ribbons of asphalt. Camels, the ships of the desert, have been replaced by Aramco tankers.

Paradoxically, television documentaries both reveal and mask what is happening. By bringing the Serengeti migration, the mountain gorillas, and the Papua New Guinea "sing-sing" to our armchairs, they imply that parts of the world remain as they were, that nature is thriving. Behind the scenes, however, directors take care to shield the camera lens from evidence of the encroachment of modernization. They are well-intentioned in focusing on what remains but, in doing so, lead us to underestimate the ferocious pace of change.

We'll probably manage to keep a few exotic specimens, but the leopard in a cage is not the leopard of the jungle any more than a river "turned on" for a few hours by the keeper of the dam is a wild river. Further, when we experience specimens in a tame environment, our response is not the same as when we meet them in their natural setting. A pygmy chieftain in London has even less stature than when at home in Zaire. And what is our sense of accomplishment when the price of meeting him is no greater than crosstown bus fare?

In other words, fine-tune your timing—but do not delay. Whatever we've missed, the world is still rich with marvels. The message is simple: go now!

DRAFTING AN ITINERARY

An itinerary, which simply means a proposed route, is the foundation for your trip and you can't draft a good one without doing your homework. When you know where you want to go, what you want to experience, how much time you have, and how much money you're willing to spend, link it all together to create an itinerary.

To a spontaneous person, the idea of a detailed itinerary may seem restrictive. Believe me, it's not. Once you're out the door with a thoughtful itinerary in hand, you're free to indulge whatever spontaneous urges arise. Having done the research, you understand the costs and benefits of each change you consider making on the road. If you were winging it, you could easily underestimate the chaos a spontaneous side trip might cause later on in the trip. Drafting an itinerary also uncovers opportunities to explore along the way. People who pride themselves on winging it miss a lot.

Here are five principles that apply to drafting an itinerary:

1. If you have a choice, schedule destinations most like your own country early in your trip so culture shock will be minimal. Having grown "salty" by the time you reach more exotic destinations, you'll cope with them easily.

2. Schedule countries with higher health risks toward the end of your trip. The odds are greatly against your getting sick but, if it happens, it's convenient for home to be on the horizon.

3. If you can handle the crowds, include music, art, and religious festivals in your plan.

4. If traveling in Canada, Europe, Australia, New Zealand, or the United States, you'll probably meet few unforeseeable obstacles. In most of the rest of the world, however, expect delays. Obstacles come in unlimited variety: a train ticket you can't get; a border closed because of a flare-up between neighboring countries; stolen travelers checks; anything. Then there are serendipitous obstacles: scuba diving so great you can't tear yourself away; the friend's friend you called who insists on taking you on a five-day trip to Bariloche;* tickets to the Bolshoi Ballet that came through—for next week. In other words, after calculating the time your trip should take, add 10 to 20 percent, depending on your destination, as a "fudge factor" to cover unexpected events, good and bad.

5. When scheduling connecting flights, leave enough time between them to keep a minor delay along the way from toppling your entire flight plan. Avoid changing planes and airlines if you have a choice and try to avoid routing yourself through airports notorious for foul-weather shutdowns (for example, Chicago or Boston).

When you've come up with an itinerary that works, calculate how many days it will take, including obstacles and rest days, and compare that with how much time you have.

Learning to create an itinerary will help you SAVE MONEY for a new reason. Some travel agents are suggesting that, to offset commission caps (discussed later), they may charge from $50 to $500 to draft a detailed itinerary for a client. And you wind up with their ideas, not yours. Do it yourself and spend that money on some far-away adventure.

To summarize:

1. On a good map, circle your intended stops and choose the cities abroad where your travels will start and end. Review the options with your travel agent. Make the most common sense connections among your circled destinations, avoiding doubling back when possible.

2. Once you've selected a preliminary route, adjust it to take into account factors such as available transport, tourist seasons, temperatures, rain, festivals, national holidays, costs, and accomplishing your objectives. Having made adjustments based on these factors, you have your basic itinerary.

---

* *Bariloche.* This is a Swiss-style ski resort in the Lake District of southwest Argentina. Located at the foot of the Andes, it's also the entrance to a spectacular national park.

3. Decide how you'll get from place to place and determine approximately how long each trip will take. A good guidebook and/or travel agent makes this easy. If you must estimate time when you know the distance involved but have no further guidance, err on the generous side.

4. List things you want to do or see along the way and attach time values to each. This needn't be tedious; in fact, it brings your trip to life. *Be realistic.* Don't plan a supertight trip. Rushing every day just to squeeze in an extra country, or even one more city, is seldom worth it. Remind yourself of your reasons for traveling and build in time for rest, a missed connection, or a little longer stay in some wonderful place.

   If you add up the days and are over your time budget, think first about granting yourself more time. When you've stretched that as far as you can, make your route more efficient and cut some destinations. But leave time to enjoy each place rather than rush, rush, rush. You have a lifetime for travel.

Drafting an itinerary motivates you to assemble information you ought to have anyway. Having an itinerary enables you to stay within your time and money budgets and to get the most from your trip. It is a servant, not a master.

RESOURCES

No one plans a trip wholly out of his or her head; we all draw on other resources. Most of us have dealt with travel agents and some of us have already used guidebooks. However, in this section we'll discuss what to ask to ensure that you find the best travel agent for your needs, identify the best guidebook for your trip while avoiding the turkeys, and take advantage of the vast amount of information available, often free, for your use.

How to Choose and Work with a Travel Agent

A volcano erupted in the world of travel agencies in 1995 and the dust is still settling. In this changing environment, travelers who don't educate themselves and learn to do their own research may pay dearly.

For decades, travel agents provided their services without direct charge to the consumer. They were compensated by receiving commissions from those whose services they sold (including airlines, tour operators, car rental agencies, and hotels). Thus, using a travel agent cost you nothing extra unless the agent was not competent or not objective in choosing among providers. To the contrary, a good travel agent could save you money and time and provide valuable advice.

However, in early 1995 many airlines changed the way they compensate travel agencies for distributing domestic tickets. In place of the common 10 percent commission, airlines set a maximum dollar amount they would pay (no matter how high the price of the ticket). The immediate result was loss of income to travel agencies. The American Society of Travel Agents (ASTA) estimated that 50,000 travel agents would lose their jobs and 5,000 to 10,000 agencies (of about 33,600) would close. As it turned out, only about 500 more agencies voluntarily folded in 1995 than in 1994, and more agencies came into business in 1995 than left it. Nevertheless, commission caps changed the nature of the relationship between airlines and travel agents, creating a certain, shall we say, distance.

Less obvious, but no less real, is the resulting change in the relationship between travel agents and consumers like you and me. The warm fuzzy days are cooling and travelers should be prepared for changes. Remember when owners started paying baseball players astronomical salaries? Before long the public had to pay more to attend games. Well, because airlines capped the amount of commissions they pay travel agencies, you and I are feeling the pinch.

Travel agencies are necessarily becoming more aware of the cost to them of each service they provide, and some are compensating for lost income by charging the consumer for certain services. By 1996, almost 30 percent of all travel agencies had begun charging service fees and another 30 percent were considering them. Although consumers can avoid these fees by dealing directly with the airlines, no one yet knows how much energy will be vented by exasperated travelers fuming at tied-up phone lines. Services that consumers won't pay for may simply disappear.

Complex, customized itineraries provided without charge by your travel agency may be a thing of the past. At present, AmEx charges for reissuing a ticket, making a refund, and retrieving records of past travel. AmEx tried to charge a $20 fee for booking air tickets that cost $300 or less, but consumer resentment was so great that AmEx decided the fee "didn't meet business objectives." However, certain other agencies have retained similar fees so far.

If you ask for a service for which an agency charges a fee, the agent should advise you in advance. However, it's worth asking about fees to avoid a misunderstanding. In practice, the situation is flexible. Many agencies don't charge fees to established customers, particularly if the customer objects. Other agencies are committed to charging no one. Shop around.

Some agents have hinted publicly that they'll make less effort to find the least expensive flights for clients. Their rationale is that small commissions on cheap flights are below the agency's cost of providing the service. Agencies handled cheap loss-leaders in the past since large commissions (at 10 percent) on expensive flights made up for the cheapies. With some of the fat commissions gone, time spent finding the cheapest flights is harder to recoup. Certain agencies might even be tempted to steer consumers to providers paying the highest commissions. In short, travelers must be more alert than in the past.

If you plan your journeys with the help of a travel agent, keep in mind that information from that agent will affect your biggest travel expenditures (airfare, fees to tour operators, and so on). A good travel agent can find the best (cheapest, if that's what you ask for) airline tickets, negotiate upgrades, get a ticket on a supposedly sold-out flight, locate discounts, and provide reliable advice. A poor agent can cost you time and money.

Since it's so important to find the best travel agency and agent for your trip, let's consider how to do that. Seek recommendations from friends, then look in the Yellow Pages and newspapers for advertisements that suggest a good fit with your travel plans.

Evaluating Travel Agencies

To make an informed choice of a travel agency, ask questions (this seems obvious but few travelers take the time):

- Are the agency's personnel knowledgeable about the kind of travel that interests you? This is especially important if you're considering adventure travel.
- Does the agency charge fees for its services? Some do, some don't. In early 1996, one national agency was charging $75 for preparing a complicated domestic itinerary and $150 for a complicated international itinerary.
- Does the agency use consolidators? It is essential that it does (see Chapter 6).
- Does the agency have International Air Transport Association (IATA) approval? To get it, the agency must be bonded. If it is, funds from you that are held by the agency are protected. Be cautious about making payments directly to an agency to prepay hotels, car rentals, and so on. If an agency asks you to make payments directly to it, see if the money will be held in an escrow account (and where). If you pay a deposit, get a receipt. Protect yourself by paying with a credit card. Although ASTA (703-739-2782) keeps records of complaints filed against travel agencies that are ASTA members, ASTA considers an agency's reputation to be clean as soon as a complaint is satisfied. That means you won't be told how many complaints there have been in the past.
- Does the agency belong to a consortium of travel agencies? If so, it may be able to offer certain services that a small, independent agency can't. For example, it might be able to transmit your travel plans to overseas consortium members that can assist you while you're in their area.
- Does the agency have its own rate desk? If not, it may send your complicated itinerary to an airline's rate desk for pricing, and the result may reflect that airline's interests more than yours.

- Does the agency have a toll-free number you can call from abroad? Can you reach it by fax?
- What materials (for example, lists of things to do and information on holidays) will the agency provide?
- Does it have a library of guidebooks, brochures, and videos from which you can borrow? Does it have the *Official Airline Guide*, Star Service, the *Specialty Travel Index*, and other resource materials?
- Will it maintain a file on you so you won't have to repeat your seating, eating, and other preferences every time you book a trip?
- Will it keep track of your frequent flyer miles?

Evaluating Travel Agents

Finding a reliable travel agency is only the first step. Next you must choose the most appropriate travel agent in that firm. Again, ask questions:

- Is the travel agent a traveler? If this sounds like a silly question, remember that there are desk-bound members of every business. You want someone who thinks like a traveler.
- How much traveling has the agent done to the areas in which you're interested?
- Does he or she seem bright and well-organized? Seek someone who listens and pays attention to details, is excited by travel, and is willing to make an extra effort on your behalf.
- Does the agent try to learn what you like and don't like?
- Do your personalities seem compatible?
- How much experience does the agent have? Is he or she a Certified Travel Counselor (meaning someone with at least five years' experience and a regular participant in professional training)?
- Can the agent give you relevant information about the recent experiences of other clients?
- Is the agent knowledgeable about obtaining free travelers checks, exchanging money, choosing travel insurance, and ordering visas?
- Is the agent paid a salary or paid by commission?
- Does the agent seek fare quotes directly or does someone else supply this information? Some simply use one airline to provide fares for all segments of your trip, including those on other airlines. For you to get the best deal, it's better if your agent looks up published routes and tariffs before checking with the airlines. You want an agent willing to keep digging, willing to look for fares not on the computer, willing to shop relentlessly for the best deal for you.
- Does the agent work with "preferred" suppliers? If so, he or she may receive additional compensation by steering business to those

airlines, tour operators, hotels, etc. That may be okay if it's the most desirable supplier and you get part of the override. If not, you may wind up with inferior and/or more expensive travel arrangements.

– Will the agent give you the names of other clients as references?

Just because a person is not the right agent for you doesn't mean they are not right for someone else. The idea is to find the right match for you.

What Else Can You Expect From a Travel Agent?

A good, full-service travel agent can do many things:

– reserve the seat you want
– identify the airport you'll use if there is more than one in a city
– tell you about penalties associated with your tickets
– ask the airline to accommodate your dietary preferences (although getting you a really good-tasting meal may be beyond anyone's influence)
– advise you of any maximum baggage weight or size limits
– find discounted lodging for stopover passengers (something that is especially useful when you'll be stuck with an overnight layover in high-priced places like Honolulu)
– list airport departure taxes charged along the way
– give you information about weather at your destinations
– tell you about frequent flyer procedures before you fly
– let you know when and how your tickets will arrive

When you've given instructions to your agent, it's up to you to follow through to make sure everything is done to get your trip underway smoothly. Remember the squeaky wheel.

It's unrealistic to expect travel agents to get the same pleasure from planning your trip as you do. When an agent provides service, he or she expects a commission from suppliers of products sold to you. No sale, no commission. Therefore, the amount you ask an agent to do should be proportional to the likelihood of your buying something. If you're only going to purchase a plane ticket or air pass (no hotel or rental car reservations, no expensive safaris, etc.), there's a practical limit on how much time he or she can devote to you. If that's the case, offer to go to their office and look up information yourself.

Sources of Information

Travel agents have access to details, and you need lots of details. They work from sources such as the following:

– *Fairchild's Travel Industry Personnel Directory* provides information on airlines, shipping lines, railroads, tour operators, government agencies, hotels, and special travel services.

- The *Official Tour Directory* (OTD) lists tour operators and world-wide destinations. Whether your special interest is botany, Buddhism, camel safaris, gorillas, panning for gold, rafting, whale watching, or wine tasting, the OTD can help you connect.
- The *Worldwide Services Manual* lists tours available around the world.
- The *Official Airline Guide* (OAG) includes information on regulations and requirements in various countries. By the way, the familiar OAG in book form is quickly being replaced by an electronic version.
- Flight schedules for most of the major airlines around the world, as well as fairly extensive information on train, bus, and boat schedules.
- Services that provide information on every country, including special tour and package deals.

Later in this chapter, we will review the wealth of information available on the Internet and online services pertaining to airline, hotel, car rental reservations, and virtually every other aspect of travel.

Rebaters

There are agencies known as "rebaters" that give clients varying percentages of the commission the agency receives from suppliers. Like discount stock brokers, they provide little substantive assistance. If you know exactly what reservations you want to make, you can use a rebater and save yourself part of the commission (which you won't save if you book directly with the airline). The following is a partial list of rebaters and a brief summary of their terms:

- All-American Travel Club (800-451-8747). Annual fee of $29.95, deducted from the first rebate. Rebates are 10 percent of what you purchase, minus a fee of $24.95 per ticket (or 5 percent rebate on cheaper tickets, with no fee).
- Pennsylvania Travel (800-331-0947). No membership fee. Rebate of entire commission minus a fee of $35 (the fee increases with the price of the ticket).
- The Smart Traveller (800-448-3338). No fee, but smaller rebates (e.g., 4 to 7 percent). Sells international and consolidator airline tickets, but no domestic airline tickets.
- Travel Avenue (800-333-3335). No membership fee. Various rebates. Consolidator tickets sold at a net price.

Explore the Options

What you want from your agent is the full range of options so you can choose the ones you want. Be clear about what you want and press to get it. Don't passively accept the first offer. If you're willing to endure some inconvenience in return for lower fares, say so. Ask whether the fare would be lower if you flew on a different day of the week. Or at a different time of day. Or if you moved the departure date a few days one way or the other (which might move you into a less expensive "season"). Ask whether there any special promotional deals available (or coming up).

Here's the bottom line as I see it. Travel agencies are caught in a changing, somewhat threatening, business environment. They must figure out how to survive in a world of commission caps, ticketless travel, and online bookings. Some feel they have to charge for previously free services or cut back on services. Some may be tempted to steer travelers to use suppliers who pay the highest commissions. At the same time, because of the weak dollar, international travel is increasingly expensive.

With all this going on, it's essential that a smart traveler choose a travel agency and agent carefully. Do your research, ask questions, and insist on getting what you need. As a prepared, enthusiastic traveler, you'll be a joy to a good travel agent.

How to Choose a Guidebook

A good guidebook can become a trusted friend. It saves time, money, and frustration, building your confidence by arming you with information. In contrast, it can also become a silken cord that binds without being noticed, inhibiting you from experimenting. The trick is to benefit from a guidebook without being constrained by it. Ensure that your feet find their own path or you'll find yourself too often in the midst of familiar faces.

Since most new guidebooks cost $14 to $35, it makes sense, while still in the early planning stage of a trip, to borrow guidebooks from friends or the library. Even out-of-date books are helpful at that point. See what various guidebooks have to say about countries that seem attractive to you. Learn what each country has to offer, whether travel there is difficult or easy, whether costs are high or low, which are the best and worst seasons for visiting. In the beginning, don't waste time figuring out where you'll spend the night in Edinburgh or eat dinner in Puerto Montt.* Review enough general information to decide whether a country appeals to you.

Buy the most updated guidebook for your trip.

When you have an idea of your rough itinerary, buy the most current edition of the best guidebook. Despite everyone's best efforts, most guide-

---

* *Puerto Montt.* This Southern Chilean port is excellent for boat trips to Chilean fiords and glaciers.

books lose accuracy quickly due to changing prices, political machinations, currency re-valuations, and so on. You need current information. While there's no guarantee that the most expensive book is best for you, choosing a book because it costs the least could be very costly.

Evaluating Guidebooks

A traveler needs facts, not fluff—solid information on how a country works. By "works," I mean prices, locations, and recommendations concerning transportation, lodging, and restaurants—but more than that. I also mean opinions on whether local public transportation is reliable, what to expect at border crossings, whether bureaucrats are a problem, and the details of daily life. You need to know that the steamboat across Lake Titicaca* leaves only on Tuesday mornings and if you miss it you'll have to wait a week in bitter cold. You want to know current scams being pulled on careless travelers, whether there's a safe black market, and what behavior would offend local customs. Are the prices of places recommended by a guidebook in the range of your budget? Is the index extensive enough to enable you to look things up quickly?

Finally, listen to the author's tone to see if it pleases your ear. If the author is a spectator, rushing from sight to sight (rather than insight), return the book to the shelf. There's a Swahili saying: *Mwenye pupa hadriki kula tamu*, or, "A hasty person misses the sweet things (referring to one who doesn't wait for the fruit to ripen)."

The Guidebooks

Quite a few series of guidebooks have developed a reputation for offering reliable, useful information. These include Baedeker, Berlitz, Birnbaum, Thomas Cook, Fielding, Fodor, Frommer, Hildebrand, and Michelin, among others. However, some of these are written for somewhat affluent travelers, those unlikely to hike independently into the deep outback.

The *Michelin Red Guides* provide detailed information about European hotels and restaurants, while the *Michelin Green Guides* focus more on European history, art, and places of interest. Michelin recommendations of accommodations and restaurants might please your aesthetic sense but consider carefully whether they please your wallet.

Fielding is very candid and well-written and seems to have changed course in recent years to include more information about off-beat destinations.

Fodor's Travel Guides has celebrated its sixtieth anniversary and there are now almost one hundred titles in its Gold Guide series. Although emphasiz-

---

* *Lake Titicaca*. Often called the world's highest navigable lake, this body of water lies on the Peru/Bolivia border. These waters are believed to be the birthplace of the first Inca.

ing the West, Fodor's Guides cover countries throughout the world. They provide information about interesting places to visit as well as practical recommendations for restaurants and hotels. These are longtime best-sellers designed to keep travelers in the middle-of-the-road.

The *Frommer* series now numbers more than one hundred volumes counting the basic Guides (to a specific country), $-A-Day (the original *Europe on $5 a Day* has become *Europe on $40 a Day,* and that only covers basic costs), Touring Guides (walking tours), City Guides, and Special Editions (home exchanges, bed & breakfast in North America, etc.). Frommer emphasizes Europe and the U.S. and is at its best when describing restaurants, hotels, and nightlife.

Baedeker's guides and maps are good for European sightseeing, but of minimal help as far as providing practical information for daily use. *Hildebrand's* Travel Guides are similar in format to Baedecker but they cover Asia and Africa. Both of these are more helpful for people on a tour than for independent travelers.

Berlitz Pocket Guides publishes pocket-size (four-by-six-inch) guidebooks helpful to people on tour, while the Berlitz Traveller's Phrase Books (twenty-five languages) are helpful to any traveler. There is also a Berlitz Complete Guide to Cruising and Cruise Ships.

Illustrated Travel Guides from Thomas Cook cover more than forty cities and countries.

Several series of books are well-designed specifically for travelers with low to moderate budgets. Some of the more popular include Lonely Planet Guides, Moon Travel Handbooks, Through the Back Door, Let's Go, Berkeley Guides, South American Handbook, Maverick Guide, and The Rough Guides.

The *Lonely Planet* series, colloquially referred to as the LP, has earned a fine reputation in the realm of worldwide budget/independent travel. Born in Australia, the U.S. address is Lonely Planet Publications, 155 Filbert Street, Oakland, CA 94607 (call 800-275-8555). Books in the LP series cover Africa, Asia, Australia, the Middle East, New Zealand, the Pacific, South and Central America. It is now expanding coverage of North America and Europe. There are five series: *Travel Survival Kits,* covering a specific country for a range of budgets; *On a Shoestring* guides covering anything from a region to a continent for the low-budget traveler; *City Guides*; *Walking Guides* (on hiking and trekking in a dozen or so countries); and *PhraseBooks* (for about fifty languages). The LP series now includes the former Soviet Union, and it has recently published *Central Asia* and *Romania & Moldova*. Enormous numbers of travelers with moderate to lower budgets—especially students, independent, and adventure travelers—carry the LP. It even shows up on tour buses. I consider it the first choice for virtually every country it covers, except that it may fall to second place for India, Indonesia, and the South American continent.

Shopper in famous market of Chichicastenango, Guatemala.

LP books are written in a personal, opinionated tone. In fact, authors of some editions have opined on local politics with sufficient candor that the book has been temporarily banned in the country covered. One caution: LP updates individual books in the LP series only every few years, so check the publication date.

The *Travel Handbook* series of forty-four books published by *Moon Publications* (722 Wall Street, Chico, CA 95928; 800-345-5473) is comprehensive and accurate (because it's updated annually) and its tone is fairly dry and reportorial. The books themselves are durable and compact. About half pertain to North America, but I like Moon best in Asia—especially India—and the Pacific. For Indonesia, the first choice is Bill Dalton's *Indonesia Handbook* in the Moon series. Dalton's obvious affection for the islands gives his commentary an appealing flavor. Although one of its newest titles is *Antarctica*, the book that really puts Moon in the vanguard is the *Moon Handbook*, an account of lunar explorations and a fantasy excursion to a hypothetical city on the moon.

Independent travelers to Europe enjoy the relaxed tone of Rick Steves' commentary in *Europe Through the Back Door*. His long-running series of *2 to 22 Days in . . .* (a certain country) has been retired, replaced by *Rick Steves' Best of . . .* Each proposes an itinerary and "must see" sights for limited European trips.

The *Harvard Student Association's Let's Go* series of over twenty guidebooks is said to be the best-selling series in the world (it's certainly under a lot of students' arms in Europe). *Let's Go* focuses on the United States, Mexico, the Middle East, Europe, and the Confederation of Independent States. Contact *Let's Go* at 1 Story Street, Cambridge, MA 02138.

A new challenger to *Let's Go* is the *Berkeley Guides On the Loose* series written by University of California students. The first four books covered Mexico, California, the Pacific Northwest and Alaska, and Eastern Europe. Those were followed by France, Germany, Britain/Ireland, and Central America. Contact them c/o Fodor's Travel Publications (owned by Random House), 201 East 50th Street, NY, NY 10022 or at 505 Eshleman Hall, University of California, Berkeley, CA 94720. An *Atlanta Constitution* review referred to this series as intended for travelers who belong to the "Order of the Translucent Wallet."

For South America, the *South American Handbook* (Trade & Travel Publications, Ltd., 6 Riverside Court, Riverside Road, Bath BA2 3DZ, United Kingdom) is casually referred to as "the bible." To reduce its size, sections on Central America and Mexico have been published as a separate volume. The series now includes fine handbooks entitled *Caribbean Islands*, *South Asia*, *Thailand*, *Indo-china and Burma*, *Indonesia*, and *Malaysia and Singapore*. Even though comparatively expensive, these books are good investments.

Other reliable guidebook series carried by budget-conscious travelers include: *The Rough Guides*, focused on college-age travelers in Europe, with some of the flavor of the Lonely Planet series (c/o Penguin Books, Ltd., Bath Road, Harmondsworth, West Drayton, Middlesex, UB7 ODA, United Kingdom); *Maverick Guides*, but some of these books are not current so check the publication date (c/o Pelican Publishing Copany, 1101 Monroe Street, Gretna, LA 70053); and *NTC Passport Books' Handbooks of the World* (some of the newest cover Sri Lanka, Nepal & Tibet, and Pakistan), *Essential Travel Guides* to more than fifty-four cities and countries, and *Trip Planners* for several European countries (4255 West Touhy Avenue, Lincolnwood, IL 60646). *The Insight Guide to . . .* series is international in scope with a strong budget travel orientation.

Among guidebooks with a narrower focus are: Linda White's *Independent Woman's Travel Guide to Europe*, of special interest to female travelers; *People's Guide to Mexico*, by Karl Franz, a venerable, humorous, practical guide for travel in Mexico; and *Traveler's Guide to Asian Customs and Manners*, by E. Devine, a guide to good behavior in Asia. *The Active Travel Resource Guide*

(Ultimate Ventures, $19.95) provides detailed annual information on over thirty-three hundred trips and the more than four hundred tour operators who offer them. This guide offers helpful information on a terrific variety of adventures. At the very least, it stimulates your imagination.

A good guidebook makes travel vastly easier. It's one of the differences between you and Columbus. But there's a downside to guidebooks. After you've been on the road for a while, you realize that many people are carrying the same guidebook you are and, therefore, going to the same places. Since some of your most powerful memories are likely to come from your time away from the tourist trail, don't let a guidebook become a tether. Get off the bus or train on impulse at a village which has no temple that rates a mention in anyone's guidebook. Take local transport, rent a bike, walk. Get into the interior of the country, into the small places where village life is still unaffected by clicking cameras or streams of gringos. Use the guidebook as a guide—not as a crutch.

More Tips

- Lonely Planet and some of the other guidebooks solicit your comments, corrections, and criticisms of their books. If accepted, they send you a free copy of your choice of their books. Earning a free book, even on your first trip, is a slam dunk if you take the time to gather a few pages of substantive information. I make notes in the margin of the book I'm using—about price changes, attitudes, services, people, new experiences and discoveries—and summarize them in a letter when I return. They'll even accept your marked-up book if you want to send that in. Sure, you're providing cheap labor for the publisher but you're also helping other travelers and saving yourself $25 or so. Besides, having a new guidebook near at hand is a great stimulus to putting it to use.
- Unfortunately, the best guidebooks are not always the lightest or smallest. After a moment of solemn hesitation, cut out any sections of a guidebook that cover areas where you won't be traveling and leave them at home for another trip.
- If you lose a guidebook or become unhappy with the one you have, it's not hard to find another on the road. You may be able to buy one "used" from a departing traveler or in a book shop or street stall along your route.
- If trying to get psyched or inspire a potential partner, try a travel video. International Video Network sells sixty-minute Videovisits and Rand McNally has a series of inexpensive thirty-minute videos covering many countries.

Internet Travel Resources

The volume of information about how and where to travel is expanding at nearly the speed of the electronic revolution. It's readily accessible and much of it is free.

Bulletin Boards

Bulletin boards can be used by anyone with access to a computer and modem. There's seldom any charge except for long-distance costs, and no need to pay for an online service or wander around the Internet.

The Electronic Traveler: Directory of Tourism Information Sources, an inventory of travel-related online information available from Marcus Endicott (P.O. Box 20837, Saint Simons Island, GA 31522; $50), suggests more than forty travel bulletin boards. Most focus on domestic travel and many are narrow in scope (e.g., a single state). *Boardwatch Magazine* also lists bulletin boards.

Worldwide Brochures has created an electronic bulletin board, accessible twenty-four hours a day, with a database of more than ten thousand maps, guides, travel brochures and booklets. The bulletin board number is (218) 847-3027. You pay the long distance charge but no online charges. Peruse the data base by using common sense key words that take you into scuba diving, sailing, cruising, or whatever. Mark electronically the information you want. For an annual fee of $12, Worldwide Brochures will send you a copy of everything you marked. If you don't have a modem, they'll sell you the database on disk for $19, plus postage; call (800) 852-6752. For those without a computer, they'll send a fifteen hundred–page printed version for $39, plus $6 postage. Worldwide Brochures is also available on the World Wide Web: http://www.wwb.com/.

Travel-Related Bulletin Boards

C.A.B.B.	(202) 647-9225	overseas advisories
Europe TBD BBS	(206) 771-1902	Europe travel info
Exlm Bank BBS	(202) 566-4699	export/import info
Gaia Passage	(912) 265-0784	travel info technology
Mexico BBS	(407) 582-7801	tips on exploring Mexico
PCTravel	(919) 831-4848	online airline reservation system
Travel Connection	(415) 691-0954	travel info
Travel Info Exchange	(508) 287-0660	updates of Lonely Planet pubs.
Travel Mates BBS	(708) 928-0195	travel companion finder
Travel Online	(314) 973-4073	international travel network

Internet

The Internet is an electronic means of communication. Through it, you can send messages (e-mail), access homepages (electronic billboards) on the World Wide Web, and download images, soundclips, or movies on various subjects. For information on travel, the Internet is already a good resource and should be fantastic in the future. To access this resource, all you need is a good computer, a modem (preferably 14,400 baud or above, although 9,600 baud will work), the right software, and a gateway to the Internet. At major universities and corporations, access to the Internet is simple and direct. Elsewhere, access is obtained through a bulletin board, an Internet service provider, or a commercial online service.

For travelers, one benefit of using the Internet in planning is that the information is likely to be current; however, there's no guarantee as to its accuracy. In contrast, although guidebooks remain valuable portable resources, they can become out-of-date quickly. From the time guidebook data is gathered, a year or more can pass before it's published.

Already available on the Internet are electronic editions of many travel magazines and guides, masses of information about prospective destinations, weather reports, lists of restaurants and hotels, and the capacity to make airline, hotel, and rental car reservations. Especially useful is the opportunity to converse electronically with other travelers about how and where to travel. You can pick up information from people around the world who have been to destinations you are considering, attract comments on your proposed itinerary, view videos and photographs of vacation sites around the world, and meet potential travel partners.

World Wide Web

Any discussion of the Internet quickly includes the World Wide Web (the Web) which uses hypertext links as a means of accessing information. Browsers such as Netscape and Mosaic assist in navigating the Web.

The Global Network Navigator Travel Resource Center (GNNTRC) is an excellent gateway to travel information. Travel stories, serializations of travel books, essays, photographs, State Department information, and comments from other travelers are available free. GNNTRC can help you reach hundreds of travel resources on the Internet. It also provides space for travel product suppliers to market their wares, a weekly travel magazine, and a map of travel sites on the Internet. To reach GNNTRC, gain access to the Web and use a browser (http://nearnet.gnn.com/meta/travel/index/html). To inquire about the service, send e-mail to info@gnn.com, or call (800) 338-6887.

Internet Service Providers

The major online services provide access to the Internet and the Web, of course, but Internet service providers (ISPs) offer a growing alternative. Be-

cause speed of data transmission is considerably faster on ISPs t
online services, overall cost may be lower with the former, especi
petition increases. If you decide to select an ISP, be sure that
provides adequate software and/or technical support to get yo
properly.

Internet Travel Databases

- Adventure Travel Society (http://www.adventuretravel.com/ats). Lists reliable operators by destination and activity.
- Adventure Travel Directory (http://www.ecotravel.com). Information about tour companies, destinations, travel gear.
- American Airlines (http://www.amrcorp.com/sabr_grp/interact/ globe.htm). Massive amounts of information for travelers, travel agencies, and travel suppliers.
- Amtrak (http://www.amtrak.com). For routes and special promotions.
- Bean, L.L. (http://www.llbean.com). You know what to expect.
- Centers for Disease Control (http://www.cdc.gov/travel/travel.html). Travel vaccines, food and water precautions, and so on.
- Dr. Memory (http://www.access.digex.net/drmemory/ cyber_travel.html). One of the best-linked travel sites on the web.
- Elderhostel (http://www.elderhostel.org/elderhos.html). Educational adventures for older adults.
- GreenNet (http://www.gn.apc.org/). Contributions from environmental, peace, and human rights groups.
- Himalayan Travel–World Adventures (http://www.gorp.com/ himtravel.htm) Offering trips to rugged destinations.
- Information on Travel in India (http://spiderman.bu.edu/misc/india/ misc/online.html).
- Internet Sleuth (http://www.intbc.com/sleuth/). Four hundred fifty indexes and databases, including travel.
- Live from Antarctica (http://quest.arc.nasa.gov/livefrom.livefrom. html). A NASA project directed to schoolchildren.
- Lonely Planet (http://www.lonelyplanet.com). Facts sheets, newsletter, travel tips, and destination comments.
- Lycos (http://www.lycos.com). Popular free directory of home pages.
- MasterCard International (http://www.mastercard.com). Current conversion table for fifty-four currencies.
- Microsoft (http://automap-microsoft.com/automap/route/ROUTE/HTM/). Offers a version of its Automap Road Atlas. There's a Microsoft Network site at http://www.msn.com/access/access.htm.
- Moon Publications (http://www.moon.com). Complement to its guidebooks.

Internet Travel Databases (continued)

- Mountain Travel/Sobek (http://www.MTSobek.com/MTS). Adventure travel company.
- Orbit Global Travel (http://www.pi.se/orbit/welcome.html). Info on Australia, New Zealand, and the Pacific.
- *Outside Magazine* (http://www.starwave.com/outside). Stories, guide-books, environmental news, gear reviews, and adventure travel spots.
- Pathfinder Travel (http://pathfinder.com/Travel). Travel deals, travel the world.
- PCTravel (http://www.pctravel.com). Online consumer booking service.
- Specialty Travel Index (http://www.spectrav.com). Lists more than six hundred special interest tour operators by destination and activity.
- TerraQuest (http://www.terraquest.com). For a virtual expedition to Antarctica via live links; later trips to Galapagos, Kilimanjaro, the Aegean Sea, and Mount Everest.
- Travel Agents Directory (http://www.ten-io.com/tad/). Listing of more than thirty thousand travel agencies.
- Travel Channel Online Network (http://www.travelchannel.com). Places, events, cuisine, Travel Talk forum.
- Travel Forums (http.//www.explore.com/Explorer_forums.html).
- Travel Gems (http://branch.com/gems/gems.html)
- Travel Library (ftp.cc.umanitoba.ca). Collection of travelogues, guides, opinions, and recommendations.
- Travel.city (http://www.travel.city.com). Air bookings, chat rooms, and destination information.
- Traveler's Tool Kit (http://www.travelers-tool-kit.com). Travel resources and tips.
- Travel Unlimited (http://www.dgsys.com/~jlantos/index.html). Newsletter on international travel.
- TravelWeb (http://www.travelweb.com). Allows travel agents to post home pages.
- Travel Weekly (http://www.novalink.com/travel). Serves as an electronic tour guide to help travelers locate relevant information on the Internet.
- Traveller Information Service Master Index (http://www.traveller.com/).
- Tripod, Tools for Life (http://www.tripod.com). Collection of travel information for students on the road.
- *USA Today* (http://www.usatoday.com/weather/wreg.html). Five-day weather forecasts.
- Vietnam Information: (http://www.well.com/www/gdisf).
- Yahoo (www.yahoo.com). Enormous free directory of homepages and newsgroups.

- U.S. State Department Travel Advisories and Background Notes (http://www.stolaf.edu/network/travel-advisories.html).
- University of California (Irvine) (http://bookweb.cwis.uci.edu:8042/Books/Moon/moon.html). Disseminates travel information, including some of the Moon publications.

Travel Discounts, a consolidator (see Chapter 6), sponsors a site on the Internet (http://www.dgsys.com/airfare/index.html) that lists discounted cruise, air, rail, hotel, and tour opportunities. It includes a database of thirty-five hundred travel agents, negotiated rates at thousands of hotels, access to more than two thousand tour operators, and access to more than a million discounted air fares on fifty carriers to three hundred destinations. A user might fill in an interactive questionnaire with itinerary and travel dates, e-mail it to an air consolidator, and receive a response outlining flight options within a few minutes. The user can ask, by e-mail, for a list of travel agents in his or her area qualified to make bookings. For more information, e-mail Travel Discounts (travel@netcom.com) or call (408) 626-1212.

Online Services

If you don't have direct access to the Internet through an institution or a service provider, call one of the online services and request a membership kit.

How do you choose among the services? If you'll be using them for a variety of purposes, the answer is beyond the scope of this book. However, we can examine the choices in terms of access to travel resources.

America Online (AOL) is the rising challenger to CompuServe as far as travel resources. AOL is comparatively user-friendly and its charges are competitive. The travel information available on AOL is especially suitable for independent, adventurous travelers. It has a good travel forum, Travel Books, a library of travel publications (including several with an emphasis on adventure), travel periodicals, weather reports, State Department advisories, and Eaasy Sabre (for airline reservations). The Outdoor Adventure Online (Keyword Adventure) service provides masses of information useful in travel planning: reviews of outdoor travel products, adventure tours, travel guidebooks, a column on visas, travel insurance, saving money, information on outfitters, and much more.

You can converse in a variety of foreign languages in the AOL International House (Keyword International Cafe) or browse though The Travel Forum (Keyword Travel Forum), which contains thousands of postings on international travel, including subjects such as consolidators, courier travel, and bargain airfares. The Traveler's Corner allows you to select profiles of scores of countries. Look at the Exotic Destinations Message Center for postings on, what else, exotic travel. The Internet Connection directs you to some very useful travel databases.

Preview Vacations Online (Keyword Vacation) enables viewers to book vacation packages. Most of these packages could be useful to first-time travelers but might be of only limited interest to more adventuresome travelers.

On Eaasy Sabre (Keyword Sabre), a traveler can check the availability of flights, select a seat, request special meals, use Bargain Finder to search for the lowest fares stored on the computer (although many consolidator fares do not appear), and make airline reservations. You can have tickets sent to you by mail, sent for pick-up at an airline office, or routed through a travel agency.

You can also reserve hotel rooms and rental cars from major companies. Computer-literate folks should be comfortable using Eaasy Sabre to make these reservations, at least for relatively simple itineraries. Others may find it a chore. Booking hotels is easy, but choice is generally limited to chain hotels near major airports.

The Official Airline Guide has almost sixty thousand listings in Europe, the Pacific, and the U.S., some of which are smaller hotels. However, you can't bargain on rates when you use OAG; in fact, you pay a surcharge for the service! The other online services have similar hotel and auto reservations capabilities.

CompuServe, the oldest mainstream service, probably leads the pack in terms of the volume of activity in its forums and it provides good navigators for access to forums. It presently also has more travel-related information than other services. Its Travel Forum (GO TRAV SIG), the busiest in the world, is divided by geographic areas of interest and by subject matter (with areas for travel agents, travel writers and publishers, trip reports on destinations and hotels, information on discount airlines and car rentals, and so on). There are more than a dozen other forums on train travel, adventure travel, and more. Adventures in Travel (GO AIT) is a library of travel articles. Hone your foreign language skills in the Foreign Language Forum (GO FLEFO). Information USA/International (GO LESKO) contains dozens of international travel files. CompuServe provides access to Eaasy Sabre, Travelshopper, the OAG, restaurant guides, the ABC Worldwide Hotel Guide (discussed later), travel advisories, and almost every kind of travel service. Using United Connection you can book a seat with any airline (although the display favors United Airlines).

The Online Services

- America Online (800-827-6364)
- CompuServe (800-848-8990)
- Prodigy (800-776-0836)

Charging over the horizon are the Microsoft Network and AT&T who could dwarf the other online services.

St. Basil's Russian
Orthodox Church, Red
Square. Moscow,
Russia.

OAG Worldwide Travel Facts includes weather forecasts for hundreds of international cities, currency exchange rates, State Department bulletins, and detailed information (hotels, health conditions, geography, visa requirements, customs, etc.) on more than a hundred countries. The OAG Lodging and Dining menu includes a hotel directory (emphasizing Europe, Asia, and the Pacific).

Traveler's Tool Kit Web Site

To provide continuing travel information to readers of this book, I maintain an updated list of ever-evolving travel resources, including new listings such as those above. This list is available on my World Wide Web site (http://www.travelers-tool-kit.com). I invite you to visit the site and sign in with your name and address. If you leave travel tips and comments on your favorite destinations, they will be shared with other travelers.

Any downside? CompuServe may be more expensive to use than other services, but it's also faster. Some users feel the software is slightly less user-friendly than other services and access to the Internet is currently somewhat limited. Each of these concerns is likely to be alleviated as competition increases.

Prodigy is in third place, fighting to gain stature. Prodigy is very user-friendly and has a travel bulletin board (JUMP TRAVEL BB) and a useful Travel Sources forum (JUMP TRAVEL). It is the least expensive, has the best access to the Internet, and utilizes a popular Web browser.

For a fee, Prodigy subscribers can access Worldview TravelFacts (JUMP WORLDVIEW) for information on exhibitions, sports, theater, festivals, restaurants, sights, and so on in more than one hundred sixty international destinations. Worldview can also be reached on the Internet via the Global Network Navigator (http://gnn.com/gnn/bus/wview/index.html). Worldview Travel Updates provides detailed guides listing events that will take place during your visit to specific places. State where you're going and select eight categories of special interests (music, sports, events, etc.). A guide costs $9.95 for one destination; $6.95 for each additional destination. They vary in length (e.g., Moscow is twenty-three pages, Istanbul and Alaska are thirty-nine pages). Call (800) 799-9609.

Whether using a bulletin board, an online service, or the Internet, keep in mind that evaluating information and comments can be tricky. They may be current, insightful, and on-target or they may be someone's ill-tempered desire for vengeance. Not surprisingly, some items are not too objective, such as recommendations made by a tour operator or gear supplier disguised as an ordinary traveler. In the overwhelming majority of cases, though, electronic resources open the world to every traveler.

Other Sources of Information

Commercial Tour Operators

Some tour operators are experienced travelers who entered the business to put their happily acquired knowledge to profitable use. Others are desk-bound managers who spent years assembling mountains of information. And, as with any business, a few operators are simply unqualified, relying on untested local contractors and shipping people to any destination for which they'll pay. Overall, though, tour operators are an excellent source of information about destinations.

So, how do you find them? Look for advertisements in the travel section of major newspapers, in travel magazines, and in special interest magazines (scuba diving, photography, and so on). Call their toll-free telephone numbers for brochures covering destinations of interest. Their brochures are helpful, even if sometimes filled with wildly enthusiastic descriptions.

There are good reasons why tour operators take groups where they do and why they follow certain routes. You may dislike the crowds that congregate at popular sites, but do you really want to skip the Temple of Karnak,* the Vatican Museum,† or the Taj Mahal?§ Even if many tour itineraries skip small, memorable places, overall they provide, as you will see in Chapter 4, very helpful information.

National Tourist Offices

National tourist offices are an excellent resource. Call the embassies of the countries that you plan to visit and ask for the tourist information office. They'll be delighted to send you information presenting their country in its best light. Ask about late-breaking information or permit requirements. Many countries also have an extensive network of tourist offices in-country that can make your travels much easier. Networks in India and New Zealand, for example, are two of the best.

Conversations

Bring up pending travel plans in conversation. You may be surprised at how frequently you'll find people who've been where you're thinking of going or know someone who's been there. Even small scraps of information can change and enrich your trip. Naturally, evaluate the information in terms of how current it is and the personality of the person who gave it to you. Ask for names of people to contact abroad, no matter how tenuous the relationship. You can make great acquaintances by calling a friend of a friend.

Public Library

Check out books and videotapes on possible destinations. A catalogue entitled Destinations On Tape lists more than 250 international travel videos (call 800-822-4604 to order a free copy).

---

* *Karnak*. The Temple of Karnak, one of the most impressive of all ancient Egyptian sites, is located in Luxor (called Thebes in the days of the Pharaohs).

† *Vatican Museum*. The Museum is located in Vatican City, a sovereign region within Rome. In addition to one of the world's greatest art collections, it contains the Sistine Chapel, built in 1473, with its famous ceiling fresco by Michelangelo.

§ *Taj Mahal*. Located in Agra, the Taj is a national symbol of India. It was built by Shah Jahan to express his heartbreak at the death of his wife in 1629. The Shah intended to build a similar tomb for himself, but was imprisoned by his ungrateful son Aurangzeb before he could do so.

Travel Bookstores

Bookstores that specialize in travel books and maps usually have experienced travelers on staff who will gladly talk with you about trip planning and destinations. An example of the next generation of travel resource stores opened in 1994 in Austin, Texas, in the form of a chain of superstores named TravelFest (800-343-3378 or 800-590-3378). They offer thousands of travel books, maps, videos, a full range of travel equipment (luggage, first aid kits, etc.), plus travel agents knowledgeable about international travel.

The Adventurous Traveler Bookstore, carrying more than three thousand guidebooks on travel in remote areas, operates by mail. For a free catalogue call (800) 282-3963.

International Video Network offers sixty- to ninety-minute videos ($25 to $30) of sites around the world. These videos were produced by Reader's Digest, Video Visits, Fodor's, and Rand McNally, among others. Call (800) 669-4486 for information.

State Department

The State Department issues Travel Warnings and Consular Information Sheets to advise against travel or describe circumstances in specific countries. Call the automated answering system at (202) 647-5225 for information on countries in which you have an interest. Alternatively, you can log onto the Consular Affairs Bulletin Board at (202) 647-9225 for warnings and information on topics including terrorism, crime rates, political disturbances, epidemics, and road conditions. Communicate by fax at (202) 657-3000.

Subscribers to CompuServe and several other services can connect with OAG Electronic Edition Travel Service at (800) 323-4000 for the text of Travel Warnings and Consular Information Sheets.

The State Department has several other useful travel-related publications, including *Your Trip Abroad*, basic advice for travelers ($1.25), *Safe Trip Abroad* ($1), and *Travel Tips for Older Americans* ($1).

Periodicals

Members of the Globetrotters Club (c/o BCM Roving, London WC1N 3XX, United Kingdom; membership $14) receive *The Globe*, a bimonthly newsletter as well as *The Globetrotters Directory*. The former is packed with reports written by travelers returning from exotic trips. The latter lists the names of members, along with offers of free accommodations and tidbits of advice. Locally, you can subscribe to *International Travel News* (916-457-3643), *South American Explorer* (303-320-0388), *Transitions Abroad* (413-256-0373), or *Outside* (800-678-1131). Then there are the glossies: *Traveler, Travel Holiday,* and *Travel & Leisure*.

The Travel Alert Bulletin is a four-page synopsis of news and reviews for international business travelers. Its companion publications, *Personal Travel*

Bulletin and *Fax Travel Bulletin*, are written for recreational travelers. Contact Nationwide Intelligence, P.O. Box 1922, Saginaw, MI 48605. See the Bibliography for further suggestions.

Literature

Understand the people of a country by reading its literature, both fiction and nonfiction. I hope you'll take advantage of the Bibliography at the end of the book. It lists some of the most authentic, well-written travel literature available.

Consider CD-ROMs such as *The Traveler* offered by Magellan Interactive Media. Compatible with IBM and Macintosh, it offers presentations on more than one hundred destinations and twenty-five activities (along with promotions by airlines, tour operators, adventure travel companies, tourist boards, hotel chains, and travel gear retailers). The disc is free but there is a $4.50 shipping fee. Call (800) 561-3114.

Maps

There's no reason to plan a trip using only a small map when there are fine maps available from AAA, *National Geographic*, travel bookstores, and even some regular bookstores. I consider a good eleven-by-fifteen-inch map atlas to be a sound investment.

If appropriate for your destinations, call Best Western International (800-528-1234) and ask for their free *North American Travel Guide* (which covers Mexico, Canada, the Caribbean, and the United States) or *European Travel Guide* (which covers fifteen countries).

If you don't have immediate access to a good source for maps, consider these: Magellan (800-929-4627), Map Link (805-965-4402), Maps Plus (800-221-3389), Map Store (800-862-7626), Powell's Travel Store (800-546-5025), Rand McNally (800-333-0136), TravelFest (800-343-3378), and Wide World of Maps (800-279-7654).

Check out *Expert Map for Windows* (about $15) that contains more than two hundred country and regional maps. Check a local computer store or call (305) 567-1516. This program is packed with useful information.

If maps inspire you, Worldwide Uniques (call 800-938-7623) offers an eight-color 8'8" x 13' world map for your wall. It can be trimmed to fit your space and you can write on it with a dry-erase marker to plan your itinerary. It costs $95 to $135.

A final thought about research. After you've gathered masses of information, cut, extract, and summarize it. Take with you only what is essential. Don't overload yourself with all the data you might conceivably need as you travel.

3

How to Decide Whether to Travel Solo
—or with a Partner

> There ain't no surer way to find out whether you like
> people or you hate them than to travel with them.
> —Mark Twain

Some people instinctively prefer to travel alone, while others wouldn't consider leaving home without a partner. All those who are undecided should be aware that traveling with someone—anyone—results in a trip very different from traveling by yourself. It's not that one way is necessarily better than the other, just that they are different. In other words, don't think first about who to travel with, think first about *whether* to travel with anyone.

Even traveling with someone you think you know pretty well may reveal how superficial your relationship has been. Years ago, I had a travel partner who flaked out just before we were to leave on a long trip. I chose a replacement at the last moment and wound up traveling with Godzilla for three months. A careless choice is a mistake I'll never make again!

Traveling with a partner is like paddling a canoe together. If you're not synchronized, paddles are likely to clash and you might even capsize. I strongly recommend a short trip before tackling heavy white water.

WHY TRAVEL ALONE?

– Traveling solo is the ultimate freedom. You set the itinerary and make all the decisions. No arguments, no second-guessing, no compromises. Cornelia Parker, a very wise woman, wrote, "Traveling with anyone is a very ticklish business. What is your thrill may be my bore. I cannot imagine what fire and pillage I would commit if someone were in a position to keep me looking at things longer than I wanted to look."

– Traveling alone is a confidence-builder. You learn that you can solve problems, get over the blues, and find hidden treasures all by yourself.

- When you're on your own, people are more willing to start a conversation with you and you may feel more like taking the initiative yourself. Local people seem more likely to extend invitations for a meal, a trip, or a stay in their home. In contrast, many people keep a slight distance from couples, romantic or otherwise.

- You have abundant time for contemplating, vegetating, or anything you want. Thomas Jefferson said, "One travels more usefully when alone because he reflects more."

- You needn't deal with someone else's mood swings, nor they with yours.

- You learn languages faster because you must.

- Then there's romance. On your own, you're free to meet someone who might turn out to be very important in your life.

- Your own personality may be the deciding factor. A person who is exceptionally independent and who has little tolerance for the idiosyncrasies of others might be happier traveling alone.

> "To be sure that your friend is a friend, you must go with him on a journey."
> —Angolan proverb

Traveling alone can be wonderful, but there are also reasons for traveling with a good partner. Of course, if you have an eager spouse, relative, friend, or lover, it may be a moot question.

WHY TRAVEL WITH A PARTNER?

- Travel almost always costs less when you travel with a partner. Since a single room usually costs at least 80 percent of the price of a double room, your lodging costs drop when you split them fifty-fifty. The same is true for expenses such as taxis, guidebooks, medicine, film, and reading material. If you're on a tour, having a partner avoids a stiff single supplement charge.

- It can be a relief to divide daily chores, such as changing money, buying tickets, finding a room, or figuring out how to get across town to see Chinese acrobats perform.

- You're probably safer if you travel with someone. Having a partner is especially helpful to women for minimizing unwanted advances.

- A companion keeps the lonesome, homesick blues at bay. If your partner has a down day, you can be a cheerful presence, and vice versa.

- Traveling with someone who speaks the local language makes daily life a little easier.

- Brainstorming with a partner sometimes leads to better choices than you get with solo decisions; even the best fantasy can benefit from a reality check.

- If a traveler becomes ill, a partner assumes the attributes of an angel.

- When the trip is history, you have a person with whom to reminisce.

Handling Money

If you travel with a partner, the last thing you need is conflict over money. Do you want to account for every cent spent? Do you prefer to split restaurant checks evenly or to pay for exactly what you ordered? Does one of you prefer to keep track of all expenditures?

Having each person pay for only his or her expenses every day is one way to avoid the problem—but it's also tedious. If you assume that from time to time you'll pay for one another and there will also be mutually beneficial expenditures, agree in advance how you'll keep track.

Discuss how you and your partner will handle money.

You'll both be consuming medical supplies, film, meals, groceries, and, possibly, liquor, but you probably won't be consuming them in equal quantities. If, for example, one of you typically has a couple of cold beers with meals and the other doesn't, it adds up over the course of a long trip.

One approach is to pool enough money for meals and incidentals for a week or so and pay joint expenses from this common wallet. To share the burden, alternate who carries these funds.

Another approach is to keep a running tally, keeping expenditures fairly even on a daily basis. Or note expenditures in a journal and settle up every country or two. Or settle up after returning home. Whichever of you is most comfortable with record-keeping can keep track of partnership finances. Whatever you agree on is fine so long as both of you are satisfied. Keep who owes whom from becoming a matter of importance or irritation. There are unavoidable stresses in independent travel, but this need not be one of them. Talk it over in advance. Adjust as you go.

Traveling with a Group

Since it's not unusual to fall in with several other travelers for a few days, perhaps to share costs renting a car or hiring a guide, I'll offer a few words about traveling with a group. Given all the decisions that must be made in the course of a day, trying to reach consensus every time can be time-consuming. Further, the possibility of jealousy or misunderstanding in an ad hoc group is quite real. If there's a burr anywhere in the interpersonal relationships, it can become the size of a bowling ball within a few days. Try not to become locked-in to staying with the group. If a problem develops, don't suffer. Bail out.

If you've decided to travel solo, that's the end of that. But if you prefer a partner, think very carefully about what kind of person you want.

CHARACTERISTICS OF THE IDEAL TRAVEL PARTNER

Finding the ideal travel partner is easier than finding the source of the Nile or safe passage around Cape Horn—but not much. The prize is definitely worth the effort, but it's a lot easier to succeed if you know what you're looking for.

The ideal travel partner is:

- *Someone you like.*

- *Someone who visualizes the trip approximately the same way you do.* Do you agree on destinations? Is one of you thinking of an active, adventure-seeking trip while the other dreams of long afternoons lying on the beach? Does one of you have a vision that includes a curling iron, a hair dryer, and panty hose while the other is thinking about campgrounds and hostels? Does one of you love to hike, while the other looks for a taxi if the restaurant is more than two blocks away? Are you likely to want to keep finding new places, while your partner would rather return every day to a known place? It's not a question of who's right. It's a matter of being certain the trip has the same shape for both of you or, if there are differences, that you identify and reconcile them before you leave home.

- *Someone who shares your feelings about taking risks.* How do you both feel about riding on top of the bus, hiking without a guide, spending the night on top of the pyramid, or visiting areas that may not be completely safe?

- *Someone who shares your feelings about the budget.* Reasonable people can become very weird when it comes to money. Do you both have the same ideas about your budget? Are you thinking of paying $12 a night for a hotel room, though your prospective partner won't be comfortable for less than $112? How do you feel about splurging when hit by an urge? If you anticipate different standards of living on the road, it may signal differences in your respective views of the whole trip.

On the easygoing tropical island of Gili Trawangan,* I met a couple from Sydney who were barely into their first vacation together. They had just moved into a clean bungalow with a bathroom, decent beds, a fan, and only fifty feet from the water—all for $5 a night. He was obvi-

---

*Gili Trawangan. A tiny island off the coast of Lombok, Indonesia, offering sunny days, snorkeling, and magic moonlight.

Fierce rapids on the Rio Futaleufú. Chile.

ously delighted by the place and the price. A few hours later, they stood on the front porch heatedly discussing her desire to return to the mainland and the comforts of the Sengiggi Beach Hotel* at $70 per night. I have a feeling that was not the last of their disputes.

That couple is a reminder that there are risks in traveling with a significant other, especially when romance is in first bloom. The occasional stresses of long-term travel can exert a little pressure on even an intimate relationship. Small irritants, if not acknowledged and dealt with, can grow to overwhelm romantic illusions.

- *Someone who operates on a similar clock.* As Thoreau put it, "The man who goes alone can start today; but he who travels with another must wait till that other is ready." The day person/night person issue has plagued more than a few travelers. If one partner dedicates himself to late night partying and the other prefers visiting local markets at dawn, there's a problem on the horizon. Partners can also fall out over the timing of meals. Do you wake ravenous, or prefer not to wait until mid-morning? Do you want three meals a day, or is catch-as-catch-can fine? Would one of you become crazed if the other were late for a meeting? A stickler for punctuality and orderliness could find the occasional chaos of the Third World rather trying. Be certain you understand one another and can adjust accordingly.

- *Someone whose energy level is similar to your own.* Be sure you and your prospective partner seek a similar pace of travel. If you don't have com-

---

* *Sengiggi Beach Hotel.* This is an upscale hotel on the island of Lombok, Indonesia. Lombok is said to resemble Bali of fifty years ago, but that's a bit of exaggeration.

patible degrees of fitness, you may not be able to travel well as a team. An upbeat, peppy partner is a real joy.

- *Someone who doesn't have health problems that would interfere.* On an easygoing trip, health is probably not an issue. For a long or arduous trip, allergies or potentially serious afflictions should be considered carefully in advance. The important thing is that both partners share the same expectations.

- *Someone who has a flexible, easygoing personality.* There are bumps in the road that will jostle anyone's cart. Travel requires solving problems and resolving uncertainties, so if you choose a partner who blows up easily, you'll be unhappy. The more remote from your own culture, the greater the challenges. Look for a partner who has a sense of humor and understands that most frustrations arise from the very differences in culture that make a place worth visiting.

- *Someone who has personal habits compatible with your own.* Do you have similar feelings about alcohol, cigarettes, and illegal drugs? If one partner spreads his gear over every available surface, will the other flip out? If one of you snores . . . well, then what? No judgments, just a reality check before the plane rolls down the runway.

- *Someone who understands how a partnership works.* Travel with someone who will share the load and keep agreements; someone you can count on.

- *Someone who recognizes the need for "quiet time."* Everyone enjoys a good conversationalist, but anyone who doesn't get enough quiet time, or time alone, to maintain equilibrium may get cranky. Many of us are simply not used to spending twenty-four hours a day within fifty feet of the same person. Unless you're into nonstop conversation, it helps if both of you are comfortable with silence. When you need quiet time, don't suffer: ask for it. Writing in your journal and reading are two ways to create quiet time. Reach agreement that the need for time alone is not a rejection of the other person. If one of you needs an occasional meal alone, a solitary walk, a breakfast-to-dinner solo day, or some parallel travel, can the other person recognize that need without feeling rejected?

- *Someone who feels the same way you do about intimacy.* Is romance on the agenda? Do you feel okay about sharing a room, or a bed? Don't make assumptions about this one.

- *Someone who is willing to communicate and solve problems.* If there's a problem, a molehill can become volcanic if not dealt with when it arises.

Agree not to store up small resentments; agree to express, calmly and contemporaneously, your feelings about your partner's behavior, the dynamics of the trip, or whatever the issue is.

There must be a mutual commitment to solving problems in creative ways. If you can't find a mutually satisfactory solution, or a practical compromise, consider a trade-off. Your partner prevails this time, you get your way next time. There is no point in silently compiling a list that demonstrates, to your own satisfaction at least, that your partner is Jack the Ripper.

> "I learned one thing."
> "What?" "Never go on trips with anyone you do not love."
> —Ernest Hemingway,
> *A Moveable Feast,*
> 1964

Choose some regular time, like Sunday breakfast, to discuss candidly how you both think the trip is going. Are you spending money at about the right rate? Are you traveling at a pace that makes you both happy? Is it time to change the itinerary or make any other changes? Are you having fun?

- *Someone you like!* Nothing is more important.

Don't lightly decide whether to travel solo or with a partner. If you'll be happier with a partner, choose that person with great care. If you're considering traveling with a nonstop talker who criticizes and complains, take a cold shower.

HOW TO FIND YOUR TRAVEL PARTNER

You've decided to travel with someone and you have a good idea of what your ideal person would be like. Now what? If you're not married to or romantically involved with a potential traveling partner, and neither family nor friends are suitable, check bulletin boards at colleges and bookstores. Review *International Travel News, International Living, South American Explorer*, and other travel periodicals in which travelers seeking partners list where they'd like to go and when.

The richest resource I know of is the Travel Companion Exchange (TCE) at (800) 392-1256 or (516) 454-0880. This reputable, fifteen-year-old service is one of the largest in the country. Its well-written, bimonthly newsletter, full of useful travel information, lists more than five hundred males and females eagerly looking for partners with whom to hit the road. Whether you're looking for a partner to avoid the single supplement charge on a tour in the south of France or to join you for a year-long stroll from Capetown to Cairo, you have a good chance at finding likely candidates through TCE. The newsletter costs $48, and a membership, including the newsletter, costs $99 for six months.

Other organizations that I am not personally familiar with but that advertise in reputable places include the following:

- Partners-in-Travel (310-476-4869), which publishes a Traveler's Directory of about five hundred singles looking for travel partners, plus a list of about one hundred fifty tour operators that offer package tours that accommodate singles. There's no charge for listing yourself in the directory, but only members ($25) receive the directory.
- Golden Age Travelers Club (800-258-8880), a travel club for persons over age fifty, which will either find you a roommate for a tour or cruise or waive the single supplement fee ($10 membership, quarterly catalogue of trips).
- Partners for Travel (800-866-5565), which charges $120 per year to help find traveling companions for those over fifty and single. However, the charge is refunded if you take one of their educational or adventure trips.
- Connecting (604-737-7791), which publishes an annual *Single-Friendly Travel Directory* listing tour operators, outfitters, resorts, cruise lines, and singles clubs whose services and pricing policies are directed toward the solo traveler. The directory is free with a subscription to *News for Solo Travelers* (bimonthly, $25 per year). Travel tips in the newsletter are oriented toward solo travelers, but it includes listings of about fifty potential travel companions.

You can also leave home alone, planning to find one or more partners along the way. While you can't be sure you'll meet someone compatible who's going your direction, it's easy to meet travelers in museums, on city bus trips, on trains, on the trail, at the beach, in hostels and restaurants, even just walking along the street. If one of these spur-of-the-moment partnerships doesn't work out, it's easy to dissolve. In other words, if you prefer traveling with a partner but don't find one at home, don't let that ground you.

Wherever you find a potential partner, run through the "ideal partner" checklist to make sure you're compatible. And when you find a great travel partner, treasure her or him. Partners who finish a long trip on a friendly basis are a good bet to be friends for life.

HOW TO AVOID LOSING YOUR TRAVEL PARTNER

Most travelers never stop to think what they would do if they and their partner were separated. As a result, the next time they meet, after considerable inconvenience and anxiety, might be back in their hometown. It's worth creating a contingency plan to get back together if you're separated. It doesn't matter much what your plan is so long as you've agreed on one before you're unexpectedly in different places. Each partner must know what the other will do in a missing-person situation. With a contingency plan, it may take a while to get together, but at least you will.

For example, you might agree that if separated while walking around town, each of you will return to your hotel. Alternatively, you can agree on a time and place to look for one another. That's easy.

It's more likely you'll become separated just as the train you were about to catch is pulling out. My agreement with my partner is that if I'm not *certain* she's aboard, I'll get off. If I don't find her after looking around, I'll wait a while hoping she'll find me. If still no luck, I'll return to our last hotel and wait. If my partner was aboard the train that pulled out without me, she'll get off at some reasonable place and try to reach me at the hotel. If that doesn't work, she'll head back.

If there's a language barrier at your hotel, you might specify that you'll meet at one of the major tourist hotels. English will be spoken and the manager should be able to help.

Some people agree to reconnect through the appropriate consulate or embassy or the central police station.

As a fail-safe preparation, keep a telephone number in your money belts that each of you will call (usually a number at home likely to be answered).

If you come up with a more fool-proof contingency plan than the ones I've suggested, I'd like to hear about it.

A final comment about travel partners. The man who holds the *Guinness Book of Records* title as the World's Most Traveled Man has been married and divorced six times. His explanation: "My wives all said they loved travel, but they were thinking the QE II and the Ritz, not riding some dirty boat from one godforsaken island to another." I wonder if this chapter would have helped.

4

The Organized Tour

> Tourists capture the image of a well-known place in a
> photo but miss its essence; the anti-tourist dismisses
> the place as a cliché and misses the whole thing;
> while the traveler grasps its majesty.
> — John Thorn

I've often heard people discuss theoretical distinctions between "tourist" and "traveler." Naturally, those who think of themselves as travelers insist on the distinction, while those who see the world on organized tours are reluctant to categorize themselves as tourists. Certainly, effortless mass tourism has inspired satire, especially in the case of tourists who think they are intrepid travelers as they're shepherded safely to places previously accessible only to daring adventurers.

Paul Fussell opined, "An explorer seeks the undiscovered; a traveler seeks that which has been discovered by the mind working in history; and the tourist seeks that which has been discovered by entrepreneurship and prepared for him by the arts of mass publicity." Another critic described tourists as people who travel primarily to raise their social status at home, to realize fantasies of freedom, or to pose as members of a social class above their own. Doesn't make you want to be categorized as a tourist, does it?

In my opinion, the distinction between traveler and tourist goes beyond destination, means of transport, length of time on the road—and even whether someone else takes your luggage down to a bus each morning. It's based on your objectives and state of mind. A traveler intends to merge with a place and its people in a way that a tourist does not wish to.

To me, the word "tourist" has a connotation different from merely describing people who travel on an organized tour. It identifies people who see well-known sights and leave a place understanding the culture only superficially. They have few friendly contacts with local people and are little changed by their trip. A tourist is a person who, whether with a tour group or not, is primarily along for the ride and doesn't get actively involved.

> "He did not think of himself as a tourist; he was a traveler. The difference is partly one of time, he would explain. Whereas the tourist generally hurries back home at the end of a few weeks or months, the traveler, belonging no more to one place than to the next, moves slowly over periods of years, from one part of the earth to another."
> —Paul Bowles, *The Sheltering Sky*, 1949

From that perspective, it would be inaccurate to categorize everyone on an organized tour as a tourist. Tour participants can be far more than tourists if they educate themselves about what they will experience, interact with local people as meaningfully as possible—and choose their tour operator wisely.

Independent travel requires endurance, a measure of self-confidence, the ability to organize, adequate health, and some control over your business and personal responsibilities. Uncertain about meeting these requirements, many people hook up with a tour, especially for their first major trip, and have a great time. If anxiety about coping with distant parts of the world might cause a person to stay home, he'd be doing himself a disservice to dismiss tours. It's far better to explore the world in whatever vehicle feels comfortable than to mildew in an armchair at home.

If taking a tour seems like a good way to get underway, the trick is to select the tour that will meet the objectives you set. That's what this chapter is about. Even if you are not interested in tours today, it's possible you'll travel with an organized tour group in the future.

REASONS TO TRAVEL WITH A TOUR OPERATOR

- *Someone else does the thinking and makes the arrangements.* Decide to travel with a tour group and that's one of the last decisions required. Before long, the mailman delivers a glossy brochure bulging with superlatives, an itinerary, a list of what to bring, an orange plastic luggage tag, and detailed instructions. Underway, courteous guides answer every question, adequate hotels and restaurants appear when wanted, and scenic vistas flow by without misadventure. If there are hassles, you probably won't even hear about them, much less have to deal with them. Participating in a tour, by the way, can teach you a lot about planning your own itinerary the next time out.

  Some people sign up for tours because they lust for luxury. For example, one banking tycoon engaged a tour operator to lease a swanky private train to take his party deep into the Gobi Desert for a sumptuous banquet brought in by camel caravan. Another client wanted to "rough it" on the Salmon River, with silver, china, crystal, and violins at night. One tour operator makes a living providing suites on the QE II that cost over $37,000 for the five-day Atlantic crossing.

- *Some countries require that visitors travel with a tour group.* For many years that was the only way outsiders were permitted to travel in China. That requirement has been generally abandoned, although permission to travel independently in places such as Bhutan, Myanmar, and North Korea phases in and out. Countries with limited tourist facilities want to be sure that big spenders are given priority. It's also easier for an inquisitive government to keep tabs on groups than on independent travelers.

  In several countries, traveling with a tour group is not mandatory, but logistics can be daunting for an independent traveler. For example, consider a group if you want to travel hassle-free in Mongolia.

- *Some tour operators include considerable educational value in their trips.* If so, you're likely to be accompanied by an art historian, a geologist, or some other appropriate expert to help satisfy your curious mind.

- *A tour can be an efficient way of moving from place to place.* Since independent travel, especially in the Third World, can be very time-consuming, a tour may be a good fit for a traveler with limited time. If you don't want company, an "air and accommodations only" tour package may be useful.

- *Some people prize the company of others.* In fact, meeting like-minded people may be part of the reason for the trip. It is not unusual to travel repeatedly with people with whom you've formed friendships on a tour.

- *Tours may increase opportunities to meet local people.* Although many tours tend to insulate tour members from local contact, some are organized specifically to permit participants to talk with educated and well-traveled local people, perhaps when they give lectures to the group.

- *Some tours actually* SAVE MONEY. For example, joining a budget safari group after arriving in Kenya will cost you much less than organizing a safari for yourself. If you don't mind staying in the places, eating the type of food, and seeing the sights that tour groups do, you can save money by joining tours and taking advantage of group rates. In fact, if you book an off-season tour not long before departure, you should get an extremely good price.

- *A tour may be ideal for persons with less than robust health.* The availability of assistance may enable someone to travel who doesn't have the reasonably robust health required for independent travel.

- *Tours free you from handling the logistics of a trip.* Running the Colorado River through the Grand Canyon or the Rio Bio Bio in Chile on your own would require acquiring and transporting quite a bit of specialized equipment and supplies. It's a lot easier to leave that to others.

- *A tour provides the opportunity to combine high adventure with low risk.* The expertise of experienced guides enables people to make difficult trips in comparative safety.

After reading a stack of tour brochures, you will realize that tourist trails around the world are deeply worn. On the other hand, if you read brochures put out by a few companies such as Geographic Expeditions, Mountain Travel/Sobek, and Turtle Tours, you may be amazed at how many remote corners of the world still await your visit. Companies like these have sought out nearly inaccessible hideaways from Mongolia to Indochina, from the sub-Sahara to Antarctica. They'll take you to Lunana in northern Bhutan, to the fabled Inner Dolpo region of northwest Nepal, across the Himalayas from Manali to Ladakh, or on an icebreaker out of Cape Town bound for the far side of Antarctica. Yes, you could arrange almost all of these trips on your own, but you'd have to do extensive research and overcome formidable logistical problems to do so. Even if you're prepared to make the rigorous effort, choosing whether to do it on your own or with a tour operator is not always an easy call.

REASONS *NOT* TO TRAVEL WITH A TOUR OPERATOR

It's interesting that some of the reasons that persuade people to sign on with a tour group are the very reasons that persuade other people *not* to. Tours come with trade-offs. Many tour operators work hard to combat the disadvantages I mention below but, to some extent, they are inherent in tours.

- *Many tours are expensive when compared to the costs of independent travel.* For single travelers, part of the extra expense of a tour is the dreaded single supplement. This is a substantial charge often added to cruise, hotel, or tour prices for people traveling alone. After all, the single traveler takes up a space which would otherwise accommodate two fare-paying people. SAVE MONEY by seeking out tour operators who don't impose this charge or who waive it if you're willing to accept an assigned roommate. Negotiate. Tell the tour operator you'll sign up only if the charge is waived. As departure date approaches, the operator may see it your way. If not, consider finding a partner (see Chapter 3).

  Because many tours are very expensive even without the single supplement, you may be interested in knowing why they cost you more than independent travel. It's because the tour operator, trying to anticipate the preferences of prospective clients, often builds upscale amenities into trips. They usually lodge you in expensive hotels all the way, or at least before and after a trek, and furnish a sociable, educated, English-speaking guide. On your own, you might stay in less expensive lodgings and get along without a guide (or with one whose English is only somewhat better than your command of his language). Beyond that, the operator pays for other helpers, local permits, fuel, equipment, food, transportation, and insurance. On your own, you might eat more simply and rely on public transportation.

Then there's overhead. The tour operator maintains a staff to provide all those pre-trip services to you. Remember that gorgeous brochure? To the high cost of producing it, add what it cost the operator to find you and mail it to you. On top of all that, at least 10 percent of the trip price is paid by the tour operator to the travel agency and another 3 percent goes to your credit card company.

The operator spends extra money to ensure that the trip is flawless—because that's what people seem to expect on tour. The independent traveler, on the other hand, is prepared to accept a glitch or two (after all, he's his own tour operator). It's up to you to understand and choose what you want.

- *Regimentation is the rule.* On a typical tour, you board the daily transportation at a prescribed time, travel a fixed path selected by others, and eat as a group when the bell rings. The tour operator sets the pace. If it's significantly different from your natural pace, you can go bananas. There is seldom any "down time." You're expected to eat, and enjoy, everything on the plate. You can struggle against the routine by skipping some of the planned activities, substituting your own, and hitting the streets every time there's a free period on the schedule. In the end, however, you're still aboard a guided missile.

- *Being with a tour group changes the nature of any experience.* A cloud-wrapped monastery, a memorable experience when seen alone, changes when twenty-five people pile through the low door and the monks scramble to peddle their crafts (and they do).

- *Unprofessional tour guides can drive anyone crazy.* Unprofessionalism ranges from not knowing the subject to paying no attention to group preferences to hitting on the clients.

> "Most travelers content themselves with what they may chance to see from car-windows, hotel verandahs, or the deck of a steamer . . . clinging to the battered highways like drowning sailors to a life raft."
> —John Muir, American naturalist

- *Your companions can make or break the tour, and possibly you in the bargain.* Noel Coward referred to tourists as " . . . monumental bores who travel in groups, herds and troupes." As a generalization that's unfair, but bores are not nearly the worst human peril you encounter on tour. A mysterious metamorphosis lies dormant in some people, seemingly triggered by paying a lot of money to a tour operator. Failing to ask the tour operator in advance for an honest profile of the group could be a serious error.

Richard Bangs, founding partner of Mountain Travel/Sobek, listed some of the clients his guides dread: The Stud—who's out to conquer the landscape and anything else available; The Ignoramus—who learned nothing about the tour destinations ahead of time and didn't bring the proper gear; The Inflexible Retentive—who has memorized the brochure and explodes when local conditions force the slightest deviation (even an otherwise understanding person may cast her cape aside and emerge as a chronic complainer); The Peacock—whose primary pleasure is parading around in the most expensive clothing available; The Snipe—who snarfs up far more than his share of whatever goodies are available; and The Grunge—who violates all rules of hygiene, endangering everyone else's health.

- *Food and hotels selected by tour operators are typically Westernized.* You could wind up missing much of the flavor of the country.

- *You meet few local people.* Those you encounter are lecturers very familiar with Westerners, or hardened traders whose primary goal is to sell you as much as possible during the brief moments you are together. They're very good at it but it's not what you would call a fulfilling experience for you.

> "The traveller sees what he sees; the tripper sees what he has come to see."
> —G. K. Chesterton

People on tour see restaurant workers, taxi drivers, and beggars who gather outside their hotel (who are there precisely because it is a tourist hotel), but have little interaction with the general populace. They don't hang out with local artists, musicians, soldiers, store keepers, politicians—or even travelers. An invisible cocoon forms around a tour, difficult to penetrate in either direction.

- *You're likely to become dependent on the lifeline of bus and guide.* Travel becomes too easy. Someone else has the answers and you become timid about venturing out on your own.

Some independent travelers may be tempted to look down their noses a bit as they see a tour bus pulling up in front of yet another temple. However, there's another way to look at it. First, that tour bus is taking people to places to which they would not, or could not, otherwise go—and that's good. Second, tour groups pay in hard currency, vitally needed by the host country—and that's good. Third, I remember standing in a blazing hot, dusty, chaotic bus yard, trying to figure out what the name of my destination might look like in Hindi. Overwhelmed by noxious fumes and the sound of roaring engines, my eye was caught by an air-conditioned luxury tour bus gliding by, stereo playing, hostess already pouring ice-cold beers. I promise you, I wasn't looking down my nose at tour groups at that moment. And that's good.

If you're feeling uncertain about what you'll encounter in some faraway land, you're not quite as fit as you'd like to be, don't want to take the time to organize a trip on your own, or just want to be coddled, consider a tour. If going on a tour will initiate a lifetime of traveling, give it a try. If you decide to take a tour, hit the road with optimism and a cheerful spirit. Make it your trip—and don't sweat the small stuff.

TOURS—HIGH COST TO LOW COST

Tours don't come just in vanilla. They vary widely in cost, services provided, and objectives. Itineraries, multiplying like a computer network, are now a great spider web covering the globe. To make wise choices, you need to understand what is available.

Upscale. On some fully escorted tours, you never lift a hand; in fact, your feet may barely touch the ground. The accommodations are five-star and the food is gourmet (although being served Chicken Cordon Bleu in Beijing may strike you as a little weird). An imported expert guides you through the sights of the day and lectures to you at night. After a nightcap, you tuck yourself into a crisp, clean bed.

Standard. On the majority of tours, you're accompanied by an escort, stay in good hotels, eat well, and listen to local guides reel off a galaxy of details. Every morning, you're rousted out early to line up your bags in the hall, ready for the next lap. These tours generally last between ten and thirty days, and prices vary accordingly.

Locally hosted packages. A guide meets you or your group as you arrive at a destination, takes care of you for a few days, then sees you safely onto transport to your next destination—where you meet your next guide-for-a-day.

Special focus. Some tours distinguish themselves with a special focus, such as Chinese celadon, butterflies along the Tambopata,* French wines, or the Namibian system of jurisprudence. Special focus tours are often organized by zoological societies, museums, cultural groups, and the like.

Adventure travel. The popularity of this type of special interest tour is rapidly expanding. I'll discuss them at greater length in the next section.

Affinity groups. These groups can be composed of anything from accountants to zydeco musicians to redheaded people named Smith. Shoppers, feeding wildly in country after country, are a common affinity group.

---

*Tambopata. This river in eastern Peru joins the Madre de Dios to flow into the Amazon. It is noted for spectacular bird life and nature preserves.

Package. You initiate a package tour by stepping into a travel agency with a general idea of where you'd like to go. You leave the agency with a package of airline/hotel/overland transport reservations and travel on your own within that framework. No escorts are provided. Hotels, airlines, and rental car companies sell blocks of space to package operators (sometimes called wholesalers) at a discount, so the cost to you can be significantly less than if you bought the individual components separately. You get the group discount without the group; not a bad deal. The accommodations will be somewhat upscale and Westernized, but at least you're on your own. A Foreign Independent Tour (FIT) is similar, usually unescorted but with occasional guide service.

Disability groups. Since international travel can be difficult for persons with significant disabilities, it's worth getting advice and assistance in advance. The Society for the Advancement of Travel for the Handicapped (212-447-7284) has a list of tour operators who make special efforts to assist travelers with disabilities. *The Handicapped Traveler Newsletter* is full of travel advice (903-677-1260). S. Gersten and J. Freedman have written a helpful book titled *Traveling Like Everybody Else: A Practical Guide for Disabled Travelers* (Adama Books, Bellmore, NY).

Not specifically fitting in the standard concept of a tour, are two other situations in which you employ someone else to show you the sights. Although local tours and local guides are passed up by many travelers, each has merits worth considering.

Local Tours

Inexpensive local tours are offered by a unit of government or by private tour operators. Most commonly, they are bus trips around a city or region lasting for one long day, although some continue for a week or more. There's usually no problem boarding just before departure, but it's safer to sign up a day ahead of time. A local day tour saves you from having to figure out how to get to and from a dozen remote sites in a city new to you. The driver or guide explains what you're seeing and is usually willing to answer questions having little to do with the tour. By the end of the day, you've identified places to which you want to return and you may have met interesting people in the bargain. I often take a local trip on my first day in a large city new to me.

It would be logical to assume that everyone on the bus paid the same for the local tour—and it would be wrong. Those who asked their hotel or a local travel agency to book them almost certainly paid much more than those who booked directly with the tour operator. If you book through your hotel, ask for a discount. If someone tries to switch you from a tour you requested to a different one, it's probably because they get a higher commission from the latter.

Local Guides

Wherever your elbow is in the world, a would-be guide will touch it to commend himself to your attention. He may dress in a shiny suit and speak a melodic upper-school English, or he may be a fourteen-year-old in a scruffy *djellaba*. Whichever, he is certain to be tenacious. He will also probably be knowledgeable, which he'll attempt to demonstrate by bombarding you with arcane info-bits before you can say, "No, thank you." He'll offer to guide you safely through the maze of the *souks* of Marrakech, protect you from being cheated by merchants, and shield you from his "not honest" competitors who are also seeking your attention.

After several experiences with guides who told me much more than I wanted to know and always seemed to have an uncle whose carpet shop just happened to be on our route, I responded by turning away every applicant. Before long, I learned better. In addition to what they've programmed them-selves to tell me, guides provide answers that help satisfy my curiosity as no guidebook can. With encouragement, they take me to remote corners I would otherwise miss. As a bonus, beneath the routine patter, many guides are interesting—proud of their knowledge and their fluency in foreign languages.

If you think a person would expect to be compensated for performing such services, you would be right. The question is, how much? Starting off without an agreement almost assures that one or both parties will be unhappy at the end. However, before discussing price, agree on exactly what services the guide will provide. That done, if he's failed to state a price, raise the subject. He's likely to respond, "Nothing, sir. Nothing at all. If you do not like my services, you pay me nothing. If I am helpful, you pay whatever you decide." Sounds fair, eh? Yes, it does—but it's a trap. Your conscience will never permit "nothing" and the guide knows it. If you pay anything less than a year's income, the guide will protest that it is too little. His protest may be quiet and courteous, as if embarrassed that you don't know any better, or he may feign shock or grief. You are vastly better off reaching agreement in advance. If you wish, talk with several prospective guides, comparing their merits and their asking prices. Or decide what a guide's services would be worth to you and offer a take-it-or-leave-it price. The price of a guide is, to put it mildly, highly elastic, reflecting how many guides there are and how many prospective clients. Only if the trip involves some strenuous activity such as climbing with you to the top of the four highest pyramids at Tikal is there likely to be an irreducible minimum price.

You often see a little knot of tourists being towed passively through a site by a fast-talking guide. Within minutes a few become hostile, but most lapse into glassy-eyed boredom. In contrast, when I set off with a guide I immedi-ately try to engage him as a person and get him to see me as an individual traveler. I let him know my special interests in the site. As we walk, I ensure that we proceed at my pace, so I can understand what I'm seeing, take photographs if I choose, and ask questions. If the guide makes a special effort, he is paid a bit more than we agreed on—and we're both happy.

HOW TO CHOOSE THE BEST TOUR OPERATOR

Before investigating any particular tour, decide where you want to go, how long you want to travel, what time of year you prefer, how much you want to spend, and the kind of people with whom you want to travel. In other words, set the initial agenda yourself. If you choose to make adjustments later to meet the specifics of available tours, at least you're following your own path.

Resources

Read travel magazine ads. If you have a special interest, such as scuba diving, bicycling, or historic preservation, review ads in magazines that concentrate on your interest. Send for every brochure that tweaks your interest.

You seldom get a discount if you book directly with the tour operator, so you lose nothing if you deal with a good travel agent. However, the travel agent is paid by tour operators, not by you, so there is some potential for a conflict of interest. Travel agents have access to thousands of brochures which they'll order for you on request. Take a look at their *Official Tour Directory*. See Chapter 2 on how to choose the best agent for your trip.

Write to the U.S. Tour Operators Association (211 E. 51st Street, Suite 12-B, New York. NY 10022) for a free copy of its *Smart Travelers Planning Kit*. This USTOA guide lists all member companies and the areas of the world in which each specializes.

Local and national business and philanthropic organizations promote tours all over the globe, as do many universities. Watch for their ads.

The American Association of Retired Persons (AARP) and other "seniors" organizations (such as the Golden Age Travelers Club, Grand Circle Travel, National Alliance of Senior Citizens, and the National Association of Retired Federal Employees) sponsor tours, as well enabling members to obtain discounts of 10 to 50 percent on many hotel and tour rates.

Tourspeak

One of the most helpful foreign languages to learn is "tourspeak." Here's a sample: If an agent (or brochure) says you will "visit" someplace, it means that the bus will stop and you'll have time to get off and look around. If the word is "view," however, there will be only a brief opportunity to take a photo or two, while "see" means that the bus might slow down as it whizzes by the attraction. If a brochure says that you "can" play golf or "will be able" to visit an amusement park, these activities are probably not included in the price. Another tricky word is "near," as in "your little cottage is near the beach." It may be near only in a taxi. Listen and read with care so you'll know what to expect.

Check Out the Tour Operator

Evaluating tour operators is a good way to avoid aggravation and yet an amazing number of people don't bother. A man was recently indicted in Alexandria, Virginia, for ripping off more than two thousand people in forty-three states. He used telemarketing to sell cheap vacation packages (e.g., $199 for two people to the Caribbean and Cancun). Requiring the would-be traveler to pay in full in advance, he would then deliver "promotional vouchers" with so many restrictions that virtually no one could use the trips. Here's the kicker. Among the aliases he used were Dusty Rhodes and Skip Town! It must be true; it was reported in *Travel Weekly*.

Several magazines, such as *International Travel News* and *Consumer Reports* (see the Bibliography), periodically publish ratings of major tour operators. Call the American Society of Travel Agents (ASTA, 703-739-2782) or the USTOA (212-750-7371) to check credentials of travel agents and tour operators.

What to Ask the Travel Agent or Tour Operator

1. *Firsthand experience.* Has anybody in the travel agent's office traveled with this tour operator? If so, were they happy? Have any clients of the travel agency traveled with the operator? Were they satisfied? Get the names of some with whom can you speak (you'll get good advice about the trip as well as inside information on the tour operator).

2. *Operator's experience.* How long has the tour operator been in business? How many tours does it handle annually? How many trips has it sponsored to the area that interests you?

3. *Protection.* Since you'll want your money back if the tour operator cancels the trip or goes bankrupt, is it financially responsible? Does it have liability insurance? Is it bonded? Does it belong to the consumer protection program (a $5 million fund available to reimburse consumers in the event of bankruptcy) of the USTOA? Details on that program are provided in a free brochure, *The Standard for Confident Travel* (call USTOA at 212-750-7371). Does your payment go into a trust account or escrow held by a third party? Can you pay by credit card? What penalties are there if you cancel? Have any complaints been filed with the state consumer affairs office against the tour operator? Naturally, you won't pay any tour operator until you've carefully read all the terms of the contract.

4. *Price.* Exactly what does the price of the tour include? If meals are referred to as European Plan, no meals are included in the price. If it is

American Plan, three meals a day are included, whether you are hungry or not. Modified American Plan (MAP) means that breakfast and lunch or dinner are included. If it's Continental Plan, you'll get a bread and beverage breakfast that may leave an echo in your stomach. Is the price firm—or does the tour operator retain the right to increase the fare after you've signed the contract? An increase of more than 10 percent or a significant change in departure date should entitle you to a refund. Are there any extra charges, such as side trips, taxes, and so on, not included in the price? Will they provide other single travelers so you don't have to pay a single supplement? To compare prices of various trips, take the total price, subtract your estimate of the airfare if it is included, then divide that figure by the number of *nights* included. That will give you a uniform price/day figure for each trip.

5. *Cancellation.* What are the cancellation penalties? Are there situations in which either you or the tour operator may cancel without penalty?

6. *Trip difficulty.* Many tour brochures grade the trips they offer in terms of physical difficulty. Seek a match with your own energy level. Don't hesitate to ask; you're in this for fun. An active person could be climbing the walls after two weeks of sitting on a bus. On the other hand, if a trip is billed as "strenuous trekking" or "high altitude," don't sign up without understanding what that means.

7. *Guides.* Who will accompany the tour group? Who exactly will be the guide? There's nothing wrong with using local subcontractors if they're well-trained and reliable. When they're not . . . well, that's when the glossy brochure turns into toilet paper. What is the ratio of guides to group members? How long have the guides been with the company?

8. *Accommodations.* What is the quality of the scheduled accommodations? Lodging differs considerably, so ask for specifics. Where is the lodging located? If it's frequently far from the center of towns, you'll waste time commuting.

9. *Group demographics.* What will be the maximum and minimum number of persons in the group? Ask about the demographics of people who have already signed up. If you have an interest in romance, find out if there are appropriate singles on the manifest.

10. *Pace.* What will the pace of the trip be?

11. *Independence.* Will there be time to explore on your own during the tour?

12. *Contacts.* Will there be opportunities to connect with local people?

13. *Materials.* What materials will the tour operator provide in advance (gear lists, maps, readings, and so on)?

14. *Extensions.* Are there side trips or extensions you can take rather than returning home with the group?

15. *Diet.* Will dietary, religious, non-smoking, and other personal preferences be accommodated?

16. *Free trip.* If you deliver a certain number of other people who sign up for a tour, will the tour operator give you a free trip, including air fare, room and board? If so, how many people would it take?

17. *Payoff.* What is there about this trip that will make it a "trip of a lifetime?"

Choosing the tour operator who can best meet your objectives is as important as deciding whether to travel with a tour group at all. It's worth doing your homework.

ECOLOGICAL RESPONSIBILITY

In the real world, few travelers are likely to select a tour operator solely or even primarily because it treats the environment gently. However, in choosing from among a group of otherwise qualified firms, ecological responsibility could be the deciding factor. Not surprisingly, you'll have to look beyond mere inclusion of some form of "eco" in a company's title. That word is meant to appeal to the public but may mean little in practice.

When evaluating a tour operator in terms of ecological responsibility, ask questions such as: Do you use wood for fires or do you use alternative fuel sources? How do you dispose of organic and inorganic waste? Are your guides sensitive to local cultures? Are your local support staff members adequately clothed, fed, and housed? Do you provide predeparture information about the ecology of the destination? Do you use low-impact transportation when practical? Do you purchase goods and services locally? Are your local facilities designed to minimize environmental damage? Do you donate money or equipment to help the local environment or protect natural resources?

Since these are like "have you stopped beating your wife" questions, not all tour operators may be candid, but their answers will give you a chance to form an opinion. Further, even a few inquiries may motivate operators to be more ecologically responsible.

Some tour operators, listed in the table on the following page, are well regarded for their efforts to provide travelers with environmentally sensitive experiences.

Other good resources on ecotourism include: The Ecotourism Society (703-549-8979); the Center for Responsible Tourism (415-258-6594); the *Alternative Tourism Resource Guide*, published by the Center for Socially Responsible Travel (415-258-6594); *Handle With Care: A Guide to Responsible Travel in Developing Countries* (800-486-7737); *Archaeological Field Work Opportunities*, which lists hundreds of sites where you can assist with archaeological work (call the Archaeological Institute of America, 800-338-5578); *EcoTraveler* magazine (see the Bibliography); and *Earth Trips: A Guide to Nature Travel on a Fragile Planet*, by Dwight Holing, which offers a lengthy list of nature tour operators.

The Ecumenical Coalition on Third World Tourism has published some considerations for travelers to keep in mind. Among them are: travel with a genuine desire to learn more about people and be aware of their feelings; listen and observe; realize that your personal time concepts and thought patterns are not universal; learn local customs; ask questions; don't expect special privileges; don't make promises you can't or won't keep; and, reflect on the experiences of each day.

Environmentally Responsible Tour Operators

Above the Clouds Trekking	800-233-4499
Actif International (British Columbia)	800-822-8438
Amazonia Expeditions	800-262-9669
Capirona (Ecuador)	011-593-6-886-614
Center for Global Education (Minneapolis, MN)	612-330-1159
Center for Socially Responsible Travel	415-258-6594
Costa Rica Expeditions (Costa Rica)	011-506-222-0333
Earth River Expeditions	800-643-2784
Earthwatch (Watertown, MA)	617-926-8200
International Expeditions	800-633-4734
Inuit Adventures (Arctic Quebec)	800-465-9474
Mountain Travel/Sobek (El Cerrito, CA)	800-527-8100
Overseas Adventure Travel (Cambridge, MA)	800-221-0814
Plowshares Institute	203-651-4304
Sierra Club	415-923-5630
Travel Links	800-648-2667
Wildlands Adventures	800-345-4453

EIGHT VERY UNUSUAL TOUR OPPORTUNITIES

Although many tours follow a basic pattern, the creativity of some tour operators has resulted in magnificent exceptions. These exceptions demand a little more of participants, provide contact with local people, and inevitably have a deeper impact on those who choose them.

Code of Ethics for Nature and Culture Travelers

1. Aspire to invisibility (observe but do not disturb natural systems);
2. Vanish without a trace (minimize your impact on the environment);
3. Seize the power of your experience (act directly to accomplish conservation); and
4. Reverse missionary zeal (respect local cultures).

(Earth Preservation Fund; 206-365-0686)

Political Consciousness/Reality Tours

Dr. Toni Hagen, a long-time trekker in Nepal, expressed the view that mass tourism has even more impact on local cultures than it does on local ecology. Some ecological damage can be reversed, but neither technological advances nor money can restore loss of cultural identity.

With that in mind, several organizations offer tours specifically intended to interact gently with local cultures while enhancing the political consciousness of travelers. *People to People International* (816-531-4701), with chapters in thirty-four countries, sends American teenagers abroad as Student Ambassadors. It also has a program that arranges for adults to meet professional peers (scientists, doctors, teachers and so on) and sit in on speeches and seminars. The idea is to explore common interests through personal contacts.

Friendship Tours (209-576-7775) sends knowledgeable lecturers with its groups and arranges meetings and interviews along the way. *Anniversary Tours* (800-223-1336) shows its guests the nitty-gritty of life in the Confederation of Independent States and Eastern Europe. *Global Awareness Through Experience (GATE;* 608-791-0462) attempts to promote change, especially with respect to equality and justice, in countries such as Peru, Nicaragua, and Mexico. Participants meet spokespersons for the poor and attend meetings of reform movements.

Perhaps the most prominent provider of "reality tours" is the *Center for Global Education* (612-330-1159). CGE specializes in trips to the Middle East, Southeast Asia, South Africa, Latin America, and various other parts of the "Two-Thirds World" (which includes two-thirds of the human population, land mass, and resources). Its objective is to expose participants to poverty, injustice, political instability, unequal allocation of resources, and the dynamics of international social change. Participants talk with poor people as well as with traditional decision makers. These are intense trips, intended to educate through frequent meetings with everyone from *campesinas* to refugees, clerics to ambassadors. The Center calls it "experiential education" and expects you to do some reading before you go. Recent trips have included meetings with refugees returning to El Salvador and Guatemala, acting as election observers in El Salvador, and exploring causes and effects of violence in South Africa.

"They shall beat their swords into plowshares, and their spears into pruning hooks; nation shall not lift up sword against nation, neither shall they learn war anymore."
—Isaiah 2:4

Plowshares Institute (203-651-4304) offers short-term (e.g., 2½ weeks) "immersion seminars" and cross-cultural experiences to promote greater global understanding on the part of North Americans. Trip members meet religious, business, government, and local leaders in Africa, Asia, Latin America and Eastern Europe. The Institute has held recent seminars in Brazil, Hong Kong, the Czech Republic, Hungary, Germany, and South Africa. They want travelers to listen to as many voices as possible so they can think more deeply about solutions to inequities. Participants must agree to do some reading before the trip and to share their experiences with others after they return. They want trip members to act on what they learn about issues of global peace and justice.

The *Center for Responsible Tourism* (415-258-6954) is another highly regarded organization whose objectives are similar to those of Global Exchange.

The goals of *Global Exchange* (415-255-7296), a relatively new group with very modest fees, include linking people north and south of the equator who are promoting social justice, democracy, and disarmament. Their trips visit Central America, Cuba, Mexico, Vietnam, Brazil, and southern Africa. Global Exchange is active in efforts such as a literacy project in Honduras, delivering medical supplies to Haiti, and sending books to schools in South Africa. They've published several very good books and will furnish speakers on request.

Trips for Women

There is a growing belief that women traveling with other women tend to behave differently from women traveling with men. A friend suggested that when women travel together, each has the opportunity to take responsibility, exercise initiative, compete less, and be herself. To provide these opportunities, some tour operators specialize in trips for women only.

Woodswomen (800-279-0555), founded in 1977, says it is the largest women's travel organization in the world. Its trips include Mount Rainier, Denali Park, Alaska, Minnesota, Nepal, Ecuador, Europe, and Africa. Woodswomen offers bicycle touring, dogsledding, backpacking, mountaineering, canoeing, snorkeling, scuba, rock climbing, horse packing, hiking, safaris, skiing, and more. Typical group size is between five and twelve women. Since one objective is to encourage the spirit of adventure through travel experiences, these are not armchair vacations. Call for a copy of *Woodswomen News* ($2).

Outdoor Vacations for Women over 40 (508-448-3331) specializes in trips for active women over forty. The group visits New Zealand, Guatemala, Belize, and Idaho's Salmon River. *Overseas Adventure Travel* (800-221-0814) offers women's cross-cultural adventures in Bolivia, Tanzania, and Nepal/Tibet (including optional homestays). *Rainbow Adventures* (800-804-8686) organizes almost two-dozen exciting international adventure trips for women over thirty.

Other women-only tour operators include: *Earthwise* (508-283-8717), *Great Horizons* (303-447-2234), *Hawk, I am Your Sister* (505-984-2268), *Women in the Wilderness* (612-227-2284), *Womanship* (800-342-9295), and *Womantrek* (800-477-8735).

Overlanders

Don't mistake an overland adventure trip or expedition for a typical general-purpose tour. The overlander consists of a heavy-duty truck transporting a group of young people who may have little in common other than a bare-bones budget and willingness to absorb hardship in the quest for adventure. These trips travel rough routes but passengers get to know the rural essence of countries they traverse. Long days of travel are broken up with camping in some idyllic spots and visits to spectacular attractions.

The typical truck carries twenty to twenty-four people, usually an amalgam of Aussies, Kiwis, Brits, Yanks, and a few Europeans. The most popular trips traverse South America, Africa, and Asia, using routes such as Bogotá to Patagonia, Tangier to Johannesburg, Cairo to Nairobi, and London to Kathmandu. Hostilities cut some of the traditional routes across Asia from time to time, but there are always plenty of trips taking off from London, or elsewhere in Europe, heading south into Africa. Three to eight months later, the survivors roll into Kenya, Zimbabwe, or South Africa. There are less challenging overland trips in Europe and Australia which use comfortable coaches on trips of four to twelve weeks.

Because these trips cover difficult terrain, people who sign on should be flexible. Some companies even discourage middle-aged travelers unless they're supernaturally young at heart. These aren't trips for people who are disposed to complain or who expect to be pampered. If an overland trip will be one of your first, I recommend signing on for only a limited time, like two weeks. If it suits you, continue with the group. If not, you'll be ready to be on your own.

The overland tour operator furnishes the vehicle, fuel, tents, cooking equipment, and a leader/driver. Some companies throw in a second driver who may also do the shopping and cooking. More often, passengers do both themselves. Lodging may be the back of the truck, tents, or basic local accommodations. The longer trips are priced in the range of $40 to $45 per day (though some are as high as $75), including food and lodging.

Trucks supplied by reputable companies are comfortable, mechanically sound, and staffed by experienced drivers. Nevertheless, I've heard tales about trips on which the truck broke down three days into the Sahara or the axle snapped in one of the monster potholes in central Zaire. On occasion, relationships among the passengers make the Middle East look peaceful. On one trip, the driver and cook disappeared for good during the fourteenth rainy night in a row. On another, the driver drove off in the empty truck, sold it, and kept going. Whichever company you choose, get a solid financial guarantee covering cancellations, breakdowns, or other interruptions.

Three heavyweights in the overland business are *Encounter Overland* (EO; 071-370-6845), *Dragoman* (0728-861133), and *Guerba* (0171-938-3939). EO uses trucks with soft tops (the sides roll up, the top rolls back) and tow a gear trailer. Seating is in a row along each side. EO accepts ages eighteen to forty. The longest EO trip is 155 days, London to Harare, for about $42 per day, including the kitty that pays for food, campsites, entrance fees, and similar expenses. EO runs dozens of trips of varying lengths in Africa, Asia, and South America.

Dragoman operates in the same areas, plus Mexico and Central America. It's longest trip is 217 days and runs the length of Africa (for about $40 per day, including food). Dragoman uses Mercedes trucks with side windows, a hard top, and forward-facing seats. Dragoman accepts ages eighteen to sixty.

Guerba concentrates on Africa. Its longest trip covers twenty-seven countries in 231 days and costs $40 per day, including the food kitty. Its trucks have roll-up sides, a hard roof, and sideways seating. Guerba accepts ages eighteen to sixty-five.

In the United States, contact all three companies through the Adventure Center (800-227-8747). This twenty-year-old California company, representing overseas tour operators who offer more than three hundred trips (safaris, trekking, overlanding, etc.) in sixty-five countries, deals with individuals as well as travel agents.

Adventure Travel

Adventure travel trips, fairly expensive and often physically demanding, appeal primarily to comparatively affluent people in their late twenties to late forties. Trips range from "gravity adventures" such as whitewater rafting, bungy jumping, and tandem skydiving, to "soft adventures" that combine the exploration of wilderness with considerable creature comforts. One operator, reflecting the spirit of many, bills itself as a "broker of your dreams."

Adventure travel tour operators, of whom there are now more than ten thousand in the United States alone, offer trips through some areas so remote or undeveloped that arranging a trip on your own would be a logistical nightmare. Some trips involve real danger, but more often guides work hard to convey the feeling of adventure and challenge without placing clients at undue risk.

Most tour operators grade their trips in terms of how physically demanding they are. Since getting in over your head guarantees an unhappy trip, pay attention to these grades. If a trip isn't graded, ask. When considering an adventure trip, get opinions from several people who have taken that specific trip.

From among thousands of adventure travel operators, I'll mention a few with which, in my opinion, offer especially high-quality trips. *Mountain Travel/Sobek* (800-227-2384) has built a fine reputation for its mountain and river trips (and its brochure is a visual treat). It charges more than most of its competitors, but superior equipment, experience, and services may justify the price. MTS sometimes invites you to join it on an exploratory whitewater expedition (the first descent of a wild river). Of course, you return the compliment by paying a considerable fee. By the time you read this, you may have missed the opportunity to join MTS on its first circumnavigation of Greenland: twenty-five days on an ice-breaker for only $19,900 (I wonder if they thought a flat $20,000 looked like too much?).

A high percentage of organized adventure travel treks take place in Nepal and neighboring Indian states of Kashmir and Ladakh. One of the best and least expensive operators in these areas is *Himalayan Travel* (800-225-2380). However, its trips extend far beyond the Himalayas, including Europe, Latin America, and Africa. *Wilderness Travel*, based in Berkeley, California (800-368-2794), is another highly regarded company, especially for trips in Nepal. It offers over one hundred trips on five continents, holding its group size to a maximum of fifteen.

Above the Clouds Trekking (800-233-4499) was first active in the mountains but has expanded to areas as diverse as Patagonia and Madagascar while maintaining its emphasis on trekking. *Journeys* (800-255-8735) offers more than three hundred trips in thirty-five countries. Several of its trips in eastern Nepal and Burma visit remote Buddhist monasteries and include instruction in meditation. Journeys also sponsors trail clean-up expeditions, monastery restoration, and solar heating projects. *Turtle Tours* (602-488-3688) offers trips from Brazil to Irian Jaya, but its unique expertise is with the cultures of Mali, Niger, and Ethiopia, including up-close experiences with nomadic tribes. *Wildland Adventures* (800-345-4453) established the Earth Preservation Fund, which supports community projects promoting environmental or cultural preservation.

Many other fine companies emphasize a specific geographic or activity niche. For example, *Earth River Expeditions* (800-643-2784) and *Outdoor Adventure River Specialists* (OARS, at 800-346-6277) specialize in highly challenging whitewater river trips and *Marine Expeditions* (800-263-9147) is a leader in trips to Antarctica (see the section on Antarctica later in this chapter).

You can organize many of these trips by yourself, possibly at a lower cost, but doing so requires considerable effort and high tolerance for ambiguity (since some arrangements can't be made until you're on the ground near where the adventure starts). You can also join local tours. Safaris in Africa are an excellent example. Joining a safari locally is not difficult—and the savings are great. Whitewater and mountaineering trips are particularly difficult to arrange on your own. In addition to logistic issues, risk goes up greatly in the absence of guides expert in the ways of the river or mountain.

The adventure travel business is generally unregulated, so it's up to you to separate experienced, reliable operators from underfinanced, uninsured companies run out of someone's basement. Ask questions and ask for references. Also take a look at the Adventure Travel Society and Specialty Travel Index Web addresses listed in the Internet section of Chapter 2.

Bicycling

Years ago, most bike trips were pretty hard-core; long days were spent in the saddle and routes demanded serious fitness. More recently, options have expanded considerably. Picture yourself pedaling south on the Carreterra Austral in southern Chile: gravel roads, few motor vehicles, milky-blue glacier-fed streams, snowcapped Andes to the east, deep blue bays to the west, crisp cool air, silence broken only by raptors conversing far overhead. Or pedaling through a landscape of fjords, orchards, alps, and rain forest on New Zealand's South Island. Or surrounded by sculptured rice paddies, Hindu temples, and friendly artisans in Bali. Or visiting cool teak forests and colorful hill tribe villages in northern Thailand. Or pedaling slowly through romantic European countryside.

You needn't spend all your time on the seat of the bike. Many bike trips include short diversions such as whitewater rafting or kayaking, elephant riding, sailing—you get the picture. Depending on the trip and the outfitter, you may camp on a beach or snuggle up with a down pillow in an elegant country inn.

Backroads (800-462-2848), based in Berkeley, California, is one of the best and largest bicycle tour operators, serving more than twelve thousand bicyclists a year. Another sound choice is *Butterfield & Robinson* (800-678-1147 is the U.S. number for this Toronto-based firm). If you prefer a boutique operator and a world of personal attention, try Aspen-based *Adventure Worldwide* (303-925-4371).

Other qualified bicycling trip operators advertise in bicycling magazines. You'll find trips designed for singles, family travel, students, pedalers over 55, women—and even for those who want to try it tandem.

Work

I haven't set out on the road specifically for a work experience, but thousands of travelers have. An English friend has been traveling for three years, stopping to take jobs once in a while to pay for her trip. She's picked fruit in New Zealand, worked in a restaurant in Hong Kong, and been a nanny in India. She always earns enough to finance her forward progress.

For $10, the Archeological Institute of America (617-353-9361) will send you its *Archeological Fieldwork Opportunities Bulletin,* which lists scores of domestic and overseas digs. Some sites sound exotic, such as Egypt or Sri Lanka, while others are less interesting. Be aware that the location affects your opportunities to meet local people so choose your spot carefully. You may pay something for room and board, but you may receive a small salary. No experience in archeology is required. Before you sign up, be clear on the nature of the work—and how hot it's likely to be.

Earthwatch (617-926-8200) will, for a fee, volunteer your services to work on a worthwhile project. These projects typically involve hard work, sometimes in challenging surroundings, but require no specialized skills. Trips include helping ornithologists in China survey native birds, analyzing artifacts to learn the role of ceremonial caves in the religion of the Maya, and seeking revelations about Stone Age settlements in Auvergne, France. Go to the Ring of Fire on the Russian Kamchatka Peninsula to find out what triggers massive volcanic eruptions. Visit the Himalayas to study avalanches; dig for woolly mammoth, camel, and giant armadillo fossils in Mexico to learn about migrations between continents; collect rare plants on Mount Cameroon to make the case for establishing a forest reserve. Not long ago, I met Earthwatch volunteers measuring water quality on the island of Roatán off the coast of Honduras. Although the volunteers seemed to be minoring in scuba diving, their valuable work may lead to a reduction in waterborne diseases among the island's population.

The *Educational Travel Directory* ($6.95) is a country-by-country listing of publications and organizations offering thousands of jobs, study/travel programs, special interest travel, and exchange living arrangements abroad.

If interested in overseas employment, take copies of your résumé on your travels and plant them where they might mature into a future full-time job. You can get a job overseas while at home but it's far more effective to introduce yourself as you're passing through. If interested in working abroad, review the discussion on work permits in Chapter 5.

Homestays

World Learning, previously known as Experiment in International Living, arranges homestays (802-387-4210). Let them know the dates and country you prefer in Europe, Asia, Latin America, or the South Pacific. The opportunity to stay in a family home, long available to students during the summer, is now available to adults throughout the year. During a homestay of one to four weeks, you gain a depth of understanding quite different from that available to a traveler staying in commercial lodgings or hopping from place to place. There's a fee to the organization (averaging less than $500 for a two-week stay), but little or nothing to the family with whom you stay. They offer their hospitality for the same reasons you would.

Soviet-American Homestays (319-626-2125) arranges homestays in about a dozen Russian cities. The cost, usually for a separate room, is about 20 percent less than for a hotel-based tour. Host families speak English and are eager to learn about Western life. Since escaping the usual tourist routes is a greater achievement in Russia than in most other countries, homestays make a lot of sense.

Servas (212-267-0252) can put you in touch with host families in eighty countries for free homestays of two to fourteen days. In turn, you have an opportunity to act as a host for international travelers under the same program.

The *Friendship Force* (404-522-9490), co-founded by Jimmy and Rosalynn Carter, sends groups of twenty to eighty people to various countries to spend a week with host families (more than 100,000 people have gone to forty-five countries since 1977). A second week is spent traveling in-country. The emphasis is on personal contact or, as they put it, "Faces, not places."

Other organizations helpful in arranging homestays include *World Learning* (different from the one mentioned above; 802-257-7751), with more than 250 programs in sixty countries, and the *Citizens Exchange Council* (212-643-1985) and *Home Host International* (612-871-0596), both of which specialize in Eastern Europe and Russia.

American-International Homestays (800-876-2048) arranges rooms with families. On a bed and breakfast basis, the price is $49 per day; for bed, meals, and a guide it's $99 per day. It operates in the United Kingdom, Western and Eastern Europe, Confederation of Independent States, China, and Australasia.

Antarctic Cruises

Since Antarctica is much larger than the United States, even when considerably reduced in size during summer, there is no way to experience all facets of the continent in the course of a one- or two-week trip. The common experience is a cruise during the Antarctic summer, December through March, concentrating on the South Shetland Islands and the Antarctic Peninsula. In these areas, temperatures are tolerable, wildlife abundant, and coastlines accessible. What such cruises miss are the jagged Trans-Antarctic Mountains, vast stretches of ice and snow, the driest deserts on earth, and the frigid

Gentoo Penguins. Antarctica.

interior where temperatures drop to minus eighty degrees Fahrenheit and the wind can howl at more than 150 knots.

Still, a trip along the coast is incredibly rewarding. Rumpled glaciers squeeze forward imperceptibly, tumbling massive blocks of ice into the ocean with a sound like sonic booms. Crabeater and Weddell seals cruise as first-class passengers on wind-sculpted icebergs whose great bulk glows iridescent blue below the waterline. You stand in the midst of more than 100,000 squawking Adelie penguins, nervously eyeing the eight thousand–pound elephant seal basking a dozen meters away in the cold sunlight.

The word "cruise" evokes images along a spectrum from Loveboat to the Queen Elizabeth II. While some of the ships sailing the Southern Ocean resemble those images, there are now alternatives. *Abercrombie & Kent, Explorer Shipping Corporation, International Expeditions, Marine Expeditions, Mountain Travel/Sobek, Quark Expeditions, Society Expeditions, Worldwide Adventures, Zegraham Expeditions*, and several other reputable firms sponsor Antarctica itineraries. These trips vary considerably in terms of ship size, itinerary and, not least, cost. Prices of $6,000 to $15,000 are not uncommon.

In my opinion, the best choices are presently offered by *Marine Expeditions*, a subsidiary of Blyth & Company, based in Toronto. Trips start at about $3,500, *including* airfare from several U.S. gateway cities. It charters excellent ships commissioned by the Russians in the late 1980s as polar research ships. These ships, now available for passenger transport because research funds have dried up, carry between thirty-eight and seventy-eight passengers. They're comfortable, tough enough to power through light pack ice and small bergs, small enough to enter constricted harbors, and are staffed with expert naturalists. They use versatile Zodiac rafts to visit one or two different on-shore sites every day. You learn about the evolution of Antarctica and its contemporary impact on the planet's weather and food chain, as well as how to identify species of whales, seals, penguins, and seabirds as quickly as though they were familiar neighbors.

For more information on cruises, see Chapter 16.

PART TWO

Getting
Ready
("Get Set . . .")

5

Going into Action

A journey of a thousand miles must
begin with a single step.
— Lao-tzu
The Way of Lao-tzu

It's time to make it happen! You've decided where you're going, the amount of time you'll take, how much money you'll probably spend, and what time of year you'll leave. Now you're ready to deal with passports, visas, plane tickets, reservations, and other nuts and bolts of travel. At this point more than a few prospective travelers skid to a halt. A process that will soon be familiar and routine can seem like an impenetrable labyrinth the first time around. This chapter will help you solve the puzzle forever.

DOCUMENTS YOU WILL NEED

Passport

What It Is

To become a citizen of the world, you need a passport. Without it, you're tethered to home base. It's like having a chocolate bar full of crunchy almonds in your pocket—awfully hard to resist.

A passport is a form of identification issued by a government permitting the holder to enter and leave his or her own country. However, if you want to enter almost any foreign country, its government will require that you carry a valid passport issued by your own country. For U.S. citizens, the main exceptions are Mexico, Canada, and many countries in the Caribbean. To be a traveler, you need a passport.

The U.S. passport has undergone significant changes in recent years. There's now a kinegram (similar to a hologram), special ink, and a security thread to reduce forgeries. A new machine-readable code enables immigration

93

officers to determine quickly whether you are an international diamond thief in disguise.

How to Get It

In the United States, the Department of State issues passports through its Passport Agency. To obtain your first passport, if you are age thirteen or older, you must apply in person at a Passport Agency office, a state or federal court, or at a post office authorized to accept passport applications.

Passport Agency Offices

Boston	617-565-6990	Chicago	312-353-7155
Honolulu	808-541-1918	Houston	713-653-3153
Los Angeles	310-575-7075	Miami	305-536-4681
New Orleans	504-589-6161	New York	212-399-7710
Philadelphia	215-597-7480	San Francisco	415-744-4010
Seattle	206-220-7788	Stamford	203-325-3538
Washington, DC	202-647-0518		

To obtain your passport:

1. Fill in a Passport Application (Form DSP-11), which you get from a Passport Agency office, post office, or travel agent;

2. Show proof of U.S. citizenship in the form of a certified copy of your birth certificate, naturalization certificate, or proof that you were a U.S. citizen born abroad. If you can't locate the necessary documents, the Passport Agency will suggest substitutes;

3. Provide proof of identity (such as a driver's license or a government or military ID card);

4. Submit two identical two-by-two-inch photographs (front view, no hat or sunglasses, with a plain light background). Vending machine photos will not be accepted. Since passport photos convey an impression of your status to a foreign official whose cooperation you may need, it's worth dressing nicely;

5. Pay the correct fee (credit cards not accepted). A ten-year passport for persons eighteen and older costs $65; a five-year passport for those under eighteen costs $40.

If you were issued a passport within the past twelve years and were older than eighteen at that time, you may renew using an Application for Passport by Mail (Form DSP-82), which you obtain from a Passport Agency office, a state or federal court, or any post office. Simply send the application, your old passport, two photos, and the fee ($55 if eighteen or over, $40 if under eighteen) to the address on the form. Normal time for issuing a passport by mail used to be about two weeks but can now be five weeks or more. If you become worried, call (603) 334-0500 to check on the status of your application. Payment of an extra $30 gets your application processed within three days, but you may have to demonstrate necessity, rather than procrastination, as the reason. If you have time, send your application in as much as three months prior to your planned departure date. Getting your passport is a big deal; why risk disappointment?

Each year, demand peaks between January and July. Mid-1985 was a record period for issuing ten-year passports. When they expired in mid-1995, there was a huge last-minute rush to renew. Hundreds of people camped for days in front of Passport Agency offices as time ticked away before their flights left.

A travel agent can handle the passport application process for you or you can hire a professional service to do it. If you use a service (see the *visa services* section below), the charge would be $35 or more for seven-day service and as much as $100 for same-day service. Plan ahead and spend the extra money on an elephant ride in Sri Lanka instead. If you think those fees are steep, a Russian who uses a service to help obtain a passport to leave his country would pay $280 for two-week delivery and $1,000 for same-day issuance.

Passport pages provide the spaces into which visas are entered, so request a passport with the greatest number of pages allowed (currently forty-eight). It costs no more and you will, hopefully, need every page. When those are filled up, use a Passport Amendment/Validation Application (Form DSP-19) to ask for an accordion page or refill section. Why do you need so many pages? First, a visa for a single country may take up a full page. Second, when you enter most countries, your passport will be vigorously hand-stamped, perhaps more than once. You may collect additional stamp imprints as you travel within a country and the stamp will strike again on your way out. To make it worse, some officials disdain putting their country's stamp anywhere except on a blank page.

Request a passport with the greatest number of pages allowed.

Use Form DSP-19 to have a passport changed to incorporate a legal name change, enclosing a copy of the document that caused the change (adoption, marriage, etc.).

Expiration

Don't let yourself be surprised by a sharp-eyed immigration officer who discovers that your passport has just expired. If you'll be on the road when

> **Store It in Your Mind**
>
> Memorize your passport number, the city it was issued in, and the dates of issue and expiration. Otherwise, you have to pull out your money belt every time there's an immigration or hotel registration form to fill in.

your passport expires, renew before you leave. Since some countries require that a passport have at least six months of life remaining at the time of entry, don't take a chance. I've heard of an occasional immigration officer raising this objection,then happily waiving it upon receipt of a small gratuity. If you arrive home with an expired passport, you're subject to a $100 fee.

By the way, the ten or fifteen minutes it often takes to reach the U.S. immigrations officer to show your passport when returning may be greatly reduced in the near future. The Immigration and Naturalization Service Passenger Accelerated Service System (all that just to produce the acronym INSPASS) being tested at JFK and Newark airports should reduce the wait to less than a minute. After enrolling in the program, you insert a plastic card into a machine, then let the machine read your fingerprints. It grinds out a receipt and you're on your way to the Customs counter.

For information about passports, order *Your Trip Abroad* by sending $1 to the Superintendent of Documents, U.S. Government Printing Office, Washington, DC 20402 (or call 202-783-3238); alternatively, call the Passport Agency (202-647-0518).

Visas

What They Are

None of us has an internationally recognized "right" to travel. Thus, a visa is a document issued by a foreign government permitting the holder to enter its country and stay for a limited period of time. A visa usually takes the form of a rubber stamp impression inked on a page of a passport, but may also be a postal-type stamp or a sheet of paper stapled or glued into the passport.

Who Needs Them

At the moment, about ninety countries require nationals of at least some other countries to obtain a visa. It's common for a country to require nationals of some countries to obtain a visa while permitting nationals from other countries to enter without one. That decision is often made on the basis of economics or politics. Citizens from wealthy countries are less likely to be required to obtain visas than are citizens of poor countries. Reflecting political motivations, for many years an Israeli visa in your passport would result in a number of other Middle Eastern countries refusing you entry. Similarly, a South African visa would cause most other African countries to exclude you. Assuming that political changes in South Africa continue and Middle Eastern countries develop better working relationships, these restrictions may disappear. Of course, knowledgeable travelers have long circumvented them by having Israeli and South African visas put on a piece of paper separate from their passport.

Generally speaking, Canada, Mexico, Caribbean and western European countries do not require U.S. citizens to have a visa. In Spring 1994, seven members of the European Union (France, Germany, Spain, Portugal, Belgium, Luxembourg, and the Netherlands) eliminated border visa and passport checks altogether. Now, travelers breeze across their borders without slowing down. Greece, Italy, Austria, Denmark, Sweden, and Finland are expected to join this group. However, because the dollar has so little buying power in Europe, many people are seeking less-expensive destinations and these countries are more likely to require visas. Therefore, a traveler should master the process of obtaining a visa.

It would be a disservice to provide a list of countries that require visas because requirements change frequently and out of date information could create serious inconvenience. To find out whether a particular country requires a visa and, if so, what its conditions are

- Order *Foreign Entry Requirements of Foreign Governments* from the Consumer Information Center (719-948-3334; or P.O. Box 100, Pueblo, CO 81009);
- Call the State Department Citizens' Emergency Center (202-647-5226);
- Call the appropriate embassy in Washington, DC.

Ask at the same time whether any special permits are required for internal travel. If you contemplate an extended stay, see if an HIV test is required (it is in more than forty countries). Foreign embassies and consulates in the United States are listed on the Internet (http://dosfan.lib.uic.edu/dosfan.html). The Automobile Association of America (AAA) is another reliable source of information about visa requirements.

If you ask your travel agent which countries on your itinerary require visas, be sure the answer is based on fact, not assumption. Of course, travelers make assumptions too. An experienced travel agent told me that any time a client of hers bought an airline ticket to a country that required a visa, she would write on the ticket: "Don't forget your visa." That worked until the client who, upon arriving in Taiwan, reached in his wallet and produced—what else?—his Visa credit card.

If you ask other travelers about visa requirements, it's better not to rely 100 percent on their answers. The information may be out of date or involve special circumstances of which you are unaware. You don't want to be standing at the border when you hear the bad news.

At the Border
Even having a visa in hand does not always guarantee entry into a country. Some countries require that you have (a) sufficient funds to pay for your stay and (b) an outbound ticket in hand. These seemingly inhospitable requirements usually are reactions to the impoverished students and joyful hippies who streamed around the world in the 1960s. Only once has a border official asked me for evidence of sufficient funds or an onward ticket. A couple of

Border Guard.
Portugal.

years ago, guards at a border crossing into Zimbabwe required all foreigners to produce onward tickets. Happening to have a Zimbabwe-to-Kenya ticket purchased in Nairobi, I lucked out. Half a dozen other travelers were left behind as our bus pulled away from the remote guard station.

Rather than an onward ticket, a few travelers carry a Miscellaneous Change Order (MCO) as a way of meeting an onward ticket requirement. An MCO is *not* a ticket and can't be used as one. It's more like a cashier's check, showing that you have a guaranteed credit in a specified amount which can be used to pay for a plane ticket. Besides meeting the onward-ticket requirement, an important feature of an MCO is that it's easily converted back into cash when you return. Be aware, though, that an MCO is almost as negotiable as cash. Lose it and your chance for a refund is virtually nonexistent. If you want an MCO, ask your travel agent or get it directly from an airline.

Although immigration officials have discretionary authority to bar a traveler from entry, that **happens only** rarely. When it does, it's almost always when arriving via an overland border crossing rather than at an airport. For that reason, think of a border crossing as a one-act play. Dress for the part by wearing your most normal clothes. Be as well-groomed as circumstances permit. Approach with a smile, say something courteous, and be patient. On the other hand, anyone with an urge to spend a few hours broiling in the sun outside a crumbling concrete guard shack on the Rwanda-Zaire border should challenge the guard's authority, throw in some vulgar language, and assert his importance back home.

Should there be a problem, stay calm and follow any reasonable instruction, such as opening your luggage. If the situation is prolonged or threatens to get out of hand, ask for the guard's superior officer.

At a checkpoint entrance to West Sikkim, a young, smartly-uniformed guard sitting at a scarred table pointed out that the visa in my passport permitted travel to Gangtok, the capital of Sikkim, but said nothing about traveling into *West* Sikkim. He was quite right. The Indian consulate official in Washington, DC, had erred and I had overlooked it. The guard had me and we both knew it. After flipping through my passport for a full three minutes, he tossed it aside on his desk without comment and dismissed me with a lackadaisical backhand flip of his wrist. I stayed within sight, but didn't press him. After about twenty minutes, I approached his table again. This time, I mentioned that I was actually *leaving* Sikkim by a circuitous route which only at the moment happened to be going away from the border. Satisfied that he had demonstrated his authority, he stamped my passport vehemently and held it out to me without a glance. We'd played the game and were satisfied.

Different Types of Visas

Visas come in several versions: transit, business, student, resident, and tourist. The three most important to travelers are the transit, business, and tourist. A *transit visa* permits only a short term visit. Its purpose is to give you time to dash into a principal city, or visit a particular sight, then continue your journey. When you present a transit visa, an immigration official may want to see your onward ticket and enough money to cover your visit. The purpose of a *business visa* speaks for itself. Some countries require that you produce an invitation from a local person or a government ministry official, or be coming for a business purpose, as a prerequisite for issuing a business visa. The *tourist visa* is what most travelers need.

The visa indicates what type it is, its length or dates of validity, and how many times you are permitted to enter the country. Normally, a visa permits a single entry. If you foresee entering, leaving, and returning to the same country, you'll need a multiple-entry visa. If you don't have a multiple-entry visa, you may be able to purchase a new visa at the border. If not, you'll have to backtrack to a major city in another country. The fee for multiple-entry is higher than for single-entry, but less than you would pay if you bought a new visa for repeated entries. The most expensive I know of is the six-month multiple-entry visa for Zaire: it's a sky-high $360 (cash only, no checks). Figure that out. I don't think it's supply and demand.

Visas are valid only for a specified length of time, usually between thirty and ninety days, but they range from a week to a year. For some visas, the period starts on the date you request. However, if the period of validity starts on the date the visa is issued, and you won't get to the country for a while, the time limit could pose a problem.

Applying for a Visa

When answering questions on a visa application, keep in mind that the government basically wants some idea why you're entering its country and where you want to go. I recommend against listing your occupation as writer or reporter, or stating affiliation with any military, government, or international organization, or anything else that could be interpreted as meaning you would be inspecting their country. Any remotely prestigious occupation is enough to establish credibility; 'teacher' seems to make officials happy.

If forms ask for a local address, officials are satisfied with the name of any moderately-upscale hotel drawn from a guidebook. Even "hotel" is usually sufficient. When it inquires about "religion," the question may be loaded in some countries. You have a choice to make. If answering "none" feels okay, that's probably safest. You could finesse the issue by putting "nondenominational" or leaving it blank. If the question feels like a challenge and you don't want to avoid it, respond as you feel you should. If a form asks about your itinerary, list everywhere you might possibly go. Under "length of stay," ask for the maximum the visa allows. Give yourself the widest latitude in case the official limits you to what you asked for. Have a passport photo handy just in case the form requires it

Don't underestimate how long it may take to obtain visas. While some are issued automatically, obtaining others can be time-consuming. You might get it in a few days or it might take several weeks. If a country is reluctant to admit visitors or is especially bureaucratic, an applicant can be in for a challenging experience. It may reduce your frustration if you realize that the United States is notorious for making it difficult for foreigners to obtain visas to visit. Here's the kicker: when you've sent your passport to one embassy with your visa application, you can't apply for visas from other countries.

If you need a fast turnaround, expect to pay more; for example, if you give a Russian consulate twenty working days to issue a visa, the fee may be $40. However, for ten-day turnaround, it might cost $50. If you want a business visa on a same-day basis, expect to cough up more than $100. Plan ahead and SAVE MONEY.

If you apply in person, a clerk will tell you when to return for the visa. If you apply by mail, the issue date is less certain. Although travel agents and tour operators are usually reliable in obtaining visas, it's your responsibility to follow up relentlessly until the visas are in hand.

In the great majority of cases, it's much easier to obtain a visa before leaving home than while on the road. You have plenty of time and don't have to deal with a language barrier. In fact, unless you're certain of the practice, it's risky to arrive at a border without a visa hoping that some official will issue a point-of-entry visa on the spot. It's possible to obtain most visas abroad, but you may have to detour to a city where the visa can be issued—and the office may be closed when you get there. In any case, your forward motion will stop while you wait (and wait and wait) for the visa to be issued. You may even discover that you just can't get the visa you want, or you can get it only by complying with some restriction, such as joining a tour group. If there is a restriction, discover it at home when you have plenty of time to dance the bureaucratic break dance, rather than on the road in the turmoil of a crowded visa office.

> It's usually easier to obtain a visa at home than on the road.

By the way, when you give up your passport abroad when applying for a visa or any other reason, always ask for a receipt.

If you decide to get your visas as you travel, find out from the appropriate consulates exactly where to get their visas abroad. Some guidebooks provide this information. Bring along extra photos in case the application requires one.

Fees

Fees for visas vary greatly. Prior to 1994, few countries charged U.S. citizens more than $20 for a single-entry tourist visa. Then in 1994, the United States initiated a $20 surcharge on machine-readable visas issued to foreign travelers wishing to visit the U.S. That provoked reciprocal increases by many other countries. While most fees currently range from $20 to $50, they may soon emulate new car prices. Ethiopia has gone from $10 to $70; Tanzania from $10 to $45; Vietnam now charges $75. Given these changes, it's important to call ahead to ensure you send the correct fee. If you send the wrong fee, your application may return unprocessed.

Visa Services

Another approach in obtaining a visa is to employ a professional service. They know current requirements and ease your mind, but you pay generously for their assistance. They charge from $30 to $100 per visa, plus postage and the cost of the visa itself. These services fill in the forms and hand-carry them, with your photos, International Health Certificate (if required), and passport, from embassy to embassy. Knowing embassy personnel helps them speed up the process.

Tell the service the date you want each visa to become effective. As I mentioned earlier, a visa has a time boundary so don't let it become effective so far in advance of your arrival that you have to cut your visit short. Give the service a date by which you want the visas returned to you. Follow up periodically to monitor their progress. When they return your passport and visas, check to ensure you received all the visas you requested. Don't discover their mistake in a Sierra Leone airport. Yes, it happens.

While many services are listed in Yellow Pages under "Passport and Visa Services," here are a few to consider:

- Express Visa Service, Washington, DC (202-337-2442)
- Global Visa Service, New York City (212-682-3895)
- Intercontinental Visa Service, Los Angeles (213-625-7175)
- Trans-World Visa Service, San Francisco (415-752-6957)
- Visa Advisors, Washington, DC (202-797-7976)
- Visa Center, New York (212-986-0924)
- Visa Expediters, Washington, DC (202-387-4789)
- Visa International, Los Angeles (213-850-1192).

Expiration

Don't overstay the expiration date of a visa. Pay a fee and get an extension, or, if you must, leave the country and return with a new visa. If you overstay, you become an illegal alien, subject to fine, deportation, and arrest. You might be lucky enough to blow by the border official on the way out without being noticed. However, if they catch you there will probably be a fine; in Thailand it's $100 a day.

Special Permits

Permits are sometimes needed to go certain places or do certain things. For example, because authorities want to keep track of who is wandering where, many treks on Himalayan trails require a permit. If you don't reappear, they know where to look. Sometimes a permit is required to take photographs. The fee is small for 35mm cameras but is often high for video cameras.

Some permits are a bureaucratic way of enforcing an unofficial policy. For example, posters throughout India welcome tourists to the eastern state of Assam. However, during periods when foreigners aren't welcome in Assam, you won't be permitted to enter without a permit, no matter how many posters you point to. And that permit will not be quickly forthcoming. In three tries I've never been willing to stay in Calcutta long enough to see if a permit would eventually pop out of the system.

Permits also are used to protect natural resources. Showing admirable restraint in light of its need for hard currency, the Rwandan government permitted only twenty-four people a day, split into four groups, to climb the mountainsides to see gorilla families in the wild. Travelers who reached

Rwanda without this permit in hand were likely to find all permits sold. Some had to wait a day, others a week or more, depending on how many no-shows there were and how long the line of hopefuls.

To sustain Milford Track's reputation as "the finest walk in the world," New Zealand officials regulate the number of people on trails and in huts. The permit is expensive and months may pass before it's issued. Arrive without a permit and you might be lucky—but you're more likely to be disappointed.

Another type of permit is the requirement in a few countries that you register with the police within twenty-four hours of arrival. This requirement is noted in guidebooks and is usually brought to your attention by a point-of-entry official. Your hotel clerk will probably take care of it for you. That service should be a freebie, but an appropriate tip is a good investment. To avoid an unpleasant surprise, in the form of a fine, when ready to leave the country, follow up to ensure that the registration occurred.

Some countries require you to register with police on arrival.

Fortunately, permits are seldom required. Many can only be obtained on the spot, but those that can be acquired at home should be.

Work Permits

If you're thinking of getting a job while abroad, find out before you leave what is required to get a work permit. It's difficult to get a permit abroad, so it would be unwise to depend on earning money you'll need as you travel. Many countries, especially those in Europe, are flooded by refugees seeking work. Regions with depressed economies generally exclude outside labor to protect jobs for their own citizens. Employers can be heavily penalized for hiring people who lack official work permits. If you want a job that would require an extended visa or formal working arrangements, expect obstacles.

Your best chance of getting a work permit is to possess a specialized skill in short supply and high demand in the country where you want to work. In addition, before you arrive you may have to find an employer who will give you a written offer of employment. Not many travelers can pull that off in advance.

How to Find a Job

Once in a country on a tourist visa, you may find temporary jobs "off the books." Although the most frequent employers of passing travelers are restaurants and farmers, many Western travelers have at least two other skills they can market in any economy. Proficiency with English vocabulary and grammar, and knowledge about business at home, are potentially valuable skills to someone wanting to export goods to your home market.

Be alert for opportunities for self-help. English-language menus, brochures, store-window signs, and other forms of advertising often contain incorrect grammar or spelling. Travelers regularly trade meals in return for correcting a restaurant's menu.

Check out trade shows as you travel. Talk with potential employers and other local people. Try to connect with the expatriate community, if there is one. As with so many things in life, success depends on taking the initiative.

Under its Work Abroad program, the *Council on International Education Exchange* (CIEE, Work Abroad, 205 42nd Street, New York, NY 10017; 212-661-1450) negotiated reciprocal agreements with New Zealand, Costa Rica, Germany, France, Ireland, England, Jamaica, and Canada allowing U.S. students to work in those countries on a temporary basis. To be eligible, you must (a) be at least eighteen years old, (b) be taking at least eight hours of classes or begin the program within six months after you were last enrolled, and (c) apply *before* leaving the United States. To work in Germany, France, or Costa Rica, you must also be fairly fluent in the national language. In five of the countries above, the work must take place within a specified four- to seven-month period, usually including summer. For a reasonable fee, CIEE will obtain your work authorization and give you a list of potential employers, general tips on employment, and information on living in the country. An on-site CIEE representative will help with job-hunting and finding lodging. If you're willing to take a subsistence-level job to support yourself and cover costs of some local travel, you should have no problem. If you want a job related to a special interest of yours, contact potential employers before leaving home.

CIEE also sponsors work camps from late June to early September in Europe, North Africa, and a few other places. You work on a local project in return for free room and board. In addition to the merits of the project, you meet people from other countries, learn some foreign language, and experience another culture. Typical projects include restoration of historical sites, well-digging, road building, housing rehabilitation, archeological digs, historic preservation, forestry, and working with children, elderly persons and people with disabilities. For most countries you must be over eighteen but need not be a student.

Many books provide guidance concerning overseas jobs. See, for example: *Teaching English Abroad* and *Work Your Way Around the World* by Susan Griffiths; *Directory to Overseas Employment* from Transitions Abroad (800-562-1973); *The Directory of Jobs and Careers Abroad* by Alex Lepinski; *The Almanac of International Jobs and Careers* by Ronald and Caryl Krannich; and *Jobs for People who Love to Travel,* Impact Publications (703-361-7300). English-language newspapers published abroad, such as the *International Herald Tribune* and the *South China Post* in Hong Kong, list job opportunities. If you meet the requirements listed for a job, the employer will arrange a work permit.

Be skeptical of ads in U.S. newspapers promising high-paying jobs abroad.

They may be legitimate—or may be the first move in a scam intended to extract money from you. If you line up a job through correspondence, satisfy yourself, perhaps through a reconnaissance trip, that you know enough about the foreign country to be sure it's worth making the commitment.

MORE BEFORE YOU GO

Rail Passes

A rail pass may SAVE MONEY, make travel easier, increase your flexibility, and enable you to lock in a major travel cost for budgeting purposes. Or it may be a waste of money. We'll discuss how to figure out if a pass would be a good purchase for your next trip.

Although rail passes are available for use in Canada, Japan, and Australia, among other places, you are most likely to consider them for use in Europe since the rail network there is comprehensive, fast, and comfortable, and the variety of passes is so great.

Think about rail passes before you go. Since rail passes are often intended to be an inducement for tourists, some must be purchased outside the country where they'll be used. For example, a Eurailpass is supposed to be purchased outside Europe—and that's the safest thing to do. However, Eurailpasses are also sold at some major European railway stations at about 20 percent more than the U.S. price. The *Eurail Traveller's Guide* lists a limited number of places where you may be able to purchase a pass in Europe and Euraid Tourist Information offices may also be able to help. Most other types of rail passes can be bought in Europe.

For much more information on determining whether buying a rail pass is a good way to SAVE MONEY for your trip, see Chapter 6.

Airline Tickets

Since airfare is such a major part of travel costs, it's one of the best opportunities to use your knowledge to SAVE MONEY. When flying domestically, most people call a travel agent and buy tickets for their whole itinerary. For international travel, the matter is not so simple since booking everything at home may cost you the opportunity of buying tickets abroad at lower prices. It may also commit you to being at certain airports on certain dates, curtailing flexibility and freedom. Whether to pack that albatross in your luggage deserves serious thought.

There are several situations in which you *should* buy your airline tickets before leaving home:

1. When you're going to an area where flights are infrequent, which means they're often fully booked. One approach is to buy fully refundable tickets in the United States for the entire itinerary, treating the extra cost of refundability as an insurance premium. If you can buy a segment

cheaper as you travel, buy it and get a refund on that segment when you get home. If you can't buy a significantly cheaper ticket, you won't be left standing in the airport.

2. When an air pass must be bought before arriving in the country in which you'll use it.
3. When you want to fly as a courier.
4. When you'll be traveling to or from a popular resort area in high season.

For much more information on buying airline tickets, see How to Choose and Work with A Travel Agent (Chapter 2) and How to SAVE MONEY on Air Fares (Chapter 6).

Travel and Health Insurance

Let's face it, insurance is not a fun topic. Nevertheless, I suggest spending a little time thinking about it because a few people do experience losses while traveling. A camera disappears, there's a bill for medical services in a foreign hospital, or it becomes necessary to cancel a trip after sending in a large deposit. The odds are highly in your favor that none of this will happen, and in later chapters we'll discuss how to make the odds even better. Still, a prudent traveler should at least understand insurance options.

As with other forms of insurance, terms of travel insurance are understood by practically no one, at least not until after a loss. Let's change that by dividing travel insurance into three types of coverage: personal property; trip interruption or cancellation; and medical.

Personal Property

You may already have some personal property coverage for losses overseas; check your homeowners, renters, or automobile insurance, or the fine print in your credit card agreements. If not, many insurance companies offer a low-cost rider to an existing policy.

If you're not covered, should you buy insurance? The answer depends on how insurance-conscious you are at home, how inherently risky your trip will be, what risks would be covered, and the premium. If you insure everything to the hilt at home, you may be disposed to buy insurance for peace of mind.

If you're undecided, consider how much you have at stake

Ask if your policy covers losses overseas.

and what risks you would be insuring against.

To provide perspective, the insurance industry reports that half of all claims relate to loss of baggage and personal effects, and, as you'll see in Chapter 13, airlines accept only limited liability for luggage they lose. If you have coverage, remember that it has a deductible. On balance, insurance that covers lost baggage alone seems disproportionately expensive to me, especially considering the exclusions.

Terms of insurance policies vary widely. Ask *exactly* what would be covered. Lost luggage? Lost cash? What about the loss of specific items, including a camera, jewelry, or other valuables? Would you need a police report to make a claim? What about costs incurred by delays? Would you be covered for harm you cause to others and their possessions, perhaps through use of a motor vehicle? What exclusions are there (if, for example, you travel through certain territories)?

The scope of coverage matters. For example, a standard policy covers luggage only if you can prove it was stolen, while an "all risks" policy covers you whatever the cause of loss. Since no insurance policy will reimburse you for loss of your journal, exposed film, or passport, the best coverage is to stay alert.

Trip Interruption or Cancellation

What are the odds you'll have a claim for trip cancellation or interruption? The National Tour Association says that only one in 100,000 individuals who book tours might be affected by failure of the tour company. On the other hand, the U.S. Tour Operators Association estimates those odds are as high as one in twenty. Figure that out. Travel Guard International, an insurer, reports that approximately 3 percent of people who buy trip cancellation insurance actually cancel a trip.

For most travelers who cancel a trip just before departure, loss might consist of hotel reservation deposits or a nonrefundable airline ticket. The bigger loser would be someone who had made a nonrefundable payment for a cruise or tour. Further, if you have to change your flight schedule midtrip, the extra cost could be substantial. Only you know how likely it is that health or business obligations might interfere with your trip and whether the odds suggest buying cancellation/interruption insurance.

Some policies bury exclusions as if they were land mines, so read the fine print. To do that, you need a copy of the complete policy, not a summary prepared by the marketing department. Take it for granted that an insurer will interpret the policy strictly against you.

Here's what you want to know. If a travel agent can't answer your questions satisfactorily, call the insurance company yourself.

- When would coverage begin and end? Coverage of some policies ends seventy-two hours before the trip starts. If you were forced to cancel after that, you'd be out of luck.

- Under what conditions would the policy reimburse you for penalties and deposits if you canceled after your deposit with the tour operator became nonrefundable? Would a personal or business conflict, or change of heart, qualify? A policy that would reimburse you in case of voluntary cancellation could be extremely expensive.

- Would you be covered if illness, injury, or death (yours or your companion's), or some other major problem at home, caused cancellation or interruption of your trip? Would proof of medical reasons be required? Would you be covered for extra trip costs incurred as a result of disaster striking a close family member?

- Would the policy cover you if a pre-existing medical condition forced you to cancel the trip? A typical definition of such a condition is "any ailment for which a person was treated by a doctor, or for which he took prescribed medication, during a specific time period." Some policies will not reimburse you if the pre-existing condition that caused the loss existed between 30 and 180 days before you purchased the policy. If you have a pre-existing condition, look for a policy that will cover you if that condition has been controlled by medication. The pre-existing exclusion applies, of course, to the traveler and companion, but is often broadened to include family members at home. Application of the pre-existing exclusion has prompted so many complaints that companies are abandoning it (this is discussed later).

- Would you be covered if unexpected problems along your route, such as a hurricane, terrorism, or a communicable disease, interfered with the trip?

- Are there other exclusions (e.g., drugs, hazardous activities, or war)?

- Would you be required to have a doctor certify your illness before you canceled?

- Could you extend the policy if you extended your trip?

- What sort of failure by the tour/cruise operator would result in payment to you? Exactly which of your expenses would be covered if the tour operator canceled? You want protection against failure to perform, not merely bankruptcy. By the way, you may get free protection against operator failure simply by paying with a credit card. If the operator fails, the charge can be removed from your account.

If an interruption is caused by the airline (say there's a mechanical problem or a pilot fails to show up sober, that sort of thing), the airline is not required to make any special effort on your behalf but it will usually do its best to speed you on your way—or feed and house you if necessary. If, however, the delay is caused by bad weather or heavy air traffic, airlines uniformly disclaim responsibility.

Trip cancellation/interruption insurance should include coverage for accidents, lost or stolen baggage, some evacuation cost coverage, and some medical coverage.

Trip cancellation/interruption insurance is not inexpensive. Premiums range from $5.50 to $8 for every $100 of coverage you want. Balance the premium for temporary coverage against what you have at stake: up-front money (e.g., a deposit on a tour, a cancellation fee charged by the tour operator if you drop out, or nonrefundable tickets) and the depreciated value of the belongings you are taking with you. And don't forget the deductible.

I've read letters to travel columnists praising trip cancellation/interruption insurance, but I've also read angry complaints that one policy or another didn't pay off. Tour operators recommend cancellation insurance because it keeps clients off their backs in case of a problem. Travel agents recommend travel insurance, but they may be earning a commission of as much as 35 percent of the premium by selling it to you.

You can SAVE MONEY if you use a travel agency that has purchased ASTA's Travel Reimbursement Protection Insurance. In that case, coverage may cost you nothing. Ask your agent or call (800) 285-1779.

There is also *package insurance* available that covers everything for a fee of about 7 percent of your *prepaid* expenses. If there are no tour costs involved, that means air fare, rail or air passes, and not much else. For tours, the premium cost of package insurance may be reasonable.

Tour operators assert that insurance supplied by them is somewhat less expensive and has more generous terms than individually purchased policies. Compare prices.

Medical

Whether overseas health insurance coverage is a good investment is such a personal decision that no general recommendation is possible. The State Department reports that of the sixteen million adult U.S. citizens who flew overseas in a recent year, twenty-three thousand were hospitalized abroad. That's 1½ out of each one thousand travelers. If we assume that a forty-five-year-old male with no specific threatening health problems is three times as likely to be hospitalized as the average traveler, he's still only likely to be hospitalized one out of every 222 trips.

Existing Coverage. If you already have health insurance, call the carrier to see what your policy covers overseas and what it doesn't. Most Blue Cross and Blue Shield plans cover some emergency care overseas and bills are sent directly to them. Medicare, on the other hand, does not cover anyone overseas.

What is Covered? Travel medical insurance typically pays for treatment of an illness incurred abroad, including prescription drugs. It may or may not pay for transportation of a family member to your bedside to assist you, for emergency evacuation, or for dental care.

If you consider buying coverage for overseas medical expenses, ask first about premiums, deductibles, and co-payments, then about possible exclusions of pre-existing conditions, sexually-transmitted diseases, injuries arising from civil war, and problems related to illegal drugs, pregnancy, and self-inflicted injuries. Ask whether travel in any particular countries is excluded.

If you have what might be considered a pre-existing medical condition, discuss the situation with the insurer. Some won't pay if you had a health problem during a specified time period prior to your trip and that condition was responsible for your later claim. Most companies that retain this exclusion use a relatively lenient sixty-day period (although some use ninety days or more and some even exclude conditions controlled by medication). Most policies provide coverage for pre-existing conditions if there have been neither symptoms nor treatment within the stated period prior to the trip; that is, for conditions that are stable or controlled.

The good news is that an increasing number of companies have recently begun waiving the pre-existing medical condition exclusion. However, they often have a requirement that coverage be purchased within twenty-four hours of payment of the first deposit on your trip. Therefore, if you want insurance coverage, you should identify an insurance company before you book the trip. Keep documentation of the timing in case you later need to make a claim.

Does the policy cover risk sports like scuba diving or skiing?

Ask the insurer whether you must call home for precertification for an elective or surgical procedure. You probably will, at least for nonemergencies. Ask whether the insurer requires a second opinion. Naturally, if you claim a loss due to health, you'll have to prove that health was the cause.

Some policies exclude coverage for injuries that arise from sports such as scuba diving, mountain climbing, and skiing. Some will include them if you pay an additional premium. The Diver's Alert Network (DAN; 800-446-2671) was established to cover divers for the costs of transportation/evacuation and treatment for the bends. DAN will also evacuate anyone, regardless of pre-existing conditions. The cost is $25 a year for an individual, $35 for a family.

If you decide to buy travel medical insurance, the amount of coverage should depend on whether your primary medical insurance will be in force. If it will, a policy for enough to cover its deductible should be sufficient. If not, premiums run about $3 to $5 per day for coverage of up to $100,000. For a small additional fee, you can usually buy lost luggage and trip cancellation/interruption riders to medical insurance.

Reimbursement or Direct Payment. Payment by an insurance company comes in two forms. In one case, you are reimbursed for expenses you've already paid, while in the other the company pays the medical care provider directly. This is an important distinction because if you incur medical expenses you are likely to be required to pay them on the spot—which will require cash, a direct-payment insurance policy, or possibly a credit card. Carrying evidence of reimbursement insurance may help delay payment, but don't count on it. If you plan to seek reimbursement for expenses, collect receipts for payments and documentation of diagnosis and treatments (these records will also assist your doctor at home).

Other Health-related Coverage

Emergency Evacuation. If you'll be taking above-average risks, such as climbing peaks in Torres del Paines, consider emergency evacuation coverage. Although most medical care abroad is fairly inexpensive, evacuation is not. From relatively remote areas of the Pacific, Asia, South America, or Africa, air evacuation could cost $30,000 to $50,000.

The Traveler's Emergency Network (TEN) will provide and pay for emergency evacuation (up to $45,000), including transport home if necessary, should a member become ill or injured when more than one hundred miles from home. They may advance you money to cover medical fees, but you'll have to reimburse them. They will also arrange reputable medical assistance, which can be every bit as valuable as airlifting you off the mountain. If you'll be hospitalized abroad for more than a week, TEN will pay round-trip expenses for someone you choose to fly to your side. TEN coverage is provided regardless of pre-existing conditions. The fee for these and other services is $30 a year for an individual, $50 for a family. For further information, call (800) 275-4836.

Medical Assistance Overseas. The MedPass program offered by Global Emergency Medical Services (800-860-1111) helps travelers connect with high-quality medical help when needed. Leave your medical records with them, call their hotline if you need assistance on the road, and they will connect you with a selected health care provider and send your records by fax. You pay for any treatment. At a cost of $75 per year plus $1 per travel day, compare it to what you get from the International Association for Medical Assistance to Travelers (see Chapter 8).

For a registration fee of $60 and an annual fee of $52, the Blood Care Foundation (Box 7, Sevenoaks, Kent TN13 2SZ, England; 44-732-742427) will immediately dispatch a safe supply of blood for transfusion to a traveler in need in any country. This could be of benefit in countries where blood is not safely screened for HIV and other diseases.

By the way, if you have a health problem that's not obvious, consider wearing a Medic Alert tag that signals medical personnel of allergies and special health conditions. The tag includes a telephone number which can be called for additional information about your condition. Call or write the Medic Alert Foundation if interested in the $35 tag (800-344-3226; P.O. Box 1009, Turlock, CA 95381).

Where to Buy Insurance

Insurance companies sell travel coverage policies directly, through travel agencies, or through tour/cruise operators (sometimes under the operator's name even though it is not the insurer). Don't make the decision on price alone. Take a close look at the breadth of coverage, the amount of coverage, the terms, and the extras. A good company will let you call collect if you need medical assistance and will provide direction to nearby medical care (and a translator if needed). It will also contact your family if you ask them to. If you decide you want health insurance, ask your travel agent's opinion as to the best carrier. Ask other travelers about their experiences.

The following are some of the better-known travel insurance companies:

- Access America (800-284-8300)
- American Express Travel Protection Plan (800-234-0375)
- Berkeley Care (800-645-2424)
- Carefree Travel Insurance (800-323-3149)
- Corporate Assist (800-756-5900)
- CSA (800-348-9505)
- Global Care (800-779-1017)
- Health Care Abroad (800-237-6615)
- Humana/WorldCare Travel Assistance (800-521-4882).
- International SOS Assistance (800-523-8930)
- Mutual of Omaha (800-775-6000)
- Nationwide (800-654-6700)
- Safe Passage International (800-777-7665)
- Tele-Trip (800-228-9792)
- The Travelers (800-243-3174)
- Travel Assistance International (800-821-2828)
- Travel Guard International (800-826-1300)
- Travel Insurance Services (800-937-1387)
- Travelers Insurance International (800-243-3174)
- TravMed/Medex Assistance (800-732-5309)
- Trip Mate (800-888-0432)

Figuring out what to do about insurance may be a minor hassle the first time around, but from then on it's easy.

On the subject of car rental insurance, please see Chapter 16.

Hotel Reservations

Most travelers venturing for the first time to foreign countries take it for granted they should make hotel reservations before leaving home. Travel agents say many of their clients make reservations for every night of the trip, while others reserve a hotel room for at least their first night out and the night before they fly home. Making reservations is common for travelers heading for an event likely to fill a city, such as Carnival in Rio or Octoberfest in Munich. Others make a reservation because they've heard that a certain hotel is so splendid they're willing to pay almost any price to stay there.

The bottom line: most people make reservations to reduce concern about the unknown. A reservation is a security blanket, ensuring there will be a room available in a safe location at an acceptable price. It also eliminates the need to spend time selecting lodgings on arrival, perhaps while struggling with an unfamiliar language.

If you decide to make reservations, consider whether you want a smoke-free room, a view, quiet, a certain floor, proximity to certain services, or whatever. If you're not dealing directly with the hotel desk, the operator may note your request but may not be able to guarantee that it will be met. Remember that you're likely to pay more, perhaps considerably more, for amenities such as a favored view.

Making Reservations

If a standard brand hotel is okay and you don't care much about the cost, it's probably easiest to let your travel agent handle the reservation. If you prefer to have a hand in the process, you need information.

- All of the U.S.-based hotel chains with international operations have *800 numbers*. However, you won't get the best deals by talking to a central 800 operator staring at a computer screen full of standard prices that don't reflect how eager a certain hotel is for your business. Nor is the operator likely to know many of the particulars of the hotel, such as the best rooms or views (let alone the location of noisy ice machines).

  Instead, call 800 information (800-555-1212) for the direct dial number of the hotel location you want. Many of the international chains based in other countries also have 800 numbers in the United States. After the hotel quotes a rate, ask about special package deals, corporate rates, and other discounts. Say you are willing to pay a certain amount and ask what they have available. By the way, listen carefully to whether you are quoted a "double occupancy" rate or a "double room" rate. The former means that each of two people pays the quoted amount; the latter is the total price of the room.

- *UTELL International* (800-448-8355) is an international reservation service that has connections with over sixty-five hundred hotels in 140 countries (about eleven hundred hotels are in the United States). Its hotels range from small independents to international chains and from tourist class to deluxe. In France you can choose from among four hundred UTELL hotels, while in Gambia your only choice is the Atlantic Hotel Banjul (hey, they say it has four stars). There's no separate fee for using this service.

- *INNterREST* on the Microsoft Network enables users to make reservations for hotels and other travel products around the world. It provides Web site addresses for participating hotels so users can access more information about each hotel chain. It also has a restaurant database.

- Call the U.S. representative of the *Tourist Board* of the country in which you're interested. Most are associated with their embassies in Washington DC. Ask for a list of hotels and also for personal recommendations.

- Good *guidebooks* list phone numbers of recommended hotels. However, these numbers are more useful if you're calling Scotland than Shanghai (the language barrier becomes a little more formidable on long distance).

- Check out lodging used by interesting *tour operators* for their tours (since they obviously approve of the property and the management). For example, the *Backroads* brochure lists a fine group of European inns at which its bicycle tours stop for the night.

- Travel agencies have *lists of hotels* overseas as well as access to a computer-based service on which thousands of hotels are listed. Fax machines minimize language barriers and let a travel agent exchange information with foreign hotels quickly and easily. Since travel agents may receive a commission from the hotel, be careful that their suggestions match your preferences.

- In *bookstores* or *libraries,* take a look at books that review international lodging (e.g., *Country Inns and Castles*).

- We discussed making hotel reservations via *online services* or the *Internet* in the Internet section of Chapter 2. To repeat, it's unlikely you'll get the most favorable prices via computer (in fact, you may pay a surcharge). Further, computer reservations don't always 'take,' which you won't discover until you arrive late on a rainy night.

Reasons Not to Make Reservations

Are there reasons not to make reservations? Many travelers suggest four main arguments against doing so.

- If a hotel abroad has spent enough on advertising to be known here and to make a reservation easy, its rates are likely to be pretty high. According to *The Wall Street Journal*, rates of "name" international hotels are setting all-time records. Even U.S. rates seem out of control: a suite at The Ritz-Carlton in San Francisco rents for $600 a night; The Mark Hotel in Manhattan is $625. It's a cinch that restaurant prices in those hotels average $50 a meal or more. Is that in your budget?

  It could be a mistake to assume that reasonably priced domestic hotel chains are equally reasonable overseas. For example, the Best Western in Paris was $180 per night for what the *Journal* described as a "room with chipped paint and no shower curtain." Quality Inn charged $160 a night in Rome and Best Western $135 in New Delhi. If you are disposed to stay in a chain hotel, don't make assumptions about the international price.

  In the end, you'll spend a lot more on hotel rooms if you make reservations from home.

- Upscale hotels overseas tend to be cocoons for well-heeled tourists, insulating them from the rich texture of local life.

- A reservation is unnecessary except in a few very popular destinations or during some special event.
- More important than the other disadvantages, a reservation is a commitment to be at a certain place on a specified date. That may not sound bad before you leave home, but it can become a serious restriction on your freedom once you're traveling.

After traveling for a while, the security of having a reservation no longer feels necessary. You know what to expect. You've learned that lodging is easy to find locally through guidebooks, tourist information offices, other travelers, and your own common sense. Throughout the world, hotels, lodges, inns, guest houses, pensions, bungalows, youth hostels, and a dozen other forms of lodging, compete vigorously for your business. Something will be available with the amenities and price that suit you. As you reminisce years from now, you'll remember the funky, family-style lodging and its proprietors, not international chains.

Exceptions

There are a few circumstances in which even an experienced traveler might want to make advance reservations:

- If you'll be flying into a city late at night and flying out early the next day, you may prefer to know for sure where you'll lay your head.

- While you don't need reservations to travel happily in Europe, you can, on rare occasions, wind up in a charmless dump without one.

- If your destination is a specific resort.

- A woman arriving solo in some destinations, especially late in the evening, may prefer to be going to a known destination.

Other than these exceptions, I recommend the freedom of winging it.

To SAVE MONEY when booking rooms, see Chapter 6. If you decide to find lodging as you travel, see Chapter 11 for an extensive discussion of how to find superior, affordable lodging anywhere in the world and how to ensure you get it at a fair price.

Adventures

By adventures, I'm referring to short-term activities such as safaris, whitewater river trips, treks, and so on. The decision you must make in the planning phase is whether to make arrangements at home, usually through a tour operator, or to do your own research to see whether you can arrange things when you get there. It's probably easier to do it at home, but that will result in a different experience and be more expensive.

People pay higher prices to avoid uncertainty when arriving in a foreign country with limited time, and that's understandable. Time is also a factor. If you set up something at home, you hit the ground running when you get there. Otherwise, you may burn a day or two getting an activity organized locally. If you want to trek in Thailand, you can set it up in the afternoon and leave with a guide the next morning. For an African safari, you might have to wait several days until the next one leaves. Raft trips in Costa Rica leave on set days of the week. Adventures like these are extremely easy to arrange locally—and considerably less expensive than if done at home.

Arranging an adventure when at or near the local site is an excellent way to SAVE MONEY. I've often saved 50 percent or more compared to what I'd have paid for a similar, though probably more luxurious, trip had I booked it at home through a tour operator or travel agent. Yet many people routinely have someone make these arrangements for them, paying dearly for advertising, intermediaries, and upscale amenities.

The time will quickly come when you'll be comfortable arranging mini-adventures while abroad. It requires a little effort but it's not nearly as difficult as it appears. In foreign countries, outfitters and tour operators seek you out, often willing to tailor their services to your desires.

If cost is the controlling factor, you're better off making arrangements locally. If time is more important, it may be to your advantage to sign up for an adventure before you leave home. If you see an adventure that appeals to you, say in a guidebook, and you want to book it at home, select a tour operator or outfitter as we discussed in Chapter 4. For a discussion of how to SAVE MONEY when arranging an adventure, see Chapter 6.

The steps necessary to go into action are very manageable. Obtaining a passport and visas is simple when you know the routine. If you want a job abroad, need a permit, or want to buy a rail or bus pass, you now know how to go about it. Making travel and health insurance decisions requires research and attention to details, but doing it once makes the decisions easy for later trips. You know the factors to consider when deciding when to buy airline tickets, whether to make hotel reservations, and when to book adventures.

What Needs to Be Done When

12 months before D (Departure) Date
__Start initial planning for your trip.
__Start setting money aside.
__Start collecting information.
__Start interviewing travel agents.
__Start studying languages, if appropriate.
__Start talking with travelers.

6 months before D Date
__Rough out your itinerary and the length and cost of your trip.
__Select your travel agent.
__Research air fares, tour options, and insurance.
__Have passport photos taken and start the process of getting a passport.
__Read literature from and about countries you may visit.
__Review guidebooks.
__Determine what shots you'll want and when the sequence should start (Chapter 8).
__If you're in marginal physical condition, begin increasing your physical activity.

3 months before D Date
__Firm up your itinerary.
__Obtain a credit card and ATM card.
__Start getting visas.
__Make decisions about your gear and begin assembling it.
__Add to your travel information file.
__Collect addresses of people to contact abroad.
__Increase your physical activity; build your stamina.
__Choose someone to look after your affairs while you're away.
__If you have a Will, update it if appropriate.

2 months before D Date
__Decide whether you want an International Drivers License, Youth Hostel card, and/or International Student ID card. Get the ones you choose.

__Take medical and dental exams.
__Start inoculations.
__Complete research and make airline reservations.
__Buy any new clothing and equipment you need.
__Decide whether additional insurance is appropriate.
__Test new equipment, especially shoes and camera.
__Set aside a place to pile travel gear; start piling.

1 month before D Date
__Buy airline tickets; get seat assignments.
__Buy film.
__Buy medical supplies.
__Make photocopies of appropriate documents and distribute them.
__Complete inoculations.
__Prepare for closing your house or apartment.
__Make financial arrangements (someone to pay bills, pay credit card charges, etc.).
__Give necessary documents to the person who will be taking care of things.

2 weeks before D Date
__Buy travelers checks.
__Organize gear for packing; see if it will fit in your luggage.
__Schedule suspension of utilities, subscriptions, and other services.
__Arrange for mail to be forwarded.

Final week
__Shut down your home (Chapter 9).
__Send your itinerary to those who should have it.
__Complete packing at least three days before departure.
__Confirm all flights; ensure you have all tickets and other documents.
__Say your good-byes.

6

Money

Not all those who wander are lost.
— J.R.R. Tolkien
Fellowship of the Ring

Would cutting the cost by $1,000 make your dream trip affordable? You'll learn how to save that much and more in this chapter. What we're about to discuss will buy you more time, distance, and adventure—yet not cost you one extra cent! This chapter is filled with suggestions about how to SAVE MONEY, prepare a reliable budget, and manage your money successfully as you travel.

If you assume that it costs a fortune to travel internationally, and money matters, you're likely to conclude that you can't afford to travel. Unless you know what you're doing, you might be right. Unhappily, it's getting ever more expensive for the uninformed to travel. In the United States, according to the Dow Jones Travel Index in early 1996, business air fares increased 43 percent in 1995 and leisure air fares went up 48 percent. During the same time period, higher occupancy rates made hotel managers more bold about charging domestic travelers close to rack rates. In other words, it's rough out there—at least for the unwary. It takes a well-informed traveler to avoid outrageous prices, both at home and abroad.

I'm going to begin this chapter with three thoughts about saving money:

1. If you have a choice, it would be a mistake to travel in the cheapest way possible. A miserly trip can exact a high price on your health and state of mind.

2. Some people assume that traveling on a low to moderate budget assures a meaningful trip. Not true. It does provide many opportunities for personal contact with local people, but it's up to you to take advantage of those opportunities.

3. When we discuss getting the most for your money, it is always in the context of accomplishing your goals for the trip and having a great time.

HOW TO SAVE MONEY

Saving Money on Air Fare

Let's start with the premise that you need never pay full fare for any ticket to anywhere. It's up to you. You may not believe that now, but I'll bet you will by the time you reach the end of this chapter.

Bucket Shops

Elsewhere in the world, savvy travelers buy airline tickets in "bucket shops," a term applied to agencies that sell normal airline tickets at heavily discounted prices. Among cities renowned for bucket shops are Amsterdam, Athens, Bangkok, Calcutta, Hong Kong, London, Nairobi, Penang, and Singapore. When you walk into a bucket shop abroad, you're unlikely to mistake it for the American Express office. The decor is usually Spartan and the clerk's manner a bit, shall we say, brisk. They know you're there because of price, not pretty paintings on the wall or small talk.

The bucket shop I used in Calcutta consisted of two desks and a computer set up on a landing halfway up the first flight of stairs in a budget hotel. That seemed a little shaky, but they handed me authentic tickets in return for my money.

By the way, if the ticket available happens to be on an airline you haven't heard of, don't assume there's something wrong with it. For example, the 747s of Air Garuda (Indonesia) and Varig Air (Brazil) can compete in service and reliability with planes used anywhere in the world. If you are concerned, call the FAA to see if an airline is on its "not permitted to land in the United States" list.

Here are a few leads, not endorsements, from among dozens of established bucket shops:

- In Singapore: GASI Travel, 12 Devonshire Road (tel. 65-734-0133)
- In Amsterdam: Malibu Travel, Damrak 30 (tel. 31-20-623-2977)
- In London: Major Travel, 28/34 Fortess Road, Kentish Town (tel. 071-482-4840)
- In Athens: Inter Trust Travel, 43 Nikis Street (tel. 30-1-322-8181).

Consolidators

Here's the great news: there's a little-known equivalent to the bucket shop in the United States. The domestic versions are called "consolidators" and they have plenty of heavily discounted tickets available. Since you pay 15 to 60 percent less than published air fare prices, buying from a consolidator is a vitally important way to SAVE MONEY. Exactly how much you save depends on your destination, the time of year, and the day of the week on which you want to leave. The deal you get also depends on the research you do, the questions you ask, and your persistence. Consolidator prices may even be somewhat negotiable; some consolidators will give up a little of their profit to close a sale. It's still a good deal for them because they thrive on high volume.

From experience, airlines know when to expect large numbers of empty seats. Since an unfilled seat is worth nothing to them, they allocate blocks of tickets to consolidators to sell at below-market prices. To avoid offending full-fare flyers, airlines don't advertise this practice. Instead, they contract with consolidators to sell tickets for prices they would never publish on the Computer Reservations System (CRS) from which travel agents draw fares. Consolidator tickets aren't sold behind the airlines' backs. They are part of overall yield management by the airlines to maximize their profits. All you have to do to take advantage of these low fares is to know how to find and evaluate them. And you're about to find out.

The airlines allocate tickets to consolidators at very low fares or simply give consolidators a high commission. In the latter case, part of the commission is passed on to you in the form of a lower fare (which is why you may have some negotiating room).

Even though consolidators' prices are consistently excellent, airlines in the midst of a price war or major promotion may temporarily make prices of certain tickets competitive with consolidator prices. However, as we've all learned, tickets available at "price war" prices may be as plentiful as hens' teeth.

Price wars can make consolidator's tickets less appealing.

Unfortunately, a few consolidators follow the same practice. When you ask for the ticket at the price they've advertised, they can't deliver. I understand that they have only a limited number of tickets and may sell out quickly, but if I sense a come-on, that consolidator never hears from me again.

If you see an ad, call the consolidator or take the ad to a travel agency and ask them to get the ticket for you at the advertised price. The majority of consolidators will deal directly with individuals, while the rest sell only through tour operators or travel agents. In either case, your travel agent can make the purchase for you if you prefer and don't mind paying a small markup. Since the fare isn't in the CRS, travel agents have to do a little more work than with standard tickets, but they get commissions from the consolidator. In the past, many travel agents haven't taken advantage of consolidator tickets even though they would benefit clients because they wanted to maintain their historic relationships with the airlines. With commission caps that may change.

Consolidators are located everywhere from a tiny office in Santa Ana, California, to substantial suites in New York City, Los Angeles, and Washington, DC. Many advertise in newspapers such as *The New York Times, The Washington Post,* and *Los Angeles Times,* and periodicals such as *Travel Weekly.* Check your bookstore or library. The best resource I know of is *Fly for Less: The Only Complete Guide to Selecting Reliable Consolidators and Wholesalers Who Offer Bargain Airfares* ($19.95), by Gary Schmidt. It's in some bookstores or you can call the publisher (800-241-9299). The Better Business Bureau of New York publishes a booklet entitled *Advisory on Ticket Consolidators* (257 Park Avenue South, New York, NY 10010; $3.50).

In addition to low prices, another potential advantage in buying a ticket from a consolidator is that its contract with an airline may permit it to waive advance purchase or Saturday night stayover requirements, a real bonus for seize-the-opportunity travelers. These tickets sometimes even count toward frequent flier mileage. The terms of a consolidator's tickets are frequently *less* restrictive with respect to penalties for cancellation or changes than a standard ticket bought from an airline at a higher price. Nevertheless, be sure you understand any restrictions and penalties. For example, it's not unusual for a consolidator to impose a "last minute" (meaning within seven days of departure) booking fee and a penalty if you cancel a ticket just before departure.

If you can't find the discounted tickets you want at home, buy them on the road. For one complicated trip throughout Southeast Asia, I bought an ordinary ticket in the United States for only the first leg of the trip. By purchasing the rest of my tickets at bucket shops in Singapore and Bangkok, I saved almost $800 over what I would have paid had I purchased regular tickets in the United States for all segments. For other trips, I've saved thousands by buying consolidator tickets for the entire trip.

You can usually pay for tickets purchased in London's bucket shops or from U.S. consolidators with a credit card. Doing so would enable you to cancel the charge if the ticket didn't arrive or the consolidator went bankrupt. A few U.S. consolidators insist on payment by cash or check in order to avoid paying the credit card discount. Others accept credit cards but add a small

Potential Drawbacks to Consolidators

There are several potential drawbacks in dealing with a consolidator:

- Occasionally you don't get frequent flyer mileage credit.
- You may not be able to get an advance seat assignment.
- Your choice of airlines and flight times may be restricted.
- The route you fly may not be the most direct. There may be an overnight stop before you reach your destination.
- Tickets often cannot be transferred or exchanged (at least not without a fee).
- If your flight is canceled, it's unlikely you will be able to transfer easily to another airline.

charge to cover the discount. In most of the rest of the world, you pay in cash. In that case, hold on to your money until you have a ticket in hand.

After you've made your reservation with a consolidator, wait a day, then confirm with the airline that it holds a reservation in your name. Avoid anxiety by insisting on delivery of the ticket well ahead of your departure date. When you receive it, check that flight numbers, times, and dates are correct. Ensure that your status is shown as "OK," which means you have a confirmed seat (rather than being wait listed). Again, confirm directly with the airline.

I haven't had a problem with consolidators or bucket shops nor do I know anyone who has. The few problems I've read about in the United States generally concern transactions between a travel agent and a consolidator which has gone bankrupt, taking ticket payments with it. Of course, travel agents, cruise lines, and airlines go bankrupt from time to time as well. Use common sense, trust your intuition, and ask questions:

- Where is your office located (street address, not a post office box)?
- How long have you been in business?
- With what airlines do you have contracts?
- Whom can I contact at the airlines to vouch for your firm?
- Is your firm accredited with the ARC and IATAN?
- Are you bonded? If so, for how much?

If you still have any doubts, call the Better Business Bureau where the firm is located, check with travel agents, or call the American Society of Travel Agents consumer affairs department.

Consolidators have formed the Airline Consolidators Association which may become a self-regulating body. They contemplate a default protection program, similar to what some tour operators have, to compensate agents and consumers if a member goes out of business.

There are two types of organizations which could be mistaken for consolidators. The first is a ticket *broker*. Unlike a consolidator, a broker has no contract with the airlines. Instead, a broker locates cheap tickets, often buying from consolidators, and resells them to the public. If a ticket broker is undercapitalized, it may be somewhat risky to deal with that broker. One giveaway is a broker who won't send you a ticket until receiving your money. The second is actually a *wholesaler*, a tour operator who will also sell "air only" tours; that is, a tour that consists of nothing but the airline ticket. They possess low-cost tickets because they buy in volume from airlines to serve their tours. If they have excess tickets, you can get an excellent price.

There are almost two hundred true consolidators (excluding ticket brokers and travel agencies who claim to be consolidators but aren't). All sell to travel agencies, while about 60 percent sell to individuals as well. The following list of consolidators excludes many of the smallest and newest, and those that are neither bonded nor accredited by ARC or IATAN. Consolidators tend to specialize in geographic regions, so seek out ones most suitable for your trip. I'm not endorsing any consolidator by including it on the list below, but I've had successful experiences with every one I've used.

Major Consolidators

Air Brokers International	(800) 883-3273	Around-the-World, South Pacific *#
Alta Tours	(800) 338-4191	Europe, Latin America *#
AmeriCorp Travel Professionals	(800) 299-5284	CIS, Asia, Africa, Latin America *#
Asensio Tours	(800) 221-7679	Latin America *#
Campus Connections	(800) 428-3235	Low fares in the United States for ages 12 to 25.
Campus Travel Center	(800) 328-3359	Europe, South Pacific *#
Centrav	(800) 874-2033	Europe, Mid-East, Latin America Africa, South Pacific. Agents only. *#
Chartours	(800) 323-4444	Europe, Mid-East, Africa, Latin America, North America #
Consolidated Tours	(800) 228-0877	Europe. Agents only. *#
Council Travel	(212) 661-1450	Asia, Latin America, Europe, United States. A travel agency that deals with consolidators; 40 offices.
D-FW Tours	(800) 527-2589	Europe, Mid-East, Asia, Africa, Latin America. Agents only. *#
Diplomat Tours	(800) 727-8687	Europe, Latin America, Asia, North America, Africa. Agents only. *#
Euram Tours	(800) 848-6789	Africa, South Pacific, Europe, Latin America, North America, Africa.*#
Fare Deals Travel	(800) 347-7006	Africa, Asia, Europe, Latin America, South Pacific #
Getaway Travel	(800) 683-6336	Mid-East, Africa, Asia, Latin America. *#
GIT Travel	(800) 228-1777	Europe, Africa, Russia, Latin America. *#
GTI Travel Consolidators	(800) 829-8234	Asia, Eastern Europe. *#
Holbrook Travel	(800) 451-7111	Africa, Latin America. *#
Interworld Travel	(800) 468-3796	Africa, Latin America, Europe. *#
J & O Air	(800) 877-8111	Europe, Asia, Latin America, South Pacific. Agents only. *#

Jetset Tours	(800) 638-3273	Europe, Australia/New Zealand, Asia, Africa, Circle Pacific. Agents only. *#
Magical Holidays	(800) 433-7773	Europe, Africa, Latin America, Asia. *#
New Frontiers	(800) 366-6387	Specializes in Europe. *
Overseas Express	(800) 343-4873	Europe, Asia, Latin America, Africa. *#
Picasso Travel	(800) PICASSO	Europe, Mid-East, Africa, Latin America, South Pacific, Africa. *#
Premier Travel Services	(800) 545-1910	Latin America, South Pacific, Africa, Mid-East, Europe. #
Rahim Tours	(800) 556-5305	Eastern Europe, Russia, CIS, China, Mongolia, Scandinavia. *#
Skytours	(800) 246-8687	Europe. *#
South Pacific Express Travels	(800) 321-7739	South Pacific, North America. *#
STA Travel	(800) 825-3001	Europe, Mid-East, Africa, Asia, Latin America, North America, South Pacific. STA offers substantial discounts to anyone under 25 and to students under age 30 (or up to age 34 on some airlines). Agents only. #
STT Worldwide Travel	(800) 348-0886	Africa, Asia, Europe, Russia, Latin America, North America, South Pacific. *#
Thompson Express. C.L.	(213) 628-9550	Europe, Mid-East, South Pacific, Latin America, North America, Africa. Agents only. #
Trans Am Travel	(800) 822-7600	Europe, Mid-East, Africa, Latin America, Asia, South Pacific. *#
Travac Tours	(800) 872-8800	Europe, Mid-East, Africa. #
Travel Center	(800) 419-0960	Asia, Africa, Latin America, North America, South Pacific. *#
Travel N Tours	(800) 854-5400	Europe, Africa, Latin America, Asia. *# Agents only.
Travnet	(800) 359-6388	Asia, South Pacific. Agents only. *#
UniTravel	(800) 325-2222	Europe, Latin America, North America, Asia, Africa. Agents only#
Up & Away Travel	(800) 275-8001	Europe, Mid-East, Latin America, North America, South Pacific.*#
Worldwide Travel	(800) 343-0038	Europe, Mid-East, Africa, Asia. *#

Note: * means the agency has bond coverage, although it may be as low as $30,000; and # means accreditation by ARC and/or IATAN

For names of more consolidators:

- look in the travel section of major newspapers,
- call any airline and ask for names of consolidators with whom they have contracts,
- send $3.50 to Travel Consolidators (Better Business Bureau of Metro New York, 257 Park Avenue South, New York, NY 10010) for its *Advisory on Ticket Consolidators,*
- read *Fly There for Less: How to Slash the Cost of Air Travel Worldwide* (Bob Martin, Teak Press; $18.95) which lists consolidators and makes a variety of money-saving suggestions, or *Fly for Less* (cited above),
- take a look at *Best Fares*, a discount air fare magazine (817-261-6114),
- order *Airline Consolidators Quick Reference Chart* which lists forty consolidators ($5 from On the Go Publishing, P.O. Box 091033, Dept. A11, Columbus, OH 43209)
- read the regular *Consumer Reports Travel Letter* on domestic and international consolidators.

Global Discount Travel Services, a relatively new agency, is said to sell TWA domestic and international (Europe and Mexico) tickets at 25 percent less than whatever TWA charges for the same ticket (even during fare wars). There are rumors that this discount, available as a result of a complex legal settlement, may drop to 20 percent. For information, call (800) 497-6678 or write 4052 South Industrial Road, Las Vegas, NV 89103.

Flightpath USA has a database of more than 200,000 airfares offered by more than thirty consolidators, which it makes available to subscribing travel agents. Using this database streamlines the process of finding the best fare, and Flightpath says it weeds out any consolidators with questionable reputations. If your travel agent is not a subscriber, call Flightpath directly (703-812-9500) for a listing of travel agents located near you who do subscribe. This service is worth looking into.

If you deal with a travel agency, remind them as often as necessary to find discounted tickets for you; not merely low published rates, but discounted rates. If your agent doesn't have contacts with consolidators, try elsewhere or buy the tickets yourself. Any traveler who doesn't learn about and utilize consolidator tickets is missing the biggest money saver of all.

APEX Fares

Advance purchase excursion (APEX) are sold by airlines and travel agents These fares are inexpensive when compared to the cost of regular tickets, but, by definition, they must be purchased well ahead of departure date. Procrastinate and you lose the APEX option. The advance-purchase requirement is usually twenty-one days, but can fluctuate between seven and thirty days.

The lower price is a trade-off for accepting certain restrictions that vary airline to airline and month to month. APEX tickets may have minimum and maximum length of stay requirements, plus restrictions on, or penalties for, making schedule changes (in departure date, itinerary, etc.) after you've bought the ticket. If you buy an APEX ticket and don't use it, you may lose the entire purchase price, or at least have to pay a substantial penalty.

An advantage of many APEX tickets is that they are "open jaw." That means the ticket permits you to fly from home to one city and return home from a different city without paying a penalty. For example, if you've flown to Nairobi and traveled overland to southern Africa, you can fly home from Johannesburg rather than returning all the way to Nairobi to leave for home. An open jaw ticket saves considerable travel time and money.

Other Bargain Air Fares

No Frills Carriers. Whether traveling to a domestic destination or connecting with an international flight, SAVE MONEY by using a no frills carrier. Expect a little less leg room and a lunch that consists of a bag of peanuts and a soft drink—in return for saving hundreds of dollars. This is an area in which a travel agent may not be your best friend because the commission for booking a cut-rate flight may not be enticing. Further, tickets for some of these carriers must be filled in by hand rather than by computer, which doesn't thrill many agents. Of course, no frills airlines such as Southwest Airlines are already in the vanguard of ticketless travel.

If your travel agent routinely suggests only the major carriers, ask for information on some of the no frills carriers listed on the following page. If it's not forthcoming, call yourself.

For flights in the United Kingdom and nine European countries, it's difficult to beat the fares of *British Midland Airlines.* However, to get the lowest fare you must purchase your ticket before reaching United Kingdom or Europe. To learn more about this reputable airline, call (800) 788-0555.

Similarly, *Icelandair* has offered low fares to generations of travelers between the United States and Europe. As a bonus, you get to see Iceland from the air. Call (800) 223-5500.

Last-minute Brokers. Distress situations are another good source of discounts. An airline or cruise ship that has vacancies at the last minute is likely to offer major discounts. To take advantage of them, you have to be flexible regarding your departure date. Here are a few of the many last-minute brokers:

- *Discount Travel International* (800-334-9294): $45 membership; claims discounts of 15 to 60 percent off published rates for international airfare and cruises; 5 percent off domestic air fare rates

Major No Frills Air Carriers

America West	(800) 235-9292	Coast-to-coast, Mexico, Vancouver, BC
Carnival	(800) 824-7386	New York, California, Florida, Caribbean
Continental	(800) 525-0280	Coast-to-coast, international
Kiwi	(800) 538-5494	Midwest, East Coast
Midway	(800) 446-4392	Midwest, Northeast
Midwest Express	(800) 452-2022	Milwaukee, Midwest, coast-to-coast
Reno Air	(800) 736-6247	West Coast
Southwest Airlines	(800) 435-9792	Coast-to-coast
Sun Jet	(800) 478-6538	Texas, California, Florida
Tower Air	(800) 221-2500	Coast-to-coast, several international destinations
USAir	(800) 428-4322	Coast-to-coast
ValuJet	(800) 825-8538	Seventeen southern cities

- *Entertainment Hot Line Travel Club* (313-637-9780): annual fee of $35; claims up to 65 percent off market prices
- *Last Minute Travel* (800-527-8646): no fee, but operates primarily in the Caribbean
- *Moment's Notice* (212-486-0500): yearly fee of $25; claims discounts of 15 to 50 percent; claims airfare discounts of up to 60 percent
- *Vacations To Go* (800-338-4962): membership $19.95; good discounts, but mostly on cruises
- *Worldwide Discount Travel Club* (305-534-2082)

Standby. Standby brokers are similar to distress brokers. I know of the following brokers:

- Access (212-333-7280)
- Airhitch (212-864-2000)
- ANZ Travel (310-379-2483)
- Encore Short Notice (800-638-8976)
- Stand-Buys, Ltd. (800-255-1488)

To take one example, you give Airhitch a period during which you would like to leave for Europe, listing several acceptable destinations. A few days ahead of time, they tell you the date of your flight and where you'll wind up. However, short notice means that finding a cheap connecting flight in the United States could be a problem.

Around-the-World. There are more than forty separate around-the-world (ATW) packages, most of which must be purchased before you leave home. Circle Pacific (for the Pacific Rim region), Pacific Air Pass, Polypass (South Pacific), Super Caribbean, Scandinavian, Discover Pacific, Visit South America, and ATW tickets can be purchased at prices well below the cost of out-and-back or point-to-point fares.

Ask about restrictions affecting changes to itinerary, flight dates, doubling back, side trips, minimum stopovers, traveling only during off-season time periods, limits on refunds, and minimum and maximum travel periods. These tickets are usually valid for six months or a year. Expect to pay in the range of $1,200 to $3,000. For a long-term "walkabout," they're hard to beat.

Consolidators who specialize in ATW tickets typically have the best prices. Among them, Air Brokers International (800-883-3273) specializes in Circle-the-Globe and Circle-the-Pacific tickets. Travel Brokers (415-398-2925) features ATW tickets, as does Pan Express Travel (212-719-9292).

Foreign Airlines. SAVE MONEY by flying on one of the lesser-known foreign flag airlines such as Malev (Hungary), Lot (Poland), Korean Air, or Cathay Pacific (Hong Kong). If you're working through a travel agent, you'll probably have to make a specific request. You can do the research by calling embassies of the countries where you'll be traveling. You get lower prices as well as a chance to talk with local people returning home, but usually won't receive usable frequent flyer miles (although an increasing number of foreign carriers have reciprocal arrangements with American carriers). Just because an airline isn't well-known in the United States does not mean it isn't reliable.

Air Passes

Air passes, which you purchase through your travel agent or directly from a foreign airline, can be an excellent way to SAVE MONEY. Passes do have certain restrictions: travel must be taken within a specified time period (typically between two and twelve weeks), sometimes you must circle back through a hub city, you must buy the pass before arriving in the country, and you may have to arrive on the sponsoring airline.

While your itinerary is in the planning stage, compare point-to-point airfare with the cost of the pass to see which is the better deal. Because distances are vast and normal tickets are relatively expensive, air passes have worked well for me in Brazil, Australia, and Indonesia.

In Europe, take a look at the *Discover Europe Airpass* (British Midland Airlines) that covers the United Kingdom, and includes almost a dozen European cities. *Discover Europe* (Lufthansa and Finnair) offers many European routes. Some of the others include: *EuroFlyer Pass* (Air France and others), *Europe AirPass* (British Airways and others), *EuroPass* (Iberia), *Passport to Europe* (KLM and Northwest), *Baltic Pass* (SAS), *LeFrance Pass* (Air Inter),

Visit Norway Pass (Braathens SAFE), and *Visit Spain Airpass* (Iberia). Some of these passes must be bought in conjunction with a transatlantic ticket on the sponsoring airline. Again, a pass makes sense only if you can use it fully without letting it distract your itinerary.

Air passes are very suitable for Latin America. One of the best is the *Sudameripass* (Aeroperu). For $999, you receive six flights, starting from Miami, Mexico City or Cancun to Lima, then on to many other South American cities. Additional international flights are inexpensive and add-ons within Peru are only $25 each. This is a great deal!

Chile, Bolivia, Colombia, Argentina, Venezuela, and Brazil also offer passes. The Brazil air pass is $440 for five flights among nineteen cities ($100 each for additional segments). Argentina offers four stops for $450.

One of the best ways to see the South Pacific is with a *Polypass* (Polynesian Airlines) for $999 starting from Honolulu. You get unlimited travel among the Cook Islands, Samoa, French Polynesia, Fiji, Tonga, New Caledonia, and Niue, plus one round trip to Auckland, New Zealand, and one round trip to either Sydney or Melbourne, Australia. Even though the pass is valid only for thirty days, it's another great deal. Other passes in the region: *Australia and New Zealand Airpass*, *Visit Australia New Zealand Airpass*, *Australia Explorer Pass*, and the *Kiwi Air Pass*.

The concept of twenty-one days of unlimited travel in India may be a bit daunting but that's what you get with a *Discover India Fare* for $400. In Indonesia, $300 buys three flights with a *Visit Indonesia Decade Pass*. The Thai Airways pass is $239 and good for four domestic flights.

On the *Discover Asia Airpass* offered by SilkAir (based in Singapore), you buy as many flight segments as you choose at either $129 or $229.

Similar to an air pass is a ticket for a *fixed* multistop itinerary sold at a price below that of the requisite one-way tickets. In Europe, these tickets may involve more than one participating airline.

Frequent Flyer Coupons

The frequent flyer program is not aging well. Intended as a marketing ploy, it worked so much better than anyone imagined that it's been converted into a house of mirrors. In addition to inspiring brand loyalty, it has set employees against employers, and frequent flyers against the very airlines that sought their business. Some employees fly odd routes at odd times just to travel on "their" airline, costing employers money in the process. At the same time, airlines set snares for frequent flyers who want to make money by selling the coupons they have earned. On top of all that, after drawing consumers into their programs, airlines restrict frequent flyer seats to only 5 percent (sometimes 10 percent) of each flight. As a result, many loyal customers wind up having to fly thousands of miles out of their way or make reservations twelve to eighteen months ahead of departure.

How to Earn Credits. The usual way to earn frequent flyer points is by—what else?—flying. However, the nonflying ways in which you can increase your frequent flyer credits are increasing daily. For example, AT&T, feeling the bite of competition, is offering a True Rewards plan (800-773-9273) which credits five frequent flyer miles to one of three airlines for each dollar you spend on long distance calls. In other words, if it takes twenty-five thousand miles to earn a "free" domestic flight, you must spend $5,000 on long distance phone calls to earn it. If you average $100 a month, that's more than four years worth of calls. MCI and Sprint have equivalent plans in partnership with different airlines. Several car rental firms have similar deals. The concept keeps expanding. A grocery chain in Texas awards frequent flyer miles in return for the veggies and bologna you buy.

> You can earn frequent flyer miles with some calling cards or credit cards.

If other terms are competitive, consider using credit cards that award frequent flyer miles in proportion to your purchases. Many airlines sponsor MasterCard or Visa credit cards, issued by various banks, that earn frequent flyer mileage credits. Use of Diners Club or American Express cards earns credit with one airline or another.

With the BancOne TravelPlus Visa card, the value of every purchase you make is converted to points that accumulate toward a free ticket. When you get enough points, the bank buys the ticket for you. Under this program, you are unaffected by blackouts or limited seat allocations imposed by the airlines. When you take the trip you've earned, it earns additional frequent flyer mileage. The BancOne gold Visa card includes car rental collision damage waiver coverage and there is no annual fee. There are some limitations, but it's worth looking into (call 800-945-2023). Keep an eye open for other deals that build your frequent flyer credits.

Flying on any of two dozen or more *foreign* airlines earns frequent flyer miles on one of the U.S.-based airlines. For example, flying Chile's Ladeco Airline earns mileage credit on TWA; flying LanChile earns mileage on Continental.

To avoid wasting mileage, join several frequent flyer programs. However, most people need to concentrate their mileage on one, or at most two, airlines to earn the minimum mileage required to earn a "free" flight before their miles start expiring.

If you fly a lot, keep track of your mileage yourself (including miles earned as bonuses from related purchases) rather than relying on the airline to keep an accurate record.

Transfers. Transfering frequent flyer coupons is not against the law, but that doesn't mean airlines don't try to prevent it. On most airlines, a traveler caught trying to use a coupon with someone else's name on it may lose it or be denied boarding (similar to the situation when a person buys a non-refundable ticket from someone who can't use it). Nevertheless, a market for coupons struggles on. If you haven't accumulated enough frequent flyer miles to earn a trip and can't find a friend who wants to share extra mileage with you, check newspaper classified ads under "ticket swap" for offers from individuals and dealers.

National coupon brokers deal mostly in first and business class tickets. Although that's where the greatest savings are, that's not how most international travelers fly. If you deal with a coupon broker, try to have the coupon reissued in your name (which may take four to six weeks). Some brokers provide you with a newly-issued ticket, not coupons, by handling the coupon transfers in-house. If the coupon won't be in your name, ask the broker if your money will be refunded if the airline won't accept the coupon (don't get your hopes up). Paying with a credit card gives you and the broker something to discuss if there's a problem.

When offered a coupon, check its terms carefully including the expiration date. Many certificates state: "Void if bartered or sold." However, some airlines permit one transfer, probably contemplating a gift to a family member. Under the Delta Skymiles program, mileage awards may be transferred to anyone you choose but, at least theoretically, not sold or bartered.

When dealing with airline personnel, naturally you won't mention how you got the coupon. However, for international travel, you must show your passport to the ticket agent when checking in. If the passport doesn't match the frequent flyer coupon and the agent makes an issue of it, the airline could confiscate it and your trip could end on the spot.

During periods when domestic airport security is tightened, the agent will ask for an ID and possibly a photo to demonstrate that you're the person to whom the ticket or coupon was issued. If they don't match, the agent may either confiscate the ticket or coupon—or decide you're a bomber. As a result of security checks, airlines have discovered so many "transferred" tickets in use that they may keep checking IDs even after security concerns are reduced. If you're not certain of an airline's policy, ask ahead of time. Coupons SAVE MONEY, but it's "buyer beware" all the way.

Cashing In. You can exchange your frequent flyer miles for a ticket directly with the airline. If you want your travel agent to handle the exchange, ask first whether there would be a charge for the service. Remember to use frequent flyer mileage credit to buy an expensive ticket, not a cheap one. Assume you spend about $.02 to earn a frequent flyer mile. If you can buy a ticket for cash for significantly less than the value of the mileage credit you've accumulated, hold onto the credit for a later day.

What the airlines promote with one hand, they take away with the other, meaning there are often restrictions on when you can take trips earned with frequent flyer points. In what was perceived by some as a cynical move,

Northwest recently offered to let its frequent flyers "buy" their way out of blackouts and various other restrictions by paying additional frequent flyer points. Of course, the restrictions were imposed by Northwest itself.

Sources of Information. There are so many frequent flyer programs and the rules change so often that the most helpful thing I can do is provide sources of current information on various programs. *InsideFlyer Magazine* ($33 a year) reports on bonuses and new programs and rates the various programs. The annual reference edition of *The Official Frequent Flyer Guidebook* ($14.99) explains all airline, hotel, car rental, and credit card programs, and lists all blackout dates. Both are available by calling (800) 487-8893. Check back issues of *Consumer Reports Travel Letter* for comparisons of the various programs.

A computer program called FTM AirMax helps travelers find the best combination of airline, hotel, car rental, and credit cards to maximize frequent flyer points. Order the $80 software by calling (800) 386-2476. Travel libraries of major online services and many travel bulletins boards offer shareware that will help you keep track of frequent flyer points and let you know when you have earned awards.

Couriers

Even most experienced travelers don't know what a courier is—so they miss a great way to SAVE MONEY. Here's the situation. Air freight companies often have rush shipments but, for security reasons, the FAA won't permit them to be sent as unaccompanied baggage on regular airline flights. To send the shipment air freight would be expensive and clearing customs on the other end could take days. On the other hand, if sent as part of a traveler's personal baggage allowance, it clears customs immediately. That's where you come in. Sending you as a courier costs them less than paying air cargo rates, especially since you partially reimburse them for your ticket.

A courier typically pays only one-third to one-half the unrestricted coach fare, although savings of 85 percent or more are possible. As shipment date approaches, the fare drops. When time is running out, the courier firm may even pick up the whole cost of your flight. As a bonus, you'll probably be entitled to frequent flyer credit for the flight.

More than thirty thousand courier flights originate from the United States each year; 90 percent depart from Los Angeles, Miami, New York, and San Francisco, and a few flights leave from Atlanta, Boston, Chicago, Houston, and Washington, DC.

Here are a few recent *round trip* courier ticket prices: New York to Singapore for $250; New York to Santiago for $375; New York to Prague for $425; Los Angeles to Sydney for $250; Los Angeles to London for $199; Los Angeles to Melbourne for $250; San Francisco to Mexico City for $125. Summer courier fares are higher than at any other time because the balance of supply and demand is working against you.

Who is Eligible? To become a courier you must be at least twenty-one years old and have a valid passport. Some courier companies charge a fee (e.g., $35 to $50) the first time you fly with them. Many require a refundable deposit (e.g., $100 to $200) to assure that you'll show up to accompany the return shipment. You also have to pay any airport departure tax (typically, $18 to $28).

How It Works. You leave from a designated city and are probably limited to carry-on luggage, although you're sometimes allowed to check one bag. In some cases, you're a courier on the outbound flight only, leaving you with a full baggage allowance for the return flight.

As a rule, it's better to book a flight one to three months before you'd like to travel. Most popular destinations require at least a two-week advance reservation, and four to six weeks is better during the summer to assure you'll get a ride.

It's normal to wonder, "What's in that baggage anyway?" meaning "Am I going to wind up in the Saigon slammer?" Courier companies insist that shipments are legitimate: canceled checks, contracts, electronic replacement parts, that kind of thing. Fortunately, it doesn't matter. For your protection

Major Courier Brokers

Go Travel	(213) 466-1126	
Council Travel	(212) 661-1450	
Courier Travel	(800) 275-2359	to Europe, the Middle East, and South America
Discount Travel International	(212) 362-3636	
Halbart Travel	(718) 656-8189	to Mexico City, London and Madrid
IBC	(310) 607-0215	to the Far East and London
Line Haul Service	(305) 477-0651	to Central and South America
Midnite Express	(310) 672-100	to London
Now Voyager	(212) 431-1616	to Europe, South America, and the Far East
Polo Express	(415) 742-9613	to Australia, Asia, London
UTL Travel	(415) 583-5074	to London and Asia
Way to Go Travel	(213) 466-1126	to Australia and the Far East

Why Don't More People Fly as Couriers?

- Almost no one knows the opportunity exists.
- The amount of personal baggage you can take is usually limited to one carryon.
- You must return home within a comparatively short time. The typical turnaround to Europe is one week, two weeks to Asia, and seven to twenty-one days to South America. However, you can negotiate with some courier companies to get a longer turnaround, even up to six months.
- You may want to fly with a companion and they don't get the courier rate. However, that may not be an obstacle because the company may need two couriers on the same day, or at least on successive days, or it may be willing to sell a ticket to your companion at a discount. Worst case, you fly as a courier and your partner flies on a commercial ticket.

and theirs, the courier generally never touches the baggage and is not personally liable for it. When you arrive, you hand an envelope containing the manifest and the claim check to the courier company's representatives. They take the baggage from the claim area and clear it through customs while you go off to play.

How to Become a Courier. Look up courier companies in the Yellow Pages under air courier service, courier service, delivery service, or freight forwarding. If your directory has no listings, visit the library and look in directories for the gateway cities listed above. Alternatively, contact a courier broker. However, if you arrange a flight through a broker, you may pay a registration fee to the broker, and the air fare may be slightly higher than if you book the flight directly.

When you've located the flight that goes when and where you want, it's time to ask the courier company or broker a few questions:

- Will I be a courier in both directions?
- What will my baggage allowance be?
- How long will I be allowed to stay?
- Will I need a visa?
- Are there any other restrictions?
- What is the cost of the ticket? Are there any extra costs I'll have to pay?
- How and when do I book a ticket?

An efficient way to find out about hundreds of opportunities is to join the International Association of Air Travel Couriers (IAATC). For $42 a year, you receive bimonthly *Shoestring Traveler* newsletters and the *Air Courier Bulletin* listing what's available. The IAATC provides a no-charge, fax-on-demand service to communicate last-minute opportunities and has a bulletin board that searches for the lowest courier and noncourier air fares. They'll even send a free audiocassette telling you how to become an air courier. For more information, call (407) 582-8320.

A monthly newsletter called *Travel Unlimited* (P.O. Box 1058, Allston, MA 02134; $5 for a single copy, $25 for an annual subscription) used to emphasize courier flights but has now broadened its interest to travel bargains in general.

Several books have been written on the subject, including the *Air Couriers Guide Book* (Owen Publications, Box 16845-A, St. Petersburg, Florida, 33733); *The Insider's Guide to Air Courier Bargains*, by Kelly Monaghan, $17.45 postpaid (Upper Access Publishing, P.O. Box 457, Hinesburg, VT 05461; or call 800-356-9315); and *The Courier Air Travel Handbook,* by Mark Field, $10.70 postpaid (Thunderbird Press, 5390-10 West Greenway Road, Suite 112, Glendale, AZ 85306; or call (800) 345-0096. Check the publication date because courier information is quickly outdated.

Flying courier won't fit the travel plans of all independent travelers, but it's a very economical way to explore the world, especially if you live in or near one of the major gateway cities.

Good Deals and Money-Saving Tips

- Check the ads in the travel sections of *The New York Times, The Washington Post,* the *Los Angeles Times*, and your local paper for *national airline specials*. These airlines often cut prices sharply to encourage travelers to visit. I recently flew from the United States to New Zealand on Air New Zealand for $650 round trip (or "return," as they say in N.Z.), instead of the usual $1,300. That ticket also allowed two additional stopovers (I chose Sydney and Rarotonga*). That's a deal to watch for.

- Ask a travel agent about *air-hotel package deals*. Special promotions offer air fare and several nights lodging for less than you might pay for regular air fare alone. Some packages are priced so low that they're worth it even if you don't stay in their hotel. These deals are common for Jamaica, Cancun, and major cities in Europe, but you may find some for more adventuresome destinations. Most of these packages are legitimate; only a few offer poorly located or maintained facilities. Ask for the names of previous travelers you can call for references.

---

* *Rarotonga.* Largest of the fifteen Cook Islands, Rarotonga is located three thousand miles due south of Honolulu. It is inhabited by Polynesians who migrated there perhaps as long ago as 500 A.D., along with a sprinkling of New Zealanders who came along considerably later. Some feel you haven't lived until you've spent Saturday night dancing and drinking Leopard Beer in the Banana Court Bar.

- *Senior Airfare Coupons* are available to travelers age sixty-two and above. You buy a book of four or eight coupons. Each coupon costs from $130 to $150 and is good for a one-way flight anywhere in the contiguous forty-eight states (note: no international flights). Companions not over age sixty-two can buy coupons at a higher, but still discounted, fare. There is usually a fourteen-day advance reservation requirement, but it's possible to fly standby as well. Typically, you must use coupons within a year after purchase, although there's a refund on unused books. These coupons save the most money on long flights.

- Many airlines have *10 to 30 percent discounts for "seniors"* (generally age sixty-two and up, but sometimes as low as fifty). Even bargain-hunting travelers fail to take advantage of this one. There are two reasons. Many of them don't know about it (and the airlines aren't going to mention it). Worse, many travelers who know about the discount so hate the idea of being considered a "senior" that they don't bring it up. Many hotels, including Sheratons, Holiday Inns, and Days Inns, offer 10 to 20 percent discounts to people as young as fifty or fifty-five. National Car Rental gives a 30 percent discount to seniors. In some cases, these discounts are available only to AARP members. If you travel with a companion, the companion may get a 10 percent discount regardless of age. SAVE MONEY.

- You'll get a discount if you have an *International Student Identity Card* and use the network of travel agencies associated with the card. Produce the card overseas, ask for a discount, and you may get one.

- Time on your hands? Book yourself on a busy flight, one likely to be full. When you check in, tell the agent that if they need to bump someone, you're willing to be bumped. If the airline has *overbooked the flight* and you're bumped you may get a cash payment and/or a free flight anywhere the airline flies.

- There are various other strategies for saving money on airline tickets, but they're a little complicated and airlines generally frown on them (not surprising, since the idea is to defeat airline restrictions). Ask your travel agent about:
  - *crisscross tickets* (round-trip super saver tickets with overlapping dates);
  - phantom or *hidden city tickets*. Book a ticket to a cheap hub destination for less than the cost of a ticket to the intermediate stop where you really want to go. Airlines don't like it, but they seldom try to intervene. Since you get off before the destination shown on your ticket, you have to travel with carry-on luggage only.

- *back-to-back tickets.* These avoid the requirement that you stay over a Saturday night to get the cheapest air fare. Buy two cheap tickets which include the Saturday night stay, the first from your home to the destination and back, the second from the destination to your home and back. Use the first portion of each ticket to go and return. Either use the second portion of both tickets for another round trip (which usually must be within thirty days) or throw them away. The back-to-back strategy will SAVE MONEY whenever the cost of the cheapest ticket is less than half as much as the unrestricted (no Saturday night stay) ticket.

• To get the cheapest fare you must ask for it. Ask again. Be absolutely clear that you want the least expensive fare and nothing else. Make sure the travel agent knows you are *flexible*. For example, can you

  - leave on any day within a period of several days?
  - stay at your destination over a Saturday night?
  - depart from a nearby airport rather than your hometown?
  - accept an intermediate stop or a change of planes?
  - accept an alternative destination? For example, you may save as much as 70 percent by flying into Louisville instead of Cincinnati, or Colorado Springs instead of Denver, or Toledo instead of Detroit, or Birmingham instead of Atlanta, among others. There is usually public or private transportation between airports.
  - fly during off-peak hours (especially overnight)?
  - fly during off-season (that is, other than June through September)?

  The more "yes" answers, the more likely you'll SAVE MONEY.

• Don't buy tickets on *weekends*. Airlines often raise ticket prices on Saturday and Sunday. If other carriers don't go along immediately, they lower prices on Monday.

• *Fare wars* often follow a major holiday. Be ready.

• Domestic coach-class *fares dip at three predictable times* of the year. Prices start down in March and hit a low from mid-May to mid-June. They rise from mid-June, then dip to a similar low about August 1. For the rest of the year, it's all uphill, except for a dip between Thanksgiving and mid-December.

• When you've tentatively selected an airline, dates, and route, review the *restrictions* carefully:

  - Are you permitted to make changes or cancel the ticket? If so, what is the charge? If not, be certain you're really ready to make the deal final.
  - Does the ticket permit you to add a stopover without charge?

- Is there a minimum or maximum stay?
- Can you make the whole trip on one airline? If so, it may be cheaper than using several airlines (unless you are buying bucket shop segments abroad).
- Are you entitled to a discount (e.g., as a student or a senior)? If you take a domestic flight to connect with your international flight, remember to seek the best deal on the domestic flight as well.

- Watch the World Wide Web. Airlines are using silent auctions to fill last-minute vacancies at prices 16 to 25 percent off full-fare prices.

Saving Money When Booking Lodging

If you choose to make hotel reservations before leaving home and want to SAVE MONEY, here are some ideas:

- Use *hotel consolidators* for rates 25 to 70 percent off rack rates (the theoretical full price). Hotels Plus (800-235-0909) specializes in Great Britain and Europe, but has some locations in Asia, Africa, and the Middle East. It represents everything from cottages to hotels and mansions. Room Exchange (800-846-7000) specializes in upscale hotels in the United States, Mexico, the Caribbean, and several European and Asian cities. The Hotel Reservations Network (800-964-6835) offers discounted rates of up to 50 percent for fairly expensive (up to four star) hotels, mostly in the United States but some in Paris and London. Luxury hotels seldom advertise specials because they don't want to antagonize their less-creative guests—but your travel agent should know about them. You'll beat the rack rate with these services, but you'll still be well above the prices charged by budget hotels.

- *"Half-price" discount programs* sound good but (a) you may not be able to reserve a room with that kind of discount on the dates you want it (the same problem as trying to book a frequent flyer ticket), (b) the rate on which the discount is calculated (the rack rate) may be an inflated rate which almost no one actually pays, and (c) the programs have membership fees of $30 to $125.

  When you enroll, you receive a directory and an ID card and make your own reservations (preferably at least thirty days ahead of time). Since the program is designed to fill empty hotel rooms during slack periods, you probably won't get a room when the hotel expects to be able to rent it for a higher price.

  These companies tend to emphasize hotels in the United States but some lists include hotels in Europe, Canada, Mexico, and the Caribbean, as well as a fair selection in Latin America. Half-price programs are not very active outside of developed countries.

The *Europe Hotel Directory* of Entertainment Publications (800-445-4137; $38 annual fee) seems to have the largest overseas selection, including at least some choices for budget travelers. ITC (800-342-0558; $36 annual fee) is more active in Asia and the South Pacific than its competitors. Several others worth considering are Carte Royale (800-847-7002; $40 annual fee), Encore (800-638-0930; $50 annual fee), Great American Traveler (800-342-0558; $50 annual fee), and Privilege Card (800-236-9732; $75 annual fee).

- Several *hotel brokers* offer rates at about 35 percent off rack rate. Of those, Vacationland (800-245-0050) and Travel InterLink (800-477-7172) have the best selection in Asia. The problem with most hotel brokers, from the standpoint of adventurous travelers, is their concentration on a relatively few large cities.

- You may be able to obtain *"preferred" hotel rates* through your travel agent. A preferred rate is one negotiated with a hotel by a travel agency, consortium (e.g., Carlson Wagonlit, American Express, U.S. Travel), or travel club (e.g., International Airline Passengers Association). Even small travel agencies offer a preferred rate program if they have signed up with independent booking services such as Thor 24 or ABC. Discounts range between 10 and 40 percent, averaging about 20 percent. Most of the hotels that participate in preferred rate programs are midscale to expensive. Ask to see your travel agent's preferred rate directory to find hotels available where you want to go, then ask the agent to make the booking. Preferred discounts may be somewhat less than half-price and broker deals, but rooms should be available at any season.

  > Ask if your travel agent can get you a preferred hotel rate.

  In evaluating these discount programs, remember that the rack rate may be fictional. The discount may sound large, but the result may be neither as good as you could negotiate on the spot nor anywhere close to the deal you could make with a smaller, independent hotel.

- When making a reservation, SAVE MONEY by asking for a discount on grounds of being a *member of a privileged category*, such as an employee of a specific corporation, a student, a travel writer, a frequent flyer, a senior, or a member of the government/military/clergy or some organization such as AAA, AARP, Encore, or anything else that seems remotely defensible. The hotel may ask for some identification, but a business card is usually sufficient to capture the corporate rate (which may be up to 20 percent off the rack rate).

- If you are a senior, say so. The minimum age for a *senior discount* varies from fifty to sixty-five. In addition, almost a dozen large hotel chains have "clubs" for seniors with discounts clustered in the 10 to 25 percent range (though some go up to 50 percent). Membership in some is free; in others $10 to $50 a year. For $10, anyone age fifty or above may join AARP (202-434-2277) and take advantage of its discount arrangements with hotel chains.

- Ask about a hotel's *promotional discounts* for weekends, two-for-breakfast, summer season (July and August are bargain times in Europe), or whatever. Ask what discount they give for making a reservation thirty days in advance (it could be as much as 30 percent). See whether they have a package deal with an airline. Don't ask *whether* the hotel has such a discount; just ask for it. If the hotel clerk expects vacancies, which is often the case, he or she will work with you to find a way to encourage your presence. It may not be as good a deal as you could make in person, but you should get some break.

- Some travel agents sell *vouchers* for hotel rooms. Before starting your trip, you buy as many vouchers as you expect to need, then pay with them as you travel. The incentive is that you're supposed to receive significant discounts by using vouchers. In some cases you do; in others, you wind up paying even more than the rack rate. The hotel chain with the best voucher deals consistently seems to be Holiday Inn (discounts are between 10 and 20 percent) but its rates are still above those of some other chains and many good local hotels. Vouchers are good for travel agents and great for hotels, but not so good for travelers.

By the way, if you can prove you made a reservation that a hotel doesn't honor, the custom is to give you a free night at a comparable hotel and transport you there. Act as though both you and the clerk take it for granted that that is the least they can do.

Saving Money on Adventures

Part of the exhilaration of travel is doing new things, unusual things, challenging things. In other words, having adventures. For the purposes of this section, I use "adventure" to mean experiences of short duration; part of a trip rather than its entirety. I'm thinking of rafting day-trips, diving, snorkeling, renting a bike, going up in a hot air balloon, taking a safari, renting a boat or helicopter, and so on.

Assuming you want as many adventures as practical, and that cost is a consideration, let's discuss how to SAVE MONEY on adventures. We know that paying someone at home to make arrangements for you in some far away place is more expensive than doing it yourself. But there's another cost that's less obvious. The service you can buy for $200 in Greece may be advertised at $400 in the United States, so that's the base price—before the agent's commission is added on. The message here: SAVE MONEY by doing it yourself.

Here's an example. By arranging my own trip to Rwanda, I paid less than $350 to visit the mountain gorillas. This amount included round trip air fare from Kenya to Rwanda, the park permit, food, lodging, and local transportation. If a United States travel agent had arranged a similar trip, the price could have exceeded $2,000. From home, I called the Kinigi Park Administrative Office in Rwanda (the telephone number was in the Lonely Planet *Africa* guidebook, but I could have gotten it from the embassy) and chose a date on which a permit was available to visit the gorillas. Next, I got a Rwandan visa, specifying the dates I wanted it to be effective. The Rwandan visa is unusual in that you must arrive in the country on the date your visa becomes effective. Because of the time constraints of the visa and the permit, I booked the Kenya to Rwanda flight while still in the United States to avoid any delays in Kenya. I waited until I arrived in Rwanda to arrange for local lodging and transportation. *Hakuna matata;* "no problems."

Another example. In Nairobi, you can sign up for a tent camping safari to Masai Mara, Lake Nakuru, Amboseli, and any of the other game parks, and pay about $40 per day for food, transportation, camping gear, cooks, guide—everything. The safari companies have offices on the main streets and their representatives roam the hotels seeking your business. Guidebooks mention recommended companies. It's worth a little shoe leather to visit several offices to compare destinations, services, prices, and personnel. To avoid this small effort, or for the comfort of certainty, many people book the trip at home and pay $200, $300, even $800 or more per person per day. For the extra money you receive an impressive brochure and stay in upscale accommodations that are considerably less authentic than a simple tent. Either way, the wild game is the same. Sign up for the safari in Kenya and save enough money to travel for an extra month—or bank a down payment for your next trip!

There are two ways to organize your adventure yourself. Do it from home—or do it when you get there. Either way, gather information before you leave. Guidebooks are good at identifying potential adventures and listing reputable operators (other sources of information are listed at the end of Chapter 2).

When you know what adventures appeal to you and have the names of several providers of services, you can contact them from home and you're also prepared to contact them as soon as you arrive.

Saving Money with a Rail Pass

Does a Rail Pass Make Sense for Your Trip?

Since the rail pass is most commonly used in Europe, let's look at the Eurailpass in its various versions. Train travel is fairly expensive in Europe, so a rail pass initially seems like a good investment. However, don't buy any pass without first doing the calculations necessary to see if it makes economic sense for your itinerary. For one thing, the basic Eurailpass may not save you any money unless you travel 1,200 to 1,500 miles within a two-week period—and that's a lot of traveling in Europe. If you travel on five days during that period, that's 240 to 300 miles a day. Another consideration is that a Eurailpass is a better value in northern Europe than in southern Europe since train tickets cost more in the north.

Ask a travel agent how much individual tickets would cost between your destinations or review the point-to-point fares in the Rail Europe brochure or the Rick Steves guide mentioned later in this chapter. Compare those costs with the cost of various rail passes.

If a rail pass makes sense, the next step is to select the one that works best for you. Here are the choices.

The Eurailpass

Of the several rail passes available for use in Europe, the most well known are the various versions of the Eurailpass. This pass, valid in seventeen countries, can also be used on ferries from Sweden to Finland, Ireland to France, and Italy to Greece. It is accepted for boats on the Rhine and Danube and on buses in Ireland.

A basic Eurailpass is good for unlimited travel during periods ranging from fifteen days to three months. If you are twenty-six or older on your first travel date, your rail pass must be for first-class space (which costs 50 percent more than second class). If you are under twenty-six, you can buy either first or second class. For example, the 1996 consecutive-day Eurailpass costs from $522 for fifteen days up to $1,468 for three months.

Other Versions. The Eurail *Flexipass* works best for people who don't plan to travel frequently. If you can concentrate your travel into a limited number of days, a Flexipass will SAVE MONEY over an unlimited pass. Travel is first class and the pass is valid for travel on a certain number of days within a two-month period. A pass valid for ten days costs $616; fifteen days costs $812.

Anyone under age twenty-six on the first date of travel may buy a Eurail *Youthpass*, which differs from the regular pass in that it costs less and you travel second class, as do most Europeans. A pass costs from $418 for fifteen consecutive days to $798 for two months.

The Eurail *Youth Flexipass*, which permits travel on any ten days within a two-month period, costs $438; if valid for any fifteen days, it costs $588.

The Eurail *Saverpass* is designed for people traveling together. Between October 1 and March 31, you must have at least two people in your group. During the peak season of April 1 to September 30, you must have a minimum of three people. The 1996 Saverpass costs from $452 per person for fifteen *consecutive* days of unlimited first class travel to $712 per person for one month. I've seen off-season Saverpass specials in which one person pays full-price and all others in the group pay only 50 percent. There's a deal!

To add to the confusion, there is a Eurail *Drive Pass* that combines first class train travel (four days) with a rental car (three days) within a twenty-one day period.

The Europass

If those weren't enough choices, there's the Europass which serves people who plan to take short trips to fewer places than covered by the seventeen-country Eurail passes. The basic Europass allows you to choose any three, four, or five countries from among France, Germany, Italy, Spain, and Switzerland. If it takes adding one or more from among Portugal, Belgium, Luxembourg, or Austria to make you happy, you can do that for an additional fee. To give you an idea of prices, the Europass for three countries costs $316 per person for five days of travel within a two-month period. Extra days cost $42 each. Europass Youth tickets for persons under twenty-six cost $210 (plus $29 for each day beyond five). When a traveler buys a first-class Europass, one partner on the same trip can buy an identical Europass for half-price. This deal does not apply to youth Europasses.

The Europass will be 15 to 20 percent more economical than the Eurail-pass if your travels will be limited to the Europass countries (rather than the seventeen covered by the Eurailpass). In addition, the Europass provides somewhat more flexibility. However, keep two principles in mind. First, if your itinerary is flexible, you may be better off with the Eurailpass so you can travel more widely if you choose. Second, the more you travel by train, the more your savings grow over buying point-to-point tickets.

Country/Regional Passes

If you'll be traveling in only one area, a country or regional pass is a better buy than a Eurailpass. Choices include: Austrian Rabbit Card, Benelux Tourrail, BritFrance Rail, Czech Flexipass, European East Pass, Finnrail, Freedom of Scotland Travelpass, Greek Railpass, Hungarian Flexipass, Italian Railpass, Polrailpass, Portuguese Flexipass, Russian Flexipass, Scanrail (extra discounts for persons over age fifty-five), Spanish Flexipass, and the Swiss Pass, among others.

VIA Canrailpass

There are rail passes in many non-European countries but the *VIA Canrail-pass* stands out. It permits twelve days of multistop travel from Nova Scotia to British Columbia within a thirty-day period. Between June and September, the price is just over $400. The rest of the time, it's about $300. The price is discounted for students (twenty-four and under) and seniors (sixty and over). It even throws in a few bells and whistles such as a free long-distance calling card worth $15, the right to purchase extra travel days separately, and cheap rental car options.

Resources

My choice as the best source for European rail pass information is Rick Steves' *Back Door Guide to European Railpasses* (call 206-771-8303 for a free copy). Match your itinerary with the Guide's map which shows individual fares among European cities and then determine whether a rail pass is a good deal for your trip. If you buy a rail pass from Steves, there is no handling fee and you receive a video on *How to Get the Most out of your Railpass*, a free guidebook, and comments on your itinerary. Add a staff that understands the priorities of budget travelers, and you have a tough combination to beat.

Call Rail Europe (800-438-7245) for its *Traveler's Guide, Eurail Sales Information* and the excellent brochure *On Track*, which lists current train schedules and fare information. The Council on International Educational Exchange (205 East 42nd Street, New York, NY 10017) is another sound resource for information. You might also consult:

- *Traveling Europe's Trains*, Jay Brunhouse. Pelican, 1994;
- *Thomas Cook's On the Rails Around Europe*. Thomas Cook, 1994;
- *Europe by Eurail*, George and LaVerne Ferguson. Globe Pequot, 1995;
- *Eurail Guide*. Houghton Mifflin, 1995;
- *Let's Go Europe*;
- *Europe Through the Back Door*;
- *Europe by Train*, Katie Wood and George MacDonald. Harper Perennial.

European railway schedules and other information are available on CompuServe (access GO RAILWAY).

Companies in the United States that represent European railroads include Rail Europe (800-438-7145); DER (800-337-8724); CIT (800-248-7245); and BritRail International (800-677-8585). They also can make reservations for the Eurostar Chunnel service, InterCity and EuroCity routes, and the high-speed trains in France and Germany.

A last word on rail passes. It's a lot of fun to be able to hop aboard the train any time you want (more on how to do that in Chapter 16)—but it takes time and a bit of study to figure out if a rail pass will SAVE MONEY. The outline above gives you a good foundation and more information is readily available from the sources I've listed. The decision is up to you.

Saving Money with a Youth Identity Card

The International Identity Card, issued by the Council on International Education Exchange (CIEE), will help you SAVE MONEY abroad. It's available for $15 by mail from CIEE, ID Department, 205 East 42nd Street, New York, NY, 10017 (call 212-661-1414); or buy it for $14 on any of more than four hundred college campuses.

Eligibility

To be eligible for the student card, you must (a) demonstrate enrollment in a study program leading to a degree at an accredited school during the year of application, and (b) be at least twelve years old and not over twenty-five. To be eligible for the GO-25 card, which costs $18, you need not be a student but must be under twenty-six. Full-time teachers are eligible regardless of age.

Benefits of the Card

The CIEE card entitles holders to discounts on transportation through Council Travel (800-743-1823), a subsidiary of CIEE. Council Travel, with dozens of offices located on or near college campuses, also offers guidebooks and information on budget travel. With the card, you receive the *International Student Travel Guide* which contains information on student discounts in sixty-five countries. The card also entitles you to discounts on selected local transportation abroad (e.g., 35 percent off on Italian train fares), as well as on some entrance fees and tickets to events. Most other ID cards are worthless overseas as far as entitling you to discounts.

The CIEE card provides insurance to help pay the expenses of accidents and injuries (up to $3,000), sickness (up to $100 per day for inpatient confinement for a maximum of sixty days), and emergency medical evacuation (up to $10,000). Card holders have access to a toll-free hotline to ask for help with a medical, financial, or legal emergency while abroad.

If all that isn't enough, CIEE sells many useful travel publications, including *Work, Study, Travel Abroad* and *Volunteer.*

Even if you don't have the CIEE card, or any card at all, ask whether there's a student discount before handing over your money.

HOW TO PREPARE A RELIABLE BUDGET

Most people are about as fond of figuring budgets as they are of figuring their taxes. As with taxes, you may pay a penalty if you fail to learn how to construct a reliable budget. Until you know how, you're flying blind, likely to run out of money in the middle of your trip. With a sound budget, you can plan well and stretch your trip to the limit. In other words, budgeting is a liberating experience.

Some travelers initially think in terms of a bare-bones trip, spending as little as they can. What that requires is some hitchhiking, cooking a number of your own meals, eating on the margins of nutrition and hygiene, living occasionally in barely habitable accommodations, and foregoing most treats. Sound like fun? Aren't your time, health, and safety worth a lot more to you than a few rupees? After all, one reason to travel is pleasure. If you make informed choices, bargain, do without a private bathroom some of the time, and skip overpriced tourist frills, you can easily have a great trip within a reasonably tight budget.

One thing is for certain: the amount of money you have available to spend is a major factor in choosing destinations. Think New York City is expensive? It ranked only fifty-sixth on a list of the world's most expensive cities. Heading the list: Tokyo (more than twice as expensive as NYC), Osaka, Zurich, Geneva, Oslo, Copenhagen, Vienna, Moscow, Helsinki, and Libreville (Gabon). Other high-priced destinations: Singapore, London, Berlin, Rome, and Paris. One hundred dollars admits you and a friend to an opera in Sydney, pays for a couple of hours on a Venetian gondola, or just gets you through the door of a geisha show in Tokyo.

Europe is no longer the inexpensive paradise it was in the Sixties. Traveling very economically in one of the least-expensive countries, such as Portugal, you might scrape by for around $20 a day (including lodging, food, and public transportation). Budgeting carefully, expect to spend $25 to $50 a day in less-expensive countries and around $75 in the higher-cost countries. With a few exceptions, it's easy to live reasonably for $25 to $30 a day in the rest of the world.

Constructing the Budget

Put together a budget by listing all the *types* of things you expect to spend money on, then plug in *times* and local *cost* estimates. With a little practice and decent information to work from, there's nothing to it.

Let's practice by assuming certain expenses for a hypothetical thirty-day trip in Asia, departing from San Francisco:

1. *Predeparture expenses.* These include the cost of visas, film and other photographic equipment, medical protection (e.g., shots, prescription medicines, over-the-counter medicines), guidebooks, information-seeking long-distance calls, clothing, and other gear. Let's estimate predeparture expenses for this trip at $350.

2. *Air fare.* To estimate air fare, first decide whether to buy all tickets at home, or to take advantage of lower prices in bucket shops along the way. For a first trip, we'll budget the higher figure, as if you were using tickets purchased at home (you'll get a bonus refund if you buy cheaper air tickets abroad). Assume a net cost for air fare (getting to Asia, traveling around, and returning home) of $1,000.

3. *Other types of transportation.* This includes trains, local buses, taxis, and other non-air transport. Your itinerary shows the segments for which you'll be buying tickets and guidebooks give you a reasonable idea of the costs. Estimate $100.

4. *Lodging and meal expenses.* Since bed and board consume a large part of your budget, it's fortunate they're costs you can control. The best cost estimates come from current guidebooks and from people who've recently returned from your destinations. Of course, before you're actu-

ally there, it's hard to know exactly how much you have to spend to buy the type of meals and lodging that make you happy. Ten dollars will rent a charming room in Thailand while a $90 room in Paris may be a dump. Nevertheless, since you have to make an estimate, here's the process:

Regarding lodging: For our thirty-day trip, subtract the number of days when you'll pay no separate charge for lodging, such as when you'll be trekking or on an overnight plane or train. Let's say there are eight of those days, leaving twenty-two days. An average cost of $15 per day (this is Asia) times twenty-two gives you $330. Adjust that upward by 15 percent to cover price escalation and an occasional splurge and budget $380 for lodging.

Regarding meals: An average cost of $12 per day for meals times thirty gives you $360. Adjust that upward 15 percent and budget $415. If that seems like a lot, compare it with what you'd spend in thirty days at home.

5. *Special experiences.* If you don't plan for them, paying for special experiences can wreck your budget. I'm referring to things like the cost of a safari, scuba diving, a helicopter flight over the Franz Josef Glacier,* sailing along the fjordland coast of Norway, trekking among the hill tribe villages in Thailand,† climbing Mount Kilimanjaro, or chartering a plane into the Okavango Delta.§ Most of these opportunities will surface during your research but you won't recognize some as "musts" until you get there. Include as many as you can in your budget.

How much do these special experiences cost? Check guidebooks, call the embassy, ask a knowledgeable travel agent, ask someone who's been there recently. If you can't turn up anything, take a guess. I suggest three rules of thumb: (a) special experiences cost more than you might expect in *developed* countries; (b) if modern technology is involved, such as a helicopter, they'll be fairly expensive even in a Third World country; and (c) prices quoted by a travel agent for special experiences will almost certainly be higher than you'll pay if you make your own arrangements abroad.

For our hypothetical trip, assume four days scuba diving off the coast of Indonesia and a four-day trek in Thailand with a locally hired guide. Estimate $350.

---

* *Franz Josef Glacier.* Located on the west coast of the South Island of New Zealand, this glacier was named for the Austrian Emperor. Hike alongside the glacier, climb up its face, fly over it, or even land on it.

† *Hill tribe villages.* Located in northern Thailand, these villages are home to several groups of people that immigrated from Burma and Cambodia and have retained their distinctive dress, language, and culture.

§ *Okavango Delta.* Located in northern Botswana, this network of waterways and islands offers some of the most unspoiled game viewing in all of Africa.

6. *Miscellaneous.* This category includes odds and ends: clothing you buy underway, souvenirs you can't live without, toiletries, beverages, books, postcards, postage, and so on. Your estimate here is a matter of personal preference and available money. Whatever your estimate, add 25 percent. For this hypothetical trip, budget $180.

If you want to fine tune your budget, find out whether your own currency has grown significantly stronger or weaker since the information you're relying on was published. Banks and stockbrokers have this information. For current exchange rates, check the Currency Trading table in the third section of *The Wall Street Journal*. In recent years the weakness of the dollar has greatly increased the affordability of Third World countries, in contrast to Europe.

To be even more conservative, add up all the categories and add 15 percent to the total to cover surprises and spontaneous splurges.

If the grand total is more money than you have, don't skip a beat. The purpose of your estimated budget is to simulate reality ahead of time to avoid surprises. Your estimate will put you on notice that you have to tighten your budget or redesign the trip a little. The estimates I've used above are relatively generous. Many travelers could easily make the same trip for 30 percent less.

In summary, avoid an absolutely bare bones budget if you can. Leave room for decent food and shelter, for small pleasures, treats, and special experiences. SAVE MONEY on big ticket items such as airfare and design lifelong memories into your budget.

CHECKLIST: BUDGET

Predeparture Expenses

$_____passport, visas, and photos

$_____international student ID card

$_____guidebooks

$_____hostel membership

$_____camera, film, filters, other photo equipment

$_____luggage, daypack

$_____new clothes

$_____travel insurance

$_____gear (binoculars, money belt, etc.)

$_____health care (medicine and shots)

$_____toiletries

$_____reading material

Transportation

$_____air fares

$_____other (trains, buses, etc.)

Meals and Lodging

$_____en route

$_____daily lodging

$_____daily meals

Special Experiences

$_____safaris, scuba diving, glacier climbing, etc.

$_____entertainment (sightseeing, tours, etc.)

Miscellaneous

$_____souvenirs, gifts, tips, laundry, etc.

HOW TO MANAGE MONEY SUCCESSFULLY

In figuring out the cost of a trip as we did above, you learn how much money you'll spend before you leave and how much to take with you. Knowing that, you have choices to make about the *form* in which you take funds with you. Your choices include currency, personal check, traveler's check, credit card, ATM card, and debit card.

Currency

Not so long ago, explorers and travelers carried their funds in truly hard currency; that is, in the form of precious metals or minerals. Everyone was relieved, although skeptical, when currency came along. Even though currency is more convenient, it's still bulky, vulnerable to loss, and uninsurable. Given the options available today, it would be a major mistake to carry all the money you need in the form of currency. So why not forget it altogether and rely on travelers checks or one of the other substitutes? There are several good reasons and I'll touch on them in the sections that follow.

How Much and Which Currency?

I generally take currency equal to 10 to 25 percent of my estimated expenditures. For the hypothetical trip above, that would be between $250 and $700.

Some guidebooks recommend carrying more than one readily-convertible currency, but I've never found that necessary. The few currencies accepted around the world for conversion into local money are the U.S. dollar, the German mark, the British pound, the Japanese yen, and, to a lesser extent, the Canadian dollar, French franc, and Swiss franc. Hotels, restaurants, and shops usually won't accept foreign currencies other than these. The U.S. dollar is the most widely accepted currency around the world, as well as on the black market.

Although carrying one dollar bills for gifts or tips makes sense, carrying change is pointless. Your coins are without value in most other countries. Tip someone with a quarter and it becomes worthless because the local bank won't give him anything for it unless he accumulates hundreds of them. Even then, the exchange rate is poor since banks don't want to transport heavy, bulky foreign coins (any more than you should).

You may want to carry a few personal checks since they're sometimes accepted in large cities or you may need them to get cash from AmEx. However, don't rely on cashing them along the way to finance your trip.

Travelers checks

Travelers checks are an efficient and safe way to transport money. They don't take up much room and you're protected in case of theft or loss. So why not take travelers checks and forget everything else? There are several good reasons:

- There may be nowhere to exchange a traveler's check for cash at the moment you need to pay for something (such as on a weekend when banks are closed). Further, many banks in less-developed countries won't accept travelers checks at all. Sad to say, some merchants won't either. They've gotten burned by accepting checks that travelers then fraudulently reported as lost or stolen to get replacements. If the issuer invalidates the check before the merchant can redeem it, the merchant bears the loss.

- You may pay a fee when you buy travelers checks and again when you exchange them for local currency.

- You may get a less-favorable exchange rate for travelers checks than for cash, although this is reversed where more money exchange offices prefer to accept travelers checks so they don't have to guard stacks of hard currency.

- Travelers checks aren't accepted on the black market, so without cash you lose the opportunity for creative financing.

The Fee

Most issuers of travelers checks will try to charge a fee, usually 1 percent of the amount you want to convert. They may imply that a fee is automatic but, if you want to SAVE MONEY, negotiate. When buying checks from a bank, point out how long you've been a customer, promise to leave your account with them for a while, or persuade them you're on your way to becoming a tycoon who will do business with, or maybe even buy, their bank. Get that fee dropped. If you belong to an organization that dispenses travelers checks (such as the American Automobile Association), you won't have to pay a fee for converting your cash into travelers checks.

> You can negotiate the fee for issuing traveler's checks.

Which Brands and What Denominations?

Carry only widely accepted brands of travelers checks such as AmEx, Thomas Cook, Citicorp, Barclays Bank, Visa, and BankAmerica. Some people recommend buying at least some travelers checks in foreign currency so you won't be stung by an unfavorable spread when you cash them overseas. I've never understood that since you're stung on the rate when you purchase them here. If you want foreign currency travelers checks and your bank can't issue them, try Thomas Cook (your travel agent can initiate the transaction online) or Ruesch International (800-424-2923).

In deciding what denominations of travelers checks to carry, the issue is bulk versus flexibility. Carrying packs of $10 checks gives you the greatest flexibility but chokes your money belt. If you take only $100 checks, you run the risk of being stuck with more local currency than you want as you're about to leave a country. I carry mostly $20s, a few $50s, and only enough $100s to pay for airline tickets and special events. If you use AmEx, you can leave home with some $500 checks and have them reissued in smaller denominations abroad. To minimize bulk, use a credit card to buy more checks as you travel.

What To Do in Case of Loss or Theft

The issuers of travelers checks promise they'll replace them if lost or stolen. And so they do, but you can make the process easier by knowing and following the rules. Sign travelers checks when you get them and sign only once. *Never* countersign a traveler's check until you're in front of the person accepting it. Most of them pay little attention, but if you draw one who does, your check won't be accepted if it's already countersigned. Further, if a check you've reported missing shows up bearing both your signature and countersignature, you'll have some explaining to do.

When you purchase the checks ask how the replacement process works, request a booklet listing local representatives where you will be traveling, and get a telephone hotline number.

When you cash a traveler's check, record the number, amount, date, and place of the transaction. If you don't keep track, a clever thief could steal a few checks and you won't discover it immediately. It's to his advantage for you to be long gone before you realize there's been a theft. You might even lose some checks yourself and fail to report them for replacement. Review your remaining checks once in a while to ensure that none are missing. If some are, you have to figure out whether you simply failed to record a transaction or the checks have been lost or stolen.

To report a lost or stolen traveler's check abroad, contact the nearest office of the issuer. If you don't have the booklet with you, look up the number in a local telephone directory (under "travelers checks," "banks," or "travel agents") or ask a local merchant or bank that accepts the checks. If you have the original receipt, or a record of the check numbers and denominations purchased, as well as those that were lost or stolen, you can expect quick replacement. Without this information, expect to wait while it's obtained. You may only get partial replacement until enough time has passed for the issuer to be sure exactly which checks are missing.

Take the receipts on the trip but *keep them separate* from the checks. That sounds obvious, but I mention it because I've heard a couple of sad stories from people who lost both their checks and receipts at the same time. I also give a copy of the receipts to my travel partner and to someone at home. That's easier than steaming in Kuala Lumpur for a few days waiting for funds to arrive.

Credit Cards

What about credit cards? Can you forget travelers checks and just take plastic? Even though credit cards are accepted in Kathmandu, and you'll find ATM machines on street corners in Marrakesh, the answer depends on where you are going. In many of the most fascinating parts of the world, credit cards are still unrecognized. And even if cards are accepted, you may not want to patronize the hotel or restaurant that will accept payment by charge card, especially when traveling on a modest budget. Still, in recent years the trend has been to rely on credit cards as the primary source of payment, at least where you can pay for almost everything with plastic, transforming travelers checks into a back-up source of payment.

Back up your credit cards with alternate sources of funds.

The credit card, recognized and accepted in many far-flung places, has become an increasingly important travel tool. In a growing number of countries, including most of Europe, many expenses can be charged on Visa, MasterCard, American Express, and, to a lesser extent, Diner's Club and Discover. In fact, it may make sense to put everything you can on your credit card if you can do so without changing the nature of your trip (e.g., eating or staying in more expensive places than you would otherwise have chosen). Since even the most experienced traveler can't calculate precisely the amount of money needed for a long trip, credit cards provide a cushion. However, even if credit cards are widely accepted at your destinations, back them up with an alternative source of funds.

Credit Card Benefits

Paying with a credit card has quite a few benefits. For example, you

- reduce the amount of cash you carry
- benefit from certain protections included in the terms of the credit card
- avoid some of the spread and commission charged when you convert cash or travelers checks into local currency
- benefit from the exchange rate you get when using a credit card (the international corporate rate is more favorable to you than the rate you get from a local bank or currency dealer)
- have some protection should there be a problem with the purchase
- possibly earn frequent flyer mileage.

More Benefits of Credit Cards

There's more. Credit card services go far beyond simply extending credit. As an example, I'll review some of the services of the lowest-fee American

Express card (to confirm the current range of AmEx services, call 800-221-7282 for a copy of the *AmEx Traveler's Companion*).

1. *Cash.* Suppose you decide on a side trip to Irian Jaya,* or you've taken a few extra scuba dives or bungee jumps, or your money belt disappears from a shelf in the bathroom. In short, you need more money. What to do? Use your credit card to get a *cash advance.* Take your AmEx card to an overseas AmEx office or one of the almost 100,000 AmEx cash dispensing machines around the world. We'll discuss using a bank card in an automatic teller machine (ATM) a few pages later.

With an AmEx card, enroll in advance in the Express Cash program and get a Personal Identification Number by calling 1-800-CASH NOW. Thereafter, you can withdraw up to $1,000 every seven days. There's a 2 percent fee per transaction (minimum fee, $2.50; maximum fee, $10). Express Cash also enables you to obtain travelers checks from American Express Dispensers and selected AmEx Travel Services offices.

2. *Check cashing.* With an AmEx card, you can cash your personal check at AmEx Travel Service Offices in more than 120 countries. You're limited to a maximum of $1,000 (up to $200 in cash, the balance in travelers checks) every twenty-one days. There's no fee for cashing a check other than a charge for the portion issued in travelers checks.

3. *Money transfer.* Using an AmEx Moneygram, someone at home can transfer up to $10,000 to you while you're traveling in any of sixty countries. Once you arrange the transaction, transfer takes only about ten minutes. You pick up the funds, usually in travelers checks, at an AmEx Travel Service Office. The catch is that fees are high. To send $10,000 by Moneygram, the sender would pay a 3½ percent fee; for $1000, the fee is 7 percent; for $100, the fee is 25 percent.

4. *Mail pick-up.* For card holders, the network of overseas AmEx offices will accept and hold mail for arrival. More on the mechanics of receiving mail in Chapter 20.

5. *Insurance benefits.* AmEx and other credit cards have certain no-extra-charge insurance benefits associated with use of the cards. AmEx provides $100,000 in accidental death and dismemberment coverage when you travel in a common carrier and have charged the tickets on your AmEx card. Benefits also include collision damage and theft insurance coverage for a rental car (up to a maximum of fifteen days). This coverage usually applies when you decline the insurance option offered by the car rental company *and* charge the rental cost on your card. This useful benefit may permit you to

---

* *Irian Jaya.* Part of Indonesia, Irian Jaya shares an island with the country of Papua New Guinea.

avoid the exorbitant fees for collision damage and theft insurance that rental car companies attempt to charge. I say *may* because some car rental companies will not accept credit card policy coverage. However, credit card coverage is intended to be effective overseas which the insurance policy on your domestic vehicle almost certainly is not. Some vehicles, such as Jeeps and RVs, are excluded, as is loss of luggage. Read the fine print.

It has become common practice for a rental car company to take an imprint of a credit card as security against possible uninsured damage to its rental car. They may then put a "hold" on part of the credit line you have available, meaning you no longer have access to that amount of credit. If that would be a problem, be certain you understand exactly what the rental car company intends to do and make your plans accordingly. Otherwise, you may be surprised at an inconvenient moment. See further discussion of rental car insurance in Chapter 16.

Purchases made with the AmEx card are covered for ninety days against theft and accidental damage up to $1,000, but only above other applicable insurance you have. This coverage includes shipment of items from overseas, but does not include items stolen from a car. The basic AmEx card provides reimbursement up to $200 for expenses caused by delayed luggage and up to $500 in excess of the airline's liability if your checked bag is lost or damaged.

6. *Legal and medical assistance.* Card holders can call the AmEx Global Assist Hotline (202-554-2639) collect from overseas for the recommendation of a doctor or help in locating an English-speaking lawyer. Global Assist will keep your family and colleagues informed about your situation and assist in transferring bail payment. For information about Global Assist, call (800) 554-AMEX in the United States.

If your credit card doesn't provide legal/medical assistance, call the nearest consulate or embassy for the same information. Embassy staff will send messages home, file a protest if you are being mistreated, and receive money sent to you from home. They won't give you legal advice and usually can't get you out of jail. A pamphlet that deals well with these issues is *A Safe Trip Abroad* (send $1 to the Consumer Information Center, Department 154 X, Pueblo, CO 81009).

7. *Other benefits.* AmEx provides information on passport and visa requirements, immunizations, and weather forecasts. It can also tell you how to replace lost documents and locate lost luggage. AmEx and some of the other cards offer free telephone translation services and will help you find a local interpreter, at your expense, if you need one. Check out the AmEx Geography Hotline at (800) 395-GLOBE.

If an AmEx card is lost, stolen, or destroyed, report it to the nearest AmEx Travel Service Office (which is easier if you're carrying the appropriate address pages from the AmEx Traveler's Companion directory). While abroad, report a loss by calling (919) 333-3211 collect. If you know your credit card number when reporting a loss, you may obtain an emergency replacement card within a day. However, since the emergency replacement card doesn't have a magnetic strip, you can't use it to get cash from an Express Cash machine.

Terms of the American Express card require that all charges be paid each month, so you might want to arrange to have this done at home. Otherwise, keep track of charges and send a check yourself. Similarly, if overseas charges, including possible purchase of airline tickets, approach the limit of a bank card, ask someone at home to make the minimum monthly payments needed to keep you below the limit, as well as to meet your card's minimum monthly payment requirement. The laws of some countries consider it fraud when a credit card holder makes a purchase that exceeds the card limit.

I've used the American Express card as an example because it has an extensive overseas network and very useful services. However, the AmEx card is more expensive and more difficult to obtain than bank cards. MasterCard, Visa, Discover, and Diner's Club now offer many of the same services, such as (a) cash advances, (b) "extended protection," meaning double the manufacturer's warranty on products you purchase, (c) "purchase security," meaning that the issuer will replace, repair, or reimburse you (usually up to $500) for eligible items of personal property in the event of theft, fire, vandalism, weather, and so on (when bought with the credit card and claimed within ninety days), and (d) rental car collision and damage insurance.

If you'll be traveling with a credit card from an issuer other than AmEx, familiarize yourself with its features. For an outline of these features for Visa, call (800) 847-2911 (outside the United States, call 410-581-9994 collect). For Mastercard, call (800) 622-7747 (outside the United States, call 303-278-8000 collect).

Credit Card Tips
- If you carry a credit card from the bank where you keep a checking account, see if the bank will use your checking account to pay any

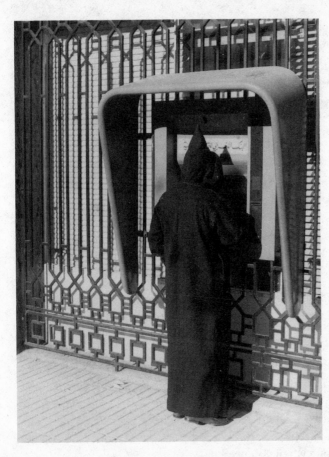

Old meets new—banker at overseas ATM. Tangier, Morocco.

charges you put on the card while on the road. That prevents interest from accruing and leaves your maximum credit limit available.

— When using a credit card, (a) read the entries carefully before signing the receipt and keep your copy to compare with the charge that later appears (just in case figures on the bank copy were altered), (b) watch that a merchant doesn't slip two sets of forms into the handpress, and (c) take the carbon or watch it being destroyed. If your credit card disappears, you may be liable for only up to $50 as long as you report the loss at once. Any merchant who accepts the card can help you report its loss.

— Using a credit card does *not* free you from paying for an item if you are dissatisfied with it, if the goods turn out to be worth less than you thought, or the vendor ships you the wrong item. You do, however, have a right to complain to the credit card issuer and withhold payment while your claim is investigated. However, you must file your complaint within the time limit stated by the issuer of the card, usually thirty or sixty days. Moreover, when goods are defective the credit card usually provides protection only to a person who purchased the item in their home state or within 100 miles of home. In other words, they aren't required to investigate claims with respect to items you bought abroad. Although many issuers make at least an attempt to investigate the dispute, the facts are often impossible to determine so they rule against the debtor (the card holder).

- If dissatisfied with the way American Express handled a dispute, you may contact the Federal Trade Commission (202-326-2222). In the case of Visa or MasterCard, contact the agency that regulates the issuer of the card.

- If you use a credit card to help finance your trip, carry more than one card. Don't let a technological glitch or plastic-eating machine bring your trip to a halt. Anticipate losing a card and have cash or travelers checks ready as backup.

To sum up, whether a credit card should be a central source of finance or merely a potentially useful supplement depends on your budget and itinerary.

ATM Cash Cards

Automatic teller machines are eagerly waiting to put cash in your hand in many corners of the world, at least if you whisper your PIN in their ears. While the ATM card reduces the importance of other forms of carrying funds, it should not become a crutch. The ATM may have instructions you can't decipher, it may not accept your card, or it may be out of money. Or you may not be able to find one when you need it.

What You Need to Know:
- Exact locations of ATMs where you'll be traveling. The Cirrus (Master-Card) and Plus (Visa) systems claim more than 200,000 locations each in almost ninety countries. Call (800) 999-5136 for a copy of MasterCard's *Shopping with Your ATM Card*. Call (800) 424-7787 for the Cirrus worldwide ATM locator service or ask your local bank for a Cirrus Location Directory. Call (800) 843-7587 to order the Visa Plus *International ATM Locator Guide* (check it out on the Internet at http:/www.visa.com/visa/).

- Whether your PIN is valid abroad. Foreign ATMs accept only numbers, not letters, and some require six numbers. Check with your bank.

- Whether overseas ATMs are open twenty-four hours a day.

- Whether there is a daily limit on how much you can withdraw.

- What fees are charged for each transaction.

An ATM withdrawal will SAVE MONEY because it clears through your bank at the commercial rate of exchange, which is 3 to 5 percent better than the tourist rate you'd get at a local bank. There should be no commission nor, since you are drawing out your own money, will you pay interest. However, your home bank probably charges a transaction fee of $2 or $3 so it's worth asking. On balance, an ATM is an efficient way to obtain cash abroad.

Debit Cards

Visa is testing TravelMoney, a prepaid travel card, similar to what is known as a debit card. You deposit a certain amount in advance with a Visa issuer and then use the card to withdraw cash from banks or ATMs until your deposit is tapped out. There probably will be no transaction fee for withdrawals and you won't be charged interest on withdrawals. You may be charged $1 if you use this card in an ATM but nothing if you use it in a bank. There's a fee for the card and, of course, you earn no interest on your deposited funds.

The European Union is now testing a debit card that permits disbursal of cash in several different European currencies. Machines are already in use in which a traveler can insert one currency, say dollars, and receive another, say marks. However, rates of exchange are typically below market. Nevertheless, diminishing national barriers and the spread of microchips are relieving monetary headaches for travelers.

Receiving Money Overseas

Suppose you're on the road and decide it's time for refueling from home. How do you get money from there to where you are? Here are some alternatives:

- Have someone send you a check payable in a foreign currency, say for thirty-five English pounds, from a U.S. bank. The typical bank will charge a fee of somewhere between $7.50 (Citibank) and $35 (Chase Manhattan), then it may charge you another $25 to wire the draft. That's quite a bit to pay just for getting less than $60 to England.

- Ask someone to buy a money order from, or take a bank money order to, Western Union who will then wire it to an overseas bank. The fees can be quite high. Furthermore, some banks abroad will insist on giving you your own money, which they received in hard currency, in local currency which may have no value beyond their borders.

- Ask someone to have a traveler's check issued in foreign currency (even if there's no fee for this, keep an eye on the exchange rate), fill in the payee, sign it and send it to you overseas (perhaps by one of the express mail services such as Federal Express).

- Reusch International, based in Washington, DC, offers an economical solution. Call (800) 424-2923 and ask for the International Division. When you specify the foreign currency and the amount you need, they'll tell you the rate of exchange and the U.S. dollar equivalent. For $2, they'll mail you a bank draft payable in the foreign funds or, for $5, they'll mail that draft to someone overseas (or wire it for $15). If the exchange rate is right, that's the best deal in town.

Exchanging Your Money

Before we discuss where and how, let's discuss situations when you're better off not exchanging money for foreign currency. The first is where you have more bargaining power when you pay in U.S. dollars. Obviously, you SAVE MONEY then by using dollars. This situation is not uncommon in Third World countries. The second is where paying in U.S. dollars would cause you to pay a premium. I think of this situation as "dollar pricing." That's what occurs when the rate a vendor, let's say a hotel, quotes is much higher in dollars than it is in local currency. The two-tier pricing enables them to extract the maximum from tourists who don't know any better. Here's an example. When the Mexican peso cratered in 1995, many tourists called travel agents to book Mexican resort vacations. What a shock they got. Prices were as high as ever because major resorts quoted their prices in U.S. dollars. Thus, resort owners, not travelers or hotel cooks, benefited from the wounded peso. At the same time, prices were rock-bottom for independent travelers who stayed in hotels off the tourist trail, ate in local restaurants, and paid in pesos. It's an important lesson.

Where to Exchange Your Money

If you fly into a country, look for an exchange window in the airport. If you arrive by train, there will probably be an exchange window in the station nearest the border or in the first large city. If arriving on foot or by automobile, you should find an exchange desk just beyond the immigration office.

If arriving in a country between midnight and dawn when the money exchange office at your point of entry may be closed, you might be wise to have a little local currency in hand. For Europe that's not hard to do, but your bank at home is not likely to have kwatcha, pula, lempira, or shillingi for you to take with you. If it does, it will charge a hefty fee and give a poor exchange rate in the bargain. It's not worth it. In my experience, where no official money exchange is available, there are always informal bankers on the street.

The only times I've entered a country carrying any of its currency were when I had some left over from an earlier visit or had bought some from another traveler (which is, since it has become worth zero to him, an opportunity to get a great deal). Only once have I gone hungry for a couple of hours as a result of having no local currency.

A few countries require travelers to change a specified amount of money at the point of entry—at the official exchange rate. Countries with this requirement usually have an artificially inflated currency and, therefore, an active black market. By clipping travelers at the border, the government ensures that it gets at least some of your money at its pie-in-the-sky official rate. Tanzania border officials made me exchange U.S. $50 at the border at a rate of 191 shillingi to $1. That was a little painful since the street rate in the nearest town was 280 to $1. Myanmar occasionally requires travelers to spend $300 to purchase local currency at a ridiculously low rate. Algeria mandates that a small amount of money be changed, but Sierra Leone sometimes requires travelers to change more money at the official rate than they'd intended to spend during their entire stay in the country. These requirements are rare and the amount is usually either a fairly modest fixed amount or an amount related to the number of days you'll be in the country.

> Wait to trade money until you know the fair exchange rate.

Hustlers at borders, including the guys outside airports and train stations, try to con you into exchanging money with them before you know what rate you should get. Since exchange rates are always poor where travelers enter a country, change only the amount you need to get into town and pay for a night's lodging and a couple of meals.

If there's no human waiting to exchange your money, there may be a machine. Automatic currency exchange machines, which resemble an ATM and are named "MultiBank," or "MultiChange," or something similar, have joined the mechanical plague spreading around the world. Increasingly common in Europe, they make exchanges among as many as fifteen currencies twenty-four hours a day. You feed the machine your currency and tell it what currency you want back. In some places, the machine's exchange rates are better than bank rates (taking bank commissions, fees, and stamps into account), but not always. Exchange the minimum amount you need until you can make a comparison. I have to admit, they're fun to play with, kind of like slot machines where you win every time.

In some countries, the only places you can exchange money are the banks. However, in Peru, Brazil, and Thailand, among others, government-sanctioned, privately owned currency exchange dealers operate in small offices along the main streets. Their rates differ from one another but are generally better than bank rates. Shop around.

Interestingly, some places in Europe post a notice offering a slightly better exchange rate if you show a student ID card. Even if there's no notice, it doesn't hurt to ask (a good rule to apply to all sorts of transactions).

The sellers of products or services, including hotels, restaurants, and souvenir shops, will almost always give you a poor exchange rate. Some will even zap you with a fee on top of that. Get your local money elsewhere.

How Much Local Currency Should You Buy?

I seldom travel with more than $50 to $100 in local currency unless I'm about to buy a ticket, or pay a hotel bill, or I anticipate some other large expense.

If you buy too much local currency, you waste money on the exchange transaction in both directions, buying and selling. Further, if you're stuck with the currency after you leave the country, it's probably a total loss. How much you need at a given moment depends on the day of the week and whether holidays are coming up. If you won't have ready access to an exchange window, exchange enough to avoid standing with an empty wallet in front of a closed bank on a holiday or weekend. You may find someone on the street who will exchange money but, if you're in a bind, you can bet the rate will reflect your situation.

To avoid winding up with excess local currency as they leave a country, partners need to keep each other current on how much local currency each is carrying.

Making the Exchange

Before you approach a currency exchange window, calculate roughly how much money you should receive in an exchange. Learn the rough relationship between your currency and theirs (e.g., you get three of theirs for one of yours), and the calculation becomes second nature. Among other things, it will keep you from being the victim of a misplaced decimal. It happens.

Things get a little complicated when you reach the window. Each foreign currency in which the dealer trades is listed, followed by several columns. The figure in the "Buying Cash" column is applicable when you are using your cash to *buy* the local currency *from* the dealer. In the "Selling Cash"

Exchanging Indian Rupees

	Buying Cash	Selling Cash	Buying Trav. Checks	Selling Trav. Checks
US $	37.00	39.00	39.00	41.00
Yen	107.00	112.00	113.00	118.00
Mark	1.50	1.60	1.65	1.75
Pound	.65	.68	.68	.71

Notes: (a) at the exchange window above, you would get a better rate for traveler's checks than for cash. (b) In a restaurant or shop, you might receive 34 rupees for $1 (a poor rate).

column, applicable when you are *selling* local currency back *to* the dealer, there's a different figure. There will always be a difference, called the "spread," between the buying and the selling rates. The selling figure will be the higher of the two. In other words, you don't get as much back when you cash out. For example, suppose you pay $10 to get 370 rupees (10 x 37). You don't use any of them, so you sell them back to the dealer. Instead of getting $10 back, you will get $9.49 (370÷39). This spread is like the house percentage in a casino, guaranteeing a profit to the dealer. Obviously, you don't want to pay that spread for any more money than you need.

The "Buying Travelers checks" column shows the rate of exchange when you are buying local currency using your travelers checks. If the dealer's ratio differs significantly between cash or travelers checks, you will want to convert at the better rate (assuming you have both cash and checks to trade).

A transaction fee may be charged when you buy local currency.

As you shop for the best exchange rate, keep an eye on the transaction fee often charged in addition to the spread. That fee may be based on (a) the total *amount* of the transaction, (b) the *number* of travelers checks you cash (the worst case I've seen was a Viennese hotel that charged $6 to cash each traveler's check, no matter what the denomination), (c) the *amount* of the checks, or (d) whether you are exchanging cash or travelers checks. Even if it sounds confusing, it becomes easy with practice.

To calculate the net result of the numbers on the money changer's signs, say to each dealer, "How many (pesos) will you give me for a U.S. $50 traveler's check (or whatever you want to exchange)?" The answers give you net figures you can compare accurately with another dealer. If the difference between dealers is small, consider whether it's really worth walking back across town to chase a few pennies.

Unfortunately, travelers can't assume that all currency exchange clerks are honest. The amount given you may not just be incorrect—it may not even be close! Some clerks play little tricks on you. In Russia, the clerk may pass you a "doll." Named after the popular Russian stacking dolls, that's a packet of money in which the top and bottom bills are real and the ones in the middle are fake. That's just one of the reasons to always count the money before taking even one step away from the counter or window. Force yourself to ignore the people in line behind you. Count the money in plain view of the clerk. If it's correct, tuck it away out of sight before you leave the window. The money is at risk as long as it's in your hand or in an accessible pocket.

Speaking of getting correct change, I think of the clerk in the post office in Kathmandu who tossed my change, a wad of rupees, on the counter. I looked down at them, made no move to pick them up, then looked at him steadily, without expression. After a few moments, he noticed me still standing there, the money undisturbed. With no comment, but looking a little disgusted, he tossed a few more rupees on the pile. I glanced down, then back at him. Twice more our little drama repeated itself, after which he refused to look up. After hi last contribution, I counted the money and found it correct. I left without a word, but with an inner smile.

In some countries in Central America, I've been almost startled to receive correct change when paying for something. The clerk or waiter often makes a small personal deduction from your change or gives you coins from a nearby country that are worth less (or worthless). I think of this practice as an informal self help or foreign aid program.

In South America, India, and a few other places, merchants play an interesting game of monetary musical chairs. When a bank note becomes torn or worn, banks will no longer accept it—which means that merchants will not accept it from you. But, oh, will they try to *give* it to you! Take a look at your change, including money you receive in a currency exchange transaction. If there is a seriously battered bill, simply hand it back with a smile. They'll accept and replace it. No hard feelings; it was just a little test to see if you heard the music stop.

Currency Declaration/Exchange Forms

Many countries require you to fill in a currency declaration form as you enter, listing the amount of money you have in cash and travelers checks. In theory they want you to show, as you leave, that your remaining money, plus receipts for money changed legally, equals your original declaration. The idea is to prevent you from exchanging money at a more favorable rate on the black market (which would leave you with more money than you should have). I've heard of only one person whose money was physically counted on arrival, so it seems you wouldn't be at much risk if you accidentally declared more than you were carrying. Doing so would make it easier to balance if you used the black market and were checked on the way out.

If your official money exchange receipts were ludicrously insufficient to have paid for basic needs, it wouldn't take Sherlock Holmes to suspect some trading on the black market. I've never been clear about what would happen at that point. I suppose you could explain that you'd stayed with friends and spent next to nothing. If that didn't fly, there might be a fine or some unofficial solution.

Keep receipts you receive when you exchange money at sanctioned exchange offices because you may need them to sell unused local currency when you leave the country. This requirement is not always enforced, but if it is and you don't have receipts, your local currency becomes a souvenir.

Some people alter official bank receipts to indicate that they exchanged larger amounts than they actually did. Since that's evidence of clear intent to deceive, I think it is a very unwise solution.

What usually happens as you leave a country is . . . nothing. If your receipts are even asked for, they're dumped in a pile without review. I can't say there has never been a thorough check, but it's not the practice. Nevertheless, it seems wise to change a reasonable amount of money legally. Moderation in all things, eh?

The Black Market

Most guidebooks avoid discussing the black market or simply say you should avoid it. Certainly that's the safest course, but I am going to discuss the black market because many travelers encounter it and many use it—or want to. If you're one of those people, you should definitely know what you're doing. You won't have to look for the black market. It will find you—in forms ranging from a discreet, eyes-averted whisper to a growling proposal from a man grasping a wad of bills in each hand.

I've heard a couple of people object to trading on the black market, feeling that doing so is harmful to the local government. It's a complex issue and I've yet to hear the pros and cons articulated convincingly. On the other hand, I suppose conservative economists applaud the black market as an inevitable operation of the capitalistic system. I've also heard people justify it on the theory that a certain government is corrupt and *should* be ripped off. On balance, I don't see it as a moral issue.

You won't have to look for the black market—it will find you.

What It Is and Why It Exists

Black markets come into being when a government insists on fixing the value of its currency higher than it would be in a free market. Besides making purchases more expensive for travelers, that makes the country's money unacceptable beyond its borders. Thus, its citizens can't travel abroad unless they somehow obtain hard currency. By hard currency, I mean coin or paper issued by a government and backed by resources adequate to redeem it at face value at any time. Its value is set by trading in the international market. In contrast, soft currency often lacks adequate backing. That's why you can't pay for a hard-money lunch in San Francisco with soft-money Indonesian rupiah. Local people also need hard currency to buy goods (from sewing machines to drugs to weapons) more cheaply in a neighboring country. Certain scarce goods may be sold only for hard currency, even within the country. The result is inevitable. To get your hard currency, local folk will give you more of their currency than you'd get at the official rate.

Of course, as we all know, not everyone is looking for money to buy a sewing machine. For many, exchanging money is their primary business and more than a few are not your most savory citizens. These black market traders profit by paying you one price for hard currency, then finding people who will eagerly pay them even more for your money.

Countries differ in how they deal with black market operations. In Brazil and Peru, for instance, most of the black market is officially tolerated. In neighboring Chile, it isn't. In Zimbabwe the government is so tough on local dealers that the black market has been forced underground (i.e., there are no street solicitors). On the bright side, if you can arrange a black market transaction in Zimbabwe it's likely to be free from shenanigans.

The reason travelers exchange money on the black market is no mystery. It's not uncommon to receive 30 percent more local money on the black market than you get when exchanging money at the official rate. The last time I was in Zimbabwe the street rate was 51 percent higher than the bank rate. In Bolivia, the black market rate has occasionally been 800 percent more than the official rate!

If the Myanmar government forces you to buy $300 worth of kyats at the airport at the official rate of six for $1, it would cost you about $150 for a cab into town. Later you can buy foreign exchange certificates (FEC) at a rate of, say, 100 kyat for $1. On the black market, you'll get 115 kyat for $1. Even where the spread is smaller, whether travel is very cheap or moderately expensive depends on how much you pay for your local currency.

Many of the major black market opportunities that previously existed in South America and Eastern Europe have diminished. However, substantial differences between the official rate and the black market rate (the spread) still exist in Algeria, Angola, China, India, Libya, Mozambique, Myanmar, Nepal, Romania, Rwanda, Surinam, Uganda, Vietnam, and Zaire. There are other countries in which spreads are more modest, say 15 percent. If there's any risk in using a particular black market, I wouldn't consider it unless the bonus is more than 10 percent.

If you're going to a country with a black market and expect to use it, you may want to carry a higher percentage of your funds in cash. If you do, be especially watchful for thieves along the way.

Risks of Trading on the Black Market

Prepare for a black market exchange as you would for a legitimate exchange at a bank. Ask other travelers what rates they've been getting and where. Listen to offers, but make no deals until you have a good idea of the best rate. If someone offers you a below-market rate and won't raise it, smile pleasantly and walk off.

Prepare for black market exchanges as you would legitimate ones.

Here's a tip that's less obvious. If offered a rate considerably *above* the usual black market rate, don't even discuss it. Leave immediately because a rip-off is underway. The high rate is the bait and you've been cast in the role of fish. Because dealers operate within a narrow range of rates, an offer significantly above the range signals a transaction that, one way or another, is never going to close at that rate.

In evaluating risk, the first consideration is the potential legal penalty; where black market trading is against the law, you might get caught. An immigration official might conclude that you've been trading on the black market if your currency declaration form and official money exchange receipts don't explain your expenditures. They could ask questions, but it never seems to happen.

A police officer might witness a street transaction and arrest you. That's not pleasant to contemplate, but I've yet to hear of a traveler being confined for a black market currency exchange. For drugs or smuggling, sure, but it seems unlikely for a street trade.

The biggest risk is that you take a chance of getting ripped-off yourself as you concentrate on beating the government exchange rate. In all the world, the risk of this is probably highest in Dar es Salaam, the capital of Tanzania. I estimate the chances of getting ripped-off in Dar are at least seven out of ten.

Picture a traveler who has just arrived in Dar after a tiring trip. The heat and humidity, along with a couple of bitter, lukewarm beers beneath a drooping umbrella at the New Africa Hotel, have dulled his brain. As he steps out into the street, two young men smoothly slip alongside like pilot fish. In well-practiced English, they offer to help find a hotel, a taxi, a safari company, or whatever else he wants. No charge, of course. They are master directors, setting the stage for the play. Before long, this prologue leads to Act One in which the traveler agrees to change money with them. If he feels a little obligated, maybe even a little friendly, he won't even feel the hook go down.

Act Two can go several ways. In the midst of the transaction, just after he's handed over his money, a police officer rushes up. The traveler's new acquaintances start running and the cop goes after them. After standing there for a minute, the traveler says to himself something like, "Gee, those guys took off with my money." Or maybe the cop stays and threatens the traveler with jail . . . unless, of course, he prefers to pay a fine to the cop on the spot. He might even take the traveler to the police station. If that happens, he's well connected and the fine will be painful. How does $500 sound?

There's another variation. As the transaction gets underway with a dealer, several of his friends appear and simply take the money, using no more than implication of force.

Sometimes the dealer mixes small bills inside a stack of larger bills, includes a few outdated bills that have no value, or uses sleight of hand to give a short count. Maybe he slips in some currency from a country even more depressed than his own.

I talked with someone who had climbed into the back seat of a car parked on a busy street in Dar because it seemed a safe place for an exchange. Unexpectedly, the car drove away, putting the traveler at something of a disadvantage. A passenger in the front seat asked for the traveler's money to "check it for counterfeit." Oh, sure! At that point, the traveler noticed that there were no inside door handles. Thinking quickly as the car stopped at an intersection, he reached out the window, jerked the door handle, and hopped out. The car drove on and the only price he paid was a hot walk back to the center of town. It was a cheap lesson if he learned it. A traveler who comes away with anything at all from an exchange in Dar should immediately try his luck in Monte Carlo.

In summary, yes, there are risks. However, thousands of travelers successfully exchange money on the black market every day. Those who are repeatedly successful know what they're doing.

How to Do It Right

The best way to control black market risk is to exchange money with business people, especially restaurateurs, hotel managers, and shop owners, in their place of business. They'll be in the same place day after day. If they were to rip you off, they'd have to face you the next day. They'd rather make their money when they move your hard currency along in the system. As established merchants, they make arrangements to prevent unexpected official visits. To make it discreet, you may just pay your bill, using hard currency, at the black market rate.

Another relatively risk-free exchange is with a local person for whom it's an occasional transaction, a person doing it to serve a goal such as study or travel abroad. Since they want to keep their accumulation of hard currency quiet, there's not likely to be a problem.

In Kigali, Rwanda, a portly man on the street offered a rate of 115 Rwandan francs, compared with the bank rate of 77. When the traveler produced his money, the man offered his personal check in return. Personal check? It was the traveler's first week in Africa and it must have showed.

If you decide to deal with a street person, control risk by setting the ground rules yourself.

- Don't initiate the transaction and don't ask the rate. Let the offer come from the trader.

- Require that the exchange occur in a place you consider safe, such as your locked hotel room or a semipublic place that you choose.

- Don't let the other person see all your money, or even where you keep it. Count out the bills you'll exchange and put them, ahead of time, in a separate pocket.

- *Insist* that he hand his money to you or your partner to count first; not *vice versa* or even simultaneously. Never buy his line that since neither of you trusts the other the exchange should be simultaneous. You know you're not going to run off with his money but you don't know what he'll do. If he runs you won't catch him. Think about it: if he couldn't run faster than an outraged client, he wouldn't still be in business.

- Count the money carefully. Separate each bill from the next to avoid counting the bills he's folded in half as two bills. If he's up to something, he'll try to distract you, perhaps with conversation. Count the money again. After you've counted it, don't let him get it back from you on some pretext. If he gets his hands on it again, he has another chance for a switch. When you're satisfied, give him your money and watch his hands. He may try to palm one of your bills and claim he never received it.

When someone won't make the exchange on your terms, smile and take a hike. Trust your intuition. As Kenny Rogers preaches: "Know when to hold 'em, know when to fold 'em, know when to walk away, and know when to run."

In making a decision about trading on the black market, ask yourself whether you feel any ethical qualms. What level of risk are you willing to tolerate? How much of your trip depends on getting the black market rate? Before you go ahead, assess the local situation. Talk with other travelers and consider the suggestions above. Never be greedy and never press your luck.

I have a fond recollection of a flight from India to Nepal. The flight attendant came to my seat and asked if my partner and I would like to join the captain in the cockpit. Surprised but pleased, we accepted instantly. Throughout the flight, the captain chatted away, identifying various Himalayan peaks, even standing the plane on one wing to point out Mount Everest. It was a fantastic experience. Only as we were on the final landing path into Kathmandu, runway racing toward the cockpit windshield, did the long, slow curve break sharply over the plate. "I say," said the captain in that melodious Indian accent, "I wonder if you would like to change a few hundred dollars for rupees? Black market rate, of course."

Bargaining—When and How

Most Westerners are convinced they don't like bargaining, at least not "street" bargaining. Perhaps underlying a cultural hang-up is the belief that they don't know how to do it. Except for unhappy episodes when attempting to buy a car, most Westerners don't do much one-on-one bargaining.

A traveler should get ready for a change of pace because in most of the world bargaining is part of daily life. In the Third World, anyone who doesn't bargain is regarded as so foolish that he or she deserves to be charged a penalty. Even in Europe it's far more common than most Western tourists realize. It would be a shame to let inhibitions or cultural differences interfere with experiencing the art and sport of bargaining. Besides, if you use tips from this chapter you'll SAVE MONEY wherever you travel. It's a skill that can also help you SAVE MONEY when you return home.

In the Third World, prices in restaurants are usually fixed—but be prepared to bargain for almost everything else, including hotel rates, transportation, guides and treks, clothing, art, crafts, and souvenirs (even small ones). You may occasionally walk into a shop and see price tags on items, maybe even a sign that says "fixed prices." Occasionally prices really are fixed, but these signs are more likely the first move in bargaining chess.

Surely you can't bargain over air fare? Oh, but you can! The offices of most major airlines won't bargain, as far as I know, but many travel agencies abroad have some latitude in what they charge for a ticket. There's a spread between what they get from you and what they remit to the airline. Since you don't bargain with travel agents at home, you may feel reluctant but give it a try. You'll be surprised at how often the agent comes up with a previously unmentioned "special." You'll never get it without asking.

To begin the bargaining process, start with your own state of mind. Loosen up. Think of yourself as writing your own lines in an amusing play.

Ideally, you should decide what an item is worth to you before you start bargaining. That's easier said than done with spontaneous purchases, especially when it's something you've never seen or heard of before. Have you given much thought to how much an antique Peruvian coca pouch is worth to you? If there's a price tag on it, ignore it. If the merchant calls out a price, ignore it. Think for a moment what you would pay to have that particular object in your home. Only then should you investigate what the item is worth in the local market. Ask several people who've bought something similar. If you ask just one person, it may be someone who paid way too much.

Don't fall in love with something the first time you see it. Check out other shops. The colorful carved fish mobile that caught your eye in Ubud, Bali, has counterparts in a dozen shops—and they differ in quality as well as the shopkeeper's view of its value. Initial prices vary from merchant to merchant. Do some preliminary bargaining to get feedback from the market. After a few rounds of light sparring, you'll have an idea of the neighborhood of the outcome. More than anything, successful bargaining takes patience. As the process continues, you keep adding to your information.

See what local buyers pay for what you want. As you walk through the market, look over their shoulders. You may not get it for the same price, but you know what the merchant can sell it for and still make a profit. That's a big edge.

The bargaining process begins as you enter the shop.

Recognize that the bargaining process begins earlier in a transaction than you think. While you're wandering around the shop, the vendor is sizing up your clothes and noting the amount of attention you give particular items. As she approaches, you'll hear: "You are from what country?" She may inquire about your occupation and where you're staying. Her bargaining strategy will be based on your responses, starting with the language in which you answer. As charming as she may be, her questions do not spring from friendly curiosity.

They're part of a highly developed socioeconomic evaluation that would make Northwestern's Kellogg Graduate School of Management proud. Answering her questions would be like showing your hole card in the middle of a hand of poker. Instead, just smile, mumble, respond with a question of your own, or act as if you didn't understand her.

It would be an expensive error to show enthusiasm for the thing you want, so bargain first for something else. Let your attention wander from one item to another, patiently letting the vendor guess what might interest you. The more time she invests, the greater her eagerness to conclude a sale at some price. I try to avoid bargaining in front of other shoppers since I don't know what affect their presence may have on the merchant.

She may try to hand you the item in which she thinks you have an interest. Just smile and nod, hands in pockets. If you accept it, you may have a difficult time getting her to take it back.

Don't hesitate to courteously criticize the item for which you're bargaining, pointing out real or imagined defects. Indicate aspects that aren't right for you or mention features of similar products elsewhere that this one doesn't have. However, I avoid implying that the shopkeeper or artisan is intentionally selling something undesirable or worthless. There's always some "face" involved and you do better by maintaining a courteous relationship. Keep the tone light, never angry. I cringe when a tourist bargains loudly and aggressively, heaping scorn on some object. Whatever the outcome, it's a disgraceful way for a visitor to behave. Similarly, if the vendor gets too aggressive, I'm out of there. I don't mind a skillful pitch, but I'm not there to be hassled. I am absolutely certain I do not want to carry an 8 x 10 carpet in my luggage, no matter how beautiful it is in the merchant's eyes. If I can't get her to stop trying to sell it to me, I leave.

Always let the merchant make the first offer. Don't respond when pressed for a counteroffer. Be cool. Keep looking around. See if the price will drop before you respond. The merchant's first price may be twice to ten times what will be accepted, so don't think of just knocking 10 or 20 percent off it. If you pay more than 60 percent of the asking price at the famous Sunday market in Chichicastenango,* the shopkeeper might light a candle in your memory. In other words, don't buy into the asking price as being somehow related to actual value. If interested, mention a figure you *might* pay; perhaps 20 percent of the reduced asking price. State your tentative counteroffer with reluctance and expect a response somewhere between incredulity and personal affront. In a rare case, your integrity or sanity may be challenged. Keep in mind that merchants are also actors with their own scripts.

Chichicastenango. This small town in Central Guatemala has winding streets, whitewashed houses with red tile roofs, and an Indian population that wears colorful traditional clothing.

If you have any expertise concerning an item, don't reveal it until you can use it to your advantage as you near the climax.

Tell the shopkeeper that you aren't a rich tourist and can't afford her price. If you're staying at an inexpensive hotel, say so. If what you say is consistent with how the shopkeeper has sized you up, perhaps a smaller profit will be more acceptable than loss of the sale.

Two people can be an effective team in a bargaining situation by playing a variation of the old "good guy, bad guy" routine. As one person bargains, the other begins to fidget, expresses disinterest in the item, checks the time, moves toward the door, and exerts pressure on the bargainer to come along. At that point, the prospective buyer mentions a price considerably lower than that at which the negotiation has stalled. The merchant, having only a few moments in which to make the deal, may yield a bit more.

If you're by yourself, suggest that you're going to leave and "look around," perhaps mentioning a competitor's prices, real or mythical. These are words that strike dread into the heart of any merchant. Once out the door, you're someone else's prey. Or say, "I'm going to see what my friend thinks." More grim words. Be sure to give the merchant a chance to make another "final" offer. It shouldn't take long. If it doesn't come, step out the door. If a merchant won't drop the price any lower as you walk out, and doesn't follow you, you're close to a fair price.

If you've reached an impasse on something you really want, tell the seller you'll pay the price if some other widget you have an interest in is included.

If you're planning to buy several of one item, such as a sarong, first negotiate a price for a single item. Then introduce the possibility of buying several. Ask for a further discount of, say, 30 percent.

It sometimes helps to pull money out of your pocket and hold it in your hand. Psychologically, it may make the seller want to reach for it—by meeting your price. More than once I've put the amount of my target price in one pocket, pulling it out at the last moment and saying, "This is what I have." It sometimes works. If it doesn't and I still want to play, I check another pocket and discover a bit more money. Remember, timing is important—and she's been through this scene thousands of times.

In countries in which hard currency has special value, you may break an impasse by offering to pay your price, but in U.S. dollars.

Prices vary from season to season. In the tourist off-season, great deals are available but when the market is pulsing with acquisitive tourists, you'll pay closer to the top of the range (but still less than the asking price). After all, the vendor knows there will be an innocent coming through the door right behind you, eager to be sheared.

It's easy to lose perspective during the bargaining process. You could find yourself getting hung up over $2, or even fifty cents. If you feel ambivalent about purchasing the item, hold firm or walk away. If it's something you want to own, and walking off doesn't produce a last-minute concession, walk back and pay the shopkeeper's last price. Don't let your own "face" stand in your way. Why chastise yourself later over having left behind something you really wanted?

What if the asking price is so cheap that you're willing to pay it without discussion? If you're talking about a few cents, it's not worth your time to bargain. But if you want to make a contribution, why not choose an appropriate charity or a needy person? Why make a donation to a shopkeeper who, in that economy, is seldom one of the needier people?

If you accept something from the merchant, such as a cup of tea or a cold drink, be aware that her primary motive is to make you feel indebted and/or friendly. I'm not disparaging her motive, only saying that acceptance of a cup of tea creates no obligation on your part. If you don't reach agreement, leave with a courteous "thank you anyway." Under the rules of engagement, negotiating, no matter how lengthy, commits you to nothing. You're ethically free to walk away anytime. If you and the merchant place a different value on something and you can't resolve the difference, that's okay. However, when a merchant accepts a price you've offered, you should pay that price. It would be bad karma to walk away at that point.

As you bargain for anything, remember that your adversary is a pro, much more experienced at this than you are. She knows her costs and the quality of the item. She won't close a sale if she won't come out all right, so don't hesitate to do your best. Stay lighthearted and friendly. Since sitting all day in a market stall on a steamy day isn't anyone's idea of a great time, a good bargaining bout may be fun for the seller. However the deal goes, leave one another with a pleasant memory.

> Remember that the shopkeeper is a pro at bargaining.

Here's a final thought about "after the sale." If it later appears that your purchase wasn't all that shrewd because of price or quality, learn what you can from the experience and forget self-recriminations. If somebody claims to have bought the same thing for less, think of it as a reminder of price elasticity that you can use to your advantage next time (and people have been known to shade the truth more than a little when discussing their own shrewd bargaining). All this may seem complicated at first, but it isn't in practice. In no time, you'll be improving on these strategies with your own flourishes.

More on bargaining in Chapter 11 (Lodging) and Chapter 21 (To Buy or Not to Buy).

7

Travel Gear

I had grown into my clothes, the way travelers do
who haven't looked into a mirror for weeks.
— Colin Thubron
Night in Vietnam

TRAVEL LIGHT!!!

That's so easy to say—and so hard to do. I hear of people who claim they can slide everything they need for a three-month trip under their plane seat every time. Or fit it all, plus the Collected Works of Shakespeare, into a daypack. But let's talk about normal human beings, people who want to travel with a good book, camera, shower shoes, maybe even a snorkel; people traveling to have fun. They too can travel light, but it takes some thought.

For my first long trip, I wanted to be prepared to dress (up) for any contingency. The predictable result: overload, a greenhorn's mistake. The fact is that local people are aesthetically-understanding about travelers. If you look clean and smile, they don't expect high fashion. Randy Wayne White, whose excellent articles appear in *Outside* magazine, observed that inexperienced travelers take too much of what they don't need, and experienced travelers take too much of what they do need. Instead of throwing or giving it away, they lug the extra stuff mile after mile to be returned unused to the closet.

There's a better way. Don't include an item just because it *might* come in handy (the deadly "just in case" syndrome). You can almost always do without it. If not, you can probably find some local equivalent. Limit yourself to what you're willing to carry without complaint up a steep hill on a hot day. If traveling with a partner, travel light enough that either of you can carry all the luggage, leaving the other free to sprint ahead to find a room or good seats on a bus.

Try to hold your personal load to twenty-five pounds. Thirty to thirty-five is more likely, and still bearable. If you leave home with more than fifty pounds, I guarantee you'll cut down for the next trip. A few extra pounds may not seem to matter much at home, but they will on the road. Besides, international airlines may charge a penalty for everything above forty-four pounds. Even if they waive the penalty, your back cannot.

Besides weight, you also want to consider the quality of your gear. There is no point wasting money in buying trendy labels, but cutting corners could become expensive if something important fails on the road. Besides, the fancier gear looks, or the more recognizable the brand name, the more it commends itself as a target for thieves. It's best to buy high-quality, durable, lightweight clothing and equipment, but don't let prices of the optimum gear keep you at home. Some people travel with the cheapest gear available and good fortune usually carries them through without a hitch.

When I tired of starting from scratch each time I prepared for a trip, I made a list of everything I'd taken on past trips and evaluated each item in terms of whether it had been needed. I then made a list of everything that had been worthwhile, and that list, tweaked to take climate and special activities into account, serves as the basis for every trip I take. It makes packing a snap.

Remember the guy who gave a speech that went on and on, boring his audience into slumber? At the end, he apologized, saying, "My speech would have been shorter if I'd had more time to prepare." Choosing the right travel gear also requires time and research. Proceeding by trial and error in haste, an inexperienced traveler will always carry too much.

CHOOSING LUGGAGE

Choosing what to carry your gear in as you wander the world is an important decision. My criteria for luggage are transportability, durability, accessibility, and security. With these in mind, let's review the strengths and weaknesses of various types of luggage: hard-sided, soft-sided, duffel bags, backpacks, daypacks, and the accessories that go with them.

Hard-sided Luggage

After watching poor quality, overstuffed luggage disintegrate in transit, baggage handlers recommend hard-sided luggage because of its durability. Of course, durability is important partly *because* of baggage handlers. However, I don't recommend a standard hard-sided suitcase for anything but a trip where you go to one place, stop, and return—a typical business trip. Weight is the major reason. A hard-sided suitcase adds an extra ten pounds or so beyond the weight of soft-sided luggage. When it's dead weight dangling at the end of one arm, you'll be ready to abandon it after the first mile.

Soft-sided Luggage

My first choice, and that of many travelers, is to carry the weight on my back. Nevertheless, some people cannot or prefer not to carry a backpack. Maybe it's a back problem, maybe an image problem, maybe just habit. If that's the case, look for soft-sided luggage made of 1,000-denier Cordura nylon or polyester. If it has wheels, make sure they are wide and sturdy, partly recessed or protected by housings (dainty little wheels won't stand up to rough surfaces and long distances), and make sure the luggage comes with a strong leash or handle. Look for a waterproof pocket and compression straps inside (to keep your gear from shifting). Good construction is important. Rivets are more durable than D-rings or screws for connecting shoulder straps and handles. Seams are usually encased in plastic for water-resistance, but casings of leather, shell fabric, or wide woven tape resist abrasion better.

The Lark E-Z Traveler Soft Piggyback (call 800-421-5275 for information) and the Samsonite Silhouette Piggyback (call 800-262-8282) have durable wheels, a retractable handle, and a strap. They're sturdy but expensive. The Lark, for example, can cost $300-$400, depending on size. An alternative is the Travelpro 727 Rollaboard (about $150), a soft-sided, roll-a-long bag small enough to be carried aboard. The Travelpro 777 (about $200) is a larger, check-in version. Although Travelpros are used by many airline crews, they have small wheels, which allow the bottom of the bag to scrape. If you'll be using the bag beyond the confines of plane and hotel, I'd consider something else.

Consumer Reports has given "Best Buy" status to the Samsonite Oyster ($90) and the Airway Atlantic Concept (also $90), even though the shells of both are only 600-denier. The TravelSmith Turbo Transit ($159) has something for everyone: 1000-denier Cordura, sturdy rubber wheels, a strong nylon strap for pulling, a leather handle, a pair of hidden shoulder straps so you can sling the whole thing onto your back, and a small pack that zips off the side for day trips. With the daypack zipped off, the Turbo Transit meets carry-on limits. Call (800) 950-1600 for the catalogue.

When you're shopping, picture yourself pulling the suitcase uphill on a winding lane in Greece. Are the wheels so thin they can't handle the cobblestones? Is the suitcase so high and narrow it will tip over every few feet? A suitcase that works fine for a European destination where it will be hoisted about by taxi drivers, porters, and bellmen (assuming you're willing to pay for their services) may be much less satisfactory where you are handling it yourself on subways and in bus stations. As you explore more deeply into the Third World, distances grow longer and the sun hotter.

Carefully examine brand name bags on sale in discount stores. Those bags are often inferior in quality to similar models sold in luggage shops. If you choose a shoddy bag, then stuff it to its limits, don't be surprised if it fails along the way. Improve the odds a bit by securing cheapo luggage with a couple of tough webbed luggage straps.

Duffel Bags

A duffel bag with a broad shoulder strap works well for some people, although, because it has no frame, it offers little protection for the contents.

Consumer Reports gave a perfect rating to the L.L.Bean Sportsman ($109). It's made of 1,000-denier fabric and weighs only half as much (4.2 pounds) as most soft-sided luggage. Call (800) 221-4221.

Eagle Creek (800-874-9925) cargo duffels and cargo gear bags are much less expensive than a good pack. Made of Cordura nylon, they range in size from 2,000 cubic inches up to 12,100 cubic inches and come with a good shoulder strap. The Eagle Creek Toy Chest (5,850 cubic inches, $149) has expandable side pockets, a comfortable shoulder strap, and lots of other goodies.

The BAD (Best American Duffel) Bag has some of the best workmanship I've seen in duffels. BAD Bags (call 800-424-2247) come in four sizes from 3,000 to 8,000 cubic inches. The 5,200 cubic inch bag sells for $104. Made of 1,000 denier Cordura Plus with a one-ounce urethane coating for water resistance, BAD Bags have two inside pockets, an outside pocket, a leather handle, a seat-belt nylon shoulder strap, two grab loops, and heavy-duty hardware. BAD Bags look great and are built to handle hard wear on the road. One model was chosen by Will Steger for his seven-month dogsled trip across Antarctica in 1990 and an Outside magazine writer wrote that "BAD Bags are the best all-around duffel bags available."

Because duffel bags hold so much, they can get very heavy. To address that problem, an interesting hybrid developed that has recessed rubber wheels on one end and a leash on the other (which, of course, makes them heavier still). If you go in this direction, I recommend getting one that has a shoulder strap. The L.L. Bean Large Ultimate Rolling Duffel (6,220 cubic inches, Cordura Plus, $140) is well made and comes with built-in fiberglass stays around the bottom. The Eddie Bauer textured nylon duffel bag with wheels has shoulder and waist straps (5,800 cubic inches, about $200; call 800-426-8020). The Briggs & Riley version looks very businesslike (about $180; 415-728-2000).

Backpacks

The days when backpacks were carried solely by hard-core hikers or hippies are long gone. They are now carried by travelers from across the entire economic spectrum. I've never grown fond of carrying a heavy weight on my back, but I consider a backpack the best choice for the type of travel I enjoy. It keeps me mobile, able to take my gear where I want to go without pulling my arm off. Using its harness, I can go farther, easier with a backpack than with any other form of luggage.

A good pack is made of tough fabric, provides easy access to its contents, can be locked up tight, and stands up to the rigors of any trip. For ten years, I had not one problem with my Kelty Kathmandu. When the main zipper finally failed, Kelty took the pack and replaced all the zippers and the back panel without charge. That's standing behind a product. To meet the criteria of, durability, accessibility, security, and transportability, I recommend a convertible, interior frame backpack. "Convertible" means that the harness suspension system can be zipped out of sight behind a zippered panel. In that mode, resembling normal luggage more than a backpack, you can walk into a hotel or a bureaucrat's office without being stereotyped as a backpacker. Oh, the concierge in a five-star hotel will probably notice, but if he's as good as he should be he'll never raise an eyebrow. Besides, who wants to plan a trip around the expectations of a concierge?

If you're going on a lengthy wilderness excursion, you may prefer a backpack with an exterior metal frame to which a sleeping bag, climbing equipment, and other odds and ends can be attached. Otherwise, an interior frame pack is superior. It's lighter, less susceptible to damage, and less likely to get hung up on an airport carousel.

just GO! magazine (which has evolved into *EcoTraveler*) gave the Eagle Creek Continental Journey pack its highest rating: sturdy construction, 3,900 cubic inch capacity, Cordura Plus nylon, internal frame, lockable YKK zippers, and a zip-off daypack (4.3 pounds, about $170). The Eagle Creek Transport I backpack ($180) is very similar, except that it's a little heavier and more upscale in appearance. Another very popular Eagle Creek model is its smaller convertible called Solo Journey (about $100). Eagle Creek's most recent products are the Switchback ($195) and Switchback-Plus ($245). The former is a convertible backpack with built in rubber wheels and a pull-frame. The Plus version adds a zip-off daypack. Consumer Reports liked the L.L.Bean Travel Pack ($99) and the Jansport China Clipper ($140). The Jansport Vagabond Travel Pack (6,240 cubic inches, $150) also gets good reviews. REI and Kelty packs also receive consistently good reviews from travelers.

Daypacks

In addition to one principal piece of luggage, I use a daypack to carry a book, journal, pens, maps, fruit, sunglasses, camera and film, medical supplies such as band aids and sunscreen, and, usually, a bottle of water; things to which I want easy access. I do *not* use it for carrying things that belong in my money belt. My daypack has one main compartment and two smaller ones, all with lockable zippers. It's a dark color and leaves home well treated with Scotchgard. Apply the same standards of quality for a daypack as for a backpack. You'll rely on it for years, so go for quality.

Some women prefer, especially when traveling in Europe, a purse-equivalent to a daypack. If that's your choice, be sure it is sturdy and defensible, with a secure clasp and a tough strap. If you can do without a purse, you should.

That leads to the topic of a fanny pack. It should never be used as a storage place for valuables. It's probably better for carrying non-valuables than a purse, but a thief may strike anyway since he won't know what you have in it. If interested in a fanny pack, they are sold everywhere. Some of the most ingenious are offered by L.L.Bean. To show how far uptown they've come,

Packs

I recommend that a pack have the following characteristics (many of which are equally applicable to suitcase, carry-on, or duffel bag):

- *Color.* Any pack gets dirty from spending time on train station platforms, the open deck of a boat, the roof of a bus, or as your seat in an ox-cart. A dark color makes the dirt less obvious.
- *Fabric.* Choose a durable fabric. One of the best materials is 1,000-denier Cordura nylon with a light urethane coating. Cordura is tough but not waterproof, so Scotchgard it before each trip. If your pack will be exposed to water, consider a rain cover (check the catalogues, $13 to $35). A large plastic trash bag provides protection and is less expensive.
- *Construction.* Look closely at the construction of luggage you are considering. On a pack, the seams should be double- or triple-stitched and reinforced at stress points. Inside seams should be taped or finished. Raw edges will soon begin to fray—and those little stringlets seek zippers like a Sidewinder missile seeks heat.
- *Handle.* It should be padded.
- *Shoulder strap.* It should be padded and wide.
- *Suspension harness.* It should be strong and easily adjustable. The stays should be aluminum so they can be fitted to the contour of your back.
- *Lumbar pad.* It should be large enough to provide a cushion where the pack rests against your lower back.
- *Waist belt.* It should be strong and padded.
- *Compression straps.* They should tighten the load to keep it from shifting around.
- *Zippers.* Plastic zippers seem to fail less frequently than metal and work more smoothly in very cold temperatures. Ensure that zippers are sturdy (such as #10 YKK) and well-sewn into the pack. Check that the zipper will re-seat itself on its tracks if it splits open. There should be a flap over the zipper to keep rain out.
- *Compartments.* In single-compartment luggage, contents can become a hopeless jumble as you paw through. I prefer a large front-opening compartment plus several smaller, lockable compartments that let you separate contents on the basis of function. If a pack has just one compartment, use stuff bags of different colors to create mobile compartments and make things easier to find.

  Some people like packs with a zip-off compartment that can serve as a daypack, but I prefer a daypack designed solely to be a daypack.

- *Expansion.* Some packs have a soft bottom (and duffels an expandable end) that opens to increase capacity by up to 1,000 cubic centimeters. This feature is handy toward the end of your trip if purchases become irresistible, but it would be a great error to fill it up as you start the trip.

there are now modular system fanny packs with zip-off gear pouches, mesh water bottle holsters, urethane-coated packcloth for water-repellency, external tie-downs (for things like a wind shell), a padded back panel, and a Scotchlite reflective strip on the back. What would Daniel Boone think?

Baggage Limits

Not surprisingly, airlines limit the size and weight of luggage they permit passengers to check or carry aboard. Since luggage is more secure and protected from loss and rough handling if you carry it aboard, you need to know carry-on size limits. Further, you need to know check-in limits so you aren't forced to leave a bag behind in some remote airport. This information should be one of the factors affecting your choice of luggage.

The bad news is that because rules differ from airline to airline and change frequently, I can only give you guidelines. You need the facts applicable to your specific trip. Learning weight and size limitations will SAVE MONEY. If your luggage is overweight at the airport, a point at which you have little bargaining power, you may pay a stiff penalty. Penalties for excess baggage start at $45 per bag and increase from there.

As a general proposition, the cheaper your plane ticket (relative to other tickets for the same flight), the more strict the limits on weight, size, and number of pieces. In the United States, weight limits are seldom a problem, except on small planes taking you to small places. Most airlines will accept bags weighing up to seventy pounds. Typically, you are permitted to check two pieces of luggage and carry one aboard. Sometimes you're allowed to check a third piece in place of the carry-on. A briefcas or collapsible luggage cart could technically count as part of your allowance but seldom does. Reading material, 35mm cameras, binoculars, and similar items are not counted.

Check the airline's size and weight limits before you go.

There are no standardized international weight or size limits, but a maximum of forty-four pounds is not unusual. For checked luggage, a total size of sixty-two inches (length + width + height) for one piece is common for economy class (with a total of 106 inches allowed for two pieces). Enforcement is erratic. In Bangkok, I've watched many passengers check four to six heavily strapped bags, each large enough to conceal a small water buffalo.

Carry-on luggage is often limited to a total of forty-five inches for under-the-seat (9 + 14 + 22), sixty inches for overhead (10 + 14 + 36), and seventy-two inches for a garment bag (4 + 23 + 45). Some airlines have a wonderfully simple solution. They place a wooden box near the gate. If you can cram your bag into it, you may carry it on board. If not, it doesn't go. I've listened to passengers scream in rage when told their bags were too large to be carried aboard.

If you're about to get socked for an overweight penalty, be creative. Reclaim your luggage. Unpack and dress in as much as you need to (there is no limit on that yet). Load up your daypack. Ask someone to treat one of your bags as theirs (which they won't do if they're cautious). If nothing else works and the circumstances are right, leave a little currency in your ticket envelope (this is not recommended in the United States, Canada, and most of Europe).

Where to Buy Luggage

Where will you find the luggage you want? If you prefer a standard suitcase, visit department stores and luggage shops. If you're considering a duffel or backpack, start by reviewing catalogues, including L.L.Bean, Camp-Mor, Magellan's, Patagonia, REI, and MountainSmith. Scan outdoor and travel-oriented magazines. Educate yourself about what is available on the market and the price ranges. Don't forget discount stores such as Service Merchandise or Wal-Mart (it's amazing how quickly features of the best luggage are copied).

When you have a feeling for features and prices, stop by a local outdoor gear store or travel superstore to find packs with the features you want. By visiting a local store, you can see and touch the product, discuss fit, quality, and characteristics with a knowledgeable person, compare competing products, and get later help fixing any glitches.

Try on different packs with the assistance of a salesperson who knows how they should fit. Learn how to adjust the suspension harness properly for your body. When you've found a pack that feels right, examine its construction and features closely.

Resist the temptation to buy a pack that has too much volume for you. Given the compulsion to fill empty space, think about the maximum weight you want to carry and keep airline size limits in mind. One traveler I admire hasn't checked a piece of luggage for years. She travels only with a bag that she can take on board and fit under the seat or in the overhead compartment. Besides eliminating the risk of losing her bag in transit, the smaller bag disciplines her to travel light.

Ask for recommendations from the sales person, especially if he or she is an experienced traveler. What are the strengths and weaknesses of the various types of luggage? Which ones have other customers liked the most? When you've made your choice, load it up and walk around the neighborhood so you know what to expect.

Shop for the best price for the luggage you want, but be cautious about buying something cheap. Quality matters. It's no bargain if you wind up with luggage that starts to disintegrate in the boonies. Good luggage will last a long time, so it's definitely a good value.

Locks

Luggage *must* be lockable. If there is only one zipper tab for an opening, there should be a ring to which it can be locked. If there are two zipper tabs, they should be designed so that one can be locked to the other. The zipper tab, which should be metal, typically has a large hole at the top and a small hole at the bottom. Buy a lock with a shackle small enough to fit through the small hole of the tab. If you lock the zippers using the large holes, the compartment can easily be opened enough to allow a hand to reach inside. Try it and you'll see what I mean.

Few little zipper locks are very strong, but avoid the cheapest ones. They're too easy to force or to pick. Small combination locks are better since thieves are less familiar with them.

Some travelers use an electrical cable tie in place of a lock. When looped through the eyes of a zipper, a thief must cut it to gain entry—and you'll know he was there. Of course, you have to cut it yourself to get in. I prefer locks. At Radio Shack, a pack of thirty ties costs about $2.

A lightweight plastic-coated bicycle-locking cable makes it easy to secure your luggage to something immovable. Eagle Creek combines an ingenious forty-two-inch retractable cable with a combination lock (3 ounces, about $14). Any store that sells sailboats can cut a length of rigging wire and weld a loop into each end to receive a lock.

Even the best lock doesn't prevent someone from slashing your luggage, nor from stealing it, but it foils the opportunist, the sneak thief who has only a few seconds to get inside and doesn't want you to know he's been there. Locks signal an observer that you're aware of his presence. Like any wolf, he'll prey on the weakest in the flock—and that won't be you.

Luggage Tags

Buy sturdy luggage tags, perhaps ones that have a leather flap to hide the name and address from prying eyes. Otherwise, put a piece of paper (not a business card) bearing only your name in the window of the tag. Your address goes on the back to prevent passersby from knowing where your empty home is. Some travelers use an office address or a friend's name and address. Don't forget to include your country with the rest of the address.

Since baggage handling can detach any luggage tag, tape your name, address, and a friend's telephone number, to the inside of your luggage. I strongly recommend also tagging, or otherwise marking, your camera, daypack, and anything else from which you may become separated.

When a lost bag is located, it is sent to the address on the tag. If that's your home, that might not be your first choice when you're in the middle of a trip. A recent innovation is a tag that asks the airline agent who locates your lost bag to read the enclosed itinerary and forward your bag to the appropriate destination. It's worth considering (Magellan's, $4.85 for two).

Use a distinctive mark on your luggage so it's easily identified.

Unless your luggage is very distinctive in appearance, you might mark it with a strip of bright adhesive tape or a colorful ribbon.

Besides being a signal to you, it keeps an inattentive fellow-passenger from taking your luggage from the baggage carousel. It happens.

Most people get a kick out of airline check-in luggage tags from exotic places but it's better to pull them off as you go if you don't want your luggage to accidentally visit one of those places without you.

HOW TO PACK

For an extended trip, start assembling clothing and equipment weeks before departure, and, this is important, complete packing at least three days before you leave. Don't fudge on that date. Details, double-checking, and last-minute purchases can be stressful. By finishing early, you avoid mistakes and walk out of the house feeling comparatively peaceful. Laying things out early allows time to figure out what you can do without. Practice packing and you'll discover that not everything can make the trip. I would urge you to leave with some room in your luggage, but no one ever does. Fortunately, it all settles after a while.

Packing Tips

- Clothes are like calories; they all add weight. After laying out all the clothes you think you need, let a few days pass. Then subtract one-fourth of the pile, maybe more.
- Use a list and check things off as you put them in the bag.
- Many travelers roll shirts, pants, underwear, everything, into cylinders, each secured with a stout rubber band. Rolling saves space and keeps clothes relatively unwrinkled (don't even think about lugging a travel iron along). When everything is rolled, searching for an elusive shirt doesn't scramble the contents of your bag. Some who don't roll their clothes, wrap them in plastic bags from the cleaners to keep them separated.
- Pack no glass containers or containers with spout tops that open easily under pressure.
- Protect breakables, such as a camera, by surrounding them with cushions of clothing.
- Keep sharp edges away from luggage fabric to avoid a tear under pressure.
- To minimize shifting, put the heaviest things in the bottom.
- Stuff small items (socks, belt, etc.) inside shoes.
- Pack only small quantities of things, such as soap, that you'll consume as you travel. They're easy to replace so there's no reason to leave home with a supply for the whole trip.
- Figure out what you can share with a partner so you don't duplicate items.

- Leave home with your luggage partly empty so you have space for things acquired along the way. Of course, when you're disciplined enough to do this, you're a candidate for the Traveler's Hall of Fame.
- Put things in approximately the same places each time you repack on the road.
- Pack essential medications in carry-on luggage. The same goes for basic toiletries if you want to look spiffy as you deplane after a transoceanic trip.
- Perhaps the most important packing tip concerns not "how" but "where." Valuables belong in your money belt, not in checked luggage. Semi-precious valuables, such as a journal, belong in carry-on luggage. The only exception may be film, which may have to be checked because it's so bulky.

CHOOSING CLOTHING

The following guidelines will reduce the weight of the clothing you take, help you stay clean and comfortable, and reduce potential problems on the road.

Equip Yourself for the Weather. It's obvious that a travel wardrobe should reflect the climate at your destinations. However, accomplishing that is not always simple since temperatures can differ quite a bit within a small area, often reflecting changes in altitude. It's not many miles from Mombasa on the coast of Kenya to the summit of Mount Kilimanjaro, but the temperature difference may be seventy degrees. A relatively short plane trip takes a traveler from midsummer in Indonesia to midwinter in New Zealand, another sixty degree temperature drop. Do the research necessary to find out what high and low temperatures (average temperatures are useless) and rainfall to expect. This information is available in some guidebooks, in libraries, from embassies, and from other travelers.

"Your true traveler will not feel he has had his money's worth unless he brings back a few scars."
—Lawrence Durrell.

Layering. The strategy of layering can greatly reduce the bulk and weight of what you take on your trip when visiting cool or cold climates. Think of layering as dressing in three distinct layers. The inner layer is a thermal layer that also draws perspiration away from your skin, rather than trapping it, and allows it to evaporate. For this purpose, a synthetic material (e.g., Capilene or polypropylene) works very well. The middle layer is for insulation. Many materials work fine and need not be bulky. The outer layer is to protect you from rain, snow, and wind. It should be lightweight and breathable, and have pockets, a hood, and zippers for ventilation. I like some combination of a light synthetic undershirt or thermal underwear, a turtleneck, a warm canvas or corduroy shirt, maybe a down vest, and a Gore-Tex shell.

Dressing in layers makes it easy to adjust during the day to changes in exertion, temperature, precipitation, and wind. Best of all, layering helps you avoid lugging around a single heavy outer garment.

On a recent visit to New Zealand, which came after three months of traveling near the Equator, I found myself in the midst of their coldest winter in thirty years. Although I had no parka, layering provided plenty of warmth, even when scrambling across the glaciers. Each morning, I put on about half the clothes in my pack, including a Capilene undershirt, turtleneck, a long-sleeve canvas shirt, and a windproof shell. Rather than carry them all the way from home, I bought a sweater, gloves, and a wool cap within hours after arriving in Christchurch.* At night I was comfortable in a flannel nightshirt and thick socks. A lightweight poncho provided fine protection from rain. A good parka would have done the job, but I didn't want to carry one for a hundred days just to enjoy it for ten.

Timing. When you absolutely need bulky clothing for severe cold weather during part of a trip, try to arrange the trip so the need comes at the beginning. I'm referring to times such as high-altitude winter weather, or hiking that requires heavy boots and specialized gear. Use the heavy stuff, then ship it home inexpensively via sea freight.

Function Over Fashion. Some travelers feel more secure if they are prepared to dress conventionally for any event that might come up. Since Europeans are more fashion conscious than the rest of the world, many travelers to Europe feel more comfortable with at least some dressy clothing. However, if most of a trip involves walking in central Africa, why worry about being a little underdressed if you drop into the famous Prague Spring Music Festival on your way home? If you go from the steamy canals of the Pantanal† to a fine restaurant in Rio, it's okay to be a little behind the fashion curve when the alternative is to carry a blue blazer through the rain forest. In other words, forget about packing clothes for every contingency.

Match the Pieces. Choose a color scheme so various items of clothing will match one another. One way to do that is to concentrate primarily on two colors. Take bottoms that will match well with several tops.

---

* *Christchurch.* The largest city on New Zealand's South Island is often described as the most English city in New Zealand. It is a departure point for the Southern Alps and some fine walks.

† *Pantanal.* One of the world's great wildlife preserves, much of this vast swampy region in southwest Brazil is accessible only by air or water.

Colors. Colors such as maroon, blue, red, black, and green don't show the grime and wounds of traveling as dramatically as light colors do. Taking much white clothing on anything other than a very warm weather or very urban trip would be a mistake. Even khaki shows dirt easily.

Avoid the Military Look. A potentially more serious mistake would be wearing clothing that looks as if it were military-issue, including olive drab or camouflage cloth. Why invite the authorities to question your mission?

Check for Good Condition. Examine all clothing you plan to take to be sure it's in good shape. Don't let a loose button or faulty seam make itself known at the most inopportune time. Nevertheless, your clothing may not be in great shape when you return. In many regions of Asia, for example, the cleaning process includes pounding clothes against a flat rock on a river bank. The laundry comes back clean, but a little stressed.

Choose Easy-to-clean Clothes. Choose clothes that resist wrinkling and are easy to care for. In the past, wool and 100 percent cotton were universally recommended but synthetics have recently found more defenders. A wet cotton shirt or socks can stay cold and damp for much longer than polypropylene and synthetic blends. The latter are lighter weight, wash and dry more quickly, and look better after being rolled up in your pack. Leave at home anything that requires dry cleaning.

Check the price of laundry service before sending anything off. It's generally not as inexpensive as you might expect. Sometimes the charge is based on weight; more frequently it's based on the number and type of pieces. Wash small pieces yourself. Minimize expense, as well as wear and tear, by taking concentrated laundry detergent along.

Try to take clothes that will air-dry overnight and minimize those that can't be washed until you'll be in one place for several days. A Ziploc bag works well for transporting things that should have dried before some departure—but didn't. If you're trekking, fasten the Ziploc bag to the outside of your pack with a large safety pin.

Rather than wringing them dry, clothes wrinkle less if you shake them, roll them in a towel, and hang them up. If you hang rumpled clothes in the bathroom, steam from the shower eliminates most of the wrinkles.

Checklist: Clothing

The following list contemplates an informal, lightweight trip. Your adjustments should reflect personal tastes, the length of your trip, and anticipated climates and activities. As a general rule, keep clothing simple and modest. If you travel with a partner, don't duplicate any clothing you can share. And remember to count the clothes you'll be wearing as you walk out the door to the airport.

For Men

1. Shirts.

__ Two **short-sleeve outdoor shirts**. Consider 100 percent cotton mesh polo shirts with collars. They are cool, wash easily, and stand up well to travel stress.

__ Two **long-sleeve shirts** with collars (depending on the weather). My favorites are medium weight cotton with front pockets that button. Smith & Hawken and Patagonia shirts are a good combination of quality and price. Depending on the trip, you may want one or two dressier, wrinkle-proof shirts.

__ Two or three cotton **T-shirts**. Buy more as souvenirs.

__ One long-sleeve **turtleneck** for cool weather. They're warm, look good, and travel well.

__ One **vest**. This is definitely optional, but can provide both warmth and a little dressiness.

2. Pants.

__ The number of pants needed depends on the trip; usually two pairs, seldom more than three. One pair should be a tough 100 percent cotton twill, suitable for rough parts of the trip. L.L. Bean offers these in several colors. If the weather will be very cold, I substitute 85 percent wool pants made by Woolrich. Smith & Hawken sells durable canvas pants in eight-ounce medium weight and $11\frac{1}{4}$

For Women

1. Shirts.

__ Two **T-shirts**.

__ Three **shirts or blouses**, as dressy or basic as appropriate. Long sleeve or short sleeve, depending on the weather, but probably not **no** sleeve. Plunging necklines should be avoided. A **jogging top** can serve as a shirt, a swimming suit top, and even sleepwear.

__ Whether you bring a **wool shirt** depends on the weather; the same for a blue jean shirt. Either layers well over a blouse.

__ For cool weather, a **turtleneck** is very desirable.

__ Besides warmth and dressiness, a **vest** also provides an extra bit of modesty in conservative countries.

2. Pants.

__ One or two **lightweight** pairs of loose-fitting pants (possibly substituting one heavier pair, depending on expected weather). Buy casual pants on the road.

__ **One or two regular skirts** for slightly dressier wear. Skirts should fit loosely and skirt length should be below the knee. In some countries, especially the Arab world, women are expected to keep their legs covered,

For Men

2. Pants (continued)

ounce. "cast-iron" weight. The second pair should be **lighter weight**, but very durable (again, 100 percent cotton).

___ One useful style has legs that zip off at mid-thigh (creating a good pair of shorts for use when the sun rises high). The TravelSmith catalog (800-950-1600) offers two useful versions of these convertible pants. The third pair should be a potentially **dressy pair of khakis**. Patagonia sells khaki pants with a cotton outer sheath and polyester inner core that make them extremely durable. For European or big-city trips, add a pair of dress slacks.

Avoid pants in which the side or slash pockets do not swing freely; that is, ones in which the pockets are sewn to the pants leg. They dump change, keys, and everything else every time you put your feet up. For security, look for pockets that button, zip, or close with Velcro, or sew metal snaps into the tops of the pockets. In fact, some pants have sewn-on security pockets big enough to hold airline tickets.

___ One pair of **hiking or gym shorts**. To reduce weight, take shorts that can double as a swimming suit.

___ On the road, consider buying colorful, lightweight pants made in the local style. They're fun to wear even though they may begin to look a little weird or start to fall apart by the time they get home.

Contrary to expectations, blue jeans don't make great travel companions. They are heavy, have no dress-up potential, dry slowly, and can bind fiercely on a long bus trip.

For Women

2. Pants (continued)

so local standards of modesty should guide your choices. Some women prefer blue jean skirts.

___ Some women recommend a pair of sturdy **leotards** or **ballet tights** for warmth.

The comments I've heard about one-piece pants suits or body suits have been uniformly negative, referring either to lack of flexibility or incompatibility with using basic toilet facilities.

___ Bring at least one pair of modestly-cut **shorts**.

For Men	**For Women**
3. Underwear.	**3. Underwear.**
__ Cotton or blended briefs in dark colors. Three pairs are plenty if you'll be able to wash them regularly. Taking nylon underwear, which doesn't breathe, to the tropics would be courting a fungal infection.	__ Three pairs of cotton or blended panties and one or two brassieres. Although silk underwear dries quickly, it's inappropriate for warm climates. There are many places where not wearing a brassiere would offend local mores and attract unwanted attention. Some women attach a runners key pouch to their bra as a hidden stash for emergency funds. You may also want a half-slip (Hidden Assets makes one with a money belt built in).

4. Socks.

__ Take three or four pairs of high quality socks. You may want some wool socks (with a little nylon) heavy enough for hiking, as well as some that are lighter but still sturdy enough for sock-footed temple visits. Some argue that the best socks are made of hydrophobic (water-hating) synthetics that wick sweat away from the foot. Two favorites are the Wigwam Ultimax and the Thor-Lo hiking model. Various colors, even gym gray, conceal road grime better than white does. By the way, if you take several identical pairs of socks, you have less of a problem when one sock wears through or floats off down the Ganges. Depending on the trip, a man might want one pair of dress socks and a woman one pair of knee-high stockings (if appropriate for your shoes).

5. Shoes.

__ One pair of **sandals.** Cheap rubber sandals or plastic flip-flops are fine for showers and the beach, but you need sturdy sandals to cushion the feet and protect them from street debris when walking around town. Teva river sandals are a favorite, but similar brands work fine so long as they are well made and have an ankle strap and fairly thick soles. Wear sandals for a while before you leave so the straps won't rub raw patches on your feet when it matters.

I used to travel with hiking boots but seldom do so any more because they're heavy and space-consuming. Well-made, lightweight, low-cut **trail/ walking shoes** are fine for all but strenuous hiking situations. Dark brown, gray or black don't show dirt and look fairly dressy. Ordinary tennis shoes are okay but they usually provide less arch and lateral support than good walking shoes do. If you're willing to spring for the cost of walking shoes, you'll probably consider it a good investment. If cost is a problem, go with tennis shoes.

Rub in Sno-Seal to waterproof shoes. I've been told that the aerosol in at least some waterproofing sprays dissolves the glue between the sole and the upper (not to mention further stressing the atmosphere).

Whatever your choice in shoes, give them a good workout before you go. Don't get underway with a pair that doesn't fit. Your feet are your wheels; if you don't pamper them a little, you'll wish you had.

For women: My recommendations are the same as for men's shoes adding, perhaps, ballet-type slippers or light leather flats for dressier wear. They're light and compress well in a pack.

6. Belt.

__ Take one sturdy belt that fits the loops of all your pants.

7. Nightshirt.

__ You need some covering for hostels, overnight trains, outdoor toilets, and to meet strict standards of modesty in some countries. A gym warm-up suit works fine but is bulkier than a nightshirt. In tropical countries, consider a **khanga**, **lava lava**, **lunghi**, **pareu**, **sarong** or whatever it's called locally. It's a rectangular piece of cloth that you wrap around knee-to-waist or chest to provide modesty consistent with local custom. It also serves as a beach blanket or towel and only costs about $2.

8. Swimsuit.

__ On some beaches in the Third World, skimpy suits are not welcome. On others, suits are not necessary at all. If you bring a suit, it should be more modest than not and be made of quick-drying material.

9. Rain gear.

__ Consider a Gore-Tex **shell** or a waterproof **poncho**. The latter takes less room and should be long enough to cover a pack on the trail. Although hot and not very durable, a cheap raincoat or rain suit that stuffs into a pocket may be sufficient. Some efficient travelers use them as bathrobes and windbreakers as well. Samsonite offers an attractive raincoat with a hood (Magellan's, $16.85).

10. Extra warmth.

__ Light, warm synthetic is a good place to start. A lightweight windbreaker, which needn't be expensive or fancy, can be extremely useful. A polyester-cotton jacket or polypropylene pile works well. A down vest provides warmth in a small package. If you'll need a light sweater, it may be worth taking one along (but less often than you might think). Buy a heavy sweater when needed rather than carrying it all the way. Find warmth through layering or endure a little chill rather than lug a heavy jacket around the world. If it will really be chilly, take thermal underwear.

11. Towel.

__ Don't expect to be furnished a towel or washcloth very often in budget hotels. If you take a towel, it should be small and thin to save space and drying time.

12. Bandannas.

__ They make good sweat bands and are generally useful, especially for women. They're plentiful in local markets.

13. Scarves.

__ A nice scarf can dress up an otherwise road-weary outfit and a warm scarf makes you snug in raw weather. In certain cultures, women are expected to cover their heads with a scarf.

14. Hat/sun visor.

__ You should have one or the other. If you don't take one, you can easily buy it on the road.

15. Gloves.

__ If heading to a very cold climate, including high altitude, take a pair of insulated gloves. For less than bitter cold, a pair of wool knit gloves is fine. If you want to protect your hands and warmth isn't a factor, cheap cotton gloves are sufficient (e.g., paddling trips and in places such as Rwanda where gloves protect your hands from stinging nettles as you haul yourself up volcanic slopes to visit the mountain gorillas).

16. Tie.

__ If something comes up that makes you think you need a tie, buy it locally. If you can't, ties won't be the custom—so forget it.

17. Blazer.

__ If you expect to do some business or visit places where upscale dress is appropriate, tuck a wrinkle-proof blazer in the bottom of your bag. However, it's not worth carrying one on the off chance you *might* want it.

Checklist: Toiletries

Use a leak-proof, soft-sided toiletries kit (not a heavy leather kit). The see-through type works well. Unless you are on your way to Antarctica, you needn't take sufficient quantities of everything to last for your whole trip. Take small sizes and restock as you go.

__ **Band-Aids**

__ **comb** (and/or brush)

__ **deodorant** (stick type preferable to aerosol)

__ **dental care items:** including **toothbrush** (preferably a travel-type with its own storage container or cap), **tooth paste**, and **dental floss**

__ **insect repellent.** DEET is very effective but since DEET is absorbed into the bloodstream, a 40 percent solution is preferable for use on a long trip. UltraThon ($6.85), a 33 percent DEET solution using a controlled-release polymer suspension, is becoming very popular. Permethrin clothing spray is also recommended (see Chapter 8).

__ **laundry detergent** (more useful than you might imagine)

___ **lip balm** (with sunscreen)

___ **mirror** (metal if you believe in, or have, bad luck)

___ **moleskin** (to prevent a blister from bringing your trip to a halt)

___ **mosquito coils**

___ **nail clippers** (or emery boards)

___ **panty liners** (if you will be doing a lot of trekking)

___ **razor and blades** (ordinary soap or shampoo can serve as shaving lather). Many travelers aren't happy with a battery-powered electric razor on a long trip, but Braun makes a compact, eight-ounce version for under $30.

___ **safety pins** (to pin keys in your pocket, pin a pocket closed, replace a button, etc.)

___ **sanitary napkins or tampons** (*not* universally available, so you may want to take an adequate supply)

___ **sewing kit**

___ **shampoo** (Johnson & Johnson Baby Shampoo can double as shaving lather and as laundry detergent)

___ **soap** (small), in a plastic soap container

___ **sun screen** (waterproof; SPF 15 is popular, but there is a trend toward greater protection)

___ **thermometer** (in a plastic case)

___ **toilet paper** (take out the cardboard tube). "Don't leave home without it." Keep some in your daypack, more in your luggage. TP is for sale most places, but it's a rarity in Third World bathrooms or hotel rooms. Ignore this advice only if you intend to follow the local custom.

___ **tweezers and scissors** (if not part of your Swiss Army knife)

Prescription and other medicines, as well as first aid supplies, are discussed in Chapter 8.

Checklist: Miscellaneous Gear

___ **Bags.** Take a couple sturdy plastic **garbage bags**, large enough to protect your pack from a downpour or salt spray, and a few sturdy, freezer-grade **Ziploc bags** (for leaky toiletries, a wet bathing suit, etc.). Plastic bags, such as dry cleaning bags, keep muddy shoes from soiling their neighbors in your luggage. Light nylon camping **stuff sacks**, with drawstrings and cord locks, are useful for organizing small stuff.

___ **Camera Gear.** Take more film than you think you'll need, a camera, zoom lens, extra camera battery, lens filters, and a lens cleaning kit. If you don't trust airport X-ray machines, carry film in lead-foil film bags (Sima Super FilmShield, $15).

___ **Clock.** Take an alarm clock that's durable and compact and ticks quietly—but has a loud, reliable alarm. I like one that also illuminates the face with a push of a button. You can find a very satisfactory clock with these characteristics for no more than $12. If you need an especially loud wake-up call and are willing to pay extra for it, consider the Braun which has a built-in flashlight and increases in volume until it hits 82 dB (Magellan's, $37.85). Whatever your choice, start the trip with fresh batteries.

___ **Eyeglasses.** Remember sunglasses, prescription glasses, and contact lenses. Bring a decent-quality pair of sunglasses (with unbreakable lenses and UV protection) since many sunglasses for sale abroad provide little protection. BassPro makes AquaVision polarized glasses ($15, 800-227-7776). Whether it seems worthwhile to bring a second pair of prescription glasses depends on how much you rely on them. At least bring an up-to-date prescription in case you need a replacement. A **hard plastic travel** case keeps glasses from being crushed in your pack (TravelSmith offers a "bombproof" case for $9.50). Bring a retainer strap for glasses.

Dust and sand in the air sometimes cause problems for contact lens wearers. Since standard contact lens supplies are bulky and often unavailable on the road, some travelers have switched successfully to disposable contact lenses. Don't forget lens solution.

___ **Flashlight.** Take only a flashlight with a switch that can't turn on in your pack. One extra set of new batteries should be sufficient. **Batteries**, except for the lithium type used in high-tech cameras, are sold almost everywhere. A compact MiniMag or a key chain flashlight saves space, but I prefer an EverReady on which the case slides up to provide a lantern-like effect. Look for something waterproof.

___ **Guidebooks** (or sections of them).

___ **Journal.** A five-by-eight-inch journal fits easily into a daypack.

___ **Locks.** For luggage, sturdy small locks are better than super-cheapies that can be picked in a second. Take enough for luggage and daypack zippers and give a duplicate set of keys to your travel partner. Code each key to match the corresponding lock (with dots of paint or nail polish) to avoid frustrating fumbling. There are also locks which, when open, retain their keys (about $4/pair).

To avoid the problem of dealing with multiple keys, some people choose small combination locks. Using the first numbers of your zip code, your birthdate, or something else obvious, helps you recall the combinations. Three-number locks on which you set the combination yourself cost $5 at Sears, $3 at hardware stores, $13 for a pair from Magellan's.

For security in hotel rooms, some travelers carry a battery-powered door stop alarm ($9.75), a wedge that fits under a hotel door. If the door moves, a shrill siren alarm goes off. A low-tech door wedge also works fine. A Travelock ($9.85) locks dresser drawers as well as hotel doors.

A Jammer is a device that sticks with a suction cup to the inside of a train or hotel sliding window. If someone tries to open the window, the Jammer is supposed to wedge in tightly to prevent entry.

___ **Maps.** Traveling without good maps is an unnecessary handicap. Some guidebook maps are good but they're small. Buy large-scale maps to help in planning your trip then take them along to assist in rerouting. Travel bookstores and AAA are good sources (see Chapter 2). Tourist offices abroad have adequate maps.

___ **Money belt and wallet.** The traditional favorite money belt is a fairly flat ten-inch pocket designed to be worn around the waist under the clothes ($12 to $17). Although shoulder-holster, hanging-from-the-neck, pin-on-the-bra, and around-the-calf styles provide good security, their capacity is usually too limited. Some travelers like a hidden-pocket that hangs inside the front of the pants or skirt from a loop belt (about $10). It's easier to reach than the around-the-waist type, but at only six to seven inches long, it may not hold all the things you must keep secure.

If you carry a wallet, cordura may be preferable to leather because the rough cordura surface makes it less likely to slip or be slipped out of a pocket. Some people prefer a three-fold wallet that attaches to the belt with a light chain. They can be purchased in motorcycle shops and truck stops.

___ **Reading material.** Starting your trip with enough reading material for the entire journey means carrying a heavy burden. New books are often more expensive abroad than at home, but you'll find plenty of used book shops that will trade two of your books for one of theirs. At the excellent bookstore on the lake shore in Pokhara,* the very literate owner will sell you *The Snow Leopard* or some other book ideal for your trek to the Annapurna Sanctuary, then buy it back for half-price when you return. Readers recognize one another so it's also easy to trade with other travelers.

Reading the literature of a country as you travel through it—whether fiction, philosophy, history, art, architecture, or culture—brings greater depth of meaning to the words and to the trip. In terms of price, variety of contents, and weight, Norton Anthologies of short fiction, literature, essays, or poetry are an excellent value. Thousands of tissue-thin pages provide hundreds of hours of pleasure. See the Bibliography for many other suggestions.

___ **Rubber bands.** Take a dozen or two for rolling your clothes and all kinds of unexpected uses.

___ **Swiss Army knife.** A knife with a couple of blades is adequate, but it's the rest of the collection that makes Swiss Army knives indispensable. One version includes scissors, corkscrew, tweezers, can opener, bottle opener, and screwdriver. One caution: a knife may be confiscated by airport security if you are carrying it in your daypack or pocket.

___ **Wristwatch.** Desirable features include a display of the date and day, an alarm, a light for the face, and water-resistance. Whatever you wear, it shouldn't look expensive.

---

* *Pokhara.* This colorful small town in central Nepal is a starting point for treks into the Himalayas.

___ **Writing materials.** A couple of long yellow pads, plus a few ball-point pens (which are easy to replace while traveling). If you have room, pens make nice gifts.

If some of the gear you want isn't available from your local outfitter, Magellan's (800-962-4943) has a catalogue filled with what they call "essentials for the international traveler." As travelers themselves, Magellan's telephone operators have used much of the equipment listed in the catalogue so they can discuss it accurately. Moreover, if you're looking for something they don't carry, they'll call you back when it turns up, even if it's a year later. That's good service.

REI, Camp-mor, and Patagonia also publish very useful catalogues. The Compleat Traveler (212-685-9007) and Traveler's Checklist (203-364-0144) are reliable mail order resources.

Some of the best resources for a wide range of travel books, luggage, and equipment are TravelFest superstores, based in Austin, Texas (800-343-3378).

Checklist: Documents to Take Along

___ **Airline tickets** (and copy).

___ **American Automobile Association membership card.** If you are a AAA member, foreign automobile associations may extend reciprocal benefits to you, including maps and travel information. You may even get free road service if you've rented a vehicle.

___ **ATM card.**

___ **Certificate of Registration** (registration of items with Customs on departure).

___ **Credit cards** (including a list of card numbers and telephone numbers for reporting a loss).

___ **Driver's license.** A normal driver's license serves as general identification and may be required to rent cars. In addition, the local American Automobile Association office sells an International Driver's License (for $10 and a passport-size photo). It is, at least in theory, required to drive in Japan, Indonesia, Thailand, Eastern Europe, and parts of Europe.

___ **Insurance.** Proof of insurance and your agent's telephone number.

___ **International Association for Medical Assistance to Travelers (IAMAT) card.**

___ **International Certificate of Vaccination** (yellow card).

___ **International Student ID card.** Widely accepted verification of student status.

__ **Itinerary.**

__ **Medical Information.** Blood type, description of special medical conditions, allergies, personal physician's phone number, health insurance information.

__ **Names, addresses, telephone, and fax numbers.** People to be contacted in case of emergency and people to contact on the road and at home.

__ **Passport** (plus copies of the first two pages of the passport), extra passport photos, and separate proof of citizenship in case you must replace a lost passport.

__ **Permits** (trails, game watching, work).

__ **Prescriptions.** Extra copies of essential prescriptions.

__ **Reservations** (for hotels, etc.).

__ **Telephone charge card.**

__ **Travelers checks** (and a separate copy of check numbers).

__ **Visas.**

__ **Youth Hostel Membership card** (See Chapter 11).

Checklist: Optional Equipment

Everything on this list could add to the pleasure of your trip and I've taken most of the items at one time or another. You could take them all at once if you want to—so long as you plan to travel with an elephant and bearers. The issues are weight and space, as well as simplicity.

__ **Binoculars.** Good ones are expensive—and attractive to thieves. They are essential for wild game viewing, but for most other purposes a zoom lens works well.

__ **Brief case.** Eastern Mountain Sports, Eagle Creek and others make a soft Cordura brief case for keeping papers and documents collected inside your pack. These are surprisingly useful.

__ **Business cards** (or travel cards you've designed for the trip). Cards make a good impression on officials and are an easy way for travel friends to keep track of your name and number.

__ **Calculator.** For about $35, you can buy a Seiko SII. It's a calculator, currency converter, metric converter, and translator between English and a selected language (about forty thousand words, phrases and idioms; most of the languages available are European). Although very small, it has sufficient memory to store travelers check numbers, flight information, telephone numbers, and so on. Simple solar-powered calculators sell for $2.

___ **Carabiners.** These small locking rings, used by climbers, are unexpectedly handy for avoiding losing things. No need to buy the high-quality type unless your life will be hanging from one.

___ **Cassette recorder/player.** There are times when familiar music is soothing, particularly when traveling alone. You may also want to record ethnic music to add magic to your memories. Some travelers use a recorder to dictate notes and record tour guides. Take only a few extra batteries (preferably the same size that fits your flashlight) and tapes since both are available on the road. If you're planning to write about your travel experiences and may be interviewing people, a recorder is a great help.

___ **Contraceptives.** They can be purchased abroad but the brands may not be ones you recognize.

___ **Duct tape.** About three feet (wound around a piece of cardboard) is enough to fix a lot of what breaks on the road.

___ **Eating utensils.** A knife, fork, and spoon kit is nice when your hands are filthy or you don't feel like eating with them.

___ **Electrical gadgets.** Another reason, beyond weight, space, cost, and karma, not to take electrical appliances that have to be plugged in is that they may not work. For one thing, your plug may not fit in the local socket. If your trip is geographically limited, you may get away with one **adapter** plug ($3 to $5). Otherwise, consider an adapter plug set (Magellan's, $11.85). Note that a videocamera battery charger may need an adapter.

Since electric current in much of the world is different (220-240 volts) from that used in the United States (110-120 volts), you are likely to need a current **converter** as well. The type of converter depends on where you're going, the kind of equipment you will use (camcorder, razor, laptop computer, CD player, etc.), and how heavy your usage will be. Converters range from $15 to $28 and weigh up to 13 ounces. Magellan's catalogue tells you what converter you would need—but you have to decide whether you really need the appliance.

___ **Film shield.** A lead foil bag that protects twenty-two rolls of film (about $13).

___ **Immersion heater.** Plug one end of this device into a wall socket and dip the other in your tea or coffee cup, heating the water in minutes. It's lightweight, inexpensive ($12), convenient, and pays for itself quickly. Choose 220V or 110V depending on where you'll be traveling.

___ **Mace.** Be aware that carrying sprays such as Mace is forbidden on many airlines (more on security in Chapter 13).

___ **Mask and Snorkel.** Although both are usually available for rent at dive sites, you can't always find a mask that fits well and has a clear lens. Fins available for rent are often weary and sized for people whose feet resemble fins less than mine do. Still, think twice before carrying bulky fins around the world. Scuba diving equipment is always available on-site but quality varies. Inspect it closely. If you doubt it, try elsewhere.

__ **Musical instruments.** Shared music is an instant introduction. I envied a Canadian with whom I traveled who had a wonderful time playing his fiddle with local bands. I carry a tenor recorder and a harmonica for my own amusement.

__ **Nylon clothesline.** Potentially useful, seldom necessary.

__ **Pillow, inflatable.** It sounds wimpy, but you'll love it on long overnighters on a bouncing bus. Consider a covered inflatable pillow (under $10) which tucks under your chin and curves around to rest on your shoulder. Some travel agents give inflatable pillows to clients.

__ **Radio.** A shortwave radio, such as the Grundig Traveller II (thirteen ounces, about $99) or the Grundig YB 305 ($129) will pull in the BBC and music from around the world. If you're more interested in listening to local music and local language, a simple AM/FM radio will do.

__ **Sewing kit.** A small one, including a few safety pins, can be useful (no more than $3). On the other hand, it's easy and inexpensive to have sewing repairs done as you travel.

__ **Sheet sack.** Since beds in hostels don't come with linen, they require you to use a sheet sack. Some hostels rent them but the cumulative expense would be fairly great for anyone staying in hostels frequently. Since a sheet sack takes up room in the pack, your decision should reflect how often you expect to sleep in hostels. You can make one, buy one from a hostel, or order one from Magellan's ($15 to $24).

__ **Sink Stopper.** A flat rubber sink stopper can be handy, especially when washing clothes (one-half ounce, $2).

__ **Sleeping bag.** Seldom necessary; carry only if you are certain to use it.

__ **Sleeping pad.** You really have to need it to make it worth carrying for weeks or months. The Therm-a-Rest brand is tough and rolls up fairly compactly.

__ **Slippers.** If you want something other than socks or sandals for showers, down-the-hall toilet trips, or the beach, consider Ultra Soles. Partially net, they come in a pouch and weigh only four ounces. Magellan's ($7.85).

__ **Travel games.** When there's nothing going on and you're not creatively inspired, break out the **cards** and start a first-to-ten-thousand-points game of gin rummy. If you draw a curious crowd, use the opportunity to meet people and learn some of the local card games. **Chess, backgammon, and**

Scrabble are available in miniature travel versions. Amuse yourself and others with any of the versions of **Trivial Pursuit** or its imitators (especially ones that focus on travel). A **Frisbee** is great for a playful spirit and a little exercise. A plastic jar of **soap bubble fluid** is an easy way to get involved with local kids.

___ **Umbrella.** I buy a cheapie on the road if I need one. If you'd rather start out with a good one, stick with an eight-inch compact version.

___ **Water bottle.** Choose a tough plastic bottle with a secure top (it's best if the top is attached to the bottle). It should hold no less than one liter, nor more than two liters (if bigger, it gets very heavy when full). TravelSmith offers an interesting collapsible canteen ($19) which holds two liters yet fits easily in a pocket when empty. It's polyurethane inside and tough packcloth outside. A wineskin served me well for several months in South America. The reason I consider a water bottle only optional is that in most of the Third World disinfected water is sold in very serviceable plastic bottles. Although a water bottle can ride happily in a daypack, Magellan's Bottle Bridle, an over-the-shoulder harness, is also useful ($9.85).

___ **Waterproof bags.** Seal Pak (800-531-9531) makes a waterproof bag that straps around your waist and goes into the water with you. It will hold a wallet, passport, or plane tickets. Similar is the five-by-seven-inch Water-Pocket from Watersafe ($13, call 800-355-1126). There is also a urethane-coated nylon Hydra-Pouch (about $10). It's a six-by-seven-inch neck pouch which keeps valuables dry. Basic Designs (707-575-1220) offers a bag with a screw top that will hold a small camera as well as valuables. It is made to be carried rather than worn.

___ **Whistle.** This could be useful for summoning help on a wilderness trek— or for security purposes.

Checklist: What Not to Take

- Breakable or leaky containers
- Electrical appliances
- Jewelry
- Illegal drugs
- Illegal drugs
- Illegal drugs
- Problems from home
- Anything you absolutely cannot stand to lose

These checklists will simplify your preparations and remind you of key items otherwise easy to overlook. Medicine and first aid items are covered in Chapter 8.

Camping

For most travelers, carrying a full set of camping equipment is cumbersome and unnecessary. I've had no difficulty renting what I needed as I went along (inexpensively, at that). For white-water trips, safaris, and similar events, equipment is available at the departure point. On most independent treks, there are villages along the way where you can find food and lodging so you needn't worry about a tent, foam pad, tarp, stove, and the rest. If you need cooking equipment, it's certainly better to rent it rather than carrying it halfway around the world. In places where a hammock would be desirable, say on a boat chugging down a tributary of the Amazon, there are plenty for sale locally.

Sleeping bags are so heavy and bulky that I've never wanted to carry one around the world. If you do, synthetic is better than down if there's any chance the bag will get wet.

Jewelry

Wearing expensive jewelry conflicts with being a traveler. In addition, good jewelry and watches, including authentic-looking fakes, are a magnet for thieves. As I was checking into a small hotel on Ipanema Beach in Rio, a woman burst in through the front door, crying, blood streaming from her forehead and one elbow. A thief had knocked her to the sidewalk as he ripped a heavy gold necklace from her throat. She's wearing a gold necklace in Rio? Of course, the same thing would have happened had her necklace been only an expensive-looking fake. Dress yourself with local crafts. Buy inexpensive jewelry from local artists. Thieves know how little these things cost and leave them alone. If you buy expensive jewelry while traveling, keep it locked up.

8

Keeping Healthy

I have traveled widely in my lifetime, having been struck
by the virus at an early age and having, as yet, developed
no antibodies to harden my resistance or immunity.
—Caskie Stinnett
Grand and Private Pleasures

Who hasn't heard stories about a vacation spent staring out the window at the beach while Montezuma exacted his revenge? More than five thousand Australians canceled vacations to Bali after a report that one Swedish visitor died of encephalitis. Thousands of travelers canceled East African safari reservations after reading stories about the Ebola virus, even though the game reserves in Kenya and Tanzania are located halfway across the continent from where Ebola struck in Zaire.

Should international travelers be concerned about their health? Yes—at least enough that they learn what the issues are and take basic preventive measures. No—if that means exaggerating the risks and staying home.

Consumers Association in England, which probably conducts the most extensive travel health surveys in the world, recently announced that only about 15 percent of all travelers get sick, and only 4 percent become sick enough to seek medical attention. Moreover, even those small numbers were affected by higher percentages in destinations such as India and Africa.

At least as important as knowing the low rate of illness is realizing what affects those who do become ill. More than half have only stomach problems and diarrhea. Next in line are sunburn, coughs, colds, ear infections, and motion sickness. Of those who do get some bug, the overwhelming majority are over it by the time they get home; a very small price for the vast rewards of travel.

About one-quarter of traveler's deaths are related to injuries, not diseases, and often involve motor vehicles and alcohol. Another substantial percentage of deaths result from underlying medical problems, such as cardiovascular disease, and have nothing to do with travel. The risk of being affected by a major health problem while traveling is probably greater than the risk of being impaled by a unicorn, but it's certainly tolerable.

The potential health problems discussed below affect only an infinitesimally small number of travelers. For example, of more than 140,000 Peace Corps volunteers, only three died of tropical diseases in thirty-four years. With the exception of malaria, the other diseases seldom even appear on lists of potential hazards published by the World Health Organization.

I feel reluctant to devote so much space to health issues for fear it will make them seem daunting. I do it *only* because it is precisely this knowledge and preparation that can enable you to travel virtually anywhere without undue concern about getting sick.

When it's so easy to stay healthy abroad, the behavior of some travelers amazes me. They assume they're bulletproof and won't get sick no matter what they do. They read an article on health risks, throw a couple of all-purpose antidotes in their toiletries kits, and never give another thought to health. Perhaps they believe that signing on with a tour group encloses them in a magic bubble. A few even convince themselves that the only way to truly experience a country is to live exactly as the locals do, eating street food and drinking tap water. These attitudes court disaster.

Good health depends on factors such as where you go, whether you take

Caveat

Since I'm not a doctor, what follows cannot be taken as medical advice. Even if I seem to state something definitively, I'm simply sharing with you the results of my research and the choices I make for myself. You must do your own research, at the time you're going to travel, applicable to the specific regions you expect to visit. I am not a substitute for your doctor. If you consult one or more doctors, ensure they are qualified to answer the questions you ask. A doctor may be expert in his or her field but inexperienced or behind-the-times concerning your foreign travel questions.

When I mention a product by brand name it's because I presently consider it to be the most effective choice. I have no interest in promoting any particular product. Any medicine mentioned in the text should be taken only by a person who is aware of its risks and possible interaction with other over-the-counter and prescription medicines. Be cautious about buying drugs over-the-counter abroad that are sold only by prescription in the United States. Ensure that you understand clearly what the possible side effects might be.

effective preventive measures, what care you exercise, what risks you take, and your state of health when you left home—plus your attitude and a little luck.

Prevention

I'm a naturally healthy person and have probably had good luck along the way, but simple preventive behavior has been the major factor in keeping me free from health problems on the road. Prevention is easy. It consists of doing a little research, exercising common sense, following a few guidelines, and getting check-ups before leaving for an extended period.

Start by considering honestly whether you have any disabilities or illnesses that should deter you from traveling independently to the countries you've selected. Evaluate the physical demands of the trip in the context of your general fitness. Keep in mind the style of travel you plan and the availability of health services. Discuss the trip with a doctor. Also remember that travel doesn't make people immune to things that make them sick at home such as heart disease, upper respiratory infection, and chronic diseases like diabetes.

Instead of staying home or taking unnecessary risks, learn: (1) which health hazards may exist on a particular trip, (2) what to do to avoid those hazards, and (3) what to do should a problem occur. This chapter is filled with that information.

Risk usually accompanies expansion of our horizons, but that didn't keep our ancestors at home and it shouldn't keep us at home either. I'll take Kenya anytime over fast foods and freeway driving.

Research

As soon as I have an itinerary, I call the *Centers for Disease Control* (CDC) in Atlanta, Georgia. The CDC has current information on immunization requirements, malaria prevalence, and other travel-related diseases in every country. Call (404) 332-4559 for the international travelers voice hotline; (404) 332-4565 to order documents available by fax. Ask for disease outbreak bulletins, information on AIDS abroad, lists of useful publications, and so on. You'll be dealing with recorded messages, so be prepared to take notes. A typical call lasts five to ten minutes.

Advice from a good *travel medicine clinic*, of which there are more than five hundred, is usually superior to advice from most general practitioners. To find a clinic, check the phone book for the subheadings Travel Medicine or Infectious Disease under the main listing for Physicians, or call a medical center or tropical medicine specialist. If you send a self-addressed nine-by-eleven-inch envelope with ninety-eight cents postage to Dr. Leonard C. Marcus (Travelers Health and Immunization Service, 148 Highland Avenue, Newton, MA 02115), he will send you a list of more than one hundred travel medicine clinics.

Prices vary considerably from clinic to clinic. Some charge a consultation fee ranging from $25 to $125 (which may include one or more vaccinations). A shot that costs $5 at one might cost $25 at another.

Most *local public health services* have exotic immunoglobulins and vaccines on hand (which doctors in private practice often do not). Their charges are reasonable and their nurses are expert at giving shots.

Among questions you should ask is whether any countries on your itinerary require visitors to have had specific vaccinations before entering. These requirements are also listed in *Health Information for International Travel* published by the U.S. Public Health Service (available from the Superintendent of Documents, U.S. Government Printing Office (GPO), Washington, DC 20402, 202-783-3238). GPO is an excellent source for overall travel medicine information.

If you'll be traveling to any place at all exotic, you'll probably need immunizations. Some immunizations consist of a series of two or three shots and some cannot be given at the same time as others. That means you can't wait until the last minute to get them. Tell the health service where you're going and which shots you want and they'll give you a schedule. Ask also about shots you should consider that are not necessarily related to travel, such as measles, mumps, diphtheria, tetanus, and influenza. If you have the time, call three months before your planned departure. If you're in a hurry, a month may be enough.

Don't wait to get your immunization shots.

Travelers are occasionally stopped at some country's border and asked to provide proof they've had some immunization or another. An *International Certificate of Immunization* (known as the "yellow card" even though it's a booklet of several pages) is accepted as proof. If you don't have it, you may be turned back or required to get an inoculation on the spot under conditions that certainly would not be your first choice. Your local public health department, or whoever gives the inoculations, has the certificate and will list required vaccinations, other shots you've received, your blood type, allergies, and the person to notify in case of an emergency. The card lets you know how long each vaccine is effective. Since the yellow card is typically the only record of your shots, leave a copy at home.

If you have access to any of the major computer online services, log on for detailed international current health advisories.

I haven't suggested asking a doctor in private practice for information pertaining to international health issues because many don't have it. They usually weren't trained for these illnesses and don't encounter them with any regularity. You can't afford information that's out of date or just plain wrong.

Medical Help Abroad

The International Association for Medical Assistance to Travelers (IAMAT) provides a world directory of English- or French-speaking doctors

> ### Advice for Health Problems
>
> If a significant health problem develops:
> - ask for recommendations from a consulate (yours or anyone's),
> - contact a university medical center,
> - call your credit card company if it offers medical assistance to travelers,
> - consult your IAMAT list,
> - check with volunteer organizations such as the Peace Corps,
> - contact the State Department Overseas Citizens' Emergency Center,
> - ask expatriates,
> - get advice from other travelers,
> - get assistance from local people,
> - get to a big city where the standard of care is higher than it is in the countryside, or
> - hop on a plane for home.

abroad who meet its standards and have agreed to charge according to an established schedule of fees. IAMAT also provides a World Malaria Risk Chart, a booklet on *How to Protect Yourself Against Malaria*, and a World Immunization Chart. IAMAT even sells a freestanding mosquito net for beds. There is no charge for the information but a donation of some amount is suggested (and needed). When you see the material, you'll feel like donating. Call (716) 754-4883.

Many credit cards have services that recommend hospitals and provide the names of English-speaking doctors to travelers abroad. They may even furnish an American doctor to consult with you or your foreign doctor.

Consider taking this chapter with you as you travel. If a problem develops, this information will help connect the symptoms with the probable disease— and thus with the appropriate medicine and other remedies.

THIRTEEN PRACTICAL TIPS

Even if some of the following tips seem obvious, I'm including them because I didn't understand them fully before I started traveling.

1. Keep well rested. Every traveler feels worn out once in a while from an overnight bus trip, several days of mountain trekking, or any number of things. Being immersed in a culture different from your own can be surprisingly wearing, especially early in a trip. You have daily tasks to do in a new environment, you're often in the midst of more people than you are at home, and you may be feeling a little homesick. All of this, plus a fast pace, can catch up with you physically and/or psychologically. If that happens, shut down for a day or two, or longer if that's what it takes. Being run-down makes you more susceptible to illness and undermines the positive attitude that helps ward off oncoming disease. Taking time to rest is a trade-off, an investment in preventing future sick days. In planning an itinerary, schedule a few days on a beach or some other peaceful place after an especially demanding adventure.

Getting enough sleep usually isn't a problem on the road. There will be days when you're out at dawn to catch a bus or train or you stay up for late night conversations and parties, but generally you turn in much earlier than at home. Away from cities, night life is pretty quiet. Where there is no electricity, yawns come early and most local people have to be in the fields or at the market at sunrise.

To ensure decent rest, find hotel rooms shielded from noise. Keep in mind that three sounds can penetrate the most determined slumber. The first is the sound of muezzins in long gray caftans standing on the balconies of minarets calling the faithful to dawn prayers. Even where a scratchy phonograph record and loudspeaker have replaced this classic figure, what has been lost in authenticity has more than been made up by an increase in decibels. The muezzin's command pierces a brick wall as if it were papier-mâché. Ask where the muezzin is and put some distance between his call and your bed. The second sound is ubiquitous. I used to think that roosters crowed only at dawn. They don't; they hold challenge matches all night long and it takes days to adapt to the raucous screeching. The third is the honking of impatient drivers in the early morning.

2. Improve your fitness before you leave, then stay within your limits. Work on physical conditioning before leaving home. Get into shape to walk three to five miles without discomfort. If your general health permits, lift weights for a few weeks to build upper body strength. Extend your limits as the trip progresses, but don't try to do too much early on. It's easy to tear up a knee by plunging down a steep, rocky mountain trail before your thighs have strengthened to share the load.

3. If you feel more than a little sick, get help. Seems obvious doesn't it? Still, I keep meeting people like a German woman who fell ill in Nepal and stayed miserably, painfully sick for a month. When she finally went to a doctor, her dysentery was cured in a few days. Why suffer? Get help.

4. Do not consume local water or food unless you are certain they are uncontaminated. Assumptions aren't good enough, especially since they tend to be wishful thinking when you're thirsty or hungry. By following the guidelines in Chapter 12, you greatly improve the odds in your favor.

5. Eat nutritiously, drink plenty of water, and take vitamins daily. When making unusual demands on your body, eat well (even when it means eating unfamiliar foods) to keep up strength and resistance. If your diet becomes unbalanced, especially due to a shortage of greens, consider multivitamins with minerals, and extra vitamins C and E. On my next trip, I plan to test acidophilus tablets, which are supposed to be a good diarrhea preventive. Clean water is a necessary investment.

6. *Keep clean.* Dress in combinations of clothes purchased in the last three countries you've visited, let your hair grow, do whatever helps you feel free—but get clean regularly. It's not for someone else or for the sake of convention, but because staying clean affects your health and state of mind. After a day in a gritty city, or coming off a dusty trail, a shower lifts the spirits. Opportunities to shower "later" evaporate all too often so I've learned to take a shower when I have the chance.

Keeping your body clean helps keep cuts from getting infected or letting jungle rot get a foothold. No one really likes taking a cold shower in cold weather or washing out of a bucket, but it's worth gritting your teeth once in a while to get clean.

Because diseases communicated by touch are more common on the road, wash your hands much more frequently than at home. The best way to avoid accidental fecal-oral transfer is keep your fingers out of your mouth and not rub your eyes or nose. In public toilets, surfaces have been touched by many hands so avoid touching anything you don't have to. Wash your hands in the morning, wash before eating, wash after visiting the bathroom. We may not wash as much as we should but we can train ourselves to wash more than at home.

7. *Treat cuts and sores immediately.* The possibility of infection is higher when you're traveling, especially in the tropics. When skin is constantly moist, microbes flourish and small cuts and sores become infected quickly. When something needs first aid, tend to it right away.

8. *If you must receive a blood transfusion, exercise great caution.* Tainted blood supplies spread HIV and other diseases. If the need for a transfusion is foreseeable, consider flying, or being evacuated, to where the blood supply is safer. If that's not possible, call an Embassy to see if it has a registry of screened donors. Make the medical facility aware of your concern. Insist on sterile needles and get someone trustworthy to supervise the process. The Blood Care Foundation in London can deliver fully tested blood by courier (if interested, write before you depart to P.O. Box 7, Sevenoaks, Kent TN13 2SZ, United Kingdom).

9. *Shield yourself from people coughing and sneezing near you.* Even if you feel like a hypochondriac, protect yourself by turning away, moving away, or covering your mouth and nose. Those little droplets travel faster and farther than you would believe. During your travels, you may be in crowds in train stations, on local buses, and on city streets. Respiratory diseases are common, so being a little defensive is better than being a lot sick.

10. *Protect yourself from mosquitoes* (not to mention sand flies, black flies, and tsetse flies). This is one of the most important ways to protect your health. If biting insects are a problem, tuck your pants legs into your socks and wear a long-sleeve shirt. Stay away from stagnant bodies of water, rivers, and lakes around dawn and dusk when mosquitoes are most numerous.

Use an effective repellent. Although a persistent underground rumor suggests that Avon's Skin So Soft works as a repellent, recent tests do not indicate that it deters mosquitoes. Vaseline Intensive Care advertises a No Burn No Bite suntan oil, but apparently the slogan means only that it doesn't *attract* bugs.

What works best is anything based on DEET (N, N-diethyl-metatoluamide), available in various concentrations up to 100 percent. However, DEET may cause adverse reactions in some children when used in high concentrations or in anyone when use is prolonged or excessive. Since pregnant women are generally advised to avoid insecticides, check with a knowledgeable doctor. For most people, there seems to be no problem with normal use of DEET, especially in a 30 to 50 percent solution. Permethrin is also an effective repellent when sprayed on clothing.

Some mosquito repellents will eat their way through your toilet kit if they spill, so transport them in a watertight container. When I look at the way they dissolve plastic, it makes me wonder what they do to skin.

Adjust the precautions you take according to the level of risk. Don't get spooked every time you hear a nasty whine, but do make an extra effort to avoid those little biters and suckers.

Since even the best prevention may not be successful 100 percent of the time, we'll discuss treatment for malaria later on in this chapter. Mosquito warfare is also discussed in Chapter 11 (Lodging).

11. *Carry good medical identification,* including notice of your blood type, allergies, and other special health characteristics (relevant medical or surgical history and names and doses of critical medication). List the name of a person to contact should you be in need. If you have medical insurance, carry evidence of it.

12. *First Aid.* The Red Cross offers a worthwhile first aid course and issues a useful first aid instruction card for travelers. They can also teach you how to perform cardiopulmonary resuscitation (CPR) and the Heimlich Maneuver, important skills at home or abroad.

13. *Coming Home.* If you took malaria pills, remember to keep taking them for four weeks after leaving the malarial area. During your first weeks back, keep an eye on your health. If there's a problem, don't ignore it. Get a check up and tell the physician exactly where you've been. If he or she is not knowledgeable about diseases in that area, find a specialist.

Minimize the effect of the relatively minor health problems on this list by washing frequently, dealing with a problem before it becomes serious, and using your head. Where I have mentioned medications, I've indicated whether the item is available over-the-counter (OTC) or by prescription only (P).

ALLERGIES

Even if not troubled by allergies at home, you might encounter something on the road that pushes an allergy button. Typical symptoms are sneezing, itchy eyes, nasal congestion, and headache. Antihistamines, such as Benadryl capsules (OTC), Chlor-trimeton (OTC), or Seldane (P) could be helpful but they have a sedative effect. *Seldane must not be taken at the same time as erythromycin.* If you have a history of asthma, bring your medicine with you and don't let your travel schedule interfere with taking it regularly.

ALTITUDE SICKNESS

How to get it. Altitude sickness comes from ascending rapidly to an altitude at which there is considerably less oxygen in the air than you're used to. For example, at 15,000 feet, the oxygen in your blood is only half what it is when you're having dinner at the Top of the Mark in San Francisco. Symptoms of altitude sickness tend to occur in situations such as when hiking in three or four days from the Tanzanian savannah at 5,000 feet to the 19,340-foot summit of Mount Kilimanjaro.

Sleeping at high altitude appears to be an important factor in causing altitude sickness. That's why mountaineers say: "Climb high, sleep low." In Nepal, a popular trekking destination, some trekkers are stricken when they ascend too quickly, sleep high, and cross 17,000-foot mountain passes before they become acclimatized. You also increase the chances of experiencing altitude sickness by overexerting yourself, getting dehydrated, and/or overconsuming alcohol soon after arrival at high altitude.

Physical fitness doesn't seem to protect against altitude sickness. To the contrary, the more fit the climber, the greater the likelihood of climbing too fast. Paradoxically, a recent medical study shows that climbers over sixty are only half as likely to develop altitude sickness as people between twenty and thirty-nine.

Symptoms. At altitudes above 8,000 feet, about one out seven people experiences shortness of breath, headache, loss of appetite, nausea, fatigue, and sleeplessness. Above 10,000 feet, the percentage may rise to 50 percent. These symptoms often indicate a mild case of altitude sickness. Symptoms develop during the first day at altitude, become most severe within the next two days, then usually subside. If the symptoms become more severe and problems with balance develop, a moderate case of altitude sickness may be developing. A dry, wracking cough can become a major problem. A friend of mine lost an opportunity to summit Mount Everest because his violent coughing fractured a rib.

Altitude sickness is no more than a minor problem for the great majority of people who experience it. However, it's important to be aware of the risk of *high altitude pulmonary edema* (HAPE), which is fluid building up in the lungs and reducing the oxygen supply to the blood, and *high altitude cerebral edema* (HACE), fluid building up in the brain.

Although pulmonary edema can occur as low as 8,000 feet, it is usually the result of rapid ascent, severe exertion, and sleeping at high altitude. A person who looks blue around the lips and develops chest congestion, wracking coughs, pink frothy sputum, rapid heart rate when resting, shortness of breath after very little exertion, persistent vomiting, serious loss of coordination, and extreme fatigue, *must descend immediately*. With those symptoms, I don't think I'd argue. Symptoms of cerebral edema include severe headache, nausea, vomiting, hallucinations, difficulty maintaining balance, and bizarre behavior. To protect life, *descent must be immediate*.

How to avoid it. Ascending slowly is the best way to prevent altitude sickness. Take at least two days to get to 11,000 feet, then another week to reach 18,000 feet. Some experts recommend not increasing the altitude at which you sleep by more than 2,000 feet a day. This becomes more important the higher you go. If you ascend more rapidly, rest a day every 3,000 to 4,000 feet.

You can take acetazolamide (Diamox)(P), unless you have an allergy to sulfa, beginning a couple of days before starting your ascent and continuing throughout your stay at high altitude. By stimulating respiration and making the blood more efficient in delivering oxygen, it helps about half who take it. It also stimulates urination, so if your urine turns dark yellow, you need to increase fluid intake.

When you exert yourself at high altitude, inhale bottled oxygen if it's available and get extra rest. Consume plenty of complex carbohydrates and go light on proteins and fats. Take in a little extra sugar, especially before you undertake strenuous exercise.

In the Andes, people drink *maté*, a tea made from coca leaves, in the belief that it provides some immunity to altitude sickness. At the very least, it helps prevent *dolores de cabeza* (headache). The best evidence it works is that local people have continued drinking it for centuries. In general, however, tea, coffee, and alcohol are dehydrators and should be avoided. Instead, drink more water than you believe possible, increasing the amount as you ascend.

For people having trouble sleeping at high altitude, there's a temptation to take sleeping pills. The problem is that sleeping pills depress respiration and diminish the amount of oxygen being received. It's better to wait it out.

Treatment. If you develop a mild case of altitude sickness, take acetaminophen (Tylenol) or ibuprofen (Motrin) as well as Diamox. It would be wise to descend and see how you feel in a day or two. If you continue to ascend, be vigilant concerning your condition. Stop climbing if symptoms of a moderate case develop. Take Diamox and oxygen if available. If you don't get better, descend at least 1,500 feet and see if you improve.

If you develop symptoms of pulmonary or cerebral edema, descend immediately. Don't wait for help (or even daylight, if descending at night is not ridiculously hazardous). Descend at least 3,000 feet; more is better. Get oxygen if you can. Don't try to tough it out. Pulmonary or cerebral edema can kill. Even if you feel better at the lower altitude, it would be better not to ascend again until an expert has evaluated your condition. For pulmonary edema, Nifedipine (P) is recommended. For cerebral edema, Dexamethasone (P). *If suffering from either, don't rely on medicine alone—get professional help.*

ATHLETE'S FOOT/FUNGAL INFECTIONS/BLISTERS

Keep your feet in good condition. Foot problems are frequent on the road and can put you out of action for days. Since high humidity and going barefoot in communal bathrooms contribute to getting foot fungus, wear shower shoes in and around the shower and dry your feet thoroughly. Don't let your socks get too grungy; change them every day if possible.

If your feet will be constantly wet, as they might be during an extended trek in Amazonia, coat them with Vaseline to ward off jungle rot. Sounds messy but it works.

If painful cracks develop between toes, treat them immediately. Tinactin (OTC), Desenex (OTC), or Mycostatin (OTC) as a powder or spray should work. If you're prone to problems with foot fungi, sprinkle Mexsana (OTC) powder in your shoes to absorb perspiration in which fungi thrive.

Wearing two pairs of socks helps prevent blisters. If you feel a blister developing, put on a band aid with a patch of Moleskin (OTC) over it. If you pop a blister voluntarily, you're inviting infection, a bigger problem. If a blister pops by itself, treat it as you would a cut. Wash it often and unless you're allergic to neomycin, try Neosporin (OTC) antibiotic. If you have that allergy, apply some other topical antibiotic. Cover the blister when you need to do so to keep it clean. The rest of the time, such as when in bed, leave it open to the air. Watch for infection. See if you can find and fix whatever caused the blister to form. It may have been something as simple as a rough spot on the inside of your shoe, or even a few grains of sand.

BIRTH CONTROL

The birth control method of your choice (if it's other than abstinence) may not be available as you travel, so you may want to take a supply with you. Both male and female travelers would be well-advised to travel with condoms unless they are certain no new relationships will transcend the platonic. Be aware that high temperatures shorten the life span of most condoms.

The effectiveness of birth control pills may be diminished when a woman is taking oral antibiotics (including ampicillin and tetracycline). If a woman has continuing diarrhea, "the pill" may not be absorbed and she may not be protected. The stimulating experiences of travel have been known to cause some travelers to neglect their regular birth control routine. Since changing time zones may throw you off the once-every-twenty-four-hour dose required for maximum protection, it is recommended that you continue to take birth control on the schedule you used at home rather than shifting to local time.

It may be useful to know that disruption of circadian rhythms and hormonal imbalances that may occur during travel can disrupt a menstrual cycle, even causing one or two periods to be skipped.

BITES/PRICKLY HEAT

Most bug bites, excluding malarial mosquitoes, are little more than a temporary irritation. If there are dozens of bites, which may be the case if that nice-looking bungalow turned out to have bedbugs or you've run into a swarm of sand flies on the trail, it takes superhuman willpower not to scratch, even though you know scratching makes the situation worse. An application of Mexsana or Calamine (OTC) lotion helps hold down the itching.

If bites are in danger of becoming open sores that can become infected, try a 1 percent Hydrocortisone cream (OTC) or oral Benadryl (OTC) for three or four days. Hydrocortisone is a topical anti-inflammatory drug that doesn't cure anything but does help control the compulsion to scratch. Benadryl is an antihistamine tablet intended for temporary relief of upper respiratory allergies, hay fever, and the common cold. In addition to their chemical effects, doing *something* to stop the itching helps control the psychological urge to scratch. If you do scratch a little, use something other than fingernails, something softer and less likely to transmit germs.

Spraying your clothes with Permethrin adds protection against pests like chiggers, mosquitoes, bedbugs and ticks. One such spray is sold in sporting goods stores as Permanone Tick Repellent.

I've read about a dermatologist who recommends wearing dog tick and flea collars around your ankles to ward off sand flies and other insects. Until they do more for my dog, I'll pass on that idea.

Lice love to play in your hair but they don't mind making themselves at home elsewhere on your body as well. They'll come to your attention as you begin to itch or, the fates forbid, experience a kind of indefinable crawling sensation. There are plenty of shampoos available abroad that get rid of lice, so it's not worth taking anything with you. To make sure they're gone, wash your clothes thoroughly with hot water and detergent. The little devils like to hide in the seams, so scrub vigorously.

Keep an eye out for ticks. They seem to be the penance demanded in return for a great walk through the bush. If one has already burrowed into your skin and is gorging on your blood, you must remove it. If you leave the head behind it can cause an infection so use the tip of a hot match, a spot of gasoline or alcohol, insect repellent, or iodine to make the tick want to let go. When the tick is gone, wash the site thoroughly with soap and perhaps apply an antibiotic cream (such as Neosporin). If you are concerned and no medical help is readily available, consider taking an antibiotic such as Amoxicillin or Doxycycline for a few days.

Who hasn't winced at the sight of Humphrey Bogart on the deck of the African Queen recoiling at the sight of leeches sucking his blood? We think of leeches in water but the land-based variety found in tropical rain forests is more common. Check your shoes and legs. If a leech has attached itself, use heat, iodine, or alcohol to remove it. Salt will also make one let go in a hurry. Wash the wound with soap and water. If it bleeds for a while because of the anticoagulant injected by the leech, apply pressure to stop the flow.

Fleas may await you in even the nicest looking bed, but DEET will keep them away. If you don't have DEET, wad up the bedding, toss it out it into the hall, and hope the mattress is relatively uninfested.

Black flies, Tsetse flies, and sand flies spread unpleasant diseases though their bites. If the risk is significant, spray your clothing with Permethrin and use DEET on exposed skin. Reapply after swimming or sweating profusely. It may be better not to use full-body applications of DEET for more than a week at a time, but doing so seems better than picking up one of these insect-transmitted diseases.

Prickly heat, caused by sweat glands getting plugged, consists of a field of red bumps that itch like the devil. A common cause is clothing that doesn't let sweat evaporate into the air, especially in the sultry tropics. To avoid it, keep dry, wear loose cotton clothing, and apply talcum powder. Air conditioning should help (of course, you tend to get prickly heat where there isn't any AC).

There are a few other things that may take a bite out of a traveler. For example, it's best not to assume that all dogs are friendly. They are often guards rather than pets, which means they are very territorial and may move in for a nip if you intrude on their space (more on this subject under "Rabies"). If there's reason for concern, carry a stick or a handful of rocks. Monkeys are notorious biters and humans should stay clear of them. Snakes are more common in the Third World landscape than in your yard, but they'll do everything they can to avoid you if you just watch where you step. Contrary to the movies, most wild animals will flee from you (although hippos do attack humans and they take no small bites). If an animal does happen to take a bite, follow the recommendations in the section on Rabies later in this chapter.

BURNS

Immediately apply cold by means of a cool cloth or an ice pack, or immerse the burned area in cold water. Remove clothing unless it is stuck to the burn and cover the burned area to keep it clean. Do not apply butter or other grease. There are good burn creams available locally but when you need one, you need it immediately so it's worth carrying one along. Silvadene (OTC) is one of the best. Small burns will normally heal without further medical attention but a large burn deserves medical help. By the way, it is the practice in some cultures to apply a poultice of dirt and dung over a burn. While I respect traditional medicine, I'd think twice about that particular remedy.

CHAPPED LIPS

The old favorites are Blistex (OTC), Vaseline (OTC), or Chapstick (OTC) in combination with an SPF 15 sunscreen.

COLDS and COUGHS

Cold viruses live in the upper nasal passages and are usually spread from the nose to the hand of an infected person then to the hand and nose of the victim, often through intermediaries such as a doorknob or telephone receiver. Improve your odds of avoiding a cold by staying away from people with colds (easier said than done), washing your hands frequently, and keeping your hands away from your nose and eyes. You are more resistant to getting a cold if you keep rested and eat well.

We haven't done well at curing a cold, but there's plenty of help available to reduce symptoms such as a stuffy nose. Sudafed (OTC) tablets, Advil Cold & Flu (OTC) tablets, and Dristan nasal spray (OTC) are decongestants that shrink mucous membranes and open up nasal passages to make your nose run (which is good because the fluid takes the cold virus with it). Aspirin (OTC) or Tylenol (OTC) help with the headache. Note that aspirin is not advisable for some small kids and Advil Cold & Flu may not be recommended for a pregnant woman.

For a congested cough that is interfering with sleep, consider Robitussin DM (OTC), which is both an expectorant and a cough suppressant. Robitussin AC (P) contains codeine, to which a significant number of people are allergic and it may also put you right to sleep. Guaifenesin (P) is the same as Robitussin. Humabid LA (P) and Hytuss 2X (OTC) are expectorants in tablet form. Water is also a very effective expectorant, as are hot beverages and soups. Cough lozenges of various types are available everywhere. If the congested cough is not interfering with sleep, concentrate on an expectorant only. For a dry, persistent cough, consider Benylin DM (OTC). In both cases, look for an alcohol-free product unless you want to knock yourself out.

Fever and thick green or yellow sputum accompanying a cough may be signs of bronchitis or pneumonia (discussed later).

CONSTIPATION

Drinking ample fluids and eating fruits (especially apples, dates, figs, and mangoes), veggies, and other fiber help prevent constipation. Should constipation not resolve itself naturally, try Colace capsules (OTC) or Senokot (OTC) for one or two days. Milk of Magnesia (OTC) is good, but bulky to transport. Use constipation remedies for a short time only. Some are sufficiently addictive and after a while your bowels won't work properly without them.

When constipated, don't just lie around. Exercise is a strong stimulant to bowel activity. Suspend taking narcotic pain medicines (since they slow bowel activity).

CUTS

Have a doctor look at serious cuts or punctures. For the nicks that come with everyday living, start with a thorough washing with soap and clean water. Betadine (OTC) is a good antiseptic solution for the initial cleansing. Unless you're allergic to neomycin, apply Neosporin (OTC) ointment. The ointment will keep the dressing from sticking to the cut and will keep it moist. To keep a cut clean, you may need to cover it with a bandage during the day. Because exposure to air helps the healing process, leave the cut uncovered at night without refreshing the ointment on it. By the way, mosquito repellent in a cut doesn't feel good at all.

If bleeding is severe, apply direct pressure (except to the head, neck, or torso), preferably with your hand on a thick clean compress. If no compress is available, use your bare hand. Raise the area of bleeding higher than the heart, but only if there is no fractured limb or neck injury. Apply pressure to pressure points in the groin and upper arms. If a cut requires stitches, clean it, close it as much as possible (perhaps with a butterfly bandage), keep it moist, and get to a doctor within twenty-four hours. Start antibiotic treatment.

Since a cut, especially in the sweaty tropics, can be a magnet for little bugs that create infection, change a dirty bandage right away and be alert for the redness that signals infection. If an infection starts, you'll probably see red streaks around it. If the streaks run in the direction of the torso, Amoxicillin (P) may be the best choice, although Cipro (P) might work. The area will probably feel unnaturally warm, swollen, and tender and you may run a low fever. If these symptoms appear, see a doctor at once.

Treat a minor abscess by puncturing it gently with a sterilized needle after you've sterilized the area with alcohol or iodine. Wash it thoroughly and apply anti-bacterial ointment. Leave it open to the air part of the time and keep it clean.

You've probably heard that there is something different about coral cuts. Well, it's true. Infection probably comes from micro-organisms living on the coral or in the water. If you clean the cut immediately and thoroughly (alcohol or hydrogen peroxide, which bubble the coral fragments to the surface, are good), and treat it as a cut (e.g., with Neosporin) and not just a scratch, you should have no problem. If you don't treat it, infection is possible. Not long ago, I was with a friend who didn't tend to a coral nick on her knee. Within forty-eight hours, her knee became enormously swollen and so painful she couldn't sleep for several days. It's worth being careful.

DEHYDRATION

Dehydration is insidious. You would expect it to be a problem in the Sahara, but it can happen anywhere, including at sea, at high altitude, and when you're sick. Prolonged diarrhea can lead to serious dehydration and even death. At home, you may get by drinking two or three pints of fluid each day but during a hike in the tropics you could lose that much through perspiration in two hours. If you lose fluid equal to 5 percent of your body weight, you'll feel thirsty. Lose in the range of 6 to 10 percent and you'll experience headache and difficulty walking or performing any work. Lose more and you're heading for delirium, unconsciousness, and possible death. Put another way, an unacclimated person working outdoors in an extremely hot and humid or hot and dry climate should be drinking ten to sixteen pints of fluid a day. That's a lot! Most people fall far short and unknowingly risk the consequences.

Water, juices, broths, and colas are good. Coffee, tea, and alcohol are diuretics, which means that they tend to increase the discharge of urine. It may help your state of mind to bolt down a cold beer after a long day in the hot sun, but you need to follow it with nonalcoholic fluids. By the way, increasing salt intake helps retain fluids.

Even better is drinking clean water into which a packet of Oral Rehydration Salts (ORS) has been mixed. The ORS replace some of the electrolytes (or salts) that your body is losing. ORS packets are available throughout the Third World.

DIARRHEA

How to get it. Microbes that cause diarrhea are transferred from person to person by contact or they enter the system via contaminated food or water. The usual reason travelers are affected is that bacteria in the digestive systems of people at their destination are different from their familiar domestic bacteria. Not better or worse, just different. In addition, taking antibiotics tends to destroy friendly bacteria. This leads to diarrhea that should cease when you stop the medication.

Symptoms. Diarrhea is the symptom. The problem is actually gastroenteritis (inflammation of the digestive tract) which accompanies many diseases. Diarrhea's intensity varies and is usually self-limiting, meaning it will go away by itself. One person may feel a little queasy for a couple of days while another may have vomiting, stomach cramps, and mild fever. Simple diarrhea should clear up without treatment in two days to a week (only 10 percent lasts longer than one week). If it doesn't, stop in to see the doc.

How to avoid it. The best way to avoid diarrhea is to make a continuous effort to avoid contaminated food and water. Eat only peeled fresh fruits and veggies, eat well-cooked foods, and don't drink water that might be contaminated (see Chapter 12). Some of the pathogens that cause diarrhea will enter your system no matter what you do, but following precautions concerning food, drink, and cleanliness will greatly increase the odds in your favor.

To prevent diarrhea, some doctors suggest taking a prophylactic such as trimethoprim/sulfamethoxazole (Bactrim/Septra; P), Doxycycline, or iproflaxin (Cipro; P). However, they can cause an adverse reaction such as hemolytic anemia, photosensitivity, or a severe rash and may actually contribute to diarrhea. At the least, they help make invading pathogens more resistant to antibiotics. The majority of doctors I've talked to do not recommend preventive medicine for diarrhea.

A less intrusive preventive would include taking two bismuth subsalicylate tablets (the old standby, Pepto Bismol; OTC) four times a day. If you do, don't be surprised if your tongue and stool turn black and you hear a ringing in your ears for a while. It's better not to take Pepto Bismol and aspirin at the same time. Some people are convinced that acidophilus tablets also help prevent diarrhea.

If you are with a group and someone gets diarrhea, concentrate on your personal hygiene and avoid contact with the affected person.

Treatment. The best way to treat simple diarrhea is to take no medicine but drink plenty of clean water or other nonalcoholic (and, preferably, caffeine-free) fluids to avoid dehydration. Fruit juice and bananas replace lost potassium; honey and sugar replace lost glucose. Bottled soft drinks are fine, especially those that are caffeine-free, since they also replace glucose. To replace salts, add a little table salt to food, juice or soda. Alcohol is not recommended in conjunction with diarrhea.

In many places throughout the world Oral Rehydration Salts (ORS) are readily available in pharmacies and general stores. Taken with clean water they are an excellent replacement for lost salts, glucose and minerals. You can make your own mixture as follows: eight ounces of fruit juice (for potassium), 1 pinch of table salt, and one-half teaspoon of honey (to help absorb the salt). With this brew, drink eight ounces of clean water into which you have mixed one-fourth teaspoon of baking soda. It doesn't sound too tasty but it works.

Eat nondairy foods, especially carbohydrates, that are easy to digest. Take aspirin, rest, and let your system have a day or two (sometimes up to a week) to clean itself out. Keep fluids coming in, even beyond the point at which you stop being thirsty. The goal is replacement. As you tentatively start eating solid foods again, remember BRAT. The acronym stands for bananas, rice, apples and toast. Your intestines will appreciate it.

Circumstances, such as an upcoming all-day bus trip, may make it temporarily preferable to prevent diarrhea from running its course, so to speak. For that purpose, Kaopectate (OTC) will give more body to the stool but it doesn't reduce other symptoms, like cramps, or reduce the frequency of the diarrhea events. For additional relief, there is Pepto Bismol. If you want *certainty* of relief from the primary symptom, the leading anti-motility drug is Immodium (OTC). Lomotil (OTC) is equally effective but more likely to cause drowsiness and retention of urine. Either will contain the problem, but neither is a cure. To the contrary, both retard completion of the cycle, meaning they cause the body to retain the pathogens. Nevertheless, take Immodium along. When you need it, you need it.

Another treatment for diarrhea is a general antibiotic such as ciprofloxacin (Cipro; P), ofloxacin (Floxin; P), or Bactrim/Septra (P). Some physicians feel it's better not to take antibiotics for diarrhea unless it is accompanied by fever. Those who do recommend antibiotics are divided on whether it's better to take anti-motility drugs before taking antibiotics, or better to start with antibiotics, or take both together. There seems to be a small majority in favor of taking the antibiotic first, permitting the diarrhea to flush out your system.

Enterovioform and Mexaform are used to treat diarrhea in some other countries but both are considered dangerous and neither is approved for use by the FDA.

Diarrhea accompanies quite a few illnesses, including dysentery. If the diarrhea doesn't disappear after a couple of weeks, or there are other symptoms (such as fever, severe cramps, blood or mucus in the stool, light sensitivity, or stiff neck), the cause may be more serious than unfamiliar bacteria. In such cases, do your best not to use the anti-motility agents such as Immodium. Try Cipro and get medical attention.

Prolonged diarrhea may also indicate Giardia (discussed later). In that case, you might try metronidazole (Flagyl; P), but be aware that some people experience nausea and vomiting if they drink alcohol at the same time. Tinidazole (Fasigyn; P) is often used outside the U.S.

FATIGUE/STRESS

Discomfort, ambiguity, concern about safety, and other stresses of travel burn considerable energy. The time a person can travel without feeling physically or mentally exhausted differs depending on personality, as well as physical and mental resilience. If you shed stress easily and have a light heart, you may coast through an entire trip without feeling fatigued. If you're less flexible, sleeping too little, or a little off your feed, daily demands can get to you. Weather can be a factor, too. A string of gray days causes most heads to droop.

Learn to recognize symptoms like crankiness, withdrawal, and lassitude for what they may indicate. Notice when little bumps in the road that would normally make you laugh don't seem amusing at all. A series of minor illnesses or accidents may be stress or fatigue related. You may find yourself thinking maybe you should cut the trip a little short.

The remedy is simple. Stop! Chill out. Spend extra money for a while. Find a place to stay that's a notch or two up from your budgeted norm. Eat well. Play. Forget errands. Get shined up. After a few days, you'll probably be your high-spirited self.

I've never gotten so fatigued that a good break didn't restore my energy but if that happened I'd take a close look at my health and nutrition. I'd certainly try several remedies before calling it quits and going home early. Besides, I like to go home feeling strong, with that last burst of speed you summon at the end of a race.

By the way, if you recognize that fatigue or stress may affect your travel partner also, you'll be a sought-after person with whom to travel.

FEVER

Start with acetaminophen (Tylenol; OTC) or aspirin (OTC), except for small children, to lower body temperature. Remove excess clothing. Increase fluid intake. If you don't know what's causing the fever, consult a doctor. If that's not possible, and the fever is accompanied by headache, chills, and fatigue, and you are in a geographic area where malaria is a possibility, consider treating for malaria first (discussed later). If there is also bloody diarrhea, treat for bacterial dysentery (also discussed later). If the temperature increases to above 104 degrees, you must take stronger action: cool the body with water, ice, and moving air. Get a doctor.

FOOD POISONING

Symptoms are usually vomiting and diarrhea, sometimes with cramps. They may start within an hour after eating the contaminated food—but may take a day or more. Take ample fluids and symptoms should disappear within twenty-four hours. Contaminated seafood can make you more ill, including neurological symptoms and respiratory failure. Along with vomiting and diarrhea, you might experience a peppery or metallic taste in your mouth and loss of coordination. If that happens, get medical help.

FROSTBITE

If frostbite occurs, warm the affected part quickly against warm flesh, immerse it in warm water, or wrap it in something warm. Do not rub the skin or it can be seriously damaged.

HEADACHE

For a mild painkiller, many people choose acetaminophen (Tylenol; OTC). Aspirin (OTC) is an anti-inflammatory drug (i.e., it helps relieve inflammation and muscle aches) as well as a painkiller. Ibuprofen (Advil; OTC) has the same objectives but is stronger than, and does not contain, aspirin. Motrin (P) is exactly the same as Advil, except stronger. You can achieve a Motrin-like result by increasing the dosage of Advil. It is better not to take acetaminophen for pain relief while consuming alcohol or for a hangover because the combination may overtax your liver.

If a headache is accompanied by a distinctly stiff neck, fever, sensitivity to light, and a general feeling of malaise, the possibility of meningitis should be considered (discussed later) and medical attention sought immediately.

HEAT EXHAUSTION

It takes several days to acclimatize to an unusually hot, humid environment. Avoid exposure during the hottest part of the day. Wear a head cover. Cool down by wearing loose-fitting natural fabrics that enable perspiration to evaporate quickly. Light colors help reflect heat.

When working or exercising in the hot sun or in high humidity, make an effort to drink clean, nonalcoholic fluids and take in extra salt. If your urine turns darker yellow, it may be a sign you aren't drinking enough water.

When approaching heat exhaustion, you sweat heavily but your skin feels clammy and looks pale. You may feel nauseated or throw up. Your muscles may cramp and you may have a headache. Your heart rate is higher than normal but blood pressure may drop. At this point, your temperature may still be only slightly above normal. Stop what you're doing, get into the shade, rest, cool yourself, and drink as much fluid as you can hold (including ORS, if available).

If you respond properly, heat exhaustion shouldn't be a severe problem but it can progress to heat *stroke* which can be fatal (discussed later). I recall a huge sign on the pier at Agana, Guam, that said, "The Sun Is Hot In Guam!" Tired of watching visitors keel over at midday, they were trying to put arriving travelers on notice.

HYPOTHERMIA

Hypothermia commences when the core body temperature drops below a certain point. What surprises people is that the cold need not be excessive or even very prolonged. I've seen hypothermia strike a person within fifteen minutes after being dumped from a capsizing raft into Idaho's Yampa River in early summer.

Initial signs of hypothermia are lethargy, loss of coordination (such as clumsiness or stumbling), numbness, confusion, and shivering. In a mild case (when the body temperature, taken in the armpit rather than the mouth, is still above ninety degrees Fahrenheit), remove the victim from the source of heat loss, including wet clothing. Dress him in dry clothing and cover his head and body with something that will help retain body heat. Get him to exercise if he feels up to it. Put him in a dry sleeping bag and climb in yourself to share your body heat.

If hypothermia is more serious (the body temperature is below ninety degrees Fahrenheit), it can cause death. The person will behave stupidly, stop shivering, and be unconcerned about the cold. Treat advanced hypothermia the same as a mild case, except that *no* exertion should be permitted. Exertion, even rough handling, can result in death. Get help immediately.

INSOMNIA

When having trouble sleeping, some people take Benadryl (OTC). Although it's primarily an antihistamine, it will induce sleep, is nonaddicting, and is unlikely to conflict with other medicine you may be taking. I have also seen increasing recommendations in favor of taking Melatonin (OTC) for insomnia (see the discussion on Jet Lag).

If you choose to take a sleeping pill, there are many possibilities. In order of duration of their effect (beginning with the shortest) they include: Serax (P), Restoril (P), and Dalmane (P). None of these drugs should be taken in conjunction with alcohol, which is also a depressant. After a week or so, the body seems to develop an increasing tolerance to sleeping pills, meaning you have to increase dosage to achieve the desired effect. That, I am told, can become the path to addiction. Sleeping pills can also interfere with the normal stages of sleep, possibly leaving you poorly rested on awakening. Some people recommend Hyland's Homeopathic Calms, or Valerian.

Consider taking rubber or wax earplugs with you. They at least reduce the uproar in the street below your window to a tolerable level.

JET LAG

Jet lag is a kind of physical and mental disorientation that may disrupt your natural rhythms when you cross three or more time zones. Symptoms include inability to sleep, fatigue, and loss of appetite and mental sharpness. However, if it's any consolation, flying on a north-south axis without crossing time zones doesn't produce jet lag.

Some people recommend alternating feasting and fasting for three days before departure, getting extra sleep, and avoiding last-minute stress as a way of combating jet lag. Even if such a regimen works, it's not very consistent with the reality of getting underway on an extended trip.

In numerous articles written about jet lag, authors suggest eating lightly, drinking little or no alcohol, and getting extra sleep during the flight. That must explain why the airlines deliver a meal every few hours, serve free alcohol nonstop, and show movies all night.

For a long flight, set your watch to the current time at your destination and try to stake out three or four seats in the center section as nap space. Realizing it's already midnight at your destination makes it easier to convince yourself to catch some sleep, even at the cost of passing up those very forgettable movies. If you're a light sleeper, this is a fine time to break in your earplugs. If it's already daytime at your destination, minimize your sleep since you'll be going to bed there on local time.

Avoid caffeine during a long flight and don't arrive at a destination with an alcohol buzz. That's a time when you need your sharpest wits about you.

Despite your best efforts, your sleeping pattern may be out of sync with local time after a long flight. Your body wants to sleep when your eyes and brain say it's time to play. Given the physical and mental energy you burned getting ready for the trip, it should be no surprise if you're a little cranky.

Adjust your schedule to local time immediately. Plan a quiet first day but don't take a daytime nap. If you can't sleep easily for the first night or two, you might try a sleeping pill. Some research suggests that spending time in the sun may also help reset your biological clock.

Here's the breaking good news: scientific tests (reported in the *British Medical Journal*, among other sources) show that taking readily-available, inexpensive melatonin capsules effectively reduces the impact of jet lag. The premise is that proper functioning of our internal body clock is dependent on a natural hormone named melatonin (a derivative of the amino acid tryptophan), which is released by the pineal gland. At present, the best dosage is thought to be five to ten milligrams taken thirty to ninety minutes before bedtime on the day of your arrival and for as many nights thereafter as you feel any effects of jet lag. Lower dosage is needed for westbound travel since it's easier to stay up late than it is to go to bed at what your body thinks is noon. Melatonin is not magic but it reduces the length and extent of jet lag and that's no small breakthrough. Side effects of synthetic melatonin can include headache, nausea, and a mild contraceptive effect in some women. Health food stores sell melatonin as a simple nutritional supplement for about twenty cents a capsule. However, these may vary in strength or purity. The drug companies working on melatonin urge consumers to wait until melatonin, meaning their proprietary version, receives federal approval. In any case, consult your doctor.

The overall impact of extended air travel is more extensive than jet lag alone. In flight, the cabin is pressurized to the equivalent of an altitude of four thousand to eight thousand feet. Therefore, passengers breathe air with a lower concentration of oxygen than they are used to. This alone can produce a slight headache, nausea, and fatigue. In addition, outside air coming into the plane is heated before being circulated in the cabin. In the process, it becomes very dry. To give you a comparison, relative humidity in the cabin of a transoceanic flight can get down to 10 percent, as opposed to 20 percent in the Sahara Desert. Since low humidity in the cabin causes your body to lose moisture, ask a cabin attendant to increase the humidity and drink extra fluids, especially water.

MENSTRUATION

Over the course of extended travel, it's not too unusual for menstrual cycles to become irregular or even stop for a while. That's one possible explanation if you miss one or more periods.

MOTION SICKNESS

Spending a week on Heron Island on Australia's Great Barrier Reef is a fine experience, but most people get there in a small boat that crosses fifty miles of rough water (the helicopter is much more expensive). There's a fabulous bus ride through the mountains of Sikkim, but it's like riding on a dragontail for eight hours. If trips like these challenge your tummy, you're susceptible to motion sickness. Despite what you may have heard, it's not all in your head. It occurs when there is a breakdown in the signal between the motion-sensing parts of the body (inner ear, eyes, and limbs) and the brain. However, your expectation of becoming sick from motion can increase the probability that you will. Motion sickness symptoms include lightheadedness, dizziness, sweat, pallor, nausea, and vomiting.

The solution is simple. Dimenhydryinate (Dramamine, OTC) or meclizine (Bonine, OTC) will stabilize your innards and your mind. Take one pill an hour or so before the onset of motion. Adults may prefer a Scopolamine patch (P) which, applied eight hours before any tummy twisting, remains effective for up to seventy-two hours. These medications can make you a bit sleepy but that's a lot better than hanging over the rail or out the window. Some physicians recommend that these drugs be avoided by pregnant women, asthmatics, and anyone being treated for glaucoma.

On a more naturalistic level, try ginger root in the form of hard candy, gingerbread or, better yet, powdered ginger root capsules to settle your stomach. It works. Green olives, green apples and crackers also help, as does Coca-Cola, and none of them make you drowsy. Many people swear by the effectiveness of a wristband based on the principle of acupressure. Its small beads pressing on the wrist do the job for many travelers. A German firm sells earrings with titanium electrodes that deliver a small electrical current to an acupressure point in the ear. Neither I nor the FDA can vouch for their effectiveness.

Whatever vehicle you're aboard, choose a seat that will have the least motion, usually somewhere in the middle. Get fresh air blowing in your face. Keep your eyes on a steady reference point, such as an object in the vehicle itself, rather than watching scenery rushing by to the side. You can't fool your inner ear, but there is no need to reinforce the sensations by watching endless switchbacks of a mountain road whiz by. If the vehicle stops, get off and walk around.

Perhaps most effective, other than medication, is diverting your mind (I know that's easier said than done). Make yourself as comfortable as possible and try to sleep. If you can't do that, focus your mind on something else or talk with the person next to you. Invite cigarette smokers to desist (pantomime the potential consequences if they don't). Watching someone else get sick is enough to put almost anyone over the edge.

If you toss your cookies, clean up as quickly as you can. Wash your face, brush your teeth, wash or put soda water on any soiled clothes. If someone else loses it, don't be upset with them. You know they would have preferred not to do it. Remind yourself that it will soon be over.

PARASITES

Worms tend to arrive in undercooked meats (especially pork) and fish. They're also quite at home in water. You probably won't see them but their presence may be advertised by diarrhea, bloody urine, muscle pain, coughing, headache, and fever. Another sign may be rectal itching, most noticeable at night. Among the diseases they cause are amebiasis, American trypanosomiasis, Bilharzia (schistosomiasis), Chagas' disease, filariasis, giardiasis, leishmaniasis, malaria, and more. If you suspect a problem, have a laboratory test your blood and a stool sample to determine whether parasites are sharing your travels and, if so, what you should do. The correct treatment, which depends on the type of disease, is usually effective.

Since you can also pick up certain parasitic worms through your feet, resist the pleasures of going barefoot, especially on dirt. Keep shoes between you and those little augers. If you wear open sandals in Africa, wear socks as well.

As usual, the best prevention is good hygiene and caution with food and water. Run-of-the-mill worms shouldn't cause much of a problem, so long as you prevent reinfection, which you can do easily after returning home.

STRAINS/SPRAINS

A strain is an injury to a muscle, while a sprain is an injury to the ligaments that hold bones together across a joint (as in a twisted ankle). Treat either by icing the area, preferably for at least a full day, and elevating it above your heart if practical. Wear an elastic bandage if you have one. Take an anti-inflammatory drug (such as Ibuprofen, OTC) to reduce swelling and pain and prepare to get some involuntary rest.

SUNBURN

Sunburn can bring a trip to a painful halt. I recently spent a full day snorkeling in a series of six spectacular bays on the island of Ko Tao.* To avoid sunburn, I wore a tank-top and plenty of sunscreen. That night, I discovered I'd overlooked a couple of spots. Both my Achilles tendons were inflamed and swollen, practically glowing. Along with the pain, severe blistering developed and there was considerable chance for infection. A friend wrapped ice cubes in a cloth and held them on the blisters to minimize the ultimate severity of the burn and the swelling. I immediately applied Aloe Vera and kept the burned area moist. Later, I treated the burns as if they were cuts, applied Neosporin, and took aspirin for the anti-inflammatory effect. As I was returning to the mainland the next day the burns didn't interrupt my travel, but I wouldn't have been putting Scuba boots on over those inflamed tendons any time soon. I learned my lesson.

Since one of my reasons for making a trip is to be outdoors, I don't expect to stay out of the sun while I travel. Nevertheless, I keep in mind that when the sun is high, a clear atmosphere lets through a lot of burning rays. On a boat or the beach, water reflecting the sun's rays multiplies the effect. The remedy: cut the time of exposure, cover up, wear a hat or a visor, and use a good sunscreen (rated SPF 15 or above). Even a waterproof sunscreen must be applied frequently—and use plenty of it. It's cheap compared to the alternatives.

UPSET STOMACH

Unfamiliar foods, robust spices, poor sanitation, lack of refrigeration, stress, or even just bacteria new to your system may give you digestive problems. For effective relief, try Pepto Bismol (OTC). It comes in chewable tablets (anyone who puts a bottle of that pink liquid inside a pack deserves what will inevitably happen sometime during the trip). Pepto Bismol contains aspirin, which I mention because some people have ulcers or are allergic to aspirin. As an antacid, consider Maalox or Mylanta (OTC); Tagamet HB (OTC) is also popular.

If abdominal pain is severe, accompanied by vomiting and/or cramps and fever, stop eating and drink a little clean water. If there is a high fever, consider taking an antibiotic. Also check the right lower part of the abdomen. If it is very tender, appendicitis is a possibility. Severe abdominal pain can accompany several problems, some of which are surgical emergencies. Get medical help.

---

* *Ko Tao.* This small island in the Gulf of Thailand has no cars, seven dive shops, and great restaurants on the beach. It's close to Heaven.

URINARY TRACT INFECTION

Bacterial urinary tract infection comes to your attention when urination produces a painful, burning sensation. Frequency and feelings of urgency increase. There may be some fever and back pain. To prevent urinary infection, drink plenty of fluids, including acidic drinks like cranberry juice, urinate frequently, minimize caffeine intake, and wear clean cotton underwear.

The indicated medications are usually Bactrim/Septra (P), Ampicillin (P), or Cipro (P). See a doctor, when you can, for precise diagnosis.

A similar burning sensation may also indicate the presence of a sexually-transmitted disease or, in men, a prostate problem.

If you also have pain deep in the small of the back, accompanied by nausea and vomiting, it could be pyelonephritis, a serious kidney infection requiring prompt medical attention. If you're in the boonies, start the Cipro.

VAGINAL YEAST INFECTIONS

When a woman is taking antibiotics (such as tetracycline for malaria), especially in a hot, muggy climate, her chances of developing a vaginal yeast infection increase substantially. Contraceptive pills may also facilitate infection. The most common symptoms are rash, itching, and some discharge. A dilute vinegar or lemon juice douche may take care of it. If not, Nystatin (OTC) vaginal suppositories used at bedtime for at least three consecutive nights, or clotrimazole vaginal tablets, are often recommended. Some women also recommend acidophilus tablets, citrus fruits, and decreasing the intake of sugar and alcohol.

Major Health Problems and What to Do About Them

Major medical problems referred to here include some from which you are generally sheltered at home but might encounter as you travel. You don't want to experience them—and you don't have to if you make a reasonable effort.

BRONCHITIS (and related respiratory diseases)

Bronchitis, an inflammation of air tubes between the throat and the lungs, is commonly caused by an infection (viral or bacterial), an allergy, or an irritation. If untreated, it can lead to pneumonia.

How to get it. Usually by inhaling airborne bacteria or viruses.

Symptoms. Because airways have narrowed, the chest feels constricted. Green, yellow, or white sputum develops, but it's the fever and dry wracking cough that get your attention.

How to avoid it. Good luck is the best ally although general fitness helps by keeping immune levels high. Treat colds and flu early. Certain people have a pre-disposition to bronchitis: smokers, alcoholics, asthmatics, and people especially susceptible to allergies.

How to treat it. Bactrim/Septra (P) or Erythromycin (OTC) are the best bets if the cause is bacterial. If viral, antibiotics won't help. In either case, breathing hot vapors will help break up the sputum and reduce coughing. Keep a vaporizer or a tea kettle going if you can find one. Try Robitussin (OTC) and drink lots of water.

CHAGAS' DISEASE

This disease is a significant cause of death for inhabitants of Central and South America. It arrives via nocturnal insects (sometimes called "kissing" or "assassin" bugs) which emerge from hiding in the walls and ceilings of rural lodgings. Typically, they drop down from a thatch roof (or palm tree if you're sleeping outside). They bite but it's their feces entering through your eyes, mouth, or the wound caused by the bite that infect you. The first sign is a small red bump at the bite site, followed in a week or two by fever and a firm swelling at the spot. Chagas' Disease can result in congestive heart failure ten to twenty years after infection. The best defenses are insect repellent and mosquito nets. Nifurtimox or Benznidazole have been recommended as treatment. Although the disease rarely affects travelers, I mention it because the symptoms could be difficult for a general practitioner to diagnose.

CHOLERA

How to get it. Cholera, currently present in more than forty countries, is caused by a toxin produced by bacteria. Humans get it most frequently from contaminated water and food, especially raw seafood such as shellfish (in which the bacteria concentrate). It can also be transmitted by infected food handlers who use inadequate hygiene, but it is not spread by inhalation. Since it usually erupts as an epidemic, travelers hear about it and can easily avoid infected areas. In the absence of an outbreak, the risk of contracting cholera is very low. However, where cholera is endemic, there is still some risk of transmission by carriers not showing symptoms. Check with the Centers for Disease Control before you travel.

Symptoms. Cholera attacks the lining of the intestines and sucks vast quantities of fluid from the cells. The victim experiences copious diarrhea, often accompanied by vomiting and cramps. This massive loss of fluids and salts destroys the victim's electrolyte balance, prevents retention of nutrients, and causes collapse of the circulatory system. If untreated, death from dehydration is a possibility.

How to avoid it. The best protection is to stay away from current outbreaks. There is a vaccine against cholera, but it only lasts from three to six months and is thought to be no more than 50 percent effective. When I might be where cholera is present, I get this vaccine anyway. It comes in two doses, one to four weeks apart. Unhappily, there is a new strain of cholera in India and a few other Asian countries for which there is as yet no effective vaccine.

Given the limited effectiveness of the vaccine, follow hygienic precautions in any area where there are known cases of cholera. Don't drink untreated water and don't eat raw seafood (specifically shellfish), uncooked fruits and vegetables, or other food prepared under unsanitary conditions.

How to treat it. See a doctor immediately and have a stool sample tested for cholera. Most cases of cholera clear up by themselves within three days, yet thousands of people die because they can't get enough clean water or other fluids to drink. Because of small body size, children are especially vulnerable to severe dehydration. A victim should rest and take nothing by mouth except fluids (that's right, no food). It is *essential* to drink vast amounts of uncontaminated fluid and get sufficient rest. Water, broth, caffeine-free colas, and sugary juices are good. Best of all are Oral Rehydration Salts (ORS) in clean water to replace salt, potassium, bicarbonate and sugar. ORS are available from Jianas Brothers (816-421-2880), from many health food stores, and at many pharmacies abroad. If ORS is not available, add one teaspoon of plain salt and five teaspoons of sugar to each quart of clean water. Combine orange or other fruit juices with salt and honey. If nothing else, drink clean water and baking soda. Avoid milk and drinks containing caffeine. Several antibiotics, such as Cipro (P), Floxin (P), Bactrim/Septra (P), help reduce the length of a cholera attack, but they kill protective bacteria as well as the ones causing cholera.

DENGUE FEVER

How to get it. The colloquial name, "breakbone fever," tells you right away that it's something you'd just as soon skip. Its most serious form is dengue hemorragic fever. It's found in tropical Asian countries, Africa, the Caribbean, Central America and South America. North Americans don't hear a lot about it, but there have been epidemics in a dozen Latin American countries in the last ten years and it is a growing public health threat. It is brought into your life by a female mosquito who takes her nips and transmits the virus usually during the day when you may not be expecting mosquitoes. Dengue hangs out in urban areas and often ventures indoors.

Symptoms. The symptoms may not show up for weeks. When they do, there are at least two stages. First, a fever develops, along with chills, headaches, and vomiting. This lasts three to five days, then goes away. Within seven days, another lighter fever begins, along with chills, vomiting, severe headaches, and wracking aches in joints and muscles. This fever lasts for about a week. The symptoms may be mistaken for malaria until a diffuse rash appears on the trunk of the body, the palms of the hands, and the soles of the feet. Most symptoms disappear within ten days. However, remission may be followed by a relapse and full recovery may take weeks. The pattern is not well understood. The good news is that it is seldom fatal. The one fatal strain causes death in about 5 percent of untreated cases.

How to avoid it. There is no preventive antibiotic or vaccine. The best defense is similar to that against malaria (except there are no prophylactics), but with increased vigilance during the day. Don't get bitten. If you hear of an outbreak of dengue fever, move on.

How to treat it. As a viral disease, neither antibiotic nor vaccine is known to cure it. Take acetaminophen (do not take aspirin), keep taking fluids to avoid dehydration, and get plenty of rest. However, if you're not sure whether what you have is dengue or malaria, treat it as if it were malaria.

DIPHTHERIA

How to get it. Diphtheria, which causes inflammation and obstruction of the nose and throat, is spread primarily by contact with an infected person, or his secretions. The mid-nineties outbreak of diphtheria in Russia, Ukraine, and other states of the former Soviet Union was the most severe in the developed world in thirty years.

How to avoid it. A diphtheria vaccine (usually combined with tetanus) provides a high degree of immunity. Almost everyone gets this vaccination as a child, but a booster is necessary every ten years. Because diphtheria germs are common, this immunization is important whether you travel or not.

DYSENTERY

How to get it. Amoebic dysentery (or Amoebiasis) is usually caused by a protozoan, E. (for Entamoeba) histolytica. Bacillic dysentery is usually caused by Shigella bacteria. Both generally enter through your mouth via poor hygiene, primarily with respect to food and water. The use of human waste as fertilizer and failure to wash one's hands after defecating contribute to contamination. Both types of dysentery can be spread by a food handler who doesn't keep his hands clean, by human contact, and by flies and other insects who have stepped in human waste before dropping by the kitchen or outdoor market. The odds are good you won't encounter dysentery if you're reasonably careful about sanitation and hygiene.

Symptoms. On the road, it's difficult to distinguish between amoebic and bacillic dysentery (in fact, it may be initially difficult to tell the difference between dysentery and plain diarrhea). If the symptoms are cramps accompanied by profuse, bloody diarrhea, but no fever, the cause is likely to be amoebic. If the symptoms are similar but accompanied by fever, the cause is probably bacteria. In either case, the abdominal area becomes extremely sore and sensitive. For certain diagnosis, the stool must be tested. The clues that point to dysentery rather than simple diarrhea are fever, and blood or pus in the stool. There may be a period of remission followed by repeated intermittent attacks or constipation. This pattern may continue indefinitely until the dysentery is properly treated.

In amoebic dysentery, the protozoa may be carried by the blood to the liver, lungs, or brain, leading to formation of abscesses. Amoebic dysentery can be lethal, but with basic treatment there's little to fear. It is, however, a high price to pay for impulsively drinking tap water or being careless about personal hygiene.

How to avoid it. Choose with care the places you eat and drink. Wash your hands frequently and don't put your fingers in your mouth. Remember, dysentery can be spread from one person to another by touch. Antibiotics can be taken prophylactically but that's not a good idea unless you need to be absolutely certain of a week or two with no problems.

How to treat it. Besides recognizing the symptoms, test the stool or the blood. Treat amoebic dysentery by drinking extra fluids and taking oral rehydration salts to replace lost fluids. When you're reasonably sure that what you have is not common diarrhea, Metronidazole (Flagyl, P), followed by

Iodoquinol (P), are recommended for amoebic dysentery. Flagyl should be avoided by pregnant women and should not be taken within twenty-four hours of drinking alcohol. Tinidazole (Fasigyn, P) is used by many, but is not sold in the United States. Bacillic dysentery is not especially dangerous and should go away within a week or so even if not treated. Drink plenty of fluids to prevent dehydration, rest, eat light, nongreasy foods, and treat with Ciprofloxin or Co-trimoxazole (Bactrim/Septra, P). If Cipro doesn't do it, try Flagyl. Symptoms should subside within ten to fourteen days and should not recur.

GIARDIASIS

How to get it. When excreted by human or animal carriers, the Giardia lamblia parasite (more recently named Giardia intestinalis) can survive for months, during which time it can easily wash into a water supply. That's one reason why even the apparently pristine rivers in the Sierra Madre mountains of California carry danger far downstream from the snowy wilderness. Besides being spread via feces in food or water, Giardia can spread from person to person via poor hygiene, which permits transfer of the infected feces.

Symptoms. Fewer than half the individuals who drink water heavily contaminated by Giardia develop infestations; 75 percent of those who do develop no obvious symptoms. The minority experience diarrhea, stomach cramps, excessive intestinal gas, and lack of energy. If the stool is foul smelling and the victim starts burping and experiencing a taste like rotten eggs, Giardia is a likely culprit. If diarrhea lasts for more than a couple of weeks, suspect giardiasis.

How to avoid it. Drink only clean water and eat hygienically prepared food.

How to treat it. Even if untreated, symptoms disappear in seven to ten days—but may recur. If treated, symptoms should disappear for good in about a week. If not treated, the victim may become a symptom-free carrier for years, capable of transmitting the disease to others.

Diagnosis is usually based on a test of the stool. The accuracy of the test depends on the number of cysts present at the time of the test, and the cyst count can vary hour to hour. Giardia can be treated with metronidazole (Flagyl)(P), also used to combat amoebic dysentery. However, according to the CDC, Giardia has been increasing its resistance to metronidazole. In any case, it should not be taken by anyone who is pregnant, nor taken in conjunction with alcohol. If there is a relapse after treatment, consult a doctor.

HEAT STROKE

How to get it. Heatstroke (or sunstroke) is a risk when you spend too much time in the sun without replacing perspiration with fluid intake. Exercise or exertion contributes to the problem, especially in high humidity when sweat doesn't evaporate efficiently to cool the body. With heat stroke, the control system that regulates body temperature has stopped working. Temperature escalates, leading to possible kidney damage, brain damage, and death.

Symptoms. You feel feverish and confused and your skin is dry, flushed, and hot to the touch. Note: unlike heat exhaustion, the victim has a high temperature and does not sweat. Pulse and breathing rate increase. As heat stroke begins, sweating stops. Unconsciousness is possible.

How to avoid it. Drink plenty of fluids in conditions of intense sun and high temperature, especially when exercising. Reduce exercise when humidity is high and pay attention to your body. If your pulse becomes unusually rapid or you begin to feel faint, stop! Get out of the sun. Drink something and consume some salt.

How to treat it. Get the victim out of the sun and lower the body temperature quickly. Undress the victim and put cold packs on groin, armpits, head and neck; even immerse the victim in cold water if possible. Fan vigorously. Massage the limbs to assist circulation. Some recommend giving the victim a little to drink, very slowly. Others, to avoid the risks of vomiting or aspiration, prefer to give nothing. When fever has subsided, cover the victim to prevent chilling and seek medical help. After the event, the victim should rest for several days, drink plenty of fluids, and, oh yes, avoid similar circumstances.

HEPATITIS

Although hepatitis is casually referred to as if it were a single disease, it comes in four designer versions: A, B, C, and E. All attack the liver, but they differ in how they're transmitted and in their effects. Those afflicted typically recover completely from types A and E, but B and C can become chronic and possibly fatal.

Hepatitis A

How to get it. Hepatitis A virus (infectious hepatitis), the least serious, is usually spread by consuming food or water contaminated with human or animal waste. Shellfish and raw fish are common sources. It's also transferred by contaminated needles and occasionally by sexual intimacy. The incubation period is two to seven weeks. Hep A is probably more common than all the more exotic diseases combined.

Symptoms. The symptoms are headache, nausea, and fatigue, similar to a case of flu that won't go away. Other symptoms include generalized aches and pains, a slight fever, vomiting, runny nose, lack of appetite, diarrhea, and upper abdominal pain. Urine becomes golden-orange. In most cases, jaundice ensues, meaning the skin and whites of the eyes turn a distinct yellow hue in five to ten days. This happens because the liver is under attack, failing to dispose of old red blood cells properly. At this point, the liver, located in the upper abdomen on the right side, is extremely tender to the touch. Lymph nodes also become distinctly enlarged. You're likely to feel sick for a couple of weeks and weak for one to three months. To check for hepatitis, get a blood test. Not everyone who gets hepatitis A, including children, shows the symptoms.

Any time you're not drinking enough water, especially if you're sweating heavily, your urine becomes more concentrated and may turn yellow. If that happens, drink several pints of fluid in a short time span. If the urine color doesn't become much lighter within a few hours, watch for other telltale symptoms of hepatitis A.

How to avoid it. For decades, many doctors have recommended receiving an immune globulin (IG) shot just prior to departure. This provides some protection but not immunity. The duration of the effectiveness of the shot depends to some extent on the dosage. A two milliliter dose is supposed to be effective for two or three months while a five milliliter dose lasts about five months. Health departments routinely give the smaller volume so if you want longer protection, ask for it.

In 1995, the FDA approved Havrix, a new vaccine already in wide use in more than forty countries, which appears to give immunity for ten to twenty-five years. The first shot should be received two to four weeks before travel, followed by a booster six to twelve months later. If you'll be traveling to a high-risk area in less than four weeks, receive IG simultaneously with the vaccine. Since 100 percent immunity is seldom certain, continue to avoid food and water that may be contaminated. The CDC and The National Foundation for Infectious Diseases recommend this vaccine. Call (800) 437-2829 for an informational brochure.

Avoidance of hepatitis A must become part of your daily routine on the road. Check out cleanliness when choosing a restaurant, drink only clean water, avoid ice, eat only thoroughly cooked foods, avoid raw shellfish, and wash your hands more frequently than you do at home. Even if food and water are not contaminated, the container they're in may be. By the way, if you hear a rumor that an alcoholic beverage will neutralize the hep A virus, it's wishful thinking.

How to treat it. If you're exposed to hepatitis A while traveling, but you're not yet showing symptoms, consider getting an IG shot immediately (but only if you can be certain the needle is clean). Antibiotics will not help and may harm your liver. There is no known cure for hepatitis A, but it's self-limiting rather than chronic. Fatality need be of concern only to very elderly or chronically ill persons. If you get it, be as certain as you can that your sources of clean food and water are reliable thereafter. Then settle in for a good rest, eat well, drink lots of fluids (except alcohol for at least three months), and be careful not to pass it on to anyone else through contact.

Hepatitis B

How to get it. The hepatitis B virus is extremely infectious. The example sometimes given is that a single drop of hepatitis B–infected blood in a large swimming pool filled with unchlorinated water can infect a swimmer. Think of it as one hundred times more infectious than AIDS. The hepatitis B virus is transmitted most commonly in the same ways, and sometimes at the same time, as HIV: by sexual contact, contaminated blood, infected needles, or even from open sores on an infected person. It can also be transferred by infected blood products and oral-fecal contact. In parts of the Third World, transfusions and inoculations are risky because not all donated blood has been thoroughly tested for freedom from HIV, hepatitis B, malaria, and other diseases, and not all disposable needles are disposed of. High-risk areas include Southeast Asia, China, sub-Saharan Africa, the Amazon Basin, and several Caribbean islands.

Symptoms. The disease manifests itself from one to six months after exposure with gradual onset of abdominal pain and loss of appetite. Jaundice, similar to that with hepatitis A, occurs in about half of all cases of hepatitis B. Symptoms can last several months, but it's possible to have hepatitis B and show none of the usual symptoms.

How to avoid it. Newly developed vaccines Heptavax B, Recombivax-HB, and Engerix-B are effective against hepatitis B. The vaccine is given as a series of three shots over a period of six months, although they can be given within two or three months if need be. The opinion of the American Pediatric Association and other medical organizations seems to be that everyone should receive a vaccine. The National Foundation for Infectious Diseases has begun an education and vaccination campaign on college campuses. Others recommend the vaccine in connection with foreign travel only for people who expect to have sexual contacts or stay for more than six months in areas such as Southeast Asia or sub-Saharan Africa where hepatitis B is endemic. The six months boundary seems a little arbitrary, so you might want to receive the vaccine even for shorter trips. The present cost is about $150 but protection may be worth it if you're going to be staying in a high-risk area.

Avoid injections (including drugs, tattooing, and acupuncture), practice good hygiene, and avoid questionable sexual contacts.

How to treat it. Receive hepatitis B immune globulin as soon as you know you've been exposed. You can eat anything, but must avoid alcohol. Unlike with hepatitis A, extended bed rest doesn't help much. Alpha interferon is said to help in some cases. There is a 95 percent probability of complete recovery and immunity, but if hepatitis B becomes chronic, as is not uncommon in Southeast Asia, it can be fatal. There is also a slight possibility that you will remain a carrier of the virus and, if so, your risk of cancer or cirrhosis of the liver increases. Anyone with troubling symptoms after returning from a trip should mention the possibility of hepatitis B to the doctor.

Hepatitis C

Hepatitis C is widespread throughout the world, including the United States. Check with the CDC or your public health service concerning your destination. It's transmitted in the same ways as hepatitis B and HIV. Disinfection of water is an essential preventive. Most people recover spontaneously but chronic liver disease, usually cirrhosis or cancer, results in about 30 percent of cases. Treatment is the same as for hepatitis B, except that the drug treatment would be beta interferon. A Japanese team has identified the virus causing hepatitis C, so an effective vaccine may be on the way.

Hepatitis E

Hepatitis E is transmitted primarily by drinking contaminated water, but can be spread in the same ways as hepatitis A. There is no vaccine against it and immune globulin probably offers no protection. The most important method of prevention is avoidance of contaminated water. Those infected generally recover from hepatitis E without any problems.

JAPANESE B ENCEPHALITIS

This mosquito-borne viral disease attacks the central nervous system. It is present in rural areas in Asia from China to Pakistan, but it's extremely rare for an urban traveler to get it. Even someone traveling in rural areas in the rainy season has only an estimated 3 percent chance of encountering mosquitoes that carry the parasite. Most infections are mild, but a severe case can cause brain damage and has a 10 percent chance of being fatal. A vaccine, approved by the FDA in 1992, administered in three doses over a three-week period, protects against the disease. Check with the CDC with respect to countries you will visit.

LEISHMANIASIS

How to get it. Leishmaniasis is present in Central and South America, Africa, central Asia, the Middle East and northern China. A quick nighttime nip from an infected female sand fly injects a tiny parasite that invades lymphoid cells in internal organs such as the spleen and liver, bone marrow, or mucus membranes.

Symptoms. Unfortunately, you may not even notice the bite until weeks or months later when it becomes a painful ulcer. Since it's difficult to distinguish Leishmaniasis from quite a few other diseases, it's important to realize that a skin ulcer may be a signal.

How to avoid it. Prevention being preferable to cure, take the usual precautions against sand fly bites, such as using insect repellent, wearing long pants, using fine mesh netting, and so on (see Malaria).

How to treat it. The problem is that most infected people wait several months before seeking treatment, then they may consult a doctor who doesn't diagnose it properly because of lack of familiarity with the disease. Tell your physician that you've been traveling in exotic places because, if left untreated, Leishmaniasis can be fatal. Treatment with Stibogluconate sodium (Pentostam, P) should cure the problem. The type of Leishmaniasis that affects the skin creates lesions and boils, often on the face, backs of hands, forearms and legs. These too can be treated with Pentostam. However, some disfigurement is possible if the parasites attack the mucus membranes of the mouth, nose or throat.

MALARIA

Malaria is present in over one hundred countries; almost two million people die from it each year, far more than die from AIDS. A child infected by one of the virulent strains of malaria can die within hours of showing the first symptoms. Of the 300 million people infected every year, only about thirty thousand are travelers. To provide perspective, only .00003 of the thirty million U.S. travelers abroad last year got malaria. That's because with proper precautions, malaria is almost fully preventable. Amazingly, some travelers in known areas of risk ignore even the basic precautions of taking preventive tablets and following simple routines to avoid being bitten by mosquitoes, the carriers of the disease.

Although early treatment of malaria is usually effective, consequences can be very serious if treatment is delayed. People living in highly malarial areas may develop partial immunity after repeated attacks of malaria but unprotected travelers are at risk.

According to the CDC, the risk is highest in tropical Africa, Amazonian South America, parts of India, Thailand, Malaysia, and New Guinea.

Travelers to Africa should take malaria especially seriously for several reasons: it's a year-round problem, not just seasonal; travelers go to Africa specifically to spend time in rural areas, which is where mosquito infestation is most severe; a higher percentage of mosquitoes in Africa than elsewhere carries the malaria parasites; and, if that weren't enough, one of the parasites they carry is the most drug-resistant strain. For comparison, the odds against getting malaria are 2,000 times more in your favor in Latin America.

How to get it. Physicians used to believe there was something about the air in swamps and sewers that caused the disease. Hence the name "mal aria," or bad air. Turns out they weren't far off. We now know that it is the female anopheline (a Latin word meaning "the hurtful ones") mosquito, a lover of swamps and sewers, who delivers malaria to us. She is merely a carrier, picking up one-cell parasites from an infected person and transmitting them, via the saliva accompanying her pesky bite, to the next person. The parasites travel to the liver of the new host, multiply, and escape into the blood stream. There, they invade red blood cells and multiply, causing the cells to burst and the parasites to flood the system like bloodthirsty pirates searching for more cells to invade.

Symptoms. Malaria symptoms usually appear between a week and a month after exposure, but can take longer. The first round of symptoms includes chills that may last from fifteen minutes to an hour, even up to eight hours. Chills are followed by several hours of high fever, then heavy sweating. These symptoms are usually accompanied by fatigue, severe headache, muscle pains, dizziness, and increasing weakness. When an attack of malaria subsides, the patient feels fatigued, but much better (how could it be otherwise?). Symptoms may recur every one to three days, depending on which species of parasite is roaming around in the blood. The parasites can also damage the brain and kidneys (in the kidneys it's called Blackwater Fever because bursting red blood cells darken the urine), which can be lethal.

In only a minority of malaria cases is there any intestinal uproar, so a person who has some or all of the symptoms listed above plus nausea, vomiting, cramps, and/or diarrhea may have typhoid, cholera, dysentery, dengue fever or hepatitis rather than malaria (now there are some great choices!). If you have an unexplained fever in an area in which malaria is common, get a blood test immediately.

How to avoid it. Prevention is the best answer. Don't get bitten. Before you leave home, review the *World Malaria Risk Chart* and *How to Protect Yourself Against Malaria*, both available from IAMAT. The CDC Malaria Branch publishes a useful booklet called *Recommendations for Prevention of Malaria Among Travelers*. Call the Malaria Hotline at (404) 332-4555.

There are a number of ways to minimize the likelihood of feeling the mosquito's sting (I *don't* mean staying at home). Be more vigilant when mosquitoes are most active—during warm months and at dawn and dusk. Be wary of water, especially if it's slow-moving or stagnant. Strong scents and body odors attract mosquitoes, so a shower at the end of a hot day is practical as well as pleasurable. For anyone disposed to take hair spray, perfume, or perfumed cosmetics on their travels, the mosquito's keen nose is one more incentive to leave those things at home.

Definitely use an insect repellent. Among those available, DEET is amazingly effective and no traveler should be without it in a malaria area. Since questions have been raised about the safety of high concentrations of DEET with respect to absorption of DEET through the skin, you might choose a 30 to 50 percent concentration for your skin, and a more concentrated solution for clothing. Rub it on thoroughly and reapply it every few hours—more frequently if you sweat heavily or otherwise get wet. By the way, DEET on one part of your body does not deter mosquitoes from biting untreated skin nearby. Some people don't like the way DEET feels on their skin, and it does have a fairly distinctive, ahem, aroma, but these are minor considerations compared to a bout with malaria.

Ultrathon is an insect repellent that uses a polymer suspension to achieve controlled-release of a 33 percent DEET solution with very low absorption through the skin. It's supposed to keep mosquitoes, ticks, flies, chiggers, gnats, and fleas at bay for up to twelve hours, and it is resistant to water and perspiration. It leaves an oily feel but has a pleasing aroma. Whatever you select, use it. Not getting bitten is by far your most effective protection. We'll discuss this further in Chapter 11 (Lodging).

Clothing fends off mosquitoes fairly effectively so, at prime time in malaria-land, wear long pants and shirts with long sleeves. Protect your neck. Army surplus stores sell light, inexpensive hats with mosquito-proof mesh that covers head and neck (don't worry if you salute when an officer of the French Foreign Legion strides by).

Tuck your pants into your shoes, especially if ticks are a problem. For extra protection, spray your clothes with DEET or, better, a Permethrin spray. Permethrin does more than repel; it actually kills the mosquitoes. It's not toxic to humans, won't melt synthetic materials, and remains effective even after the clothing has been washed several times.

Where mosquito nets are needed, you'll usually find them provided in your hotel room or for sale on the street. The most common type of net hangs from overhead, covering the entire bed. If there are holes or tears, tape them closed or tie the net around them into a small knot. If you can't seal the holes, ask the clerk for a better net. If you decide to take a net with you, there are some good nets available. The SleepScreen brand rests on the bed or ground and consists of a small dome over your face and a net that stretches down the bed. Weighing only ten ounces, it costs about $30 (or twenty-three ounces and $40 for a double).

When mosquitoes are around, light mosquito coils at the head and the foot of the bed. After you're in, tuck the net under the mattress all around. Think of yourself as the favorite entrée on some mosquito's evening menu and act accordingly.

Virtually all knowledgeable travelers take a *malaria prophylactic* (I know you know that we're not talking about a condom here). Note that the word "prophylactic" means "to defend against," rather than "to prevent." At present, no drug regimen guarantees complete protection against malaria. What drugs do is suppress multiplication of the parasites in the liver, thus preventing their spread through the body to become full-scale malaria. However, even a person who's taken no antimalarial pills is unlikely to contract malaria from a single bite, so don't panic if one little dive bomber slips through. We seem to have at least a limited natural immunity but, since that immunity is minimal, protection remains very important.

Quinine protected Enrico Caruso when he sang grand opera fifteen hundred miles up the Amazon at the turn of the century and Dr. Livingstone as he trudged through the jungle trying to find the headwaters of the Congo, but it may not work for you. That's because malaria parasites have developed a gene that resists the effects of quinine. The areas in which these parasites are most resistant to chloroquine, the quinine-based drug everyone used to take, are the northern half of South America, virtually all of sub-Saharan Africa, and most of Asia from Afghanistan across to Papua New Guinea. The malaria parasites along the borders of Myanmar and Cambodia have become resistant to almost all drugs.

Some degree of chloroquine resistance has been reported everywhere malaria occurs except for Mexico, Haiti, the Dominican Republic, Central America north of Panama, and most of the Mideast. Not long ago, the CDC was suggesting that where parasites are resistant to chloroquine one ought to take Mefloquine (Lariam. P). The CDC recommends Fansidar as a means of suppressing malaria symptoms long enough to reach proper medical treatment, but doesn't recommend it as a prophylactic.

Some well-regarded antimalarial pills are not sold in certain countries. For a trip I took to central Africa, the most appropriate antimalarial drug appeared to be Proquanil (Paludrine). It wasn't sold in the United States but was available over-the-counter in England. I took a daily Proquanil and a weekly chloroquine pill and didn't get malaria. Of course, a friend relied on carefully selected Chinese herbs as antimalarial protection for the same trip and she didn't get malaria either. What can we conclude from that?

Since there may be some side effects with a malaria prophylactic, ask a doctor what to expect in connection with the one you choose. For example, if my palms and the soles of my feet started scaling, I'd feel better if I knew it was just a side effect of Proquanil. Check also with the CDC International Traveler's Hotline (404-332-4559). Select information you want from document numbers they give you, enter your fax number, and they'll fax you right back with current vaccination and other recommendations.

I cannot recommend a specific antimalarial pill because that choice should be determined by where you're going, how much time you'll be spending in rural areas (where mosquitoes are most dense), and any drug allergies you have. You need current medical information to connect the best protection with your itinerary.

The usual drill is to begin taking the pills two weeks before you enter an area where there's a malaria risk. As perhaps some slight evidence of global consciousness, almost every traveler I know who takes a weekly pill takes it on Sunday. To avoid an upset stomach, take it after a meal. Continue taking the pills at prescribed intervals during your travels and for four weeks after you are last exposed to any risk of acquiring malaria. The objective is to kill any parasites that may still be lounging around your liver. If, for example, you're going to New Zealand after you leave the Philippines, the four week period would begin the date you left the Philippines.

Women in their first trimester of pregnancy should be extremely wary of antimalarial drugs. Neither they nor young children should take these drugs without advice from a knowledgeable doctor.

A person who has taken any antimalarial drug is not permitted to donate blood for three years thereafter. The explanation I've heard is that the drug may mask the presence of the malaria parasite in the liver for many months. Since one might be hosting malaria parasites without knowing it, blood banks don't want to take the risk of passing them along in donated blood.

A few words about what does *not* work. Studies do not support the belief that Vitamin B1 is an effective mosquito repellent. Gadgets that project sound waves do not work. Avon's Skin So Soft acts as a temporary physical barrier because of its mineral oil, but is only about 50 percent effective as such and only if reapplied every ten minutes or so. As a Saint Joseph's Hospital (Atlanta) Travel Advisory put it: none of these alternatives will hurt you, but relying on any of them to prevent malaria "would border on lunacy."

How to treat it. In the 1700s, South American natives taught strangers how to use powder made from the bark of a tree to relieve malaria symptoms. That was good advice at the time, but if you believe you have the symptoms of malaria, see a doctor. If you must minister to yourself until you reach a doctor, take an increased dose of whatever prophylactic medicine you've been taking. The number of pills you should take depends on the dosage and contents of your tablets. When you buy the drug, ask "What dosage should I take if I experience symptoms of malaria?"

If you get malaria, a blood test will determine which type of parasite is involved. You then take a drug designed to kill that specific parasite and there should be no recurrence of the symptoms. In other words, malaria is curable. The danger is in failing to get treatment. Without treatment, one type of malaria parasite can be lethal. Other types are unlikely to be lethal but can cause recurrence of the symptoms and damage to assorted internal organs if untreated. The message should be clear.

If you see a doctor after you return from a trip during which you took antimalarial drugs, be sure to mention that fact. If you think you may have malaria, tell the doctor where you've traveled. Also ask him to consider the other diseases your research said might be out there. If you're concerned that your doctor may not be current on malaria and these other diseases, find an infectious disease specialist right away.

The bottom line: (a) with reasonable efforts, you can probably avoid mosquitoes and thus avoid malaria; (b) protective medicine greatly reduces the chances that full-scale malaria will develop; and (c) if you get malaria, proper treatment should cure it.

MENINGOCOCCAL MENINGITIS

In this disease, bacteria infect the membranes that line the spinal cord and brain. Because bacteria are spread by coughing and sneezing, people in crowds are most at risk. Fortunately, most adults have developed an immunity to meningococcal bacteria, but if a person is stricken, it's usually fatal.

There is a vaccine, effective for three years, that is often recommended for travel in sub-Saharan Africa, the Middle East, northern India, and Nepal. A flu shot is also a good idea since being sick with the flu makes it easier for the meningococcal bacteria to enter the body. Symptoms include high fever, chills, headache, stiff neck, nausea and vomiting, and sensitivity to light. When meningitis is suspected, penicillin is often the recommended treatment.

POLIO

Polio, transmitted by oral-fecal contact or contaminated water, is common in underdeveloped countries and is still present in parts of Europe, especially around the Mediterranean. Even though polio hasn't been completely eradicated in the United States, some children do not receive the vaccine.

If you've never had the polio vaccine, consider getting it before traveling in underdeveloped countries. Even if you have, consider a booster dose prior to travel. Ideally, you should start the course several months before your planned departure, but this can be cut a bit if necessary. Public health departments seem to recommend the Salk dead vaccine (received by inoculation) as slightly safer than the Sabin live vaccine (taken orally).

RABIES

Rabies (also known as hydrophobia) causes prolonged suffering and death. It's present in most countries, including Europe and the United States. Rabies is found in raccoons, jackals, wolves, bats, cattle, cats, and dogs, among other animals.

Although symptoms usually appear within two to eight weeks, one nasty characteristic of rabies is that it can take up to two years to show up—long after the victim has forgotten the incident that caused it (which could be a bite or getting infected saliva in a wound). To be cautious, receive the Human Diploid Cell Merriaux Vaccine in two not particularly painful injections before you travel.

As you travel, don't pet an animal that can bite you and get out of the way if you see an animal behaving strangely (with erratic motions, howling bark, frothing mouth, and jaws fixed open). Rabid animals are fearless and will attack without provocation.

If bitten, or even licked on a wound by an infected animal (since the virus travels in the animal's saliva), wash the wound immediately with soap and clean water. Pour in some hydrogen peroxide. If no clean water is available, use alcohol, tea, or even carbonated soda. You are attempting to wash the virus from the wound, so wash vigorously and repeatedly. See a doctor to help decide whether to receive the vaccine if you haven't had it. The decision is much easier if the offending animal is caught and tested.

SCHISTOSOMIASIS (also known as Bilharzia)

More than 200 million people carry this parasite which exists primarily in sub-Saharan Africa, the Middle East, Japan, China, the Philippines, Indonesia, Thailand, tropical South America, and the Caribbean islands. If you'll be traveling in one or more of these places, you should know the precautions to take.

How to get it. Schistosomiasis is caused by trematode parasites that live inside fresh water snails. After metamorphosis, they enter the water, seeking their next host (and humans are very hospitable). If these parasites are present, a person is at risk when swimming in, bathing in, drinking, or even just walking through water. Parasites can enter a host through the skin (a break in the skin, such as a cut, isn't required) or when ingested orally. They reproduce and attack the bowel, bladder, liver, and colon, ultimately appearing in the stool or urine. When parasite-contaminated excrement later enters the water source, the process begins again as the parasite seeks out the snail.

Symptoms. The first sign might be a brief rash where the parasite entered the body. Appearing three to ten weeks after infection, symptoms include abdominal pain, tender and enlarged spleen and liver, headache, chills, fever, diarrhea, blood in the stool or urine, nausea, aches, body rash, coughing, and loss of weight. Remission may occur two to eight weeks thereafter. In advanced cases, schisto has caused blindness, epilepsy, and even death. The diversity of symptoms make it very hard to diagnose.

How to avoid it. Don't swim in rivers or lakes where schisto is a possibility, especially in stagnant water, immediately downstream from a city, or anywhere along the Nile. Even brief exposure can result in infection. If you must cross fresh water in a schisto-infected area, wear shoes and cover your ankles. If you get wet, rub your skin dry immediately; use alcohol if you have it. Boil, filter, or treat water with iodine to disinfect it for drinking or bathing. If you can do nothing else, wash with soap. Prevention is important because schisto can do considerable damage before being detected.

How to treat it. You may need to be tested more than once because a test soon after having been exposed may be misleadingly negative. Schisto can be diagnosed by a urine or stool test and can be cured by a drug regimen. Praziquantel (Biltricide, P) is sometimes recommended, but the appropriate drug depends on the specific type of parasite involved. The dosage necessary to be toxic to the parasite can cause side effects and the drug regimen should be administered only under a physician's supervision.

SEVERE PAIN (broken bones, kidney stone, etc.)

If you're going to be days away from outside medical help, take a heavy-duty painkiller along in case of serious injury. It won't cure anything, but it makes it easier to endure pain until reaching help. If you have an adverse reaction to codeine, consider Demerol (P). As a narcotic, Demerol should be treated with care and should not be taken in conjunction with alcohol. The bottle should be labeled to avoid any problem with customs. For lesser pain, ibuprofen (Advil, OTC) is an effective analgesic and anti-inflammatory drug.

SEXUALLY-TRANSMITTED DISEASES

Acquired Immunodeficiency Syndrome (AIDS).

How to get it. AIDS, caused by the human immunodeficiency virus (HIV), is epidemic in at least ten African countries, India, Thailand, the Philippines, and is a growing problem in many other countries. Good news: you do not contract AIDS just from being in certain places. Nor is it spread by casual contact, coughs or sneezes, food or water, toilets, or any of the usual suspects that cause many diseases. Whether you contract AIDS is determined primarily by your own behavior; it is not an inherent peril of being on the road.

AIDS is transmitted primarily by sexual intercourse or, euphemistically, by transfer of body fluids. It can be contracted during a single sexual contact. You get no free swings (so to speak). HIV infection can also be transmitted via a needle—while taking intravenous drugs, getting inoculations, getting a tattoo or an ear pierced, undergoing acupuncture or a blood transfusion, or when accidentally jabbed.

> "Your next sexual partner could be that very special person. The one that gives you AIDS."
> —Public Health Notice in Zimbabwe.

Symptoms. The symptoms are too complex—and well known—to bear repeating here.

How to avoid it. To avoid deterring tourists and business people, some governments low-ball the number of known HIV-positive cases in their countries. That means you should not rely on published information about the prevalence of AIDS in a given country. Unless you're skiing across Antarctica, assume HIV is present.

The local people travelers meet most frequently are those who make their living on and around the tourist trail. Unfortunately for all concerned, this puts them in a high-risk group. Among those at highest risk are intravenous drug users, prostitutes, and guys who prowl the tourist trail hoping to seduce female travelers. Keep in mind that other travelers who have sex with local people can, if infected, pass it on to you. You must not let blood, semen, or vaginal secretions from an infected person enter your body.

It's pathetic that your life may be on the line when you're considering a sexual relationship with an enchanting person as you travel—but that's the way it is. How many unexpected births must there be before we concede that condoms are scarcely fail-safe as protection. The odds overseas seem prohibitive to me unless both people have been tested and the relationship is exclusive.

If you haven't traveled extensively in faraway places, you may not be able to predict how you'll respond to the stimuli of romantic settings and attractive companions (ones about whom, unfortunately, you may not know a lot). Could a prospective partner be unaware of his or her AIDS status? Or could someone even lie to you about their status or sexual behavior? If you are uncertain about what choices you might make as you travel, you would be well advised to take latex nonoxynol-9 spermicide condoms along. Although latex doesn't remain impervious to tropical heat for long, animal skin condoms are too porous.

Anyone who uses a questionable needle to inject recreational drugs or otherwise pierce one's skin in a foreign country has a death wish, one that may be accommodated. Stay away from tattoos and acupuncture unless you're certain the equipment is sterile (which is highly unlikely). If you require an inoculation, be certain that a new, still-in-the-package, disposable needle is used. Don't take anyone's word for it. *See* the package opened—or go elsewhere. Some travelers carry a syringe and needle along in case of injury in countries where AIDS is common.

A related issue is whether the blood supply available for transfusion is contaminated. Most underdeveloped and developing countries still can't ensure that their blood supply is free from hepatitis, AIDS, or other diseases, so travelers should do everything possible to avoid receiving a transfusion. In an emergency, consider the use of plasma extenders. If you're traveling with a partner, or a small group, you might compare your blood types and HIV status to determine who could be donors for whom should the need arise. If the need for a transfusion arises and you have the choice, buy a plane ticket. Fortunately, the odds against needing a transfusion at the moment you are in a high-risk AIDS country are massively in your favor.

How to treat it. There is no known vaccine for protection against AIDS, nor is there any known cure.

Herpes

Since herpes is transmitted by direct contact with herpes sores on an infected person, the primary preventives for herpes are abstinence or use of a condom. Herpes manifests itself through small blisters on the lips or genitals which burst to form sores that last for a couple of weeks. If the herpes virus is already present, the blisters may be induced by exposure to intense sunlight or unusual stress.

There is presently no known cure for herpes. However, if herpes sores develop, treatment with acyclovir (Zovirax, P) may reduce the severity of symptoms. It is available in ointment and capsule form, but dermatologists consider the capsules to be far more effective. Some dermatologists also recommend Ambesol Gel (OTC). Even Blistex (OTC) is said to have some effectiveness in reducing the symptoms of oral herpes. Do not touch the herpes sores and keep the area around them dry. Wash your hands often.

Syphilis, Gonorrhea, and Other Sexually-transmitted Diseases (STDs)

STDs are more prevalent in the Third World than in developed countries and they do not affect local people only. Nevertheless, more than a few travelers have rolled the dice, making an intimate decision based on a spontaneous evaluation of someone's personality or appearance. Abstinence is the best preventive medicine, followed by having sex only with a partner who has no sexually-transmitted disease. Condoms come in a distant third. If you decide to go forward, use a latex condom and a vaginal spermicide. In addition, check for sores or discharge, wash the genitals of a prospective partner with soap and water, and urinate after intercourse. Sounds pretty romantic, doesn't it?

Common STD symptoms include penile or vaginal discharge, urination that leaves a burning sensation, and lower abdominal pain. There may also be a rash and fever. Men generally experience the first symptoms of gonorrhea within two to twenty days but it may be weeks before a woman feels symptoms—if ever. However, some STDs, especially gonorrhea in Asia, are asymptomatic. It would be prudent to assume that you might have been infected and practice safe sex until receiving negative results on blood tests. If you think you may have an STD, let partners know, avoid sexual contact, and start medication immediately.

Where gonorrhea has not become penicillin-resistant (as it has in parts of southeast Asia and Africa and a few other places), try ampicillin. If you are allergic to penicillin, try tetracycline or doxycycline. In the case of a penicillin-resistant strain, take ciprofloxacin (Cipro, P). Ceftriaxone (Rocephin, P) should also be effective but it is presently available only as a shot (and that is not desirable in some countries).

Treatment for chlamydia, which may be the leading cause of infertility, is doxycycline, tetracycline, or ofloxacin.

Women may experience a pelvic inflammatory disease, often caused by gonorrhea or chlamydia. Treatment usually includes cefoxitin and doxycycline (for non-pregnant women only).

Syphilis announces its presence with a sore on the genitals or the lips, fingers, or anus. Although the sore is painless, it is highly contagious. It disappears without treatment, but the disease continues to grow in the person affected. If untreated, syphilis may cause serious problems, including heart disease and insanity. When an unexplained sore appears in one of these areas two to ten weeks after sexual contact, get medical help (including penicillin).

Treatment for STDs can be complicated, so see a doctor as soon as you can.

SHOCK

Symptoms of shock include a weak, fast pulse, pale face, perspiration, fainting, clammy skin, dull eyes, and nausea. Shock often accompanies major trauma (e.g., a large burn, severe illness, extensive blood loss), but can occur in other situations as well. Keep the victim lying down and elevate the legs higher than the head. Use blankets to conserve body heat. Giving the victim water or ORS (not alcohol), may help, but there is some risk of vomiting or aspiration. If the victim is unconscious, turn him on his side so he won't choke. Keep mouth and throat clear. Because blood is not flowing to vital organs, shock can kill. It is essential to get medical help immediately.

SLEEPING SICKNESS

Tsetse flies hang out around livestock, lakes, and river banks in central, west, and parts of southern Africa. Bites become red and swollen and lymph glands become tender. DEET and Durathon are good repellents, and it apparently takes several bites to infect a human.

Symptoms include high temperature, sleeplessness, and sharp headaches. Drugs are available to treat sleeping sickness but the choice depends on careful diagnosis. Failure to get treatment leads to lethargy, depression, and apathy (as in "sleeping")—and can lead to death.

SMALLPOX

Even though smallpox has been officially eradicated, a few countries in Africa still require evidence of a smallpox vaccination. If you'll be visiting one of them and have a smallpox vaccination entered on your yellow card, no problem. If you don't have or don't want the vaccination, ask your local public health department to give you a "certificate of contra-indication," meaning you don't need the vaccine. That should get you past the border. In only two countries has anyone even asked to see my yellow card and in neither case were the entries examined with any care.

TETANUS

How to get it. Tetanus (sometimes called lockjaw) microorganisms are omnipresent and can infect someone through any break in the skin. Tetanus may invade through puncture wounds from splinters, thorns, and almost everything else. Remember your mom warning you not to step on a nail? It's a serious problem, but one that can largely be prevented through immunization.

How to avoid it. The Tetanus vaccine (usually combined with the diphtheria vaccine) provides a high degree of immunity. Almost everyone gets this vaccination as a child but a booster is necessary every ten years (or within five years of your last immunization if you've had a dirty scrape, cut, or skin ulcer). Because tetanus germs are so common, this immunization is important whether you travel or not. Clean and cover any wound. If it's large, get medical attention.

TRAUMA

Trauma is a wound or shock produced by a physical injury. Travelers are more at risk of experiencing traumatic injury than of being affected by almost any of the exotic diseases on this list.

Traumatic injury can occur in many forms, but I have two suggestions that will provide considerable protection. First, be careful in traffic abroad because (a) the traffic flow may be the reverse of what you're used to, and (b) the pedestrian seldom has the right of way. Look both ways before stepping into the street. Too often, drivers, especially drivers of big trucks, are careless of human life.

Second, if you're riding in a vehicle and the driver seems drunk, get out— or off. It's amazing how many canyons are littered with the remnants of buses because a cannonballing driver didn't see a curve in time. Don't assume, as you might at home, that the driver must know what he's doing and will get you safely to the barn. A high correlation between alcohol and accidents prevails around the world. Listen to your intuition.

I don't drive a car in Third World countries when I can avoid it. As much as I enjoy the convenience, it's like trying to dance when you don't know the steps.

If someone is injured in an accident, see if he or she is breathing, then check for a pulse. If CPR seems necessary, put to use those lessons you took before leaving home. If you think there's a broken bone, apply ice, immobilize the area with a splint, elevate it, and find a doctor. Be careful not to aggravate a neck or back injury by unnecessary movement. If movement is unavoidable, immobilize the injured area with a splint first. You can splint an arm by strapping it to the chest. Bind legs together. Use a tree limb, anything, to keep broken pieces from moving freely.

If there is serious bleeding, control it by applying pressure to the wound or to the artery supplying blood to that extremity. If a person is unconscious and you can do nothing else, place the person on her side with her head lower than her chest so fluids can drain away from her lungs and exit her mouth.

TUBERCULOSIS

Tuberculosis (TB) has never ceased being a problem in underdeveloped countries. Recently, it's being spread by people who got it as a result of diminished immune systems due to AIDS. New forms of TB are increasingly resistant to standard drug treatment. Three things you can do are: keep yourself in good health, avoid letting people cough on you, and get a TB skin test if you may have been exposed. A vaccine is available for anyone who anticipates prolonged exposure to tuberculosis.

TYPHOID

How to get it. Consuming food and water contaminated by Salmonella typhi bacteria is usually how people contract typhoid. High-risk areas for typhoid, which is highly infectious, include areas of Africa, Asia, Central and South America.

Symptoms. It begins like a cold or the flu and progresses to extreme fatigue, chills, high fever, coughs, bloody diarrhea, headaches, and loss of appetite. A telltale sign is that your pulse gets slower when your fever increases. After a week or so, there may be pink spots on the body and some delirium.

How to avoid it. Be alert to sanitation in places you eat and drink, especially in villages and rural areas. In 1994, the FDA approved Typhin Vi, a single-dose vaccine said to be effective with no side effects. The vaccine is received in two shots, four weeks apart, then a booster is required every three years. A live oral vaccine against typhoid has been reported to be as effective as an injection and is, of course, painless. Typhoid is still common in underdeveloped countries so it's worth keeping this immunity current.

How to treat it. There should be no long-term complications if you get extended rest and take one of several antibiotics (Bactrim, Cipro, Floxin).

TYPHUS

How to get it. Bites from or the ingestion of contaminated feces from lice, fleas, mites, ticks, and rats are the primary source of infection. Typhus exists mostly in the highland areas of Africa, Asia, the Middle East, Mexico, Peru, and Ecuador.

Symptoms. There may be days or weeks of fever, chills, severe headache, coughing, pains in the chest and back. There may also be a rash on the trunk of the body that lasts for up to a week. Typhus carried by lice and mites may progress to pneumonia after about a week. The severity of typhus depends on the specific bacteria involved.

How to avoid it. Watch out for lice, fleas, mites, ticks, and rats. Bathe frequently and wash your clothes in very hot water. Use insect repellents and a shampoo like Kwell (OTC). If you hear of an outbreak, go somewhere else.

How to treat it. Tetracycline (P) and Doxycycline (P) are considered effective.

YELLOW FEVER

How to get it. As with malaria, yellow fever is brought into your life by a mosquito. However, as with dengue fever, this one bites during the day.

Symptoms. Jaundice (yellow skin and eyes) gives this illness its name. There is an initial fever with rapid pulse. The fever ebbs, then returns with a slower pulse, perhaps accompanied by bleeding from the mouth and stomach, headache, loss of rationality, and possibly coma.

How to avoid it. Yellow fever is still present in most of Central and South America, Africa, and the Caribbean, especially in rural areas. If you may be in a yellow fever area, get a single shot of live virus vaccine before you go, then a booster every ten years. If a country requires evidence, as a condition of entry, that you've had this vaccination, you must have received it at least ten days prior to your arrival and had it entered on your Yellow Card. Countries that require evidence of the vaccination are all in central and west Africa, plus French Guiana. Note that the yellow fever vaccination must be separated from a cholera vaccination by at least three weeks.

How to treat it. There is no effective treatment, but medical assistance is necessary to provide IV fluids, monitor kidney functioning, and control gastrointestinal bleeding.

TRAVEL MEDICINE KIT

With this litany of unpleasantness in mind, it's obvious why a traveler is well-advised to carry a thoughtfully prepared travel medicine kit. I'm no hypochondriac, but I carry more medicine when I leave the country than I ever keep on hand at home. I've never had to use even one of the major treatments and don't expect to.

If you don't take this chapter with you on your trip, consider taking at least the medical Checklists in the back of this book to help properly match the remedy with the problem.

You may have seen ready-made portable medicine kits for sale. Some may be okay for minor first aid but I don't use or recommend them. Because they're designed for use anywhere, they're incomplete and expensive. It's better to think carefully about what you might encounter and design your own kit.

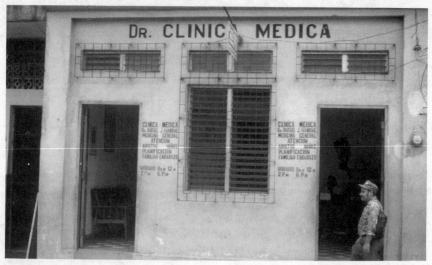

Medical clinic. San Pedro de Sula, Honduras.

If you prefer a kit, check the catalogues or call Medex Assistance (800-537-2029; kits at $35 and $100).

Medicine Kit Tips

- Transport medicine in a watertight case or sturdy Ziploc bag.

- Leave glass containers at home.

- When pills come in an unnecessarily large container, transfer them into a smaller one, along with the prescription information. Make sure all containers are clearly labeled.

- When you have a choice, take a capsule rather than a liquid. Even things that shouldn't spill sometimes do.

- Since medicines-of-choice change frequently, write on separate slips of paper what illness each medicine is intended for and its major symptoms. Put each slip in the appropriate container. Symptoms don't announce themselves with labels, so you have to be able to connect them with the appropriate remedy.

- Take copies of prescriptions and their generic names. If filled abroad, ensure that proper weights, presumably metric, are used. Have the pharmacist include the expiration date of each prescription medicine on the label so you'll know when it's time to throw something out.

- Don't rely on prescription medicine that is nearing its expiration date.

- Take most medicines along rather than planning to buy them while traveling. Otherwise, you might need a medicine where there is no source or when you have a problem communicating your need. In addition, some drugs sold abroad contain impurities. If you buy abroad, beware of brand name drugs being sold at absurdly low prices. Make sure the label looks authentic (misspellings, for example, don't inspire confidence).

- Take essential medications in your carry-on luggage (so they won't be lost if your checked bag is).

- Consider taking a brief first aid manual with you.

- Confer with your doctor before buying the components of a travel medicine kit. This is especially true for pregnant women; mothers who are breast-feeding; persons with asthma, glaucoma, diabetes, or hypertension; persons with kidney, heart, thyroid, or prostate disease; or persons with autoimmune or chronic disease. Review all drug doses and the circumstances in which you should take them with the doctor who prescribes them.

Checklist: Shots to Get before You Go

What shots you need depends on (a) where you're going, (b) the current status of your inoculations, and (c) the requirements of the countries you'll be visiting. Obtain annual information on the prevalence of specific diseases in specific countries, along with immunization requirements, from *Health Information for International Travel* (HIFIT). This information is available on a current basis in the semi-monthly *Summary of Health Information for International Travelers* issued by the Centers for Disease Control. Call the CDC hotline at (404) 332-4559 for information.

Because some shots interfere with others and some shots are given as a series, you can't drop into the health department at the last minute to get all shots at once. Besides, it's nice to have some time to recover from any adverse reaction. Although it would be ideal to receive the full series of immunizations over a four- to eight-week period, the pace can be accelerated if need be.

- **Cholera:** Vaccine four to six weeks before you leave. If practical, it should not be received at the same time as the yellow fever vaccine. Check with the CDC to determine whether a cholera certificate of vaccination is required to enter any country on your itinerary.

- **Diphtheria:** Vaccine six weeks before you leave. Booster every ten years.

- **Hepatitis A:** One week before you leave, take immune globulin to increase immunity. Since this is a blood-based product, it would be risky to get this shot in any country where blood is not screened and treated. Alternatively and substantially more expensive, there's Havrix, the newly approved hepatitis A vaccine. The first shot is taken two to four weeks prior to departure; the second, six to twelve months later.

- **Hepatitis B:** Ideally, the three-shot vaccine (Recombivax) takes six months.

- **Influenza:** Vaccine anytime. Especially important for people over sixty-five.

- **Japanese B Encephalitis:** Three shots over a three-week period. Since there is a possibility of severe reaction after each vaccination, the series should begin at least six weeks prior to departure.

- **Measles, mumps, rubella:** Vaccines six weeks before you leave. If born after 1956, it is recommended that you receive a measles vaccine even if you've had an earlier shot.

- **Meningococcal meningitis:** Vaccine five weeks before you leave.

- **Polio:** Even if you were vaccinated as a child consider getting this oral vaccine several months before you leave.

- **Rabies:** Begin Human Diploid Cell Merriaux Vaccine series four to six weeks before you leave. It may be repeated every two years if desired.

- **Smallpox:** Vaccine eight weeks before you leave.

- **Tetanus:** Vaccine (combined with diphtheria vaccine) six weeks before you leave. Booster every ten years or after a puncture wound or major laceration.

- **Typhoid:** If you take the standard vaccine, get the first shot eight weeks before departure, the second shot four weeks later. The oral vaccine may be preferable, but should be kept refrigerated and must be taken as directed. Booster every three years. Alternatively, take the newly FDA-approved single-shot vaccine, Typhin Vi.

- **Yellow Fever:** Vaccine three weeks before you leave. Booster every ten years.

My public health service advises that yellow fever and immune serum globulin can safely be given at the same time, even though that isn't their first choice. The same is true for immune globulin and oral polio.

Enter each shot on your yellow card. Keep a copy in a safe place since it's probably the only record of what you've had and when.

If you are interested in studying potential health problems abroad in greater depth, I've included helpful resources in the Bibliography

Health Reminder

If a health problem emerges after your return, including unexplained weight loss, which you suspect might be related to your travels, tell your doctor where you've been and your ideas about possible causes. If symptoms are severe, find a specialist.

9

When It's Time to Go

> I travel not to go anywhere, but to go.
> I travel for travel's sake. The great affair is to move.
> —Robert Louis Stevenson

Just before I go—I decide not to go. There's too much to be done. I won't be ready in time. I'm very well-organized at getting ready for a long trip, and I still can't avoid stress as my departure date grows imminent. Fortunately, I've gotten used to these feelings, so I get a grip and make the plane every time.

The trouble is that when you're stressed, you tend to forget things. Even when your checklists report that you've packed all your clothing and equipment, you still have to remember all your last-minute tasks and make arrangements for everything that someone else has to do for you while you're away. I've solved that problem by creating two checklists; one for me, one for my Guardian Angels.

Guardian Angels are what I call the relatives, friends, business associates, and significant others who pay my bills, care for my home, screen the mail, handle taxes, feed the animals, and do all the other tasks that keep my home life together while I'm away.

My absences can be a burden for my Guardian Angels. They have a lot of responsibility if a problem arises, especially since I seldom call home. For that reason, I shower them with postcards from far away. When I return, I bring them exotic presents and do whatever else is appropriate. I'll always be in their debt.

These checklists are intended to avoid that moment when, lying on the perfect beach on Bora Bora,* I sit up, snap my fingers, and say, "Damn, I forgot to . . ."

---

* *Bora Bora.* The most beautiful and magical of the Society Islands (of which Tahiti is the best known) in the South Pacific.

Checklist: Last-Minute Tasks

__ **Appliances.** Before you walk out the door, make sure you've turned off, set, or unplugged everything that runs on electricity (check whether your brand of refrigerator should be unplugged). Don't forget the computer. You don't want a power surge to zap your tools and toys.

__ **Bills.** Pay everything outstanding. Open a special checking account with a Guardian Angel as a signatory, and put enough money in it to cover all foreseeable bills. Arrange to have incoming checks deposited. Sign and date checks for monthly rent or mortgage payments and put each in a separate stamped envelope to be mailed each month. Leave a petty cash fund so your Guardian Angel won't have to pay expenses out of his or her own pocket.

__ **Cable TV.** Depending on the length of your trip, you may SAVE MONEY by disconnecting cable service.

__ **Car.** Ask a Guardian Angel to start your car every week and roll it a foot or two to keep the tires happy. SAVE MONEY by transferring your car to "storage status" for insurance purposes (meaning you retain comprehensive but not liability coverage).

__ **Documents.** Give a Guardian Angel copies of important documents including: (a) the first two pages of your passport; traveler's check, credit card, and ATM numbers; reservations, airline tickets, and your itinerary; (b) a list of AmEx mail service offices along your route and approximate dates on which you expect to pass them; (c) telephone numbers of people to call if there's a problem at home for which repairmen might be needed, as well as telephone numbers for your attorney and accountant; and (d) access to insurance policies, stock certificates, mortgages, or other documents, if needed.

__ **Fax machine.** Consider using call forwarding to forward incoming faxes to someone else's machine or ask your Guardian Angel to check the output of your fax machine.

__ **Fireplace.** Close the flue with the damper.

__ **Freezing weather.** Ask your Guardian Angel to let the water faucets drip if freezing weather hits.

__ **Growing things.** Arrange for someone to cut and water the lawn and other green things. Lend indoor plants to people who will care for them. If you leave animals behind, obviously you'll arrange to keep food and water flowing, and leave the name of a veterinarian and authority to get care if needed.

__ **Keys.** Give house and car keys to people who need them. Hide a set outside and/or take one with you.

__ **Legal matters.** Consider giving someone a General Power of Attorney, enabling them to take action necessary on your behalf. Tell someone where your Will is located.

__ **Mail.** File a change of address form with the post office, redirecting mail to a safe haven. There's no reason to discuss your impending absence with post office personnel nor to indicate a return date on the form. Ask the recipient of your mail to trash junk mail, set personal letters aside, forward bills to your designated bill-payer, and open the rest.

__ **Personal care.** Get travel clothes cleaned and mended. Consider a last-minute haircut.

__ **Security.** Lock all doors and windows. Use several automatic timers with multiple on and off settings for the radio (perhaps the best justification for talk radio) and a light or two. If the trip is a long one, a Guardian Angel might change the timer settings occasionally to conform to sunset and should reset everything after a power outage. Alternatively, consider the VersaTimer (less than $100; call 800-835-1515). Plug it into your computer, install a simple program, and set up to three devices for as many as 672 weekly "power events." You can even change the schedule remotely via modem. It should work if a prospective burglar will just pay attention.

If you have a burglar alarm, let the operator know you'll be on a trip until further notice and tell them who to notify in the event of a signal.

Put new bulbs in the lights just before you leave (with spares nearby). Draw back side curtains but leave some open in front. Close some doors leading from one room to another. Leave enough clutter to make your home look lived in.

Tell your neighbors you'll be away and ask them to keep watch. Make sure no signs of absence are allowed to accumulate (including flyers, doorknob hangers, and shoppers newspapers that appear from time to time). Invite someone to park in your driveway once in a while.

People differ on whether to notify the police that they'll be away. I don't, nor do I let tradespeople know. I'm less worried that someone will guess that the house is unoccupied than I would be if strangers knew for certain.

__ **Subscriptions.** Suspend newspaper and magazine subscriptions unless you really plan to plow through the pile on your return. The publisher is supposed to add the period of suspension to the end of your subscription period but you may have to follow up to make it happen. If you've forgotten to suspend any subscriptions, ask your Guardian Angel to suspend them as they arrive.

__ **Taxes.** If property taxes are your responsibility and will become due while you're away, arrange for payment rather than suffer a penalty. Arrange for an income tax extension if necessary.

__ **Telephone.** If your trip isn't too long and you anticipate nothing urgent, an answering machine may do the job. Otherwise, consider "call forwarding" to connect calls with some other number. If you subscribe to other special services (e.g., "call waiting"), SAVE MONEY by suspending them. Ask whoever receives your calls not to discuss your absence with callers unless it's someone known to them as a friend.

___ **Trash.** Anything you don't dump could be a health hazard by the time you return.

___ **Utilities.** This is a great time to start over in the refrigerator and freezer. Give away what you can and store frozen food with someone else. Depending on manufacturer's recommendations, unplug them or turn settings to a high temperature. Those innocuous-looking boxes gulp electricity like a parched camel hitting a water hole.

Don't leave the water heater standing ready to provide steaming hot water on demand. Turn it off or set it to its lowest setting. Turn heating and air conditioning systems off unless the weather is likely to be extreme. If you leave them on, set the thermostat at a level that may leave the house uncomfortable but prevent extremes in temperature. Turn off inside water taps tightly but not the main valve at the street. In case of cold weather, you want your neighbor to be able to let the faucets drip for a while.

Make sure utility bills will be paid in your absence. If you must, leave money on deposit with the utility company.

___ **Valuables.** If you have valuables that should be safeguarded, hide them, store them with someone, or drop them into a safe deposit box. If concerned, store your computer, TV, and stereo with a neighbor. This is a good time to back up your computer hard drive and tuck disks away in a safe deposit box.

___ **Do you have everything?** Confirm that you've packed everything on your checklist. Double-check that you have packed tickets, passport, cash, credit cards, and travelers checks and that you've given copies to your Guardian Angels if appropriate. Does this sound too cautious? My partner on one trip to South America didn't discover until he got off the plane in Lima that he'd forgotten his travelers checks. I won't describe the repercussions except to say that investing a few extra minutes just before leaving is much better than wasting hours or days ten thousand miles from home.

Checklist: Guardian Angel

___ **Bills.** I've opened a special checking account (# _____ at _____ Bank) and you are a signatory. Please deposit incoming checks and pay incoming bills. Please mail, on the ____ of each month, one of the signed and dated checks for my monthly mortgage (or rent) payment. I left extra money in this account for you to use as a source of petty cash for unforeseen expenses.

___ **Car.** Please start my car every week and roll it a foot or two to keep the tires happy. Since this car is in "storage status" for insurance purposes (meaning it has no liability coverage), it must not be driven.

___ **Documents.** I've given you (a) copies of the first two pages of my passport, reservations, airline tickets, and my itinerary and the numbers of my travelers checks, credit cards, and ATM card; (b) a list of AmEx mail service offices along my route showing the dates I expect to pass them; and (c) a list of telephone numbers of repairmen to call if there's a problem, as well as numbers for my lawyer and accountant. If you need information from my insurance policies, mortgages, and so on, they're located _____.

__ **Fax machine.** Please check incoming messages on my fax machine from time to time. If that's inconvenient, you can use my call forwarding to forward incoming faxes to another machine.

__ **Freezing weather.** Please let the water faucets drip if freezing weather hits.

__ **Growing things.** I've put my indoor plants in your care and have arranged for _____ (at _____) to cut and water the lawn and other green things. If there's a problem, please hire someone else to keep things looking well-tended. Please fill food and water bowls for _____ each morning. I've left an adequate supply of food in the pantry. If _____ needs care, the vet is Dr. _____ (at _____). You have my full authority to obtain whatever care _____ needs.

__ **Keys.** I've given you two sets of my house and car keys.

__ **Legal matters.** I've given you a General Power of Attorney, which gives you authority to take any action necessary on my behalf. Should you need it, my Will is located at _____.

__ **Mail.** Please trash junk mail, set personal letters aside, pay the bills, and open anything that looks as if it might deserve attention.

__ **Security.** Please occasionally change the timer settings on the three automatic timers to conform to sunset, and reset everything if there's a power outage. The burglar alarm is activated and I've given you the code. If you need to reach the operator, the number is _____. Please replace any light bulbs that burn out on the lights on timers (spares are in the kitchen cabinet). I've left the doors and curtains as they are intentionally. Please make sure no signs of absence accumulate outside (like flyers, doorknob hangers, and shoppers newspapers). Feel free to park in my driveway.

__ **Subscriptions.** I think I've suspended all subscriptions, but if anything arrives please call and have it suspended.

__ **Taxes.** If I'm not back by_____, please mail the income tax extension I've given you. Please pay the property tax bills when due.

__ **Telephone.** If my answering machine memory fills up with calls, please empty it and make a list of calls received. If you receive a call for me, please don't discuss my absence unless it's someone you know well.

__ **Valuables.** I've stored my _____ with _____, so don't be alarmed if you notice they're missing.

Last Minute

As the countdown reaches its end, remember to line up someone who can take you to the airport. Call the airline a day or two prior to departure to confirm your reservation, and call again a couple of hours before your flight to ensure the plane will depart as scheduled.

Allow more time than usual to get to the airport. During periods when airport security is increased, airlines suggest that you check in an hour and a half before flight time. That requires quite an adjustment if arriving even thirty minutes early seems extravagant. Increased security means that cars arriving at the airport may be inspected by guards, parking lots nearby may be closed, and supersensitized metal detectors cause longer lines by detecting insignificant pieces of metal. No need to start a long trip with jangled nerves or, much worse, by missing a flight.

Check in right away and make sure the seat assigned is the one you want. When your ticket envelope is handed back, see that all the correct tickets are still in it. Then take a deep breath and stride toward your adventure with a bounce in your step.

PART THREE

On the
Road
("Go!")

10

The Day You Get There

One of the gladdest moments in human life, methinks, is the departure upon a distant journey into unknown lands. Shaking off with one mighty effort the fetters of Habit, the leaden weight of Routine, the cloak of many Cares and the slavery of Home, man feels once more Happy.
— Sir Richard Francis Burton
Journal entry, December 2, 1856

Through the Airport

It's happening! Twenty hours and three connections after taking off, having ignored at least half of the prescriptions for preventing jet lag, you stagger off the plane, burning eyes squinting in the bright sunlight.

The immigration officer smiles pleasantly, examines your passport, and looks for a visa if one is required to enter the country. She may ask to see a ticket proving you have the means to move on, but that's rare. After a discreet glance down at her computer screen to see if you are on Interpol's "most wanted" list, she welcomes you to her country, nods to the next person in line, and you're on your way.

Your next stop is the Customs counter. If you've filled in a customs declaration form, the official will take a look at it. If he hands it back, you're expected to keep it to show when you leave. Most countries are concerned about people secretly bringing in items they might sell to local citizens. Some countries also have absolute prohibitions against bringing in items such as alcohol, explosives, pornography, and anything that might carry a plant or animal disease. Unless smuggling is your game, don't enter a country without declaring weapons or unusual amounts of drugs, currency, or valuables. The Customs officer may ask you to fill in a currency declaration form, especially if there's an active local black market. Most people are a little nervous about going through Customs but it's generally painless. Before you know it, you're waved along with a smile.

Even if you can't read the signs, follow the crowd to the baggage area. In minutes you've claimed your gear and are ready to start on a few tasks. The first stop is the currency exchange counter, where you change just enough money to last for a day or two. If there's a Tourist Information counter, collect all the information that might be useful, including how to get into town. Then stop by the airline counter if you need to reconfirm a flight or do any other business.

Before long, you're ready to head for town. This is when you need to shift into "traveler's mode." You will seldom be as vulnerable to theft as you are at this moment. Your self-protective reflexes, soon to be fine-tuned and automatic, are still abstract and untested. Up shields!

The Ride into Town

The intense beehive hum you hear just outside the terminal comes from a zillion transport entrepreneurs seeking your patronage. And each one of those taxi drivers is hoping you have no idea of the fair price for a ride into town. Your job? Educate yourself on the correct price before you get to the curb. Ask people on the plane. Ask at Tourist Information. Ask a friendly local person. Before leaving the baggage claim area, try to line up a small group to ride together and split the fare.

If an airport has a system through which you buy taxi tickets at a booth inside the terminal, use it. Otherwise, a taxi driver will know he has a greenhorn who is about to help him pay for a new television set.

If there's an airport shuttle bus or local bus that stops near your destination, either will be much cheaper than a taxi. The local bus may cost less than one-tenth as much as a taxi. No matter where the bus drops you in town, the cost of transport from there to whatever hotel you choose will be far less than airport taxi rates. Ask at the airport about bus transportation.

At the curb, listen to what drivers are charging local people. Take advantage of competition. Get quotes from several drivers, then invite everyone to beat the best offer. Nine times out of ten, someone's self interest will overcome the group's attempt to maintain a monopoly price. As you bargain, keep in mind that if the taxi driver doesn't get your business, he may have to drive back to town empty. When you get an acceptable price, climb in and enjoy the ride.

Some travelers relax the moment they see a meter. No bargaining, they think, just pay what the meter says. Things are seldom that simple when there's a taxi involved. First, the mere presence of a meter doesn't mean the driver intends to use it. He might prefer to start bargaining with you somewhere away from the airport. Second, if the meter is working, make sure it wasn't accidentally already running before you got in. Third, if the meter is "broken," there's a reason—and you won't like it. Strike a deal before the wheels roll. And last, even if the meter is flipped on as you get in, and it works, make sure you aren't charged a night rate for a day ride.

Some cities fix the rates taxi drivers can charge to take you to certain destinations. Those rates are supposed to be posted in the taxi. Unfortunately, some taxi drivers print their own official looking cards showing inflated fares to certain destinations. If a rate card looks homemade, climb right back out.

In a large airport where departure and arrival points are separate, try the area where *departing* passengers are dropped off. After dropping off a passenger, a taxi must go to the end of a long line waiting for arriving passengers to take back into town. Or, he can pick you up immediately—for a considerably discounted fare, of course.

As a final word on taxis, consider a couple of entreaties: (a) don't let yourself be separated from your bag before getting into your chosen taxi, and (b) never get into a taxi before you've settled on a fare.

Master this simple process of getting into town on a cost-effective basis and you'll SAVE MONEY for the rest of your travels.

Tourist Information

After you get to town, arrange lodging (more on this in the next chapter), then visit the local tourist information office. Its location is probably in your guidebook. If not, your desk clerk or a police officer or someone on the street will know where to find it. Watch for the international "I" symbol on street signs.

> "Afoot and light-hearted I take to the open road, Healthy, free, the world before me, The long brown path before me leading wherever I choose. Henceforth I ask not good fortune, I myself am good fortune, Henceforth I whimper no more, postpone no more, need nothing, Done with indoor complaints, libraries, querelous criticisms, Strong and content I travel the open road."
> —Walt Whitman, *Song of the Open Road,* 1856

Someone in the tourist office is likely to speak some English and will gladly answer your questions. Even if no one speaks a language you know, you'll find brochures, posters, and maps—a gold mine of information. If you give the tourist officer a list of places you'd like to see, she can help organize your visits and suggest additions. She'll tell you about special events taking place while you're around, and she may even sell you tickets and arrange transportation. If the newspaper isn't in one of your languages, it's easy to miss what could be a fascinating experience. Friendly tourist information officers have told me about a ceremonial burial that was about to take place in a village in central Sulawesi,* an elegantly costumed

---

* *Sulawesi.* This mountainous, K-shaped Indonesian island contains a remarkable blend of Islamic and animistic-Christian cultures. The ship-shaped architecture and death rituals of Toraja-land are unique.

dance performance celebrating the Hindu poet Rabindranath Tagore's birthday in Calcutta, a gathering of tribes performing ritual dances in northeast Botswana, and, in Prague, the best chamber music I've ever heard.

During your full first day, climb aboard one of those see-it-all-in-a-day tour buses. They're an inexpensive, efficient way to cover long distances in a new town to find what merits a visit. When you get tired of being herded, hop off. If you're lucky, you'll meet another traveler using the tour the same way.

Overcome the temptation to take taxis everywhere. They cut you off from local people and spontaneous experiences. Instead, learn to use local public transportation right away. Before long, you'll be flagging down brightly decorated *matatus* or *collectivos* or *jeepneys* or whatever the transit vehicles are called where you happen to be. Getting around the way local people do is definitely the way to go.

11

Lodging

You fly off to a strange land, eagerly abandoning all the comforts
of home, and then expend vast quantities of time and money
in a largely futile effort to recapture the comforts that you
wouldn't have lost if you hadn't left home in the first place.
—Bill Bryson
Neither Here Nor There

You never forget places where you lay your head as you travel. Some are
wonderful, some make you laugh, and there are always a few that, well, make
great stories. In this chapter, you'll learn how to find lodging that will suit you
anywhere in the world.

I understand why new travelers feel uneasy about being able to find satisfactory places to stay as they venture abroad. As I began planning my first trip
to Africa, I had little idea what to expect in terms of lodging. On arrival in
Nairobi, surrounded by people offering shelter, I quickly learned how naive
my concern had been. The reality is that providing lodging for hire is a leading
means of economic survival in most of the world. Good lodging abounds and
there is plenty of competition for your business.

In major cities and tourist centers anywhere in the world, you'll find
upscale hotels that equal or exceed the opulence of those in your home country. Most are nationality-neutral and English is commonly spoken. You can't
miss the logos of international hotel chains with their cookie-cutter amenities. They charge extraordinarily high prices because they provide a reassuring cocoon and know that most Western travelers, especially those on business or on tour, expect to pay high prices. These are "world" prices, usually in
dollars, that have no relation at all to prices in the local economy.

Virtually everywhere you'll find pleasant, locally owned midscale hotels
in which comfort and character outweigh occasional dings. Although their
prices may be above the budgets of some independent travelers, they're very
reasonable by North American and European standards.

Then there are the legions of lower-priced hotels with which many travelers become intimately familiar. They range from a concrete box ruled over by Quasimodo's ill-tempered brother to an architectural masterpiece gently supervised by an elderly couple whose mission in life is your daily happiness. At the lowest end of the rate scale, some hotels are best enjoyed with a measure of good humor and recognition of where you are. You may be pleased to know that shortcomings are more often in the nature of rickety furniture, or fixtures that don't work, rather than dirt or bugs.

Satisfaction with lodging depends in part on a good state of mind and realistic expectations. Here's an example: In the late seventies, when China had just reopened itself to strangers, tourist facilities were not highly developed. Our group (visitors then were required to travel as a group) stayed at the venerable Peking Hotel. Although it had a kind of Addams Family ambiance, it was the best hotel in Beijing at that time and had an excellent location near the Imperial Palace. It turned out that there were a few, although generally small, holes in the walls. Some in the group were outraged by the holes and complained regularly. The rest hardly noticed and had a great time. It was a matter of state of mind.

Many North Americans leave home with a mental image of two queen-size beds, a private bath with operational tub and shower, air conditioning, good soundproofing, and reasonable prices, all in a large room with a view. Internationally, these expectations will be met and exceeded at the higher end of the price scale. Overall, however, expect some differences. For example, you'll find one large bed or two monastic singles, but seldom two large beds. Air conditioning is more the exception than the rule. Tubs become a distant memory. Soundproofing? Maybe if you block the window with a pillow. What you often get is character and an exciting new world just outside the front door.

> "I dislike feeling at home when I'm abroad."
> —George Bernard Shaw, English writer

Even if you start off with hotel reservations in hand, this chapter will be of benefit. After a few days on the road, you may decide to choose lodging that has more local character or better suits your pocketbook. Or you may find that the flexibility of traveling without reservations has become more important than it seemed at home.

HOW TO FIND GREAT PLACES TO SPEND THE NIGHT

How do you find lodging? No problem; it often finds you—through a tug on your sleeve. When you arrive in a new place, you're approached by *people representing low and midpriced hotels* (known as a *losman, ryokan, hospadaje, pension, residencial,* and many other names). If you're at the airport, touts spring forward to solicit your business, flashing photographs of hotels and their rooms. They may offer free transportation into town in return for your agreement to "just take a look" at the hotel. Ask questions. If a hotel sounds attractive and is located near where you want to stay, the offer is at least a good way to get into town and may result in a good room.

Your trusty *guidebook* is more reliable than the eager tout, at least as to quality. Providing information on hotel prices, amenities, and management is one of the ways a good guidebook justifies its price. It sometimes suggests real treasures and at least keeps you from running around town looking at dogs. On the other side of the ledger, guidebook favorites fill up early (and they will have raised their rates as soon as they were mentioned in the book).

Don't fall into the habit of thinking there are no alternatives to guidebook suggestions. Once you have your travel legs, you'll be perfectly capable of finding your own special places. Pretend you're writing a guidebook for a friend coming next year. Just go out and look around.

Ask *other travelers*. A strongly positive recommendation usually leads to a memorable stay. On only a few occasions have I reached a hotel someone raved about and wondered if the guy had been taking hallucinatory drugs. On the other hand, always pay attention to a warning about a specific hotel.

"To awaken in a strange town is one of the pleasant sensations in the world. You are surrounded by adventure. You have no idea what is in store for you, but you will, if you are wise and know the art of travel, let yourself go on the stream of the unknown and accept whatever comes in the spirit in which the gods may offer it. The tourist travels in his own atmosphere like a snail in his shell and stands, as it were, on his own perambulating doorstep to look at the continents of the world. But if you discard all this, and sally forth with a blank and leisurely mind, there is no knowing what may happen to you."
—Freya Stark,
Baghdad Sketches

Many *tourist information booths* in or near airports, train stations, and bus depots offer a room-finding service. You may pay something for this service, either as a fee at the booth or in a slightly higher room rate, but it can be very helpful on a cold, drizzly night. Unfortunately, the least expensive lodgings in town are seldom on lists provided by these booths. However, the clerk may know about places that have yet to appear in any guidebook.

Ask a *hotel clerk*. If you've stopped into a place that has no vacancy or you just can't agree on price, tell the clerk what you're looking for. It's common to get helpful directions.

If you have several possibilities in mind, call to check for availability and prices. Crisscrossing town after a long day on the road is no one's idea of fun.

Lodging and Fellow Travelers

Other travelers become competitors at certain moments. When a bus, train, or boat pulls into a small place with limited accommodations, you're all in competition for a bed. In such cases, one partner should go ahead unencumbered to find lodging while the other waits to collect and watch the luggage.

Telephoning is particularly useful if you're competing with a group of arriving passengers for scarce space in choice lodgings.

If no assistance materializes, it's no big deal. Find that special place *all by yourself*.

HOW TO CHOOSE LODGING THAT'S BEST FOR YOU

According to surveys, what most travelers look for in lodging is clean appearance, reasonable price, convenient location, good service, and security—in that order. After staying in a hotel, people are usually satisfied with location and price, but they remember dirt, lack of security, and noise forever.

Location

When you first arrive in a country, you may want to choose a hotel that has a reputation as an information node, a gathering place for travelers with interests similar to yours. These hotels are usually reasonably priced, but more important is the opportunity to learn quickly how the country works from people with current experience. Guidebooks sometimes note such hotels; if not, ask around.

If gathering information is not the primary objective, look for lodging located near some of the sights you'll be visiting, near public transportation routes, and within shouting distance of a restaurant.

Amenities

What amenities matter? Start with comfort and beauty. Memories grow from quiet courtyards and views of the Parthenon from your balcony. Of course, sometimes the only amenity that matters is a "vacancy" sign.

The level of amenities differs from continent to continent. Generally, Asia and South America offer better value, or at least more aesthetically pleasing rooms, than do Africa or Central America. Don't take specific amenities for granted:

- What's the *shower* situation? For openers, is there a shower at all? If so, is it in the room or is it down the hall? Is there a separate shower stall or does the whole bathroom become the shower stall? Since a private bath-

Five-dollar beach cabins. Ko Tao, Gulf of Thailand.

room can double the room rate, the more frequently you do without a shower in your room, the more you SAVE MONEY. Is there hot water? If you care, don't take anyone's word for it. Test the temperature. That will also tell you whether the water pressure is more than a symbolic drizzle. Don't assume that hot water is available twenty-four hours a day. In fact, it may be available for only six to eight hours a day. Forget to check these hours and icy water will greet you at a moment guaranteed to make you unhappy. When the plumbing doesn't work as represented, which is not uncommon, at least you'll hear some wonderfully inventive excuses.

When I checked my room at a lovely two-story stone lodge on the crest of a mountain ridge in Kalimpong,* no water flowed from the shower nozzle. However, the charming proprietress assured me that hot water would be available at 7 P.M. Given the chill Himalayan air, I watched the clock eagerly. Right at seven, the hot water arrived as promised—at my door, in a bucket.

You may be startled to see water being heated by electric coils bolted loosely to the wall above the shower head. This arrangement seems a little dangerous, but I haven't heard of anyone being fried.

I've missed a few showers when I really wanted one and taken some in water that promised frostbite. Overall, though, there have always been enough showers at just the right times to make me remember showers on the road with pleasure.

---

* *Kalimpong.* Located in the foothills of the Himalayas in West Bengal, India, it is known for its orchids and access to Sikkim.

- What about the *beds*? Are they clean? Are they soft enough? Finding a firm bed is seldom a problem. Length? If you're tall, you learn to be comfortable in short beds.

- Is the room *secure*? Does it have sturdy locks on the doors and windows? For more on hotel security, see Chapter 13.

- Are the lobby and the room *clean*? Is there evidence that bugs might be a problem?

- Will the room be *quiet* enough for sleep? Don't trust the hotel clerk on this one. Either he's genuinely stopped hearing the racket or he's not going to tell you. It may be stone quiet when you check in at dusk. Then, about the time you're settling in, the disco next door roars to life for an all-nighter. Check out nearby bars, road traffic, muezzins, roosters, and thin walls—and hope there aren't too many noisy guests. If you suspect a problem, ask for a quieter room higher up or at the back of the building. Don't wait until 4 A.M. to discover the truck depot below your window.

- Any discussion of amenities must include *toilets*. I know one person who won't leave the United States because of her aversion to any toilet she believes to be inferior to what she's used to. Given the strength of her feeling, she's made the right choice. Fortunately, most people are more flexible.

  The toilet may be in your room, down the hall, or in a different building, and the price of the lodging will reflect the proximity of the toilet every time. Toilets come in quite a few forms. At the low end, so to speak, the toilet is a hole in the floor of a small room and waste drops into a fertilizer-collection room below. Squat toilets are common in Asia. On each side of a hole there's a place to put one foot, which may be a little ceramic footprint or nothing more than a plank worn smooth over the ages. They're easy to use. Well, maybe not the first time, but there's nothing to it once you learn to watch the relative position of your trousers.

  Western-style toilets have become increasingly common in hotels that cater to international travelers. Of course, in some of the least expensive places, toilet seats are sometimes missing and toilet paper is a rumor. If the room you're looking at has a Western-style toilet that's supposed to flush, see if it does. The flushing device may not be the familiar handle; look for a knob, a push button, a pull chain, a pedal, or even a bucket of water. If it doesn't flush, ask the clerk to help.

  Not all toilets are plumbed to accept paper. If there's a trash can nearby, that's where used paper should go. Otherwise, it will probably clog the pipes, distressing all involved. If toilet paper hasn't been provided, ask for it. The clerk may smile and say, "Sure," but you may have to follow up. The majority of the world's population doesn't use toilet paper, which is the main reason you don't see people eating with their left hand. Your best bet is to carry your own supply of TP (including the high-quality stuff you borrowed from the upscale hotel where you stopped for a beer).

- When traveling through an area in which *malaria* is a problem, ensure there is some barrier between you and mosquitoes. This usually means screens on the windows or a mosquito net over the bed. If you take a mosquito net with you, buy one impregnated with Permethrin or spray it yourself. If there are neither screens nor a net, you may have to sleep with the windows closed. Although that turns a tolerable night in the tropics into a sweat bath, a hot night is a lot cooler than malarial fever.

  On tropical islands, windows are fitted only with rough hurricane shutters and no glass. That's part of the charm. About all you can do is fire up a green mosquito coil at both ends of your bed and sleep under a light sheet. I take a couple of packets of coils with me but they're brittle and hard to use when broken. When you're in mosquito-land, coils are generally available in the stores (if there are stores).

  Speaking of insects, hold your shoes upside down and shake them before putting them on. Give scorpions, spiders, or whatever a chance to live another day.

- Ask whether *breakfast* is included in the price and, if so, what it is. You're likely to find it surprisingly spare, usually of the bread and coffee variety. Find out where and when it's served. It's no fun to drop into the dining room with high expectations just after they've stopped serving. If breakfast doesn't appeal to you, perhaps you can negotiate a slightly lower room rate.

- I'm hooked on lodging that exemplifies an *ethnic architectural idiom*. I'm thinking of places like a *ryokan* in Japan with painted shoji screens and scented tatami mats, a *losman* in Bali with incense burning at Hindu shrines in manicured gardens, or a white-walled *posada* in Portugal nestled against the gray stones of a castle wall with views of red tile roofs and distant fields of corn.

- A *smiling, knowledgeable owner or clerk* who looks me in the eye and makes me feel welcome overcomes shortcomings elsewhere.

- My decisions about some amenities depend on the circumstances. *Air conditioning* is an example. It raises the room rent quite a bit and may seem a little decadent after you've been on the road for a while. On the other hand, when you're coming off a hot trek neither of those objections matter one whit. Air conditioning is not standard internationally, so if you're interested, be sure to ask.

  When the sun is high in tropical latitudes, a *ceiling fan* greatly aids a good night's sleep. Even a small oscillating table fan can make a humid night bearable. Besides cooling your body, the breeze from a fan keeps mosquitoes away.

  With the southern India solar furnace operating at full blast, I gratefully paid a premium to stay in the only hotel in Tiruchirapalli* that had a *swimming pool*.

  If it's not too hot, it's too cold. It was so cold one Christmas season in Ladakh, above ten thousand feet, that I rented a potbellied stove and had it set up in my room. It cost more than the room itself, but was worth ten times what I paid. If a room heater isn't available, pile on blankets and hibernate.

- I love to waken to a *great view* out the window. When I can find a room with a balcony and a panoramic view, I pay extra every time.

Price

Lodging that ranges from satisfactory to terrific is available at reasonable prices almost anywhere. What do I mean by reasonable prices? The Residencial Las Mercedes in Arequipa, Peru, has a formal sitting room with a stately grandfather clock and a stylishly furnished wood-paneled dining room. Each morning I ate breakfast on a sunny flagstone patio with a view of two volcanoes. That double room cost $8. At Pouso de Chico Rey in Ouro Prêto, Brazil, a double room in a home filled with Portuguese colonial antiques and tapestries rented for $13. My room in the Colonial Palace in Cuzco, Peru, had a fifteen-foot vaulted ceiling with a skylight. It overlooked a courtyard containing a fountain and orange blossoms. All that for $8.

---

* *Tiruchirapalli*. "Trichy" is located in the state of Tamil Nadu in southeast India. It is known for the Rock Fort Temple on a massive plateau that towers over the city and for the extensive temple complexes of Srirangam and Sri Jambukesjwara.

A lovely Balinese-style *losman* in Ubud, Bali, decorated with carved ceremonial masks and prints of scenes from the *Ramayana* cost $7.50 for a double four years ago. A private bungalow, just off the beach on the island of Ko Tao, had a bathroom, fan, verandah, and world-class view and cost $7 for a double. Prices may have gone up slightly, but you get the idea. Even better, these prices weren't the lowest available. Travelers were staying in those towns for half what I paid.

There's no shortage of pleasant, affordable lodging in South America and Asia. Much of it even has some style. Throughout most of Africa, lodging is more basic, less charming, but still very inexpensive. As a generalization, a decent double room might average $14 and there are plenty that are cheaper—much cheaper.

In Europe, the supply and variety are immense, but prices in large cities are similar to those in New York and Los Angeles; in other words, hotel rooms are expensive. However, a little searching will turn up affordable lodging even in Europe. The 350-unit Campanile chain charges about $57 for a double in France, $70 in the Netherlands, and $82 in Belgium. In Germany, a *zimmer frie* averages about $45 for a double. In Norway, you'll pay $75 to $150 for "budget" hotels. Still, in 1996 a determined budget traveler could often find adequate shelter for $25 to $50. Note that where hotel prices are high, food prices are high. How about $60 for a bottle of undistinguished whiskey in Norway?

There's a cardinal rule in renting a room: *see the room before you accept it.* For one thing the reality may be very different from the clerk's description. For another, you can't bargain as effectively until you've seen the room. If you are traveling with a partner, one of you checks the room while the other watches the gear. If a clerk goes with you, she'll probably be carrying keys to more than one room. No matter what you've said you want, the clerk will open the bidding by showing a Western traveler the hotel's most expensive room, the local equivalent of the Emperor's Suite. Even if tatty, it's sure to be huge. Although the air conditioner pumps out more noise than cool air and the radio has only one channel, that room will cost at least 500 percent more than the room you said you wanted. They know Westerners are crazy. No problem, just smile and ask to see other rooms.

> See the room before you accept it.

Cheap rooms don't always start out cheap. The clerk states the room rate as if it were fixed, but that doesn't mean it is. Feel free to bargain on the rate:

- when you'll be staying three or more nights,
- in off-season, or when something (bad weather, a riot, a coup) has curtailed tourism,
- when you see a lot of room keys hanging on hooks behind the clerk,
- maybe every time, unless clearly inappropriate.

The cost of lodging is a large part of your budget. If you bargain effectively on lodging prices, you'll definitely SAVE MONEY. If you don't, lodging will still be affordable but you'll spend more than you need to.

When the clerk states a price, you say it's too expensive, that you'd like a room that costs no more than "x" francs or rupees, or whatever. Actually, you have even more leverage if you call ahead and say you'd like a room for "x" francs. At that point, the clerk has no chance for your business unless she agrees. Cite prices at a competitor's lodging. Ask for a special rate on grounds of being a student, a teacher, an archaeologist, an old person, a young person, or anything else you can think of. If you have a business card or a membership card, lay it on the counter. Reality doesn't matter; the desk clerk doesn't care. The point is to persuade her that you won't stay in her hotel unless you get a discount of some kind. Then give her a theoretical reason for granting it.

Try not to look too exhausted from the day's travel and never let your luggage go to a room until you've agreed on a price. As she calculates her offer, the desk clerk is evaluating whether you have enough energy to try another hotel. If she senses your energy waning, she'll become Gibraltar.

Be firm but pleasant, never argumentative. It's poor strategy to disparage the accommodations being offered. Why behave like a person the clerk wouldn't want under her roof? Further, the clerk probably lives in worse conditions than the room you're discussing.

If you can't get the room rate reduced, ask for a better room at the same price. If the clerk offers a lower rate but for a less-desirable room, offer to pay the lower price for the room you really want.

If you're one of a group of people traveling together, occupying several rooms, insist on a group rate discount, all or none.

You should receive an almost automatic discount of 10 to 30 percent if you'll be staying at one place for three or more days.

If you've reached a temporary impasse, ask if the clerk "can do any better." Ask her for an alternative. If nothing happens and you're not satisfied, say you've decided to look around at other hotels, but leave slowly

Be certain you and the clerk agree on the final price.

enough that she has a chance to make another offer. You're likely to hear a call from over your shoulder. On the other hand, if your bargaining doesn't achieve what you want, don't let pride send you away if you really want to stay there or if you'll collapse if you don't inhale an ice cold beer in the next sixty seconds.

Make sure that the room will be available to you for as long as you want it or at least until a certain date. Otherwise, you could be evicted unexpectedly.

In the end, be certain to agree with the clerk on a *total* price. Don't set yourself up for miscellaneous charges and taxes that were never mentioned. At the upper end of the price scale, it is becoming more the rule than the exception to add various luxury taxes and service charges. Ask the clerk to write down the total price on a piece of paper or enter it on the ledger,

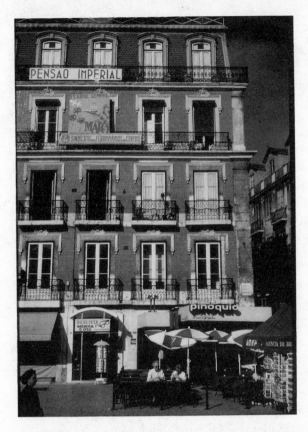

Lodging. Lisboa, Portugal.

anything to ensure that no misunderstanding arises at checkout time. Be certain what time period is covered by the price (especially in India). Get it all straight on the front end so you can part friends when you leave.

When you've reached agreement, pick up a hotel business card. Some have a map on the back and all have the address in the local language—which is how you get home after you've forgotten the name of the hotel and how to get back to it. One night I took a series of buses across Beijing, guided through two transfers by a Chinese acquaintance who spoke a bit of English. She showed me where to get off to attend a performance by a famous troupe of acrobats and continued. When I emerged from the theater hours later, I realized I had no idea which bus to take, let alone how the transfers worked. If I hadn't had the hotel card, I'd probably still be circling Beijing like Charlie on the MTA.

A last thought: *always check behind before you check out.* Look under the bed, in the closets, on the shelves, everywhere. Did you leave anything drying on an outside line? Even if you find an about-to-be-forgotten piece only once every twenty times, it's worth checking. Do the same thing in a restaurant. As you're about to leave, take a quick check for daypack, camera, and journal. It's an easy routine. If you leave something behind, either you won't be able to get back for it or it won't be there when you do. Take the easier way.

OTHER INNOVATIVE CHOICES

Hostels and Elderhostels, YMCAs and YWCAs, the Gray Circuit, Backpacker Hotels, Formule 1, and Homestays were specifically designed to help you SAVE MONEY. They're also fine places to meet other travelers and local people.

Hostels

Hostels, especially in Europe, are the financial salvation of budget travelers. However, many people who can afford to pay more for lodging seek out hostels because of the ambiance. They're good places to meet like-minded travelers, find a temporary traveling partner, and gather information.

Where will you find hostels? They're everywhere in Europe (slowly expanding into Eastern Europe) and you'll find some in northern Africa (Egypt, Sudan, Morocco, Tunisia and, if you're feeling adventuresome, Libya). In sub-Saharan Africa, there are a few hostels in Kenya, Zimbabwe, Lesotho, and South Africa. In the Middle East, there are hostels in Israel, Syria, and Saudi Arabia. Traveling east to Asia, look for scattered hostels in Pakistan, India, Nepal, Sri Lanka, Thailand, Malaysia, South Korea, and the Philippines. Although there are many hostels in Japan (more than six hundred), Australia, and New Zealand, there are comparatively few in the United States and hardly any in Central and South America.

How much do hostels cost? In the United States, you'll pay from $5 to $22. In Europe, hostels cost in the range of $10 to $15 a night. Prices are lower elsewhere and many hostels offer excellent family rates as well.

Joining *Hostelling International—American Youth Hostels* (HI-AYH), a member of the International Youth Hostel Association, gives you access to almost six thousand affiliated hostels in more than seventy countries. A twelve-month membership in HI-AYH costs $10 for a person seventeen years or younger, $25 for a person eighteen to fifty-four, $15 for anyone over fifty-five, and $35 for an entire family. A lifetime membership costs $250. Purchase membership at any hostel or from any HI-AYH office (the main office is located at 733 15th Street NW, Washington, DC 20005; 202-783-6161).

Here's the most important point. Despite the word "youth," there is *no maximum age limit* (except in Bavaria) and more than 10 percent of hostellers are over age fifty-five. There is also no minimum age limit except that a person under eighteen may be asked to provide parental permission and very small children may not be accepted by hostels that don't have appropriate facilities for them. All you have to be is young in spirit.

In the past, youth hostels had requirements such as getting in before curfew, being locked out most of the day, and doing some household tasks. In urban hostels, these limitations have largely disappeared, although guests are expected to clean up after themselves. In rural areas, some hostels still close during the day (since the manager may have a day job elsewhere) and residents are sometimes asked to sweep a room or take out the trash. Hostels may limit the length of stay to five days during busy seasons.

Hostels range from clean, basic shelter to architectural or cultural marvels. For example, you can stay in a castle in Altena, Germany or aboard a three-masted sailing ship in Stockholm. In the United States, there's a Spanish Village built as a bohemian artists' community in Miami; an old Longshoremen's Hall in Seattle; a Greek revival farmhouse in Peninsula, Ohio; a turn-of-the-century home in Redwood National Park, Klamath, California; a lighthouse in Cape Vincent, New York; and a former lifeguard station in Nantucket, Massachusetts. *Historic Hostels*, which describes hostels in historic buildings, is available from HI-AYH for $3.

Some hostels serve hearty, inexpensive meals, while others permit you to cook your own meals. Besides being a great way to SAVE MONEY, hanging out in the kitchen is a good way to meet other travelers. It's not unusual to find a pool table, a library full of well-worn books, or a piano with which to amuse yourself.

Traditionally, sleeping accommodations have been dormitory-style, segregated by sex, although the trend is toward rooms with four to six beds. The hostel furnishes blankets and pillows, but you need a sleep sheet, which you can bring, rent, or buy. Carrying a sheet is a small burden, but if you expect to stay in hostels frequently, renting would be expensive. Expect to pay $15 to $25 to buy a sleep sheet.

> Hostels are a great way to meet fellow travelers.

Making advance reservations at popular hostels may be a good idea during peak seasons in Europe. In most other places it usually isn't necessary. If you choose to book ahead, send a letter about six weeks before your arrival giving the date of arrival, number of beds (or private rooms) desired, and length of stay. Enclose a deposit for the first night's stay. Otherwise, you can call a day or two ahead of arrival, or even the same morning if you won't get there until later in the day. Some hostels provide reservation envelopes that you drop through the mail slot if the door is locked during the day. You can also make reservations abroad through any HI-AYH office. The majority of travelers just drop in with their fingers crossed.

By paying a slightly higher nightly rate (usually about $3 more), nonmembers may be permitted to stay in a hostel. If this extra charge applies to the membership fee and you stay a week or so in the same place, you pay for membership on the spot. Naturally, members receive priority over nonmembers for beds.

HI-AYH offers "discovery tours" to help people learn about different cultures, experience new environments, and make new friends. These groups usually consist of ten or fewer travelers. Since they sleep in youth hostels, prices are modest.

Two handbooks tell you what you need to know about hostels: *Europe and the Mediterranean Budget Accommodations* and *Africa, America, Asia and Australasia Budget Accommodations*. The International Youth Hostel Federation in England (44-707-332487) publishes both. They can also be obtained from HI-AYH or any of its thirty-eight regional offices. Good guidebooks also describe hostels, and tourist information offices usually have pamphlets published by local youth hostel associations.

Elderhostels

Elderhostel programs are for people over the age of sixty (who may be accompanied by a younger spouse or companion). These programs combine inexpensive lodging with classes at more than nineteen hundred universities and other educational institutions in the United States and forty-three other countries. Participants stay in residence halls or nearby youth hostels. The emphasis is on studying interesting subjects and meeting like-minded people. Elderhostel has recently introduced Service Programs through which participants provide volunteer service to worthwhile causes (such as Habitat for Humanity) around the world. Call (617) 426-7788 for a free Elderhostel catalogue.

YMCAs and YWCAs

The Ys offer travelers lodging in almost three thousand locations in nearly one hundred countries. They are often a little higher priced than most budget places but uniformly clean, pleasant, and friendly. Unlike hostels, cooking is seldom permitted. To find information about YMCA lodging around the world, obtain a copy of the *World Alliance Directory* ($11) by calling the YMCA Program Store at (800) 747-0089. Call the Y International at (212) 760-5869 for a catalog of YMCAs and YWCAs. Call (212) 614-2700 for the YWCA *Worldwide Directory* ($10).

The *U.S. and World Wide Travel Accommodations Guide* ($16.95 from the Campus Travel Service, 800-525-6633, P.O. Box 5486, Fullerton, CA 92635, and many campus and retail bookstores) includes information on YMCA lodging, home and farm stays, home exchange opportunities, more than seven hundred colleges worldwide that rent rooms (costing between $10 and $30 a night) when school is not in session, and more than seven thousand economy and moderate hotels and motels.

The Gray Circuit

For decades, security regulations required travelers to the former Soviet Union and Eastern European countries to stay in designated high-priced tourist hotels and restricted the flow of travelers to fit the number of hotel rooms available. When the borders opened, there were far too few hotel rooms to serve the flood of business and pleasure travelers so the entrepreneurial profit motive immediately spawned the "gray circuit."

When you arrive in Moscow, you're quickly contacted by representatives of the gray circuit, the unofficial housing service. Someone, probably claiming to be a student, will approach you and invite you to see a small apartment they represent. One way to tell if it's good, and cheap, is if it's already crowded with other travelers. Since these places are typically in large apartment blocks, staying in them is a good way to meet Russians.

In Eastern Europe, tourists commonly pay $200 to $300 for a hotel room with only basic amenities. However, because of the economic crunch and the rise of budding capitalists, renting a room in a family home has become increasingly common. Prices are much lower, although they are rising (partly because of utility costs). In Prague, for example, a room that went for $20 just after independence might be in the $50 to $70 range today. Top Tour (42-2-232-1077) and AVE (42-2-2422-3226) are agencies in Prague that find rooms in this range. On the other hand, people with space will approach you outside American Express, the post office, the train station, or as you're walking along the sidewalk. The situation is similar in Budapest, Bucharest, and other major cities. I've heard of nothing but good experiences from renting rooms in these unofficial places.

Backpacker Hotels

In New Zealand, even basic motels are moderately expensive. Youth hostels are a budget option but they aren't always easy to find. To fill the void, an extensive network of excellent backpacker hotels has sprung up, most of them old centrally located hotels that have been spruced up and given a few new amenities. They radiate charm and good vibes—and you can often stroll downstairs to a pub and restaurant. Rooms seldom cost more than $8 per person and you needn't arrive with a backpack. This sort of alternative is growing in Australia and elsewhere.

Formule 1

Formule 1 hotels, which style themselves the "McDonald's of the hotel industry," have become very popular with travelers in Europe. There are already about 450 of them (approximately 400 in France, the rest in Germany, Belgium, and the United Kingdom) and the concept is spreading quickly throughout Europe (and heading for Australia and South Africa). Since they are usually located on the periphery of cities and towns, they best serve people who have their own transportation.

You can check in at the front desk or by slipping your credit card into a slot in a reservation machine. Your credit card also opens your door, but only for as long as you reserved the room when checking in.

The private rooms are only eight-by-twelve-feet with a double bed and full-size bunk bed, sink, desk, and color TV. Very clean bathrooms are down the hall. They don't offer much style or ambiance, but at about $28 are an affordable alternative to overpriced dumps.

Homestays

When you have an opportunity to stay with a family, whether for free or fee, take a chance. If you'd like to set up something before you hit the road, try one of the organizations described in Chapter 4 which specialize in arranging trips where the focal point is a homestay. If you haven't arranged anything in advance, ask around until you find a family who'll take you in for a while. Don't let uncertainty about what it might be like dissuade you from accepting a family's invitation. The odds are good that it will be an experience you'll remember with affection.

If an opportunity to stay with a family arises from hospitality rather than a commercial motive, be sensitive to what's needed to fit in. Despite its good intentions, the host family may not really be able to afford the food and drink it lavishes on you. Some travelers become sponges, accepting hospitality as though it were their due and overstaying their welcome. Instead, reciprocate by making some contribution. They probably need money, but it may feel awkward to offer it. If a gift seems okay, buy something such as groceries, cloth, or tools (a simple rice thresher costs only a few dollars in Indonesia but greatly eases a family's workload). In some situations, it may be better to do some tutoring or other useful work for the family. Ask others about the local customs concerning hospitality as a guide to what you should do. Without fail, send a card or letter to the family later in your trip or when you get home.

This discussion has been about choosing lodging that pleases you at a price you're willing to pay. If price doesn't matter or you feel an urge to splurge, arm yourself before you go with the results of polls which rate "the world's best" hotels (take a look at Traveler Online at http://www.cntraveler.com). Here are some of the best—and their rates: Claridge's (London, $405–$466 for a double); Cliveden (Berkshire, $332–$625); Hotel de Crillon (Paris, $653–$714); Hotel Ritz (Paris, $714–$851); Villa Cipriani (Asolo, Italy, $188–$250); Hotel Hassler (Rome, $389–$564); Hotel de Paris (Monte Carlo, $388–$449); Mt. Kenya Safari Club (Kenya, $285–$530); Bora Bora Lagoon Resort ($634–$964); The Peninsula (Kowloon, $337–$492); The Regent (Kowloon, $285–$453); Four Seasons (Bali, $425–$2,000); The Regent (Singapore, $245–$260); Shangri-La (Bang-kok, $211–$279); and The Ritz-Carlton (Sydney, $194–$233).

Turn About

When you meet people from faraway places traveling in your home country, remember the hospitality you received when you were on the road. Be sensitive to how expensive it is for most foreigners to travel in the West (think of the feeling you get when you price a new car—or new tennies for that matter). Be generous. Pick up that tab. Take them to see your local wonders. Provide a secure pillow when you can.

12

Eating and Drinking

> If you are lucky enough to have lived in Paris as a young man,
> then wherever you go for the rest of your life, it stays
> with you, for Paris is a moveable feast.
> —Ernest Hemingway
> *A Moveable Feast*

Pleased to see a sign advertising a Mexican restaurant, I dropped in for a meal. The first clue I wasn't in Acapulco came when the waiter urged me to, "Try the enchilada with our special monkey gland sauce." That restaurant, in Bulawayo, Zimbabwe, was owned by a Maltese and a South African, neither of whom had been within four thousand miles of Mexico.

Even though the local version of some dish isn't prepared the same as it is at home, can you find food you like as you travel? The answer is an emphatic *yes*. In fact, good food is one of the rewards of travel. Europe is renowned for culinary excellence, of course, but you'll easily find high-quality restaurants throughout the world. If local cuisine isn't to your taste, Chinese, Indian, and Italian food are almost universal. In one country after another, you'll discover a new symphony of tastes. Many local dishes are so delicious you'll seek them out when you return home. That's important to know because if you're worried about whether you'll find what you like to eat in some faraway place, you may not go. I've known that feeling.

HOW TO FIND FOOD YOU REALLY LIKE

Picture yourself walking into the little town of Pokhara, Nepal, after a three-week trek in the Kali Gandaki Gorge alongside towering Annapurna. You crave a pizza. What are the chances? Actually, they're great. A little place with a view of Lake Phewa serves a pizza that could hold its own in Chicago. Next door, travelers crowd in to chow down on water buffalo burgers. Take your choice.

A typical meal of rice and condiments. Myanmar.

Except in parts of Europe, good meals are also inexpensive. At your table on a balcony in a restaurant in Cuzco, lean back against the finely chiseled stones of an old Inca wall and listen to *El Condor Pasa* played on Andean flutes. A meal of delicately spiced grilled fish, several vegetables, whole-grain bread, and a large Cuzquena dark beer might cost $4. On the island of Roatán, off the north coast of Honduras, marinated tuna filet, French fried potatoes, salad, and a couple of Salva Vita beers, served on a deck extending over the moonlit Caribbean, could run $5.

For dining tips before departure, clip references from travel magazines. Once you're abroad, check your guidebook and ask other travelers. Hotel clerks and taxi drivers eagerly offer recommendations, but the kickback they get may be more appealing to them than the food. Glance through windows of places filled with smiling local diners. Most restaurants post their menus outside, making it easy to check out dishes and prices as you stroll.

"Street food," not common in the United States, consists of snacks, a single dish, or a simple meal that you buy from a streetside stall or cart. Often, the food is fried, grilled, or tumbled in a wok as you watch. Street food can be tasty, cheap, fast, convenient, and ethnically authentic. *It may also be hazardous to your health*. Although the high temperature of bubbling fat sterilizes the wok, food may sit on greasy plates in the sun for hours while flies feast. The hands that go with the smiling face may not have been washed all day.

Considering that the gastronomic pyramid ranges from street stalls with plumbing and a roof to establishments that serve the finest cuisine, I offer two cautions. Although some hotel food ranks among the finest in the world, too often you get only high prices and little character. Why stay cooped up in the hotel when you can have dinner aboard a teak sailing junk moored in Hong Kong Harbor or in a candlelit garden at the edge of a cascade of terraced rice paddies in Bali. Similarly, avoid restaurants that market themselves vigorously to tourists. Why settle for the same food and faces you find at home?

Shopping in local markets can provide good, cheap meals. If there are no posted prices, watch what local people pay for what you want. Don't be bothered by being charged a small premium, but avoid being badly ripped off. It could be a mistake to hold out a handful of money and invite the lady to take what she wants for her tomatoes. If you have no idea, hand her what you think might be right. If a little more is due, she'll ask. After you've stocked up, you're ready for a terrific picnic.

In New Zealand and quite a few other countries, lodging frequently includes common cooking facilities. It's fun to cook in a kitchen with other travelers, sharing tales of the road.

Finding food you like becomes easier as you add appropriate food words to your vocabulary. Draw on a phrase book, ask questions, and take notes.

How to Order

You've found the perfect restaurant, but the menu is in a language you can't read. Now what? The daily special is always popular and cheap, but until you're certain of your tummy's tolerance I'd review the ingredients before placing an order. If you see someone else eating a meal that looks appetizing, stroll over to their table. After a friendly greeting, ask what's on their plate. If there's a language problem but the food looks good, take a chance.

If communication is a problem, point to an item on the menu as you pronounce it. When you sense it's needed, use your fingers to show the waiter how many of an item you want to order. Be sure you and the waiter understand each other. If in doubt, ask that your order be repeated back to you.

Check prices carefully. They're usually clear but there are exceptions. The fish you order in that picturesque little cafe overlooking the Danube may seem affordable until you get a monumental bill. That's when you discover that the menu price was for a serving of one hundred grams and you just enjoyed a very expensive four hundred-gram fish. Ouch!

Before you receive the bill, figure out roughly how much your meal should cost. You may be surprised at how frequently there are "mistakes" in the bill. Just in case the cashier assumes you are unfamiliar with the currency or are fabulously wealthy, count your change. No point in getting annoyed. It's part of the game.

Exotic Dishes

There aren't many foods my stomach can't handle, but I'll admit there are many local favorites my mind can't take. How about roasted locusts, toasted silkworms, bull penis soup, stewed grasshoppers, dog kabob, roasted tarantulas, stir-fried termites, deep-fried scorpions, broiled rat, pig snout, anaconda head, pan-fried palm grubs, and sea slugs? Makes chocolate-covered ants sound almost appetizing. Becoming a part-time vegetarian as you travel shields you from giving offense if you decline well-intentioned offers of food that you find too challenging.

HOW TO EAT HEALTHY

It's far better to return home raving about newly discovered spices and food preparations than to start raving on the road as a result of what you ate. Travelers find delicious-looking food almost everywhere in the world, yet as in the melancholy folk song about the lemon tree, not all is as edible as it appears. Fortunately, this paradox is easily resolved. If you understand the risks and know what to look for, eating will be a pleasure to remember. Be careless, even once, and you may be, as was that balladeer from the sixties, "a sadder man but wiser now."

"Lemon tree very pretty, and the lemon flower is sweet. But the fruit of the poor lemon is impossible to eat."
—Will Holt

Outside of Europe, Australia, New Zealand, and a few other destinations, the rule is: *If it's not boiled, peeled, or cooked, forget it.* While that's easy to remember, it's also a little simplistic. It takes more than that to safeguard your health on the road. How cautious you should be varies greatly country to country. The fact is that outside of developed countries, you must limit your food choices. Virtually all travelers who follow a few basic rules come home in perfect health. The major issues to consider are preservation and sanitation.

Preservation

Restaurants should store perishable food at temperatures of less than 45 degrees or more than 140 degrees and keep dairy products refrigerated. However, in many countries, scant attention is given to proper preservation, sometimes even in upscale restaurants. Consequently, meat and fish spoil quickly, exposing unwary diners to parasites, dysentery, hepatitis, and other food-borne diseases. Because local people eat food not kept at proper temperatures, they often have the very problems you want to avoid.

Where proper refrigeration is improbable, seek very hot food such as vegetables stir-fried as you watch. Avoid any food that has been sitting around for more than a few minutes. If everything were cooked well-done and served immediately, most of the risk would be eliminated. Too often, that isn't what happens.

If you choose meat, be certain it's cooked well-done. Beef (or pork, buf-

Street market. Lisboa, Portugal.

falo, venison, etc.) may be a higher risk than chicken since the chicken may at least have been killed on the same day it's served.

Seafood is typically sold soon after being caught or has been dried so thoroughly it looks like shoemaker's scraps. Either way, it's relatively safe. However, many travelers skip raw fish and shellfish because they are often associated with outbreaks of cholera. Perhaps it's a blessing that so much of the seafood around the world is served fried.

In Darjeeling, a German fellow told me that he'd been traveling in India for five months, eating street food and drinking tap water. He said it with some pride, asserting that he was experiencing the real India. I was impressed by his hearty constitution or his extraordinarily good luck and felt like a wimp for the care I'd been taking with what I ate. "You mean you never got sick?" I finally asked him. "Yeah, well, when I was in the hospital for malaria, they found out I had roundworms and Giardia. That was kind of a bummer." Maybe he was experiencing the real India, but I like my way better.

Sanitation

Poor sanitation practices are another health concern. In street stalls, there is seldom even a gesture toward sanitation (not too surprising since there's no running water), which raises the risk of contaminating serving utensils as well as the food. It's also hard to become comfortable with the sight of a stringy length of unidentifiable flesh dangling above a bloody counter, swinging from a rusty hook like a slow pendulum in the sun, a mobile buffet for flies.

Food handlers may themselves be transmitters of diseases, especially hepatitis. The farther away the source of clean water, the less likely it is that

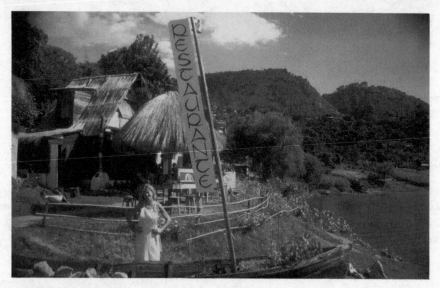
Lakeside village restaurant. Lake Atitlan, Guatemala.

hands get washed during the course of a day.

If a cook uses a knife to cut a raw fish then slices your potato, you may be about to ingest anything that was wrong with the fish. Similarly, if your tea is served in a cup used by someone else, then swirled around in a pail of murky wash water, you may be about to swallow someone else's problem. The solution: keep your eyes open and be impolite rather than becoming indisposed.

When I eat street food I choose my spots carefully, eating only well-cooked vegetarian food like vegetable tempura or boiled corn. Even though freshly deep-fried food is pretty well disinfected, I can't tell if fragments of meat or fish have been cooked clear through. Food can also become contaminated if it sits around on an open shelf for a while after being cooked. Keeping snacks such as fruit, bread, and nuts in your daypack helps avoid yielding to street-stall temptation.

Since a diner's hands can also transmit disease, they should be washed thoroughly before every meal. In a few countries, it is the custom to eat with your fingers. If you're comfortable with that custom, give your hands an extra scrubbing. Otherwise, ask for silverware. If it comes wet, dry it off or pour some hot tea over it. If you really don't want to do without silverware, carry a Scout-type metal set or plastic utensils. Whether you use silverware or not, in some countries it is the custom not to eat with one's left hand (see Chapter 17). If there is no napkin, you'll probably be given a bowl of water in which to dip your fingers at the end of the meal.

In most less-developed countries, do not eat fresh green salads. Except in Europe, avoid fruits and vegetables unless they have been peeled or cooked. They may have been fertilized with human or animal waste, or irrigated with contaminated water. Bacteria or pesticides that aggregate on the skin are no problem once the skin is removed. Thorough cooking kills the bacteria, but merely rinsing vegetables off with water does not eliminate the problem. If the rinse water is contaminated, it adds to the problem. Adding sufficient chlorine or iodine to the rinse water helps make food safe.

Ice cream, cheese, and other dairy products are on the forbidden list in most less-developed countries. The reason is use of unpasteurized milk and contaminated water. Travelers have reported health problems from ice cream even in Europe. Just because you see local people eating ice cream doesn't mean it's safe for you. Watch out for mayonnaise and cream sauces too. **Generally, avoid dairy products in less-developed countries.**

Fruit will become an important part of your diet. Luscious fruits with earthy, lascivious tastes are abundant in the tropics. You will enjoy some so much that you will miss them at home. Bananas and pineapples can keep you going over some long stretches.

Bread is generally a safe, tasty way to fill up—unless it bounced off the cart onto a Calcutta street on the way to your table. Yes, I saw that happen. Of course, you may have second thoughts after seeing a bare-chested deliveryman, sweating in the oppressive heat, walk into your restaurant with a load of pita bread tucked under his arm. Ever wonder why some pita tastes so salty?

By the way, adding fresh lime juice or lemon juice to your food may overcome minor contamination.

Just when your health should be at its best, you may be unbalancing your diet. Respond by eating lots of peeled fruits and well-cooked veggies. Consider starting vitamin supplements before your departure and taking vitamins as you travel.

The Bottom Line

Remember that, like the lemon tree, not everything is as desirable as it looks. There's no reason to be obsessed or overly concerned; just know and follow the basic rules. Knowing what to watch for and making thoughtful choices enables you to eat wonderful food around the world.

HOW TO DRINK HEALTHY

The moment you enter many countries, you are sentenced to carry a two- to three-pound weight with you every day. You're on the honor system, but it would be wise to abide by the terms of your sentence. The weight I'm talking about is a bottle of potable water.

You see labels that say water has been "boiled," or "treated with ozone," and others that claim "natural water from mineral springs" (meaning nothing was done to purify it because it came from a supposedly safe source). A label in Sulawesi, Indonesia, proudly declares that the bottle contains "Mississippi Mountain Spring Water." If you've counted the mountains in Mississippi lately, you may not find that one too reassuring. But that's what they sell, so that's what I drink.

In most European countries, tap water is potable. Nevertheless, if you drink it you may feel queasy simply because the bacteria cocktail is new to your system. When I'm in Europe for a short time, I stick with bottled water. If I'll be there for a longer time, I drink local water and let my stomach adjust.

In hot, humid weather, especially when exerting yourself, your body needs much more water than you normally drink. Yet not having ready access to clean water and having to pay for bottled water leads too many travelers to cut back on consumption. That's a mistake. Cutting back can result in exhaustion, urinary tract problems, or even a kidney stone. One way or another, you'll get sick. If you stop urinating for several days, or your urine attains a golden hue, gulp down a quick liter or two of clean water and increase your daily intake.

Keep well hydrated when traveling.

If troubled by a minor bout of diarrhea, replace the fluids you're losing. If safe water isn't available, drink other nonalcoholic fluids. Keep in mind that alcohol, as in the cold beer that tastes so good, is a diuretic. In other words, your output will ultimately be greater than your intake.

Illness at home is often a well-tended inconvenience, maybe even a respite from your job, but illness on the road is unpleasant and expensive (in terms of risk and time). Your body needs water to function well, especially in hot climates. Pour it in and daydream about free, plentiful, pure water at home.

Learn to drink healthy and you can be a happy traveler.

Prevention

Some travelers say they drink water in restaurants, even tap water, with no ill effects. Maybe so, but isn't that like playing Russian roulette? Sooner or later, you're going to lose.

Don't assume that water served in restaurants, including expensive restaurants, is safe. In regions of the world where water safety is doubtful, ask for bottled water, bring your own, or drink something else. I've never noticed any restaurant staff appearing offended by someone drinking water they've brought with them (bought in a store for half the restaurant price).

Bottled water is better than tap water only if it's not just tap water. Some unscrupulous merchants take used bottles and refill them with unpurified water from the local spigot. In India, vendors invite you to sell empties back to them, one more reason to ensure that what you buy has a factory seal. Since they usually can't or don't reseal the bottles, make sure bottles you buy are firmly sealed. If you order bottled water in a restaurant, you should be the one to open it at the table. Ensure that the bottle is filled to the customary level, with an air space at the top. If it's filled all the way to the top, suspect a backroom refill. It's safer to drink carbonated bottled water since it's hard to replace the little bubbles at home. Drink contaminated water and you may spend a lot of time in one place.

Here's a hot secret: ice is water. When you order a drink, you must specify "without ice" (*sin hielo, en Español*). Otherwise you'll be leaving untouched drinks behind or figuring out how to discreetly dispose of the ice cubes you've hastily hauled out of your glass. If some ice has already melted in the drink, give it a pass. The bugs that can harm you aren't much bothered by having their environment reduced to zero degrees centigrade and the alcohol in your drink will affect you much more than it will them. Further, your ice cubes may have been little chips on a large block that was carted or dragged through the streets to the restaurant.

Prudent travelers brush their teeth with bottled water and don't drink shower water. Many avoid tap water even aboard an airplane.

In Ngorongoro Crater,* I met a Scottish couple on their honeymoon. They had just dragged in from Zaire where they'd spent a week lying sick in the back room of a nearly empty general store in a ramshackle village. Their temperatures and the temperature outside on the dusty road had both hovered around 104 degrees Fahrenheit. They ruefully acknowledged that they'd gotten careless about water. Not surprisingly, they'd made some resolutions.

How to Disinfect Contaminated Water

When planning to filter, boil, or chemically treat water drawn from natural sources, draw from the safest sources possible. Look for wells, springs, water upstream from human habitation, swiftly running water, clear water, or water running over a rocky or sandy bed. Avoid water that is stagnant; water downstream from human, industrial, or animal contamination; and water that is smelly, scummy, or muddy or contains decaying vegetation. Seems obvious, doesn't it?

---

*Ngorongoro Crater. This version of paradise is located in northern Tanzania, close to the Serengeti, Olduvai Gorge, and Lake Manyara. Wild game roams the crater floor of this extinct volcano (twelve miles across and two thousand feet deep). In the early part of the century, it was often called a "Garden of Eden."

Boiling

Suppose you're going to travel by dugout canoe in the Okavango Delta and you can't bring enough bottled water along for a two-week trip. One solution is to purify what you need by boiling. Boiling requires a container, time, and fuel and is somewhat dependent on weather and altitude, but it works so long as the water is brought to a rolling boil. When the surface of heated water begins to be disturbed and vapors rise, the water is not boiling and may not have reached the temperature lethal to the bacteria, viruses, and parasites that concern you. Although it consumes sometimes scarce fuel and water, let it boil for several minutes.

Filtering

Filtering is generally thought of as an alternative to boiling, but let's look at what we want to avoid in contaminated water:

 - Suspended solids, such as decaying vegetation and mud, are usually not very harmful and are easily removed by a filter.

 - Worms, larvae, and similar large organisms can be filtered out.

 - Protozoa, single-cell organisms that cause illnesses such as amoebic dysentery and Giardiasis, can be removed by a fine filter.

 - Chemical contaminants, which can make water unpleasant to taste and smell and are sometimes dangerous, can be removed by only some filters.

 - Bacteria, small single-cell organisms that cause cholera, typhoid, bacillary dysentery, salmonella, and diarrhea, can be removed only by very fine filters.

 - Viruses, including the type that causes Hepatitis A, are too small for even the finest filters to capture. They are, however, susceptible to boiling and chemical treatment.

The most basic kind of filtering might be called do-it-yourself. Merely pouring contaminated water through a finely woven cloth removes many large contaminants. If that's all you can do, do it. You can make your own rough filter by filling a container with clean sand and poking a few holes in the bottom. Pour water gently and slowly, discarding the first water through. Another approach is to let water sit undisturbed in a container for forty-eight hours or more. Some contaminants will settle to the bottom and others will die. Draw water from the surface without disturbing the sediment.

Portable water purifiers, available in catalogues and from outfitters, claim to filter out bacteria and parasites, but do not remove the threat from viruses unless a lethal chemical ingredient has been added. Another limitation of filters has to do with capacity. If a manufacturer states that its filter is effective for one hundred gallons, how do you know when that limit has been reached? To solve that problem, select a filter that clogs and can't be used when it's reached capacity.

Katadyn (call 800-950-0808) makes high quality portable filters. The eight ounce MINI is a ceramic microfilter (.02 microns) designed to remove bacteria and protozoa without using chemicals. It costs about $150 and needs a $70 replacement filter after two thousand gallons.

The MSR (Mountain Safety Research) WaterWorks (call 206-624-8573) filter uses a carbon/membrane microstrainer, weighs eighteen ounces, and costs about $125. Replacement of its key components runs about $75. It is designed to remove bacteria, protozoa, and organic chemicals.

Recovery Engineering's Pur Explorer purifier (800-845-7873) combines a 1.0 micron filter with a tri-iodine resin matrix. It weighs twenty-five ounces and sells for about $140 (plus about $40 for the replacement cartridge needed after processing five hundred gallons). Recovery Engineering also offers the Scout version for about $70 (replacement cartridge for about $35). It is designed to remove bacteria, protozoa, and viruses.

Basic Designs (707-575-1220) sells a ceramic filter designed to get rid of bacteria and protozoa. It costs about $30 (plus replacement filter after five hundred gallons).

The General Ecology First Need filter costs about $60 (replacement filter needed after one hundred gallons) and weighs about sixteen ounces. It is designed to eliminate bacteria, protozoa, and organic chemicals.

The Timberline filter weighs only six ounces, will disinfect more than four hundred liters before replacement, and costs about $20 (plus $14 for replacement). The filter can be used separately as a straw. The hitch is that the filter is 2.0 microns, so it doesn't remove bacteria or viruses (although it does take out Giardia and other protozoa).

Simpler and less expensive is the Water Tech purifier, a plastic cup weighing four ounces, with a clip to hook it onto your belt. It disinfects by use of a resin material impregnated with penta-iodine, represented as being lethal to all protozoa, bacteria, and viruses. The cup will process one hundred gallons (three thousand cups) and disinfects much more quickly than iodine tablets. The disinfected water passes through a carbon stage to remove any taste and odor from the penta-iodine. At about $25, this cup is very satisfactory for low-volume use. The same company also makes the Oasis Portable Water Purification System, which resembles a bicycler's water squeeze bottle and uses similar technology. Good for about one hundred gallons, it may be even better than the cup (about $30).

If you take a filter, remember that (a) weight and size matter, (b) you must follow instructions, including keeping it clean and not using it beyond its capacity, and (c) it can't protect you when you don't use it.

Iodine

Suppose it's the middle of the night and you've just checked into a hotel in Xi'an.* There's a container of water on the night stand but you have no idea whether it's been boiled. Even though you're very thirsty and have no filter, it wouldn't be good for international relations to build a fire in the middle of the floor. A 2 percent tincture of iodine solution from any pharmacy is one answer. It will kill parasites, bacteria, *and* viruses. Mix the iodine solution with the water and let it sit for ten to thirty minutes to ensure that disinfection has taken place. If the water is cloudy, let it sit long enough for most of the suspended particles to settle *before* adding your iodine. If the water is cloudy or cold, make the iodine solution up to twice as strong and let it stand twice as long. Even better, let the mixture sit overnight.

To eliminate the risk of spilling iodine solution in your pack, carry a bottle of fifty iodine tablets (Potable Aqua, about $6, in the United States, or Aquapur in other parts of the world). Give the tablets twenty to thirty minutes to do their job. Since the tablets deteriorate over time, toss them out after a year. There is also a crystalline iodine product called Polar Pure. A $10 bottle will disinfect about two thousand quarts of water, so it's very economical. Both are available in camping goods stores and catalogs.

If anticipation of the taste of iodine gives you involuntary shivers, you'll be delighted to learn that Potable Aqua now sells PA Plus (about $10) that removes the yellow-brown color and singed-iron taste from iodine-treated water. PA Plus is made mostly of Vitamin C, so you could substitute lemon juice or your own vitamins to remove the taste.

Think of iodine as back-up purification. If you are considering using it as your primary disinfectant for an extended trip, consult your doctor.

---

* *Xi'an.* The largest city in central China, Xi'an is one of the world's oldest populated areas (established in 6,000 B.C.) and is considered the cradle of Chinese civilization. It was the Chinese anchor of the Silk Road and is now visited by those eager to see the recently excavated terra-cotta figures from the tomb of Qin Shi Huang Di, the first emperor of unified China.

In the market. Sulawesi, Indonesia.

Chlorine

Chlorine (bleach) also disinfects water. Check the label for the percentage of chlorine contained in the solution. If it is 1 percent, add ten drops per quart of contaminated water. If it is 4 to 6 percent, add two drops per quart of water. If it's 7 to 10 percent chlorine, add one drop per quart of water. Let the mixture stand for thirty minutes before drinking.

Whether it's worth taking iodine tablets, chlorine, or a filter with you depends on what part of the planet you visit. When I'll be in remote country for a week or more, I take the purifier cup and a handful of iodine tablets. They're cheap and light and will handle anything I'm likely to encounter.

Problems are not limited to contaminated water. You may also have to give up *milk* in many countries. If you can't be certain that the milk has been properly pasteurized, assume it hasn't been. Even a legend on the container claiming that the milk has been pasteurized is less than conclusive in some countries. Why risk tuberculosis or brucellosis? If milk is brought to a boil before being served in tea or coffee, it should be safe. Unfortunately, restrictions on milk extend to milk products, including *cheese* and *ice cream*.

Beer, wine, soda, and *bottled soft drinks* are okay. You encounter an incredible variety of beers as you travel, often local brews in which people take great pride. Watch for brands such as Ohlsson's Lager in Botswana, Three Horse in Madagascar, Tusker in Kenya, Primus in Zaire, Cuzquena Malta in Peru, Brahma Chopp in Brazil, and Polar in Chile.

There are a couple of drawbacks to beer. Besides being a diuretic, it's often served warm (because there is no refrigeration and the ice melted two days ago). If a bottle of beer is served with a glass, chances are the glass has been swished through tepid contaminated water at best. You are better off drinking from the bottle after wiping its mouth. A straw is a good solution for some beverages, but it's hard to maintain your poise sitting in a bar drinking beer through a straw.

In less-developed countries, wine is much less common than beer, more expensive, and seldom memorable. At the Alcove Restaurant in Dar es Salaam, a headwaiter in a rumpled tux offered me their featured wine: Thunderbird.

Tea and coffee made from boiling water are safe. Highland nomads in western Nepal say, "Tea is the horse of the traveler." I agree and drink huge quantities of tea wherever I go. Loaded up with sugar, a few cups of tea will get you through the coldest morning. But remember, an otherwise safe liquid can be infected by a contaminated container or prolonged exposure to air. In practical terms, that means the tea is fine but the teacup may get you. Take your own cup, clean what's available, take a chance, or go without.

To summarize: use bottled water and break the seal on the bottle yourself. Otherwise, boil water, filter it, or drop in those little iodine tablets, and avoid containers that may be contaminated. It takes only a little thoughtfulness to be a healthy traveler.

13

Safety and Security

Toto, I've a feeling we're not
in Kansas anymore.
—Dorothy
from Frank Baum's *Wizard of Oz*

"**Y**ou've got to be crazy!" That's what I hear from friends when I say I'm heading for some distant place they perceive as dangerous. While it's normal to wonder how you'll be treated in Johannesburg, New Delhi, Santiago, or any other place you don't know much about, I've been met with overwhelming friendliness on every continent. People smile, call out greetings, offer to help, and want to talk. They welcome travelers to their country and their homes, proud of their culture and their kids. Friendliness is the rule.

Having said that, it's still true that traveling does present certain risks. However, it's important to know that risk abroad is very different from the drug-related crimes and armed robbery featured in our daily newspapers. In fact the most frequent problems afflicting travelers abroad are stubbed or broken toes (apparently from stumbling around in dark hotel rooms), lost luggage, being bumped from an overbooked flight, and diarrhea acquired from contaminated water. These risks should deter no one from traveling.

Although physical assault is very rare, opportunistic nonviolent theft *should* be a concern. The traveler is an inviting target unless he or she knows what to expect and is prepared to avoid or respond to any problem. Many of the people you meet have seen the United States depicted on television as a land of unimaginable luxury. The fact that you're in their country tells them you have enough money to travel beyond horizons they'll never approach. As some associate you with what they've seen, you'll sense admiration—but perhaps a little envy too. The possessions you carry may be worth more than the average annual income in their country, so to a few people you represent an opportunity for a little informal redistribution of wealth.

A *Condé Nast Traveler* poll revealed that 42 perent of its readers who responded had money, clothing, or jewelry stolen while traveling (by the way, most of them were in Europe). Almost half of those who had lost something said it was taken from their hotel rooms; 26 percent experienced street theft (mostly by pickpockets); and almost 30 percent encountered some scam such as the basic taxi rip-off, a tricky currency exchange, or a slippery purchase. Virtually all of those losses could have been avoided with a little knowledge and preparation.

Since 33 percent of those who responded to the poll had been victims twice, that group must have included some slow learners or very unlucky folks. There's a clue in the fact that only 36 percent reported carrying their money in a money belt.

Being prepared reduces risk. Here's an example. Suppose I know that anyone who comes up to me on the street, says the word "baput," and counts to one hundred, will then demand that I hand over my money. What will I do if that scenario actually begins to unfold? Obviously, I'll leave the scene long before the count reaches one hundred. What if I also have a description of the kind of person who says "baput" and know where he's likely to approach me? The risk of that person surprising me would be pretty slim, wouldn't it? Well, that's what this discussion is about: knowledge, preparation, and good habits.

Knowledge and preparation reduces risks.

To a lurking thief, a traveler wandering down the street looking lost or pre-occupied appears the way a limping gazelle does to a hungry lion. Now turn that image around. Picture a traveler walking with an air of self-assurance and purpose. I don't mean acting arrogant or 'tough,' just confident and alert, aware of his or her surroundings. Since that person doesn't look like easy prey, especially if in the company of others, the thief will look elsewhere.

Remember that old joke about two guys who are suddenly confronted on the trail by a grizzly bear? The grizzly rears up and roars, about to charge. Ben cries, "My gosh, what shall we do?" His partner Scott says, "I'm getting out of here!" "You're crazy," shouts Ben as the bear starts its rush, "you can't outrun that bear." "I don't have to," Scott calls back over his shoulder, "all I have to do is outrun you!" That's all each of us has to do as a traveler; we must simply make sure we're not the thief's first choice.

It's your job to know whether you need to be especially alert in the places you'll be visiting. Overseas, as at home, crime is most common in cities and where tourists congregate. High-risk areas include train and bus stations, streets around tourist hotels, and nightlife areas. There are also a few cities where it might be wise not to wander the streets at night under any circumstances. These include Bogotá, Dar es Salaam (Tanzania), Kinshasa (Zaire), Moscow, and Rio.

Some guidebooks offer good advice concerning security risks at your destinations, but it's worth taking advantage of other resources as well. Review Consular Information Sheets or Travel Warnings (see the next section) and talk with experienced travelers before you leave home.

Talk with other travelers as you approach a country. Seek guidance from the desk clerk at your hotel. Question local people. Adjust your alertness based on what you hear and see. If a situation requires caution, be cautious. No lapses.

We don't worry much about certain risks at home because we know how to avoid them. Abroad, however, risks are more real for anyone who doesn't "know the territory." Unprepared tourists are right to worry—because they don't know how to protect themselves. Knowledge prevents problems. When the simple routines in these columns become automatic, you can travel the world without fear.

WHICH COUNTRIES TO SKIP

Are there countries you should skip? There certainly are and you should identify them while drafting your itinerary. However, since it's hard for reporters to get the facts, let alone evaluate them, disturbances in a distant country are frequently reported as being worse than they are. And, of course, a little sensationalism never hurts sales.

Unfortunately, when talking with returning tourists, we tend to hear from the one person who had a problem, not from the dozens who had none. By analogy, when someone has a bad meal in a restaurant, he's likely to talk about it, and the meal gets worse with each telling. Almost anyone who has traveled has succumbed to the temptation of telling, and embellishing, some adventure. After all, stories about a coup or riot sound pretty exciting when repeated at home. Nevertheless, even taking sensationalism and exaggerations into account, there are always a few places, changing year to year, that a traveler should leave off the itinerary.

How do you identify which countries to skip? Start with the countries the U.S. government forbids its citizens to visit. Beyond those, it's a matter of research and common sense. News reports, even if unnecessarily alarmist, signal places that deserve careful review before inclusion on your route.

U.S. Department of State *Consular Information Sheets* describe crime and security conditions, political disturbances, and areas of instability in every country. They also include addresses and emergency telephone numbers for U.S. embassies and consulates. If conditions in a country are considered particularly dangerous, or a major demonstration will occur on a specified date, the State Department also issues a *Travel Warning*. These publications tend to be extremely cautious because "hostage" is not a welcome word around the State Department. To get this information, call the State Department Citizens Emergency Center (202-647-5225 or 202-647-3000) and follow the prompts you hear to have Sheets or Warnings faxed to you. Both operate twenty-four hours a day. If you prefer the computer/modem route, dial the Consular Affairs Bulletin Board at (202) 647-9225. You can also obtain them via

CompuServe (GO STATE) or America Online (keyword TRAVEL). Once you're abroad, this information is available from embassies and consulates. The State Department Bureau of Consular Affairs publishes *Tips for . . .* (name of country), which offer advice on travel to various countries. Ask a travel agent if there are any warnings applicable to your route.

If you ask the embassy of the country about local safety, keep in mind that their response may be subjective. If there's an internal problem, one government may want to keep foreigners away so they don't see it. Another, more dependent on tourism, may minimize danger so tourists won't cancel.

A recently returned traveler is a good source of information provided you can evaluate his frame of reference. Here's what I mean by frame of reference. A bunch of us were talking one evening in a Bangkok cafe as it bobbed gently on the Chao Phraya river. Those of us who had just arrived from South India saw Bangkok as intimidatingly modern and distressingly westernized. An Englishman, just arrived from vacationing in New Zealand, saw the same Bangkok as dirty, disorganized, and distressingly Asian. That's frame of reference, the eye of the beholder.

There are, however, real problems, ones that have to do with civil war or terrorist attacks. Terrorists sometimes pressure a government by attacking places that attract tourists. If bombs are being set off in an airport or scenic destination, even occasionally, go elsewhere. If hostage taking is in a cycle of local popularity, it's a good idea for travelers not to attract attention by looking affluent or dressing in pseudomilitary clothing.

There are many wonderful places to visit which go through periods when they belong on no traveler's route. I'm thinking of parts of Angola, Colombia, India (Punjab, Jammu, Kashmir), Sudan, Sri Lanka, and Uganda, the Kurdish section of eastern Turkey, the Philippines (northern Luzon, Mindanao), and various fragments of the former Yugoslavia. I'd skip Nigeria, Liberia, and North Korea for the foreseeable future and be cautious about traveling by train or private car in Cambodia.

On the other hand, some places have a fearsome reputation but feel very different when you're there. For example, Thailand's notorious Golden Triangle, long reported as the epicenter of battles among opium-trade warlords, seems disappointingly normal when you get there. In fact, it's now distinguished by a resort hotel where sweating tourists beam beneath a masonry arch while having their photograph taken with the muddy Mekong River in the background. You can hardly find a warlord anymore, unless you count the one who owns the resort.

There are a few precautions you should consider when traveling in a genuinely high-risk area. Tell people at home what they should do in case you find yourself in an emergency situation. Check in with your embassy on arrival. Don't discuss your itinerary with strangers. Leave nothing controversial in your hotel room. Watch for people who seem to be following you. Keep a mental note of potential safe havens and develop a plan of action should a dangerous situation arise. If shooting starts, take cover and don't pick up a weapon (forget Rambo!). Sit someplace out of sight and try to remember why you came.

The bottom line: some places should be off limits from time to time, left for another day. Do the research. Find out whether a place is as forbidding as it initially sounds. If it's a close call, trust your instincts. If you decide to go, get updates from other travelers when you arrive. In making decisions, the frequency of random violence and attacks directed toward tourists, and the attitude of the government, should be given considerable weight.

HOW TO PROTECT YOURSELF WITH A MAGIC CLOAK

Standing in a crowded bus station in San José, Costa Rica, I heard a tourist complain loudly that someone had just snatched his passport from his shirt pocket. He kept it in his shirt pocket? Anyone who does something like that has to be brain dead. There's no reason to be a victim when thievery can be avoided so easily. Knowledge and preparation form a *magic cloak* which, when followed without exception, makes a traveler almost invulnerable.

Perhaps the most important part of the routine is a mind-set you establish before you leave home. That is, deciding that you won't defend your dignity or property at risk of injury or life. Suppose you're walking along a street in Tangier and some guy standing in a doorway with his buddies makes a nasty comment about you, your partner, or your country. Fortunately, you've already decided not to be provoked by a meaningless, gratuitous insult. Does it make sense to play someone else's game on their home field? So you walk on without feeling bad in the slightest.

In the serenity of an easy chair, it's easy to agree that the possessions you carry aren't worth trading your life to protect. It's more difficult to imbed that principle so deeply that you won't make a different decision in the heat of the moment or after several beers in some exotic port. That decision should become the first of your routines.

Money Belt Routines

Some of the most important routines concern your money belt.
- Keep all your valuables (passport, credit cards, driver's license, immunization record, airline tickets, and most of your cash and travelers checks) in a money belt. *Always.* It's a small hassle to get them out when you need them, but it keeps them from disappearing unexpectedly. A money belt can take many forms: a belt around your waist, a pocket hanging inside your pants from your belt loop, a pouch dangling from your neck, a shoulder holster, and so on.

- Whatever the form of your money belt, it must be *inside* your clothing, riding comfortably without signaling its presence. Although its fabric may be water-resistant, it won't keep out rain or the perspiration generated during a long hike, so keep the contents inside a Ziploc bag. Transporting valuables in a pouch outside your clothing, including the often-seen fanny pack, may be comfortable and convenient but it puts them at great risk. Fanny packs can't be protected effectively and get clipped off every day. That's when the wearer realizes that carrying valuables in one was a mistake.

- Lock your money belt in your luggage at night unless you feel you're in a high-risk area. If you are, keep the belt with you while you sleep.

- You find lots of things on the beach—sea shells, a volleyball game, maybe even a new friend—but you can lose things too. When heading for the beach, leave your money belt in the hotel safe if you trust it. If you don't, lock it in your luggage in the hotel room. If you take it to the beach, ask a friend to wear it while you're swimming, or take it in with you in a waterproof pouch.

  On a beach such as Copacabana in Rio only about 20 percent of the sharks are in the water. Don't even think of hiding your money belt under your towel or digging a hole for it. As an acquaintance put his money belt under his towel, I noticed a teenage guy stroll by. He eyed us obliquely and kept going. Several minutes later he eased down just behind us, only a few feet away. I watched in fascination as his foot slowly snaked across the sand until his toes could probe under my friend's towel. I yelled. He scrambled to his feet and tore off down the beach. My friend had underestimated the caliber of the competition.

- Keep a small amount of cash and travelers checks in your luggage to avoid being cleaned out if a thief were somehow to get your money belt. For the same reason, it's prudent for partners to split up cash, travelers checks, and credit cards between them.

Making the small effort to follow these simple routines will make your trip a happier one. Convince yourself that the very first time you're careless with your money belt, it will disappear. Why learn the hard way?

Wallet Routines

- Make it routine to put your wallet in a secure front pants pocket, a buttoned or Velcro-closed thigh pocket, or some other inaccessible place. Some travelers use a wallet attached by a loop to their belt. I grimace when I see a traveler stuff a wallet into a rear pants pocket, an inside jacket pocket, or a purse—all predictable places. When a thief knows where to look for your wallet, he's halfway to his goal.

I met a documentary filmmaker in Ternate* who had a special pocket sewn on the inside of his pants, opening at the waistband, in which he kept his wallet. It worked. Then he left his hotel room door unlocked in Sengiggi Beach, Lomboc, and someone walked off with his backpack. He forgot there's more than one routine to follow.

- If your wallet is vulnerable, make it "sticky" by wrapping it with rubber bands.

- Act as if the thief can get your wallet wherever you put it. On that assumption, keep only business cards, a few dollars, and a couple of travelers checks in it. Everything else belongs in your money belt. Sure, it's a little inconvenient, but it's a lot easier than canceling and replacing credit cards, wiring home for money, and suffering the anxiety of a major loss. Travel is supposed to be fun.

Luggage and Daypack Routines

The objective is to prevent anyone from opening your luggage and removing what he wants—or walking off with the whole thing. These routines can foil his plans.

- Keep your luggage locked most of the time. If you have something valuable in your daypack, such as your camera, lock it when in crowded places or when you check it at a museum.

- Bus and train stations and, to a lesser degree, airports, attract people who admire your possessions. While waiting, keep your hand or foot through your luggage strap, lean against it, or otherwise keep in physical touch with it.

  David, an Israeli as hirsute and bulky as a bear, asked if I would watch his pack one afternoon at a bus station in Pisco, Peru. I agreed. When he locked his pack to my belt with a chain, I knew he was an experienced traveler. That was his not-so-subtle way of saying he expected me to watch his pack as closely as he would watch it himself.

- When you check your luggage, ask the agent for the letter designation of your destination. See, don't assume, that the right tag is attached. In addition to inadvertent errors, I heard of a ticket agent who purposely mis-tagged bags, sending them to another city where a

---

* *Ternate.* Portuguese and Dutch forts on this tiny volcanic island in northeastern Indonesia are a reminder of the glory days when Ternate was at the center of the spice trade (it was one of the world's few sources of cloves). Sir Frances Drake stopped by in 1579.

confederate waited to claim them. Clever, eh? Watch your luggage depart toward the plane and watch as it's loaded on a bus.

- If your bag gets lost in transit, you have to prove it was in the custody of the carrier. That's much easier if you have a baggage claim check (try getting one at a Guatemalan bus stop).

- Your luggage can go astray on arrival. Not all the folks watching the bags clunk around the carousel are passengers. Some are official porters who promote their services by snatching your bag and guarding it until you see it and come over. Then there is the unofficial porter who picks up your bag if it looks unattended. If you see it happen, he smiles and acts like a porter. If you don't, he's out the gate. I'm sure you've seen those warning signs that say, "Bags look alike." It must be true. To a thief, your bag looks like his.

   Station yourself close to the point where bags enter the baggage claim area. That way you'll get first shot at your bag. If you're farther down the line, chatting with someone you met on the plane, your bag may leave the airport before you do.

   At the airport in Trivandrum, India, I was waiting for my backpack to roll into sight when a slightly built young man swooped down like a fish eagle on the daypack at my feet. His boldness probably meant he had confederates nearby to whom he planned to pitch my pack on the run. As always in a crowd, I was standing with my size thirteen shoe firmly planted through the pack's strap. When the pack didn't come away in his hand as he expected, he slid sprawling across the floor. I'm sure he was back the next day.

- Vulnerability increases in crowded places such as a train station. After a long trip you're tired and a little disoriented, thinking about the town, talking about lodging, maybe looking for a friend, and you're not concentrating on the present. Zap! You've been stung. Theft may be nonviolent but that doesn't mean it's polite. Even if you see the person who raced by and grabbed your daypack out of your hand, you have little chance of catching him. Be alert in crowded places, watch the people around you, and keep in touch with your gear. Force the thief to look for an easier target.

- If you have much walking around to do, or you'll be waiting for hours, consider storing your bag in a locker or the "left luggage" room.

- Suppose you're in a public place and can't store your bag and can't stand taking it with you while you run errands. If you ask someone reputable-looking to watch it, set it clearly within their territory.

Reduce the risk by locking it to something with your bicycle lock. Make sure you are communicating with one another about how long the person will be there.

- If you sleep in a public place, lock your bag to something or use it for a pillow. Even lacing the straps through a bench or around a stanchion will foil someone running by.

- When traveling in a group, help one another. Leaving the train platform in Puno,* passengers are jammed together as they're funneled through a single exit gate, a perfect situation for thieves. The architect of that place must have been a member of the Pickpockets & Pack-Slashers Union. As our group of six approached the exit, we formed a circle, packs in the center. Does that sound overly cautious? Well, that train station has a terrible reputation—and our little merry-go-round formation didn't lose a thing.

- If you have a compartment on a train, keep the door locked when you're out of the room and lock your bag to the washstand or something else built in. If that won't work, lock two bags together. If you have an open berth on the aisle, use your bag as a cushion between yourself and the wall while you sleep, or lock it to something.

- Bus travel tests your vigilance. When your bag is traveling on the roof of a bus, secure it to a rail with a bicycle chain-lock. That keeps it from falling off on a curve or being pitched off into waiting hands.

- If you have your bag with you in the rest room, take it into the stall with you.

- A hotel room is not always a safe zone. As you're leaving the room, take a moment to lock up things you'd rather not contribute to the local economy.

- The locks on your hotel room door and windows won't help a bit unless you use them.

- Believing them easier targets for grab-and-run theft, thieves target women. A woman should wear her shoulder bag strap diagonally across her chest rather than hanging off one shoulder. When a man is walking with a woman, he should walk between her and the street to guard against someone making a grab for her shoulder bag.

---

* *Puno.* High, cold Puno is located in the southeastern corner of Peru on the shore of Lake Titicaca. It has a fine market for llama and alpaca wool articles and offers excursions to the floating reed islands and the island of Taquile (to see Inca ruins and fine textiles).

- If you have your daypack on your back in a crowded bus, beware of busy fingers trying to get inside. If you tend to carry it over one shoulder, be alert against a grab-and-run. Each time you set it down, keep in touch with it; keep your hand on it or your foot through a strap. Keep it out of reach of passing hands. If you put a camera in your daypack, be especially alert.

- Carry a local language newspaper prominently under your arm if it will help you pass as a local.

- Be alert when someone offers to help, especially when you didn't know you needed help. An offer needn't make you defensive, just alert. Similarly, don't be too quick to volunteer to help someone else. Don't suppress your friendly instincts, but take a moment to size up the situation.

The comments above are not meant to make travel seem daunting. It's just that knowing what to expect, following the simple routines I've described, and using the information in the rest of this chapter provides a magic cloak to guard your travels.

WHERE TROUBLE COMES FROM—AND HOW TO AVOID IT

We've talked about protecting your money belt, wallet, luggage, and daypack from theft. Now we're ready to discuss other potential safety and security problems a traveler might encounter. You can learn to recognize and sidestep every one.

Political and Religious Discussions

As we all know, discussions of politics, sex, or religion can become very spirited. They are especially tempting topics on the road because a vigorous discussion can generate cultural insights you might otherwise have missed. The problem arises when what seems like stimulating give-and-take to you may be personal and confrontational to others. Tempers can flare even more when controversial subjects are combined with alcohol.

If you want to stir things up, try converting others to your way of thinking or insist that your country's political system is the only rational one. Voice your opinions about the merits and demerits of local persons of the opposite sex, and throw in a few complaints about the inconveniences you've encountered in their country. Then get ready for fireworks.

I'm not suggesting that you avoid discussions of politics, sex, or religion; I'm only suggesting that it's better to ask questions than to preach. Be open-minded and sensitive to the mood of the group. Keep it light and humorous. Should the mood sour, pay for a farewell drink for your new acquaintances, if appropriate, and bail out. The bottom line: there's no upside to getting into an argument in a bar.

Alcohol, Drugs, and Firearms

Alcohol

Alcohol is as much related to problems of safety and security when you're abroad as it is on highways at home. After a few drinks, you become a shade inattentive. You fail to recognize a problem developing or you take a risk you'd otherwise have avoided. Suddenly you're face-to-face with an unpleasant situation. If you gulp down a couple of beers after a hot afternoon of trudging through the temple grounds of Prambanan and Borobudur,* or add a cool bottle of white wine to your dinner in Rio, stay a little more alert to your surroundings than you might at home.

Drugs

I have one word of advice about drugs: DON'T! Don't buy them, don't sell them, don't use them, and don't transport them in or out. This isn't about morality. It's about safety and security. Using exposes you to impure drugs and can put your life on the line. Anyone who buys or sells drugs may be dealing with an informer or a cop. Sneaking illegal drugs through customs might work . . . except when it doesn't. More than one-third of all U.S. citizens incarcerated abroad for any crime are in on drug charges, many with very long mandatory sentences. **Avoid drugs at all costs.** Anyone busted on drug charges learns quickly how very different the legal process is and how much more severe penalties are in most foreign countries. Maybe you saw the movie *Midnight Express*?

Some drug sales are setups from the beginning. The seller has tipped off the cops or is a cop. The buyer is arrested during or immediately after the deal goes down and the drugs are confiscated—probably for recycling. Naturally, the buyer's drug money disappears. Somewhere along the way to the police station, a large amount of money may be mentioned with the implication that its receipt might be related to the buyer's freedom. If not, the buyer may be held without trial for years. Under the legal systems of many countries, a person under arrest is considered guilty until innocence is proved. Perfunctory trials and harsh sentences are common. On bulletin boards in La Paz hotels, I've read pitiful notes posted on behalf of foreign prisoners begging for someone to contact a relative. Roadside billboards in Malaysia promise execution as the reward for trafficking in drugs!

---

* *Prambanan and Borobudur.* The Hindu temple complex at Prambanan on Java, built A.D. 700–900, is the largest in Indonesia. After being destroyed by earthquakes, restoration has been ongoing since the 1930s. The Buddhist temple at Borobudur, near Prambanan, is the largest ancient monument in the Southern Hemisphere. It is a five-story pyramid, over four hundred feet on a side. Buried for a thousand years by volcanic eruptions and tropical vegetation, it was discovered by chance in 1814. Its restoration, the largest such project since Abu Simbel in Egypt, began in 1973.

A traveler who expects the embassy to intervene, give them a good scolding, and put them on a plane for home, should have a chat with the State Department ahead of time. Embassies have neither the ability nor willingness to do much more than provide a list of lawyers and notify next of kin.

If a new acquaintance asks you to take a package home as a favor, agree or not as it suits you, but don't actually accept it without opening and inspecting the contents carefully. Whatever reasons are given for not opening the package, they're not good enough. If it contains drugs or other illegal goods it is you who must answer to the law.

Sadly, drugs also mean that travelers must be thoughtful about accepting apparent hospitality. Whether you accept food or drink from someone should depend on the circumstances. If the offer is from someone you have reason to trust, no problem. If an offer comes from a new acquaintance or seems inappropriate in some way, be cautious. Bus and train stations are special-alert zones. If you have the slightest doubt about an offer, turn it down. You can decline on grounds of being a vegetarian, a nondrinker, having an upset stomach, or give no reason at all. Be polite, but put your own welfare first.

I recall a twenty-two-year-old Japanese student who accepted an orange soda from a person he met in a bus station in Tanzania. He awakened thirty-six hours later in a hospital to which some kind passersby had taken him. After the drug wore off and his headache subsided, he asked about his backpack. The nurses shook their heads and shrugged their shoulders.

The State Department reports that no U.S. citizens have been arrested abroad in connection with prescription drugs they bought in the United States and took along for personal use in labeled containers. However, you can get into trouble by legally buying large amounts of certain drugs, such as tranquilizers and amphetamines, in one country and attempting to take them into other countries where they are illegal. The same goes for attempting to return with them to the United States if the quantity is such that Customs might suspect commercial intent.

Firearms

Sentences for illegal possession of firearms abroad can be very harsh, at least by U.S. standards. How does thirty years sound? Don't consider taking a weapon to another country without first obtaining a permit from its embassy. A little political instability can make border guards, police, and other officials convinced that your weapon indicates your intent to help the insurgents. What could follow would not be pretty.

Prohibited Photographs

Since we'll discuss this subject more thoroughly in Chapter 22, I'll mention only briefly that a traveler can get in trouble by taking photographs of forbidden objects. What's forbidden? Fortunately, there's a standard list: bridges, airports, harbors, military personnel and installations, and some temples. After watching me take a couple of photographs of Calcutta Harbor, an officer of the law gave me a sharp warning and definitely wasn't interested in whether I thought the regulation was reasonable. If there's the slightest doubt about who might be watching, skip the shot. I don't know what the actual penalties might be, but no harbor is that picturesque.

Encounters with the Law

Few people arrive in a foreign country intending to cross the law, but it can happen anyway, usually because of ignorance or carelessness. Common problems involve visas, currency violations, customs violations (bringing in or taking out something prohibited), being in a traffic accident, or violating a local statute, such as entering a restricted area. Buying, selling, using, or transporting drugs is by far the most effective strategy for winning a trip to jail. Being drunk or disorderly in public comes in second. Carrying a weapon may or may not protect you, but it will get you stopped at the border of every country in the world.

You are governed by the laws of the country you are in.

When visiting a country, you are governed by its laws and they may be based on principles of jurisprudence very different from those in your own country. The differences relate to the issue of whether an individual's rights or the government's rights have primacy. In most places, the government wins hands down. For example, detention for a week or more without being formally charged and with no showing of probable cause is common. There may not even be a right to immediately contact anyone outside jail. Bail may be denied and right to trial by jury is far from being universal. The best plan is to obey local laws.

When your path collides with officialdom, your behavior can make all the difference in how things turn out. Don't be disrespectful or show anger. That's easier said than done, but it's essential. There is a saying in Ghana that goes: "Once you have crossed the river, you can be rude to the crocodile." That wise counsel needs no explanation.

Suppose there's no question of guilt? You did what they say you did and you both know it. No matter how silly the regulation seems that you're being charged with breaching, don't criticize it. Express naive surprise. Apologize immediately. Promise that, now that you know the law, you'll never commit this offense again. However, if you did not commit any offense, I wouldn't say otherwise.

If detention is prolonged or the interpersonal dynamics are deteriorating (e.g., the guard is getting drunk or you're losing your cool), call for a superior officer. If appropriate, request a representative of your embassy or consulate. They probably won't get you out of jail, but someone from the consulate should visit you and put you in touch with a well-connected lawyer, preferably one who speaks your language (although maybe that won't matter if he's connected well enough). They will also notify your family and/or traveling partner, help get money transferred from home if you need it, and arrange for food and bedding (which usually doesn't come with the jail cell).

I've heard a couple of people say they responded to difficulty by offering a bribe. That's not a solution that comes naturally to me and it entails some risks. We'll discuss bribes at greater length in Chapter 17.

In India, it's fine to be persistent but if you decide to employ assertiveness or anger, brace yourself to encounter the full weight of an infinite bureaucracy. In Africa, the odds that your display of temper or threats will intimidate a nineteen-year-old private holding a submachine gun are infinitesimally low—off the board, I'd say. At the same time, the chances that your show of anger will escalate the situation to your disadvantage approach 100 percent. The slightest hint that you deserve special treatment *because* you are a foreigner will provoke special treatment all right, but perhaps not in your best interests.

It's important to keep such encounters in perspective. During one somewhat hectic three-month journey in Africa, I passed through a total of fifty-four immigration and customs stations and had not one problem. At almost every station, I was passed through with a friendly wave. At the others, I did as I was asked, which usually meant opening my pack to be searched. I asked and answered questions politely. Not wanting to appear nervous or say the wrong thing, I volunteered little information. When asked why I was there, I said, "To see this beautiful country." If you're calm and patient, you can out wait most problems.

At a police checkpoint in Tanzania, a guard ordered me to put my journal away. "No writing at this police station," he said. The police station in question was a card table in the paltry shade of a scraggly baobab tree. Curious, but not wanting to debate the wisdom of his requirement, I smiled and buried my journal in my daypack.

> In Prague, I discovered I'd used up my multiple visa for Hungary. To return, I needed another visa. They told me at the Hungarian Consulate that they didn't issue visas on Saturdays, meaning I'd have to delay my trip for two or three days. Prague is a great place to spend a weekend but I was scheduled to catch a flight out of Budapest the following Monday. I calmly asked to see a higher official. After a long delay, a man appeared who coldly agreed to issue the visa but only if I paid a "special service" fee of $80. Swallowing my retort, I asked to see the most senior officer on duty. He turned out to be an erudite, sophisticated person who spoke fluent English. After a friendly conversation lasting over an hour, mostly about new business opportunities in free Hungary, he issued the visa, stamped "diplomatic courtesy," at no charge.

I am not advocating that you present yourself as a person who can be taken advantage of. That could be a mistake. Instead, try to establish some person-to-person contact with the official. Ask personal questions. Establish eye contact—difficult if the guy is wearing shades or one of those stiff army hats with a black visor. If you ask for his help or advice, he may transform himself into an individual human and show you how to solve the problem. Reasonable flattery works in every language.

As you travel you will interact with more officials than you normally do at home. Most will be pleasant human beings. Only a very few will be tight-lipped, self-important creeps. If one starts to give you a problem, it's your job to keep the situation under control. It's not difficult when you're prepared.

Disturbances

What do you do about disturbances that spring up while you're on the scene? Fortunately, most of them aren't nearly as dangerous as they appear from a distance. Take the 1985 coup in which the commanding general of the army deposed the president of Bolivia. The newspaper reports made La Paz, the capital, sound like the last place in the world you'd want to be. The militia fired a few machine-gun volleys into the air, imposed a curfew, and shut down transportation for three days. That was all there was to it—for me, at least. The outgoing president, on the other hand, was awarded a lifetime vacation in a remote village in the steamy lowland jungle. There weren't even any T-shirts commemorating the event.

Friends told me of watching a riot from their hotel room window in Caracas while seeing the same scenes televised on CNN.

I was in the Perinet* forest searching for lemurs while a military coup was attempted in Antananarivo, the capital of Madagascar. With radio and telephone shut down, news finally reached us along the railroad line. By the time we heard about the battle, the shouting, if there had been any, was over. No problem, except that it looked bad in newspapers at home. If friends and family know you're in an area in which a disturbance is taking place, they need your reassurance.

I recall one disturbance that didn't seem threatening until it suddenly burst out of control. As I stood in a shop doorway in a Chilean town talking with the shop owner, a street intersection a few yards away filled with students. Before long, they were shouting angrily as fiery speakers demanded that the government reveal the whereabouts of students who had "disappeared." Squads of heavily armored policemen arrived, looking menacing but not interfering. Without warning, someone threw a stone through a storefront plate glass window. As the glass shattered, so did détente. In an instant, clubs were swinging and rocks were flying in every direction. I ducked into

---

* *Perinet.* This forest reserve, located in central Madagascar between Antananarivo and Toamasina, is home to the rare Indri Lemur.

the shop just as the owner hauled down his steel mesh security curtain with a clang. If I hadn't made it, I'd have been trapped in the furious crowd. As it was, shots cracked a few feet away from where we crouched under the counter. I sometimes learn the hard way, but I don't recommend it. Since that day, I've kept my distance.

Whether it's a student protest meeting, police breaking up a strike, or an all-out coup attempt, no traveler should let curiosity lead him into the middle of it. The rule is simple: *stay away from trouble.* If there's a flare-up when you're around, don't go to watch. If you go anyway, thinking you'll keep your head down, you may too late find yourself caught in a mob. Stay in your hotel. If there's action in the street below, stay away from the windows. Pull the curtains or blinds to stop flying glass. Store some food and water if you have time. Just in case water is cut off, fill the bath tub or whatever containers you can find. Keep your flashlight nearby in case power goes off. Know where the fire escape is. If there's a curfew, obey it. An ice cold beer on a hot night isn't worth getting shot.

If it looks as if the situation may continue or deteriorate, ask the hotel manager to help you slip away. For a price, someone is ready to accommodate virtually any need.

Theft: Scams, Pickpockets, and Sneak Thieves

The vast majority of theft is so cunning it reminds me of the definition of true sarcasm: a blade so keen the victim doesn't know he's been struck until he turns to walk away and his head falls to the ground. Victims don't know the thief has struck until they discover something missing. I have grudging admiration for the creativity that thieves put into separating people from their belongings, but not enough to reward it. Having learned what to watch for, I'm prepared for them.

The magic cloak of routines we discussed at the beginning of this chapter are excellent protection against standard brands of theft. However, an elite group of thieves have concocted some especially clever ways to take possession of your valuables. When you're in their neighborhood, you can't afford even a short lapse of attention. However, when the simple routines we've discussed become automatic, anxiety disappears.

As you read the examples below, it may be hard to believe they could be real because they're so different from your daily experience. But they are, every single one of them. And there are dozens of variations in all languages. If you read and remember them, they'll remain nothing but amusing anecdotes to which you will add your own.

Scams

The variety of scams is as infinite as the imagination. A few scams have even achieved the status of classics, informally inducted into a Travelers Hall of Fame. Fagin would be proud of his successors. As a neophyte traveler begins to tell the story of what just happened to him, his more experienced listeners exchange wry smiles and nod their heads in recognition after the first few lines. It's like hearing a couple of bars of an old familiar song. Here are some of the scams out there.

People who want to do something for you. A smiling, always smiling, young man appears at your elbow offering to help load your luggage into a taxi, guide you to a hotel, find you a discount, get tickets for you, anything. If he's legitimate, he'll provide a helpful service and earn a small tip. Nothing wrong with that, but if he's not legitimate his offer may not be quite what it appears. A yellow caution light should go on when a stranger offers to help.

The first hustler you meet may be an official in an impressive looking uniform at the airport or the train station. He takes you in hand, guides you through the baggage-collection process and toward a car waiting at the curb. If you get into that car, you're signing up for an expensive ride—and will wind up at an expensive hotel. It has to be to cover his kickback. And, of course, he's no more an official than you are.

You're standing on a street corner in Athens, lost, looking for the Plaka district. Someone comes up and asks if you need help. "Oh, no problem, I'm going that way myself," she says. Somewhere along the way, it's your wallet that gets lost.

"Ten baht, ten baht," cries the smiling *tuk-tuk* driver. He's offering to drive you to three temples for a fare of ten baht (forty cents). What can you lose?— so you hop into his canopied three-wheeler and he chugs off to a nice temple. After seeing that temple, he stops in front of a large gem store, which he begs you to enter "for few minutes only." If you go inside, the store gives him a coupon valid for five liters of petrol plus a commission on anything you buy (which, of course, raises its price to you). As you leave the store, he takes you to another temple. When you come out, he's long gone, crying "ten baht" somewhere else. No big deal. You've gotten more than your ten baht worth.

Then there's the taxi driver who tells you that the Royal Palace, where you just asked him to take you, is closed today. Ever helpful, he offers to take you to the last day of the "Special Gem Exhibition." Guess what, the "Special" exhibition runs forever, the taxi driver is hoping for a commission on what you purchase, and the Royal Palace is open.

Selling you something that isn't what it's represented as being. If it *were* ivory, a rhino horn, an elephant hide (anyone trying to buy any of these deserves to be swindled), gold or jade, it would be a great buy at the price— a "steal," you might say. You would have done the impossible: outsmarted the local merchant. Of course, if it turns out to be plastic or cowhide, the price is pretty outrageous and your new treasure has zero resale value. How many times have you heard someone say, "If it sounds too good to be true, it probably is?" or "There's no free lunch?" Clichés, yes, and so true.

You can definitely buy satisfying souvenirs in foreign countries at prices far below anything comparable at home, if there were such things at home. You can even buy authentically valuable items at bargain prices. However, if something is represented as handmade, antique, rare, or as having unique value, and those qualities are *not* reflected in the price, STOP! Think "no free lunch!" Make sure the claims are true before you buy. If you can't, recognize the risk.

Let's go back to that gem store and suppose that a beautiful emerald catches your eye. The ever-so-soft-spoken salesperson whispers, "This small stone will be worth three times more in your country. Sell it there and pay for your trip." You smile evasively and think, Oh, sure. . . . But you wonder if it just might be true. With practiced timing, the salesperson goes on, "If you can't sell this stone for at least 100 percent more than you pay here, you can take it to our embassy in your country and they will give you a 50 percent profit. Same day. No questions. Just show them the sales slip." Well, now, you think, if that's true, I could really clean up with a more expensive stone. "How much is that one over there? The big one." To help set the hook, he produces a fancy Certificate of Guarantee. If your yellow caution light isn't glowing brightly by now, you're in big trouble—and not just in this gem store. Do I need to tell you that the embassy will greet you with a stonewall when you state your request for 50 percent profit, even though they've heard the same sad story many times and know you're about to hit the roof? Of course, by the time you're talking to the embassy, you've already found out what the Certificate of Guarantee is worth.

Watch the ball all the way into the basket. After you've made a purchase, keep your eye on it until you leave the store. Let's say you've just bought a piece of batik art. Try not to let it be taken out of your sight to be wrapped. If it is and you can't go with it, inspect the package before you leave the shop or at least the city. It's disheartening to discover a switch when you're thousands of miles away.

Nothing at all for your money. Read the Letters to the Editor columns in a few travel magazines. They're full of laments about goods received that weren't what was ordered and purchases that never arrived. If you're having things made and shipped, such as Indian furniture, Hong Kong suits, or a Tibetan rug, it's not unreasonable for the merchant to ask you to pay in full at the time of purchase. It's not unreasonable for you to decline. Compromise. Advance enough money to cover the merchant's costs. If that won't work, offer to leave the balance at a local bank with directions to release it on receipt of shipping papers. The best deal is to pay the shipper when you pick up the goods. The worst deal is to pay for something that never arrives—because it was never sent. Using a credit card may protect you if nothing arrives. See the credit card section in Chapter 6.

Every item I've taken to a post office myself, and everything I've had a merchant ship via sea freight, has made it home. Of course, two colorful rugs from the Tibetan Refugee Centre in Darjeeling didn't arrive until nine months after I did. On the other hand, I know a fellow who's still waiting for the brass and teak silverware he purchased. Well, it's only been four years.

If the purchase price seems small and you really want an item, why not take a risk? Be as satisfied as you can of the merchant's legitimacy and try to pay a balance on delivery.

Students. You'll meet a lot of students as you travel. They're curious about you and want to practice speaking your language. They may dream of visiting your country and would love to have a contact. They can be engaging and interesting and introduce you to local life. The only thing wrong is that some of them aren't students at all.

What they want from you is the trust engendered by their proclaimed status. After some conversational groundwork, they may ask for money to get them home to see their parents or to support some political refugee project. Perhaps they are reluctantly willing to part with their family's cherished antique opium pipe or sake set or seal ring or whatever. They assert student status to persuade you to drop your defenses, including your common sense. The bottom line: when approached by a self-proclaimed student, be as open as you usually are but be alert.

Can you help me? A smiling young man approaches you on the street and says, "Excuse me, sir. Do you speak English? Will you do me a great favor? At our shop, we have an important document that we have translated into English. Would you be so kind as to tell us whether it is grammatically correct? It will take only a moment." Being a considerate traveler, you agree to help. You are taken to his uncle's store and wind up spending the next hour being shown gems, carpets, or carvings while waiting for the document that may or may not appear. The whole thing is a ruse to get you into the store. Hardly the end of the world, just a little off-putting.

Another approach begins when a pleasant looking middle-aged man asks for help finding his way. He produces a map and asks you to take a look. Get deeply involved in his map and something you own may be taking a trip without you.

Morning price. You are offered a special "morning price" because you are someone's first potential sale of the day. In the past, it was considered good luck for a merchant to break the ice with an early sale, so they'd drop their price to make it. The superstition may be gone but the come-on lingers. No problem, as long as you don't really believe it's either a first sale or a special price just for you.

Times two. Somewhat less amusing is the "times two" hustle. The local vehicle driver (taxi, collectivo, rickshaw, whatever) agreed on a price to take you and your friend to the soccer match. When you arrive, he demands double the price you agreed to, insisting that the price quoted was for one. In your generosity, you may think there was a misunderstanding. There wasn't. To keep discussions like these on an even footing, always remove your gear from the vehicle before commencing the payment ritual. Sometimes it helps to take out paper and pen and ostentatiously take down the driver's license number. Mention the tourist police. Move the discussion off the street and into a store or hotel lobby. Whatever your style in handling matters like this, actually losing your temper could turn by-standers against you.

> Regardless of the circumstances, losing your temper is never a good idea.

Keep perspective. The small amount of money involved does not justify spoiling your day or risking escalation into a serious dispute. I'm not suggesting that you routinely give in; just that you acknowledge that taxi drivers (a) are not representative of the rest of the population, (b) live a pretty hard life, and (c) still don't earn very much. About the best you can do is try to reach clear agreement before you get into the vehicle, then stay calm if a disagreement arises. If you want help, ask a shopkeeper to call a police officer.

Post office. A particularly annoying form of petty theft occurs when a postal clerk accepts your postcards, planning all the while to steam off the uncancelled stamps and turn your postcards into wall decorations. This trick happens all over, but Kathmandu is notorious for it. What to do? Ask that the stamps be hand-canceled. Don't accept a promise; stand there until you see it happen. They know the reason for your request. It's part of the game.

Be reluctant to give a hotel desk clerk money in return for her promise to buy stamps and post your mail. I know better than to create such a temptation, yet recently did just that. Is six months too soon to expect post cards to arrive from Buenos Aires?

Pigeon drop. This threadbare hustle is alive and working around the world. Someone "finds" some money, a watch or anything else of value (in Rio, the favorite is a fat book of lottery tickets) on the street just as you pass by and calls it to your attention. Get ready: the curtain is going up. You are being invited to participate in a masterful performance. Before long, as a condition to sharing in some great benefit, you are asked to put up some "good faith" money. That may sound ridiculous as you read it, but for many people it somehow seems to make sense when the scam is underway. Go along for a while if you want some amusement and can stay in a public place, but be ready to fold the hand fast.

Take my picture, mister? The teenager walks up with a smile, hands his camera to you, then retreats a dozen yards away to stand in front of a tourist attraction. Always a good neighbor, you snap his picture. He not only doesn't come back for his camera, he sprints off into the distance. Puzzled, you turn around—to discover that his accomplice has slipped up behind you and disappeared with your daypack, camera, or whatever you set down to do the favor. After all, you were chosen precisely *because* you were carrying something you'd have to set down. His camera? It's defunct or a $10 cheapo.

I may write an entire book devoted to *Street Scams Around the World*. Not only would it help travelers avoid problems but it would reveal the true creativity of the human mind. As you have experiences you'd like to see in the book, I hope you'll let me know.

Pickpockets

Pickpockets abound the world around. Some are five-thumbed fumblers while others are such proficient artists they can score on anyone. Fortunately for travelers, Fagin's descendants tend to concentrate in predictable places and strike at predictable times. Like the bank robber Willie Sutton, pickpockets go where the money is. Knowing those places and times, you're better prepared to foil their quick hands. For example, travelers not alert for pickpockets in Rio, Tangier, and Saigon would do better to mail their money to a charity and stay home.

In Italy, several cute young girls approached four elderly tourists. The smallest youngster shyly held up a ragged piece of paper covered with drawings she said were hers. The tourists smiled, clucked approvingly, and leaned forward to admire her work. The other cute little girls, also very talented with their hands, busied themselves by picking the pockets and purses of the four art-lovers. Those thefts were not even discovered until the group got back to the hotel.

One spring afternoon, strolling along the Vltava River in Prague, a man in a well-pressed suit with an expensive topcoat draped over his right arm, walked up to me. Given his distinguished appearance, I was a little surprised when he said, "Sir, you would like to change money?" He named an exchange rate substantially above the normal black market rate. Since money-changers' rates stay within a fairly tight range, his offer immediately raised my guard. He stepped closer, speaking in a quiet, almost confidential tone. I never felt his right hand, concealed beneath his topcoat, as it slithered into the side pocket of my pants but, because I was expecting his move, I caught his wrist in a tight grip. We stared at one another. When I let go, he slowly backed off then walked briskly away. His gimmick was to distract me by arousing my greed, diverting my attention. Later that same afternoon, I was walking back along the river and spotted the same man standing close to a young woman. I yelled and ran toward them, calling out a warning. The man strode away looking disgusted. I imagine he still patrols the river every afternoon.

Pickpockets seek easy marks. Favorite targets include obvious green-horns, people wearing or carrying something expensive, and anyone whose attention can be distracted or who's had too much to drink. Here are some examples of where they flourish.

- Walking through the colorful market, you stop in the midst of a jostling crowd to watch the camel auction. Later you start to pay for a carved bone necklace and . . . guess what? When in a crowd, especially when your attention is attracted to things around you, leave valuables behind or in your money belt. If you're carrying your daypack, keep it locked or in front of your body. Instead of carrying your camera or purse hanging off one shoulder, wear the strap diagonally across your chest. Keep your hand on it, not on the strap. If you're wearing a jacket, keep your purse under the jacket.

  A fanny pack extends the same invitation as a dangling purse. Since it's almost impossible to protect, it should never contain your valuables. If you wear a fanny pack, a thief doesn't know what's in it so it may serve as a lure anyway.

  No experienced traveler carries a wallet in an insecure back pants pocket unless it's a decoy to send a pickpocket on his way. A front shirt or pants pocket that can be buttoned, snapped, safety-pinned, or zippered is more secure. A Velcro closure helps but will yield to a determined hand. When I carry my wallet in a front pants pocket, I stick my comb into it or put several rubber bands around it, either of which make it more difficult to pull from the pocket. Whenever you take your wallet out of your pocket, it's vulnerable.

- Every time you pay for something, you show a pickpocket where you keep your money. That gives him a big edge—and gives you another reason to keep most of your cash separate from the money you need immediately. Keep telling yourself: if you put it where they can get it, they will get it.

- Some tourist destinations post a sign that warns tourists to be wary of pickpockets. The result is similar to what happened when Sherlock Holmes used an alarm of fire to trick a lady into revealing where she'd hidden a valuable letter. When she heard the alarm, she promptly ran to save the letter—and he had her. Upon reading the warning sign, most people touch their wallet to be sure it's still there. If it is, both they and the pickpocket now know it. Similarly, when someone shouts "Purse snatcher!" almost everyone will touch his or her valuables. Then the thief's accomplice begins his harvest.

- Taking your belongings becomes child's play, sometimes literally, through skillful use of diversions. Someone "accidentally" bumps you fairly hard, but a bystander is there to keep you from falling. The hands of one or the other are about to lighten your load. A drunk lurches into you, maybe drops a bottle at your feet; a deformed beggar clutches your clothes; a loud noise or a fight attracts the attention of the crowd. In the jostling as the crowd presses forward to see what's happening, wallets find a new home.

  As a group of colorfully dressed teenage girls runs up to several tourists, offering trinkets for sale, one drops her handful of coins to the cobblestones. Responding to her cry of alarm, the tourists obligingly start picking them up. As they help, they're stripped as quickly as if by piranhas.

  Sometimes it's a team effort. A person stands behind a card table on the sidewalk, demonstrating sleight-of-hand tricks. As the crowd watches his hands, the other half of the team, the real expert, explores their pockets.

  What should you do? Protect yourself from being a victim by accepting a very simple premise: a skilled pickpocket can get whatever you keep in your pockets or purse. Your response? Keep in your pockets only what you can afford to lose.

Sneak Thieves

- In many restaurants and bars, you're vulnerable to sneak thieves. You set your camera and daypack on the chair next to you and when you look again, they're gone. Instead, put your stuff on the table in front of you or on your lap. If you put your daypack and camera on the floor, put your foot through the straps. Use the chair next to you only if it's shielded by your body, out of reach of a snatch-and-run thief. If a couple of people sit near to you and begin to argue loudly, watch your gear.

- Many of us enter a semi-hypnotized state as we enter the fascinating experiences of the day in our journals or share experiences with our friends via postcards. In that stuporous condition, we're as defenseless as a deer on the road staring at oncoming headlights. You needn't abandon your literary efforts. Just tuck your goodies out of sight.

- When you're exchanging a large amount of money, write down the amount you want and show it to the clerk rather than announcing it to listening ears behind you. Put your money securely away before leaving the bank. Cornelia, a German botanist friend, exchanged her marks for Madagascar francs, which she stuffed into her breast pocket as she walked down the steps of the bank. Quick as a trout striking a lure, a guy reached over her shoulder from behind and left her poorer but wiser.

- In Lima, during a very early morning walk to catch a bus to Nazca, Peru, a middle-aged woman approached and pointed to my daypack. I looked over my shoulder and saw a patch of nasty-looking yellow goo on the side of the pack. She produced some toilet paper and offered to help me clean it off. Not wanting to miss the bus, I decided to wait and clean it off at the station. I thanked her and kept going. A block or two farther on, a stocky man caught up with me and pointed. He, too, offered toilet paper. This apparently coincidental profusion of toilet paper registered even on my sluggish early-morning mind. I stepped away from him, just as several young men emerged from the shadows and converged on me. As they neared, I bolted for a nearby church. They followed me inside, but stopped short of the front pew where I was surrounded by people attending Mass. After a few minutes, the men drifted away to play their tricks elsewhere.

  I mention this experience as an example of diversion. The goo had been lathered on my pack by someone who was trying to get me to stop, take the daypack off my back, perhaps even hand it to the Good Samaritan to clean. Within seconds the wolves would have swooped down and that pack would have had a new owner. This particular trick and its sophisticated variations are on their way to achieving classic status around the world. A couple of years after it happened to me in Lima, local thugs, armed with mustard or ketchup, began using it at Kennedy Airport against Japanese tourists.

- Sneak thieves love trains. An old woman in an alpaca shawl stands outside your window offering a carved stone replica of an Inca figure. As soon as she has your attention, her accomplice runs down the aisle and scoops up your camera. Between cars, she tosses it to a buddy. From then on, you'll be buying picture postcards. You can prevent it so easily by knowing what to expect. You'll know you're a seasoned traveler if, when a distraction occurs to your right, you look first to your left.

The long list above may seem pretty complete—but it's not. As you travel, you'll come across variations or even something new. I hope you'll share them with me so I can pass them on to other travelers.

Muggers

Although theft encountered by tourists is almost always nonviolent, there are a few places in which theft by force is not uncommon. I'm thinking of

Maputo (Mozambique), Kinshasa (Zaire), Tangier, Lima, Bogotá, some beaches in Spain and, increasingly, Rio de Janeiro. Even in those places, I consider the risk low enough that I won't skip them—but I am extra careful.

How to Avoid the Problem

As always, preparation and common sense are your greatest protection. If you're new in town, ask the manager of your hotel about areas to avoid, or times of day when there might be increased risk. Don't make yourself a target by having too much to drink too far from your hotel, wearing an expensive watch or ring, flashing wads of cash, or hanging around where people make you feel creepy. Pay attention to your intuition. Don't walk down dark streets. Take a taxi if you feel uncomfortable.

Don't act bewildered or lost. In other words, don't behave like a first-day tourist. Any mugger is going to choose the easiest and wealthiest looking target, and that's not the person striding along with an air of confidence or the person drinking his nightcap at the hotel.

If you feel someone walking toward you looks suspicious, walk in another direction. Walk in the center of the sidewalk, away from alleyways and parked vehicles.

If a male traveler decides to woo a local woman he's met in a bar, he'd be wise to keep an eye on his drinks (among other things). Otherwise he may meet some new friends on the way home.

A recent study indicated that the chances of being mugged are reduced by 70 percent just by walking with one other person; by 90 percent if with two people. Makes sense to me.

How to React

If you're walking in a high-risk zone and are approached by someone seeking something (the time or whatever), step away and casually go to "yellow alert." That's a sad commentary on human relations, but a good way to avoid a problem.

Decide how you'll respond if confronted by someone who looks as if he's armed and/or willing to use force. Stay as calm as you can. Try to make the other person relax a little. Act self-possessed, but don't argue or show anger. Cooperate and disengage as quickly as possible. The idea is to escape without violence. Depending on the situation, it may be best to drop or throw your wallet or jewelry or whatever on the ground, then back away. If he stoops to pick it up, be ready to flee.

I've heard a suggestion to carry a second, or dummy, wallet with just a few dollars in it to surrender to a mugger. That may be a way to protect another wallet loaded with cash, but you shouldn't have that kind of money in a wallet anyway. Even if you did, would you want to risk your life to protect it?

If an assailant demands that you come with him, it's only to give him greater advantage. Do not go with him. Pretend you don't understand. Act like you think he's joking. If that doesn't work, yell, throw your wallet, and run in the opposite direction.

If you feel you must fight, use every weapon you have: keys spread between your knuckles, a pen, or a bottle; even a daypack loaded with books swings a lot of weight. Fight all out! Yell for help as loudly as you can. Shout "Fire!" Bite, pull, try to break a finger, go for the genitals (a grip is better than a knee). Act like you've gone crazy.

There are very few places where someone will threaten a traveler's personal safety unless the traveler

- takes foolish risks,
- gets involved with people of a type he would avoid at home,
- uses drugs or alcohol to excess in public,
- doesn't do his basic research and puts himself in places he should have avoided,
- loses his temper and provokes a confrontation,
- values his possessions too highly, protecting them by risking his safety,
- behaves in ways inappropriate to the culture.

Hotel Security

Ask other travelers about a hotel's security. You can learn a lot about hotel security before you ever walk through the door. Hotels that have earned reputations for poor security are sometimes noted in the guidebooks. Ask other travelers about the hotel you're considering. Notice whether there are people hanging out in front of the hotel who you wouldn't want to pass after dark. A shabby lobby may be a clue that the owners make their money less by pleasing guests than by ripping them off.

While checking in, keep in touch with your gear. When you go to look at a room, take your bag along unless you're confident there's no risk in leaving it untended.

Since the hotel staff and other guests will see the register after you sign in, a woman may be well advised to use initials.

Don't let anyone see your valuables as you check in.

An ordinary door lock is almost worthless for security purposes. What television bad guys do to locked doors with a credit card also happens in real life. Even if it bars the general public, the lock on your door won't keep the hotel staff out. One security expert estimates that 85 percent of hotel room theft is committed by dishonest hotel employees. Besides, who knows how many room keys are floating around in the hands of former staff, or former guests for that matter?

If someone knocks on the door claiming to be a hotel employee, call the desk to confirm if you have the slightest reason to be concerned.

I assume that someone will be in my room while I'm out and that I can't outsmart anyone but a thief-in-training by hiding my valuables in some cranny. Therefore, I lock in my pack anything I'd rather not lose. When I have reason for concern, I lock the pack itself to something secure. Fortunately, most hotel staff members, baggage handlers, bus drivers, and the like don't have lock-picking skills. Even a tiny lock requires forcible entry, which you can spot immediately, and many people won't steal when they think you'll notice right away that you've been ripped off. Locks also communicate that you're not a goose passively waiting to be plucked.

Assume someone will be in your room while you are out and prepare accordingly.

For effective security in a hotel room, you need a dead bolt or a chain-and-slide bolt. Even a hasp on which you can use a padlock will work. The Portabolt door lock (800-999-3030; $19.95) attaches easily between any door and its frame to provide security similar to a dead bolt.

Some travelers carry Travel Guard, a battery-operated alarm about the size of a pager that combines a detachable flashlight and alarm clock with a smoke detector and vibration sensor ($50 from Immcon; 800-829-5044). If the door moves while Travel Guard is hanging on a doorknob, an 85-decibel alarm goes off. When you pull a pin out of the Companion Personal Alarm (also from Immcon), a 110-decibel siren sounds.

Radio Shack sells a combination personal alarm/motion detector that has a built-in flashlight ($14.95). Safety Zone (800-999-3030) offers a wide variety of travel safety items. If you prefer low-tech, jam a simple plastic wedge under the door or brace a chair under the handle. If there's no way of securing the door, change rooms or hotels unless the circumstances convince you there is no risk at all.

A thief doesn't always politely enter a room from the hallway, so don't build a Maginot Line at the door only to forget the windows and balcony door. Can the windows be locked? Are there bars on them? Could anyone get into your room by climbing through the window? If an arm can reach through the bars, keep your gear well out of reach. Lock the windows when you leave. If the hotel rises higher than two stories, a room on the third to the sixth floor at least puts you above outside-entry thieves with a fear of heights.

Hotel smoke detectors are almost nonexistent in many parts of the world. If that concerns you, consider the Traveler Portable Smoke Detector, a palm-sized detector that emits an 85-decibel alarm (call 800-962-4943; $24.50). If you leave the key in the lock when you go to sleep, you won't have to search for it if there's a fire. If you hear a fire alarm, touch the door knob. If it's hot, call the desk or see if you can escape out the window. If trapped in your room, use a wet towel to block the space under the door, shut off fans or air conditioners, and try to signal from the window. If the knob is cool, take your money belt, lock the door behind you (if you recall the little boy who cried "Wolf!" you know there's not always fire where there's an alarm), and head for the fire exit. Don't try to use an elevator to escape from a fire. If there's smoke, crawl under it.

If there's a Do Not Disturb sign in the room, I may hang it on the door knob when I go out to mislead anyone wandering the hallway. I usually don't leave my room key with the desk clerk when I leave for the day. That won't keep the staff out of my room, but it does keep the presence of my key in the box from advertising to others that I'm away. It also keeps passersby from reaching across the counter and snatching the key in the clerk's absence. Key control is often a joke.

Make sure the safe truly is.

What about leaving your valuables in the hotel safe as you start on a ten-day trek in the tropical heat? Good idea, except that not everything called a safe is what you think of as a safe. Be sure the safe is someplace secure to which only the owner or manager has access. Otherwise, the "safe" might turn out to be a desk drawer or a space under the cash register drawer.

An Englishwoman in Zanzibar gave all her money to the obliging desk clerk to put in the hotel safe. When the day came to catch a boat back to the mainland, she went to reclaim her money. The clerk denied having received anything from her. The manager shrugged his shoulders. That's when she realized she had no receipt.

Present your valuables in a sealed envelope with your name written across the flap. A reliable safe-keeping operation should have a printed receipt form. If your hotel doesn't, get a written receipt from the manager or owner. If they try to evade giving you one, don't leave your valuables. Think twice about staying in the place at all.

Suppose you want to leave your bag behind while you take a trek through the rain forest or a side trip to the beach. Leave it with the hotel manager if you can, with instructions to release it only to you. Ask for a receipt. Find out if it will be locked up, rather than left behind the front desk day and night. Even in a storage room, I lock my bag to something with my bike chain lock. Since your belongings will be stored with those of other travelers, it's not impossible that something of yours might be picked up by someone else if not secured. When you return, check the contents. When the hotel staff sees that you are treating security of your bag seriously, they'll be more inclined to do so as well.

Being anxious about safety and security would be a waste of time and detract from the pleasure of your trip. Instead, don your magic cloak. The routines become automatic. I've never lost a single item to a thief as I've traveled and I believe most knowledgeable travelers can say the same.

LOSING YOUR VALUABLES

Lost Airline Ticket

Treat an airline ticket as carefully as if it were cash. If it leaves your possession unexpectedly, call or go to the nearest office of the issuing airline and submit a Lost Ticket Application. This process will be much easier if you know the ticket number, flight numbers and dates, and the amount of the fare. Since few of us memorize this stuff, it helps to have a copy of the ticket along. It will cost you time and money if you have to call home to your travel agent to get this information.

One U.S. airline states clearly on its ticket that it will give no refund for a lost ticket. Others charge a fee of $50 to determine whether your ticket has been used. If it has, you get nothing. If it hasn't, the ticket may be reinstated or you may get a credit for the price, minus the search fee, against the price of a ticket for some future flight. However, you may be asked to sign a form agreeing to pay for the replacement ticket if someone uses the lost original. The message here is to act fast before someone can use or exchange the stolen ticket. At best, airlines typically wait ninety days or more before issuing a refund.

If you lose your ticket while overseas, you'll probably have to buy a new ticket for the rest of your route. That would be very bad news because you would lose whatever discount you got on the original ticket (e.g., APEX, round trip).

To avoid the whole problem, keep that ticket safe in your money belt and keep a copy stashed somewhere else. Actually, the possibility of the loss is another reason to buy plane tickets as you go. You can't lose what you're not carrying.

Lost Credit Card/ATM Card

If a credit card disappears, call immediately to cancel it. The telephone numbers when calling from overseas are as follows: American Express (919) 668-5271; MasterCard (314) 275-6690; Visa (410) 581-9994; and Discover (801) 568-0205. When a card is stolen, report it to the police and get a copy of the report. If fraudulent charges show up on your bill later, you must notify the card issuer in writing within sixty days of receiving the bill to limit your loss to $50.

If your ATM card disappears, notify the issuing bank and get a new card. You are only liable for up to $50 for fraudulent use of your card if you report the loss within two days. Some banks will hold you liable for as much as $500 after that.

Lost Passport

According to *Money* magazine, only three out of every one thousand travelers have their passports stolen. That doesn't count the ones who lose them in various creative ways. How to prevent it? Keep your passport in your money belt when it's not in use. If you have to let it out of your possession, such as when turning it over to a hotel clerk to register with the police, get a receipt. Never leave town without checking that you've tucked it safely away.

Since having a copy of the first two pages of the lost passport greatly speeds replacement, make three copies of the first two pages of your passport before leaving home. Put one in your money belt, put one in your luggage, and leave one with someone who can fax it to you.

If you lose your passport, get a police report and take it, along with four two-by-two-inch photographs, to your embassy or consulate. They will re-

Make copies of your passport to facilitate replacing it.

quire a copy of your birth certificate. If you haven't brought it along but have left a copy with someone who can fax it you, you're in great shape. If you overlooked that detail, they may accept an affidavit from someone else (who must be able to prove their own American citizenship) vouching for your citizenship. The replacement passport will be good for only one year but when you arrive home, you can trade it in for a new permanent passport.

Lost Luggage

A traveler can lose luggage anywhere, but it's at the airport where we most often put it out of our sight and control, trusting that it will rejoin us thousands of miles away. And that's a reasonable expectation since, according to the National Institute for Aviation Research, only one out of every two hundred bags checked with major U.S. airlines is reported lost. Whether you consider those odds acceptable may depend on whether you've ever been the "one."

Rather than focusing on ways to be reunited with your luggage after it's lost, follow a routine to keep it from getting away in the first place. Whether you're traveling by plane, train, or bus, check in well ahead of departure time, make sure your bag is marked for the correct destination, and remove any old destination tags. Take off the shoulder strap and zip away the backpack harness so the bag won't get hung up in baggage-moving mechanisms. Watch it as far as you can to ensure it is put on the right vehicle.

If you take a bag aboard a plane and there's no room for it, don't just hand it over to an attendant. Take out any valuables, then get a claim check for it. Be ready to collect it promptly at your destination.

Suppose it's not there? First in frustration then with mounting concern, you search for it as other passengers drift away. Check the lobby area and baggage storage room in case your bag arrived before you did. If it's not there, fill in a form describing the bag and its contents. Put the form and a copy of your ticket and baggage claim check in the hands of the most senior person you can find. Get that person's name and keep a copy of the form. If you give up your claim check, get a receipt.

Tell them that your name and address are on a luggage tag securely attached to your bag and that your itinerary is inside. Let them know where to reach you while you're waiting for the bag and where to deliver it when they find it. Motivate the carrier to find that bag.

If the delay is more than a few hours, they should reimburse you for reasonable expenses, such as basic clothing and toiletries. If the carrier's representative doesn't offer to do so, ask for authorization before making purchases, but do so in a courteous tone that takes it for granted. Keep receipts as a basis for reimbursement. If the lost bag delays your onward progress, ask the carrier to pay for a hotel. After you leave the terminal, call with regular inquiries.

It's reasonable to think that if a carrier lost your bag and couldn't find it, they'd pay for it and its contents. Reasonable, yes; reality, no. Under regulations which the airlines were active in drafting, their liability to you is very limited. The maximum reimbursement is $1,250 (which may soon be raised to $1,850) on a domestic flight and $9.07 per pound for checked luggage ($400 for unchecked luggage) on an international flight. In practice, rather than record the weight of each bag, international airlines assume the maximum (thirty kilos) and consider the limit of liability to be $640.

The airlines reimburse you on the basis of the *depreciated* value of your luggage and its contents, not replacement value (what it will cost you to replace what they lost). Then they unfurl a list of items excluded from coverage altogether: currency, cameras, camcorders, expensive jewelry, medication, and similar items. If that would be a problem, ask the airline in advance about Excess Valuation Insurance. The cost is from $1 to $2 per $100 of coverage up to $5000. Note that these policies may exclude something you want to cover: breakables, antiques, musical instruments, art, and computers.

Your household insurance or personal effects policy may cover whatever loss is not covered by the airline's insurance. Further, that reimbursement may be based on replacement value, which is in your favor. See "travel and health insurance" in Chapter 5.

Even when it's clear a bag has departed for luggage heaven, the airline may still take three to twelve weeks to reimburse you. In other words, carry your valuables in your money belt, your camera in your daypack, and nothing irreplaceable in your luggage.

14

Woman on Her Own

> All travel is a quest, conscious or
> unconscious searching for something
> that is lacking in our lives or ourselves.
> — Freya Stark

Who hasn't heard of a woman who was pinched on a bus in Rome or hassled in Morocco by some creep who just wouldn't get the picture? Fear of sexual harassment deters too many women from traveling on their own. It's a fear with some basis, but it shouldn't, in the opinion of many women travelers, keep anyone at home.

Thousands of women travel independently, and successfully, every year. Most travel in groups of two or three, but a great many travel solo. Since knowledge routs paranoia and controls risk, this chapter will discuss what a woman alone or with other women can expect and how she can minimize or eliminate potential problems.

Many women praise the benefits of traveling alone, most of which are the same as those treasured by any independent traveler. However, one benefit is unique. It's easy for a woman on her own to escape stereotypical male-female roles, including standard divisions of responsibilities. Responsible for coping, her self-confidence grows. The ways in which she interacts with people, locals as well as other travelers, are different from when she's in the company of a man.

The most common problem a woman may have to deal with is the hassle of low-grade sexual harassment. It doesn't happen everywhere, but there are certain countries in which a woman should be prepared for being hassled by local males. The hassling may consist of a suggestive comment, a call, a whistle, a touch, or more aggressive intimidation—anything to test the woman's interest. This problem seems most persistent in certain countries where there's a strong religious presence—places such as Spain, Morocco,

Italy, Sicily, Greece, Egypt, Turkey, Saudi Arabia, Oman, Yemen, Pakistan, and Mexico.

There seems to be a relationship between offensive male behavior and generally repressed, unrealistic attitudes about relationships with women. In some countries, men are raised with the idea that women are subordinate; women are expected to bend to the male will. Trash television has further shaped male attitudes about Western women, especially when they see foreign women act in ways that would result in anything from ostracism to stoning in their own society. Soap operas don't do female travelers any favors. With this background, some men feel it's their right to make advances, and they expect them to be welcomed. These attitudes are diminishing, but they're not gone yet.

And what of concerns of bodily harm? Statistics show that rape is far more common in industrialized nations, such as the United States, than in underdeveloped countries. Unfortunately, that's a little misleading. A female traveler is more visible than local women on whom the statistics are based, and she's likely to be penalized by attitudes of local men toward Western women. Further, when a woman is in an unfamiliar culture, she may be unaware of behavior that might be taken as provocative by local males. She's also likely to be less knowledgeable about dangerous areas she should avoid.

HOW TO TRAVEL SAFELY

A woman who hasn't traveled alone may ask, "Will I be safe?" The answer is "Yes!" or at least, "Yes, if . . ." Women travelers are not obliged to free men from their cultural ruts, but there are many things a woman can do to insulate herself from unwanted attention. Here are some suggestions, many from women who have traveled alone.

- Observe how local women dress and try to follow that pattern. In cultures that retain old traditions, a local woman covers most of her body with clothing and tends to stay out of public view. In that context, a female traveler who wears tight shorts and a provocative T-shirt will quickly become conscious of the effect she's having, attracting some observers and offending others. Loose-fitting clothing that covers arms and legs is usually appropriate. It's easy to copy local customs, even without wearing local-style clothes.
- Minimize eye contact with men. If a friendly smile can be misinterpreted, a wink can start a war. Dark sunglasses are an excellent way to avoid eye contact.
- Common courtesies such as thanking a man for opening a door for you can lead to being followed. An impassive nod may have to be sufficient.

- Pay your own way so that neither of you feels that one of you is indebted.
- Drinking alcohol or smoking cigarettes in public may be considered provocative. It's not a question of right or wrong; it's a case of "When in Rome . . ."
- Many women elect to hook-up with other women travelers when passing through a zone of possible annoyance. Others ask a male to accompany them for a while, being up-front about the reason. A little hand holding in public goes a long way. A show of a relationship discourages unwelcome attention, even more so abroad than at home. Even an imaginary boyfriend or husband who is "on his way over" can help.
- Don't let a strange man touch you, except during a handshake or when giving help you've requested. Even an apparently neutral touch may be a way of testing your limits. In Europe, among other places, a man may take advantage of a crowded place to press against a woman in an offensive way. The consensus is that she should raise hell, pushing him away with a shout. At the same time, be prepared to accept being squashed in a crowd as part of travel.
- If a man forces his attentions on you, don't just shake your head, smile, or say "No, thank you." Rather than behaving in an apologetic way, respond immediately and directly, saying "No!" or "Stop!" loudly and firmly, preferably in the local language since you may not be understood in English. Frown fiercely and let bystanders know there's a problem, calling on them for help if necessary. Your plea should be addressed to one person (another woman is best) rather than to the crowd. Tears help to engage bystanders. Being firm and determined is better than being rough or violent.
- In a new town, ask the desk clerk, manager, or owner of your lodging to identify parts of town to avoid. Ask for suggestions of restaurants where a woman traveler will feel comfortable. At the same time, be cautious not to let a male member of the hotel staff think you are flirting.
- In restaurants, reading a book or writing in a journal helps discourage men from approaching.
- Keep your hotel room door locked. Otherwise, in some places, staff people with legitimate business walk right in. Be alert when a male member of the hotel staff enters your hotel room. Stand up. Let your body language show that you're on guard. Watch him. If a problem develops, call the front desk. If there's no phone, step into the hall and shout for help. Don't admit anyone until you're satisfied about who they are.

- Don't accept gifts from strangers. That sounds obvious but some offers may be superficially appealing, such as taking you snorkeling, hiking, surfing, or on some other attractive local adventure.

  After two years in the Peace Corps in East Africa, Luanna met a young local man at a restaurant in a beach resort and accepted his offer to spend the day with him on his sailing dhow. She was cautious enough to insist that they not go alone. "No problem," he said. "My mother lives in a village just down the coast. We'll sail down and pick her up." No village. No mother. Bad trip! If you feel a need for a chaperone, start the trip with one. Don't be lured beyond the range of help.
- On trains, try to find a compartment occupied by a family or by several women.
- On buses, sit next to a woman rather than a man.
- Beaches tend to attract men who may become a problem.
- If something in the environment is making you feel uncomfortable, hire a taxi instead of walking.
- Some women travel with a fake wedding ring. If a conversation becomes overly personal, they refer to an imaginary husband, perhaps producing a photograph to back up the story. Note that wearing an expensive-looking ring could present temptation of a different kind.
- If a situation is becoming uncomfortable, mention that you have a specific communicable venereal disease.
- I've yet to meet anyone who has used Mace, but it may offer a feeling of security in an extreme situation.
- Don't be drawn into discussion of controversial topics, especially male/female relations.
- Be wary of any local lothario who prowls around tourist attractions. He's experienced in approaching foreign women and has had plenty of opportunities to develop his "line." He may say he wants a chance to practice his English, or he may pretend to be a guide—anything to get you into a conversation. If you don't want his attention, don't answer even the first question.
- Study self-defense before leaving home. The self-confidence you project as a result of this training sends a signal to many who might otherwise approach you.

Resources

As a starting point for learning the extent to which females may be hassled in any country, consult a guidebook and ask other travelers. *Women Travel: Adventures, Advice and Experience*, edited by Miranda Davies and Natania Jansz, discusses comparative levels of potential sexual harassment in seventy countries. One of Thalia Zepatos' objectives in writing *A Journey of One's Own: Uncommon Advice for the Independent Woman Traveler* was to help women feel more confident about traveling on their own.

Other useful resources for women travelers include *Travelin' Woman*, a monthly newsletter intended to help prepare women to travel; a newsletter called *Solo Travel International* (602-748-2092); *The Independent Woman's Guide to Europe* by Linda White; and *Traveler's Guide to Asian Customs and Manners* by Kevin Chambers. A free newsletter called *Women & Travel* lists even more books by and for women travelers (call 800-358-6013). American Express publishes a free guide entitled *Travel Smart for Women* (Women's Travel Booklet, American Express, 200 Vesey Street, New York, NY 10285).

The Bibliography contains many books by and about woman travelers.

Women's Wire, which commenced operation in 1994, is the first interactive computer network devoted to women's issues. In addition to a travel-related database and the opportunity to ask questions and exchange travel tips online, Women's Wire lists women interested in travel. Fifteen dollars a month entitles the subscriber to two hours online. Rates start at $2.50 per hour for usage beyond that. Call (415) 615-8989.

If a woman chooses not to be offended by stares, whistles, and comments in a few places, she can keep that part of her trip from being spoiled. It's a shame anyone should have to alter their behavior because of someone else's offensive actions, but a little caution prevents many problems. A few women travelers I know recall the exasperation and anger they felt at being made the center of attention when they wanted to be left alone. The majority, however, have felt safe and relaxed throughout their journeys.

15

Language

> The treachery of the phrase book ... is that you cannot begin to follow the answer to the question you've pronounced so beautifully—and worse still, your auditor now assumes you're fluent in Swahili.
> — Pico Iyer

The Peugot taxi dropped me off in front of a new, but already shabby, shopping mall somewhere near the center of Gaborone, capital of Botswana. I looked around for the only hotel in town listed in the guidebook as charging less than 65 pula, about $40, per night (I like the fact that the name of the currency in Botswana, which is 85 percent desert, is also the word for "water"). No hotel in sight. Despite knowing how to say almost nothing in the Setswana language, I knew it was time to ask for help.

Using my phrase book and exchanging gestures with a helpful soldier, I deduced that the hotel I was looking for had been torn down to make room for the shopping mall. The soldier pointed vigorously down the road. Always hopeful, I decided that he might be indicating another hotel. Of course, he was also pointing toward South Africa. There being no public transportation in sight and no other source of information, I swung my pack onto my back and started down the road.

Twenty minutes later, I arrived at a sleazy roadhouse. That the "DISCO" sign dwarfed the "Rooms 70 pula" sign communicated the management's priorities. After some spirited sign language to convey the thought that I was more interested at the moment in sleeping than dancing the night away, and wasn't looking for a companion, I was taken to a room modeled after a Devil's Island original. I figured the mosquito coils and the aerosol bug spray cans in the room would probably be useful since the cow standing outside the window had pushed her head into the room through the screen. Nevertheless, I had overcome a language barrier.

HOW TO OVERCOME A LANGUAGE BARRIER

Many people worry, and I was one of them, about the so-called language barrier. As it turns out, there's no reason to be intimidated. Not being able to speak a local language causes difficulties, but nothing insurmountable. Learning to pronounce twenty to one hundred words of vocabulary will get you through anywhere. Even a dozen words, an expressive face, and two hands go a long way. Okay, you could probably get along with nothing but English and your arms in a strait jacket.

In vast reaches of the world, you'll encounter English, Spanish, French, or Arabic. Even in Africa, with its multitude of local languages and dialects, you can communicate most places using one or another of those four languages, maybe adding a few words of Swahili. Given the limited language skills of many First World travelers, it's fortunate that the English planted their flag as widely as they did a few centuries ago. Since English is spoken in varying degrees around the world, at least for a few meters on either side of the tourist trails, you can often get by without learning anything else. But why do that? In return for a little effort, you make more friends and fewer mistakes. The first step is to overcome the embarrassment of stumbling in a language strange to your ears.

People like to hear you speaking their language. At least as important, you feel a part of the country and a sense of accomplishment when you master some of the basics of the language (well, "master" may be overstating it a bit).

No one need have language-related apprehension about traveling in Europe. If you studied a European language, no matter how long ago, you remember more than you think; at least your eyes will, if not your tongue. In **People like** metropolitan areas there may be a bit of a language gap in **to hear you speak** some budget hotels, restaurants, and taxis, but nothing **their language.** troublesome. If you need help, drop into an upscale hotel. You encounter plenty of people who speak English when you need it. Even in the countryside, local folks who don't speak English have seen enough foreigners to know what their needs are. Picture a non-English-speaking person entering a restaurant in your country. One way or another, he or she would be served something pleasing. So will you.

How to Learn

If you're out of school, how do you get started learning a new language? Simple: join a regular class, enroll in a school language lab, or hire a tutor. Take yourself to study in places as pleasant as Paris, Madrid, Antigua (Guatemala), or San Miguel de Allende (Mexico). Check out international travel-study programs through the American Institute for Foreign Study (203-869-9090), explore immersion classes in the United States at The Language Schools (802-388-3711), or gather information from the National Registration Center for Study Abroad on schools abroad offering language classes (414-278-0631).

Teach yourself using one of the series of good language books I mentioned in Chapter 2. The Passport Books *Just Enough Series* is one of the best. Small dictionaries are good. Take a look at the very useful *BBC Phrase Books* (also Passport Books) that include built-in dictionaries. The better guidebooks include a section of basic vocabulary and phrases. Laminated cards (four-by-eight inches) provide frequently used words and phrases in a handy, practically weightless form. Don't forget handheld electronic translators. Besides being helpful, they endlessly entertain bystanders.

Dorrance Publishing Company (643 Smithfield Street, Pittsburgh, PA 15222; 800-788-7654) publishes the *Traveler's Pictorial Communication Guide* ($6.95) based on the principle of, as they put it, "One picture is worth ten thousand words." This book is packed with illustrations of clothing, menu items, lodging, transport, various services (e.g., barbers, medical help), and many other aspects of daily life. You point to the picture—and the idea gets across. *The Wordless Travel Book* (Ten Speed Press, 1996, $4.95) and a book titled *Point It* work the same way: just flip open the book, point at an icon—and you're communicating.

For a language in which pronunciation is difficult, reading alone may not be adequate. Hear the language spoken on cassettes, records, or videotapes. Let your computer help through CD-ROMs and foreign language software. Here are some of the better choices: Berlitz Think 'n' Talk (about $200), Learn to Speak 4.0 (about $180), PictureIt! (About $70), The Rosetta Stone (about $400), and Video Linguist (about $100).

It's easy to learn basic words by listening to daily conversation, pointing to things, and asking questions. Pronouncing words as you would in your own language may not be correct in another language. Listen carefully to how local people say things. If you use the same pronunciation, they'll have some meaning. Otherwise, you'll earn some blank looks.

Connect conversation with actions. Learn more than the basic five or ten words that most travelers learn. As soon as you enter a new country, make a list of useful words, the words of daily commerce. Practice that new vocabulary out loud without letting fear of mistakes slow you down. Don't get hung up on verb tenses.

What to Learn First

Here are some key words and phrases that every traveler needs to know. Rather than fumbling through a phrase book, write down or memorize these appropriate words and phrases.

- greetings and expressions of courtesy such as hello, good day, goodbye, please, thank you, pardon me, "my name is . . . ," and "what is your name?"

- yes and no
- directions (few phrases are as useful as "where is . . .")
- toilet (if you ask for the washroom, bathroom, rest room, or little boy's or girl's room, you may mystify the listener)
- food-related words (including, "May I have the bill, please?")
- lodging-related words ("Do you have a room with two beds?")
- transport words (including airport, bus station, train station, subway station, and gasoline)
- phrases for bargaining in the marketplace ("How much is . . ." and "That's too much.")
- personal pronouns
- numbers
- time of day
- the verbs "to be," "to have," and "to go," when combined with personal pronouns (I am, he is, etc.)
- pleas for help such as "I don't understand," "Please speak more slowly," "Help!" "Go away!" and "I need a doctor."

There are some sure tests to show whether you've become operational in a language. If the bus to your destination is leaving a busy station in ten minutes and you can buy a ticket and find the bus in time—you're a linguist. When you can make small jokes in a language—you're a linguist.

WHERE TO GET INFORMATION AND ASSISTANCE

If your trusty phrase book fails you, it's a setback, nothing more. It merely means it's time to get some help. That's easy if you know where to look.

- Look for young people, on the theory they might be students studying English.
- Expensive or Western clothing suggests that a person may be well-educated or in business, either of which may mean some training in English.
- Many countries have excellent tourist information centers whose addresses are listed in good guidebooks. In most countries, someone on the staff speaks a little English.
- Talk with local travel agents to find out what's going on in the area and transportation options. Let them know what you want and ask for suggestions. It seems as if "for only $5 . . ." someone's cousin's son is always willing to give you a lift up to Portillo* the next morning.
- Your embassy or consulate can help. A considerate staff person in the

---

* *Portillo*. North of Santiago, Chile, Portillo offers the best skiing in South America.

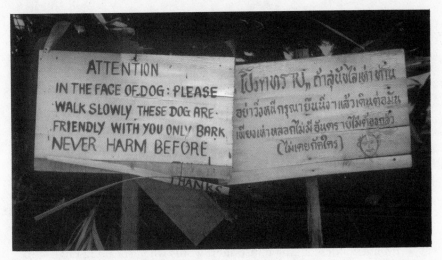

English is not always the easiest language. Chiang Mai, Thailand.

Citizens Service Section of a consulate may give you useful information on a person-to-person basis.

- Drop into the local office of the United States Information Service (USIS), the overseas network of the USIA. The typical USIS office has travel advisories, summaries of international news, and a great library. The air-conditioned libraries of various USIS offices are fine sanctuaries from tropical heat.

- The staff at your hotel can provide helpful information, especially if you develop a friendly relationship with them. They can direct you to banks, shops, doctors, tourist attractions, and restaurants, or find you a cab, opera tickets, a boat for your snorkeling trip, or even a mountain guide. They can tell you fair prices for local transport, popular types of clothing, and almost anything else. Of course, price information should be taken with a grain of salt since it may be biased toward the home team. If your own hotel can't help, try an upscale or chain hotel. Either the staff will be able to communicate in your language or there will be a travel agent in-house who can.

- Draw on other travelers. When you meet someone who has recently visited a coming stop on your itinerary, ask about accommodations, restaurants, transport, exchange rates, everything. The guidebook I use in Indonesia highly recommended a small hotel on the island of Ternate. That's where I planned to stay until I talked with a Dane who had stayed there a week earlier. He said the hotel was as nice as the guidebook said, except that it was crawling with bedbugs. I was pleased to avoid learning that the hard way. A couple I met in Chobe National Park in northern Botswana was so enthusiastic about mighty sand dune formations deep in the Namib Desert in Namibia that I drove eight hours out of my way to find them. Not only was the drive through spectacular scenery but the couple had understated the beauty of the dunes.

The corollary to seeking assistance from others is that you should take time to give information to others. It's one of the karmic laws of traveling.

WHEN SPEAKING ENGLISH

Speaking English in countries in which it's not the primary language has made me more aware of its complex and confusing structure. If your local vocabulary isn't getting the job done and you need to try English, tailor it to the situation.

- It's not condescending to use short words when speaking English to someone for whom it is a second or third language. Pronounce words clearly and speak in short sentences. Make one point at a time. Gentle repetition is fine.
- Speak slowly but not so deliberately that it sounds patronizing. Speaking rapidly makes anyone hard to understand.
- If phrasing a sentence one way doesn't work, try it a different way.
- Use expressions in your language that are similar to ones used in the local language.
- Use plenty of gestures.
- Contractions, slang, idioms, jargon, and abbreviations don't translate well.
- Watch the listener's eyes to see if he or she is following what you're saying. Ask whether you are being understood.
- Avoid raising your voice as if speaking to a child who is hard-of-hearing, and avoid mimicking the accent of local people speaking English.
- Be polite and patient and take responsibility for your own shortcomings in speaking the local language.

HOW TO ASK QUESTIONS

When language is a problem, a traveler must learn the art of asking questions in ways that elicit helpful answers. Otherwise good-hearted people are likely to give you an answer intended to please you, even if they have to guess what that might be.

Approach with a smile. Hold your hands in sight, and let your body language convey a peaceful, friendly intent. Don't be aloof or demanding. If all this sounds obvious, remember that the other person may be smaller than you and uncertain of what to expect.

Begin a question by saying, "Good day" or "Pardon me" rather than impolitely intruding with your desire to get an answer.

If you have no language in common, think of yourself as a preacher who has lost his tongue or a writer whose commandment is "show, don't tell." Use

When Translation Isn't

As a reminder of the significance of nuance, here are a few of the many signs, apparently in English, that may make you smile as you travel.

- "Because of the impropriety of entertaining guests of the opposite sex in the bedroom, it is suggested that the lobby be used for this purpose." (Zurich hotel)
- "Ladies are requested not to have children in the bar." (Norwegian cocktail lounge)
- "Please leave your values at the front desk." (Paris hotel)
- "Please take advantage of the chambermaid." (Japanese hotel)
- "Our wines leave you nothing to hope for." (Swiss restaurant)
- "The manager has personally passed all the water served here." (Acapulco hotel)
- In Russia: "There will be a Moscow Exhibition of Arts by 15,000 Soviet Republic painters and sculptures. These were executed over the past two years." and "If this is your first visit to the USSR, you are welcome to it."
- "Specialist in women and other diseases." (Rome doctor)
- "Fur coats made for ladies from their own skin." (Swedish furrier)
- "Is forbidden to steal hotel towels please. If you are not a person to do such thing is easier not to read notis. Please do bathe inside the tub." (Tokyo hotel)
- "Drop your trousers here for the best results." (Bangkok laundry)
- "Ladies, leave your clothes here and spend the afternoon having a good time." (Rome laundry)
- "Order you summers suit. Because is big rush, we will execute customers in strict rotation." (Tailor shop in Rhodes)
- "In face of dog, please walk back with slow. This dog are friendly with you. Only bark. Never harm before you." (Thai garden)
- Then there's the sign in the lobby of the Jambo Inn in Dar es Salaam: "Women of immortal turpitude are strictly not allowed any room." I swear it's true. I saw it every evening as I headed upstairs.
- A breakfast menu in India offered me "stress lemin, juices tin, tasty cult lates, choice omelet, con flakes, paper poasted, solid curmel custid." On top of all that, they promised to bring "bad tea" to my room.

your hands, paper and pen, even the dust at your feet. *Perform* your question. Build a picture of what you want.

Avoid asking questions in which you imply the answer, especially when asking directions. Avoid questions that can be answered by "yes" or "no." Questions such as "Is the train station down that street?" or "Does the train leave at eight o'clock?" contain the seeds of disaster. The local person, only partially understanding, is likely to nod affirmatively or even say "Yes," when there may not even be a train. Instead, say "Where is the station?" and then, "What time does the train leave?"

If you lack confidence in an answer, follow up with a contradictory question. If a person has pointed to the left to indicate the direction of the train station, ask, "Is the train station that way (pointing some other direction)?" Whatever the next answer, it will tell you something.

A map does wonders to overcome pronunciation difficulties. If you have a guidebook or map that has the name of your destination in it, show it to the other person.

Always be patient. The person with whom you're talking doesn't exist merely to answer your questions. She wants to help and she's doing you a favor. She's not ignorant and speaks her language well. It's your language she's having trouble with or your pronunciation of her language. Let her answer in her own way, never implying that the difficulty is somehow her fault

The bottom line: language is only a speed bump, not a barrier.

16

Transportation

Going from point to point in other countries,
one follows a thin line of road, railway, or river,
leaving wide tracts unexplored on either side.
— Amelia Edwards
A Thousand Miles Up the Nile

Picture yourself in Provence[*] drifting along a quiet river bordered by vineyards; aboard a scraggly, spitting camel lurching along the dusty road to the airport in Varanasi;[†] swaying toward a Thai hill tribe village balanced on a crusty elephant back; or crossing Calcutta in a tattered rickshaw. Imagine cramming yourself into an Indonesian minivan called a *bemo*, or relaxing in a stately Austin Fairway taxi as you head for a gin and tonic in the faded luxury of Nairobi's Norfolk Hotel.

Fly into the heart of the Okavango Delta in a five-passenger *Cessna,* then transfer to a hollowed-out log canoe to glide along waterways lined with watching crocodiles. Perch on bulging sacks of grain as a water-buffalo cart carries you down dusty roads in sight of the Himalayas. Roll through the Indonesian hill-town of Tomohon in a two-wheeled surrey called a *bendi,* soothed by the cloppity-clop of hooves on cobblestones. Settle back in a twenty-five-foot outrigger canoe sailing from Manado for a ten-mile voyage to some of the best snorkeling in the world.

---

[*] *Provence.* Provence is located in southern France, bisected by the Rhone River, and bordered on the south by the Mediterranean. It includes Marseilles and Avignon, the spectacular Gorges d'Ardeche, and Mount Ventoux. Bright and sunny, its extraordinary light attracted Cezanne, Van Gogh, and Picasso—and has attracted legions of tourists ever since.

[†] *Varanasi.* Misnamed Benares by the British, Varanasi is located in eastern central India. On the sacred Ganges River, it is one of the most important Hindu pilgrimage destinations. Bathing ghats (steps) and burning ghats line the river bank. This picturesque city has also been a center of learning for more than two thousand years.

Here's a fundamental truth: transport in the rest of the world is very different from what we're used to at home. It's far more than just a means of getting from one place to another; it's part of the essence of travel.

Although Third World transport is often picturesque, it's not always comfortable. Travelers love to tell stories about agonizing overnighters on third class, hard seat Indian trains. Then there's the local joke that goes, "What's the maximum capacity of a Guatemalan bus?" The smiling answer: "One more." On many local buses, blaring music, too little leg room, and animals pecking at your toes are pretty standard. If there's too much character and too little comfort, paying more will make any trip easier. Even in less-developed countries, there is always a veneer of upscale transport in which passengers are sheltered from the hurly-burly of the environment.

Taking local transport means talking with people, seeing the countryside close at hand, and discovering unexpected adventures. Even when things don't go quite right, it always works out, bumps and all, if you remember that "the trip is the trip." Travel is more than destinations, and transport is more than just a means of getting from one place to another.

> "Your road is everything that a road ought to be ... and yet you will not stay on it for half a mile, for the reason that little, mysterious roads are always branching out from it on either hand, and as these curve sharply also and hide what is beyond, you cannot resist the temptation to desert your chosen road and explore them."
> —Mark Twain, American writer

TRAVELING BY BUS

The elite fly, the burghers take the train, and the people ride the bus. At home, buses come mostly in vanilla, but in the rest of the world there's a wide range of flavors. Even when the vehicle is sufficiently comfortable to pamper the most demanding traveler, traveling by bus is almost always an excellent way to SAVE MONEY while seeing the nitty-gritty of a country. For example, you can ride every mile of every bus route in the kingdom of Sikkim for less than $15.

Some trips combine spectacular scenery with luxury. The air-conditioned Scania superbus that cruises twelve hundred miles from Santiago to Arica, Chile, has a bar, a bathroom, three movie screens, and a smiling hostess. As the sleek bus hums across the moonscape of the Atacama Desert, you spy huge boulders balanced on barren mountainsides. In most climates, rain and erosion would long ago have tumbled these hot air balloon-sized rocks into dry canyons below. In the desert stillness, they hang suspended for centuries. As heat waves shimmer outside the window, cool air breezes across your face and the hostess

Local transport—a taxibus. Antananarivo, Madagascar.

sets an ice-cold beer at your elbow. At night, your seat reclines to nearly horizontal, a leg rest pops out, and you're in bed. All that for about $40.

On the double-deck luxury bus from Windhoek,[*] Namibia to Cape Town, South Africa, the attendant serves near-gourmet meals and fine South African wines. When the splendid landscape fades into dusk, she appears at your side with soft pillows and warm blankets.

Another fine double-decker travels the Garden Route along the south coast of Africa from Cape Town to Port Elizabeth (about $33). For eight hundred kilometers this bus passes through small towns and rainbow arches of blooming flowers crossing the road. Your partner sits across a table from you, sharing tea and conversation.

For rugged beauty, it's hard to top the two-day cliff-hanger in the Himalayas from Srinagar, Kashmir, to Leh,[†] or the seven-hour trip west from Gangtok[§] to the foot of Mount Kanchenjunga,[‡] or the nine-hour trip from the humid lowlands of Ujung Pandang up to the cool plateau of exotic Toraja-land.[**]

To be candid, I should mention that the buses on these last three routes are

---

[*] *Windhoek.* Clean and modern, the capital of Namibia could pass for Wichita, Kansas.

[†] *Leh.* This small town, capital of Ladakh in far northern India, was an important trading stop on the ancient Silk Road from China to Europe. Its many active monasteries and gentle Buddhist culture make Ladakh a fascinating place to visit. The road in from Kashmir and the flight across the Himalayas from New Delhi are "don't miss" experiences.

[§] *Gangtok.* The capital of Sikkim, Gangtok has gorgeous views of the Kanchenjunga range.

[‡] *Mount Kanchenjunga.* The world's third highest peak is located on the border of Sikkim and Nepal.

[**] *Toraja-land.* Located on the island of Sulawesi, Indonesia, this province is noted for its ship-shaped homes and unusual death rituals.

rolling wrecks. In fact, many Third World buses are rust-holed and thread-bare, seats torn and metal surfaces shiny from the momentary grips of a million hands. Either the windows won't open or they won't close, fans haven't worked in living memory, and overhead light fixtures are shadowy holes. Shock absorbers and springs don't. One thing that always works is the horn; shrill, penetrating, and every few seconds. Another piece of equipment that works is the boom box, usually the size of a suitcase. If you're lucky you'll get local music. If not, you'll discover what happened to the worst U.S. rap and disco tapes. Desperation hits when you find that your ear plugs are tucked away in your luggage instead of nearby in your daypack.

It may not be fair to say that all bus drivers are aggressive, but once I saw a bus driver, reflexes programmed to blast away at any obstacle, honk furiously at a speed bump in the road.

Nuts and Bolts of Bus Travel

Unlike train stations, few bus stations are architectural marvels. In fact, "yards" would be a more apt description. Picture dozens of buses parked helter-skelter in a dusty plaza. Travelers mill around, loaded with everything from briefcases to small animals to heaping baskets of fruit. Vendors weave though the crowd as conductors shout and engines race. The word cacophony captures the essence of this scene but doesn't begin to describe how captivating it is.

There's probably a relationship between where a bus is parked and where it's going but, if so, few travelers are likely to figure it out. Most buses display their ultimate destination on a tattered piece of cardboard in the front window. Of course, if you're not going to the end of the line, or are transferring to some other bus along the way, it won't be your destination that's displayed. No problem. Stay calm and keep asking and you'll soon be directed to the right bus. Then ask the driver to be certain. Since it's easy to confuse place names in a language strange to your ears, write the name on a piece of paper and show it to the driver. If you already have a ticket, show that to him. When you start wondering where to get off, enlist the aid of your fellow passengers. You get so much help, you feel like a member of the family by the time you wave good-bye.

When buying a ticket, try for an express bus. On a short trip, it doesn't matter much, but a long-distance *local* bus sometimes lurches forward only a few hundred meters at a time, stopping to pick up anyone who waves from the roadside. If you buy your ticket anywhere other than from the bus driver, find out exactly where the bus departs. It may be right outside the ticket office, or somewhere across the bus yard, or even blocks away. Make an assumption and you may be making new plans.

Keep your ticket; it may be checked several times throughout the trip.

When you give the ticket to the driver or conductor, it will be torn or punched, or you'll get a receipt. Keep it. The ticket or receipt may be checked several times in the course of the trip and collected as you get out. Even though the driver may toss it out the window after you give it to him, he may not let you off without it.

The most pressing problem on a bus is leg room. A tall person's knees are driven into the seat ahead, scrunched up to his chin, or forced out into the aisle. That's when you find that your extended knee is a tempting place for someone to sit. For any trip over an hour, reserve a seat in the first row. If reservations aren't accepted, the driver may informally reserve a seat if you tell him about, or pantomime, the leg-room problem. If you can't reserve a seat, get to the door of the bus early and, when it opens, take no prisoners.

If you think your comfort level may differ from that of a high-altitude llama herder, get a window seat so you get first choice of whether the window is open or closed. Think about which side of the bus will be receiving the force of the sun and whether you want to be toasted.

The roof of a bus is sometimes preferred seating in terms of space, fresh air and electrifying views. Riding the roof also lets you keep an eye on your luggage and avoid watching the driver getting progressively drunk. So you can't be turned down, just climb to the roof without asking permission and snuggle out of sight amid packs and baskets. Speaking of electrifying, watch for wires hanging low over the road.

No matter the time or temperature, few buses in the Third World willingly depart while even one seat is unoccupied. At the Yogyakarta (Java, Indonesia) station, for example, touts leap off incoming buses to solicit passengers with piercing cries, even trying to capture people who had no thought of going anywhere. When the driver gives up on filling every seat, he gets underway, accelerating like a race car, careening wildly around corners. The idea is to pass the bus that left just ahead of him, thereby getting first crack at prospective passengers along the road. Since stopping to pick up a passenger would leave a bus vulnerable to being overtaken by the bus speeding along behind it, the conductor hauls newcomers (often a mother with a baby and a basket of groceries) aboard as the bus slows to a fast roll. Anyone wanting off the bus is ejected as soon as the bus slows to a sprint.

Only when the bus is full does the driver relax. Of course, "full" has different meanings in different places. Usually it means that the aisle is packed with produce, baggage, livestock, and farm equipment and not one additional fare-paying life form can be leveraged into the vehicle.

People jammed together in the aisle edge over a millimeter at a time until they're almost on top of you. As you're settling in, the baby is handed to you by the woman perching on the back of your seat and an unseen fowl pecks at your shoelaces. Try to defend what you consider your personal space and your trip can be, shall we say, strenuous. If you see the humor and go with the flow, it will be memorable instead.

Except in Europe and Japan, a bus usually reaches a destination faster than a train— unless, of course, the bus breaks down, which happens frequently. Because of all the practice they get, drivers can repair virtually any mechanical failure on the spot. On the mountain road to Rumtek Monastery,* an explosion blew a ragged hole in the floorboard of our bus. An Israeli traveler in front of me turned calmly to his friend and said, "Car bomb!" It turned out that the rear tire of the bus had detonated with such force that a large chunk of rubber had blown through the floor. The driver nonchalantly parked on a steep uphill curve, replaced the tire and adjusted the clutch, all in thirty minutes. Of course, you still had to watch your step in the back of the bus or you'd become axle grease.

Since a bus may come to an unplanned, extended halt far from any human habitation, wise travelers carry a snack. Peanuts, fruit, bread, and a little water can help make a pit stop pleasant.

The price of a bus trip increases disproportionately if the bus crosses a national border. You will almost always SAVE MONEY by buying a ticket to the border, crossing on foot, and hopping on another bus on the other side. In some cases, because of time of day, remoteness of the border crossing, or a mis-match in schedules, attempting this could be a false economy.

Security

Near Chitwan,† an agile young man drops from a tree limb to the roof of a passing bus. After a furtive glance around, he grabs three of the many bags stored on the roof and tosses them off the back. As the bus slows for an uphill climb, he swings down to the back bumper, hops off, and sprints back to collect his loot. The question is: was one of those bags yours?

Let's face it, travel abroad requires a little more caution than is necessary in the United States. From Peru to the Philippines, it's up to you to make sure your luggage doesn't go astray.

Lock your bags when they're placed on a bus' roof. If joining your bag on the roof isn't your idea of fun, lock it to a roof rail with a light, plastic-coated bicycle chain. This little chain also keeps it from sliding off as the bus rounds a curve. On a mountain road near Darjeeling, India, that thin chain saved my friend's pack from yielding to centrifugal force and becoming airborne over a thousand foot drop. On another trip, I met an American in Manuel Antonio Park, Costa Rica, whose backpack had bounced off the roof of a bus, taking with it his passport and travelers checks. How many mistakes can you count in that picture?

If rain is a probability and your bag is on the roof, make sure it's com-

---

* *Rumtek Monastery.* In eastern Sikkim, across the valley from Gangtok, this brightly restored monastery is the seat of the Kagyu-pa sect of Tibetan Buddhism.

† *Chitwan.* A game preserve in southern Nepal, famous for rhinos.

pletely covered by a tarp or inside a waterproof pack cover or garbage bag. Once you're rolling, the driver is unlikely to stop to do this little chore.

As fast as the helpful driver shoves tourists bags into the bus storage compartment that opens from both sides, someone may be pulling them out the other side. Now that's a bad way to start a trip. If someone is planning to snatch your pack, they're watching you—so you must be watchful too.

When the bus lets someone off, see that your pack doesn't go along. Get off to stretch your legs—and watch. When the bus stops for lunch or a toilet break, don't leave anything valuable aboard even if the driver says he'll lock the doors.

If you're likely to sleep along the way, keep your daypack strap looped around your foot and keep everything else between you and the side of the bus. If your luggage is overhead, lock it to the rack. Of course, your real valuables are—where?—around your waist. A friend puts her pack on her lap and rests her head on it to sleep (like an ersatz air bag). These precautions may seem a little excessive, but they quickly become part of a comfortable, even amusing, routine.

Bus Passes

With a bus pass, you pay a fixed amount for unlimited travel on a bus network for the duration of the pass. In a large country, a pass can be a major money-saver. While some passes must be purchased outside the country, most can be bought on the spot. A pass usually puts you on a comfortable coach run by an established company. In fact, upscale bus services in many countries abroad use Mercedes or Scania coaches that are considerably more luxurious than buses in the United States.

Eurobus

The Eurobus, whose air-conditioned, non-smoking Volvo motor coaches visit more than twenty cities in twelve European countries, has quickly be-

The U.S. Alternative

Though primarily a U.S.-based company, the Green Tortoise offers wonderful trips in Central and North America. The Green Tortoise offers a nine-day loop through the Southwestern desert ($229 + $61 for food), nine days in the Grand Canyon ($349 + $61), sixteen days though various western national parks ($499 + $121), and twenty-eight days in Alaska ($1,500 + $250). It has recently added trips from San Francisco to Antigua, Guatemala ($649 + $151; twenty-eight days), Antigua to San José, Costa Rica ($599 + $131; twenty-one days), and other routes in Central America. Call (800) 227-4766.

come a popular alternative to rail travel in Europe. You can buy a Pass at home, in London, or anywhere along its route. Approximate Eurobus Pass fares are $189 for two weeks, $260 for one month, $325 for two months, and $400 for four months. However, if you're under twenty-seven, you can buy each pass for about $75 less (and a two-week pass costs only $139; take that, Eurailpass!). If you reserve a seat seven or more days before departure, the seat is guaranteed. If you seek a reservation within the seven day period and a seat is unavailable, you are wait-listed. If a seat doesn't turn up, you receive a small accommodation credit while you stand by. With a Eurobus pass, you can visit each city as many times as you choose and get on and off as often as you like. If you board in London, the price includes a bonus—free passage across the English Channel.

Eurobus travel times between cities are sometimes faster, sometimes slower than Eurail but the difference is seldom significant. Eurobus, which stops at a selection of budget hotels rather than bus stations, has been especially popular with women because of that perceived safety factor.

Each bus shows travel videos, carries a library of travel books, and provides trained tour guides with knowledge of local history and places of interest. For additional information, call (800) 517-7778.

> "Anything is possible on a train; a great meal, a binge, a visit from card players, an intrigue, a good night's sleep, and strangers' monologues framed like Russian short stories."
> —Paul Theroux, *The Great Railway Bazaar: By Train Through Asia*

Other Alternatives

New Zealand has the Magic Bus and the Kiwi Experience. After paying an initial fee based on your preferred route, you hop on and off the colorfully-decorated buses at will as they cruise around the country connecting you with a network of backpacker hotels. When you're ready to move on, call a toll-free number and reserve your spot on the next bus through town. It's a great way to travel.

Buses are an excellent way to see the countryside, meet people, and learn about local culture. You immerse yourself in conversations with local people of all ages, trying to ignore the driver chatting with the conductor as the bus leans around yet another curve in the sky. The way you know it was a truly great trip is if you swear, as you get off, never to ride a bus again.

TRAVELING BY TRAIN

In the Western world, trains have become an anachronism, remembered mostly by seamed-faced farmers who watched them puff across the prairies of their youth. In the rest of the world, trains are still woven into the fabric of daily life, aesthetically worn still mechanically valiant.

On a train, you travel close to the land, slowly enough to absorb what's going on, with as much privacy or contact with people as you choose. You sleep wonderfully, rocking along to a soothing rhythm, waking to a new vista emerging with each dawn.

From a train window, the world is a visual banquet. I feel as if I'm stationary, watching a panorama of lives flow past. I remember a young woman watching from her kitchen window leaning on her elbows, holding my eye until the train rounded the bend.

A train passes through time as well as space. The train north from Singapore leaves the city's futuristic mirrored-glass towers behind and within an hour is clacking through a Malaysian countryside little changed since man discovered he could plant and gather his food.

Throughout the world, there are thousands of routes along which travelers are transported in reasonable comfort. Of them, a dozen or more have trains worth a detour of many miles to ride. Writers in posh travel magazines rhapsodize about super-luxury trains, but my favorites are old-fashioned trains that maintain the style of a half century past. I like trains that leave stations reeking of character (among other things) to pass first through inhabited areas which reveal how urban people live, then slowly through landscapes of mountains and forests, clear lakes, and curious faces.

I want to share with you a few very special train trips from around the world. Some are special because of stylish furnishings, but more often it's the landscape that makes these trips unique. When you anticipate a ride on such a train, ask someone knowledgeable whether it will be daylight when you pass the most spectacular scenery and on which side you should sit.

Chile. Chile's Ferrocarril del Estado serves the seven hundred–mile Santiago to Puerto Montt run, passing through towns settled by groups as disparate as Temuco Indians and fifth-generation German immigrants. The compartments in the sixty-year-old coaches are masterpieces of faded elegance: gold-brown velvet-nap seats, carved dark wood furnishings, and etched glass. The wash basin has a brass spout and porcelain handles decorated with tiny red and yellow painted flowers. Craggy Andean peaks and snowcapped crowns of volcanoes dominate the view to the east. The twenty-two hour overnight trip costs about $35 for a comfortable private seat and cozy upper berth with crisp linen.

Peru. In southern Peru, nine coaches painted orange with a broad horizontal yellow stripe are pulled across the high desert by a near-antique engine.

Lonely tracks stretch from the "white city" of Arequipa* past mountains from which flow the birth waters of the Amazon River. Isolated shepherds' villages stand as sentinels on the high plains. Vast herds of sturdy brown and white alpaca and graceful vicuña warily lift their heads at the labored breathing of the passing machine. The conductor sways down the aisle carrying a black rubber balloon filled with oxygen for use if a passenger has difficulty breathing the thin air. Ten hours later, the train pulls into Puno on the shore of Lake Titicaca. When you've explored Lake Titicaca, the legendary birthplace of the first Inca, continue on by train to Cuzco, capital of the Inca empire.

Another Peruvian trip, lauded by train buffs as one of the seven wonders of the railway world, travels from Lima to Huancayo.† The train zig-zags its way from coastal plain to mountain heights, crossing more than sixty viaducts spanning black-walled gorges and tunneling through the frozen hearts of the mountains. Where it can't cross over or bore through, it creeps along a track chiseled into a near-vertical precipice. Even the most intrepid passengers stop looking over the edge. Climbing at an average of fifty feet a minute, it's not long before gasping passengers signal the conductor for a whiff of oxygen. Reaching 14,800 feet, this may be the highest passenger train in the world.

Mexico. In northwestern Mexico, board the *Chihuahua al Pacifico* for the comparatively short journey from Chihuahua through the Copper Canyon to Los Mochis, a small fishing resort in northwest Mexico. This has been called the most dramatic train ride in North America, a claim based on canyons carved more than six thousand feet into the earth's surface. Passengers may visit Cuauhtemocto, a community of German-speaking Mennonite ranchers, and get off at Divisadero or Bahuichivo to hike down into the Copper Canyon. If you have a few extra days, take the opportunity to experience the unusual culture of the Tarahumara Indians, people renowned for their endurance as long-distance runners.

Morocco. A fine track loops from Tangier, down to Casablanca, Marrakesh and back. On this trip, the attraction is as much the people you travel with as the destination. I shared a compartment with a woman who wore a deep blue gown, a gold-embroidered veil, heavy mesh stockings, and ornate gold rings on eight fingers. Her young daughter wore white leggings, pink T-shirt, a scarlet sweater, scuffed blue loafers, and a short-sleeved black leather jacket. Who could resist the Marrakesh Express?

Arequipa. Located near the Chilean border at the foot of snowcapped Volcan Misti, six hundred miles south of Lima, Peru. Arequipa is called the "white city" because so many of its buildings are constructed of pearly white volcanic material.

† *Huancayo.* Large city located at almost eleven thousand feet altitude, east of Lima, Peru. It has a fine Indian market.

Kenya. The train drops from Nairobi, on its mile-high inland plateau, into the sultry coastal heat of the ancient trading port of Mombasa. Although first class (about $19) costs twice as much as second, many visitors prefer it; in second class passengers are segregated by sex. As sometimes happens, "first" is relative. In some compartments, half the lights don't work, shades on the windows won't close, and the doors refuse to lock. Of course, the smiling Train Captain assures the passengers that everything will be fixed before the next trip—or at least "sometime." But the disheveled interior doesn't matter at all when the tracks enter Tsavo National Park where ostriches, giraffes, elephants, and antelope graze against the backdrop of Mount Kilimanjaro's snowy summit. This trip is often the only way to see Tsavo since the park frequently closes as rangers battle the poachers.

Zimbabwe. A steward in a crisp, white shirt, gold cuff links, and a homey blue cardigan sweater settles you into a comfortable wood-and-leather compartment. Right on time, the ten-car train, pulled by a bright yellow engine, chugs out of the Bulawayo station bound for Victoria Falls (about $12). Homes in some villages along the way have grass thatch roofs; in others, homes resemble those in a typical Kansas town. Night falls as the train enters Hwange National Park, renowned lair of black leopards. In the morning, you are dropped off on the front lawn of the colonial-era Victoria Falls Hotel.

South Africa. From Port Elizabeth on the South African coast, this train sweeps northeast for twenty-one hours across Orange Free State and the Transvaal to the urban sprawl of Johannesburg. The price is extremely reasonable considering the linen and silver in the dining car, comfortable overnight accommodations, and the idyllic landscape. We added to the amenities by bringing a picnic lunch and bottles of excellent South African Columbard and Riesling.

The internationally famous *Blue Train* covers 1,001 miles from fashionable Cape Town to big-city Jo'burg in twenty-six hours and high style. However, the hand-painted china and sparkling crystal come at a fairly high price: $639 and up, way up; not to mention having to dress for dinner. When I was in Cape Town, the Blue Train was sold out for eight months.

Australia. The modern *Indian Pacific* crosses the Nullarbor desert (which means "no trees," if I remember my Latin) to connect the west coast city of Perth with Sydney, almost 2,400 miles away. A one-way economy ticket costs around $200. This is a comfortable trip, but has none of the ethnic intensity and scenic variety found in Asia and Africa. You get an idea of the topography from the fact that one 297-mile stretch is the longest straight run of track in the world. Still, it's worth seeing the sunbaked nineteenth century mining towns, the Australian outback, and the sun rising from the desert like an explosion of orange flame.

New Zealand. A thousand miles across the Tasman Sea, you roll south from Auckland* on the *Northerner* (previously the *Silver Fern*) past volcanoes, ski slopes, blue-green mirror lakes, and rivers bursting with trout. For most travelers, the destination is "Windy Welly"† on the Cook Strait, but you needn't stop there. The train boards the Picton Ferry, crosses the Strait, and continues two hundred miles south to Christchurch. At that point, you can turn west and cross the mountainous spine of the South Island, alternating between spindly viaducts and pitch-black tunnels until you emerge in Greymouth on the rocky west coast. Or, if you'd rather, board the *Southerner* for a four hundred mile trip to the tip of the South Island. The branch line from Invercargill to Bluff bills itself as the southernmost public railway in the world.

Europe. Europe is a treasure chest full of fine train trips, although they're considerably more expensive than their counterparts in the Southern Hemisphere. Since 1883, except for an interruption or two, the royal blue coaches of the *Venice-Simplon Orient Express* (VSOE) have been bearing people across the European continent in luxury. Even before you add the cost of formal clothes (about half the men wear black tie), a one-way ticket from London to Venice costs over $1,500, double occupancy. If you start the trip in London, you cross the Channel to Boulogne, France, and drive on to Paris to board the elegant VSOE with its polished wood, Lalique crystal tulip lamps, Limoges and Wedgewood china, Irish linen, French soap, and gourmet meals. After sipping champagne in the bar car to the music of a tuxedoed pianist, you may dine on caviar, duck breast and foie gras, French cheeses, and wine. Mata Hari, Princess Grace, or Nikita Krushchev may have sat just where you're enjoying your Courvousier.

Other examples of excellent European routes are the *Chopin* (Vienna-Moscow), the *Nord-West Express* (London-Copenhagen), the *Ost-West Express* (London-Moscow), the *Sud-Express* (Paris-Lisbon), the *Remus* (Vienna-Rome), the *Lusitania* (Madrid-Lisbon), the *Britannia* (London-Munich), the *Rembrandt* (Amsterdam-Stuttgart), the *Citalia* (London-Rome), and the trip from Bergen to Oslo. And for a fabulous short trip, try the *Brunig Panoramic Express* which passes through a magic land of lakes, forests, and alpine peaks from Interlaken to Lucerne, Switzerland.

Although political changes have opened rail-riding opportunities in Eastern Europe, coaches are worn and long stretches of landscape are industrial-

---

* *Auckland.* Located on the North Island of New Zealand. Surrounded by water and volcanic hills, Auckland's population is approaching one million (including the largest population of Polynesians in the world).

† *Windy Welly.* Wellington is located on the southern tip of the North Island of New Zealand. The capital of the country, it is swept by brisk (sometimes gale force) winds from the Cook Strait.

ized and polluted. On the other hand, it's a chance to travel slowly in countries newly-opened to the world. For an afternoon's amusement in Budapest, take a leisurely twelve-kilometer trip through a peaceful forest aboard one of the red and silver cars of the *Pioneer Railway*. This little railroad is staffed by children dressed in formal blue uniforms bearing red epaulets.

Thailand. Many travelers enjoy the one and one-half day/two night train from Bangkok to Singapore (an ordinary berth costs about $85). The coaches are comfortable and the route traverses pleasant scenery. However, an alternative has emerged fairly recently. The founder of the Orient Express hotel chain refurbished the old *Silver Fern* carriages (that used to run from Auckland to Christchurch) with teak, brass, crystal, silver, and fine fabrics, and christened the result the *Eastern Orient Express*. To travel the same twelve hundred mile stretch of track I traveled for $85, passengers now have the option of paying $1,170 to $2,950 to ride on the EOE. Of course, premium tea from a silver pot is served in delicate china cups on the *Express* while on the other train tea was handed through the window in a clay tumbler.

Aboard the train from Bangkok to Chiang Mai in northern Thailand, crew and passengers frequently stand, salute, and sing the national anthem at major stops. Now that's something you don't see just anywhere.

China. Another luxury-liner, the *Marco Polo Express*, made its debut in 1993. The nine-day, two thousand mile long trip runs from Beijing to Urumqi, a city farther from an ocean than any other city in the world. It tracks a portion of the ancient Silk Road on which Chinese silks were carried across Asia to Venice and Rome. A two-berth compartment, complete with mahogany writing table, a plump easy chair, and a heavy brass reading lamp, costs about $5,500 *per person*, plus another $1,000 or so for side trips and return by air to Beijing. Are the Chinese catching on to capitalism?

On standard Chinese trains, there are sometimes no reserved seats. To give foreigners a chance, the clerk allows them a running head start though the gate for the train. Seconds later, the local crowd bursts from behind the barriers like the first wave at the New York marathon. The cars are so crowded that you may have to climb out the window when it's time to get off.

India. The Indian train system has been described as "exhilarating anarchy." Its coaches, many pulled by the world's largest fleet of old-fashioned steam locomotives, carry more than ten million passengers every day.

The Darjeeling-Himalayas train, known affectionately as the "toy train," click-clacks uphill from New Jalpaiguri in North Bengal to Darjeeling in the foothills of the Himalayas. Its miniature steam engine slowly pulls four reduced-scale passenger cars on narrow-gauge tracks through dozens of small towns and manicured tea plantations. After seven hours, passengers disembark in Darjeeling, a favorite hill station of the English raj. It's great fun even though the train is always crowded, has head and knee room suitable for Munchkins, and takes twice as long as the same journey by road.

The apogee of Indian train travel is the *Palace on Wheels* (even though it's been renamed the *Royal Orient*) whose deluxe saloon cars once transported the maharajahs and viceroys of an earlier India. Departing from New Delhi, *Palace on Wheels* visits some of India's most colorful cities, including Rajasthan's Jaipur, Udaipur, Jaisalmer, and Jodhpur, then turns east to Sawi Madhopur, and finally back to New Delhi. Travel is at night so passengers can be taken to historical sights each day. This trip takes eight days and is priced with Western tourists in mind. Tour operators charge $1,400 for twin sharing, $2,450 for a single, but you can beat that price by making arrangements yourself. The burnished teak, polished brass fittings, crisp linens, fine food, constant service, and exotic itinerary make this trip a good investment for many. Here's the bad news: There's a rumor that the government plans to convert Indian tracks from meter gauge to broad gauge. If that happens, the *Palace on Wheels/Royal Orient* may roll no more.

Other recommended long-distance trips in India: the *Rajdhani Express* (Delhi-Calcutta), the *Gitanjale Express* (Calcutta-Bombay), the *Frontier Mail* (Amritsar-Bombay), and the *Taj Express* (Delhi-Agra).

Russia. The eight day, six thousand mile trip aboard the Trans-Siberian Express (the correct name is the *Russia Express*) from Moscow to Vladivostok is by far the longest train trip in the world. I can't give you prices since Russian currency fluctuates so much, but it's generally cheaper to buy the ticket in China. While the Trans-Siberian has a certain *Dr. Zhivago* romantic appeal, a week is a lot of time to commit to counting millions of trees filing slowly past your window (at forty miles per hour top speed, this is not the world's fastest train). At long intervals, the tracks pass gray industrial cities filled with concrete apartment towers standing mute in the vast silence. At least there's plenty of time to sip vodka and talk with Russian and international passengers. There's even time to hop off for some quick exercise during brief stops, except from November to March when the bone-numbing Siberian cold could turn you into a seasonal platform monument.

Nuts and Bolts of Train Travel

With all these exceptional train trips in mind, it's time to consider the practicalities of train travel.

Cost

In most countries, train travel is inexpensive, much cheaper than flying. A berth always costs more than a seat, but it's much more comfortable for overnight travel. How much more it costs depends on whether the berth is in a private compartment, a shared compartment, or lengthwise along the aisle. However, when you travel at night, the cost of transportation includes the cost of lodging.

It's seldom wise to buy the cheapest ticket available. Third-class, hard-seat trains are a rough way to travel in almost any country. Unless you're determined to see a country on $2 a day, are writing a book on ultimate hard-core travel, or practicing extreme self-mortification in contemplation of reincarnation, do yourself a favor: skip third class hard-seat. If you do try it, I'll wager it will only be once.

In a private compartment, which costs only a few dollars extra, you're comfortable, free from cigarette smoke if you choose to be, and your luggage is relatively secure. You may even reach your destination fairly well rested. If you forego a berth and sit up the whole way, you can save a few dollars, but that could be a foolish economy on a long trip. The downside is that if you travel in a two-person compartment you miss fine opportunities for conversation. When I'm in the mood for company, I travel in large compartments or in open seating. When I need solitude, I try for a small compartment.

Where to Buy Your Ticket

Don't expect a travel agent to tear a ticket with your name on it from a computer printer. That would be far too easy. More likely, you'll have to go to the train station to buy the ticket. That, by the way, requires finding the correct station. Don't learn too late that the city you're leaving has more than one station—and it's not the one where you're standing.

The Ticket Line

If you travel by train, you'll find yourself standing in line. Realizing that you haven't moved forward for ten minutes, you notice that people are joining the line ahead of you. Maybe they're relatives of people in line, members of the same cavalry unit, travel agents, who knows, but try to avoid expressing Western-style complaints about people who cut into lines. You'll probably be understood, but neither appreciated nor helped. To avoid treading water, you can circle around and join the front of the line where it resembles a rugby scrum, or pleasantly ask someone for help. I was once taken out of the line by a fellow ticket-buyer directly to the office of the ticket master who personally handled the transaction.

Buying Your Ticket

When you reach the ticket agent's window, be your usual courteous self. Greet him (it's almost always a "him") with a friendly smile and a cheerful "hello" or "good day." After all, he's been getting a lot of pressure all day. Make sure you know the name of your destination as spelled in the local language. Ask for the seat you want, which is surely a window seat, and specify whether you prefer a nonsmoking car (don't underestimate the impact of rolling clouds of unfiltered smoke on your lungs).

Before you leave the line, confirm that the ticket handed you is what you asked for, count your change, and, oh yes, be sure the guy pressing against you isn't picking your pocket. If all is okay, thank the clerk for helping you. Wouldn't you like him to tell his family at dinner about how courteous people from your country are? Maybe as a result of your courtesy, he'll help the next traveler who has no idea what's going on.

By the way, quite a few countries require that foreigners purchase first class tickets with hard currency. If you want to SAVE MONEY, buy second class tickets with local currency, then upgrade once on board, again using local currency.

The Tourist Quota

Getting a ticket may be more difficult than you expect. In fact, you may not get one unless you know about the special ticket lines and quotas set aside for foreign travelers. Suppose it's just under one hundred degrees so you ask for a seat in an air conditioned car. The ticket agent snaps, "Finished" (which means "You must be crazy; air con sold out sixty days ago"). A little grumpily, you decide to settle for a compartment with a fan. Again, "Finished." Okay, you think, I'll sit up and sweat all night—but those seats too are "Finished."

You feel frustrated but, as a knowledgeable traveler, you aren't even close to giving up. That's because you know that a "tourist quota" of tickets has been reserved with you in mind. If there were no quota, and you tried to buy tickets only a day or two ahead of departure, you might never get a ticket, especially in countries like India. The tourist quota may not get you into first class or air con, but it will probably assure you a berth if you want one, and almost certainly a seat of some kind. So you stroll over to the Information booth—there is some kind of information source in most train stations—and ask for the location of the "foreigner's window." That's where you'll find the clerk who dispenses tickets under the tourist quota.

In Madras, India,* the foreigners window is at the end of a line designated "VIP, handicapped, ladies, freedom fighters, and senior citizens." Because the train we wanted was sold out, we were sent upstairs to see if the "big man" could help. After two hours in a sweltering office, during which time we witnessed a flurry of fists between a ticket agent and a prospective passenger and sat through two black-outs due to power failures, the big man permitted us to buy tickets for a non–air conditioned, shared compartment.

Baksheesh

A bribe, or tip, has many names around the world. A common one is *baksheesh*. Beyond cultural reluctance to try it, there are practical questions of to whom and how much. Find the lowest-ranking person who can provide what you want, starting with the conductor. The lower the rank, the less the amount of *baksheesh* required. Start by saying, "Isn't there some other way to handle this?" or, "Isn't it possible to pay an extra fare?" These classic expressions translate into any language.

The amount of *baksheesh* required is always a guess. Factor in the cost of the ticket, the standard of living in the country, and how much getting what you want is worth to you. One approach is to put a small amount of money in one pocket and a back-up amount in another. Empty the first pocket and, if that doesn't fly, pull out the back-up stash. Try to avoid getting out your wallet. If you offer too little, it may be ignored. More likely, you'll receive some clear, non-verbal signals that you need to up the ante. It works.

Sometimes a bribe can help find a previously "filled" seat.

Confirming Your Space

If you buy your ticket ahead of time, find out when you are expected to confirm your reservation—and do it. If you don't confirm when you're supposed to, someone else's seat will be in yours.

Using a Rail Pass

The following information pertains to using a rail pass in Europe, although using a pass is similar in most countries. Plan to arrive at the train station at least thirty minutes ahead of departure time. You won't need that much time unless there's a problem, but if there is you may need every minute.

Before your first ride, validate your ticket at the ticket window in the train station, not with the conductor (who may charge you a penalty). From then on, skip past the ticket lines and hop on the train.

A rail pass allows you to board the train but is not a reservation. That is, it doesn't guarantee a seat, couchette, or sleeper. In western Europe (except

---

* *Madras.* This is the capital of Tamil Nadu in southeastern India. Although India's fourth largest city, it's also one of the most pleasant. It is the point of departure for visiting the fabulous temples of South India.

Austria, Benelux, and Germany), high speed and premium trains require reservations. Reservations must also be made for sleeping accommodations and are recommended for trips lasting more than three hours and for TGV, ICE, EUROSTAR, and certain InterCity trains. Lines that require a reservation are clearly marked (with an 'R') in the *Thomas Cook European Timetable*, in national rail timetables, and on departure sheets posted in stations. If you want to travel on EuroCity or international express trains over the weekend or on holidays, you risk disappointment if you don't make reservations.

At the height of the tourist season, some travelers purchase a reservation ($3 to $10) to ensure they won't have to stand. On the other hand, if you have to stand it's only until the next station. There, you simply out-hustle boarding locals to the vacated seats. When a reservation isn't required, most people don't bother.

If you plan to sleep on a train, you have four choices. You can sit up all night in a regular train seat and greet the morning with hollow eyes. You can try for a fold-out seat and hope there's room to fold it out. You can pay a little extra for a couchette. Or you can splurge on a sleeper. The couchette provides a bunk in a tiny six-bunk, co-ed dormitory room. It costs about $20 extra. The sleeper compartment contains two or three beds and a sink and costs an extra $40 to $100. Sleeping aboard saves the cost and hassle of finding a hotel and frees the day for exploration.

While traveling, keep the rail pass safely tucked away to avoid loss or theft. If it's lost and you have a police report, you may be able to get a partial refund when you return home. In the meantime, you'll have to buy a replacement ticket. You can't get a refund after the ticket has been validated (stamped the first time) or beyond one year after the date of issuance, even if unused.

Wherever you're traveling, a good map lets you know where you are on a continuous basis. Beyond adding interest and showing you how place names are spelled in the country, a map prepares you to get off on arrival (some trains don't tarry long in a station).

Finding the Right Train

On the platform, don't rely on direction signs alone. Ask other passengers where the train you're about to board is going. If you have a general seating ticket, assure yourself that the car you board is going to your destination. Otherwise, you may be unexpectedly shunted onto a siding as the rest of the train continues on. When you hear an announcement over the loudspeaker that you don't understand, watch how others respond. If they all start packing up and moving toward another track, ask questions quickly.

Finding the Right Seat

If you have an assigned seat, its number should be printed or written on your ticket. If it's not, your name will be on a bulletin board near the proper track. Join the scores of other passengers searching for their names on one of the sheets of the passenger manifest, squinting at erasures, insertions, and cross-outs. The cross-outs, by the way, include those people who didn't believe it was really necessary to confirm their reservations.

Changing Seats

If you've been assigned a bad seat, say facing backwards or receiving the full blast of the sun, move to a better seat immediately. If someone appears with a legitimate claim, smile and move on.

Meals

If you'll be aboard long enough to become hungry, ask whether there is a dining car. There is often no food service on overnight trips, but stewards sometimes walk the aisles selling sandwiches and drinks. At unpredictable intervals, a porter may come around with inexpensive meals, usually on tin trays.

Local vendors may clamor below your window at every stop, but taste is likely to surpass hygiene. To serve health and preferences, wise travelers generally boards a train with ingredients for a picnic on wheels, including beverages.

TP

Assume that the train will have no toilet paper—or if it does, it will run out soon after you leave the station.

Security

With respect to security, you can't automatically trust the train crew or even your fellow passengers, so it would be a mistake to leave your daypack behind when you leave your seat. If you ask someone to watch your gear, make it someone you trust, not a passing acquaintance. Don't leave your luggage unlocked or your daypack accessible to anyone else at night. Lock both to something secure while you sleep. See Chapter 13 for more on security.

When you travel by train abroad, stations become part of the memory. Some are remarkable works of art, such as the soaring iron masterpieces of Gustave Eiffel. Others are massive, cold, and depressing. In some countries, they're a microcosm of the entire culture.

Walk into the New Delhi station just before midnight and there will be hundreds of people camped out, perhaps resembling the rear guard of Shah Jahan's army. Vendors cry the merits of their dosas and samosas, steaming mounds of dal, and assortments of unrecognizable fried . . . things. Extended families have made themselves at home on the long concrete platforms between trains, cooking meals on flaming braziers. Gold-thread saris and crimson tikas glow as women hover around the flames. Old men perch on burlap bales and baggage bound with twine; others squat on their heels, eating, talking, gesturing. There are Sikhs and Punjabis, Rajasthanis and Kashmiris, in turbans, beards, dhotis, and beautifully-cut business suits. Cows wander at will, munching dinner leftovers and baggage. Stations like this are very much part of the trip.

Trains are one of my favorite ways to travel. I love the beat of the iron wheels clacking rhythmically across junctions in the track and the slow pace that allows me to recharge my batteries and center my thoughts. Train travel connects me with the mellowness of an earlier era. I have yet to be ready for a journey to end.

TRAVELING BY AIR

At home we can choose among airlines on the basis of ticket price, departure times, and destinations—even friendliness of passenger agents and on-board personnel. Flying in Europe is similar, but most of the rest of the world is quite different. Your planning should acknowledge the differences. There are far fewer choices and you may have to take whatever flight you can get. In most countries, airlines have few planes, customarily fly with all seats occupied, and visit some destinations only infrequently. They are definitely not always "ready when you are."

On the positive side, flights are so inexpensive in some places that you wonder how they pay for fuel. In Honduras, for example, you can fly most of the way across the country for $30.

How Safe Is It?

Most airlines keep their planes well-maintained and provide great service; some do not. Flying on international airlines such as Thai Air, Air New Zealand, Varig, Swiss Air, and Singapore Air is a real treat. On an Air Madagascar flight from Antananarivo to Nairobi, the flight attendant appeared in the coach section bearing smoked kingfish, veal, Camembert and baguettes, a crisp white Bordeaux, and Taittinger champagne.

In contrast, on my first flight on CAAC, the Chinese national airline, the pilot cranked the engines and the passenger cabin immediately filled with dense blue-gray smoke. When the attendants didn't even take notice, I assumed it must be a common occurrence. In the early Nineties, the Chinese government licensed dozens of new airlines to serve newly-mobile masses. The sharp increase in flights has resulted in high accident and hijacking rates (ten flights diverted to Taiwan in one year alone).

Aeroflot, once the largest airline in the world, never won a warm place in anyone's heart. Its fatal accident rate for the past twenty-five years was the worst of all major airlines. On flights that made it, service was atrocious. It's hard to believe, but the situation has deteriorated from there. Aeroflot has been split up among the former Soviet republics. As a result, maintenance and air traffic control systems are more stressed, planes are overloaded, and pilots are poorly trained. So many of the old Aeroflot planes are being operated beyond their guaranteed lifetime that the U.S. State Department has instructed its staff to avoid flying on domestic Russian airlines.

In what may be a first, passengers on the Sahara India Airline flight from Bombay to Delhi recently refused to board until an official from the Civil Aviation office inspected the plane and declared it safe to fly. Those passengers may have known that fatal airline accidents occur in India at ten times the rate in the rest of the world.

As of 1995, airlines from Belize, Dominican Republic, Gambia, Ghana, Honduras, Nicaragua, Paraguay, Uruguay, and Zaire were banned from landing in the United States. Airlines from Bolivia, El Salvador, Guatemala, and the Netherlands Antilles are currently allowed to land but are on probation.

That's the bad news. To put it into perspective, the FAA reports the "death risk per flight" as 1 in 200,000 for Aeroflot, 1 in 1.5 million for Air Canada, 1 in 3 million for British Airways, 1 in 20 million for El Al, and zero for Singapore Air. Compare these odds with findings at the University of California (Berkeley) that odds of death from a coast-to-coast automobile trip are 1 in 14,000, from a bicycle accident 1 in 88,000, and from lightning 1 in 1.9 million. In the U.S., roughly ninety-five people are killed each year in plane crashes. Compare that with 112 people killed each *day* in auto accidents. Overall, the odds of death from a commercial airline accident are put at 1 in 10 million.

Nevertheless, it's worth paying attention to those monotonous instructions the flight attendants recite at the beginning of each flight, at least when they talk about where the nearest exits are. A smiling attendant for Southwest Airlines introduced the three attendants by name, then recited the familiar information. As usual, he was ignored. At the end he held up a $100 bill and said, "I'll give this to the first person who can tell me our first names." No one got that $100—but I'll bet every one of those passengers pays more attention to the instructions when they fly Southwest in the future.

Nuts and Bolts of Air Travel

To make air travel a happy experience, a traveler should follow a few basic routines.

Buying Your Ticket

- Make reservations further ahead of departure than you may be used to.
- Check your ticket to see that it is completely correct. It's risky to take accuracy for granted when the ticket includes several flights, countries, and airlines.

For the first time in years, getting a seat to Asia or Europe may be difficult unless you plan at least a month ahead. Taking advantage of the weak dollar, German, French, and Japanese tourists are filling the seats to and from the United States. Further, although demand is up, airlines have been cautious about increasing service. The clear message: plan ahead.

- Most airlines will assign seats up to thirty days in advance of the flight so you're better off making an informed seat selection before arriving at the airport. For one thing, having an assigned seat reduces your vulnerability if the flight is overbooked. The next obvious reason is to get a seat that suits your preferences. If two people traveling together select an aisle seat and a window seat, there's a chance that the middle seat will not be assigned. If it is, it's easy to arrange a switch. On the other hand, if you book seats next to one another, leaving an aisle or a window vacant, it's likely to be assigned to someone else. Keeping that middle seat empty adds a lot of comfort to a long trip.

  If you crave a view, ask the agent to look at the seating configuration for the plane on which you'll be flying and assign you a window seat that is not over the wing. If the agent doesn't look at the configuration, he or she may be guessing and you may wind up staring at shiny sheet metal for several hours.

  On most planes, the best leg room comes with the front seats, just behind the bulkhead. Sometimes bulkhead seats are held for unexpected handicapped passengers, families with children, or airline personnel. If one is empty when the cabin door closes, I leap for it, sometimes after checking with the flight attendant. The trade-off is reduced storage space and a rather oblique view of the movie screen (the latter is seldom much of a loss). Seats in the mid-cabin exit row also have extra leg room and the seats in the row ahead may not recline, another blessing.

  If being seated in the no-smoking section is important, ask to be seated far from the transition row. Fortunately, there is an increasing trend for flights to be 100 percent nonsmoking.

- If you want special meals, such as vegetarian, diet, low-sodium, diabetic, religious, or children's, place your order when you buy the ticket. Avoid heavy meals.

- Ask about departure taxes you may encounter and in what currency you must pay them. If permitted, buy the tax stamp from the travel agent to save time.

- At home, we often think of being "wait listed" as nearly equivalent to having a reservation. Overseas, it's definitely not the same. A very low wait list number may have a fighting chance. If given a high number, forget it unless providence intervenes—but you may be able to give providence a jump-start. If circumstances warrant, ask whether a small additional payment might help you move up the wait list. In Manila, I engaged a travel agent, for a small fee, who got me moved from number 37 on the wait list to a seat on the plane ten minutes before departure. He said he reminded the clerk that, as a foreigner, I would be paying in hard currency. Who knows, there may even have been a more personal, micro-economic explanation for my good fortune. Take it for granted that others on the wait list will also be invoking providence on their behalf.

When I decided to go to the Andaman Islands[*] to scuba dive, I got a reservation to depart Madras the following day. As I was leaving the travel agent's office, she mentioned casually that I was wait listed, not confirmed, for my requested return date. I was so eager to get to the Andamans that I barely remembered to ask "What number am I on the wait list?" The answer was, "One hundred and fifty one. The first date we can confirm your return is, hmmmm, let's see, thirty-two days from now." It turned out that school holidays had begun earlier in the week and hundreds or thousands of Indian families had already flown to the Andamans. Even with my good travel luck, I decided not to toss those dice.

- Confirm and reconfirm flight reservations. Fail to confirm and your paid-for ticket will probably be canceled and someone else will sit in what you'd been thinking of as your seat. You may get your money back someday, but in the meantime you'll be standing on the ground growling as you watch the once-a-week flight leave without you. If the ticket doesn't tell you when to confirm, do so at least three days (seventy-two hours) before the flight. It's sometimes worth dropping by the ticket office on the day of the flight before going to the airport to ensure that departure time hasn't changed—or that the flight hasn't been canceled. It happens.

- Ask airline clerks for a copy of their route maps and schedules to help with your on-the-road planning. There may only be one or two flights a week to remote destinations.

At the Overseas Airport
- Get to the airport on time. Airlines in Europe typically ask you to be at the airport an hour and a half ahead of scheduled departure time. In the

---

[*] *Andaman Islands.* A group of islands in the Bay of Bengal, between India and Thailand. The Andaman Islands are noted for fine beaches and diving.

Third World, it's more often two hours. You may feel this is unnecessary, and sometimes you would be right. In the United States, I roll in fifteen minutes before departure. Overseas, I'm there two hours ahead of time. If you arrive later than the time indicated, you may lose your reservation.

Remember that the trip starts, not at the airport, but at your hotel. Check out the night before if practical. If you're leaving from a large city, anticipate traffic accidents, breakdowns, and gridlock—expect the unpredictable. Allow twice as much time to get to the airport as you think you need. I have a friend whose taxi was immobilized in downtown Bangkok traffic for so long that the driver fell asleep. A bus to the Warsaw airport was halted for almost an hour by security forces accompanying a motorcade bearing Lech Walesa. In Gaborone, Botswana, the taxi driver who promised to pick me up at my hotel at 6:30 A.M. never showed. I barely made that flight by hitching a ride in the back of a pickup truck. In Calcutta, I walked out to the street at 7:30 A.M. with plenty of time to catch a taxi to Dum Dum Airport. That's when I discovered a general transportation strike had started at 7 A.M. I finally found a private "pirate car" willing to risk running a possible bus drivers' blockade, but his improvised fare schedule could have been drafted by Jean Laffitte.

Airport officials don't care at all when you *arrived* at the airport. They only care whether there is time for you to get through the process. Plan for lines at the ticket counter, the currency exchange window, the tax stamp window, and customs. In some airports, officials stop accepting passengers a half hour before flight time if it will take longer than that to clear customs. If you arrive at one of those airports twenty-five minutes before departure, you're out-of-luck. Because there are more airlines than check-in counter spaces at the Warsaw airport, the ticket agents for a departing flight yield their counter space to another airline thirty minutes before takeoff. Arrive after that and there's not even anyone with whom to plead your case.

> Airport officials don't care when you arrived, only if there is enough time to check you in.

Suppose you're running late and there's a long line at the check-in counter. If you wait in line, you'll miss your flight. Go to the front of the line and, as calmly as possible, explain the situation to the agent. Try to enlist the sympathy of the person next in line. If your karma is good, they may make space for you. If everyone in line is also anxiously hoping to board the same flight, sprint for the gate. Sometimes the agent on that end will check in your bag and have it carried directly to the plane.

As another motivation for early arrival, there is a strong positive correlation between luggage checked in close to flight departure time and lost luggage. If you check in late, your luggage may not make your flight but it will probably go *somewhere*. Rush the ticket agent and you're asking for a luggage tag that says SLC (Salt Lake City) instead of SCL (Santiago, Chile).

There is also a direct relationship between the time you check in and what your rights are, if any, if you get bumped because the flight was overbooked.

— Immediately after checking in, ensure that the agent pulled only the correct coupon. If he or she has accidentally taken two coupons, you will have an untimely problem somewhere down the line.

— Stay alert while waiting in the terminal for your flight to depart. The announcements that are so difficult to understand may be telling you that the departure gate has been changed. Ask around. Watch other passengers. Bury your head in a book and you may have more than enough time to finish it when you look up.

On Board

— Drink eight ounces of water each hour (coffee, alcohol and carbonated drinks, dehydrating diuretics, don't count). You need to compensate for the extremely low humidity in the cabin.

— Contact lenses, especially the thin disposable kind, can adhere to the cornea in the low humidity. Have eyedrops available or consider leaving your lenses in their case during a long flight.

— If you have a cold or an allergy, changes in cabin pressure may cause ear or sinus problems. Consider using a decongestant an hour or so before departure. If your ears bother you, try chewing gum, yawning, or pinching your nose shut, closing your mouth, and blowing gently.

— Get some exercise during a long trip. Roll your head and shoulders, twist your body, reach over your head, tighten the muscles in your buttocks, lift your thighs and rotate your feet. Propping your feet up relieves pressure on the back of your thighs. Walk around the cabin and get off during layovers.

— Take a blanket and pillow from the overhead bin when you board. Otherwise, they may have been claimed by the time you feel a need.

— If you're airborne when you discover you may miss a connection, see if the attendant can fix the problem before you arrive. If it will help, ask the attendant to arrange transport to the another gate by electric cart or try to delay departure of the other flight. If the attendant cannot help, move near the exit so you'll be one of the first at the ticket counter. Be creative and determined, but always courteous with the customer service person (who is beginning hours of hell dealing with angry people demanding attention).

If there's a long line at the ticket counter, don't get buried there. Minutes matter. Head for other airline counters to find alternatives or for a telephone to call toll-free reservation numbers or your travel agent to get booked on the next best flight. The airline on which were scheduled is more likely to help you than any other.

Even if it looks from the monitor as if it's too late to catch a flight, sprint for the gate anyway. You never know. If no alternative can be found, ask the ticket agent for a hotel room and meals at airline expense—in a way that implies that both of you take it for granted.

Overbooking, Delays, and Diversions

Airlines do not guarantee their schedules, nor does the law. In the event of delay or cancellation, your remedies are governed by airline policy, which means they're negotiable. If *cancellation* of a flight was not caused by a so-called act of god, an airline agent will offer to rebook you on another of their flights. Some may offer you a free coupon for a similar flight, but you may have to ask for it. If they divert your flight to an alternate destination, they may offer you a hotel room.

When a flight is *delayed*, an airline may provide meals and pay for telephone calls unless the delay was caused by bad weather, in which case you feed yourself. Airlines will not reimburse ticket holders for inconvenience, financial losses, or broken romances related to a delayed arrival.

Your rights are different in the case of *overbooking*, which is quite legal. If you don't want to get bumped, check in early. Being somewhere in line when they fill the last seat does you no good, nor does holding a boarding pass mean you'll be allowed to board. You must receive a boarding *assignment*; that is, you must be checked in.

If a flight is oversold, the clerk will call for volunteers to be bumped. If you're willing to trade your time for money, tell the clerk ahead of time that you'll agree to be bumped, but only if there is an alternative flight acceptable to you and they pay for meal, hotel, and phone call expenses. In addition to a free flight, they can also offer some combination of an upgrade, a temporary pass to a first-class lounge, and/or a cash payment in the range of $200 to $500. It's all negotiable.

Suppose you don't volunteer and they bump you anyway? For flights in and originating from the United States, the policy of U.S. airlines is that if they can put you on another flight that arrives at your destination within an hour of when you were originally scheduled to arrive, you receive no compensation. If you will arrive more than one hour late but less than two, you are entitled to a cash payment equal to the amount you paid for your one-way ticket or one-half the cost of your round-trip ticket, up to $200. If the delay is more than four hours on an international flight, the airline doubles the payment, up to $400. Plus, of course, the airline must still get you to your destination. The airline may try to get you to accept free air travel in the future in place of the cash payment. You may accept, but you don't have to.

Here's the joker. If you checked in *after* the deadline shown on your ticket jacket, you may receive no compensation at all. And, of course, late-arrivers head the list of bumpees. Even for me, a chronic late-arriver, the lesson is clear.

The policies of foreign carriers with respect to overbooking are consistent with European Community regulations which are similar to U.S. regulations. The policies of U.S. carriers pertaining to flights originating outside the U.S. are, so far, inscrutable.

When the starboard engine on our Madrid-to-Atlanta flight failed over the Atlantic, the pilot dumped fuel and returned to Madrid. The airline put us up in a five-star hotel, wined and dined us royally, and doubled our frequent flyer miles. The next morning, I requested an upgrade to Business Class from a friendly clerk—and got it.

To summarize, re-confirm your ticket repeatedly and get to the airport early. Avoid stress and disappointment and take advantage of a little journal-writing time. If a problem comes up, being prepared will reduce its impact on your trip.

You'll find additional information on air travel in Chapters 5 and 6.

LOCAL TRANSPORT

As music reveals the character of a country, so do its small vehicles. In the same way taxis and subways reflect the nature of Manhattan, collectivos in Lima and motor scooters in Rarotonga capture the spirit of those places.

European public transportation systems are extensive and efficient. Since they're familiar to us, we use them with little hesitation. However, modern transportation systems have few equivalents in the Third World. Instead, small entrepreneurs take over—and their solutions are wondrous to behold. Local transport is inexpensive, often uncomfortable, and almost always fun. **Don't be intimidated by local transport.**

Because it's unfamiliar to them, some travelers are initially intimidated by local transport. With a little experience, though, they soon hop aboard all kinds of vehicles with confidence and a smile. They're at home in a VW van decorated with colorful murals, a pickup truck with a striped metal awning above bottom-polished wooden benches, or a horse-drawn cart with a fringed roof and a honey jar filled with fresh flowers.

River taxi on Chao Phraya River. Bangkok, Thailand.

Local transport includes bemos, bendis, bicycles, camels, canal boats, collectivos, elephants, jeepneys, makoros, matatus, minivans, motor scooters, oplets, outrigger canoes, ox-carts, poda podas, pouse-pouses, taxi-brousses, tongas—and many more. Since they are so common around the world, I'll comment here on taxis, minivans, subways, and bicycles. The others will come as a series of happy surprises.

Taxis

In a taxi, you travel in comfort and with a reasonable likelihood of reaching your planned destination, sometimes paying a considerable premium for the convenience. Unfortunately, taxi drivers, as a group, seldom create a favorable impression. The problem is money. You have it and they want as much of it as they can get. Hope for a working meter or, from an airport, a fixed fee. Otherwise, bargain on the fare.

Since taxi drivers are experienced in dealing with travelers, you'll pay dearly unless you strike a bargain before the wheels roll. If you bargain in advance, you can ride for an hour and a half in a Madagascar taxi-brousse for eighty-five cents, even less in a rickshaw called a *pouse-pouse*. If you don't bargain, the sky's the limit. Bargaining with taxi drivers as an art form is discussed in Chapter 10.

When it's time to pay, first get your luggage out of the taxi, then give the driver the exact fare agreed on. That way, in the event of a difference of opinion, your luggage can't be held hostage. If you have only a large bill, state the amount of the fare before handing it over. Otherwise, with your bill in his pocket, he may claim that the fare was higher than you agreed. Regardless, he may claim he has no change, hoping you'll be in too much of a hurry to wait. With a little forethought, you can avoid this scenario.

Before your hotel clerk calls for a taxi, ask whether the call will result in an additional charge by the driver. In Athens, for instance, the charge for being summoned can exceed the charge for driving all the way to the airport. You may prefer to walk to the curb and handle it yourself.

Since it's not unusual for a taxi driver to levy a supplemental charge based on how many bags he puts in the trunk, keep at least small pieces of luggage in the car with you.

In many cities, rates increase dramatically at night. Local law may permit charging double the fare on the meter. Spare your blood pressure a peak experience by asking in advance.

Minivans

Picture yourself standing on the curb as a minivan skids to a brakes-locked stop in front of you. It has an end-of-the-line destination sign in its window, which is probably not the name of the place you want to go. You aren't sure what the fare is or what you're supposed to do next, and you have only seconds to decide whether to board. Confused, you step back and look for a taxi. After learning that taxi rides aren't exactly problem free and cost twenty times more than the "people's transport," you try again.

When you board the minivan, you find all seats occupied, the roof too low to permit standing upright, and fifteen people looking at you. Since you have no idea what the twelve-year-old fare collector is saying, you're reduced to holding out several coins. He takes what he wants. Fortunately, it's usually less than ten cents.

You had a general idea of the direction in which you wanted to go when you got in, but after ten minutes of turning corners you're not so sure. Seeing a street name that looks about right, you climb out, shoulder your daypack—and realize you're lost. It really doesn't matter; it's part of your adventure. You can't go very wrong. When you've looked around, you catch another minivan, craning your neck to see out the window, thinking surely you'll see something familiar. Maybe you do, maybe not. Either way, you get home, or somewhere.

Before long, you realize how willing other passengers are to help. If your

Right of Way

As you stroll to roadside to find a ride, repeat to yourself: PEDES-TRIANS DO NOT HAVE THE RIGHT OF WAY. Soft-shell humans must yield to trucks, buses, cars, ox-carts, camels, bicycles—everything. Not only will vehicles not stop, most won't even swerve. To make things more interesting, traffic moves on the "wrong," or driver's left side, of the road in many countries. As a rule of thumb, if a reasonable amount of English is spoken in a country, look to your *right* before you step into the roadway.

destination is some distance from the minivan route, someone may even jump off and show you the way. Because systems are so similar, your new knowledge will serve you everywhere in the world.

In most cities, local minivans race endlessly like slot cars around their circuits. You summon one with a wave as it approaches. For transportation from one town to another, there are established, even if not marked, stations from which the minivans set out. If there's no schedule, minivans won't leave before their seats are full. Touts will try to steer you toward the van that employs them. They'll say they are just about to leave, that theirs is the only van going where you want to go, or anything else they think might work. They'll try to get you to take a seat—and pay for the trip in advance.

Since the driver expects foreigners to be impatient by nature, he may try to get you to convert his van into a private taxi by buying all unoccupied seats. If he asks if you would like to leave at a time when the van is still only half-full, find out what the deal is. There is no free lunch.

You might expect that the van with the most passengers already in it would be the next to leave. Instead, it's common for a driver to get his buddies to sit in his van to pass the time, hoping that you'll see his van nearly full and choose it. After a while, you notice that every time a real passenger climbs in, someone else gets off—and the van goes nowhere. If the vans are filling up fast, take a seat. Otherwise, think of it as an opportunity to stroll around nearby, perhaps finding someone to talk with, until you see a van actually getting ready to go.

Inter-city minivans have set fees for local people, but the driver may ask you to pay whatever he thinks you're good for. If you've learned some vocabulary, ask another passenger what the fare is. Even better, watch what someone else pays, being aware they may not be going to your destination. If you're carrying luggage, you may have to pay an extra fare, certainly if it's taking up a passenger's space. Don't pay until the vehicle is about to leave. That way, if another cranks up to leave first, you're free to switch to it if you want or need to. As you start to get out, the driver may offer you a reduced fare. Let them bid for your business.

Since drivers' incomes depend solely on fares, they let everyone aboard who can cram themselves in, and then they drive as fast as they can for as many hours as they can stay, more or less, awake. Exhausted, driving without speedometers or any other dashboard indicators, sometimes buying off official or unofficial interference with bribes hurled out the window, it's no wonder that little problems crop up.

Minivans are ubiquitous, cheap, and almost always fun—and no traveler should fail to give them a try.

Subways

Many people travel to the great metropolitan areas of the world and never experience the metro, underground, or whatever the local subway system is called. That's understandable. If you don't travel by subway at home, a foreign system can appear pretty intimidating. However, because subways are fast, convenient, and inexpensive, it's worth overcoming any hesitation. Some subways, Moscow's is a prime example, are even architectural or artistic marvels.

A route map, which you can get from a tourist office or from the ticket seller, makes riding subways a lot easier. Although the first map I saw in Paris looked like a plate of spaghetti, I figured it out and now feel confident on any subway system in the world. Let's see if I can explain how subway systems work.

There are two stages in navigating through subways. The first is when you look at the map and figure out which line or lines you need to ride and where the nearest station is. The second is in the subway station as you figure out where to go to board the right car. The second stage is made more interesting by the common need to transfer midride to another line.

The first stage is simple. On the map, locate where you are and the station at which you'll start your journey. Then locate your destination and note the names of the line(s) you'll ride. Each line is named for the *last* station at both ends of the line. For instance, the line you'll board might be named, in English, "Airport–City Hall." If it's not clear from the map, ask at your lodging, ask the ticket seller, ask another passenger, or just trust your intuition.

Let's say you want off at the "Art Museum," and that's the name of one of the stations listed on the Airport–City Hall line. Look for a sign in the subway station that directs you toward that track. As you near it, you decide from the map whether the Art Museum is in the direction of the "Airport" or the "City Hall." That decision determines on which side of the track you stand and, therefore, in which direction the car will be going. A map on the inside of the subway car shows all the stops, letting you know when the Art Museum stop is coming up. It's a lot harder to describe than it is to do.

If Art Museum isn't the name of one of the subway stations on the map, note the name of the nearest station and get off there.

Now, suppose the line you first board doesn't go past the Art Museum and you have to change lines to get there. It's not difficult since each line on the map is numbered or depicted in a distinctive color. Identify the station at which the line you're on and the line to which you want to transfer intersect. When you get off at that intersection, you'll see a sign directing you to the line you want and the right direction. When you change lines, you'll usually walk up or down a level in the station. On the platform, you have an opportunity to check the route map on the wall or confirm your plan with someone.

On the subway, as on many other types of public transportation, lots of folks are pressed together in a confined space so it's wise to keep part of your mind on security. Keep your daypack in front of you. If you have a camera, keep it out of sight or keep your hand on it. Carry nothing you care about in an insecure pocket.

Bicycles

Few means of local transportation provide the pleasure that comes from exploring on a bicycle. It's cheap, relatively safe, gives you great range, lets you see things at a gentle pace, and gets the kinks out of your legs. A few travelers sign up for a bike tour and some plan a bike trip on their own, but too many forget that renting bikes locally is an option.

In Europe and a few other places, you can rent bicycles as multigeared and lightweight as you want. Elsewhere, expect a single gear and a handlebar bell. In most cities around the world, it's not hard to find places that rent bikes. Ask around. If there's nothing organized, it's not hard to find some local person delighted to earn a little money by renting his bike.

Riding local transport produces some of the finest and funniest memories from any trip. Seek it out, the more exotic the better. Ride a yak or a camel or an elephant; listen to the sounds of the creaking leather harness of the pony cart late at night; stand at the rail of a freighter as the Andes glide by in the moonlight. Using local transport is a great way to SAVE MONEY, but it does much more. It helps transform a tourist into a traveler.

CAR RENTAL

In the United States, Europe, and Oceania, we rent a car without a second thought. In much of the rest of the world, doing so deserves several second thoughts. Make no mistake, renting and driving a car abroad can be a challenging and sometimes perilous experience.

In less-developed regions, rental cars are often very expensive, especially when you add in high-priced petrol, insurance, tax, theft protection, drop-off fee, airport location, and mysterious surcharges. Reflecting irregular maintenance, mechanical problems are not infrequent and breakdowns seldom occur at convenient places. Worse, driving may expose you to considerable liability, not to mention turning your nerves into banjo strings. Automobile accidents are one of the leading causes of injury or death for overseas travelers.

The flexibility of having your own car can be very appealing.

Why discuss car rental at all? First, because the flexibility and freedom of having your own transportation is very appealing. Second, sometimes you need to rent a car to get where you want to go. Third, a rental car makes it easier to stay in hotels far removed from expensive downtown hotels in Europe. Since some number of travelers will rent a car abroad, this chapter will help make it a successful experience.

Driver's License

Ask the rental agent, in advance, what kind of driver's license you need to rent their car. In most of Western Europe, your own state driver's license is sufficient. Among common tourist destinations, Spain, Hungary, Russia, Thailand, Japan, Argentina, Brazil, Chile, and Venezuela nominally require either an International Driving Permit (IDP), available from any AAA affiliate for about $10, or a translation of your license into the local language. However, many travel agents say that a passport and your own driver's license are sufficient. If you go without an IDP, then decide to rent a car in one of the few countries that nominally requires one, it's likely you can make an "arrangement" that will cure the problem. In my experience, the IDP has become little more than a souvenir.

When to Rent

If you decide to rent from an *international company*, one way to SAVE MONEY (as much as 50 percent) is to reserve and pay for a car *before* you leave home. If you walk up to an international car rental counter in Europe, expect to pay much more than if you'd made the arrangements at home. You might get an even better rate from a small local company but, on your first trip to a distant destination, you may prefer the security and convenience of knowing there'll be a car waiting.

Several companies, including Kemwell, permit you to buy vouchers in the United States and choose your rental days after you arrive. Doing so adds flexibility while retaining the big savings over renting from the same companies locally.

Rental rates are higher in some countries than in others. For example, you could pay almost twice as much for a car in Italy or France as you would in the United Kingdom or Germany. If it fits your plans, rent the car before entering one of the more-expensive countries.

When you reserve a car, the clerk will ask what time you'll pick it up. After you state a time, find out how long they'll hold the car if your arrival is delayed. Some companies flush your reservation after thirty minutes, others give you until closing time, and some will wait patiently for up to twenty-four hours. If a rental agency has your flight number, it should know if your flight is behind schedule. Nevertheless, if you'll arrive later than expected, let them know.

If you've made a reservation and find you won't be able to honor it, cancel as early as possible. Not only does your courtesy free the car for another traveler, but it may enable you to avoid a cancellation fee. Rental companies are beginning to charge no-shows a fee, often $25, but it could be for the entire amount of the rental contract.

From Whom to Rent

Can you afford a rental car on a modest budget? It's difficult if you rent from one of the heavily-promoted international companies, but for convenience and out of habit, that's what most people do. If you plan to rent from an international company, SAVE MONEY by comparison shopping. Prices charged by car rental firms differ widely. For example, you can get substantially better rates from firms such as Auto Europe (which has more than four thousand locations in Europe and claims to beat anyone else's rate; call 800-223-5555), Budget (800-527-0700), Europe by Car (800-223-1516), European Car Reservations (800-535-3303), or Kemwell (800-678-0678), than from companies such as Hertz or EuroDollar. In a 1995 *Condé Nast Traveler* readers poll, Kemwell was voted as having the best rental rates overseas.

The following examples are based on fact, but are only for illustration since quoted rates fluctuate frequently. In England, you would have paid $189 for a subcompact for a week rented from Europe by Car compared with $303 for the same car and term from Hertz. In Germany, European Car Reservations charged $182 while EuroDollar charged $291. To rent a car for a week in the Czech Republic you could have paid $225 to AutoEurope or $580 to Avis. By the way, most western Europe rental companies will not let you take their autos across a border into eastern Europe.

Prices charged for car rentals vary, so shop around.

SAVE MONEY by renting from the foreign equivalent of Rent-A-Wreck. What do you care about a few dents when you're driving across South Africa?

You almost always SAVE MONEY if you skip the car rental counters at the airport whose rates reflect the taxes and fees they pay the airport. If you don't see signs advertising away-from-the-airport rental agencies, try the yellow pages. They'll usually come for you. If not, go into town and rent from the bus driver's friend, a local rental company, or even a local travel agent.

Here's an obscure way to SAVE MONEY. Ask a local agent if it has a car to be returned to another location. If you appear responsible, you may get the car without charge, paying only for the gas. I did this in New Zealand and the agent even left a sack of freshly picked apples on the front seat for me.

Anyone with a blemished driving record, especially by a recent DUI or accident, may not be allowed to rent a car from certain companies. Rather than learning about this restriction as you're trying to take delivery of the car, call ahead to find out what the policy is. Also, most agencies require a renter to be at least eighteen years old, but for some the minimum age is twenty-one.

The Terms of the Deal

Special rates. If you call because of a special rate you saw advertised, don't assume that the clerk at the reservation counter will offer you that rate. Since you may have to ask for it, perhaps even insist on it, it's good to have the ad with you or be able to cite the code number in it. Car rental agents also have a pocketful of deals they can offer on their own, but they won't do so unless you prompt them.

Bargaining. SAVE MONEY by bargaining. Ask for a discount on the basis of your occupation, your membership in some organization (such as a corporation, automobile association, frequent flyer club, church group, or the Mouse-keteers), your age, your credit card, anything you can think of. Bring up competitor's prices. State how much you're willing to pay. Ask about week-end, by-the-week, and other discounted rates. You can sometimes get a better deal simply by walking from one counter to the next in full view of all the agents. When you get a quote from one, invite another to beat it. It's a very competitive business, so they'll often take what they can get.

Price. Determine exactly what is included in the quoted price and what isn't. Don't let yourself be surprised by "extras" such as an airport pickup charge, state or city surcharge, late return charge, additional driver fee (which could be $5 for each additional driver per day), under-age surcharge, VAT (value added tax, which adds up to 18 percent in some European countries), extra equip-ment charge (e.g., a baby seat), one-way drop-off charge (which can be astro-nomical), collision/loss damage waiver (which runs $3 to $15 per day), theft protection (mandatory in some countries), charges for road service, and so on.

If asked for a deposit, use your credit card. If an agent demands a large cash deposit, you may return to discover it locked up or otherwise unavailable when you want it—and of course you're getting on a plane in a couple of hours.

Ask whether you get a price break when renting for five days or more. It can be less expensive to rent for six days than for four. Similarly, if you plan to use a car for more than seventeen days, see whether the company has a lease option. If so, you'll SAVE MONEY over a straight rental.

Features. Don't assume that air conditioning and automatic transmission are standard; in many countries they are not. Nor are seat belts. If you care, ask whether the car has any of the new high-tech features. For example, the Avis computerized navigational device has a video screen that shows the car as a moving dot on a map; after the driver chooses a destination, the system gives verbal prompts. The Hertz system provides a detailed printout of directions.

Before leaving the airport, get a map or directions to your first destinations and find out where to drop the car on your return. Be sure you know what time the rental office closes where you'll return the car.

If you rent a car in Europe, you might read *Motoeuropa* ($19.95; Eric Bredesen, Box 1212, Dubuque, IA 52004) which provides country-by-coun-try detail about renting, driving, or buying a car. *Autorental Europe* ($14.95; Bill Meier, Lansing Publications, Box 1887, Pleasanton, CA 94566) is another useful resource.

Thrifty and National Interrent offer automated check-out and check-in systems that resemble ATMs. The machine scans your driver's license and credit card and spits out a rental agreement for your signature. Is this getting a little spooky?

Size. The size of car you choose is important. Ask how many passengers it can transport in comfort. Lower fuel efficiency (kilometers per gallon) in large cars means the petrol bill will be high. If an agent offers you a car larger than you need, be wary. That large car may be available precisely because it's a gas-guzzler. On the other hand, be cautious about renting a micro-compact in Germany, Italy, or other places with high-speed highways where it may be blown away by drivers doing 200 kph. If you reserve a small car, as many people do, and the agency is out of that size when you arrive, it should either upgrade you to another of its cars or obtain a similar car from another company without charge to you.

Read the Contract

If there's a problem, *it does no good to claim ignorance of a provision in the rental contract.* Here are some things to look for in the contract:

- Does it define exactly what your responsibilities are?

- On the basis of the blank credit card slip you signed, does the company tie up part of your credit line as security for damage to the car? It may not be just the rental amount; it could be all or part of the value of the car. You need to know whether your credit line is about to be tapped out.

- How do they compute charges if you return the car before or after the end of the agreed-on rental period?

- Do you get unlimited free kilometers or is the rental fee based on the number of kilometers driven? If you pay more every time the little odometer numbers click, you may not feel free to explore as many mysterious detours.

- Does the rental agreement contain instructions about what to do if the car breaks down? Is there a phone number to call in case of a problem? If you feel compelled to make repairs before receiving authorization, get receipts to support your request for reimbursement.

- Are you required to return the tank full of fuel? If so and you fail to do so, you'll be charged at a rate substantially above market price. In some countries, rental companies deliver the car to you with the tank full and instruct you to return it completely empty. That's so they can charge you an inflated price for that first tank of petrol. Since it's a little perilous for most travelers speeding to catch a plane to skid into the parking lot on the last drop, the company gets the petrol left in the tank as a second bonus. Slick, eh?

– Are you permitted to drive the car into another country? Be alert to this one if you intend to drive from western to eastern Europe.

Insurance

The moment comes in every transaction when the clerk asks whether you want the collision insurance offered by the rental company. Note that this insurance covers only damage to the rental car, leaving you on your own as far as other liabilities. It is so overpriced and profitable to the rental company that the clerk has been trained to urge you to buy it. His compensation may depend on how successfully he peddles this product. Therefore, he may even insist that whatever alternative insurance coverage you offer is invalid.

To respond rationally, you must know ahead of time whether you already have insurance that covers damage to the rental car and whether this company, as opposed to what the clerk may say, accepts it. Because they don't know those answers, far too many travelers pay a high price for collision insurance they don't need.

Ask your agent if there is coverage available for rental cars overseas.

Most *domestic automobile insurance policies* offer an option providing collision coverage for cars rented in the United States, but *not* for rental cars driven abroad. Call your auto insurance agent and specify where you expect to be driving. If there is coverage, ask whether (a) the amount of coverage is limited to the value of your personal car (which might be less that the value of the rental car), (b) additional drivers would be covered, (c) it covers unusual vehicles such as RVs or trucks, (d) there is a limit on how long coverage is valid overseas (e.g., thirty days), (e) your regular deductible applies, and (f) the policy provides liability coverage for injury to persons and property. If your domestic policy provides coverage, obtain acknowledgment from the car rental company in advance and carry evidence of the policy.

If you intend to use the insurance protection of your credit card (see the discussion in Chapter 6), call the credit card issuer to be certain its coverage is in effect where you'll be traveling. Then ask the car rental reservations agent if the credit card coverage will be accepted where you pick up the car. Since it is not universally accepted, insist that they check with their *local* agent. Since a local agent may still tell you on arrival that your credit card coverage is not valid, verification in writing may come in handy. If they still balk, call a regional office for confirmation. If you were to pay for the collision damage waiver (CDW) at that point, it would probably cost even more than if you'd paid for it with your prepayment for the car. If you must pay for it to get the car, write on the contract that you are doing so at the clerk's insistence and seek a refund when you return home. If a country's laws require renters to purchase local insurance regardless of credit card coverage, you will have discovered it in advance.

Note that neither the car rental company's collision insurance nor your credit card collision coverage is liability insurance covering damage you may do to people or property. If you have domestic automobile liability insurance, read your policy or ask your agent whether it's effective when driving a rental car abroad. In the United States, state law requires car rental companies to carry various levels of liability insurance. Overseas, the situation varies.

If your own automobile liability insurance does not cover driving a rental car abroad, or you have no automobile liability insurance, investigate buying "non-owner" liability coverage. Alternatively, consider buying $1 million in liability coverage from the rental car company for the trip.

Most European border stations require that you present a "green card," proving you have insurance coverage, before they'll let you drive a rental car into their country. Travelers who don't know about this requirement before they reach a border are about to do a U-turn.

Insurance coverage may be invalidated when the driver (a) was not listed on the rental contract, (b) was intoxicated at the time of the accident, or (c) violated a geographical limitation in the rental contract, such as by taking the car across a border or on specified roads. The company will probably never know that you violated the limitation—unless you have a wreck in the forbidden zone. Then they'll know and you'll get the bill for damages.

Don't take any risks with insurance. Travel magazines are full of letters lamenting horrendous situations as a result of an accident for which the writers were not insured.

Inspect the Vehicle

My cardinal rule when renting a car anywhere other than a big city franchise situation: SEE THE VEHICLE before handing over any money. Otherwise, there may be a shiny car parked nearby as a lure, but it won't be the car in which you depart the next morning amidst grinding gears and acrid smoke. If the agent tells you that "your" car isn't available for inspection at the moment, it may be off hauling a load of swine and turnips. Ask that it be brought to your hotel before you sign up. If the car promised isn't the one that shows up the next day, be insistent. They may discover something more suitable or drop the price as you drop your standards.

Inspect the car for damage before you leave the lot. In some countries, it may already look like the loser in a destruction derby. On the other hand, some European rental agencies are very picky and returning with a tiny dent or scratch could result in demand for payment on the spot. If there are dings, get a witness or have the agent note them on the contract. When you return, take a look at the car yourself. It's seldom the policy of a rental company to inspect at the moment you return, but you may want to have the clerk note on the contract that there is no damage. Damage "discovered" after you've left may be charged to your credit card.

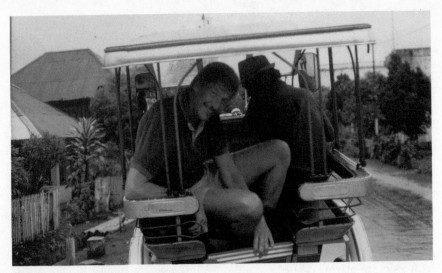
Author scrunched in a *bendi*. Tomohon, Indonesia.

Check the lights, air conditioning/heater, horn, windshield wiper, seatbelt, and brakes. Make sure there is a spare tire and jack. If the tires aren't safe, change tires, change cars, or change companies. While you're inspecting, make a note of the license number, make, model, and color of the car. If the car is stolen while in your custody or you misplace it in a crowded parking lot, you'll feel foolish if you can't identify it. If you'll be driving the car for an extended period, ask for an extra key. If one isn't forthcoming, consider having one made. Solving a lost key problem is much more time-consuming in Bulgaria than in Baltimore.

See the vehicle before handing over any money.

Before you roll away, be sure you understand how to operate all switches, knobs, gears, and repair equipment. Ask whether the car has an electronic anti-theft device. If so, have it demonstrated. Otherwise, you may wind up with a car that won't start or whose shrieking alarm won't stop.

If the tank is supposed to be full, see that it is. By the way, if you drive in Europe you should be aware that gas stations charge for services such as cleaning the windshield or filling the tires. Of course in the United States, you either get no service or it's built into the price of the gas.

While planning a trip from Victoria Falls, Zimbabwe, to Chobe National Park in northern Botswana, then on to Etosha National Park in Namibia, I found no evidence of public transportation along that stretch. I figured we could hitch from Vic Falls to Chobe and on to Katima Mulillo, a village at the northeastern tip of Namibia, but since the several hundred miles of sand and sagebrush beyond that point seemed uninhabited, hitching farther it seemed impractical. Then my partner discovered that a small resort in Katima Mulillo was a lonely outpost of an international car rental agency. It had a grand total of one car for rent and we reserved it instantly. When we arrived at the resort months later (amazingly, on the date agreed), the owner was distressed to learn that we intended to take his little Toyota all the way to Windhoek, the capital. For all its sheltered life, his pet Toyota had been confined to short scenic excursions. Nevertheless, waving our reservation, we rented the Toyota and didn't see another car for the next eight hours. All told, we put about two thousand hard kilometers on that little car before turning it in. I understand the resort abandoned its affiliation with the rental company soon afterward. Can't say I blame them.

Safety

For safety reasons, it's better not to stop if anyone other than a police officer tries to flag you down. The "good Samaritan" scam involves someone waving at you, apparently to alert you to a problem with your car. Perhaps another car pulls alongside and a passenger points at one of your tires with an expression of alarm. While you and the Samaritan check out the imaginary problem, his confederate empties your car.

If you are rear-ended, a favorite ploy in southern France, don't get out of your car if you have the slightest doubt about the situation. That little bump may be an informal introduction; the equivalent of "What's your sign." The thief wants to know you better. If you can, drive to a service station or some other well-lighted public place. Otherwise, stay in your locked car and wait for the police.

Someone who has access to your car, say in a service station, may start a slow leak in a tire. I've seen a hand-crafted blade that attaches to the toe of a shoe for exactly that purpose. When the tire goes flat later, someone will be there to help you out—and help himself. It's sad to say but anytime you accept help, you or your partner should keep an eye on the helpers.

Be alert for thieves who may try to snatch something from your car when you stop at a traffic light. In Buenos Aires this has gotten to be such a problem that many drivers slow a bit, combine a quick sideways glance with a prayer, and cruise right through red lights. Keep those doors locked and, if circumstances warrant, windows up. In some places, it's better to keep your gear on the floor of the car than on the front seat. Don't leave a tempting target for a quick hand slipping in an open window.

Be alert when driving in an area that seems risky. If someone approaches your car, perhaps indicating he wants to ask directions, be prepared to drive away immediately. If caught off-guard by someone who demands your keys, consider tossing them to him—but missing. Escape as he retrieves the keys.

If an unmarked car with a flashing light signals you to stop, drive to a well-lighted place to do so. Unless you are certain it's the police, keep the car doors locked and roll the window down just far enough to show your license. Ask for identification. If not satisfied, refuse to get out of the car and ask to be escorted to a police station.

If you believe you are being followed, make a series of turns. If the other vehicle is still with you, look for a police station or a busy petrol station.

A rental car company sticker is an invitation to thieves, so ask for a car without one. If there is one on the car, remove it. Remember the glee you felt as a child when you saw Christmas presents under the tree? That's how a thief feels when he spots a rental car. It's a giant stocking stuffed with cameras and luggage.

Park in well-lighted areas and don't leave any belongings visible. Assume that a rental car will be broken into and never leave anything expensive in the car overnight. Think of it as wheels, not as a secure place to leave your gear. Locking something in the trunk is better than leaving it on the seat, but even that provides little real protection.

You may have an opportunity to make the car temporarily secure by engaging the services of a car guardian. In places such as Mexico City and Naples, the offer from scruffy adolescents to guard your car is straight-forward blackmail. They're offering to guard it from themselves and, frankly, it's a good investment of a few pesos or lira. Elsewhere, it's a coin flip.

Driving conservatively is good practice since traffic can be quite chaotic and foreign rules of the road, both official and informal, may be unfamiliar to you. Reading signs in a foreign language takes your attention off the road for a few extra seconds. Besides avoiding an accident, driving conservatively helps avoid a traffic ticket. If you get a ticket in Europe, you pay a fine on the spot (asking for a receipt early on may help keep the fine in line with the official schedule). In other parts of the world, when and how much you pay is more likely to be a matter of negotiation on a very uneven playing field.

Besides slowing reflexes when needed the most, being intoxicated while driving can lead to jail. In Europe, penalties for driving under the influence are severe. Further, "influence" is defined as a blood alcohol level only one half to one quarter what it is in the United States. Roadblocks with Breathalyzer tests are not uncommon.

In almost a dozen countries, cars drive on the left-hand side of the road. You can learn to do it—but it will take a few hours (or more). So how do you avoid trashing the car during that time?

- Consider renting a car with an automatic transmission.
- Locate all the gadgets (horn, lights, wipers, signals) before leaving the rental lot (you'll wish you had if you need one of them halfway through a round-about!).
- Take a practice spin in the rental lot or on some nearby bunny-slope.
- Avoid starting off in rush hour.
- Take advantage of a partner who can handle the map, read street signs, and watch for bogies.

In the end, driving on the "wrong" side of the road isn't the hard part. The hard part is the constant embarrassment of walking up to the wrong side of the car, then trying to pretend you're just there to check the tire pressure.

Stress

Monetary costs of car rental seem modest compared to the mental havoc some people experience when driving a car in less-developed countries. Roads are jammed and the horn takes the place of the brake. If you aren't used to sharing a narrow road with massive trucks and with rattle-trap cars lurching along without benefit of headlights, and if you don't find pleasure in weaving through throngs of bicycles, rickshaws, horse carts, camels, and basket-laden pedestrians, forget it!

From Rwanda to Sri Lanka, I've rented cars that come with a driver. This is not an extravagance. The cost for the driver is, after a little bargaining, minimal when balanced against the guidance and tranquillity he provides. At the end of the day, he helps find suitable lodging for you before curling up in the back seat of the car or a back room of the hotel. It's not unusual to hire car and driver from a nontraditional source, such as a travel agent or desk clerk, for considerably less than you'd pay for the vehicle alone from a heavily promoted car rental firm.

Traveling in Your Own Car

For people tempted to buy a vehicle in, or take a vehicle to, a foreign country, I'd mention several considerations. First, staying in your own vehicle can isolate you from local life as effectively as being on a regimented tour. Second, in many countries the roads are in such terrible condition they can reduce your vehicle to scrap. Third, the difficulty of finding spare parts and experienced mechanics is multiplied by the square of the distance from your auto's country of origin. Fourth, every time you cross a border you may have to buy a bond, guaranteeing you won't sell your car while in the country. Fifth, to get your car across some borders you may have to pay significant bribes. Sixth, traveling a long distance with a fully loaded vehicle means accepting considerable risk of theft.

Despite all these objections, I bought a ten-year-old Citroen 2CV at the beginning of a two-month post-graduation trip in Europe. It was broken into once and run into twice but provided great flexibility and enormous fun— and I made $100 when I sold it to an arriving student.

If you'll be in Europe for a month or more and are determined to drive, look into a purchase/repurchase deal (the rough equivalent of a lease) with one of the car rental companies. You pay for maintenance, fuel, repairs, and other "owner's" expenses, but are not charged for mileage. At the end of the period, the rental company repurchases the vehicle for a price that makes the net cost to you less than a straight rental.

TRAVELING BY WATER

Freighter Travel

One of the great freighter trips I've taken was aboard the *Evangelista*, sailing the Chilean "inside passage" between Puerto Montt and Puerto Natales.* A tiny stateroom and three meals cost about $40 a day. In addition to incomparable views of the Andes and glaciers, the Captain allowed me to take the helm for hours at a time. Navimag (tel. 56-2-2035030 or 56-065-253318), which owns *Evangelista*, and a company named Transmarchilay, offer comfortable, inexpensive trips from Puerto Montt to the island of Chiloe, the small towns of Chaiten and Chacabuco at the base of the Andes, glaciers spilling into Laguna San Rafael, and to Puerto Natales. These trips take from one to six days.

Opportunities for freighter travel in the traditional sense have diminished substantially over the past several decades. That was due, in part, to regulations that require a doctor on board if there are more than twelve passengers. However, after hitting a low in the mid-1980s, capacity for passengers on freighters is again on the upswing. Increased mechanization has freed more officers' staterooms for passengers. And when cargo tonnage drops, shipping lines are delighted to earn revenue from passengers. Some of the more popular trips from the United States sail to East Africa (sixty to seventy days), Australia (seventy to seventy-five days), and South America (thirty-five to fifty days).

Freighter travel isn't as cheap as it was in the past, but it's still possible to travel in a first class freighter cabin for around $90 a day, considerably less than many cruise ships (and there are discounts for off-season travel). Some charge as little as $70 per day. Cabins are likely to be more spacious than those on cruise ships and there are often accommodations for singles with no surcharge. Most are outside cabins with large windows, comfortable sitting areas, and private facilities. Because the best cabins go to those who reserve first, some travelers make plans a year or more in advance.

You will spend more time at sea in freighters than in cruise ships.

Wholesome meals, included in the price, are usually served in the officers' dining room. Depending on the carrier, these meals may be very ethnic so make sure you know what to expect. There won't be a dance band or over-the-hill entertainers in shiny tuxedoes, but there will probably be a sun deck, VCR, library and, perhaps, a saltwater pool. The crew is there to work, so you'll have plenty of time to write the novel that's been waiting to spring to life.

Freighters travel slowly, providing more time at sea than you'd have on a cruise ship—and that's exactly what most freighter travelers are after. Because

---

* *Puerto Natales.* This tiny port town in southern Chile is a departure point for trips to the Chilean fjords, Torres del Paines National Park, and Punta Arenas.

freighters are working ships, they may not adhere to their planned schedules. If you're kept at sea extra days because the ship detours to an unexpected port to capture a cargo, there's no extra charge.

Generations of young men have told fond stories of working their way around the world as deck hands on freighters. Sadly, there are no longer jobs for U.S. citizens aboard foreign-flag freighters and long lines of professional merchant seamen stand idly in hiring halls waiting for scarce jobs aboard U.S. flag carriers. There's no room before the mast for adventuresome youths to holystone teak decks in return for passage.

I don't know how Joseph Conrad would feel about modern freighters, but they can be a fine way to travel if you're flexible and seek the ultimate in relaxation. To investigate a trip, try the following:

- *ABC Passenger Shipping Guide* provides detailed listings of ships, capacities, itineraries, fares, and sailing frequencies of passenger-carrying freighters all over the world (ABC International, Dunstable Beds, LU5 4HB, England).
- *Ford's Freighter Travel Guide* lists scheduled freighter trips ($14.95; 818-701-7414).
- *Freighter Travel News* is a well-established source of information about opportunities for freighter travel (3524 Harts Lake Road, Roy, WA 98580, $18/year).
- Freighter World Cruises represents sixteen shipping lines and twenty different itineraries. It publishes *Freighter Space Advisory* biweekly (818-449-3106; $33 per year). Fares range from $75 to $125 per day and trips are generally from thirty to seventy-five days.
- Pearl's Travel Tips is a well-known agent specializing in freighter travel (813-393-2919).
- TravLtips Cruise and Freighter Travel Association provides information about freighter routes and publishes reports from freighter travelers. For a $15 annual membership fee, you receive *TravLtips*, a bimonthly newsletter. As a travel agency, it can book trips for you (800-872-8584).

Freighter lines that don't charge a single supplement include Bank Line, CAST Lines, Egon Oldendorff Line, Ivaran Lines, Mediterranean Great Lakes Line, Mediterranean Shipping Co., Mineral Shipping Co., and Reederi Bernhard Schulte. Try also Lykes, Columbus (212-432-1700), Pace, and Navaran Lines.

Ferries and Small Passenger Ships

Unfortunately, taking a ferry is not quite as carefree an adventure as it might sound. On modern, well-maintained ships, ferry travel is fun. Then there are all the other ferry lines, the ones that provide lifesaving gear for about one-quarter of the passengers and consider maintenance an extravagance. Maybe you've seen a few of those two-inch newspaper filler stories reporting ferries that rolled over, drowning four hundred people.

After taking a long look at a ratty-looking, jammed-beyond-capacity ferry about to make an eight-hour rough water crossing to Zanzibar, I let my instinct persuade me to skip it. That particular boat made it but another, about a month later, didn't. On the other hand, many other ferries, such as the one from Brindisi, Italy, across the Adriatic Sea to Corfu, or the one from Buenos Aires to Uruguay, are terrific. Give the ship a close look, locate the lifejackets, and sit near an exit.

The MV Ilala II is a forty-five-year-old ship that sails the length of Lake Malawi in central southern Africa. Although it carries more than four hundred passengers in third class, most Westerners aboard for the entire six-day trip are happier in one of the six top-deck cabins. The scenery of distant mountains, tropical shoreline, and the walls of the Great Rift Valley is spectacular. The ship's motorboat putts ashore to visit villages and some of the resorts catering to European vacationers. The cost is about $400 plus meals. Contact the Malawi Tourist Office for more information.

Try the Bergen Line whose steamers sail north from Bergen, Norway, every day all the way up the fantastic coast of Fjordland to Hammerfest above the Arctic Circle. Call (800) 323-7436.

Don't miss traveling the canals by boat in Venice, Bangkok, and Amsterdam, or the beautiful rivers of England, France, Germany, and Hungary. Of course, in modern Europe the Danube is "Blue" only in song.

The Inside Passage in southeast Alaska is another premier trip with views of fjords, thousands of islands, and mountainous coastlines. Plenty of cruise ships make that run, but why not hop on one of the Alaska Marine Ferries? For a schedule, call Alaska Marine Highway at (800) 642-0066 (or 907-465-3941 in Juneau). The popular trip from Bellingham, Washington, to Skagway, Alaska takes 2½ days and costs $246 (not including meals). Although these ferries have been known to run late or even break down once in a while, they are an excellent way to meet other travelers and the views are spectacular. Service extends far beyond the Inside Passage, even up to Dutch Harbor at the tip of the Alaska Peninsula.

Facilities aboard ferries and passenger ships in less-developed countries vary considerably. Assume that the trip will last longer than planned and bring sufficient food and water aboard. Reserve space in the highest class accommodation your budget will allow. Lock your cabin door and window and lock your gear to something immobile. If conditions warrant, take a mosquito net and plenty of repellent. Expect a great experience—and that conditions will be inferior to what you hope for.

Cruises

The purpose of taking a cruise is not simply to be transported from one place to another, so the topic doesn't fit easily in this chapter. Still, because cruises are another way to touch the rest of the world, I want to provide some information about them.

Because the cruise industry advertises in every medium and travel agents love to book cruises, you'll have no difficulty obtaining information about cruise opportunities anywhere in the world. But while many brochures feature couples looking romantically into one another's champagne-glazed eyes, they're a little short of the kind of details you need to know about. When you find a cruise that seems to fit your objectives, ask for a copy of the contract and read it carefully.

Be sure you receive answers to the following questions:

- *Price.* What is the published price and precisely what does it include (for budgeting purposes, don't forget airfare and meals ashore)? Rates for cruises are similar to hotel rack rates in that there's no need to pay them. Try for a big discount by signing up early, or late, or because you can't afford the listed price, or for any other reason you think of. Like an airline seat, a cabin is a dead loss if it's empty when the ship sails. If the cruise operator can't fill it, you'll probably get a discount, but only if you ask for it. Give the operator a price to beat. Invite them to find a basis on which you qualify for a discount. If the price is inflexible and you're willing to pay it, ask for an upgrade at that price. Is there a single supplement charge—and will they waive it? Is cancellation insurance included in the price? If it's not, it may be worth considering if there is a reasonable possibility you might miss the sailing.

  Expect to pay extra for things such as laundry service, alcoholic drinks, tips, and on-shore excursions. Ask the operator for a list of expenses not included in the price. One common add-on is referred to as port fees/taxes/charges and can increase the cost considerably.

- *Cabin.* What is the size of the cabin and what does it include (e.g., bathroom, bunk beds, desk, window or porthole, view)? A cabin with a porthole or window may cost twice as much as an interior cabin. Since you pay for space, decide how much time you plan to spend in the cabin. Make sure it's not next to the bar, restaurant, or engines.

- *Shipmates.* What will be the ages and nationalities of your shipmates and how many will there be? If the group is too large, time ashore may be reduced and meal service slow. See if the cruise tends to cater to a particular age group and, if so, whether it's one with which you would be comfortable. Ask whether any large groups or organizations would be on the cruise. If so, might they set a tone for the trip that could make you unhappy?

Discounted Cruises

If interested in a cruise, SAVE MONEY by contacting a discount cruise specialist. The following are a few of the many companies that sell cruises at a discount:

Cruise Central	(800) 500-0033
Cruise Directors	(800) 348-0009
Cruise Line, Inc.	(800) 777-0707
Cruise Market Place	(800) 826-4333
Cruise Shoppe Operations	(800) 338-9051
Cruises of Distinction	(800) 634-3445
Cruiseworld	(800) 321-2784
CSAA Travel Agency	(415) 565-2141
Travel Company	(800) 367-6090
VIP Tours and Travel	(800) 847-4386
White Travel Service	(800) 547-4790
World Wide Cruises	(800) 882-9000
1-800-BEST CRUISE	(800) 237-8278

– *Scheduled activities.* Are there any? Will lectures be in a language you understand?

Useful resources include (a) *Berlitz Complete Guide to Cruising and Cruise Ships* (Douglas Ward. Macmillan, 1994. $17.95), (b) *How to Book a Perfect Cruise, Cruising for the Handicapped Traveler,* and *Protecting Your Travel Dollar* (800-882-9000), (c) *Answers to the Most Asked Questions about Cruises* (call Cruise Lines International Association in New York City), and (d) *Fodor's Cruises and Ports of Call: Choosing the Perfect Ship and Enjoying Your Time Ashore* (Andrew Collins, ed. Fodor Travel Publications. $18).

Sailing

Serving as crew for a transoceanic or Caribbean cruise sounds pretty romantic. After all, it's a free ride to exotic ports, isn't it? Yes and no. The volunteer crew may pay no money but they will contribute plenty of work. Still, it can be a fine trade off. Ship captains are looking for experienced sailors, but you may be accepted if you can cook, provide medical services, or record the trip on film or in writing.

One way to find a ride is to frequent marinas that cater to ocean-going yachts. Introduce yourself to owners and captains and mention your availability. Present yourself as a person who will be a pleasure to be with for several weeks in a very confined space. Put a notice on yacht club and marina bulletin boards and give your phone number to marina personnel. Watch local newspaper ads as well as those in boating magazines.

Whitewater Rafting

I suppose whitewater adventure trips are not strictly considered "transport," but I want to include a few words about them. Just because an outfitter is in business doesn't mean its staff knows what it's doing. Ask who the guides are and how much experience they have on the river you have in mind, as well as on others. Ask about safety equipment. Do they provide helmets? Are the life jackets in good condition? Will safety kayakers accompany the trip? Will the river be at a safe level? Are the rafts self-bailing? Do the rafts have foot cups? If wet suits are needed, will they be provided? By the way, a good outfitter should ask you some questions in return about your experience and physical condition.

The importance of the answers to these questions varies depending on how challenging the particular river is. If a river is ranked I, II, or III, there's little to worry about. If it has class IV or V rapids, you should be listening closely to the answers. If it's ranked VI, binoculars are all you need. If whitewater trips were completely safe they wouldn't be any fun. After all, you're in it for the thrill and the challenge. Still, if you are relying on the skill and equipment of an outfitter and its guides for your safety, don't take much for granted.

I've listed several books in the Bibliography that provide a keen sense of what river travel is about. Romanticize about the Amazon, Congo, Niger, Nile, Omo and other great rivers, but know what you're getting into before you sign up for a week or more.

HITCHHIKING

There is so much public transport available around the world, and it's so much fun and so cheap, that hitchhiking should be avoided unless absolutely necessary. Where there's no public transport, there is often almost no private transport either and hitchhiking may become a necessity. If you don't accept rides with drivers who are drinking, hitchhiking may not be very risky—but who ever knows for sure?

Hitchhiking can be educational. One summer day in southern Africa, I spent hours waiting in the shade of an acacia tree. Finally, a Toyota van appeared and the white passenger allowed her black driver to pick me up. In the course of conversation, I asked her how many people lived in her town. She said "About a hundred." When I expressed surprise at how small it was, she added, "Oh well, there are about 3,000 locals." I got the picture of how she saw the world.

On a trip from Botswana to Zimbabwe, two friendly middle-aged men picked me up. They had some difficulty squeezing my backpack into the trunk of their car because the trunk was already stuffed with appliances, tools, and several bulky, taped-up bags. When they told me that a sewing machine costs $400 in Botswana but $1,700 in Zimbabwe, I understood why they'd been shopping in Botswana. At the border, the driver took my passport, bypassed dozens of people waiting in line under the blazing sun at the Customs house, and returned in two minutes with the proper stamps. When the car was waved through the barricade without inspection, I suspected I was in the company of a couple of pros.

Fifteen Tips for More Successful Hitchhiking

Hitchhiking can be fun or it can be frustrating. These road-proven tips should help speed you on your way.

- Early in the morning, when trucks start their journeys, is usually the best time to hitchhike. Stroll out after a leisurely breakfast and you may have missed the wave. Ask local people. Be hesitant about hitchhiking after the sun falls below the yardarm and alcohol flows more freely. Besides, you may not want to fall asleep with some stranger driving.
- Stores, petrol stations, border posts, restaurants, and other places at which drivers stop are ideal for picking up a ride. Local people can tell you whether there's an informal depot for hitchhikers in town or whether it's better to walk to an out-of-town intersection.
- If several people are waiting for a ride, it's the universal custom for the most recent arrival to take the position farthest down the road from approaching traffic. In other words, the early bird gets the Mercedes. A couple of times, I've been standing in the middle of an ad hoc line of local people waiting to catch a ride when a driver stopped and beckoned to me to get in. He may have wanted English conversation or believed that he could charge me a higher fare, but I won't cut in front of local people who've been waiting longer.
- If not waiting in a line, give the impression that you're walking, not just standing by the roadside. Drivers like to think you're making an effort to get somewhere on your own.
- In choosing a spot, make sure oncoming drivers can see you clearly and have a safe place to pull over. Stand far enough off the road that you can't be clipped by a load hanging off the side of a truck.
- As a car approaches, make eye contact with the driver (which means no dark glasses). Smile and look like someone a driver would like to talk with. Make your gear look clean and compact.
- There is no universally correct hitchhiking signal. The traditional closed fist with upraised thumb, so natural in most of the Western world, is an obscene gesture in some places. In Indonesia, you raise

and lower your open palm, holding it face down and parallel to the road. In other places, point your index finger and shake it up and down at the place where you'd like the vehicle to stop. Some hitch-hikers hold up a sign with their destination written on it (as spelled in the local language, which is not necessarily how the name is spelled on your map). Some prefer not to use a sign because it somewhat commits them to ride with a driver whose company they would rather do without.

- Some hitchhikers make an obscene gesture toward a vehicle that didn't pick them up. Not only is that offensive behavior by a guest, especially one seeking a favor, but it's a disservice to other hitchhik-ers. Giving a smile or a wave will work out better for you and for other travelers.

- I recommend against a single woman hitchhiking alone. She's likely to get picked up quickly, but then what? It's much safer to hitchhike with a companion. A male and female together will have good luck, especially if the woman stands at roadside and the man stands at a distance, approaching after the vehicle has stopped. I know it sounds a little deceptive . . . well, I guess it is.

- Be cautious about accepting a ride with more than two men. I'm not saying not to do it; just to be careful.

- Some people won't accept a lift from anyone who speeds by then turns around to offer a ride. Their eagerness may indicate a motive other than hospitality.

- Before getting in, ask the driver's destination before mentioning yours. If you have any reason for concern, courteously decline the ride. The world is not as gentle as it once was.

- If it's practical, keep your belongings next to you in the car. In the situation I described above, I felt vulnerable with my backpack in the trunk.

- The driver who picks you up may expect some pay, which is not unreasonable given relative economic circumstances. You might bring up the subject before you climb in, or at least early on, to make sure there's no disagreement later. If local people pay, there may be fairly standard fares for certain distances but a traveler will probably be asked to pay a small premium. I sometimes buy the driver a snack.

- Don't buy alcohol while underway. It's common for drivers to drink and it causes a lot of fatal smash-ups. If you feel you should depart, say you're sick or have to relieve yourself. Living is more important than courtesy.

17

Etiquette

> Wherever you go, you will receive impressions
> of the places you see and the people you meet.
> Do not forget that those people will
> receive impressions of you.
> —Broughton Waddy,
> *A Word or Two Before You Go*

Etiquette, tradition, and custom exist because they help make people comfortable in their relationships with other people. We know intuitively that to be welcomed as guests we have to know and observe local ground rules. Given the subtleties of the thousands of different ceremonies and rituals on this planet, can any traveler get up to speed? Actually, it's less of a problem than it seems. In this chapter, we'll focus on issues likely to be touchy in quite a few cultures

Before starting your trip, read about customs in other countries. When you arrive, be especially alert to how local people behave in the key areas of eating, personal space, punctuality, sanitation, gestures, and relationships between genders.

Travelers of a few nationalities are held in "minimum high regard" (as they say in the U.S. Senate) around the world. They've earned criticism by their self-centered, jingoistic behavior and unwillingness to respect local culture. We can do much better than that.

Cultural intrusion of the West has already become incredibly far-reaching. Gezing is a small town in the Sikkimese foothills of the Himalayas, just down the mountain from the venerated Pemayangtse Monastery. Strolling through town late at night, when fires had been banked and lanterns shuttered, I came across a dozen kids in a lopsided shack enthralled by a row of battery-run video games. Few of those kids will become educated monks of the monastery, or even remain in their home town much longer. Unlike Johnny Appleseed, we should avoid sewing seeds of our culture as we travel.

— *The language of courtesy.* As a nonlinguist, I'm proof that anyone can quickly command the few words necessary for basic courtesy. Learn the local words for hello, please, thank you, and excuse me, and use them often. Travelers too often begin an encounter by peremptorily barking a request, such as "Where is the Post Office?" It's far better to speak first in the other person's language even if all you can say is "good morning." It shows respect and has a positive effect on what happens next. Go out of your way to create a good impression as you travel.

— *Greetings.* In many countries, greetings are exchanged more frequently than in our country. It becomes fun to call out a greeting in the local language and exchange smiles. On the tiny island of Gili Trawangan,* as you head for the coral reef you say good morning to your neighbor with *Selamat pagi* (it's *Pagi-pagi* if it's very early, but I seldom had the opportunity to use that one). Everyone walking along Himalayan trails in Nepal smiles, makes eye contact, and sings out *Namaste,* saying, more or less, "I salute the spirit within you." Throughout the Arab world, you'll be greeted with *Salaam alaykum.* In Israel, *Shalom* is said both on arriving and departing. A respectful traveler has appropriate words ready to greet people.

"If an ass goes traveling, he'll not come home a horse."
—Thomas Fuller, English clergyman

In much of Asia, it's traditional to greet a person by bringing the palms together, fingertips anywhere from chest to eye level depending on the level of respect being conveyed, and inclining the head forward a little. In Thailand, this gesture is known as the *wai* and is still common in small towns and the countryside.

The handshake, ubiquitous in the West, is less common in the rest of the world. Follow the local person's lead. As a rule, don't extend your hand to a woman unless she initiates the gesture. Zambia and several other African countries add a nice touch: your left hand grips your own right wrist as you extend your hand. Primarily in Latin America, but in many other countries as well, be prepared to receive a hug and one or more kisses on the cheek, regardless of the gender of the other person. Respond in kind.

Remember that personal space is cultural and try not to feel invaded if the person you're talking with stands closer than you are used to.

---

* *Gili Trawangan.* This tiny island lies off the coast of Lomboc, Indonesia. It offers sunny beaches, snorkeling, and spectacular moonlight.

Since people in other countries are more formal when first meeting than are people in the United States, be hesitant to address new acquaintances by their first name unless requested to do so. In fact, you may be expected to use an academic or honorary title with their last name. Unfortunately, it's not always easy to know what the last name is. For example, when you see a written name in China, the surname is first and the given name last. In Latin America, except Brazil, many names are a combination of the father's and mother's surnames. Thus, you would address Sr. Fidel Romero Santamaria as Senor Romero, using his father's surname. If uncertain, ask the other person how he or she would like you to address them rather than give offense unintentionally. Similarly, when a person says his name, ask that it be repeated until you have it right. You'll be respected for knowing, or wanting to learn, the custom.

- *Nuance.* When people for whom English is not the first language speak to you in English, they may not understand the exact nuances of what they're saying. For example, if someone calls out "Hey, you!" or "Hey, mama!" there is probably no intention to be rude. They are seeking your attention, but have a limited vocabulary on which to draw. Keep this in mind and you're unlikely to be offended.

- *Be discreet when speaking to other travelers.* Don't offend someone or embarrass yourself by saying something inappropriate on the assumption that local people around you don't understand English, or whatever language you're using.

- *The national honor and other hot topics.* Citizens of most countries are very sensitive about their national honor. This feeling is intense in Latin America, as well as in countries governed by any form of monarchy (some African quasi-monarchs are more than a little touchy as well). Don't show disrespect for a national flag, criticize a national leader, or comment publicly about controversial aspects of the society. Avoid discussing religion, politics, and border conflicts. And I assure you that no one wants to be reminded that their country receives foreign aid from your country. As a guest, err on the side of discretion.

Street vendor selling
bread. Istanbul, Turkey.

- *Hospitality.* In many cultures, and Arabic cultures are good examples, hospitality is taken very seriously. You risk giving offense if you don't accept a sincere offer of food, shelter, or assistance. Nevertheless, be very circumspect in the Arab world when talking to or about someone else's wife. Hospitality does not extend that far and your comment could be taken more personally than you intend. Remind yourself of the penalty for thieves and extrapolate.

  On the other hand, be cautious about expressing excessive admiration for someone's property, say a gold watch. He may insist that you accept it as a gift. If you refuse, you risk giving offense—but you might be expected to reciprocate.

- *Dress in accordance with local custom.* Assuming you won't be dressing exactly as local people do, at least modify your normal dress to fit local standards. Not surprisingly, restrictions on dress affects women more than men (see Chapter 14). For women, local custom often means dressing in loose clothing and covering shoulders and legs. Watch local people. In many temples, head and legs must be covered and feet must be free of shoes. Even though toplessness, and sometimes total nudity, are acceptable on quite a few European beaches and various isolated spots around the world, wearing a skimpy bathing suit is a poor idea unless you're certain it won't offend local sensibilities.

If unsure about a particular custom, ask.

It's unusual to see local men or women wearing shorts in Asia or Latin America, but male travelers can wear shorts without giving offense (except that they may not be admitted into some temples). However, female travelers in shorts may attract unwanted attention anywhere. The double standard is international.

- *Left hand.* Because toilet paper is sometimes not readily available in non-Western countries, some local people use the left hand as a substitute (in conjunction with a bucket of water when it's available). Even assuming that you carry TP with you, make it a practice not to eat with your left hand. If you forget, your dining neighbors will consider you uncivilized, not to mention unclean.

- *Shoes.* It's common in the non-Western world to remove one's shoes prior to entering certain spaces, including homes and temples. Watch others. If in doubt, slip your shoes off at the door.

- *Feet.* In some places, such as Thailand, it is offensive to point the soles of your feet, with or without shoes on, toward another person. You may need to concentrate on this one for a while to avoid doing it without thinking. Speaking of your feet, don't step on the low sill at temple doorways; step over it because good spirits live under the sill.

- *Thank-you.* In many countries you should arrive with candy or flowers or some other small gift if invited to dinner in someone's home. However, a gift of flowers demonstrates the complexity of local customs. In various places, you should not give an odd number of flowers, nor thirteen flowers, nor chrysanthemums or purple flowers (both of which may be suitable only for funerals), nor roses (which may have an overly personal romantic connotation). How to know? Ask. When someone does you a favor, send a thank you note. Give them something tangible to let them know they didn't drop out of your thoughts the moment you left.

- *Punctuality.* Punctuality is less prized throughout Latin America than in Europe, but it's hard to generalize about punctuality in the rest of the world. Two tips will see you through. First, if you arrive at the scheduled time, you're unlikely to give offense. Second, if the other person arrives significantly later than you did, hold your tongue and temper since his arrival may be consistent with local protocol.

- *Eating.* In some countries, the custom is to finish everything on your plate. In others, you're expected to leave a bit, indicating that the host was so generous you couldn't finish. You please any host by sampling some of everything. If something doesn't look palatable, it is better not to ask what it is since the reply is unlikely to improve the situation. Beyond all else, don't eat anything that might jeopardize your health, not even to be courteous.

- *The elderly.* Elderly people are treated with special respect in non-Western countries. In a group, treat the oldest person as spokesperson for the group.

- *The head.* In some places, such as Thailand, the head is considered the seat of god in a person. Therefore, avoid touching anyone's head. If you do so accidentally, offer an immediate apology. In various places, including in temples and at religious ceremonies, a woman is expected to cover her head.

- *Monks.* A woman should not touch a Buddhist monk. Step aside if necessary to avoid doing so. It is polite to give your seat to a monk who's standing, although not all local people do so.

- *Public affection.* There is little public display of affection in many countries. With the modern tide inundating the world this inhibition is diminishing, but travelers should respect the local custom. Holding hands is fine, whether from affection or as a self-defense strategy, but holding more than that may not be.

- *Servers.* Being demanding of a serving person in a restaurant is impolite. Besides, what seems like poor service may be consistent with a custom unfamiliar to you. For example, it may be customary to serve dishes in what seems an odd sequence. If you're polite, perhaps the server will point out the things on your plate that are garnishes, not intended for consumption. Otherwise, she'll just watch as you gulp them down with a grimace (yours, not hers).

- *Body language.* In parts of southeast Asia, standing with hands on hips as you address someone projects hostility. This is a good posture to avoid when dealing with an official.

- *Curiosity.* You're likely to be the object of considerable curiosity, often undisguised. I have a photo in which I'm walking down a narrow lane in Darjeeling in the midst of a group of striking tea workers carrying placards. The cause of the strike appears momentarily forgotten as every marcher stares at my 6'4" figure. Unusual height, blond hair, anything different from local appearances may attract considerable curiosity. Learn to accept it graciously.

- *Business cards.* Business cards are taken more seriously in other countries than in the United States and are offered at even a cursory meeting. You can get along without them, but you'll gain status if you bring some along. They also help avoid errors in pronunciation and help new friends keep in touch with you.

- *Littering.* Whatever your habits at home, tossing litter, even a cigarette butt in some places, can result in arrest and a fine. Malaysia, Singapore, and Australia are some of the countries that do not regard themselves as an ashtray.

- *Face.* Publicly embarrassing a person can give grave offense, especially in Asia. "Face" is taken seriously and offenses are not lightly forgiven. Public displays of temper should be avoided altogether.

- *Humor.* Few local people are amused by a traveler's jokes about local cuisine, government, and so on. What they might say among themselves, they resent hearing from an outsider, no matter how humorous the intent.

- *Home habits.* Since Europe is considerably more formal than the United States, habits that are acceptable, or at least accepted, in the United States may give offense. I'm thinking of things like chewing gum in public, interrupting when another is speaking, and slapping someone on the back.

- *Gestures.* Familiar gestures may not travel well. For example, the thumb and forefinger "OK" sign you flash in a friendly way in Chicago refers to an intimate part of the anatomy in Brazil. In Britain, giving someone a "V" sign with your palm facing inward is the equivalent of the middle-finger sign in the U.S. To wave good-bye in France, hold your palm up facing the other person and wave your fingers up and down; wave your arm side-to-side, as in the United States, and you'd be saying "No." In Peru, as in Europe, pointing to the corner of an eye means "Be alert; keep your eyes open."

   If you thumb your nose at someone in Europe, be ready to step back. Beckoning someone by crooking your finger at them is an insult in Asia or the Middle East. In parts of South America and Europe, slapping the back of one fist with the other hand conveys your wish that the other person undertake an improbable activity. In Greece, an upward nod of the head means "No," whereas tilting the head to one side means "Yes." If you raise an open hand to refuse something offered to you in Greece, your gesture may be understood as "go to hell." In that connection, be warned that a Greek may smile when angry. In India, emphatic wagging of the head side-to-side doesn't mean "No." It might mean "Yes," or any number of other things.

- *Religion.* Although it is just impressive architecture to you, it may be a holy place to someone else. If in doubt about the appropriateness of taking pictures, obtain permission or don't do it. Don't let your conversation interfere with someone else's worship. Activity in countries where Islamic customs prevail will come to a complete stop for prayers five times a day. While you're not expected to participate, you must not interrupt or show impatience.

Observing the customs I've described in this chapter will ease your way a great deal, but I can suggest two books that provide more comprehensive guidance. They are *Do's and Taboos Around the World* and *Do's and Taboos of International Trade*, both edited by Roger Axtell (John Wiley & Sons).

In addition, I recommend *Culturegrams*, published by the Kennedy Center for International Studies at Brigham Young University (call 800-528-6279 or 801-378-6528). The Center publishes annually updated four-page Culturegrams on at least 140 countries. Each provides a comprehensive background on a country and describes what to expect in terms of language, religions, attitudes, local food, tipping, holidays, customs and courtesies, and visa and inoculation requirements. The price is $4.50 each, but you can also buy a cut-rate set covering all countries of a continent or all countries that speak a single language. Culturegrams are a bargain.

BEGGING

Beyond the borders of developed countries, travelers are often shocked and saddened by the number of excruciatingly poor people they see. Most are not beggars, just people struggling to survive. But in some places there are beggars, and they congregate, naturally, where there are tourists. Children are forced to beg because their parents have learned that children arouse tourists' compassion. Stories persist of parents or master beggars who cripple children horribly to make them more pathetic, and therefore more successful as beggars.

As a traveler, you must come to terms emotionally with beggars and develop a mind-set that permits you to be neither constantly depressed by their condition nor constantly annoyed by their appeals. At the same time, their existence should never come to seem acceptable.

Akha tribe family in the northern hill country. Thailand.

Since tourists like to give candy to children, small shops near scenic attractions sell candy for just that purpose. Some tourists who know better than to dispense candy feel okay about handing out pens, maybe on the idealistic theory that a pen will permit a poetic genius to emerge. Catching on quickly, kids ask for pens, then sell them.

It's probably impossible to assess the authenticity of a beggar's condition is. A woman with a child on her hip came up to me on a Calcutta street. Asking not for money but for milk, she guided me a block or so to a small shop where I bought her a carton of milk. I left feeling that I'd made a good choice. Did she sell the milk back for cash as I turned the corner? I don't know. Should I care, or is it her right to use the best device she can to secure money for whatever she determines are her most pressing needs?

Some tourists use skepticism to mask inherent stinginess. Others give something to every supplicant for a while, then nothing to anyone. I have a friend who, each time she visits India, selects a reputable charity and makes a contribution, but doesn't give to individual beggars.

If you are moved to respond to the ubiquitous "Hey, mister" from a child tagging along behind you, one choice is to personalize the experience by giving a postcard that features your hometown. You might show photographs of your house or your significant other. I know a guy who carries an inflatable globe. He puffs it up and shows kids the world and their place on it. Another traveler plays tunes on his harmonica and lets kids experience the magic of his zoom lens and a magnifying glass he carries. Balloons, tops, and sleight-of-hand tricks draw a crowd in seconds. These things solve no fundamental problems, but they let kids be kids for a while in a hard world.

If you give to even one person while in public view, you are marked and memories are long. A generous person could probably return to Bombay after an absence of ten years and be remembered for her generosity.

Before you leave home, consult your feelings about responding to beggars. A traveler wants to be liked, but leaving a trail of trinkets behind scarcely enhances a person's image in the eyes of local people. We should face the reality that begging often changes values and lowers self-esteem. Of course, it may also keep a family alive. Whatever you decide, the reality of deformed, emaciated children will strike you like a stinging slap in the face.

TIPPING

Tipping protocol in Europe is similar to that in the United States. Travelers commonly tip airport baggage handlers, porters, room service waiters, waiters and wine stewards, tour guides, taxi drivers, and almost everyone associated with a cruise. The total of these tips can be substantial enough that you should include them in your budget. If you arrive in a country with none of its currency, don't worry. A $1 bill is readily accepted as a tip almost everywhere.

In many European countries a service charge is added to your bill. In France, for instance, the menu will probably say *Service Compris,* meaning they add a percentage, usually 15 percent, to your bill. In that case, the establishment expects you to tip no further. Of course, the waiter may still try for a tip from anyone whose travel clothes look fresh off the rack. Waiters used to tourists are likely to work them for a tip regardless of local custom and pressure them with evident displeasure if they don't get one.

When you tip, the chance of it reaching the intended recipient is much greater if it comes directly from your hand rather than being left on the table.

If you plan to tip after a service is provided, you might award part of it at the beginning to send a message and start good service flowing right away. On cruises, some experienced passengers tip half of the anticipated total on the first day or two, another half about half way through, and award a sincere smile on the way down the gangplank.

Extremely low wages in most underdeveloped countries are a motivation to be generous in tipping, certainly by local standards. Along with a tip, I look the person in the eye and say, "Thank you for helping me."

In Russia, China, Scandinavia, some of the Pacific islands, parts of Asia and Southeast Asia, and most of Africa, tipping is discouraged except at upscale establishments that cater primarily to tourists. If you're unsure, check your guidebook and ask several people outside the tourist industry. If it's not the local custom to tip, don't impose a foreign custom.

BRIBES

Despite euphemisms such as *baksheesh, dash, wairo*, and *mordida* (the last means "little bite"), what we're going to talk about is, if I may be so indelicate as to call it by its true name, a bribe. Since bribery is not a custom most of us grew up with, it makes us nervous.

In many countries, a bribe is considered proper.

The first thing to know is that in many countries a bribe is not always considered improper, let alone illegal. It's often looked at as a just reward for having wiggled oneself into some minor, underpaid bureaucratic job from which a little leverage can occasionally be exerted. The problem is that once an official has learned that a few Westerners will pay extra for his services, he makes demands on all who follow. At the same time, in some other circumstance, offering a bribe could offend someone or lead to legal trouble.

Although I've probably missed a few subtle signals, only once has an official made it clear to me that he expected a bribe. That was at the U.S.-Mexican border and it involved getting permission to take my car into Mexico. I thought I had the upper hand and there was little risk to my safety, so I ignored his demand. He backed off and nothing happened.

Twice, a customs official has asked me to give him something from my backpack. The first asked for several film canisters, which he probably intended to sell. The other boldly asked for my camera. The first I pretended not to understand; the other I refused with a laugh as if we both knew he was joking. Nothing happened.

When I tried to buy a train ticket on the midnight special out of New Delhi, three clerks told me the tickets were "finished." Not willing to give up, I casually laid a few dollars on the desk of the senior ticket master. Giving my offering the briefest glance, he repeated that there was nothing he could do for me. As I was leaving, he called to my attention that I had left something on his desk, indicating the bills with a one-eyebrow-raised nod. Sheepishly, I picked them up, feeling as if I'd been caught with my hand in the cookie jar. Twenty minutes later, a Sikh acquaintance straightforwardly bribed a porter to let us board the train. A second bribe gained us icy-cold metal berths. I spent most of the night reading Shakespeare and drinking Indian Army rum to keep warm. We got to Udaipur in time to hear an Elvis Presley imitator perform at a New Year's Eve party at the famous Lake Palace Hotel. That was *baksheesh* well spent.

If an impasse develops between you and an official who won't do what you need unless you pay him, ask to see a superior official. If the first guy is trying shakedowns on his own, you may get help. If everyone is in on it, you may be stuck.

Obviously, there's no formula for calculating the amount required to make something happen. It seems to be related to the service you need, the grandeur of the official, and whether someone has sized you up as impatient or a wealthy pigeon. In one situation, you might offer a small amount to a low-ranking official right away. Another time, you might be better off going to the person in charge. If time permits, start with a small amount then pull incremental amounts from different pockets as needed. The ultimate amount will reflect the relative value of money in the official's life and the urgency of your desire to make something happen.

When offering a bribe, be discreet. Use ambiguous words when making an offer. Ask if there "isn't some other way" to handle the problem. For example, perhaps you could pay a small "fine" to the official on the spot, or buy an unspecified "permit." If you do the deal in silence you can, as politicians put it, maintain deniability. Don't let other officials see money change hands and never let anyone see how much money you have.

DOING FAVORS

Someone may ask you to have an application form sent to him from a university in your country. Another may ask you to make a telephone call to her relative in the States or to send a copy of the photograph you took of her family at the dinner table. Since a traveler receives so much help while on the road, doing favors is essential to balance the scales. Further, the favor one traveler does for someone may motivate a kindness to some other traveler. Or it may just be the right thing to do. You don't have to agree to do everything anyone asks, but when you promise to do a favor, do at least what you promised and more if possible. By extension, when you meet a foreign traveler in need of assistance in your home country, you are honor-bound to help. It's part of the traveler's code of ethics.

18

Meeting People

> Travelers are often advised to take a long book
> on their journeys, but who would devote his attention
> to a book when he can turn the dog-eared pages of a
> total stranger whom he may never meet again.
> —Quentin Crisp
> "Riding with a Stiff Upper Lip," *The New York Times*

MEETING LOCAL FOLKS

Long after temples, dive spots, and mountain trails have merged in your mind, you remember the guide you talked to while walking through the rain forest, the family you stayed with in Oslo, and endless conversations on Indian trains. You remember the people and they remember you. They remember whether you liked their country, whether you were polite, and whether you were sincere. Meeting local people is the essence of independent travel.

Travelers too often base their opinions of local people on the few who make their living working the tourist trail, selling food, products, and services (including, unhappily, taxi drivers), relationships that are commercial, superficial, and sometimes adversarial. That's why it's worth the effort to meet normal people outside the areas frequented by tourists. Even if you feel inhibited by language or fear of rejection, it's worth doing. You learn about family life, politics, religion, cooking local specialties, symbolism in arts and crafts, their view of your country, and who knows what else. You may be permitted to witness special rituals or be taken to places you wouldn't otherwise have found. And you make genuine friends.

One easy way to meet local people is via an introduction from a friend, including the ever-helpful "friend of a friend," especially if they'll send a note in advance of your visit. Another way is to ask your alumni office whether any graduates of your high school or university live where you're going. Ask for a

Women in traditional dress. Cairo, Egypt.

letter of introduction from your place of worship to counterparts abroad with which it has relationships. Get names from professional associations (lawyers, florists, anything).

If your city has a sister-city abroad, the sister-city organization will have names and addresses of contacts. Overseas members of your local social and business clubs will be delighted when you look them up. I've seen Rotary, Kiwanis, and Lions signs in some pretty far out places. Your branch of the Friendship Force, the Council for International Visitors, Girl Scouts, and Boy Scouts can give you addresses of international visitors who have been in your hometown.

Make contact by joining in an athletic contest. Volleyball, soccer, table tennis, and badminton are enjoyed worldwide. Get out your Frisbee and invite someone to toss it with you. Attend local sporting events. Ride local transportation. Walk through residential neighborhoods. See if the local tourist office introduces travelers to local people.

It's not enough to return home and rave about how hospitable "they"—the locals—were. While still with them, leave favorable memories behind. You'll almost always have more money and time than they, so put both to good use.

MEETING OTHER TRAVELERS

When I first started traveling, it felt great to meet travelers for whom English was their first language. I felt comfortable with them, perhaps because we had so much in common. Over the years though, having become more at home away from my hearth, I've discovered the immense rewards of meeting travelers from distant lands, people with whom to share and from whom I learn. It's more than worth the struggle to communicate.

Travel is an opportunity to be more extroverted.

Although I understand, it saddens me now to see some travelers from certain countries relentlessly seek out fellow countrymen, forming a clique, creating an artificial home away from home. They miss so much.

Travel is an opportunity to be more extroverted, taking the initiative to meet other travelers. The potential for learning, for a good conversation, or a long-term friendship makes stretching worthwhile. Here are just a few of the benefits you can expect from making friends with other travelers:

- *You collect information that improves your trip.* Travelers are like reliable, interactive up-to-date guidebooks, talking about trustworthy places to buy cheap airline tickets and where to find the best safari company. If a guidebook lists ten places to stay in Ubud, Bali, they'll be filled with people who've read that book. But from other travelers you'll get opinions about the other sixty-five places to stay in Ubud. The best information is on the travelers grapevine.

- *You may feel a sense of security from traveling with others.* For example, when trekking among the hill tribe villages in Northern Thailand, you definitely feel more secure in a small group than wandering on your own.

- *You can negotiate better rates* for rooms, a vehicle, or a guide than one person can on her own.

- *You enjoy the refreshing equality of friendships formed on the road.* Since travelers are stripped to essentials, employment, possessions, and education are unknown and irrelevant—and they no longer determine status. In order to base my feelings about other travelers on the present, I avoid asking personal "background" questions that could lead to generalizations.

- *You're likely to have many shared values.* After all, you all made the effort to bring yourself to the distant place at which you've met. Having experienced similar obstacles and marvels along the way, you feel a special camaraderie and bond, a good foundation for friendship.

- *You have someone with whom to share tales of the open road.*

- Traveling on your own can get lonely and there are times when *companionship provides an emotional lift.*

Crowd and musicians making Andean music.

That leads to the issue of how to go about meeting other travelers. In most towns, there are areas notable for the density of accommodations for budget travelers. The Thamel section of Kathmandu is an example, as are Khaosan Road in Bangkok and Sudder Street in Calcutta. Walk around the Boul Mich in Paris, the Piazza San Marco in Venice, Jalan Sosrowijayan in Yogyakarta, and similar crossroads all over the world and you'll find as many travelers as you seek.

Sometimes the primary hangout is a specific place, like the well-known Iqbal Hotel and the Thorn Tree Cafe in Nairobi, the Hotel Uzbekistan in Tashkent, or the Ayllu Cafe on the Plaza de Armas in Cuzco. Many are mentioned in guidebooks; others you find on your own. Travelers congregate in train and bus stations, airports, restaurants, and scenic attractions. All you need is a smile, a friendly greeting, and a ready question.

When traveling as a couple, you have to initiate conversations with other people. Otherwise, they'll tend to keep their distance. Older travelers may need to take the initiative as well. Why remain separate just because you're twenty-five years older than travelers around you when you can close the gap so easily?

Somewhere along the way, you may meet expatriates. Although the word expatriate has literal connotations of banishment and exile, most expats live voluntarily in some country other than their own. Some are military personnel who end their careers while stationed overseas. They've become accustomed to a pleasant lifestyle and may no longer have intimate ties at home. Ex-Peace Corps volunteers are known for developing attachments to "their" countries and remaining for years after their formal service ends. Many North American oil company workers retire in northern South America. Thousands of people who have long-term jobs with multi-national corporations move from country to country like lonely satellites. Some people who work for humanitarian organizations become stateless, circling the globe for life. From Ecuador to Honduras to Malawi to Laos, missionaries remain away from home for decades, some of them helping local people obtain justice.

Relationships between expats and their adopted countries vary. Some expats involve themselves in local life while others live in near-isolation. Almost all know their way around the place in which you meet them, share a language with you, and can be a fine source of information. A traveler who accepts their hospitality should bring something to the table besides conversation. Buy the beer, help with the cooking, or fulfill a request to send something from home.

Two final thoughts about meeting other travelers. First, you'll inevitably meet people who have traveled longer and farther than you have. Learn what you can from them, but never let their exploits diminish your trip. Second, when sharing travel anecdotes, it's important to share air time as well. The other person has at least as much interest in sharing her experiences as you do in listening to yourself talk.

ROMANCE ON THE ROAD

Let's face it: travel can be an aphrodisiac. Not only is the trip a terrific high, but you're meeting other travelers with whom you share some important values. And you have time. In addition, there are all those exotic, attractive local people. Ah, if only life were so simple. The fact is that engaging in a relationship (okay, sex) on the road deserves some serious thought.

Your Partner's Feelings

If you're traveling with a partner, would your involvement with another person cause your partner a problem? How would you feel if your partner became involved with someone else? Could a third person join your partnership comfortably? Would your partner just as soon spend a little more time alone? A good traveling partner is not to be offended thoughtlessly. If there could be a problem, talk it over honestly early on, before you have to meet to split up the partnership's assets.

Other Travelers

Given all that time in sensual settings, romances on the road are hardly unknown. It's easy for travelers to get to know one another quickly through the candor and vulnerability that emerge in remote places. A relationship may develop that will bridge oceans and international datelines—or last at least until paths diverge.

In no case, however, does the magic of an exciting new relationship confer immunity to sexually-transmitted diseases. Some of these afflictions are annoying, some are serious, some are fatal. You can't know your new friend's previous sexual history at home nor with travelers or local folk while on the road. Each of us must make his or her own decision about abstinence, but the imperatives of safe sex are worldwide. If you don't drink the water, does it make sense to carelessly take a risk of a much greater magnitude?

Local Contact

One of the reasons to travel is to meet local people. If your pace is slow and your senses tuned, you may be emotionally and physically attracted to a local person. That's the good part. The bad part is that in many countries sexually-transmitted disease is widespread. That's especially true with respect to local people associated in some way with the tourist trail. At the very least, condoms and hygienic caution are a must.

There are many lovely people in the world and you may develop a genuine, loving relationship with one. If so, be aware that other cultures differ from yours so don't unintentionally create expectations that won't be met. For example, if you fall in love and the relationship is to continue, one of you will have to learn to live in a new culture. The ramifications deserve serious thought.

There can be a darker side to a relationship with a local person. No one has more than anecdotal information about the frequency with which travelers are seduced for reasons that are more mercenary than romantic, but it does happen. In other words, something other than love may be requested or taken.

19

How to Get the Most Out of Your Trip

> The journey not the arrival matters
> —T. S. Eliot

At times on a trip I feel like Theodore Dreiser's leaf floating along on the surface of a stream, completely out of control. Other times, I have at least the illusion of being in control. Fortunately, there is one vital variable I can always affect, one that can make or break my trip. That's my state of mind.

STATE OF MIND

Days and nights are filled with new experiences: art, architecture, exotic and perhaps erotic dance, theater and music, magnificent landscapes, physical challenges, and new friends. What a great way to live!

At the same time, everything is different. Language and food may be difficult to digest. Everything has to be bargained for. Something set down unattended can disappear in the blink of an eye. Decisions must be made all day long. Travel is an excellent investment, but like most investments, it's not completely free from stress.

Any traveler who expects plans to work out as smoothly as they do at home, or is determined to force them through despite unexpected circumstances, will be unhappy. To enjoy the trip, give yourself permission to change course, to go with a better idea when it comes along. When it starts raining and the trail turns to mud, you have to be ready to find the humor. Feeling that the rain god has a personal grudge against you will only make the mud deeper.

You chose your destinations for the very reason that they are different from your country. Take pleasure in the differences. Leave generalizations, preconceptions, and stereotypes at home.

Patience

The airline insisted that passengers turn up two hours ahead of flight time, then didn't allow us on board until half an hour beyond the scheduled departure time. After baking on the sun-scorched runway for thirty minutes, we were told to climb back off the plane. Milling around under the blazing sun, we discovered that this was happening because someone forgot to load the life jackets required for the flight. I'm human so I felt a little exasperated but I've learned to look automatically for the humor in situations. Lifejackets? For a flight across Saudi Arabia?

I watched a traveler radiate exasperation as he turned from the clerk in a Jakarta hotel and snapped to his partner, "He doesn't even understand plain English." Sure, the traveler was hot and tired, but that didn't excuse his behavior. If he'd seen the clerk as a person he would have acknowledged that the young man wanted to help. It was the traveler who was falling short. He hadn't learned the basic utilitarian phrases in Bahasa Indonesian and didn't have a phrase book handy. When his request in English didn't communicate, he lost patience. To restore calm, his partner responded, "Be or be one." By that he meant, as they both knew, be patient or you'll soon be a patient.

Officialdom

If officialdom in the Third World had a family crest, it would feature a hand-stamp. When you need something from an official, whether you get it may depend on your state of mind. For example, if you convince yourself that a bureaucrat has intentionally singled you out to ignore, you may feel justified in becoming angry. On the other hand, if you understand that time is treated differently than in your country and that waiting is part of life for everyone, it's easier to remain a little detached. Visualize yourself as bamboo swaying in the wind. If there's something you can't change, go with the flow. Learning to accept things calmly conserves vast amounts of energy.

When I see a traveler leaning angrily over an official's desk, demanding some privilege on grounds of being a foreigner, I assume he must value self-indulgence over peace of mind or success.

When you can pass by an official anonymously, do so. If he's an obstacle, or you need assistance, try to make him *want* to bend a regulation. Look him in the eye, smile, make personal comments, and compliment his country, the weather, anything. If you can't persuade him to do what you want, ask him to suggest a solution himself. Realize that sometimes you just have to take "no" for an answer.

People Who Want to Sell You Something

State of mind makes a big difference when dealing with people selling things. Persistent peddlers can test your sanity unless you settle on a way of dealing with them. I was blissfully strolling across the sunny *plaza de armas* in Pisco* when a woman started following me, pestering me to buy one of her handwoven belts. Snapping at or ignoring her would have been unfair, not to mention abrasive. I tried to connect with her urgency by imagining that she was supporting a large family and remembering that for eight months of the year there are no tourists to whom she can sell anything. I still didn't want to buy another belt so I looked at her and said, pleasantly but firmly, "*No, gracias.*" She wouldn't go away. I stopped walking and said, "*No tengo dinero* (I have no money)." That discouraged without offending her. If a merchant just won't stop, I go about my business but without getting annoyed.

Expectations About Time

Expectations about time will make a big difference in the serenity of your travels. Think of travel as resembling a marathon rather than a sprint. You have to pace yourself, even losing a little time here and there. Traveling too fast is a prescription for burnout.

Most of the world's population takes the longer view of life, not being too concerned when things don't happen precisely when scheduled. This attitude may be related to feelings of powerlessness. At home, you believe you can affect your environment and so you attempt to do so. In much of the world, people view themselves as objects on which the system acts as it will. If you're obsessive about punctuality, independent travel will either be a liberating experience or leave you a quivering heap. Your choice. Think of getting stressed as similar to getting sunburned. It can spoil your trip, so why not avoid it?

Persistence

I wanted to see the interior of an elegant theater in Oaxaca† but the massive front doors were locked. I tried the doors on one side, then at the rear—both locked. It was a rainy, dreary day and I was about to give up and head for cover. Then I thought, I'll just take a look around that last corner. Sure enough there was an open door and a man with a peg leg, probably in his eighties,

---

* *Pisco.* The name of this port 145 miles south of Lima in southern Peru is known in bars around the world—for "pisco sours." The Bay of Paracas, just south of Pisco, is one of the best marine reserves in the world and a short boat trip takes you to the Ballestas Islands to visit sea lions and penguins.

† *Oaxaca.* Located three hundred miles south of Mexico City, Oaxaca is noted for architecture and Indian culture. It's near Monte Alban, ancient captital of the Zapotec culture.

emerged to show me around. As he thumped along, he reminisced about the past glories of the theater then lapsed into whispery tales of the Aztecs, breathing life into the past. Since then, I've characterized persistence in terms of always turning one more corner. That means asking one more question, walking a little farther, seeing if there isn't some way to make something happen. I'm not talking about being obsessed or bullheaded. I mean that with just a little more effort, turning one more corner, you're likely to get more of what you want.

Context

Travel has helped me understand peoples' behavior in its own context, rather than in mine. Seeing hundreds of Chinese crouched beside a roadside using hand tools to break boulders into piles of pebbles, I felt critical of the government for not having provided a more mechanized way of doing the job. Miles farther down the road, I realized that machines would throw those hundreds of people, and perhaps millions more, into unemployment. That's what I mean by seeing things in context.

I've also learned not to generalize about an entire country because of an unfortunate experience with one person. That taxi driver was just a taxi driver, not a national symbol.

Attitude

I traveled with a partner who was so relentlessly positive she was almost other-worldly. She'd find the single ray of light in the gloomiest sky. When I asked how she was feeling after an incredibly hot, jolting all-day bus trip, she responded with praise for some beautifully-shaped acacia trees she'd noticed along the way. She knows that happiness is not a destination, it's an attitude.

In many countries it's a serious loss of face to display anger. It follows that the hot temper of a traveler will be met with glacial resistance. Ralph Waldo Emerson advised us that a man should behave "so that, on whatever point soever of his doing your eye falls, it shall report truly of his character . . ."

It's no myth that there *are* obstacles in the road over which a traveler may stumble. A train you planned to catch has been discontinued, your bus misses a connection, a border post closes early. You're grounded when transportation workers strike in Sydney. The power blackout in Manila snuffs out the air conditioning for which you paid double room rent. Your snorkel snoozes in its stuff sack while a mystery bug scrambles your intestines. Things happen. I prepare myself to accept, genuinely accept, discomforts as I travel. Temporary discomfort is part of the price of admission to the rest of the world. You can control how unhappy you want to be. In my opinion, the hard bed is softer to a relaxed body.

When there's a situation you just can't influence, take it in stride. Be open, not defensive. Follow your own path, not one that might meet someone else's approval. Act with intensity when you must, but let your trip be characterized by calm.

GIVE YOURSELF A TREAT

In their efforts to stay within a budget, some travelers live at a scruffier level than makes sense. Even though you've prepared yourself for a standard of living lower than at home, excessive frugality is not a virtue. If carried to an extreme, it may make you forget the reasons you decided to travel in the first place.

On the island of Lamu, I met a young couple from Australia. They'd rented a single-room hut in the middle of the island reached by a long walk across rock-strewn fields. Their paradise had one lantern, a concrete-like mattress, an outdoor toilet and shower, no protection from mosquitoes, and they had to fight off snapping dogs every time they put a foot out the door. They'd chosen that lovely cottage solely because it cost only $5 a night. On the other hand, I had a large room with attached bathroom, an overhead fan, and a balcony overlooking the sea and the social life of the village, for which I paid $9. I believe that couple had lost perspective.

> "If you can keep your head when all about you are losing theirs ... wait and not be tired by waiting ... fill the unforgiving minute with sixty seconds worth of distance run, yours is the Earth and everything that's in it...."
> —Rudyard Kipling, If

There is usually some correlation between cost and sanitation. If paying $2 less rents you a crop of bedbugs or a mosquito net full of holes, it's time to remember why you're traveling.

Throughout these chapters, I've made suggestions on how to SAVE MONEY and how to connect with the world in which you are traveling. The idea of giving yourself a treat does not contradict these suggestions. My point is to avoid false economies, to avoid being "penny wise, pound foolish." Ask yourself which is the better choice: renting a cheap room directly across from the bus station and staying awake all night or finding a quieter place for a few more dollars? Would it be wiser to book a berth than sit up all night on a long train trip? Don't you deserve an air-conditioned room after a trek in the steamy jungle? Every once in a while, check to see if you're treating yourself well enough.

The Regent Hotel in Kowloon is a masterpiece of satiny black marble and gleaming brass. Beyond the soaring glass wall of the bar, a zillion lights twinkle from Victoria Peak, and yellow lanterns swing from bowsprits of hundreds of junks in the harbor. Standing at that bar, I imagined standing on the bridge of the Starship Enterprise looking into the galaxy. You owe yourself an evening in that bar even though a mai tai costs five times what it would a few blocks inland.

The old-fashioned Oriental Hotel on the bank of the Chao Phraya River in Bangkok ranks among the very best in the world. Treat yourself to afternoon tea at Noel Coward's favorite table. Listen for echoes of conversations between Somerset Maugham and an Oxford-educated Thai prince; imagine Joseph Conrad grumbling about the waiter too slow returning with a mug of rum.

In Nairobi, the venerable Norfolk Hotel was the scene of the wild social excesses of colonial Kenya. If you happen to see a party going on, watch for an evanescent Karen Blixen or Beryl Markham across the room. Perhaps the grizzled old man wearing the bush hat and pulling on an icy Tusker can tell you stories of guiding Scott Fitzgerald or Teddy Roosevelt on safari. When you hear Churchill's booming laugh behind you, you may have had one whiskey and soda too many.

Feast at the all-you-can-eat braai (barbecue) under the stars at the Victoria Falls Hotel in Zimbabwe. The thunder of falling water plays a million-year old bass behind the string dance band. It's a fine splurge after you've been minding your budget.

As a kid, I tried out for a Little League baseball team. Incredibly nervous my very first time at bat, I was relieved when the umpire called the first three pitches balls. The next two were strikes. Hoping I'd get on base with a walk, I let the last pitch go by without swinging. The umpire called it a strike and I walked away dragging my bat in the dust. I've never forgotten that experience and never let it happen again. I decided not to let life whiz by without taking a swing, a full swing. For me, that includes involving myself wholeheartedly in whatever appeals to me as I travel.

When it's time, bust that budget. After all, when planning your trip you built in a little surplus for that very purpose. Think about what turns you on. Tickets to the Bolshoi Ballet in Moscow? Front row seats for an outdoor performance of the "Ramayana" in the full-moon shadow of an ancient Hindu temple? A whitewater raft trip down the Zambezi? A helicopter landing on a New Zealand glacier? Since you can experience some things only when you're there, is the price really so high? How would you value the same amount of money at home? It may seem expensive at the moment but don't let being on the road rob you of perspective. Treating yourself well creates life-long memories.

20

How to Stay in Touch with Home Base

The way Ken Kesey saw it, each of us is either "on the bus," or "off the bus." What he meant was that we either make a commitment or we don't; we can't have it both ways. You have to make choices, and one of mine is to be completely where I am, not halfway somewhere else. I've found that too much contact with home during a trip pulls me back down the steps of the bus. However, if you want to or need to be in touch with home, it's much easier if you understand the systems. That's what this chapter is about.

TELEPHONES

In parts of South America, it's a challenge to *find* a telephone, let alone use one. In Vietnam, you may have to make a reservation two days in advance to place your call. On the other hand, in tiny San Pedro La Laguna on the north shore of Lake Atitlan in Guatemala, an operator in a two-room adobe hut connected me with San Francisco in seconds. From a pay telephone in Te Anau, New Zealand, you hear your friend's voice in Atlanta as clearly as if she were a block away. Overall, improvements in communications technology make international calling much simpler than it used to be.

There's no need to be intimidated by a foreign telephone system. Even though it's different from the one at home, you can figure out how it works. If instructions on the wall of the booth are not in one of your languages, the illustrations should get you through. If there are neither instructions nor illustrations, look closely at the instrument. Are there buttons that invite you to push them? If necessary, ask a passerby to show you how it works.

The sound of the dial tone is not universal. It may be the sound you're used to, or it may be a sound you associate with a busy signal. Don't hang up; they're all dial tones.

In Europe, Japan, New Zealand, Australia, and an increasing number of other countries, debit phone cards are sold in post offices, hotels, gift shops, railroad stations, and similar places. Using them is quicker and cheaper than calling home collect. When you insert the card in the telephone box, a screen shows you the monetary value remaining on your card, then counts down as the amount is reduced. Some U.S. companies have begun to sell these debit cards for use in the United States and some other countries. These include: AT&T's "Teleticket;" World Telecom Group's "Amerivox;" Sprint's "Instant Foncard;" and Global Telecommunications Solutions' "Global Card." Since charges vary wildly, some are a bargain and others are not.

Here are several useful tips for using telephones overseas:

– To SAVE MONEY, a lot of it, avoid having a hotel operator place your call. If you feel disposed to make your call from a hotel anyway, find out in advance how much the surcharge will be. The hotel surcharge, referred to as a rip-off in traveler's circles, often adds 40 percent to the cost of the call and one London hotel routinely charges guests five times the actual cost of the call. By the way, watch out for substantial charges for local calls and even for access to calling card and 800 numbers. Don't lift that phone until you know the rules.

– A less expensive way to place a call is to find a public telephone booth. To place an international call, you need the international access code and the country code of the country you're calling. To that, add the area code and local number you want. Using a pile of local coins or a debit card is usually the cheapest method. You can call collect if permitted, or you can call home and reach an English-speaking operator who will handle the domestic portion of your call. The latter avoids any language problem and the charge goes on your monthly phone bill. To do this, you must be carrying the appropriate telephone charge card and international access code numbers.

With AT&T's *USA Direct* you can reach the United States from about 148 countries. Simply dial (not through the hotel operator) the toll-free access number assigned to the country from which you are calling. When connected with an English-speaking operator, give your AT&T Calling Card number or say you want to call collect. To phone someone in another foreign country while abroad, use the same access number to call back to the United States. Your call is then rerouted to any of about one hundred foreign countries. As you might guess, the latter is an expensive service. For more information on how this works and the access telephone numbers for individual countries, contact AT&T at (800) 331-1140.

A similar MCI call-home program, named *Call USA*, is operational in over one hundred countries. *WorldPhone* is the MCI service for calling among about thirty foreign countries. For access codes and information, call MCI at (800) 444-3333. The MCI International Travel Guide is full of information and tips on saving money.

Sprint Express is operational in almost eighty countries; for information, call (800) 767-4625.

Here's an interesting wrinkle. If you're in a country not served by your call-home program, you can call your program's access number in a nearby country and, essentially, call home from there. That will save the long-distance charge home and enable you to make the connection quickly.

Note that using one of the three cards above to call among foreign countries is not always the cheapest option. Before using a phone card, check the charges.

Check out the American Travel Network (ATN; call 800-477-9692), which is linked to the Computer-Assisted Variable International Automatic Redialer (CAVIAR) system. Dial in your calling card number and security code. Your card number tells CAVIAR what country you're from and you receive instructions in that language. The ATN card may or may not be cheaper when calling the United States from abroad, but it is often cheaper when calling within a country. Within the United States, ATN long-distance service offers a flat rate of 17.5 cents per minute any time of day for calls away from home. At the moment, ATN is considerably cheaper than major carriers during prime time and about even during off-peak times.

— Many travelers call from a government international telephone office because there are no surcharges. It's often located near or within the central post office (often referred to as the PTT for Postal, Telephone & Telegraph). Your hotel clerk will know where it is. If you're out for a stroll when the urge to phone hits, look for a microwave tower on top of a building that doesn't have a lot of people in military uniforms standing around.

At the PTT, you give the clerk the telephone number you want and are assigned a booth while the clerk makes the connection. The length of your call is metered. If you left a deposit with a clerk, return after completing the call to pay the balance of the bill (although sometimes the connection is broken after the time you've paid for is up).

— SAVE MONEY by placing your call during hours when rates are lowest.

- Figure out local time at the place you're calling so you don't reach an answering machine or someone groggy with sleep.

- Calling collect, which is not always permitted, is very expensive. If that's the only choice you have, SAVE MONEY by making a one-minute call and having the other person call you back.

- If the call is about something specific, it helps to make a few notes ahead of time so you don't leave things out in the excitement.

- In countries where the government operates with a heavy hand, your call may be monitored, which should affect whether you criticize the country or the government.

If there's an emergency at home, your friend or relative can contact the Office of Overseas Citizens Services at the State Department (202-647-5225), which will relay a message to the appropriate U.S. embassy on your itinerary. Embassy personnel will attempt to locate you.

MAIL

The challenge is to enjoy the pleasure of sending and receiving mail without letting the process disrupt your trip. For some travelers, writing home frequently can draw too much attention from the present, so they write home in bursts, days or weeks apart. If you keep an informal log listing the date of the most recent burst, you'll know where to pick up geographic descriptions when you write next.

American Express

Many travelers use the American Express client letter service as a convenient way to receive mail (not packages, registered mail, or telephone calls). To pick up mail, you're supposed to have an AmEx card or AmEx traveler's check, and some identification. However, many offices will allow a traveler to pick up mail merely by paying a small fee.

When giving your itinerary to pen pals at home, include addresses of appropriate AmEx mail drops. A complete list of foreign offices is available from AmEx, but choose only those offices marked as mail drops. Since most of the offices also have fax machines, include those numbers too. A fax via AmEx is a fast, reliable way to reach a traveler in case of emergency at home.

Remind your correspondents that it takes two or three weeks for a letter to make its journey. Note on your itinerary the date by which a letter should be mailed to reach an AmEx office before you do. On the itinerary, type a reminder to CAPITALIZE your last name and underline it. To reduce the chance of mis-filing, ask the writer not to include your middle name or initial.

When you stop in for mail, ask the clerk to check under the first letter of your last name AND under the first letter of your first name. If you're not sure you are communicating, write out your name. Since your eye is more likely than hers to recognize your name, lean over the clerk's shoulder if you can.

Rather than wasting a day or more or detouring for miles to check in with a mail pickup point, ask friends to send a copy of each letter to the next mail stop down the line on your itinerary. That will prevent regrets about a wonderful letter left behind.

If you arrive at a mail pickup point ahead of schedule, ask that mail for you arriving there later be forwarded to an office farther along your itinerary. They'll do it for a small fee. When you depart from the itinerary you left with friends at home, tell the AmEx office where to forward mail that might arrive in your wake. An office will usually hold your mail for thirty days.

I've used AmEx as an example, because I greatly prefer it over receiving mail via local general delivery. If you decide to use general delivery, advise your correspondents to address letters to your name, "c/o Poste Restante, General Post Office" in a specific city and country. No further address is needed.

By the way, give your cards and letters a fighting chance of getting home by starting them on their way from a city rather than from a village. Take your postcards and letters to the post office rather than leaving them in the hands of a hotel clerk.

FAX MACHINES AND ELECTRONIC MAIL

Fax Machines

The fax machine has circled the globe with the speed of rock music. You can send a fax from Nairobi to San Francisco even when Nairobi residents can't reach one other across town by telephone. Don't leave home without a list of fax numbers for people you may want to reach. If a friend at home doesn't have a fax, take the fax number of a nearby business office or quick-print office.

Where to find a fax machine? In international cities of any size, signs advertise fax services on almost every downtown block. The fax machine itself may be located in an upscale travel agency or in the back of a bakery next to a grandmother dozing with a lap full of knitting.

The owner of the fax pays a fee for use of the phone line, then charges you what competition will permit (meaning there may be room for a little bargaining). It usually works out to less than you'd spend on a long distance call. They also charge a minimal fee when you receive a fax. Include the fax number from which you are sending so the person you are contacting can reach you later.

The fax is a good way for home folks to reach you in case of emergency. They may send a fax to an AmEx mail drop office, your hotel, or through one of the fax services. For example, AlphaNet Telecom (619-736-7070) offers a service called FollowFax. In return for an initiation fee (about $20) and a monthly fee ($10 to $30), a traveler is assigned a permanent personal fax number. Any fax sent to that number is held in a confidential mailbox. You access the AlphaNet system from a local fax machine, enter your PIN, and download any waiting faxes.

Electronic Mail

E-mail isn't yet well-developed for travelers, but it will be before long. The price of e-mail communication should be very reasonable since it consists of local calls from network to network. The number of networks is increasing at, shall we say, electronic speed.

If they know your Internet e-mail address, friends at home who have no idea where you are at the moment can leave a message in your e-mail box. You then access it at your leisure. In contrast to a telephone call, you can send an e-mail message without worrying about what time it is at the destination.

All that is needed for e-mail is a computer and modem at both ends. Assuming you don't have a computer tucked under your arm, where will you find one? For the moment, that's a small problem. A few universities and some businesses have been willing to let travelers use a computer for a few minutes. Before long, though, the grandmother in the fax shop will be dozing next to a Pentium chip powerhouse.

21

To Buy or Not to Buy:
That *Is* the Question

> But there is one priceless thing that I brought back from my trip
> around the world, one that cost no money and on which I paid
> no customs duty; humility, a humility born from watching other
> peoples, other races, struggling bravely and hoping humbly
> for the simplest things in life.
> —Felix Martí-Ibanez
> *Journey Around Myself*

As I write this, I'm sitting in the midst of yak-wool pouches from Kashmir, Masai bead work, Peruvian flutes and textiles, jewelry from Tibet, and more—all things I couldn't resist buying. Even though I'm no shopper, who can resist magnificent craftsmanship, not to mention spur-of-the-moment infatuations? And no one should miss the colors, sounds, and aromas of local market days. Virtually everyone who travels comes home with mementos. Although this chapter will be of greatest help to those who take shopping more seriously, some points are relevant to anyone who buys anything abroad.

I have to confess my personal view that shopping is not traveling. I flinch when casual acquaintances ask me to bring home "something wonderful" for them. I resist the pressure of having to shop because I don't want to be concerned about theft or breakage, and I don't want to tote that extra weight. So why is it that I arrive home from every trip laden like a trans-Saharan camel?

Note that I don't consider cost an inhibition to buying. Except in Europe, prices usually are so reasonable in relation to the quality of products that much of what you see seems very affordable. Travelers encounter art, crafts, clothing, jewelry, carvings, precious metals, antiques—a mercantile smorgasbord for sale at very reasonable prices. Of course, the original cost may not be the final cost. Consider how much you'll have to spend on your purchase after you get home. For example, a professor friend paid $6 for lovely amber beads in Moldova, then spent $120 in the United States to have them strung with tiny gold beads. I bought a magnificent piece of batik fabric art in Yogyakarta for about $15, but spent more than $100 at home to have it properly mounted. Buy a jewel at a bargain price and you may pay much more to have it put into an appropriate setting. Bargains are bargains only if they're bargains after you've spent the additional money needed to use and enjoy them.

I remind myself of two things as a method of keeping purchases under control. First, it's possible and sometimes preferable to enjoy things for themselves rather than having to possess them. Second, many things look terrific in their own context but lose all appeal when transported to a domestic coffee table; ethnic hats become moth-eaten relics at home and the lederhosen bought in Munich mildew at the bottom of a drawer.

There are two kinds of travelers who, if they don't shop, won't consider their trips successful. The first is the knowledgeable collector. She's studied the symbolism of masks in Sierra Leone and wants to own some. The second is the compulsive shopper. Unlike diarrhea, compulsive shopping is not self-limiting.

The temptation to buy is at its most feverish when one first rolls into a country. Try a cold shower instead, then shop around, comparing quality and price. After a few hours, you'll notice substantial differences in workmanship that weren't evident at first. Buying during the last few days of a trip also minimizes problems of breakage, theft, and weight.

HOW TO PREPARE YOURSELF BEFORE BUYING

If you might shop, SAVE MONEY by beginning the process before you leave home. Make a list of clothing sizes of people for whom you plan to buy gifts. It helps to know sizes in inches or centimeters since size codes at home have little in common with those abroad. Think about whether gifts will relate to a holiday, birthday, wedding, love, friendship, or whatever. Decide how much you feel comfortable spending and build that amount into your budget.

If a country you'll be visiting is renowned for certain items, do the research needed to evaluate quality and prices. Take a list of what you're interested in and what it sells for at home. This research is especially important if you're considering buying jewels or electronic or photographic equipment. Travelers who fail to do advance research often wind up buying something that isn't quite what they wanted and paying more than they would have at home. But they do get to lug it around the world, then pay duty on it.

Bargaining, which we discussed in Chapter 6, should be in the forefront of your mind, especially if you intend to visit local market days when a cornucopia empties handcrafts from the countryside into town. The initial price quoted may be twice or up to ten times the price at which the merchant will eventually sell. It's up to you to get the price down.

As part of your preparation, decide *not* to buy certain things. For ethical and legal reasons, don't buy coral, wild bird feathers, marine mammal fur, endangered animal skins, ivory, live or stuffed birds, or sea turtle products. The U.S. Customs Service can provide a list. Further, if you arrive at the U.S. border with fresh fruit, endangered plants, or live animals, prepare for an exciting afternoon trying to avoid confiscation and/or a fine. A traveler discovered with an unapproved antiquity may be considered a thief, no matter what the obliging dealer said as he pocketed the cash.

HOW TO TELL IF IT'S THE REAL THING

There are bargains and there are ripoffs. High quality cannot be assumed. If you're thinking of buying something, inspect it more closely than you would at home because you won't be able to return it for a refund. For example, many people buy colorful clothing in Bali only to discover later that some of that lovely fabric is so thin it won't last long enough to be worn on the plane home. Cheap thread and careless stitching can result in unexpected vents at inconvenient moments. If you pay $6 for a pair of lightweight loose-fitting pants to wear for a couple of weeks, you probably won't care whether the patterns are machine-printed or will fade in the first wash. If you do care, take a closer look.

> Inspect all purchases closely; you won't be able to return them for a refund.

Authenticity is always a question. Is it batik or print? Elephant hair or black plastic? Leading the list of substitutes are phony designer labels. Of course, when you see foreign track shoes labeled "Niko," it makes you wonder about the quality of the shoes. If an item is offered to you as an antique, be cautious. If you like it for what it is, fine; just don't pay the price for an antique that isn't.

Jewels are difficult purchases. Unless you can tell whether a gem is genuine and, if so, know what it would cost at home, you're just off the turnip truck in the showroom of the gem dealer. If a dealer offers to authenticate a jewel or some precious metal, take it for granted that he'll provide test results that will appear to prove his representation. If the price is substantial, get an outside expert. For high-ticket items, try to buy from a merchant for whom you have a positive reference, perhaps from someone at home. *Caveat emptor* was never more true than at your friendly jewelers.

Before snapping up a reminder of some far-away place, try to find out if it comes from where you think it does. One example: tourists who fly to Antarctica routinely buy souvenirs without realizing that what they bought arrived in Antarctica on the same flight they did.

According to *Condé Nast Traveler*, most complaints from readers about foreign purchases involve electronic equipment bought in Hong Kong, artwork in Italy, glassware in Venice, jewelry in Bangkok, and rugs in Turkey. That's good information to remember.

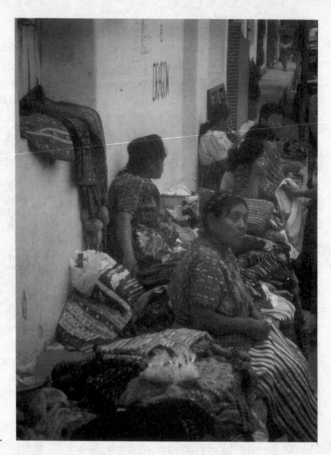

Guatemalan market.

HOW TO GET WHAT YOU BOUGHT

When you make a purchase, guard against a switch while it's being wrapped in the back room. Yucatan* hammocks are famous for their quality, but the one you examine in the front of the shop may be higher quality than the one later handed you in a plastic bag. Either stick with your purchase or examine it before you leave the shop. If you don't do that, check it as soon as you're back in your hotel.

Before you pay for something, figure out how much change to expect and count what you receive. Watch out for coins from a neighboring country which have no value for you. If a merchant intends to pull a scam with the change, he'll also be doing something to divert your attention so you won't notice. Be alert.

---

* *Yucatan.* A flat, humid, hot peninsula in Southern Mexico, rich in Mayan sites. Chichen Itza, Uxmal, and Tulum are the best known sites but there are many more.

HOW TO GET IT HOME

If you're not going to wrestle purchases all the way home, you'll have to figure out how to ship them. Choices include the merchant, the post office, courier and air express, freight forwarders, sea freight, your concierge, and homebound travelers. An established merchant, especially in Europe, can arrange for shipping by whatever means you specify. This is a helpful service but you're taking some risk if you've already paid in full.

The local post office, the most common choice, is much less expensive than courier and air express services. In some countries, however, you must prepare your purchases for shipping. In India, I had to hire a tailor to wrap my purchases in burlap until they resembled a mummy. Only then would the New Delhi post office anoint them with its elegant red wax seals. A few helpful post offices sell packing materials to help you along.

Federal Express, DHL, and UPS offer fast, reliable service—at high prices. Another alternative is a local freight forwarder. Its representative will pick up your purchase from the vendor, pack and ship it. Its counterpart at the port of entry will handle customs and forward the item on to your home. This, too, can be an expensive service.

The charge for shipping by sea, usually based on size rather than weight, is reasonable but delivery may take months. Look up shipping firms in the telephone book.

A knowledgeable concierge can handle shipping for you, but a $15 room usually doesn't come with a concierge.

On rare occasions, destiny delivers someone you can trust, heading toward your home, and willing to carry your purchases. Sometimes you find that person by asking around. Whatever your choice, consider insurance if the cargo is particularly valuable.

VAT/GST REFUNDS

A value-added tax (VAT), the equivalent of a sales tax, is added to most of your purchases in Europe. In some other countries, such as Canada and New Zealand, it is called a goods and services tax (GST), but the effect is the same. Because the tax averages about 20 percent, and can be 33 percent, it's worth knowing the rules.

Since these taxes are intended to apply to national residents, travelers can obtain refunds on certain purchases. VAT/GST paid on goods and services purchased for consumption in the country, including meals, hotel rooms, and rental cars, are not refundable. However, you can usually get a refund on taxes you paid on items purchased to take out of the country—but only if you ask for it. Some countries allow you to avoid the VAT/GST if the merchant mails the purchase to you at your home.

There are a couple of common ways to obtain refunds. Ask for a tax-refund form from the merchant, have it stamped by the customs officer as you leave the country, and then mail it back to the store. The merchant then sends you a refund check or credits the amount to your credit card account. A refund check in the currency of the country where you made the purchase will be expensive to convert. Better, try to obtain a refund directly from customs as you leave the country.

If you make a purchase at a store with "tax free for tourists" signs, your purchase is sealed and you get a VAT/GST refund check immediately from the merchant. You can cash it at a service desk or window at most airports and train terminals (look for "Tax Free Shopping"). Of course, they charge a fee for this convenience.

One final complication: you usually have to make a minimum purchase, for each transaction, to be eligible for any refund at all. This minimum may range from $35 to $250, and is often about $100. No refunds are given on purchases below the minimum.

CUSTOMS

At most borders, you'll meet a customs official who wants to see what you're bringing in—and sometimes what you're taking out. Customs agents look for items acquired abroad on which duty is payable, and for items not allowed in their country at all. However, unless a traveler is intentionally smuggling or recklessly carrying firearms, illegal drugs, or the body parts of endangered animal species, passing through Customs should mean no more than a slight delay.

Certificate of Registration

Outbound from your country, you can obtain a Certificate of Registration from Customs confirming that your camera and other named expensive items are leaving the country with you. This certificate ensures that you won't have to pay duty on these items on your return. For expensive new camera equipment or jewelry, a certificate might be worthwhile. Otherwise, few travelers bother.

Searches

Searches are not nearly so random as one might believe. The agent sizes up people as they wait in line. Sometimes informers mingle with incoming passengers, hoping to pick up suspicious behavior. Anyone fitting a certain profile or behaving in an unusual way is in for a search. If an agent is getting an assist from a drug-sniffing dog, do not attempt to pat him (dog or agent).

If stopped by an agent, remain calm. Even if you think you may have committed a minor violation, don't hesitate to open any bag when asked.

Volunteer no information and don't try to bluff your way through by blustering or threatening. An agent has been through this drill many times and won't be intimidated, but you can make one angry if you try. If a problem develops, ask what your rights are. Call a lawyer if necessary.

In some countries, customs agents have been known to steal from bags as they search them, so don't let your attention wander during the search.

Favors

If someone you don't know asks you to clear a bag through customs while he changes money or does some other chore, don't do it. Getting caught with illegal drugs can put you in the slammer for a long time. Don't wait until the dog starts barking before you realize your mistake. At that point, the person for whom you were doing the favor will be long gone.

Don't clear a stranger's bag through customs.

I have several times met people who were about to fly home and practically begged them to take stuff home for me. I sent seventy rolls of film and several journals home with a guy I met scuba diving in Indonesia. We were both cautious. I gathered enough information so I could find him if delivery was delayed. He looked in my film canisters to be sure they contained nothing but film. When he did that, I knew he was an experienced traveler and would make the delivery.

Duty

When returning home, you'll be asked to fill out a customs declaration listing your purchases. Misrepresentation or failure to declare something can result in penalties, seizure and forfeiture, and even imprisonment. Heck of a way to end a trip; who would give your slide show?

Customs agents have a pretty good idea of the market value of what they see. If one challenges your valuation, it's helpful to have a receipt. Of course, the concept of a receipt would make vendors in local markets shake their heads. If an inspector discovers an item not listed on your declaration, you may be given a chance to amend the declaration. If you decline, he can impose a fine and increase the duty. If an agent catches a traveler concealing something or using a falsified receipt, he can increase the duty up to 600 percent.

A returning traveler owes no duty on the first $400 worth of goods he or she brings home. This exemption can be used only once every thirty days. The goods must be for personal use and must be in your possession. This exemption increases to $600 when returning from about two dozen countries in Central America and the Caribbean. Duty kicks in at 10 percent on the first $1000 above the $400 exemption. Above that, the amount of duty is determined by what the item is and where it came from.

Since special interests have made duty regulations look like Swiss cheese, I can only provide a broad outline. To generalize, items such as china tableware, leather goods, jewelry, and furs have been singled out for special treatment. You would pay 27.5 percent on silver jewelry, but only 6.5 percent on most other jewelry. Duty on cut jade is 2.1 percent while that on set jade is 21 percent; crystal ranges from 6 to 20 percent, and wool sweaters from 7.5 to 17 percent. If you expect to make expensive purchases abroad, ask the Customs Service what duty percentages apply. Duty, which must be paid on your return home, can be paid by cash, personal check, or traveler's check (in some of the larger ports of entry, a credit card is also acceptable).

The largest exception, called the Generalized System of Preferences (GSP), is granted for purchases made in less-developed countries. To help them export their goods, the United States permits many purchases made in about 125 countries to come in free of duty. If you'll be traveling in the Third World and plan to do considerable shopping, call the Customs Service for specifics or check with the American consulate on the spot. Ask for a leaflet named *GSP & The Traveler*.

You owe no duty on a gift you mail home if the value is less than $100 and you send it to someone other than yourself. Duty is owed if the addressee receives more than one gift a day. Write "unsolicited gift; value less than $100" on the package. A customs inspector may open these packages before they reach the recipient. Gifts that you carry back with you are subject to duty unless they fit within your exemption.

Unique works created by a professional artist are admitted free of duty. However, mass-produced items and the work of craftsmen are subject to duty.

An item must have been made at least one hundred years ago to be considered an antique. If so, the good news is that it may be admitted free of duty. The bad news is that you may have violated the laws of a foreign country if you removed it without an export permit. If you purchase an authentic looking reproduction, obtain a written statement from the vendor confirming that it's a reproduction. That will help you get it out of the country but makes it subject to duty at home.

Duty Free

Have you thought about what "duty-free" means? It only means that goods are being sold without addition of a local sales tax or import duty. That means low prices, right? Very seldom. In fact, duty-free shops often sell imported luxury goods at inflated prices. The absence of local tax is almost immaterial. These shops are traps for wealthy and/or inexperienced tourists. A duty-free purchase may make sense if you have foreign currency left that you can't exchange back before leaving the country. The fact that you bought something in a duty-free shop overseas has no effect at all on whether you owe duty on it when you return home.

Items not permitted into the United States include plants (except that cut flowers carrying no bugs may be allowed through), fresh fruit, vegetables, meat, illegal narcotics, switchblades, poisonous items, and hazardous articles such as fireworks. Drugs and medical devices sold overseas but not approved by the FDA are not permitted to enter even though purchased legally. You can return with firearms so long as you can prove, by prior registration with Customs or the Bureau of Alcohol, Tobacco and Firearms, that they are they same ones you left with. Otherwise, unless you are a licensed firearms importer, firearms will be confiscated.

Samples of or items made from ivory, tortoise shell, coral, leopard fur, hides, shells, and feathers or teeth of an endangered species are also prohibited and you may be fined for attempting to bring them in. Don't think that just because the vendor assured you there would be no problem that Customs will permit you to keep them.

Copies of brand name merchandise ("knock-offs") probably violate someone's patents or trademarks. If the customs agent spots a fake Rolex or pirated cassette tapes or computer programs, he's likely to confiscate and destroy them. All you can do is grin and bear it. After all, you only paid that guy on the beach $20 for the "Rolex."

If you contemplate returning home with a live animal, or any wildlife product, discuss the subject with customs or the U.S. Fish & Wildlife Service before you go or with an embassy or consulate overseas. Otherwise, you may run into an expensive quarantine.

For more information on customs regulations, including current duty rates, contact a customs official at one of the more than forty district offices in the United States (check government listings in the telephone book under U.S. Department of Treasury, U.S. Customs Service, District Director). Also obtain a copy of *Know Before You Go, Customs Hints for Returning Residents* from the U.S. Customs Service (P.O. Box 7407, Washington, DC 20044, or call 202-566-8195). Also helpful are *Your Trip Abroad* (#141Z, $1.25) and *Custom Tips for Travelers* (#454Z, $.50) from the Consumer Information Center, P.O. Box 100, Pueblo, CO 81002.

IMPORTING

"These are great," he says. "I could sell a million of them back in Chicago." He's looking at a papier-mâché box in Kashmir or maybe a commode in New Zealand that has half-flush and full-flush buttons to conserve water. Last week, he talked with another traveler who planned to pay for his entire trip by collecting old watches to sell in London.

Most travelers come across items for which there might be a market back home. Many never recognize the opportunities; others do, make notes in their journals, and never follow up. But a few are serious. They come home determined to import thousands of something or other and make a fortune. Well, it's been done and it can be done again, but being successful in the import business is no slam dunk.

This discussion isn't a course on starting an import business, but I can pose some questions that will reveal how serious you are. You could answer some of them before you go, but at that point your entrepreneurial spirit won't have yet become inflamed by some item that begs to be imported. However, answering them while still on the road will make your travel time more productive.

Basic Questions

- What do I want to achieve through importing?
- Why do I think I'll succeed?
- Am I an entrepreneur at heart? Am I willing to work hard enough to get a new business going?
- How much money am I prepared to put at risk?
- Do my skills match those needed by this business?
- Do I have the time?
- Do I have correct information about suppliers, a distribution system, prices, transportation, and financing?
- What's the competition?
- What are the demographics of potential buyers?
- What are the trends in the market I'd be entering?
- How many units can I sell? How many must I sell to make a profit?
- What is a reasonable rate of growth for sales?
- What governmental regulations will affect import and sale of the product?
- Can I get a trademark or patent to protect my product from competition?
- Do channels of distribution exist to get the product to market?
- If the product will require service, can I supply it?

Check the Importing section of the Bibliography for good resources, most of which are free. If you think you might be interested in importing, it would make sense to review some of them before you depart.

Determining Effective Demand for your Product

The impulse to import strikes a surprisingly large number of travelers because they see so many appealing items they've never seen before and "they're so cheap!" They believe they know their home market, and being personally captivated by an item, they assume it will appeal to the general public. If that assumption turns out to be wishful thinking, the business is

Masks for sale. Chichicastenango, Guatemala.

about to become an expensive hobby. It takes good research as well as intuition to answer the question of whether there's a sufficient market for a product.

For demand to be effective, potential buyers must be willing and able to pay the price you have to charge to cover overhead and make a profit. The item you want to import may cost very little to purchase, but to that you must add your personal expenses, freight (land freight overseas, international air or sea freight, and domestic freight), freight forwarders' and customs brokers' fees, duty and bond charges, costs of financing, advertising, communications, insurance, and commissions to your sales representatives. When you add an acceptable profit, you have the price at which you can sell to a retail outlet. After the retailer doubles that price to the public, will your product sell in acceptable volume?

Run these numbers before making serious commitments. If they're acceptable, establish relationships with suppliers and commit to buy a small number of the product. When the product arrives, test the market to determine whether demand is as strong as you thought or whether you've just purchased your Christmas presents for the next fifty years.

Evaluating Suppliers

Importers sometimes fail to ensure that their suppliers can furnish the number of products desired while maintaining the required level of quality. People who live on the tiny island of Taquile on Lake Titicaca produce blouses of outstanding quality and design. At the low prices they charge for their fine work, you feel guaranteed of a profit when you resell the blouses at home— so you buy all the embroidered blouses on hand. You guessed right and there is an eager market. Confident you can sell ten times the quantity you bought the first time, you write the weavers in Taquile asking them to substantially increase their output. Perhaps they're delighted, send you more first-quality blouses, and everyone is happy. But, not being compulsively materialistic, they may decide instead not to increase production. Or they may try to increase output, but quality suffers and they wind up shipping you inferior blouses. You run the risk of having built market demand that you can't meet without delivering inferior quality. There goes the business.

Whatever the product, production shouldn't start until you and your suppliers are in agreement about standards of quality. Ability to maintain the original quality at increasing levels of demand is essential to success.

Until you identify reliable suppliers who consistently meet quality and quantity standards, plan to return with some frequency to the country in which your product is made. Alternatively, hire a local agent if you find one you trust and with whom you have good rapport. Someone on site helps overcome misunderstandings.

The next issue is delivery. Your imported blouses become such a hit that you land a big contract with a chain of women's boutiques, committing to deliver the blouses three months after signing the deal. Although it seemed an easy commitment to meet, it turns out that because of a drought some of the natural dyes are no longer available, or religious holidays interrupted production, or increased income enabled the weavers to award themselves more leisure time. For one reason or another, you miss the contract date. You can't do that very often and retain credibility, especially if your customers have been advertising the product. Be realistic in determining whether your suppliers can meet agreed-upon delivery dates.

Capital Required

Few suppliers are going to ship their products thousands of miles to you on consignment (i.e., letting you pay for them after you've sold them). Therefore, you have to pay for the goods in advance or on receipt. This creates the classic cash flow crunch. You can use your own money as initial capital, but more often importers arrange for a letter of credit to pay for goods. Banks charge a fee for this letter of credit and require that you have a good financial reputation. Later, after a year or two of reliable performance, suppliers may give you a short (e.g., thirty day) grace period after delivery before you must pay.

If an importer engages in wishful thinking when projecting the rate of sales, undercapitalization can lead to catastrophe. An otherwise sound business idea will fail because the company can't sustain itself until the rewards of success arrive. Be realistic and prepare for the long haul.

Learning the Business

The best time to learn the mechanics of importing is before you leave home. It's not essential, but you'll have a better idea of what information to gather and which contacts to make while abroad. It's a world of bills of lading and other shipping documents, customs forms and procedures, international financial arrangements, insurance, duties, and quotas. New terms and symbols, such as FAS, FOB, C&F, and CIF, must become part of your vocabulary. Success or failure of your business may depend on how well you learn the regulations that apply to your imports. For example, the amount of customs duty charged can depend on facts as minuscule as in what country care tags or buttons are sewed on. Happily, the U.S. Customs Service is helpful in explaining its regulations.

Other government organizations will help with importing, although they're considerably more enthusiastic if you're exporting, as will international trade departments of commercial banks. In addition, hundreds of world trade and import/export clubs provide information and hold regular meetings and seminars. Books, magazines, and newsletters on the subject are legion. Freight forwarders, the transportation experts who get your goods from there to here, are an excellent resource. Consultants and experienced friends can help. Then you learn by doing.

Years ago, most U.S. rugby clubs ordered their team jerseys at the beginning of each season from manufacturers in New Zealand or England. Since it took months for orders to be filled, many team members had to play in old sweatshirts. Seeing an opportunity, Rex, Tony, and I started Leather Balls, Ltd., to import Canterbury rugby jerseys from New Zealand. This was long before yuppie pseudo-jerseys clogged the catalogues. Because we maintained a large inventory and were able to deliver within a week of receiving an order, we soon dominated the rugby club market. As business expanded, we signed up a few trade reps ("Good morning, I'm the rep with Leather Balls.") and developed markets in ski shops and department stores. Although we were successful, I realize now that our lack of market research exposed us to much more risk than necessary.

Importing initially seems attractive because it provides a reason to return to a country you enjoy. Unfortunately, a business trip is very different from a pleasure trip. When doing business you're constantly rushing, bargaining, and unraveling red tape. There may be time for pleasure, but if pleasure comes first it could be a costly trip. Earning a profit from your travels is quite possible but don't spend money on a romantic fantasy while believing it to be a business. Of course, if you *know* it's a romantic fantasy and you want to spend money on it, that's fine.

22

Remembering

> Like all great travellers, I have seen more than I remember,
> and remember more than I have seen.
> —Benjamin Disraeli

No trip ever really ends. Memories can become faint glimmers over the years or they can remain vivid and rich. It's up to you.

By far the best way to gather memories is by being completely present where you are, immersing yourself in the experience, imprinting conversations, colors, sounds, and breathtaking views into your cells. Maps, handcrafts, coins, receipts, literature, and souvenirs all contribute to memories, but being 100 percent present is my highest priority. That requires not thinking about what's going on at home or what things will be like when I return. It means not reading international editions of magazines or newspapers as I travel. "News" usually isn't, and when I return, little of substance will have changed.

Being 100 percent present means stopping often to appreciate where I am—seeing more by seeing less. It means taking risks, making an effort, and reaching out to people. Being 100 percent present is not for spectators; it's for participants.

KEEPING A JOURNAL

Since memory is so fallible, mental images benefit from backup systems. One backup is a good journal. A journal also helps you share your experiences with friends, including those you won't meet for twenty years after the trip. A journal packed with reports of people, emotions, events, and ideas provides information and insights for years.

Accuracy and truth are requisites of a worthwhile journal. Accuracy is a matter of practice and paying attention. The truth is sometimes hard to write when dealing with issues close to the bone, such as when you didn't meet a challenge as well as you wanted to. Still, those are the very truths to record. It may be easier to explore emotions on paper if you intend no one else to read your words. When traveling with a partner, journals should be explicitly confidential.

I keep track of observations by scribbling occasional notes on a piece of paper during the day. Otherwise, with so much sensory input, I'd lose a lot before I had time to record it all in my journal. When I miss a day or two of journal writing, daily notes help me catch up.

> "To lose a passport was the least of one's worries: to lose a notebook was a catastrophe."
> —Bruce Chatwin, The Songlines

Drawings capture details that might otherwise be missed. A trek across western Nepal became even more interesting after I sketched the subtle ways in which construction and design of buildings in each mountain village differed from those in neighboring villages, though separated by less than a mile.

Make observations about people you see or meet, record your feelings about what you did, and include changes in your perspective and plans for the future. Explore similarities and differences among cultures in terms of religion, architecture, art, agriculture, and language. Attempt to capture the spirit, as well as the form, of a temple, landscape, or person.

Someone said, "Ixion breakfasted with the Gods and remembered only the pattern of the tablecloth." That's how I feel when I record only facts. Dry reporting doesn't retain the flavors. Try to make that journal sing with impressions, reactions, and reflections.

I walked for a while with an older man I overtook on the Milford Track in New Zealand. Each time the trail turned a bend and a new panorama unfolded, he'd lift a small tape recorder to his lips and whisper, "Beautiful, beautiful," or "Spectacular," or something similar. Not once did he draw a verbal picture of what he saw, nothing from which to later recreate the beauty he was experiencing.

Are you interested in publishing articles related to your experiences? If so, read a book on travel writing (perhaps one of those in the Bibliography) before you leave to learn the type of information to collect as you travel. If you fail to collect what you need, you may regret a missed opportunity.

Here's another way to SAVE MONEY. If you write with publication in mind, you may be able to deduct some or all of your travel expenses on your income tax return. If that's a possibility, keep track of expenses to support the deductions you claim. The guidelines for deductibility are pretty straightforward. Ask a lawyer, accountant, or the IRS.

Giraffe in the Masai Mara Reserve. Kenya.

TAKING FINE PHOTOGRAPHS

Why do we bother taking photographs? After all, the right photographic equipment takes time to gather, adds weight, and takes up precious space in the bag. Equipment, film, and developing add significantly to the cost of the trip. You have to guard the equipment and care for the film. Finally, shooting pictures may change the nature of a trip, slowing its pace, perhaps even intruding between observer and experience. However, most of us brush these objections aside because we intend to return home with photo-memories.

That being the case, a little preparation can help ensure high-quality photographs. Here are a few preliminary tips:

- Be clear on the purpose of your photos. Will they accompany a story you plan to sell? Join a series of images gracing your walls? Reside in an album, waiting to be called on to stimulate your memory years in the future? Prove to your friends that you stood your ground within the leap of that black leopard? Having a clear purpose, or even more than one, gives your photos coherence.

- A photographer who simply snaps away each day is likely to discover, when she reviews newly developed prints or slides, that she's totally failed to capture the essence of a country or culture. Before you leave a place, consider what characteristics best represent it and see whether you have them on film.

- If your objective is to tell a story, think about the type of photographs required and keep your objective in mind all day. If you simply want fine individual photographs, your task is much easier because one shot need not be linked to another.

- If you plan to sell your photographs, contact newspapers, travel magazines, and special interest publications to find out whether they prefer (or insist on) black and white or color, slides or prints. Even if your photographs will be published in black and white, some publishers will accept color slides since new computer scanning equipment produces clear images (and has reduced the cost of the conversion process). In other words, shoot with your market in mind.

- Keep good notes about each photo. Don't lose a sale because you can't identify the subject matter or location.

- Imagine yourself at Versailles. One photographer after another stands in the footprints of those who came before, each snapping the obvious shot. If you want to record something pleasing for the bedroom wall, standing where everyone else does is fine. Similarly, if you're taking the shot to accompany a story, the editor probably wants a familiar image that readers can identify. If, however, your goal is personal interpretation, you must stand where others have not, or capture the image under unusual conditions. See the subject with sight unique to yourself.

- Sometimes the shot of the year requires incredible patience, waiting for perfect light or the ideal cloud formation. It can also be captured by a photographer who recognizes opportunity and knows the equipment well enough to take a well-composed shot on three seconds' notice. It rarely emerges from ignorance or luck. If you're not already experienced, consider a course on outdoor, or existing light, photography. Check out a good book on photography and practice.

- If you are thinking of buying photographic equipment overseas, research the item you want, including domestic prices, before you leave. Some overseas "bargain" prices aren't bargains. When buying photographic equipment abroad, be sure you get authentic, new equipment. Watch out for warranties that require the equipment to be returned to Hong Kong, Singapore, or some other far away place for repair. If you wait to buy your trip camera abroad, you'll be depending on a camera with which you haven't practiced, and one that may turn out to be defective.

Equipment

If you're going to buy a camera for the trip, buy decent equipment, learn how it works, and *use it before leaving*. It's too common for someone to buy a new camera, toss it in the bag, and jump on the plane. Unless you're a masochist-in-training, read the manual, then shoot and critique a couple of training rolls before you leave. Solve problems at home where you can get advice easily. By the way, if you haven't used a camera for several months give it a trial run to check its mechanical integrity before leaving.

> "Many beautiful sights are impossible to transfer onto film; rather than intrude my camera into an experience for no purpose, I simply enjoy them."
> —Galen Rowell, *High and Wild*, 1983

Cameras

For easygoing photographers, an ultra-light, fully *automatic camera* with a built-in flash, compact zoom lens, and auto-focus is quite adequate. Although lack of manual control of lens speed and aperture and, therefore, of depth of field limits the effects that can be achieved, beautiful images are still possible. Nevertheless, these cameras can be fooled by light conditions and may not be appropriate for travelers seeking pictures of publishable quality. At least try to find one that has a backlight feature that compensates for a subject brightly lit from behind.

Serious photographers travel with at least two *35mm single lens reflex (SLR)* camera bodies and several interchangeable lenses. I've sometimes wished I had two cameras with me so I could be ready with both color and black and white film or film of different speeds, but never enough to lug that much weight around. Fortunately, Kodak and friends have come up with Advanced Photo System film. More about that under "Film" below.

One 35mm SLR camera that operates in both manual and automatic modes is quite sufficient for my purposes. Professional photographers seem to favor Canon, Nikon, Pentax, and Olympus, but there are so many fine cameras you can hardly go wrong if you keep weight, size, and durability in mind. Check consumer magazines and photographic trade publications for help in evaluating the alternatives.

If you want to take photographs underwater, choices include an expensive *underwater camera* (such as a Nikonos), a mid-range camera (such as a Vivitar), a cheap throwaway (which works fine for shallow snapshots), or a waterproof camera housing (EWA-Marine has a good series for SLRs and camcorders; call 800-257-7742).

Batteries

Superautomatic, multigizmo cameras are extremely dependent on batteries and suck energy like crazy. The biggest guzzlers are the auto-winder and auto-focus features. Besides dramatically reducing battery life, they also make the camera vulnerable in especially cold temperatures. When it's really cold, it helps to keep your camera inside your jacket when practical, and to keep spare batteries comparatively warm.

Extreme heat at a Mayan site. Mexico.

If your camera goes into an electronic coma in Europe, you can find a replacement battery within an hour. In much of the rest of the world, your camera might be disabled for quite a while. Further, the battery that costs $10 to $15 at home may sell for $50 in Kenya (and you'll have to pay it). Although many SLRs operate several manual shutter speeds without electric power, the lesson is clear: if your travels take you outside relatively modern cities or to very cold weather, always carry a couple of spare batteries.

Zoom Lens

Many photographers consider at least one zoom lens indispensable. When I see someone with a gigantic telephoto taking a close-up of the left eye of a rhino two hundred yards away across the savannah, I tell myself they're on a tour, have three bearers to cart their camera gear, and are only seeing the world through a camera lens—and I'm still envious. I usually carry a 28–80mm, a 70–300mm, and a telextender. Consider a lens with macro capability for extreme close-ups (including bugs and plants).

Filters

I take two filters. The first is ultraviolet, whose principal purpose is to protect the lens from being scratched. Pros substitute an 81A filter that produces a slight warming effect. The second is a polarizing filter, needed only occasionally to cut glare and reflections and intensify colors. However, a polarizing filter cuts flexibility because it consumes about two f-stops of light, requiring a slower shutter speed to avoid losing depth of field. Further, if you don't align a polarizing filter properly with each shot, it actually makes the picture worse. Don't leave it on the lens when there's not a specific reason to use it. Using a polarizing filter in conjunction with a wide-angle lens may create dark areas on one side of the sky in your frame but not on the other (seldom a desired effect).

Lens Cover

Since a lens cover is an incorrigible escape-artist and difficult to replace on the road, attach it to the barrel of the lens with a "keeper," an elastic band designed for that purpose. You might even consider taking a spare.

Lens Hood

A collapsible rubber lens hood or a screw-on lens hood shields the lens from glaring sun, as does a well-placed hat or hand casting a shadow on the lens.

Flash

A flash is worthwhile for capturing places like interiors of temples or tombs, gloomy rain forests, and nightlife. If your camera doesn't have a built-in flash, the nature of your trip determines whether it's worth bringing one along.

Tripod

The steadiness with which you hold your camera, especially in dim light, affects the sharpness of your photographs. A tripod solves that problem, but if a full-scale tripod seems too cumbersome, consider an 18-ounce monopod with a ball head or a tripod about five inches tall with a C-clamp on one end. If you decide against a tripod, finding something to brace against, maybe cushioned with a shirt or bandanna, helps. For a particularly long exposure, try setting the camera on a stable surface and using the auto-timer.

Cleaning Stuff

A simple brush, lens cleaning solution, and soft lens tissues help keep the lens spotless. Microfiber cloths sold in camera shops are excellent. Q-tips are good for cleaning the view finder and the perimeter of the lens. Avoid using your handkerchief to clean a lens.

Camera Bag

A camera bag is useful at home, but it's bulky and a target for sticky fingers when abroad. A stuff sack or army surplus shoulder bag keeps the camera out of sight and shielded from dust. Even a Ziploc plastic bag provides good temporary protection. Camera equipment should be protected from heat, cold, grit, and moisture (especially salt spray)—and rapid changes in temperature which can cause condensation. When camera or lenses are riding in luggage, cushion them well with clothing.

Film

Slide or Print

You have a choice to make between slide film (transparency) and print film. Slide film is less expensive to develop, but you have to add in the cost of a screen, projector, and slide trays. Slides are noted for excellent color and sharpness and it's exciting to see a life size lion yawning in your living room. On the other hand, because slide film is less forgiving of incorrect exposure settings, shooting slides requires more skill than shooting prints. In addition, less can be done in the lab to improve incorrectly exposed slide film. If you shoot slides but want something to hang on the wall, you can have prints made from your slides (although the process is relatively expensive).

Color or Black and White

People shoot black and white either because it's for a publication that insists on it—or because it's the best way to express a personal vision. If you're using black and white for a publication, they'll probably want you to submit prints, not negatives. If you don't do your own black and white processing, obtaining prints will either be expensive, if you pay someone for a custom job, or result in unremarkable images, if the drugstore does it on a machine. In other words, go with color unless you have a special purpose.

The new Advanced Photo System film developed by Kodak offers a very useful midroll interrupt feature. That means you can switch between film of different speeds, print or slide, black and white or color rolls easily, without losing a lot of unexposed film.

Brands

Different brands of film yield somewhat different color values. Fuji is known for emphasizing greens and blues, Agfa for yellows and oranges, and Kodachrome for reds. Any custom photo lab can show you comparisons to help choose what pleases your eye.

Kodachrome ISO 25 is said to be the sharpest and least grainy slide film easily available. The problem is that except on sunny days you have to shoot at slow shutter speeds and get little depth of field. ISO 50 provides more flexibility. I usually choose ISO 100 for outdoor photography, trading the ultimate in sharpness for greater flexibility. I also carry rolls of ISO 200 and 400 for lower light situations. Some people love Fujichrome Velvia (ISO 50) and others prefer Kodak Ektachrome Lumiere 100X. However, neither is ideal for photographing people because they do odd things with skin tones.

Black and white photography has become fairly rare, but it can convey mood hard to attain with color film. If you don't have access to a professional lab, you may want to shoot Ilford XP2 400 film that can be developed by color processing.

Kodak also offers a film specially designed for use underwater.

Number of Exposures

To cut down on bulk and frequency of reloading, carry rolls with thirty-six exposures. Even if you like to use every frame, make an exception when a particularly photogenic event is coming up. Sacrifice several unexposed frames and load a new roll ahead of time, especially if you can load in some sheltered spot instead of aboard a sailboat or in the midst of a camel race.

Where to Buy Film and Equipment

High volume outlets sell film and cameras at prices local retail stores can't match. Check the back pages of Popular Photography or other photography magazines for advertisements. When ordering film from one of these outlets, ask about the expiration dates of the film they're offering. As film draws close to its expiration date, outlets sometimes cut the price in half. That's a great way to SAVE MONEY since you'll expose it within the next few weeks anyway. Whatever film you buy, store it the refrigerator or freezer in Ziploc bags.

How Much to Buy

The amount of film to take depends on how much space you have and on your personal style. Do you fire away all day, hoping to capture a few wonderful images, or do you take a few carefully thought out shots? It also depends on where you travel, in that some places are much more scenic than others. On average, I take enough film to shoot one-half roll a day; a friend takes enough to shoot two rolls a week.

There are at least three good reasons to over-stock: (1) exposing film is cheap compared to the cost of reaching some remote place; (2) film is less expensive at home than in remote places; and (3) film you buy abroad may not have been well cared for.

Film Care

Don't leave either camera or film sitting in direct sunlight or in a space likely to become very hot. When there's film in your luggage, follow the same rules. If necessary, wrap film to shelter it from extreme cold. When film is very cold, prevent condensation by warming it gradually before loading it into the camera.

The National Association of Photographic Manufacturers evaluated the effects of baggage X-ray machines on various types and speeds of film and.

Buddhist temple.
Chiang Mai, Thailand.

concluded that the effects are negligible, even after film was exposed to the machine as many as 100 times (note: NAPM still suggests that you avoid putting films faster than ISO 400 through the machine). That conclusion may be reassuring in the United States, but when I go through an airport X-ray security station abroad I pass my camera and the film in my daypack around the X-ray tunnel. Even if the attendant insists there's no danger, it makes me feel better.

I use a double-thick lead-laminated pouch to protect rolls of film. Pouches are available in several sizes from camera stores (Sima Super FilmShield, $15).

Throw the cardboard boxes in the trash, put the plastic film canisters in the lead foil bag, and pack the bag in the center of your luggage. Because luggage may be zapped by a powerful X ray on the way to the belly of the plane, some professional photographers insist that every roll of film be examined by hand. By the way, X rays have no effect on video cameras.

Developing

I have yet to have a single roll of film developed while I travel. Everything I've heard and seen persuades me that processing is of higher quality and is less expensive at home. Rather than drugstore processing, try one of the reputable mail-order labs for higher quality at much lower prices. I've successfully used several: Seattle Film Works (206-283-9074), Kodalux (800-354-6873), Fuji Tru Color (800-224-5227), and Mystic Color (800-367-6061).

My last comment may be one of the most important. Anytime you'll be away from where you store your film, *check to see that you have plenty of UNEXPOSED film in your pocket or pack*. Don't wait until you're face to face with a silverback gorilla before discovering you're out of film.

Tips for Taking Fine Photographs

A great photograph sometimes just happens, but it's rare. Even given good equipment and a fine subject, superior results come from skill and thought on the part of the photographer. In this section, we'll discuss ways to add to the quality of the shots you bring home.

- See the subject of your photograph for itself, independent of your momentary presence. Take time to look at it, to enjoy it. When you snap a hurried picture without really seeing the subject, that distance shows in the result.
- When you know the subject matter is wonderful, consider bracketing. That is, take the first picture at the exposure and shutter speed you or your camera think is correct. Then take a photograph at the next smaller f-stop and one at the next larger (or you can bracket by changing shutter speed instead). Of course, if your camera is fully-automatic, it will neutralize your aperture change by changing the shutter speed. If you can, switch to manual. Bracketing is more important when shooting slides than prints. Sure, bracketing eats film but how many times will you see the Taj Mahal under the full moon?
- Look at the subject through the viewfinder with your camera horizontal, then with it vertical. The difference can substantially change the mood of a picture, as well as avoid clutter.
- The lens loves clouds and shadows and the gentle light of early morning and late afternoon. At noon on a clear day the light will be flat and results will lack drama.
- To avoid shooting cliché photographs, experiment by shooting from unusual angles to get different effects. If you're about to take a picture that would look good on a postcard, change your angle (or forget it and buy the postcard). The most important photographic equipment is your legs. Get out of the vehicle. Climb up the hillside. Scout

alternative points of view. See what the shot would look like from one knee or with your elbows on the ground. Avoid the common standing eye-level shot, but don't let the quest for an unusual angle lead you into taking foolish risks. Wild animals will charge—and it won't be a photo-fee!

– The closer you are to the subject, the better your photograph. I reached Kaladeo Bird Sanctuary in Bharatpur, India, just as rare white Siberian cranes arrived at the end of their long migration. Excited, I fired off most of a roll as they glided onto the far bank of the marsh, soft late afternoon light illuminating their snowy backs. On another occasion, trudging in a steady downpour through Perinet forest in Madagascar, my guide pointed up at several cat-like Indris lemurs high in the tree-top canopy. Snapping quickly to minimize raindrops on the lens, I got a half dozen shots before being driven undercover. Can you guess what those two sets of photographs had in common? Both featured bland scenery against which you could see, if you looked closely, several white dots in one set and several brown dots in the other. Only the photographer could have the slightest idea why anyone had bothered to snap the shutter. The image you see in your mind's eye is not always what shows up on film. Move closer or zoom in.

> The closer you are to the subject, the better your photograph.

– Photographing wildlife is harder than it might seem. If the subjects don't virtually fill the frame, the photo may be disappointing. Timing is also critical. When animals see you, they get nervous and start to move away. If you're slow, what you get is a wastebasket full of discarded photos of hind ends. Approach as near as you safely can, preferably downwind from the animals, and settle in. Stay still, not looking directly at them. In a short time, they'll return to grazing or playing and you'll have your shot.

– Most beginning photographers center the subject in the viewfinder. It's called bull's-eye vision. There's another method, sometimes called the "rule of thirds." Imagine drawing a tic-tac-toe grid on your viewfinder, creating nine squares. Placing your subject at one of the four intersections on that grid may create a more interesting photograph.

– Placing the horizon in the middle of the frame produces a predictable picture. If the sky is your reason for taking the picture, place the horizon in the lower third of the frame to improve the effect.

– When composing a shot, try to do three things every time: (a) Look beyond your subject to examine the background for anything that would detract from the shot, such as electric wires, advertising signs, Western tourists, and anything else that conveys a mood different from the one you're after. Since the background can make or break the picture, keep it as uncluttered as you can. (b) Look at the subject directly, not through the viewfinder, with one eye closed to see if your composition changes. After all, the camera has just one eye. (c) Just before you shoot, take your eye away from the viewfinder to see whether something is about to move into the picture. This small precaution reduces the number of photos that include the front bumper of a bus or half of some pedestrian's face.

- Try framing a distant subject by using something in the foreground. Shoot through an arch or use a tree trunk and branch or anything else that's handy. The idea is to add a sense of scale and dimension to the shot.

- Choose action shots over posed shots. Catch people doing something. Capture excitement.

- To be ready to take a shot quickly when using manual focus, focus your camera ahead of time at a selected point. When your subject arrives at that point, all you'll have to do is bring the camera up and shoot. Similarly, when you want to take a shot unobserved, adjust the focus on some object that's about the same distance away from you as the real subject, but in a different direction. You can then turn and shoot instantly.

- There's no reason you can't take a good photograph while moving, such as when aboard a train. Choose a fast enough shutter speed to freeze the subject. For most situations, 1/500th of a second is fine. The odds against a blurred photo are better if you shoot while the subject is coming toward you or receding into the distance.

- Using a reflection can produce a superior photograph. On the other hand, reflections can be an obstacle. When shooting through glass, say a car window, try to get the sun behind you. Hold the camera close to the window but don't allow it to touch. If it does, vibrations from the vehicle may blur the picture. A polarizing filter can help eliminate reflections off glass.

- Try shooting unusual architecture from odd angles and extremely close-up.

- Many captivating prints or slides are of people, the closer the better. It's easy to photograph monuments, and they do help recall where you were, but they can quickly become boring in your living room. Photographs of local people keep a trip alive. Next best are slices of everyday life, the shots that capture the essence of what a place felt like as you walked along.

- Recording the subject and the camera setting of each shot as I take it would drive me crazy. Still, if you're shooting dozens of temples, monasteries, or pagodas, they tend to blend together. I compromise by taping a number to each film container. As I use one, I enter that number in the back of my journal, indicating locations where I started and finished the roll. Another solution is to photograph something easily identifiable, such as an historical marker, to serve as a fingerprint of the location.

- Good equipment and good technique help, but developing an eye for what constitutes a memorable photograph is essential. We learn from feedback, so study your own photographs and those in good travel books until you have a feel for what works. Develop your own style. Take photographs that capture your point of view, that capture an essence, or that contain a message. The more you study the art of photography, the better you'll do. Toward that end, I've included several fine books on photography in the general section of the Bibliography.

- And of course, keep that light source behind you.

When To Shoot and When Not To

How would you feel if an odd-looking person speaking a strange tongue suddenly pointed a camera at you? Some people are fearful of, or offended by, being photographed. For some, it's modesty; for others, it violates spiritual beliefs. Some may be embarrassed by their poverty, aware of the contrast between their society and yours. Almost everyone responds in one way or another to being photographed and that reaction appears in the picture. If someone objects, your slide will show a person holding up a hand, or half-turning from the camera with a displeased expression. It's better to ask permission. Most people don't object to having their picture taken if treated with respect and friendliness rather than as a trophy.

Try taking a photo or two near a person before approaching her directly. If she notices your interest, lower the camera, wave, and walk closer. If you look guilty and retreat, you communicate that you were doing something wrong. Make eye contact, nod, smile, and take an interest in the work she's doing; try to indicate that you see her as an individual, not a curiosity. Then ask permission. If she agrees to be photographed, you have time to get an honest result. If she says no, that's the end of it. If tempted to take a picture notwithstanding protestations, imagine yourself in the place of the subject. It's a matter of respect.

On the other hand, some people enjoy being photographed because it makes them feel special. They pose, smile, and shake your hand. There are also people who enjoy it because they expect to be paid. If you don't mind paying, go ahead. The amount is almost always negotiable, at least before you take the picture. If you don't want to pay in that situation, don't take the picture.

Temple. Khajuraho, India.

I was sitting on a small hill in the Masai Mara Game Preserve watching some Cape Buffalo when a white Toyota minivan stuffed with tourists stopped nearby. The tourists were pointing excitedly toward a half dozen Masai shepherds. Each of the elegantly tall Masai, resplendent in bead necklaces and animal skins, stood balanced on one leg gripping an iron-tipped spear. As the tourists slung their expensive equipment into position for a photographic orgy, the Masai clearly indicated they wanted to be paid. The tourists snapped away, ignoring increasingly vocal demands. Then the van started to move, photo-satiated tourists now indifferent to the Masai. In seconds, the Masai raced forward, surrounded the van, and repeatedly thrust their nine-foot spears into its body. The driver spun off down the gravel road, panicked tourists screaming. Those tourists have a story to tell—but did they understand the lesson?

There are also *things* you should not photograph. General prohibitions include airports, bridges, harbors and military installations, but you must watch for specific situations. If you take a picture of those fifty-year-old destroyers tied up across the Huang Po River from Shanghai, snap a shot of the decrepit harbor of Dar es Salaam, or record on film that old bridge crossing the Moskva River in Moscow, cross your fingers. Current relations between the country you're in and your own may determine whether you'll go straight to jail—or merely have your camera confiscated. That choice won't be yours. The "No Photographs" signs outside certain temples in the Royal Palace enclosure in Bangkok are draped with rolls of exposed film. Subtle, eh?

For local guidance, check your guidebook. Read local handouts. Watch for signs. Ask someone. If you're not being watched, you may get away with it. Of course, you may be betting your camera or your freedom.

Let common sense prevail with respect to photographing *events*. If in doubt, ask. If there is no one to ask, consult your sense of appropriateness. If you decide to go ahead, watch peoples' response. Your Ladakhi hosts may accept your presence as the funeral procession winds up the barren mountainside behind their village, but they will surely object to your taking pictures as the deceased is folded into the circular cairn in which she will rest.

Slide Shows

If you've accepted invitations to see friends' slides of their last trip somewhere, you know how mind-numbing and eye-glazing a truly amateur production can be. Even if you don't want to take the time to create a professional quality show, a few suggestions will result in a show that pleases your friends.

Start by editing ruthlessly. Cut slides that evoke memories for you but would be meaningless to a detached observer. Then arrange the slides into a sequence that flows rather than one that follows your exact itinerary. Concentrate on communicating information and creating an appealing visual impact rather than presenting a literal itinerary.

Pace is important. Plan for between five and fifteen seconds per slide. If you're courageous, put the slide advance remote in someone else's control while you give your commentary. If you lag or digress, they can increase your pace without a word (or yawn).

Some conscientious maestros take the time to add printed titles to slides. A more subtle way of identifying transitions between places is by taking an occasional photograph of an airport or a street sign. While visiting a series of remote Maya sites last summer, I knew it would be hard to tell one location from another so I asked my friend to photograph me as I identified each site by using my body to form the first letter of its name.

A written outline of your commentary aids in gathering significant facts and commenting accurately on the slides. It cuts rambling, too, especially after a glass of wine. Having a large map handy, or showing slides of maps, also helps keep viewer interest high.

If you've recorded some folk music or bought tape cassettes during the trip, use them to set the mood for the show. Otherwise, find something in the library, a local record shop, or your own collection that's ethnically-related to your trip.

Plan a show that will last an hour at most, which means 350 to 450 slides. Keep another tray or two on stand-by just in case the audience is really hooked. Of course, the trick is to be sure it's not just you who's hooked.

Video Cameras

Video cameras have become light and easy to use, but improvements won't eliminate appallingly bad post-trip videos unless people learn how to use their new toy before they travel. That includes shooting a few test tapes at home, then critiquing the results. Almost any videotape requires severe editing before a public screening.

Bring with you all the blank tapes you plan to shoot. If you buy tapes abroad, you won't get a picture if the image registration system of the tape is different from your camera's system. As a case in point, the system in general use in Europe is PAL which is different from the NTSC system in the United States. If you buy a tape abroad, be sure you're getting a match.

In many places, a substantial fee is charged for a permit to use a video camera. Tourist attraction officials seem to assume that people with a video camera are either shooting film for commercial sale or are wealthy tourists.

Be cautious about substituting a video camera for a 35mm camera. Until you are expert with it, it is at best a supplement.

There is an affinity between shiny-new, high-tech video cameras and quick-handed thieves. Carry the camera with care and try not to get completely absorbed in the filming.

REMEMBERING PEOPLE AND PLACES

You meet a lot of people as you travel; people in whose homes you stay, people you travel with for a few days, or people who accompanied you diving. Some are casual acquaintances; some you come to know well.

Most travelers keep a list of names and addresses, but as time passes, a list alone may not be enough. To help keep each person fresh in mind, I add the date, location, something about the circumstances, and sometimes a brief physical description.

Near the end of a trip, with better perspective for comparisons, I list places that turned out to be extra-special. This list also helps friends in planning their next trips.

Not long after I'm home, I reflect on how I feel about the trip, what I learned, what I'd do differently. This is actually the first step in planning my next adventure.

Each of us has his or her own ways of keeping images vivid for years. But even if I were to travel with neither camera nor journal, the images would stay alive so long as I'd been 100 percent present each day on the road.

PART FOUR

The
Finish Line
("And The
Winner Is...")

23

Home Again, Home Again

> A boat was leaving in about ten days and the
> knowledge that I would be on that boat had
> already brought the journey to an end.
> —Henry Miller
> *The Colossus of Maroussi*

It's easier to leave than to return. However frequently I travel, I forget how strange it feels to come home. I avoid being met at the airport because I don't want to stand around the baggage claim area trying to sum up for someone the feelings and experiences of weeks or months on the road.

I feel a little lonely as the cab crosses the city, but that's outweighed by my desire to greet the familiar feelings of home alone. I hang my weary khakis and well-worn canvas shirt on a corner of the door and pull a collar-to-ankle *djellaba* over my head. As I move to set my money belt on the bureau, the routine kicks in and I drop it out of sight in a drawer. I pause, realizing I won't wear it again for . . . who knows how long? I'll miss it in the morning; it's been next to me every day of the trip.

I turn on the hot water heater, build a fire in the fireplace, put on some ethnic music, open a bottle of wine, and start thumbing through the mail my neighbor piled on the piano bench. My eyes wander to mementos of earlier adventures: framed photographs covering the walls, a hand-braided belt from Taquile, a midnight blue and scarlet rug from the Tibetan Refugee Center, a silver pipe from Kashmir, and ceremonial masks from the Amazon.

I don't call anyone, sometimes not for days, because I'm not ready to be back, let alone to begin telling trip tales. I want to ease back into my old world at my own pace, extending my time to think about new commitments and changes in priorities. Habits and rituals will exert their grip all too soon.

I feel stressed for a while after a long trip. There's so much to catch up on and the pace of life is always faster than I remembered. I feel a reverse-homesickness, missing being on the road, missing people I met along the way.

On the road I was unique, a foreigner, a person who stood out in a crowd, whose opinions were sought, who was from the wealthiest nation on earth. At home, I'm just one of a quarter of a billion people. It's hard not to notice the difference.

Having accepted the risks of the high seas and navigated safely back to home port, I return with new perspectives and knowledge. Physically, I'm fit and my spirit is revitalized. Yet before me is the daunting challenge of bringing to my everyday life the energy and spirit of adventure I felt during my travels. I must continue to seek the unknown, to take chances, to stretch my mind and body. Above all, I must reject ruts and the trap of the comfort zone. In other words, I have to align my behavior in daily life as much as I can with my behavior on the road. That is every traveler's challenge.

> "Traveling is not just seeing the new; it is leaving behind. Not just opening doors; also closing them behind you, never to return."
> —Jan M
> *The Silk Road*

Although I'm different from the person who left colleagues and friends behind, those colleagues and friends don't see it. They comment on my tan, maybe mention I've lost a little weight. One may ask, "Where was it you went?" but, on hearing unfamiliar, almost alien, names, his eyes soon begin to glaze. Where I've been is so far away it's not quite real to them. If you understand that, you protect yourself from disappointment.

Seldom does anyone ask, "How are people reacting to freedom in Namibia (or Hungary, Lithuania, Chile, or anywhere)?" There's little chance of substantive questions about life on distant shores. You may return bursting with thoughts about how the world ought to operate and feelings about the wonder and tragedy of what you have seen, but you may not have many chances to share them. Speculate aloud about the heroic efforts to control AIDS in Rwanda, or the bloody tribal warfare between the Hutu and the Tutsi that has retarded that beautiful country for decades, and the most informed response will probably be some reminiscence about *Gorillas in the Mist*.

After you've been back a few months the trip is still resonating in your mind but your colleagues may have forgotten you were ever away. Remain too enthusiastic about your just-completed odyssey and you risk becoming a conversational black hole, the bane of hostesses. It's a reminder of how important it is to travel to satisfy your own goals, not the opinions of others

When I feel a compelling need to share what I've experienced, I seek out other travelers. Like me, they're willing to watch anyone's slides from anywhere; they're eager to discuss politics and whitewater rivers, mountain treks and hanging out on remote beaches. Beyond that, I write, using word pictures to re-create the rumbling thunder of the mighty Zambezi River cascading over the ledge at Victoria Falls.

When I've been home about a month, I find myself reading articles and clipping stories from the newspaper. Without realizing it, I've begun planning my next adventure. As the Roman poet Martial said, "So, Posthumous, you'll live tomorrow, you say; too late, the wise lived yesterday."

> "Here I am, safely returned over those peaks from a journey far more beautiful and strange than anything I had hoped for or imagined—how is it that this safe return brings such regret?"
> —Peter Matthiessen, *The Snow Leopard*

When you return home, I urge you to write me about your trip. I'd love to hear about special places you found and anecdotes that illustrate points in this book. I'd also like to know what you found most helpful about *Traveler's Tool Kit;* about anything you feel I should have included or didn't get quite right. I'll be pleased to acknowledge your contribution in the next edition. Until then, may the wind be always at your back.

24

Rare Destinations

> Allah has laid out the earth for you like a vast carpet
> so that you will travel its endless roads.
> —*The Koran*

The more you know about special places waiting to give you pleasure, the more likely you are to get there. I invite you to join me on a magic carpet to visit some of the world's rare destinations. We'll stick with our magic carpet most of the way, but take local transport when that's more fun.

Before we leave, let me say what our trip is not. It's not a trip limited to well-known, "must see" places. Nor will we visit special places in western or eastern Europe, the Confederation of Independent States, the Middle East, the United States, or Canada—in fact, we'll visit very few places in the Northern Hemisphere. Our trip skips supermacho experiences such as plummeting down Mount Everest on one ski while blindfolded, or trekking solo across the Australian outback pushing an ice cream wagon—because that's not what most people do when they travel.

Instead, we'll concentrate on less-developed countries where our money will enable us to go farther and stay longer than it will in industrialized nations. Our magic carpet will visit rare destinations within the reach of almost everyone as far as physical effort. Most of them are perfectly suitable destinations for people new to international travel, although a few might be more fun with a trip or two under the belt. You needn't have been born with a backpack attached to your body to be able to visit these places. The information in Traveler's Tool Kit brings virtually any destination you dream of within your reach.

Let's leave our hometown behind, step aboard our magic carpet, and head for Africa, a continent almost one-third larger than North America. Although almost never the continent Westerners visit first, we start in Africa because it's a symbolic threshold for bold international travel. Because people know comparatively little about Africa, it seems distant, challenging, maybe even vaguely threatening. Yet Africa was home to some of our earliest civilizations, perhaps even the birthplace of human kind. In Africa, we see farthest into our past—as well as into our future. Either its enormous productive capacity or its profound human problems, or both, will bring Africa increasingly to our attention.

We stop first in Egypt. Even though its marvels seem familiar to us from photographs and films, reality surpasses expectation. Since the great pyramids of Giza are symbolic of Egypt, let's climb inside and clamber to their tops. Afterward, we sail up the Nile in a small *felucca* of ancient design. In Luxor, we walk through the temples of Karnak, the monumental cumulative effort of perhaps seventeen dynasties. Awed, we fly farther up the Nile to Abu Simbel near the southern border with Sudan. Before us rise the mammoth sculptures erected by Rameses the Great to warn intruders from the south that his power was more awesome than they dared confront. After a stop in a desert oasis, we flee Egypt before the heat fries our temperaments.

We instruct our magic carpet to take us south the length of the continent to the desert country of Namibia, modern in some respects yet also home to Bushmen, Hereros, and other traditional cultures. We land in Etosha National Park which consists of hundreds of square miles of desolate salt pan, barren for months but now exploding with life rehydrated by torrential rains. Free to wander on our own without guides or tour groups, we stake out one of the waterholes and watch herds and prides and flocks until our senses are satiated.

A short flight to the northeast and we're in Zimbabwe, the former Rhodesia. Our rubber raft slides into the Zambezi River just below Victoria Falls (locally named Mosi-oa-Tunya, or "smoke that thunders") to begin our descent of this world-class whitewater river. The experienced boatman makes it pretty certain we'll survive, but that doesn't detract from the pure excitement of running the raging rapids. Whitewater behind, we relax on the flagstone terrace of the moonlight-white Victoria Falls Hotel, one of the few remaining monuments to the era of Empire. The polished marble floors and staircases curving grandly to the mezzanine are a sharp contrast to our camp by the Zambezi where we fell asleep to the roar of the rapids.

In Hwange National Park, just down the road from Victoria Falls, we have the rare treat of seeing the elusive black leopard. Just before leaving Zimbabwe, we take a day-trip to Matopos National Park to see the unforgettable landscape of eroding boulders balanced in gravity-defying columns.

We cross the border to visit the Okavango Delta in Botswana, eager to visit this oasis of afona matata ("no problem" in the Setswana language) before it's over-run with visitors. We stop at the Duck Inn in the parched desert town of Maun on the eastern edge of the Delta. It's a traveler's crossroads where we ease into a conversation with some Peace Corps volunteers while savoring chilled beers on the screened porch. Refreshed, a five-passenger plane carries us above the lush wetlands of the Delta to Oddball's Palm Court Lodge. We pitch our tent near the open-air dining room nestled into a forest clearing.

Annual flood waters flowing from the north have created a lacework pattern in the Delta, forcing the wild game onto hundreds of newly-formed island habitats. With a local guide poling our dugout canoe (called a *makoro*), we slip silently into the labyrinth, gliding along narrow waterways bordered by tufted papyrus reeds. Swarms of butterflies and an occasional saddlebill stork come to see who's calling. Suddenly, a crocodile-shaped blur lunges explosively from its nest on the bank, diving darkly beneath our *makoro*. His massive corrugated mate watches us from the bank, her yellow eyes following us through narrow slits.

Several times a day, we climb ashore to stroll among curious giraffes, barking baboons, prowling lions, and ponderous elephants. One afternoon, we emerge from behind a termite mound and encounter a solitary Cape Buffalo bull less than one hundred yards away. Spotting us, he leans our way, deciding whether to charge. His eyes narrow and he begins to lope in our direction, quickly reaching a speed faster than we can run in the tall grass. About fifty yards from us, he runs through a family of satiny brown antelope hidden in its grassy nest. They scatter and he curves off to his right, continuing into the forest. This unobstructed proximity to wild game is what makes the Okavango Delta one of the most appealing destinations in Africa. At night, we sit by a campfire sharing freshly roasted fish, vegetable curries, ginger snaps, and beer cooled in the flood waters, and we talk of writing books about our adventures.

From Botswana our magic carpet takes us north up the spine of Africa to Rwanda where we head immediately for Volcano National Park. Surrounded by a ring of looming volcanoes, the park headquarters lies in ruins, bungalows collapsing, restaurant roofless, walls covered with graffiti denouncing the incumbent regime. It's a troubled time to be here. Before crawling into our tents, we take a short hike to villages occupied by pygmies wearing cast-off Western clothes. Just after dawn, we climb through bamboo forests, nettle fields, and lobelia plants to find the day's nesting place of a mountain gorilla family. Dian Fossey was murdered for her defense of these incredible primates, and we feel her spirit walking with us on the foggy slopes.

Crossing the border to the east, we stretch out on the grassy floor of Ngorongoro Crater in Tanzania. It takes little imagination to feel the rumble of volcanic eruptions, hear the echo of dinosaur screams, and envision our predecessors as they clumsily rose erect. In the present, lions, rhinos, and elephants watch us watching them.

Not far from the Ngorongoro Crater, Lake Manyara resembles a Rousseau painting, an earthly paradise for animals. The animals live together in harmony except when hunger intrudes. We see the famous tree-climbing lions lying motionless on shady limbs overhanging game trails . . . waiting.

A short distance away we stand on the rim of Olduvai Gorge where Louis Leakey searched under the scorching sun for twenty-eight years before he discovered the skull of "homo habilis." Mary Leakey scratched the earth for twenty years more before finding the 3½ million-year-old footprints that demonstrate man became a biped far earlier than we previously knew. We reflect and speculate in the silence.

The next leg of our trip takes us to Mount Kilimanjaro. Climbing to its volcanic lip, even when porters carry the food and heaviest gear, requires all of our strength and will. We need no climbing skills, but it's a long way up from the flat African savannah to Uhuru Peak at 19,340 feet. At the summit, we stand on the highest point of all Africa.

From Kilimanjaro, our magic carpet takes us east across the Mozambique Channel to Madagascar where we hop on a train to Perinet Nature Reserve to seek the rare Indris lemur in the towering tree canopy. Furry, shadowy elves accompany us along the path under the full moon.

Next, north to Lamu, is a small island off the coast of Kenya. Its mud-walled structures are architecturally unchanged from centuries ago when Lamu was an Arab trading post. We snorkel, sail, stroll down narrow lanes in the company of Abyssinian asses, and toss back liters of Tusker beer at Tetley's Inn after dusk. Lamu is an ideal place to rest after climbing Kilimanjaro.

> "There is something about safari life that makes you forget your troubles and feel the whole time as if you had drunk half a bottle of champagne—bubbling over with heartfelt gratitude for being alive."
> —Isak Dinesen

Our carpet takes us back to mainland Kenya to visit Masai Mara National Park where sweeping savannah flows through bulky hills highlighted by thorn tree sentinels and flaming sunsets, home to vast populations of wild animals. Since Masai Mara is no secret, we're lucky to be here when it's not tourist season.

Not far away, we walk the paths of Amboseli National Park, fascinated by the incomparable sight of elephant families silhouetted against the snow-capped profile of Mount Kilimanjaro. Around the campfire, we talk with other travelers about everything from powder skiing to perestroika.

Before leaving Africa, we spend an evening in the bar of Nairobi's white stucco Norfolk Hotel, epicenter of the decadent turn-of-the-century white society of East Africa. Listening closely, we imagine conversations between Scott Fitzgerald and Ernest Hemingway after a hunt. Beryl Markham, an intrepid Kenya-based aviator who knew intimately everyone from Denys Finch-Hatton (played by Robert Redford in Out of Africa) to crowned heads of Europe, summed up Africa beautifully when she said, "Africa is never the same to anyone who leaves it and returns again. It is not a land of change, but it is a land of moods and its moods are numberless." With that insight in mind, we ask our carpet to take us east along the equator to Asia.

As if with a will of its own, our carpet turns north to India and its diverse and complex people. It's a country of contrasts: a modern industrial powerhouse astride hundreds of millions of impoverished people. In this home of nonviolence, great religions are locked in timeless combat. Tradition and chaos share the same space. Visiting India requires endurance and tolerance for ambiguity, but with a healthy sense of humor, we enjoy its rich rewards.

Our first stop in India is the famous Taj Mahal in Agra. Sure it's a major tourist stop, but we'd be crazy to miss it. Beyond aesthetic brilliance and fine craftsmanship, it embodies the romantic legend of Shah Jahan, his beautiful wife Mumtaz, and the Moghul Empire. After we've seen the Taj at sunrise and beneath the full moon, our knowledge of India begins to take shape.

Just down the road is the skeleton of a town called Fatepur Sikri, given life by an emperor following a mystic's counsel that building a new capital city would assure birth of a male heir. Its delicate minarets, high-ceilinged halls, and water-cooled bed chambers were sumptuous quarters for the royal court and the royal heir—but were suddenly abandoned. Centuries later no one knows why this beautiful city stands silent.

> "India reacts very strongly on people. Some loath it, some love it, most do both. . . . The place is very strong and often proves too strong for European nerves. . . . Everyone likes to talk about India whether they happen to be loving it or loathing it. . . . All the time I know myself to be on the back of this great animal of poverty and backwardness."
> —Ruth Prawer Jhabvala

Our carpet whisks us to Srinagar in the cool Vale of Kashmir in the northwest corner of India where we treat ourselves to an evening on the verandah of a houseboat, sipping cardamom and cinnamon tea, gazing across a serene blue lake. Our 120-foot floating home has a carved dining table for eight, silk tapestries, brass lanterns, chandeliers, stained glass windows, and downy beds with velvet spreads and hot water bags for our toes. After a couple of nights aboard the houseboat, we head to a nearby mountain village for some skiing. We leave Kashmir abruptly when crowds erupt into the streets over a religious dispute.

Heading east, our magic carpet trip to Leh, capital of the ancient Kingdom of Ladakh, is unmatched on this planet. We can almost touch the icy, wind-whipped summits of the Himalayas. Below us, the Indus River is only a thin, rocky stream giving no hint of the immensely powerful river it will become in Pakistan. Under the increasing influence of visitors, the Tibetan Buddhist culture of Ladakh is yielding to Westernization but its monasteries are still bustling with activity. Monks move briskly as they perform ancient rituals in the pure light of dawn. Twisting wreaths of smoke from pitch torches, generations of prayers, and eons of idols fill the cavernous stone chambers of the Hemis, Sheh, and Thikse monasteries.

East again and we're in Kathmandu, Nepal, a flask that may hold your personal genie. Because of its gentle people and breathtaking views, a trip to Nepal is a success even without climbing Chomolungma, Mother Goddess of the Snows (Mount Everest). Some say that if you were going to see only one sunrise in your life it ought to be from the village of Dhulikel on the southern ridge of the Kathmandu Valley. Impressed, we shiver all night on a stone bench, rising once in a while to stir the fire, eager for the sun to rise over the Himalayas. When it does, it is so spectacular that the chill is forgotten and no one speaks.

We travel overland west to Pokhara, then trek to the inspiring peaks of Annapurna, passing beneath towering Dhaulagiri and its stony friends. Our walk takes us high along the slopes of Kali Gandaki Gorge, called by some the deepest valley in the world (not to be confused with Colca Canyon in Peru, which may be the deepest canyon). We visit Ghandrung, Ghorepani, and Muktinath, picturesque villages finely constructed from the scales of the mountain. Since our lungs and legs are holding up, we walk on to Jomsom and the long-ago kingdom of Mustang. We step gingerly across swinging bridges, dodging ponies with brass bells around their necks and red plumes rising from their harnesses. We talk with sturdy old Gurkha soldiers dressed in tattered uniforms, grip cups of hot tea with near-numb fingers, and listen to the raspy sound of our breath when we reach the crest of a hard-won pass. Back in Pokhara, we rest in a flower-filled garden near the lake, sunshine on our faces, looking up through the clouds at the vertical fin of Machhupuchhare and reliving the footsteps of our trek.

From Pokhara, we whisk ourselves down to Chitwan National Park in southern Nepal to ride high on an elephant's back through cool dark forests and across fields of golden mustard blossoms. Our traveler's luck holds and we see a one-horned rhino and two Bengal tigers.

Next, we ask our magic carpet to fly us across the mountains to Quilin, China, and the Li River where fantastic karst (limestone) mountain spires show the ethereal artistry of nature. As our small boat drifts along the Li toward the panorama of Seven Horse Mountain, we try to ignore chickens squawking as they sacrifice their lives to become our water-borne lunch.

We arrive next at the excavation site of the terra cotta warriors outside Xi'an, where hundreds of finely-modeled soldiers stand patiently row upon row. Although they are a legacy to us from one of China's most progressive rulers, I wonder how many of the originals lost their lives willingly to build this monument to the emperor.

The Forbidden City, home of emperors, is well worth enduring the crowds. After almost a full day of wandering its paths, we rent a bike for a ride though the life of modern Beijing. Standing in front of the Great Wall, with its serpentine coils embracing steep hillsides, I think of the enormous effort and intrinsic folly involved in building it. In the end, as is so often the case, the fatal danger to the Emperors came from forces already within their wall. We don't stay long because, at the points most accessible to visitors, the Wall is so crowded it might be Disneyland Far East.

Hong Kong, resting on China's edge, has its feet firmly planted in two distinct, even adversarial, cultures. Millions of people pack the city, urgently seeking success or survival in the final days of this star of the British Empire. At the same time, we can almost hear the patient breathing of Hong Kong's billion Chinese neighbors. Brilliantly lighted skyscrapers broadcast the power of the economy, even if it rests on quicksand. Rio is close in grandeur, as are San Francisco, Sydney and New York, but Hong Kong remains queen.

Leaving China reluctantly, we fly southwest down to Thailand. Because visiting Thailand is so easy, inexpensive, and rewarding, we immediately encounter swarms of travelers. In northern Thailand, we hire a guide in Chiang Mai and set off into the hill country, sleeping in bamboo and thatch houses in villages of different tribes. These tribes, who fled Burma or Laos decades ago, retain their original language and culture and resist assimilation into Thailand. The people dress in bright colors, harvest opium poppies during the day, and gather around our fire in the evening, open in their curiosity. We ride elephants from one village to another and pole along placid streams on crude rafts of bamboo poles lashed together with vines.

Our final flight in Thailand takes us to the tiny island of Ko Tao (Turtle Island) in the Gulf of Thailand. The presence of seven dive shops confirms that the scuba diving and snorkeling are excellent. Ko Tao has fine beaches, good restaurants, and a laid-back atmosphere. We spend about $10 for a private bungalow with a porch, toilet, and fan. Ko Tao may be close to paradise.

We reboard our magic carpet for a short flight to the south to Indonesia where we find diversity in culture, food, architecture, and art matched by few other countries. We ride a double-outrigger canoe out of Manado Bay, at the northeast tip of Sulawesi, to the small volcanic islands of Manado Tua and Bunaken to enjoy some of the best snorkeling and diving in the world. The coral is pristine and vigorous and ours is the only boat. When a massive fish rises from the two thousand–meter depths and swims toward us, it's time to continue our trip elsewhere.

Still on the island of Sulawesi, we visit mile-high Toraja-land and its picture-perfect rice paddies. Fields the radiant green of a van Gogh canvas are accented by gray-black boulders either too massive or too aesthetically perfect to move. Homes cluster at the edge of the manicured fields, the roof of each shaped to resemble the upswept bow of a ship poised to return to the ancestral homeland in Southeast Asia. In Toraja-land, the dead reside in narrow caverns carved into cliff faces. Tau-taus, fully costumed three-foot effigies of the deceased, watch us from balconies wedged into natural crevasses near the base of the cliffs.

From Sulawesi we fly to Bali to enjoy its renowned artistic culture, then move on to Papua New Guinea. On this half-an-island (shared with Irian Jaya), we visit remote valleys between slopes of towering volcanoes to meet some of the most primitive tribes in the world. Before World War II, large numbers of Papua New Guineans had no idea that an "outside" world existed. Since then, war, missionaries, commerce, and tourism have eroded that innocence. When the tribes gather at Mount Hagen for a "sing-sing" in elaborate costumes, customs of mountain life come alive. We're lucky to be here before the unique character of PNG is lost.

Flying into Oceania from Papua New Guinea risks serious culture shock. In Australia and New Zealand we return to Western societies and customs. In New Zealand we stop first on the North Island, visiting sunny bays in the pseudo-tropical north, boiling geysers and snowcapped volcanoes in its midriff, and the windswept piers of Wellington on its southern tip. For adventure we go on to the South Island. The forested mountain ridges, stony islands, and hidden coves of the Marlborough Sounds, followed by the art colony of Nelson nestled in the midst of apple orchards and vineyards, don't prepare us for the stormy west coast. Behind the blue-white Fox and Franz Josef Glaciers cascading into the Tasman Sea, we see the peaks of the majestic Southern Alps. We spend four days hiking the Milford Track, christened by National Geographic as the "finest walk in the world." That's so much fun, we walk the Routeburn, Heaphy, and Abel Tasman trails as well, even stopping once in a while to take one of the short walks that begin at roadside trail heads and lead off through the bush to emerald lakes or mountain passes.

We enjoy the Shotover Jet boat out of Queenstown, but add the longer jet-boat trip up the pristine Dart River. From Queenstown we visit Milford Sound and Doubtful Sound, the most well-known of the glacier-carved fiords. Before we leave, we take a few runs on the Coronet Peak ski slopes above Queenstown. Our last evening is spent, of course, in a pub full of friendly people and hearty beer.

Our last stop in Oceania is the Great Barrier Reef, the longest reef in any ocean. It's still a world-class attraction, despite damage at the hands of starfish and humans. The vast continent of Australia deserves more of our time, but we have to hurry along to reach Antarctica during its brief "warm" season.

We step off our magic carpet in Ushuaia, Argentina, and board a small passenger ship to sail across the Drake Passage to the Antarctic Peninsula. The shoreline is a seamless white glacier, white without features, white that is less a description of color than a blank between ocean and overcast sky. Twice each day, a Zodiac inflatable boat takes us ashore to wander among dozens of Elephant and Weddell seals and millions of Adelie, Gentoo, Macaroni, and Chinstrap penguins. Wandering Albatrosses watch with cocked heads far overhead. We spend one morning in Hope Bay, the site of one of the largest penguin rookeries in the world. The next afternoon we drop anchor off Cuverville Island, probably no larger than two hundred acres and consisting primarily of one steep, snow-covered mountain. Its magnificent bay is patrolled by wind-sculpted icebergs. Small wood huts shelter three female scientists from the Scott Polar Research Institute at Cambridge.

At Paradise Bay, one of the most beautiful harbors in the world, a black rock cliff face is brightened by streaks of blue-green copper ore, orange lichen, and emerald green moss. Bergie bits in the bay are manned by crews of seals and penguins. We celebrate Christmas Eve with a party on the fantail of our ship, singing Christmas Carols and exchanging toasts with champagne and hot spiced wine as ancient glaciers glow under the midnight sun. Even though not nearly the end of our magic carpet trip, Paradise Bay truly feels like the "end of the world."

The landscape of Antarctica is unique. Seeing it is like being permitted to visit the Ice Age—comfortably. It radiates immense power, vastness, and indifference. If lost unprotected, there would be no hope. There are billions of krill (shrimp-like food for whales), millions of penguins, huge numbers of seals and seabirds, a few whales—and not much else. Since there are no trees, no bushes, and no weeds, even tiny growths of lichen, algae, and moss are celebrated. Antarctica is a spectacular visual treat, but before long we yearn for diversity. It's time to leave for the abundant flora and fauna of South America.

Our magic carpet takes us to Punta Arenas on the southern tip of Chile, across the channel from Tierra del Fuego. A half-day overland we arrive in Paine National Park to trek along the Grey Glacier, accompanied by guanacos and scrutinized by condors. It would be hard to feel more distant from normal life than when sitting on the shore of a pristine glacial lake surrounded by vertical granite crags. Our next adventure in Chile is paddling the Bio Bio and the Futaleufu, rivers unequaled for beauty and danger.

From there, north to Puerto Montt, the starting point for a trip by small boat and bus across the Lake Country to the ski slopes of San Carlos de Bariloche in Argentina. The view always includes a lake, a mountain, or a forest—and often all three. Back in Puerto Montt, we board the S.S. Evangelista to glide serenely among the islands of Chile's "fiordland" (a term shared with Norway and New Zealand) down Last Hope Sound to Puerto Natales. Glaciers glow blue-white on the port beam while, thousands of feet above us, the Andes rise like jagged teeth in the cloudless sky.

Having been entertained by natural scenery for a while, we fly northwest across the Andes to another of the world's great cities. Rio de Janeiro, Brazil, where we're instantly swept into the life of the *cariocas* (as Rio's residents call themselves). The foul water in the Bay doesn't attract us to swim, but Copacabana and Ipanema beaches are made memorable by thousands of beautiful people, most wearing revealing "thong" bathing suits. We join a boisterous beach volleyball game, one of perhaps a hundred along the beach, and play until dusk. Energized by the physical setting, which ranks in splendor with Hong Kong, San Francisco, and Cape Town, we throw ourselves into the intense night life. Money flows, voices are raised, future-lovers are recognized, and tomorrow's labor has no reality. In the mornings, though, we're aware of hundreds of thousands of poor people living in the shadows whose daily struggle for survival leaves little time for contemplation of beauty.

In a remote village outside Salvador,* we visit a condomble, or religious-magic, ceremony, sitting for hours in the midst of more than a hundred local people in a dimly lit room whose boundaries are lost in shadows. Chanting trance-dancers whirl mindlessly, flinging sweat-spray over the crowd. While white-gowned healers minister to the faithful with clouds of ceremonial cigar smoke, a relentless booming drum sets the beat of our hearts.

We cannot fully experience Brazil without visiting the Amazon. Villages are interesting but few remain free of influence from the industrialized world. The rain forest, on the other hand, still retains unimaginable diversity and majesty. After threading our way through the forest we understand emotionally, not just intellectually, its role at the heart of our global ecosystem and the impact of its loss on the future of our species.

We fly above the forest canopy to the state of Mato Grosso to see the Pantanal, the largest natural wetland in the world. A guide with a small boat helps us explore this vast swamp that shelters millions of birds, mammals, and reptiles.

Our magic carpet takes us on up the Amazon to Iquitos, just inside the Peruvian border, where we hire guides for another trek into the Amazonian forest. We camp with Quechua Indians, wander quiet paths, build rafts to cross rivers along the way, and play catch with kids in river bluff villages.

Wanting to learn more about the rain forest in Peru, we use Explorer's Inn on the bank of the Tambopata River as a base. On our first hike into the forest, we stumble onto a dugout canoe on the shore of an oxbow lake and paddle slowly for hours, playing hide-and-seek with giant river otters. Dozens of butterflies cover our bodies, nibbling bits of salt.

It's only a short flight from the Tambopata to Cuzco, one of the world's more agreeable towns. Most visitors pass through quickly on a whirlwind tour to Machu Picchu and the sacred valley of the Urubamba, but we settle in

---

* *Salvador.* This port city in northeast Brazil is the capital of Bahia. It is noted for *Capoeira,* a foot-fighting dance, and *candomble,* magical-religious ceremonies.

for a while, becoming part of daily life. We talk with vest-makers and weavers of belts and women who mop the steps of the cathedral. A professor from the the Inca outpost of Machu Picchu, no matter where we are we'll summon a vision of that mysterious stone settlement on a narrow ridge in an ocean of peaks . . . and wonder.

We head south to see the amazing Nazca Lines. The huge figures carved into the dry coastal plain may have served as astronomical aids to farmers or landing signals to extraterrestrials (as Erik von Daniken thought), or they may have served some purpose we've yet to imagine. Whatever the lines were for, their existence confirms the intelligence of their creators.

Next, south to the "white city" of Arequipa and up to the altiplano (high plain) to the village of Chivay where Inca heritage lives in the faces of the villagers. We sit on a stone wall, the border of a terraced field first furrowed a half-millennium ago, that runs to the very edge of the ten thousand–foot deep Colca Canyon. Our senses relax and time slows as condors glide across the silent sky.

It's time to leave South America, but we have time for just a few more stops before returning home. Having gotten to know the Inca, it's time to meet the Maya.

Flying thousands of miles north, we cross the Equator and settle in the Maya city of Copan on the western border of Honduras. Spreading canopies of towering trees rooted in the heart of the ruins shelter the past from the blazing sun. As we watch, archeologists lift the shrouds from a twelve hundred-year-old society.

Just a short distance north in Guatemala, we drop in on Livingston, a Caribbean coastal town inaccessible by road (but easily reached by magic carpet) to cruise up the Rio Dulce in the company of manatees, toucans, and the seldom-seen quetzal. Continuing west, still in Guatemala, we reach incredibly beautiful, mile-high Lake Atitlan in the central highlands. Atitlan winds for more than ten miles in the shadow of terraced mountainsides and volcanic cones. Along the shore of the lake, which Jacques Cousteau calculated to be almost three thousand feet deep, we visit a dozen villages in which traditional dress and customs still prevail.

Our last stop in Guatemala is Tikal. Rising above the far northern jungle, the pyramids and temples of Tikal are the most impressive of all Maya sites. We climb to the top of Temple IV to watch the sun set over a vanished empire. Our last stops before heading home are in Mexico at three of the most impres-

"I cannot rest from travel; I will drink Life to the lees; all times have I enjoyed Greatly, have suffered greatly, both with those That loved me, and alone; I am become a name; For always roaming with a hungry heart Much have I seen and known . . ."
—Alfred Lord Tennyson, *Ulysses*

sive of the Maya city-states, Palenque, Uxmal, and Chichen Itza. The Yucatan peninsula is a great place to relax and reminisce about our tour of some of the world's rare destinations. Thanks for coming along. I enjoyed traveling with you.

By the way, when not traveling by magic carpet, one of my personal special places is a window seat on an airplane. I love views, so I always ask ticket agents which side of the plane has the best views and which seats aren't over the wing. Some of the finest views from airplanes are on flights from Punta Arenas north along the Andes and past Mount Aconcagua's icy cone before settling into Santiago; north from Lima across Ecuador along the Andes; a Society Islands puddle-jumper from Tahiti to Huahine, Raitea, and Bora Bora; the flight from New Delhi into Kathmandu, watching the panorama of the Himalayas unfold ahead; flights winding among the Southern Alps of New Zealand and setting down on a glacier snow field; and almost any inter-island flight in Indonesia with views of coral reefs and fuming volcanoes.

Looking back at our tour of special places, I could easily have included Angkor Wat, the temples of Pagan, the ancient city of Petra, Baltoro Glacier, Aswan, Ellora and Ajanta, and any number of other places. What about trips along the Silk Road from Xi'an to Venice, the Salt Road from Fez to the Haggar Mountains in the Sahara, the Burma Road from Rangoon to Kunming, the road from St. Petersburg to Yalta, and the length of the Pan American Highway? And what about a horse trek across Mongolia or hikes in the Italian Dolomites, the Zagoria region of northern Greece, the Brooks Range, or Glacier National Park? What about fishing for salmon in Russia's Ponoi River, for steelhead in the lower Dean River in British Columbia, or fly fishing in Patagonia? What about canoeing Lake Titicaca, sea kayaking around Ellesmere Island in the Arctic or along Hawaii's Na Pali coast or in Glacier Bay Alaska, or sailing the Turkish coast between Gocek and Marmaris? Yes, they're all special places—and that makes my point. The number of special places is very large indeed and they're all out there waiting for you. It's time to go.

Travel Information Form

(Leave a copy at home and take one with you.)

1. Credit card numbers: _____

2. Driver's license number: _____

3. Traveler's check numbers: _____

   _____

4. Contacts abroad: _____

   _____

   _____

   _____

   _____

   _____

5. Medical information: _____

6. Airline ticket information: _____

   _____

7. Address of bank: _____

8. Travel/medical insurance policy

9. Copies of first two pages of passport

10. Copy of itinerary

Checklist: Budget

Predeparture Expenses
$_____ passport, visas, and photos
_____ international student ID card
_____ guidebooks
_____ hostel membership
_____ camera, film, filters, other photo
equipment
_____ luggage, daypack
_____ new clothes
_____ travel insurance
_____ gear (money belt, etc.)
_____ health care (medicine and shots)
_____ toiletries
_____ reading material

Transportation
_____ air fares
_____ other fares (trains, buses, etc.)

Meals and Lodging
_____ en route
_____ daily lodging
_____ daily meals

Special Experiences
_____ entertainment (sightseeing, tours, etc.)
_____ safaris, scuba diving, glacier climbing, etc.

Miscellaneous
_____ souvenirs, gifts, tips, laundry, etc.

Checklists: Clothing

The following list contemplates an informal, lightweight trip. Choices will reflect personal tastes, the length of the trip, and anticipated climates and activities.

For Men

I. Shirts
_____ Two short-sleeve outdoor shirts
_____ Two long-sleeve shirts with collars
_____ Two or three 100 percent cotton T-shirts
_____ One long-sleeve turtleneck

2. Pants
_____ One pair tough 100 percent cotton twill or canvas (or 85 percent wool), one lightweight pair, one dressy pair of khakis (optional: pair of dress slacks)
_____ One pair of hiking or gym shorts

3. Underwear
_____ Three pairs of cotton briefs

For Women

I. Shirts
_____ T-shirts plus two or three shirts or blouses, a jogging top, turtleneck, vest

2. Pants
_____ One or two lightweight pairs of pants (possibly substituting one heavier pair, depending on expected weather)
_____ One or two skirts (optional: pair of panty hose or ballet tights)
_____ One pair of shorts

3. Underwear
_____ 100 percent cotton panties, brassieres

Checklists: Clothing, (continued)

For men

4. Socks
_____ Three or four pairs of high-quality socks (optional: one pair of dress socks)

5. Shoes
_____ One pair of sandals
_____ One pair of lightweight, low-cut trail/walking shoes (optional: hiking boots or tennis shoes)

For women

4. Socks
_____ Three or four pairs of high-quality socks (optional: one pair of knee-high hose)

5. Shoes
_____ One pair of sandals
_____ One pair of lightweight, low-cut trail/walking shoes (optional: hiking boots, tennis shoes, ballet-type slipper)

For men and women

6. Belt
_____ One sturdy belt

7. Nightwear
_____ One nightshirt (optional: warm-up suit, sarong)

8. Swimsuit
_____ One quick-drying swimsuit

9. Rain gear
_____ Gore-Tex shell (optional: waterproof poncho, light rain suit)

10. Extra warmth
_____ One lightweight windbreaker (optional: jacket of polyester/cotton or polypro pile, down vest, light sweater, thermal underwear)
_____ One good scarf

11. Towel
_____ One light towel

12. Miscellaneous
_____ Bandannas
_____ Hat/sun visor
_____ Gloves
_____ Tie
_____ Blue blazer

Checklist: Toiletries

_____ Band-Aids
_____ comb (and/or brush)
_____ deodorant
_____ dental floss
_____ insect repellent (DEET, Ultra-Thon, Permethrin clothing spray)
_____ laundry detergent
_____ leak-proof toiletries kit
_____ lip balm (with sunscreen)
_____ mirror
_____ moleskin
_____ mosquito coils
_____ nail clippers (or emery boards)
_____ panty liners

_____ razor blades and shaving lather
_____ safety pins
_____ sanitary napkins
_____ sewing kit
_____ shampoo
_____ soap; soap container
_____ sunscreen
_____ thermometer
_____ toilet paper
_____ toothbrush (with storage container or cap)
_____ toothpaste
_____ tweezers and scissors

Checklist: Miscellaneous Gear

_____ Bags (garbage bags, Ziploc bags, stuff sacks)
_____ Bicycle-locking cable
_____ Camera gear (film, camera, zoom lens, extra camera battery, lens filters, lens cleaning kit, lead-foil film bags)
_____ Clock (and batteries)
_____ Door stop alarm (or Travelock or Jammer)
_____ Eyeglasses (sunglasses, prescription glasses and prescription, contact lenses, lens solution, hard plastic travel case, retainer strap)

_____ Flashlight (and new alkaline batteries)
_____ Guidebooks
_____ Journal
_____ Locks (luggage and daypack)
_____ Maps
_____ Money belt
_____ Reading material
_____ Rubber bands
_____ Swiss Army knife
_____ Wallet
_____ Wristwatch
_____ Writing materials (pads, pens)

Checklist: Documents to Take Along

_____ Airline tickets (and copy)
_____ American Automobile Association membership card
_____ ATM card
_____ Certificate of Registration
_____ Credit cards (including card numbers and telephone numbers for reporting a loss)
_____ Driver's license (optional: international driver's license)
_____ Insurance (proof of insurance, agent's telephone number)
_____ International Association for Medical Assistance to Travelers (IAMAT) card
_____ International Certificate of Vaccination (yellow card)
_____ International student ID card
_____ Itinerary
_____ Medical information (blood type, special medical conditions, allergies, personal physician's phone number, health insurance information)

_____ Names, addresses, and telephone and fax numbers
_____ Passport (plus copies of the first two pages of the passport), extra passport photos, separate proof of citizenship
_____ Permits (trail, game watching, work)
_____ Prescriptions
_____ Reservations (hotels, cars, etc.)
_____ Telephone charge card
_____ Traveler's checks (and separate copy of check numbers)
_____ Visas
_____ Youth Hostel membership card

Checklist: Optional Equipment

_____ Binoculars
_____ Briefcase
_____ Business cards
_____ Calculator
_____ Cassette recorder/player
_____ Contraceptives
_____ Duct tape
_____ Eating utensils
_____ Electrical items (adapter plug, converter)
_____ Film shield
_____ Immersion heater
_____ Inflatable pillow
_____ Mace

_____ Mask and snorkel
_____ Musical instruments
_____ Nylon clothesline
_____ Sewing kit
_____ Sheet sack
_____ Sink stopper
_____ Sleeping bag
_____ Sleeping pad
_____ Slippers
_____ Travel games
_____ Umbrella
_____ Water bottle
_____ Waterproof bags
_____ Whistle

Checklist: Shots to Get before You Go

What shots you need depends on (a) where you're going, (b) the current status of your inoculations, and (c) the requirements of the countries you'll be visiting. Obtain annual information on the prevalence of specific diseases in specific countries, along with immunization requirements, from *Health Information for International Travel* (HIFIT). This information is available on a current basis in the semimonthly *Summary of Health Information for International Travelers* issued by the Centers for Disease Control. Call the CDC hotline at (404) 332-4559 for information.

Because some shots interfere with others and some shots are given as a series, you can't drop into the health department at the last minute to get all shots at once. Besides, it's nice to have some time to recover from any adverse reaction. Although it would be ideal to receive the full series of immunizations over a four- to eight-week period, the pace can be accelerated if need be.

- **Cholera:** Vaccine four to six weeks before you leave. If practical, it should not be received at the same time as the yellow fever vaccine. Check with the CDC to determine whether a cholera certificate of vaccination is required to enter any country on your itinerary.

- **Diphtheria:** Vaccine six weeks before you leave. Booster every ten years.

- **Hepatitis A:** One week before you leave, take immune globulin to increase immunity. Since this is a blood-based product, it would be risky to get this shot in any country where blood is not screened and treated. Alternatively and substantially more expensive, there's Havrix, the newly approved hepatitis A vaccine. The first shot is taken two to four weeks prior to departure; the second is taken six to twelve months later.

- **Hepatitis B:** Ideally, the three-shot vaccine (Recombivax) takes six months.

- **Influenza:** Vaccine anytime. Especially important for people over sixty-five.

- **Japanese B Encephalitis:** Three shots over a three-week period. Since there is a possibility of severe reaction after each vaccination, the series should begin at least six weeks prior to departure.

- **Measles, mumps, rubella:** Vaccines six weeks before you leave. If born after 1956, it is recommended that you receive a measles vaccine even if you've had an earlier shot.

- **Meningococcal meningitis:** Vaccine five weeks before you leave.

- **Polio:** Even if you were vaccinated as a child consider getting this oral vaccine several months before you leave.

- **Rabies:** Begin Human Diploid Cell Merriaux Vaccine series four to six weeks before you leave. It may be repeated every two years if desired.
- **Smallpox:** Vaccine eight weeks before you leave.
- **Tetanus:** (Combine with diphtheria vaccine.): Vaccines six weeks before you leave. Booster every ten years or after a puncture wound or major laceration.
- **Typhoid:** If you take the standard vaccine, get the first shot eight weeks before departure and the second shot four weeks later. The oral vaccine may be preferable, but should be kept refrigerated and must be taken as directed. Booster every three years. Alternatively, take the newly FDA-approved, single-shot vaccine, Typhin Vi.
- **Yellow Fever:** Vaccine three weeks before you leave. Booster every ten years.

My public health service advises that yellow fever and immune serum globulin can safely be given at the same time, even though that isn't their first choice. The same is true for immune globulin and oral polio.

Enter each shot on your yellow card. Keep a copy in a safe place since it's probably the only record of what you've had and when.

Checklist: Matching Medicines with Minor Annoyances

_____ Aches, sunburn, headache: aspirin, acetaminophen, ibuprofen

_____ Acid stomach: Maalox, Mylanta, or Gelusil

_____ Allergies, poison ivy, rash, etc.: hydrocortisone cream, diphenhydramine (Benadryl), chlorpheniramine (Chlor-Trimeton), Hismanal

_____ Altitude sickness: acetazolamide (Diamox)—do _not_ take if allergic to sulfa drugs; dexamethasone (for severe symptoms); ibuprofen; acetaminophen

_____ Athlete's foot: tolnaftate (Tinactin powder), clotrimazole (Lotrimin AF), undecylenic acid (Desenex), Mexsana, Lotrisone

_____ Birth control: birth control pills, nonoxynol-9 condoms, other personal choices

_____ Blisters: moleskin, Band-Aids

_____ Burns: Silvadene

_____ Chapped lips: Blistex, Vaseline, or Chapstick

_____ Colds: Advil Cold & Flu for chest congestion; pseudophedrine (Sudafed), Benzedrex Dry Inhaler, Afrin, or Dristan; acetaminophen

_____ Constipation: docusate (Colace), bran tablets or natural bran

_____ Contaminated water: iodine tablets

Checklist: Matching Medicines with Minor Annoyances

_____ Cough: Robitussin DM syrup (or Guaifenesin capsules), or Naldecon DX (expectorants in tablet form); cough lozenges

_____ Cuts, blisters: Neosporin, Betadine (liquid antiseptic), or aloe vera gel; Cipro for infections; Band-Aids, gauze squares, adhesive tape, wound closure strips

_____ Diarrhea: Pepto Bismol (bismuth subsalicylate), Kaopectate, Lomotil, or Immodium; Oralyte (oral rehydration salts)

_____ Eye problems: eye drops; for contact lens wearers, contact lens solution and Sulamyd antibiotic eye drops

_____ Fever: acetaminophen, aspirin; thermometer

_____ Headache and general cold symptoms: aspirin, acetaminophen, or ibuprofen

_____ Herpes sores: Ambesol gel; acyclovir (Zovirax)

_____ Infection: Neosporin antibacterial ointment

_____ Insect bites: 1 percent hydrocortisone cream, Benadryl

_____ Motion sickness: Dramamine, Bonine, Phenergan, or Scopolamine patches; acupressure wrist bands

_____ Sleeplessness: Benadryl, Serax, Melatonin

_____ Strains and sprains: Ace bandage

_____ Sunburn and other minor burns: SPF 15 (or higher) waterproof sunscreen and aloe vera; Silvadene; Neosporin; ibuprofen

_____ Toothache: eugenol (oil of cloves)

_____ Unbalanced diet: vitamins

_____ Upset stomach: Pepto-Bismol tablets

_____ Urinary tract infections: ciprofloxacin (Cipro), Ampicillin, or cotrimoxazole (Bactrim/Septra)

_____ Vaginal yeast infection: Nystatin vaginal tablets, vaginal suppositories

Checklist: Matching Medicines with More Serious Problems

_____ Bronchitis: Amoxicillin (avoid if allergic to penicillin), cotrimoxazole (Bactrim/Septra), erythromycin, ciprofloxacin (Cipro)

_____ Dehydration: oral rehydration salts

_____ Dysentery: metronidazole (Flagyl), ciprofloxacin (Cipro), cotrimoxazole (Bactrim/Septra)

_____ Giardia: metronidazole (Flagyl)

_____ Malaria: Mefloquine (Lariam), sulfadoxine (Fansidar), chloroquine phosphate, doxycycline, DEET, Ultrathon, Permethrin (one version is sold as Permanone Tick Repellent), mosquito coils. NOTE: It is essential that your malaria-related regimen be based on the places you visit and resistance patterns at that time

_____ Severe pain: Demerol; ibuprofen or acetaminophen for lesser pain

_____ Sexually-transmitted diseases: condoms with nonoxynol-9, disposable needles

_____ Typhus: Tetracycline

BIBLIOGRAPHY

This bibliography contains periodicals and books I have found particularly enjoyable or helpful. I have marked with a # sign those books that may be hard to find but are too good not to bring to your attention. The dates given are of the most recent edition of which I am aware (i.e., not the copyright date, which may be much earlier). When there was a choice, I listed the paperback edition because it's cheaper and lighter.

PERIODICALS

— *Access to Travel.* Published by the Society for the Advancement of Travel for the Handicapped. Call (212) 447-7284. $13 for 4 quarterly issues. It serves travelers who have a broad range of disabilities.
— *Best Fares Discount Travel Magazine.* P.O. Box 171212, Arlington, TX 76003. Call (800) 880-1234. $58 for 12 monthly issues (but ask for a 10 percent discount). Discount rates for airlines, hotels, car rentals, and cruises.
— *Condé Nast Traveler.* P.O. Box 57018, Boulder, CO 80322. Call (800) 777-0700. Good all-around travel magazine, but with a tilt toward the upscale traveler.
— *Consumer Reports Travel Letter.* Call (800) 234-1970. $39 per year. Objective critical evaluations of the travel industry in the tradition of *Consumer Reports.*
— *Diabetic Traveler.* P.O. Box 8223, Stamford, CT 06905; call (203) 327-5832.
— *EcoTraveler.* Skies America. Call (800) 334-8152. $11.95 for 6 issues.
— *Escape.* P.O. Box 5159, Santa Monica, CA 90409. Call (800) 738-5571. $18 for 4 issues. Emphasis on adventurous journeys, foreign cultures, and the "thrill of escape."
— *Explorers Journal, The.* Quarterly publication of the Explorers Club (46 East 70th Street, New York City, NY 10021). Reports on expeditions, scientific discoveries, and exploits of hard-core travelers.
— *Going Solo: The Newsletter for People Traveling Alone.* P.O. Box 123, Apalachicola, FL 32329. $29 per year.
— *International Living.* 824 E. Baltimore Street, Baltimore, MD 21298. $29 per year.
— *International Travel News.* 2120 28th Street, Sacramento, CA 95818. Call (916) 457-3643. $18 for 12 issues. Down-to-earth reports by contemporary travelers. Strong on practical, current information.

— *Islands.* P.O. Box 51303, Boulder, CO 80321. $19.95 for 6 issues. Each issue is a "wish list" for island travel.

— *Journal 'n Footnotes.* Quarterly newsletter published by Wonder Women, a travel and adventure network for women over 40. Membership is $29 per year. For a sample copy of the newsletter, send $1 to 136 N. Grand Avenue, #237, West Covina, CA 91791.

— *Journeywoman Magazine.* 1703-50 Prince Arthur Avenue, Toronto, Ontario, Canada M5R 1B5. Call (416) 929-7654. $20 per year. Information on female-friendly destinations and travel tips for women.

— *National Geographic.* National Geographic Society, P.O. Box 2895, Washington, DC 20077. $21 for 12 issues. Not much on "how to," but they don't get any better than National Geo on "where to." Its stories and photographs have probably gotten more people on the road than any other publication in history (except maybe draft notices).

— *Outside.* P.O. Box 54729, Boulder, CO 80322. Call (800) 678-1131. Excellent writers provide fascinating information about our planet as well as report the exploits of people who seek the ultimate in outdoor challenges.

— *South American Explorer.* P.O. Box 18327, Denver, CO 80206. Call (303) 320-0388. Quarterly publication specializing in Latin America with in-depth stories about trips, explorations, and historical events. Well suited to independent travelers. With a $25 annual membership, you receive the magazine, use of the clubhouses in Lima and Quito, and access to thousands of trip reports.

— *Thrifty Traveler.* P.O. Box 8168, Clearwater, FL 34618. Call (800) 532-5731. $28 per year. This eight-page newsletter reports on events, health, saving money, and other issues of interest to travelers.

— *Transitions Abroad.* P.O. Box 344, Amherst, MA 01004. $18 for 5 issues plus an Educational Travel Resources Guide. Articles on alternative traveling, living, working, and studying abroad.

— *Travel Books Review.* Mark Baffert (call 404-634-5874). A sixteen-page quarterly review of travel books and publishers. $19.95 per year.

— *Travel Companions.* P.O. Box 833, Amityville, NY 11701. Call (516) 454-0880. $36 per year for a monthly newsletter filled with travel tips and bargains for solo travelers. For an additional fee, join Travel Companions Exchange and receive hundreds of listings of males and females interested in finding travel companions.

— *Travelin' Woman.* Nancy Mills Communications, 855 Moraga Drive, #14, Los Angeles, CA 90049. $48 per year. Call (800) 871-6409. This ten-page monthly newsletter advertises itself as a "know before you go guide for women travelers."

— *Traveling Healthy.* 108-48 70th Road, Forest Hills, NY 11375. $29 per year. Call (718) 268-7290. Bimonthly newsletter covering general health topics.

— *Walkabout.* Box 5143, Portsmouth, NH 03802. $12 for 6 issues. Mostly reader-written newsletter for independent travelers.

— *We're Accessible: News for Disabled Travelers.* 32-1675 Cypress Street, Vancouver, BC, Canada. $15. Call (604) 731-2197. Newsletter for travelers with disabilities.

CATALOGUES

— *Camp-Mor.* Call (800) 526-4784 to order a catalogue. Wide variety and good prices.

— *Christine Colombus.* Catalogue of clothing, luggage, and travel accessories specifically for women. Published by Destinations, Lake Oswego, WI.

— *Eddie Bauer.* Call (800) 426-6253 to order a catalogue. Reliable outdoor clothing.

— *L.L. Bean.* Call (800) 221-4221 to order a catalogue. Fair prices for a wide range of reliable outdoor clothing and equipment.

— *Literate Traveler, The.* An excellent catalogue of the finest in travel literature. Call (800) 850-2665.

— *Magellan's.* Call (800) 962-4943 to order a catalogue. Describes its products as being "for more comfortable, safe, and rewarding travel."

— *Patagonia.* Call (800) 426-4737 to order a catalogue. Durable sports-related clothing and equipment.

— *Smith & Hawken.* Call (800) 776-5558 to order a catalogue. High-quality outdoor clothing.

— *47th Street Photo.* Call (800) 221-7774 to order a catalogue. Excellent selection of film and cameras at very competitive prices.

GENERAL

— *Aviation Consumer Action Project. Facts and Advice for Airline Passengers.* 1992. P.O. Box 19029, Washington, DC 20036. $2.

— Axtell, Roger E., Ed. *Do's and Taboos Around the World: A Guide to International Behavior.* Compiled by Parker Pen Co., 1993. $12.95.

— Bergen, Theresa. *Vegetarian Asia: A Travel Guide,* Noble Poodle Press, 1994. The author, a vegetarian and experienced traveler, suggests specific restaurants and dishes in each Asian country. $9.95.

— Biestman, Margot S. *Travel for Two: The Art of Compromise,* 1986.

— Bueler, William. *Mountains of the World: A Handbook for Climbers and Hikers,* 1970. A quick review of the best-known and the most difficult climbs around the world.#

— Cahill, Tim. *Pecked to Death by Ducks.* 1993. One of the best contemporary travel writers tells tales of Kuwait, Baja California, Guatemala, and Australia. Humorous and perceptive. $23.

— Chatwin, Bruce. *What Am I Doing Here.* Penguin Books, 1990. A collection of stories, profiles, and travelogues from Nepal, Afghanistan, Hong Kong, Algeria, China, Chile, and more. $9.95.

— Davidson, Robyn. *Tracks*. Pantheon, 1983. Excellent descriptions but perhaps insufficient to inspire many to duplicate her trip across Australia by camel. $12.

— Dennis, Lisl. *How to Take Better Travel Photos*.#

— Department of Transportation. *Fly Rights: A Guide to Air Travel in the U.S.* Consumer Information Center, Dept. 131Z, Pueblo, CO 81009. Fifty-eight-page pamphlet full of useful tips for those who travel by air. $1.

— Dickerman, Pat. *Adventure Travel Abroad*. H. Holt, 1986. A description of trips to 350 out-of-the-way locations. Good information for independent travelers.#

— Dickerman, Pat. *Eco Tours and Nature Getaways*. Crown Publishing Group. Call (800) 733-5000. Lists tour operators and trips around the world, with an emphasis on nature. $17.

— Fagan, Brian M. *The Great Journey: The Peopling of Ancient America*. Thomas Hudson, 1987. The leading research on how "Indians" arrived on the North American continent. $19.95.

— Fisher, Frederick. *Successful Travelling Abroad*. Culture Shock series. Emphasis on trip planning and budgeting. $12.95.

— Garfinkel, Perry. *Travel Writing for Profit and Pleasure*. Penguin Books, 1988. $10.

— Gray, William R. *Great Highways of the World*. Rand McNally, 1996. Journeys on twenty-five ancient and modern routes. $29.95.

— Gray, William R. *Voyages to Paradise: Exploring in the Wake of Captain Cook*, 1981.

— Greenburg, Laura and Jonathan. *If You Can't Remember Your Last Vacation, You Need This Book*. Thunder Publications, 1993. Lists of outfitters for ballooning, fly fishing, photo expeditions, safaris, sailing, bicycling, kayaking, heli-skiing, etc. $19.95.

— Grotta, Daniel and Sally J. Grotta. *The Green Travel Sourcebook: A Guide for the Physically Active, the Intellectually Curious, and the Socially Aware*. Wiley, 1992. Descriptions of eco-tours available (less helpful for independent travelers). $14.95.

— Hedgecoe, John. *The Photographer's Handbook*. Knopf, 1992. $19.

— Heilman, Joan R. *Unbelievably Good Deals and Great Adventures That You Absolutely Can't Get Unless You're Over Fifty*. Contemporary Books, 1990. Discounts on airfare, hotels, car rentals, and other aspects of travel. It also suggests adventure trips, tours, and cruises for those over 50.

— Iyer, Pico. *Falling Off the Map: Some Lonely Places of the World*. Knopf, 1993. $20.

— Iyer, Pico. *Video Night in Kathmandu: And Other Reports from the Not-So-Far East*. Knopf, 1988. $19.95.

— Jansz, Natalia and Miranda Davies, eds. *More Women Travel,* 1995. Rough Guides, $14.95

— Jansz, Natalia and Miranda Davies, eds. *Women Travel: Adventures, Advice and Experience.* Penguin Books, 1993. Among other topics, this book discusses potential for sexual harassment in more than seventy countries. $12.95.

— Lansing, Alfred. *Endurance: Shackleton's Incredible Voyage.* Carroll & Graf, 1986. Portrayal, drawn from the diaries of Sir Ernest Shackleton's Trans-Antarctic Expedition. $9.95.

— Leocha, Charles. *Travel Rights.* World Leisure Corp., 1994. Good outline of the rights of credit-card holders, car rental clients, and airline passengers. $7.95.

— Lewis, Norman. *A Dragon Apparent.* Eland Books, 1993. Travels in Vietnam, Laos, and Cambodia almost half a century ago by a sensitive, discerning traveler who is also a fine writer. His Golden Earth captures the spirit of Burma. Lewis is a traveler's traveler: intrepid, living unobtrusively like a local, always open to new experiences. His name is, as you might have noticed, an anagram of "New is normal." $12.95.

— McMenamin, Paul. *The Ultimate Adventure Sourcebook: A Complete Resource for Adventure and Sports Travel.* Turner Publishing, 1992. $39.95.

— Mead, Margaret. *Coming of Age in Samoa.* Morrow, 1971. Study of youth in a primitive society. How many times has this book been recommended over the years? $12.50.

— Melchett, Sonia. *Passionate Quests: Five Modern Women Travellers.* Insights into the experiences and motivations of five extraordinary travelers/travel writers.

— Morris, Mary. *Maiden Voyages.* McKay, 1993. Excellent collection of travel stories by female authors. $14.

— Morris, Mary. *Nothing to Declare: Memoirs of a Woman Traveling Alone.* Penguin, 1989. Her examination of the cultures of Mexico, Honduras, Guatemala, and the Caribbean. $9.

— Morris, Mary. *Wall to Wall: From Beijing to Berlin by Rail.* Penguin, 1992. $10.

— Morris, Jan. *Journeys.* OUP, 1985. $21.95.

— Murphy, Dervla. *Cameroon with Egbert.* Overlook Press, 1992. A report on her trip around Cameroon with a horse (and daughter), usually walking. $13.95.

— Murphy, Dervla. *Full Tilt: Ireland to India with a Bicycle.* Overlook Press, 1987. Imagine the courage and spirit it took to make this trip solo on a bicycle. To hear her tell it, she did it as a lark. $10.95.

— Murphy, Dervla. *Muddling Through in Madagascar.* Overlook Press, 1990. Dervla Murphy can inspire any procrastinating traveler. $9.95.

— Neumann, Karl Dr. and Maury Rosenbaum. *The Business Traveler's Guide to Good Health on the Road.* Chronimed Publishing. Travel medicine and more. $15.95.

— Newby, Eric. *Short Walk in the Hindu Kush.* Penguin Books, 1987. $16.95.

— Newman, Steven M. *Worldwalk.* Avon, 1989. $5.95.

— *1995 Alternative Travel Directory.* Transitions Abroad Publishing, 1995. Eclectic collection of topics pertaining to living and traveling abroad. $19.95.

— *Norton Introduction to Literature.* W.W. Norton & Co. The Norton series includes fiction, poetry, essays, drama, and so on. These paperbacks, which run 1,500 tissue-thin pages or more, are, pound-for-pound, the best value I've found for a long trip. They're fulfilling and stick with you.

— *Presence & Protocol.* The Registry Group. Call (203) 322-9292. A comprehensive catalogue of books, bulletins, and audio tapes on the cultures, taboos, protocols, and business practices of more than 100 countries.

— Preston-Mafham, Ken. *Practical Wildlife Photography.* For committed photographers interested in botany and wildlife.#

— Rand-McNally. *Almanac of Adventure.* Descriptions of more than 50 adventures, many suitable for independent travelers.

— Rowell, Galen. *Vision: The Art of Adventure Photography.* Sierra Club Books. Explanations of how he produces outstanding outdoor photography. $25.

— Rowlands, Peter. *The Underwater Photographer's Handbook.* Includes a guide to dive spots around the world.#

— St. Aubin de Teran, Lisa. *Indiscreet Journeys: Stories of Women on the Road.* Faber & Faber. Tales by twenty-six women about travels on six continents during two centuries. $12.95.

— Savage, Barbara. *Miles from Nowhere: A Round-the-World Bicycle Adventure.* The Mountaineers. Story of her two-year, 23,000-mile bicycle trip. $12.95.

— Savage, Peter. *The Safe Travel Book.* Free Press.#

— Schmidt, Gary. *Fly for Less: The Only Complete Guide to Selecting Reliable Consolidators and Wholesalers Who Offer Bargain Airfares.* Travel Publishing. At some bookstores or call (800) 241-9299. This is a great guide to consolidators. $19.95.

— Schwartz, Brian M. *A World of Villages.* 1986. Interesting account of his six-year trip through Africa, India, Nepal, Indonesia, China, Tibet, and the Middle East.#

— Sereny, Gail Rubin. *Ms. Adventures: Worldwide Travelguide for Independent Women.* Guide for women traveling solo.#

— da Silva, Rachel, ed. *Leading Out: Climbers Reaching for the Top.* Seal Press. Excellent stories by and about unique female climbers. $16.95.

— Simmons, James C. *The Big Book of Adventure Travel: 500 Great Escapes.* 1990.#

— *Smart Travel.* Ziff-Davis Press, 1995. Using computer-accessible resources to plan your trip. The book comes with a CD-ROM disk and $15 worth of online time. $24.95.

— *Specialty Travel Index.* Alpine Hansen. Call (800) 442-4942. Published twice a year, the Index lists over 600 tour operators who emphasize adventure travel (cross-indexed by activity and destination).

— Speight, Phyllis. *The Traveller's Guide to Homeopathy.* Beekman Pub., 1990. Alternative suggestions for maintenance of health on the road. $12.95.

— Teison, Herbert and Nancy Dunnan. *Travel Smarts: Getting the Most for Your Travel Dollar.* Globe Pequot Press, 1995. From Travel Smart newsletters. Emphasis on domestic and European travel. $12.95.

— Theroux, Paul. *The Great Railway Bazaar.* Ballantine, 1981. $2.95.

— Theroux, Paul. *The Mosquito Coast.* Avon, 1983. $5.95.

— Theroux, Paul. *The Old Patagonian Express: By Train Through the Americas.* Houghton Mifflin, 1989. $9.70.

— Theroux, Paul. *Sunrise with Seamonsters.* Houghton Mifflin, 1986. Consists of short stories and essays written during a twenty-year period, including stories set in Africa and India. $8.70.

— *Travel Buying Guide.* Consumer Reports. Typically informative; each chapter a compilation of articles from *Consumer Reports Travel Letters.* $8.99.

— *Travel for the Disabled: A Handbook of Travel Resources and 500 Worldwide Access Guides.* The Disability Bookshop; call (800) 637-2256. Excellent tips for travel by disabled persons, plus lists of accommodations free of barriers. $19.95.

— Twain, Mark. *Following the Equator.* 1897. Memoirs of a sharp tongue cruising from British Columbia through the South Seas to Australia and New Zealand. $13.

— *Ultimate Adventure Sourcebook.* Turner Publishing. Detailed listing of many of the best action-sport experiences and destinations around the world. $29.95.

— Waugh, Evelyn. *Remote People.* Ecco Press, 1990. $8.95.

— Waugh, Evelyn. *When the Going Was Good.* Little, 1985. Ironical excerpts from the best of Waugh's travel books. $8.95.

— Weaver, Frances. *This Year I Plan to Go Elsewhere (Last Year I Went Around the World).* Fulcrum Publishing, 1989. Journey by a (self-described) midlife woman traveler.

— Williams, Anita and Merrimac Dillon. *The 50+ Travelers' Guidebook: Where to Go, Where to Stay, What to Do.* St. Martin's, 1991. $12.95.

— Windsor, Natalie. *The Safe Tourist.* Corkscrew Press, 1995. Mostly for domestic travel but many tips are useful for international travel. $8.95.

— *Without a Guide: Contemporary Women's Travel Adventures.* Hungry Mind Press, 1996. Seventeen female writers recounting memorable adventures. $16.

— Zepatos, Thalia. *Adventures in Good Company.* Eighth Mountain Press, 1994. A guide to women's tours and adventure trips. $17.95.

— Zepatos, Thalia. *A Journey of One's Own.* Eighth Mountain Press. Does a fine job of taking fear out of independent traveling for women.

— Zobel, Louise. *Travel Writer's Handbook: How to Write and Sell Your Travel Experiences.* Surrey Books, 1992. If you're an aspiring travel writer, don't miss this one. $11.95.

AFRICA

— Adamson, Joy. *Born Free, Living Free.* Pantheon, 1987. $11.95.

— Barboza, Steven. *Door of No Return: the Legend of Goree Island.* Cobblehill, 1994.

— Bowles, Paul. *Midnight Mass.* Black Sparrow, 1983. Collection of short stories.

— Bowles, Paul. *Points in Time.* Ecco Press, 1991. Vivid portrayal of Moroccan landscape and people.

— Bowles, Paul. *Sheltering Sky.* New Directions, 1949. Bizarre physical and psychological journey in the Sahara.

— Boyle, T. Coraghessan. *Water Music.* Little Brown, 1981. Adventures of Mungo Park as he explored the Niger river. Fine insight into an earlier Africa.

— Brandenburg, Jim. *Sand and Fog: Adventures in Southern Africa.* Walker, 1994.

— Chatwin, Bruce. *Far Journeys: Photographs and Notebooks.* Viking. Photographs and journal jottings from travels in East Africa and Afghanistan. $35.

— Conrad, Joseph. *Heart of Darkness.* St. Martin's, 1989. Immerses the reader in the essence of the African experience. $8.

— Dinesen, Isak. *Letters from Africa, 1914–1931.* Univ. of Chicago Press, 1984. First-hand descriptions of decadent European society in Kenya early in the 20th century. $16.95.

— Dinesen, Isak. *Out of Africa.* Random House, 1989. Memoirs of Baroness Karen Blixen's life on a coffee plantation early in the 20th century. $10.95.

— Fage, J.D. *A History of Africa.* Unwin, 1989. Outstanding one-volume narrative history.

— Fitzgerald, Mary Anne. *Nomad: One Woman's Journey into the Heart of Africa.* Viking. Insightful discussions of politics in sub-Saharan Africa. $21.

— Flaubert, Gustave. *Flaubert in Egypt.* Flaubert's bawdy and humorous report of his 1849 trip along the Nile.

— Forbath, Peter. *The Last Hero.* Simon & Schuster, 1988. A fictionalized version of Stanley's rescue of Emin Pasha.

— Forbath, Peter. *The River Congo.* Houghton Mifflin, 1977. Excellent account of the grim history of the Congo, told with a journalist's flair.#

— Fossey, Dian. *Gorillas in the Mist.* Houghton Mifflin, 1983. Her report of thirteen years among mountain gorillas in the rain forest.

— Gide, André. *Amyntas*. Ecco Press, 1988. Report of his five years in Tunis and Algiers.
— Gordimer, Nadine. *The Essential Gesture: Writing, Politics, Places*. Knopf, 1988. Reflections on South Africa and apartheid. Ms. Gordimer has also written fine novels about Africa in general and South Africa in particular.
— Gordimer, Nadine. *Livingstone's Companions*. Viking, 1970. Excellent short stories about Africa.
— de Gramont, Sanche. *The Strong Brown God*. Houghton Mifflin, 1975. Stories of the obsessed explorers who revealed the mysteries of the Niger River.#
— Harden, Blaine. *Africa: Dispatches from a Fragile Continent*. Norton, 1990. A *Washington Post* reporter's essays on six countries in "the Nth World." $22.50.
— Harris, Eddy L. *Native Stranger: A Black American's Journey into the Heart of Africa*. Viking, 1994.
— Heminway, John. *Africa Journeys: A Personal Guidebook*. Warner Books, 1990. $12.95.
— Heminway, John. *The Imminent Rains*. Little, Brown, 1968. Unhurried conversations with old-timers in the bush.#
— Heminway, John. *No Man's Land*. Warner Books, 1989.
— Hibbert, Christopher. *Africa Explored: Europeans in the Dark Continent, 1769–1889*. Norton, 1982. He walks with Mungo Park, Speke, Stanley, Livingstone, and others.
— Hudson, Mark. *Our Grandmothers' Drums*. Grove Weidenfield, 1990. Study of the lives of African women in an isolated village.
— Huxley, Elspeth, ed. *Nine Faces of Kenya*. Viking, 1991. An anthology of Hemingway, Churchill, Dinesen, and others. Huxley's own writings, *Murder on Safari*, *Flame Trees of Thika*, and *Out in the Midday Sun* are vibrant descriptions of East African life.
— Lamb, David. *The Africans*. Vintage, 1985. Excellent combination of travelogue and contemporary history by a *Los Angeles Times* correspondent. $7.95.
— Lamb, David. *The Arabs: Beyond the Mirage*. Random House, 1988. $13.
— Markham, Beryl. *West with the Night*. North Point Press. Memoir of her remarkable life in East Africa. She was a flyer in every sense. $12.50.
— Marshall, Richard. *Strange, Amazing, and Mysterious Places*. Collins. Mystic places of the earth linked as inspiration to the spirit. $45.
— Matthiessen, Peter. *The Tree Where Man Was Born: The African Experience*. Dutton, 1983. Impressions from Sudan to Tanzania.
— Mazrui, Ali. *The Africans: A Triple Heritage*. Little, 1986. Discussion of Africa as a transmitter of Islamic, Western, and indigenous cultures.
— Michener, James. *The Covenant*. Fawcett, 1987. Five hundred years of

South African history told from African, Afrikaans, and English perspectives. It helps explain the intensity of the struggle in South Africa. $6.95.
— Naipal, V.S. *A Bend in the River*. Random House, 1989. $9.
— Naipal, V.S. *India: A Million Mutinies Now*. Viking Penguin, 1992. $13.
— Nolting, Mark. *Africa's Top Wildlife Countries*. Globe Travel, 1990. Lists top 10 countries for wildlife, with maps, photos, safaris, and other practical information.
— Paton, Alan. *Ah, But Your Land Is Beautiful*. Scribner, 1982. Social protests against apartheid.
— Paton, Alan. *Cry The Beloved Country*.
— Shoumatoff, Alex. *African Madness*. Knopf, 1988.
— Shoumatoff, Alex. *In Southern Light: Trekking Through Zaire and the Amazon*. Simon & Schuster, 1986.
— Stengel, Richard. *January Sun: One Day, Three Lives, A South African Town*. Simon & Schuster, 1990. Fascinating story of three disparate lives through the course of a single day.
— Turnbull, Colin. *The Forest People*. Simon & Schuster, 1987. Turnbull describes the lives of pygmies in Zaire. $11.
— Turnbull, Colin. *The Lonely African*. Simon & Schuster, 1968.
— Van Der Post, Laurens. *The Heart of the Hunter*. Harcourt Brace, 1980. Excellent description of the Bushmen's way of life—and apartheid. $9.95.
— Van Der Post, Laurens. *The Lost World of the Kalahari*. Harcourt Brace, 1977. $9.95.
— Winternitz, Helen. *East Along the Equator*. Grove-Atlantic, 1987. Fine report of the infamous river trip from Kinshasa up the Zaire River to Kisangani, then overland to Goma on Lake Kivu. $9.95.

ANTARCTICA

— Amundsen, Roald. *My Life as an Explorer*. Doubleday, 1927. The hero of the Antarctic.
— Beaglehole, J.C., ed. *The Journals of Captain James Cook on his Voyages of Discovery: The Voyage of the Resolution and Adventure, 1772–1775*. Cambridge University Press, 1961.
— Campbell, David G. *The Crystal Desert*. Houghton Mifflin, 1992. This biologist makes science poetic. He describes the evolution of the continent, seabirds, penguins, seals, plankton, krill, whales, the weather—and throws in tales of early explorers. Possibly the best modern book on Antarctica.
— Chapman, Walker, ed. *Antarctic Conquest: The Great Explorers in Their Own Words*. Bobbs Merrill, 1965. A fine anthology.
— Cherry-Garrard, Apsley. *The Worst Journey in the World: Antarctic 1910–1913*. Carroll & Graf. Personal account of heroism and determination on

Capt. Scott's polar expedition as well as a trip between Cape Crozier and McMurdo Sound. A classic. $13.95.

— Huntford, Roland. *Scott and Amundsen*. G.P. Putnam's Sons, 1980. A comparative biography of the men engaged in the great race for the South Pole.
— Land, Barbara. *The New Explorers: Women in Antarctica*. Dodd, Mead, 1981.
— Lansing, Alfred. *Endurance, Shackleton's Incredible Voyage*. McGraw Hill, 1959. Excellent story of Shackleton's two-year ordeal.
— May, John. *The Greenpeace Book of Antarctica*. Macmillan of Canada, 1988.
— Naveen, Ron, inter alia. *Wild Ice: Antarctic Journeys*. Smithsonian Press, 1990. Excellent photographs of the continent.
— Quigg, Philip W. *A Pole Apart: The Emerging Issue of Antarctica*. McGraw Hill, 1983. A review of political and scientific issues.
— Parfit, Michael. *South Light*. Macmillan, 1986. Discussion of the U.S. Antarctic program.
— Porter, Eliot. *Antarctica*. E.P. Dutton, 1978. Splendid photographs.
— Pyne, Stephen J. *The Ice: A Journey to Antarctica*. University of Iowa Press, 1988.
— Scott, Robert Falcon. *Scott's Last Expedition*. Smith, Elder & Co., 1913.
— Shapley, Deborah. *The Seventh Continent: Antarctica in a Resource Age*. Resources for the Future, 1986.
— Simpson, George G. *Penguins, Past and Present, Here and There*. Yale University Press, 1976.
— Steger, Will and Jon Bowermaster. *Crossing Antarctica*. Dell Publishing, 1991. An incredible 220-day dogsled trip across 3,700 miles. Six determined men from different countries emphasize the unique international nature of the continent.
— Weddell, James. *A Voyage Toward the South Pole Performed in the Years 1922–24*. David and Charles Reprints, 1827.

ASIA

— Akutagawa, Ryunosuke. *Rashomon*. Liverwright, 1970. Japanese short stories.
— Blum, Arlene. *Annapurna: A Woman's Place*. Sierra, 1983. Candid description of a successful, but tragic, women's expedition on Annapurna. $8.95.
— Bohnaker, William. *The Hollow Doll: A Little Box of Japanese Shocks*. Ballantine, 1990. Negative impressions of modern Japan.
— Bonavia, David. *The Chinese*. Viking Penguin, 1993. The *New York Times* correspondent reviews what he calls "The most forthrightly materialistic value system in the history of mankind." $7.95.
— Bonnington, Chris. *Everest: The Unclimbed Ridge*. Heartbreaking story, by one of the great climbers, of a disastrous Everest attempt in 1982.#

- Bonnington, Chris. *I Chose to Climb*. Ulverscroft, 1985. $15.95.
- Braganti, Nancy and Elizabeth Devine. *The Traveler's Guide to Asian Customs and Manners*. St. Martin's Press, 1986.
- Buck, Pearl S. *The Good Earth*. OUP, 1982. A Pulitzer Prize–winning description of China in an earlier era. One of the best. $4.95.
- Cameron, Roderick. *Australia: History and Horizons*. Columbia Univ. Press, 1971. Australia in the 18th and 19th centuries.
- Chambers, Kevin A. *A Traveler's Guide to Asian Culture*. John Muir, 1989. $13.95.
- David-Neel, Alexandra. *My Journey to Lhasa*. Beacon Press, 1988. This remarkable French citizen was the first European woman to enter the forbidden city. $13.
- DeGaury, Gerald and H.V.F. Winstone. *An Anthology of Writings on Asia*. Macmillan, 1982. Travel writing by the best.
- Dingle, Graeme and Peter Hillary. *First Across the Roof of the World*. Have you been waiting for the right time to walk the length of the Himalayas? Too late, it's been done. These two were apparently the first.#
- Fleming, Peter. *Bayonets to Lhasa*. OUP, 1986. Fleming's seven-month, 3,500-mile travels on the Silk Road from Peking to Turkistan. $9.95.#
- Fleming, Peter. *News from Tartary*. Tarcher, 1982.
- Forster, E.M. *A Passage to India*. Knopf, 1992. Insight into the Indian psyche; best read in India. $15.
- Gandhi, Mohandas K. *An Autobiography*. Greenleaf Books, 1984. Look into the mind and values of one of the more evolved humans in history. $5.
- Harrer, Heinrich. *Return to Tibet*. Schocken, 1985.
- Harrer, Heinrich. *Seven Years in Tibet*. Tarcher, 1982. Harrer, imprisoned in India at the outbreak of World War II, escaped, crossed the Himalayas, and became a confidant of the Dalai Lama. Excellent report of Tibetan life before the arrival of Chinese forces. $9.95.
- Herzog, Maurice. *Annapurna*. Dutton, 1952. First ascent by the leader of the French team.#
- Hulme, Keri. *The Bone People*. LSU Press, 1985. Insights into the Maori culture.
- Iyer, Pico. *The Lady and the Monk*. 1991. Report on Kyoto, Zen, and passion. $12.
- Jenkins, Peter. *Across China*. Fawcett, 1988. $5.95.
- Jhabvala, Ruth Prawer. *Heat and Dust*. Harper Row, 1976.
- Jhabvala, Ruth Prawer. *Out of India: Selected Stories*. Simon & Schuster, 1987. Fifteen short stories. $9.
- Johnson, Tracy. *Shooting the Boh: A Woman's Voyage Down the Wildest River in Borneo*. Vintage. She faced a cobra-infested river—and middle age. $11.
- Lee, C.Y. *China Saga*. Weidenfeld, 1987. Family saga from the Boxer Re-

bellion through the Cultural Revolution.

— Lewis, Norman. *An Empire of the East.* Henry Holt, 1994. Tribal war games, Stone Age agricultural practices, and the consequences of multinational copper mining in Sumatra, East Timor, and Irian Jaya. $25.
— Maraini, Fosco. *Karakoram: The Ascent of Gasherbrum IV.*#
— Matthiessen, Peter. *Snow Leopard.* Penguin, 1987. Adventure and anthropology in the context of George Shaller's search for the seldom-seen snow leopard.#
— Miller, Luree. *On Top of the World: Five Women Explorers in Tibet.* Mountaineers, 1984. Great stories of five intrepid women who explored Tibet in the 1800s.
— Morrow, Patrick. *Beyond Everest: Quest for Seven Summits.* Firefly Books, 1986. $19.95.
— Naipal, V.S. *Among the Believers: An Islamic Journey.* Random House, 1982. $14.
— Naipal, V.S. *India: A Million Mutinies Now.* Viking, 1991. Great guide to understanding castes and political parties.
— Narayan, R.K. *The Ramayana.* Viking, 1972. Modern version of the great Indian epic.
— Natwar-Singh, K., ed. *Tales from Modern India.* 1966. Twenty fine stories by some of India's best writers.#
— O'Hanlon, Redmond. *In Trouble Again.* Random House, 1990. $11.
— O'Hanlon, Redmond. *Into the Heart of Borneo.* Random House, 1987. Trip up the Baleh River and to the summit of Mount Batu Tiban. $11.
— Portway, Christopher. *Indian Odyssey: Around the Subcontinent by Public Transport.* Impact, 1993.
— Roberts, Joe. *Three-Quarters of a Footprint.* Bantam, 1994.
— Roberts, Paul William. *Empire of the Soul: Modern Travels in Ancient India.* Stoddart, 1994.
— Ronay, Gabriel. *The Tartar Khan's Englishman.* 1978. The story of an English diplomat-adventurer on whom the grandson of Genghis Khan was dependent as he hurled Mongol armies against Christian Europe.# A good companion piece is *The Travels* written by Marco Polo in 1298.#
— Spence, Jonathan D. *The Death of the Woman Wang.* Penguin, 1979.
— Spence, Jonathan D. *The Search for Modern China.* Norton, 1990. Four hundred years of history leading up to the violence in Tiananmen Square.
— Thubron, Colin. *Behind the Wall: A Journey Through China.* Atlantic Monthly Press, 1988. Mandarin-speaking author writes of the small places.
— Wintle, Justin. *Romancing Vietnam: Inside the Boat Country.* Pantheon, 1991. Insights into a country now at peace, striving to develop an identity. $25.
— Wolpert, Stanley. *India.* Univ. of California Press, 1991. Superbly written synopsis of Indian civilization.

MIDDLE EAST

— Bar-Zohar, Michael. *Facing A Cruel Mirror: Israel's Moment of Truth.* Scribner, 1990. Israeli politics and society from 1967 to the Intifada through the eyes of a member of the Knesset.
— Browning, Robert. *The Byzantine Empire.* Scribner, 1980. History of 1,000 years of empire.
— Burton, Sir Richard. *The Arabian Nights.* Regal Pub., 1992. $31.95.
— Burton, Sir Richard. *Personal Narrative of a Pilgrimage to Al-Madinah and Mecca,* 2 volumes. Dover, 1893. Burton traveled in disguise to holy cities in Arabia forbidden to non-Muslims under pain of death. $9.95 each.
— Durrell, Lawrence. *The Alexandria Quartet.* Dutton, 1957–60.
— Edwards, Amelia B. *A Thousand Miles Up the Nile.* Tarcher, 1983. Classic tale of an Englishwoman's 19th-century trip up the Nile in high style.
— Elon, Amos. *Jerusalem: City of Mirrors.* Little Brown, 1989. Modern Jerusalem from the perspectives of various religions.
— Friedman, Thomas L. *From Beirut to Jerusalem.* Doubleday, 1990. Short history of the Middle East, especially helpful to understanding the complexity of conflicts among various religious factions. $12.95.
— Goldschmidt, Arthur J. *A Concise History of the Middle East.* Westview Press, 1987. Conversational history from 7th to 20th century.
— Heude, William. *A Voyage Up the Persian Gulf and a Journey Overland from India to England in 1817.* Garnet, 1993.
— Holden, David and Richard Johns. *The House of Saud.* 1981. The history of the rise and rule of the most powerful dynasty in the Arab world.#
— Lamb, David. *The Arabs: Journeys Beyond the Mirage.* Random House, 1988. Excellent review of human aspects of Arab culture and history.
— Lawrence, T.E. *Seven Pillars of Wisdom.* Doubleday, 1991. Journal of an Englishman deeply involved in a revolution in Arabia against the Turks. Philosophy and anthropology written with great style. $15.
— Manley, Deborah. *The Nile: A Traveller's Anthology.* Sterling, 1991. Journeys along the Nile by more than eighty authors.
— Mansfield, Peter. *The Arabs.* Penguin, 1985. Social and political history from nomadic times to the present.
— Michener, James A. *The Source.* Fawcett, 1986. $6.99. An archaeological dig in Israel serves as the basis for recreating the history of Israel and Judaism.
— Nightingale, Florence. *Letters from Egypt: A Journey on the Nile.* Grove-Atlantic, 1988. Beautiful writing by an inquisitive traveler. $24.95.
— Stark, Freya. *Baghdad Sketches.* Marlboro Press, 1992. $11.95.
— Stark, Freya. *A Peak in Darien.* Transatlantic Press, 1977. $16.95.
— Stark, Freya. *Valley of the Assassins.* Tarcher, 1983. A report of her travels

across Syria, Iraq, and Iran through a world of castles, treasures, and murderers. $9.95.

— Thesiger, Wilfred. *Arabian Sands*. Viking Penguin, 1985. For forty years Thesiger crisscrossed the deserts of Arabia, Iran, Iraq, Ethiopia, and Yemen with a will so fierce that his companions were left behind in the sand. "I have had a hard life;" Thesiger said, "this was from choice. It was also an inexpensive one; this was essential." $8.95.

— Thesiger, Wilfred. *The Last Nomad*.#

— Thesiger, Wilfred. *The Marsh Arabs*.#

— Uris, Leon. *Exodus*. Doubleday, 1958. History of Palestine and Zionism from the 1940s.

SOUTH AMERICA AND CENTRAL AMERICA

— Allende, Isabel. *House of Spirits*. Knopf, 1985. Chilean saga from the early 20th century through the overthrow of Allende in 1973.

— Allende, Isabel. *Of Love and Shadows*. Knopf, 1987.

— Alvarado, Elvia. *Don't Be Afraid, Gringo*. 1987. A campesina's view of why the Honduran farmers fight and how they've learned to work the system ("The foreigners love to fund women's projects. So the campesino groups respond by creating women's projects.")#

— Borges, Jorge L. *Borges: A Reader*. Dutton, 1981. Excellent survey of the writing of one of South America's finest authors.

— Bradt, George N. *South America: River Trips*. Description of some of the best river trips on the continent and how to prepare for them. Bradt also publishes a useful series of guidebooks for various South American and African countries.

— Branston, Brian. *The Last Great Journey on Earth*. 1970. Journey up the Rio Negro from Manaus, across a 200-mile natural channel to the Orinoco, and over dangerous rapids to the Venezuelan coast. Discusses parallels between treatment of indigenous people in Brazil and the United States.

— Chaplin, Gordon. *The Fever Coast Log*. HarperCollins, 1992.

— Chatwin, Bruce. *In Patagonia*. Viking Penguin, 1988. A classic in which Chatwin describes his close-to-the-ground travel across Patagonia. Nice report of his conversation with Borges. $8.95.

— *The Cloud Forest*. Penguin, 1987. The high point is the section on running the Pongo de Mainique rapids of the Rio Urubamba.#

— Coe, Michael D. *The Maya*. Thames & Hudson, 1993. This book represents the cutting edge of archaeological investigations. $14.95.

— Elder, Norman. *This Thing of Darkness: Amazon Notebook*. 1979. Tale of a Canadian explorer's experiences with two tribes of Indians in the Amazon basin.#

— Fleming, Peter. *Brazilian Adventure*. Tarcher, 1988. Fine writing.#
— Garcia Marquez, Gabriel. *One Hundred Years of Solitude*. Harper Row, 1970. Seven generation family saga set in Colombia—except that nothing is quite as it seems. His whole body of work merits review.
— Greene, Graham. *The Power and the Glory*. Penguin, 1977. Priest on the run from an avenging army.
— Greenwood, James. *No Guns, Big Smile*. Pelham Books, 1993.
— Kandell, Jonathan. *Passage Through El Dorado: The Conquest of the World's Last Great Wilderness*. Avon, 1991. Detailed description of how lust for profits from rubber, gold, and cocaine ("cocadollars and corruption") in the Amazon basin led to exploitation of Indians.
— Kane, Joe. *Running the Amazon*. Knopf, 1990. A 4,200-mile boat trip from source to mouth of the Amazon. Ten started, four finished. $19.95.
— LaFeber, Walter. *Inevitable Revolutions: The United States in Central America*. Norton, 1983. Essential to understanding the past and present of Central America: why it is so violent and how commercial interests created the system of dependency. $12.95.
— LaFeber, Walter. *The Panama Canal: The Crisis in Historical Perspective*. Oxford Univ. Press, 1990.
— Lawrence, D.H. *Mornings in Mexico*. Peregrine Smith, 1982. Study of the Mexican Indian.
— Lawrence, D.H. *The Plumed Serpent*. Random House, 1955. Study of the Aztec culture.
— Lewis, Oscar. *The Children of Sanchez*. Vintage, 1979. Biography of a proud, desperate laborer and his more modern children as they survive in Mexico City's slums. $16.
— Marnham, Patrick. *So Far from God: A Journey to Central America*. Transaction Pub., 1987. Fine description of travel in contemporary Central America. $16.95.
— Matthiessen, Peter. *At Play in the Fields of the Lord*. 1965. The book is much better than the movie.
— McGuire, Stryker. *Streets With No Names: A Journey into Central & South America*. Atlantic Monthly Press, 1990. Human reality of life as seen during a 20,000-mile trip.
— Moore, J.H. *Tears of the Sun God*. 1965. Unusual story of botanists' trip through the savannah and jungles of Guiana, then via various tributaries to the Rio Negro to Manaus, Brazil, followed by some challenging climbs in Ecuador and Bolivia. Very tough trip.#
— Murphy, Dervla. *Eight Feet in the Andes*. Overlook Press, 1986. Adventuresome woman following Pizarro's route through the Andes.
— Nott, David. *Angels 4*. 1972. Eight-day ascent of 3,282-foot Angel Falls in Venezuela. Oddly, the waterfall was named for Jimmy Angel, a pilot who crash-landed on the plateau from which it originates.#

— O'Hanlon, Redmond. *In Trouble Again: A Journey Between the Orinoco and the Amazon*. Atlantic Monthly Press, 1989. Four-month trip up the Orinoco and across the Amazon Basin. Entertaining, perceptive writing.

— Parris, Matthew. *Inka-Cola: Traveller's Tale of Peru*. Ulverscroft Books, 1992.

— Paz, Octavio. *The Labyrinth of Solitude*. Grove, 1983. Brilliant analysis of Mexican life and thought.

— Peters, Daniel. *Tikal: A Novel About the Maya*. Random House, 1983. Hypothesis for the abandonment of the greatest capital city.

— Plotkin, Mark. *Tales of a Shaman's Apprentice: An ethnobiologist searches for new medicines in the Amazon rain forest*. Viking, 1993.

— Reed, John. *Insurgent Mexico*. International Publishers. Better known for his adventures in Russia, Reed's account of his days with Pancho Villa's army during the Mexican Revolution reveals the common clay and the convictions of the revolutionaries. $6.95.

— Simpson, Joe. *Touching the Void*. Harper Collins, 1990. Incredible story of a catastrophic fall during a climb in the Cordillera Blanca of the Peruvian Andes. This story embodies enormous courage and generosity of spirit.

— Stephens, John L. *Incidents of Travel in Yucatan*, 2 volumes. Dover, 1843. Classic travel tale of systematic exploration of Mayan sites in the Yucatán. $5.95 each.

— *Stolen Continents: The Americas Through Indian Eyes Since 1492*. Houghton Mifflin, 1993. $12.70.

— *Time Among the Maya: Travels in Belize, Guatemala, and Mexico*. Henry Holt, 1991. $14.95.

— Vargas Llosa, Mario. *The War at the End of the World*. FS&G, 1984. Turn of the century revolution in northern Brazil.

— Wilson, Jason. *Traveller's Literary Companion to Central and South America*. In Print, 1993.

— Woodward, Ralph Lee. *Central America: A Nation Divided*. Oxford Univ. Press, 1985. One of the best Central American histories written in English.

— Wright, Ronald. *Cut Stones and Crossroads*. Penguin Travel, 1984. Trip from the Cordillera Blanca to Lake Titicaca, tracing the Inca and the history of Peru. $7.95.#

HEALTH

— *Altitude Illness: Prevention & Treatment*. The Mountaineers Books, 1995. An 80-page pocket guide on preventing, diagnosing, and treating altitude sickness. Call (800) 553-4453. $8.95.

— American Red Cross. *Standard First Aid and Safety*.

— Benenson, Abram S., ed. *Control of Communicable Diseases in Man*. American Public Health Association, 1990. $15.

— Bezruchka, Dr. Stephen. *The Pocket Doctor: Your Ticket to Good Health While Traveling*. The Mountaineers Books, 1992. This light, small-format guide is packed with useful reminders of how to treat yourself when underway and when to seek help. $4.95.

— Bryson, Dr. Lawrence. *The Travel Health Clinic: a Pocket Guide to Healthy Travel*. Silvercat, 1996. $13.95.

— Dawood, Richard. *Travelers' Health: How to Stay Healthy All Over the World*. Random House. Excellent reference although a bit hefty for a backpack at over 600 pages. $18.

— *Diabetic Traveler*. Quarterly newsletter. $18.95. Call (203) 327-5832.

— *Emergency Medical Procedures for the Outdoors*. Menasha Ridge Press. Excellent information on lifesaving procedures and treating medical complaints and injuries. Good book to learn from or take with you. Call (800) 247-9437

— Forgey, Dr. William W. *Travelers' Medical Resource: A Guide to Health & Safety Worldwide*. ICS Books, 1990. $19.95

— *Health Information for International Travel (HIFIT)*. Centers for Disease Control or U.S. Government Printing Office, Washington, D.C. 20402.

— Howarth, Dr. Jane W. *Bugs, Bites & Bowels*. Sensible information delivered in an entertaining tone (maybe the title gave that away). $9.95.

— *Physicians Desk Reference*. Medical Economics Co.

— Rose, Dr. Stuart R. *International Travel Health Guide*. Travel Medicine, Inc. About half of this book is devoted to a review of health risks in individual countries. It's too comprehensive to carry in your luggage but contains very helpful pretrip material. $16.95.

— Rubin, M. R. and B. L. Dessery. *The Medical Guide for Third World Travelers*. KWP Publications.#

— Schroeder, Dirk. *Staying Healthy in Asia, Africa, and Latin America*. Moon Pub., 1993. $10.95.

— Sullivan, Donald L. *A Senior's Guide to Healthy Travel*. Career Press, 1995. $14.95.

— *Travelers Health: How to Stay Healthy All Over the World*. Random House. Sixty-six physicians opine on every imaginable health hazard.

— *Travelin' Talk Newsletter and Network*. For handicapped travelers. Call (615) 552-6670. The Society for the Advancement of Travel for the Handicapped also publishes a quarterly newsletter. Call (212) 447-7284.

— *Travel Medicine Catalogue*. Contains over fifty products designed to protect travelers from disease-causing insects, contaminated water, and medical emergencies. Call (800) 872-8633.

— *Travel Medicine Specialist Directory*. Travel Directory, Connaught Laboratories, Dept TC, 1645 Oak Street, Lakewood, NJ 08701. Free listing of physicians who specialize in travel medicine and offer health care before and after international travel.

— Weinhouse, Beth. *The Healthy Traveler: An Indispensable Guide to Staying Healthy Away from Home.#*
— Young, Bob. *How to Stay Healthy While Traveling: A Guide for Today's World Traveler.* Ross-Erikson, 1980. $4.95.

IMPORTING/EXPORTING

— *Basic Guide to Exporting.* Superintendent of Documents, Government Printing Office, Washington, D.C. 20229. Call (202) 783-3238.
— *Business America.* U.S. Department of Commerce. Monthly, $60 per year.
— *Commercial Agency: A Guide for Drawing Up of Contracts.* ICC Pub. Call (212) 206-1150. $8.
— *Directory of Latin American Importers and Exporters.* Centro Internacional de Promocion Industrial, P.O. Box 73, Centro Colon, San Jose, Costa Rica. Call 33-86-97.
— *Encyclopedia of Business Information Sources.* Gale Research Company, Book Tower, Detroit, MI 48226. Ask for information related to the area of trade in which you are interested.
— *Export Marketing for Smaller Firms.* U.S. Dept. of Commerce. Available from GPO.
— *Foreign Business Practices.* U.S. Dept. of Commerce. Available from GPO. Emphasizes legal aspects of international trade.
— Green, Mary. *How to be an Importer and Pay for Your World Travel.* Ten Speed Press.
— *A Guide to Export Documentation.* Educational Development for International Trade. Call (513) 276-5995.
— *Guide to Incoterms.* ICC Pub. Definitions of shipping terms.
— *Handbook on International Trade/Shipping Digest.* Call (212) 689-4411.
— *How to Make a Fortune in Import/Export.* Reston Pub. Written for individuals starting out in international trade. Call (201) 767-5054.
— *Importing into the United States.* U.S. Customs Service (GPO).
— *Network.* World Trade Institute, One World Trade Center, New York, NY 10048. Call (212) 435-8284.
— *Sourcebook.* Unz & Co. Good description of documents used in international trade. Call (800) 631-3098.

INDEX

ABC Passenger Shipping Guide, 386
ABC Worldwide Hotel Guide, 50, 140
Abercrombie & Kent, 89
Above the Clouds Trekking, 80, 85
Access, 128
Actif International, 80
Active Travel Resource Guide, The, 43–44
Advance purchase excursion (APEX), 126–127
   open jaw ticket, 127
   time requirement, 126
Adventure Center, 84
Adventures
   arranging from home versus site, 115–116
   cost cutting on, 141–142
Adventures in Travel, 50
Adventure tours, 84–85
   tour operators, 84–85
   web site for, 86
Adventure Travel Directory, 47
Adventure Travel Society, 47
Adventure Worldwide, 86
Adventurous Traveler Bookstore, 54
Advisory on Ticket Consolidators, 122, 126
Affection, public displays, 396
Affinity groups, 73
Africa
   climate factors, 24, 25
   sights of, 460–461
Africa, America, Asia and Australasia Budget Accommodations, 280
AIDS, 245–246
   prevention of, 245–246
Air Brokers International, 129
Air Courier Bulletin, 135
Air Couriers Guide Book, 135
Airhitch, 128
Air–hotel package deals, 136
Airline Consolidators Association, 123
Airline Consolidators Quick Reference Chart, 126

Airline tickets, 105–106
   advance purchase excursion (APEX), 126–127
   air–hotel package deals, 136
   air passes, 129–130
   around–the–world (ATW) packages, 129
   auctions on Web, 139
   back–to–back tickets, 138
   bucket shops, 120
   consolidators, 120–126
   couriers, 133–136
   crisscross tickets, 137
   fare wars, 138
   fixed multistop itinerary ticket, 130
   flexibility and cost cutting, 137–138
   foreign airlines, 129
   frequent flyer coupons, 130–133
   hidden city tickets, 137
   last–minute brokers, 127–128
   losing, 325
   national airline specials, 136
   no frills carriers, 127, 128
   pre–buying, 105–106
   seasonal price dips, 138
   senior discount, 137
   standby brokers, 128
   student card discount, 137
   ticket brokers, 123
   weekend versus weekday fares, 138
   wholesaler, 123
Air passes, 129–130
Air travel, 362–369
   at airport, 365–367
   buying tickets, 363–365
   on–board guidelines, 367–368
   overbooking/delays/diversions, 368–369
   safety of, 362–363
Alarm clock, 193–194
Alarms, personal alarm, use of, 323
Alcohol, avoiding problems, 306–307
All–American Travel Club, 38

Allergies, 211
Almanac of International Jobs and Careers, The, 104
AlphaNet Telecom, 419
Alternative Tourism Resource Guide, 80
Altitude, 24
Altitude sickness, 211–213
  avoidance of, 212
  symptoms of, 211–212
  treatment of, 213
Amazonia Expeditions, 80
American Airlines, web site of, 47
American Association of Retired Persons
  (AARP), 76, 140
American Express
  benefits of, 153–155
  client letter service, 418–419
  dispute resolution, 156
  lost/stolen card, 156
  weather reports, 25
American Institute for Foreign Study, 334
American–International Homestays, 88
American Society of Travel Agents (ASTA),
  34–35, 77
American Travel Network, 419
America Online (AOL), travel information,
  49–50
AmEx Traveler's Companion, 153–154
Amtrak, web site of, 47
Animal bites, 215
  rabies, 243–244
Anniversary Tours, 81
Answers to the Most Asked Questions about Cruises, 389
Antarctica, sights of, 466–467
Antarctica cruises, 88–89
  companies for, 88–89
ANZ Travel, 128
Archaeological Field Work Opportunities, 80
Archeological digs, 87
Archeological Fieldwork Opportunities Bulletin, 87
Arequipa, 352
Around–the–world (ATW) packages, 129
Arrest, handling of, 309–311
Arrival at destination, 263–264
  customs, 263
  tourist information, 265–266
  travel to lodging, 264–265
Asia, climate zones, 24
Athlete's foot, 213
ATM cash cards, 158–159
  ATM locator services, 158
  losing, 325
Australia
  sights of, 466
  train travel, 353

Australia Explorer Pass, 130
Australia and New Zealand Airpass, 130
Automobile Association of America (AAA)
  maps, 55
  taking card along, 196
  on visa requirements, 97
Autorental Europe, 376

Back Door Guide to European Railpasses, 145
Backpacker hotels, 281
Backpacks, 178–179
Backroads, 86
Back–to–back tickets, 138
Baedecker guides, 40
Baggage. *See* Luggage
Baltic Pass, 129
Bargaining, 169–174
  car rental rates, 376–377
  hotel rates, 275–277
  process of, 175–178
  in Third World, 168–169
Batteries, for camera, 439–440
BBC Phrase Books, 337
Beer, cautions about, 296
Begging, 400–402
Berkeley Guides On the Loose series, 43
Berlitz Complete Guide to Cruising and Cruise Ships, 41, 389
Berlitz Pocket Guides, 41
Berlitz Traveller's Phrase Books, 41
Bicycles, exploring on, 374
Bicycling tours, 86
Birth control, 213–214
Black flies, 215
Black market, 30, 164–169
  guidelines for use, 167–168
  nature of, 164–165
  risks related to, 165–167
Blackwater Fever, 239
Blisters, 213
Blood Care Foundation, 209
Blood transfusions, cautions about, 209
Blue Train, 353
Boardswatch Magazine, 45
Body language, 398
Boiling water, for disinfection, 291–292
Books, as information source, 20, 54
Bookstores, travel specialty, 54
Bora Bora, 255
Border, crossing and visas, 97–99
Borobudur, 307
Botswana, sights of, 460–461
Brazil, sights of, 467–468
Bribes, 403–404
  to get train ticket, 359, 403
  method for offering bribe, 403–404
Britannia, 354

British Midland Airlines, 127
Brokers, ticket brokers, 123
Bronchitis, 229
Brunig Panoramic Express, 354
Bucket shops, for airline tickets, 120
Budget for trip, 146–149
    expenses, estimates of, 147–148
Bulletin boards, 45
    travel–related, listing of, 45
Burns, 216
Business cards, exchanging, 399
Business visa, 99
Bus travel, 344–350
    break–downs, 347–348
    bus passes, 349
    comfort factors, 344
    Eurobus, 349–350
    luxury travel, 344–346
    security, 348–349
    Third World, 346–347, 348
Butterfield & Robinson, 86

C.A.B.B., 45
Calculator, 197
Call USA, 417
Camera equipment, 193, 440–444
    batteries, 441–442
    camera bag, 443
    cleaning materials, 443
    film, 444–446
    filters, 442–443
    flash, 443
    lens cover, 443
    tripod, 443
    types of cameras, 441
    video cameras, 453
    zoom lens, 442
    See also Photographs
Camping equipment, 199
Cancellation of trip, insurance for, 107–109
Car rental, 374–384
    companies for, 375
    contracts, contents of, 378–379
    cost cutting, 375–379
    with driver, 384
    driver's license, 374–375
    information sources on, 376
    insurance, 154, 379–380
    price, 377
    reserving car, 375–376
    safety and security, 382–384
    vehicle inspection, 380–381
Carry–on luggage, 181–182
Carte Royale, 140
Cash advance, 154
CD–ROM, on travel, 55
Center for Global Education, 80, 81

Center for Responsible Tourism, 79, 80
Centers for Disease Control (CDC), disease–
    related information from, 205, 241
Center for Socially Responsible Travel, 80
Certificate of Registration, 428
Chagas' Disease, 226, 229
Chapped lips, 216
Check cashing, with AmEx, 154
Chichicastenango, 171
Chihuahua al Pacifico, 352
Chile, 21
    sights of, 467
    train travel, 351
China
    sights of, 464–465
    train travel, 355
Chitwan, 348
Chlorine, to disinfect water, 295
Cholera, 230–231, 253
    prevention of, 230, 253
    symptoms of, 229
    treatment of, 230–231
Chopin, 352
Christchurch, 186
Chunnel, 352
Circle Pacific, 129
Cirrus system, 158–159
Citalia, 3545
Citizens Exchange Council, 88
Climates of the World, 25
Colds, 216
Commercial tour operators, 52–53
Communication with home
    E–mail, 422
    fax machines, 421–422
    mail, 420–421
    telephones, 417–420
CompuServe, travel information, 50
Computer–Assisted Variable International
    Automatic Redialer (CAVIAR), 417
Computer Reservations System (CRS), 121
Computer resources, 45–52
    bulletin boards, 45
    CD–ROM, 55
    frequent flier miles program, 133
    Internet, 45–49
    language learning, 335
    maps, 55
    online services, 49–52
    safety/security information, 299
    of state department, 54
Computers, finding abroad, 422
Condé Nast Traveler, 25
Condoms, 213–214, 245
Connecting, 64
Consolidators, 120–126
    for around–the–world tickets, 129

Consolidators (*continued*)
  drawbacks related to, 122
  for hotel reservations, 139
  information resources on, 121–122, 126
  listing of, 124–125
Constipation, 217
Consular Affairs Bulletin Board, 54
Consular Information Sheets, 299
Consumer Reports, 77, 177, 178
Consumer Reports Travel Letter, 126, 133
Continental Plan, 78
Coral cuts, 217
Costa Rica Expeditions, 80
Cost cutting
  on adventures, 141–142
  on airline tickets, 120–139
  on car rental, 374–377
  cruises, discounted, 388
  guidebooks for low/moderate budget
    travel, 41–44
  on hotel reservations, 138–141
  International Identity Card, 145–146
  on rail pass, 142–145
  on rental cars, 375
  and telephoning, 417–418
  train travel, 357–358
Cost of trip, 28–30
  and black market of country, 29–30
  budget for trip, 146–149
  and choice of destinations, 28–29
  and currency differences, 29
  decision–making methods, 28
  and tours, 69, 70–71
  and traveling with partner, 58–59
  weak and strong currencies, 29
Coughs, 216
Council on International Education Exchange,
  104, 145–146
Courier Air Travel Handbook, The, 136
Couriers, 133–136
  courier brokers, listing of, 134
  eligibility requirements, 134
  information sources on, 135–136
  ticket prices, examples of, 133
Credit cards, 152–158
  benefits of, 153–156
  and frequent flyer miles, 131
  lost/stolen, 155, 318
  tips for use of, 156–158
Crisscross tickets, 137
Cruises, 388–389
  Antarctic cruises, 90
  discounted cruises, listing of, 389
  information sources on, 387
Cruising for the Handicapped Traveler, 389
Culturegrams, 400

Currency, 150–151
  amount to take, 150
  currency declaration forms, 164–165
Customs, 428–431
  Certificate of Registration, 428
  duty, 429–431
  information sources, 431
  items not admitted into U.S., 431
  process at, 263
  searches at, 428–429
Custom Tips for Travelers, 431
Cuts, 209, 217–218

Dairy products, cautions about, 289
Daypacks, 179, 181
  protection against theft, 304–306
Debit cards, 159
DEET, 192, 210, 215, 239–240
Dehydration, 218, 230, 232
  protection against, 290
Dengue fever, 231
  prevention of, 231
  symptoms of, 231
Destination, factors in choice of, 19–26
Destinations on Tape, 53
Diarrhea, 218–220
  cholera, 230–231
  dysentery, 232–233
  food poisoning, 221
  giardiasis, 233
  prevention of, 218–219, 290–291
  treatment of, 219–220, 290
Diner's Club, benefits of, 156
Diphtheria, 231–232
  prevention of, 232, 253
Directory of Jobs and Careers Abroad, The, 104
Directory to Overseas Employment, 104
Discount Travel International, 127
Discover Asia Airpass, 130
Discover Europe Airpass, 129
Discover India Fare, 130
Discover Pacific, 129
Disturbances, handling of, 311–312
Diver's Alert Network (DAN), 110
Documents for travel
  listing of necessary documents, 196–197
  passport, 93–96
  permits, 102–103
  visas, 103
Do's and Taboos Around the World, 400
Do's and Taboos of International Trade, 400
Double occupancy, meaning of, 113
Double room rate, meaning of, 113
Dragoman, 84
Dress, appropriate dress and culture, 396–397
Drive Pass, 143

Drivers, hiring of, 384
Driver's license
    and car rental, 374
    as identification, 196
Driving
    buying car abroad, 384
    car rental, 374–384
Drugs, illegal, cautions about, 307–308, 428
Duffel bags, 177–178
Duty, 429–431
    duty free, 430
    Generalized System of Preferences (GSP),
        430
Dysentery, 220, 232–233

Eaasy Sabre, 49, 50
Earth River Expeditions, 80, 85
*Earth Trips: A Guide to Nature Travel on a
    Fragile Planet*, 80
Earthwatch, 80, 86–87
Earthwise, 83
Eastern Europe, lodging, 280–281
Eastern Orient Express, 355
Eating customs, 398
Ecological responsibility, of tour operators,
    79
Ecotourism, 79–80
    information resources on, 79–80
    tour operators, listing of, 80
Ecotourism Society, 79
EcoTraveler, 80, 179
Ecumenical Coalition on Third World
    Tourism, 80
Educational Travel Directory, 87
Egypt, sights of, 459–460
Elderhostels, 280
    web site of, 47
Electrical current converter, 198
*Electronic Traveler: Directory of Tourism
    Information Sources*, 45
E–mail, 422
Emotions, and travel, 11–12
Encephalitis, 237
Encore Short Notice, 128, 140
Encounter Overland, 84
Entertainment Hot Line Travel Club, 128
Environment, disappearance of natural
    phenomenon, 30–31
Escape, and travel, 11
Essential Travel Guides, 43
Etiquette
    affection, public displays, 398
    and begging, 400–402
    body language, 398
    and bribes, 403–404
    business cards, 399

    doing favors for others, 404
    and dress, 396–397
    eating customs, 398–399
    eating with left hand, 397
    and elderly, 398
    face, 399
    foot direction, 397
    gestures, 399
    greetings, 394–395
    hospitality, 396
    information sources on, 400
    littering, 399
    and monks, 398
    national honor, respecting, 395
    nuance, 395
    punctuality, 397–398
    shoe removal customs, 397
    thank–you gifts, 397
    tipping, 402
Eurail Guide, 145
Eurailpass, 143–144
    Drive Pass, 144
    Flexipass, 143
    Saverpass, 143
    Youth Flexipass, 143
    Youthpass, 143
Eurail Traveller's Guide, 105
Eurobus, 347–348
EuroFlyer Pass, 129
EuroPass, 129, 143–144
Europe, train travel, 354–355
Europe AirPass, 129
Europe by Eurail, 145
Europe Hotel Directory, 140
*Europe and the Mediterranean Budget
    Accommodations*, 279
Europe TBD BBS, 45
Europe Through the Back Door, 41, 145
Europe by Train, 145
Eurostar, 355, 360
Evacuation insurance, 111
Exchanging money, 160–162
    amount to exchange, 162
    black market, 169
    currency exchange machines, 161
    place for, 160–162
    process of, 162–164
    transaction fees, 162
Exotic Destinations Message Center, 49
Exotic travel, and first trip, 23
Expatriates, 408–409
Experiment in International Living, 87
Expert Map for Windows, 55
Explorer Shipping Corporation, 89
Express Cash program, 156
Eyeglasses, 194

Face, etiquette, 397
Fairchild's Travel Industry Personnel Directory, 37
Fare wars, 138
Fatigue, 220–221
Fax services, 421–422
Fax Travel Bulletin, 55
Federal government, weather information, 25
Federal Trade Commission, credit card disputes, 158
Ferry/passenger ships, 386–387
Fever, 221
Fielding, 40
Film, 444–446
and X–ray machines at airport, 446
Filtering water, 292–294
portable filters, 292–294
Filters, for camera, 442–443
Firearms, cautions about, 308
Fleas, 215
Flexipass, 143
Flightpath USA, 126
Fly for Less: The Only Complete Guide to Selecting Reliable Consolidators and Wholesalers Who Offer Bargain Airfares, 122, 126
Fodor's Cruises and Ports of Call: Choosing the Perfect Ship and Enjoying Your Time Ashore, 387
Fodor's Travel Guides, 40
FollowFax, 422
Food
alcoholic beverages, 296
average cost for, 147
dairy products, 289
exotic dishes, 285–286
fruit, 289
green salads, 288–289
included in tour, 77, 79
local markets, 285
meat, 286
ordering, 285
refrigeration/storage of, 286–287
sanitation/food handling, 287–289
seafood, 287
shellfish, avoiding, 230, 234, 287
street food, 284, 288
on trains, 361
water, drinking, 289–296
Food poisoning, 221
Ford's Freighter Travel Guide, 386
Foreign airlines
buying tickets through, 129
earning frequent flier miles, 131
Foreign Entry Requirements of Foreign Governments, 97

Foreign Independent Tour (FIT), 74
Foreign Language Forum, 50
Foreign language. *See* Language
Formule 1 hotels, 281
Franz Josef Glacier, 148
Freedom, and travel, 12
Freighter Space Advisory, 386
Freighter travel, 385–386
information sources on, 386
Freighter Travel News, 386
Freighter World Cruises, 386
Frequent flyer coupons, 130–133
Friendship Force, 87–88
Friendship Tours, 81
Frommer travel guides, 40
Frontier Mail, 356
Frostbite, 221
Fruits, 289
FTM AirMax, 133
Fungal infections, feet, 213

Gaia Passage, 45
Gangtok, 345
Generalized System of Preferences (GSP), 430
Geographic Expeditions, 70
Gestures, examples of cultural differences, 399
Giardiasis, 220, 226, 233
prevention of, 233
symptoms of, 233
treatment of, 233
Gili Trawagan, 60
Gitanjale Express, 356
Global Assist Hotline, AmEx, 155
Global Awareness Through Experience, 81
Global Discount Travel Services, 126
Global Emergency Medical Services, 111
Global Exchange, 82
Global Network Navigator, 52
Global Network Navigator Travel Resource Center (GNNTRC), 46
Globe, The, 54
Globetrotters Club, 54
Globetrotters Directory, The, 54
Golden Age Travelers Club, 64, 76
Gonorrhea, 246
Goods and services tax, 427–428
Grand Circle Travel, 76
Gray circuit, 280–281
Great American Traveler, 140
Great Horizons, 83
GreenNet, 47
Green Tortoise, 349
Greetings, cultural factors, 394–395
Group travel, disadvantages of, 59–60
Guatemala, sights of, 471

Guerba, 84
Guidebooks, 39–44
    best books, listing of, 40–41
    evaluation of, 39
    for moderate/low budget travel, 41–44
    special topic books, 44
Guides
    local guides, 75–76
    tour guides, 78

Habitat for Humanity, 280
Handbooks of the World, 43
Handicapped traveler
    cruises for, 389
    tours for, 74
Handicapped Traveler Newsletter, The, 74
*Handle With Care: A Guide to Responsible
    Travel in Developing Countries*, 80
Harvard Student Association's Let's Go series,
    43
Hawk, I am Your Sister, 83
Headache, 222
Health Information for International Travel,
    206, 253
Health insurance, 109–111
Health issues
    allergies, 211
    altitude sickness, 211–213
    birth control, 213–214
    blisters, 213
    bronchitis, 229
    burns, 216
    Chagas' Disease, 226, 229
    chapped lips, 216
    cholera, 230–231, 253
    colds/coughs, 216
    constipation, 217
    cuts, 217–218
    dehydration, 218, 230, 232
    dengue fever, 231
    diarrhea, 218–220, 290–291
    diphtheria, 231–232, 253
    dysentery, 220, 232–233
    fatigue, 220–221
    fever, 221
    food poisoning, 221
    frostbite, 221
    fungal infections, 213
    giardiasis, 220, 236, 233
    headache, 222
    health–preserving guidelines, 207–210
    health problems, steps to take, 207
    heat exhaustion, 222
    heat stroke, 233
    hepatitis, 234–237
    hypothermia, 222

immunizations, 205–206, 253–254
insect bites, 214–215
insomnia, 223
Japanese B encephalitis, 237
jet lag, 223–225
leishmaniasis, 226, 237–238
malaria, 207, 210, 226, 238–243
medical help abroad, 155–156, 206–207
medical kit, contents of, 251–253
meningococcal meningitis, 243
menstruation, 225
motion sickness, 225–226
pain, 245
parasites, 226
polio, 243, 254
pre–trip immunizations, 205–206, 253–
    254
prevention, 205
prickly heat, 214–215
rabies, 243–244
researching travel–related diseases, 205
schistosomiasis, 244–245
sexually transmitted disease, 245–248
shock, 248
sleeping sickness, 248
smallpox, 248
strains/sprains, 226
sunburn, 226
tetanus, 249, 254
trauma, 249–250
tuberculosis, 250
typhoid, 250
typhus, 250–251
upset stomach, 227
urinary tract infection, 228
vaginal yeast infections, 228
yellow fever, 251, 254
Heat exhaustion, 222
Heat stroke, 233
Hepatitis A, 234–236
    prevention of, 235, 253
    symptoms of, 234–235
    treatment of, 235–236
Hepatitis B, 236–237
    prevention of, 236, 2523
    symptoms of, 236
    treatment of, 236–237
Hepatitis C, 237
Hepatitis E, 237
Herpes, 247–248
Hidden city tickets, 137
Himalayan Travel, 85
Himalayan Travel–World Adventures, web
    site of, 47
Historic Hostels, 279
Hitchhiking, 390–92

Hitchhiking (*continued*)
  and safety, 392
  tips for, 391–92
Holidays, local, and choosing destination, 26
Home Host International, 88
Homestays, 87–88, 282
  organizations for, 87–88
Hostelling International–American Youth Hostels, 278
Hostels, 278–280
  historic, 279
  information sources on, 280
  reservations for, 278
Hotel reservations, 112–115
  consolidators for, 139
  cost cutting methods, 136–141
  escalating costs, 114–115
  half–price discount programs, 140
  hotel brokers for, 139
  information resources on, 113–114
  as member of privileged category, 140
  no reservations, reasons for, 114–115
  preferred hotel rates, 140
  promotional discounts, 141
  purposes of, 115
  senior discounts, 140
  vouchers, 141
  See also Lodging
Hotel Reservations Network, 139
Hotel security, 322–324
  hotel safe, 324
  locking valuables, 323
  personal alarm, use of, 323
  smoke detectors, 323–324
Hotels Plus, 139
How to Book a Perfect Cruise, 389
How to Get the Most Out of Your Railpass, 145
How to Protect Yourself Against Malaria, 207, 239
Hypothermia, 222

Ice, cautions about, 291
Icelandair, 127
Immigration and Naturalization Service Passenger Accelerated Service System, 96
Immunizations
  listing of, 253–254
  pre–trip, 205–206
  yellow card, 206
Importing, 431–435
Independent Woman's Guide to Europe, The, 333
Independent Woman's Travel Guide to Europe, 43
India
  sights of, 462–463
  train travel, 356

Indian Pacific, 353
Indigestion, 227
Indonesia, 60
  sights of, 465
Influenza, prevention of, 254
Information USA/International, 50
INNterREST, 113–114
Insect bites, 214–215
  prevention of, 192, 210, 214
  treatment of, 214
Insect repellent, 192, 210, 239–240
InsideFlyer Magazine, 133
Inside Passage, 387
Insider's Guide to Air Courier Bargains, The, 136
Insight Guide to... series, 43
Insomnia, 223
Insurance
  AmEx benefits, 154
  car rental, 154, 379–380
  evacuation insurance, 111
  health insurance, 109–111
  insurance companies, listing of, 112
  package insurance, 109
  for personal property, 106–107
  trip cancellation, 107–109
International Air Transport Association (IATA), 35
International Association of Air Travel Couriers (IAATC), 135
International ATM Locator Guide, 158
International Certificate of Immunization, 206
International Expeditions, 80, 89
International Health Certificate, 101
International Herald Tribune, 104
International Living, 63
International Student Identity Card, 137, 145–146
  benefits of, 145–146
  eligibility for, 145
International Student Travel Guide, 145
International Travel News, 54, 63, 77
International Video Network, 44, 53
International Youth Hostel Federation, 280
Internet, 45–49
  travel databases, listing of, 47–49
  World Wide Web, 46
Internet Connection, 49
Internet Sleuth, 47
Inuit Adventures, 80
Iodine, to disinfect water, 294
Irian Jaya, 154
Itinerary, drafting of, 31–33

Japanese B encephalitis, 237
  prevention of, 237, 254
Jet lag, 223–225

melatonin for, 224
prevention efforts, 223–224
Jewelry, cautions about, 200
Jobs for People who Love To Travel, 104
Journal keeping, 437–438
*Journey of One's Own: Uncommon Advice for
the Independent Woman Traveler*, 330
Journeys, 85
Just Enough, 337

Kalimantan, 21
Kalimpong, 271
Kenya, 26
sights of, 462
train travel, 350–351
Keyword International Cafe, 49
Kilimanjaro, 22
Kiwi Air Pass, 130
Kiwi Experience, 350
*Know Before You Go, Hints for Returning
Residents*, 431
Ko Tao, 227

Lake Titicaca, 39
Lamu, 26
Language
asking questions, 338–339
choosing destination, 23
communication methods, 23
computer products for learning, 337
finding assistance, 338–340
learning new language, 336–338
speaking English, guidelines for, 340
Language Schools, The, 336
Last–minute brokers, 127–128
listing of, 128
Last Minute Travel, 128
Laundry service, 187
Leaving, last–minute tasks, 256–260
Leeches, 215
LeFrance Pass, 129
Legal assistance, through AmEx, 155–156
Leh, 345
Leishmaniasis, 226, 237–238
Let's Go Europe, 145
Let's Go guides, 43
Library, travel resources, 53
Lice, 214
Live from Antarctica, 47
L.L. Bean, web site of, 47
Local guides, 75–76
Local tours, 74
Locks, luggage, 182–183, 194
Lodging
backpacker hotels, 281
bargaining for price, 275–276
best hotels, rates of, 282

breakfast at, 273
in Eastern European countries, 280–281
Elderhostels, 280
Formule 1 hotels, 281
homestays, 282
hostels, 278–280
local information sources on, 268–270
location factors, 270
price factors, 274–276
room ventilation/cooling, 274
showers in, 270–271
toilets, 272
YMCA/YWCA, 280
See also Hotel reservations
Lonely Planet
Lonely Planet guides, 41
web site of, 47
Lost valuables, 325–327
airline tickets, 325
AMT card, 325
credit cards, 325
luggage, 326–327
passport, 325–326
Luggage
backpacks, 178–179
baggage limits, 181–182
buying of, 182
carry–on, 181–182
daypacks, 179, 181
duffel bags, 177–178
hard–sided, 176
insurance on, 112
locks on luggage, 182–183, 194
losing, 326–327
protection against theft, 303–304
soft–sided, 176–177
tags, 183–184
See also Packing

Madagascar, sights of, 462
Magazines, 25, 77
Magellan maps, 55
Magic Bus, 350
Mail, 420–421
American Express services, 420–421
Malaria, 207, 210, 226, 238–243
high rate areas, 238
information sources on, 239
prevention of, 239–242
and protection at lodging, 273
symptoms of, 239
transmission of, 239
treatment of, 242–243
Maps, 194–195
resources for, 55
Maps Plus, 55
Map Store, 55

Marco Polo Express, 353
Marine Expeditions, 85, 89–90
MasterCard International, 47
Maverick Guides, 43
Medical assistance
    sources of, 206–207
    through AmEx, 155–156
    See also Health insurance; Health issues
Medic Alert tag, 111
Medical kit, contents of, 251–252
MedPass, 111
Meeting people, 405–409
Melatonin, for jet lag, 224
Meningococcal meningitis, 243
    prevention of, 243, 254
Menstruation, 225
Mexico, train travel, 352
Mexico BBS, 45
Michelin Green Guides, 40
Michelin Red Guides, 40
Microsoft, travel web site, 47, 113
Milk, cautions about, 295
Minivans, for local travel, 371–372
Miscellaneous Change Order (MCO), 98–99
Modified American Plan (MAP), 77
Moment's Notice, 128
Money
    ATM cash cards, 158–159
    bargaining, 169–174
    black market, 165–169
    credit cards, 153–158
    currency, 150–151
    debit cards, 159
    exchanging of, 162–164
    receiving money from home, 154, 158–
      159
    traveler's checks, 150–152
Money belt, 195, 301–302
    guidelines for use, 301–302
Moneygram, AmEx, 154
Money, saving. See Cost cutting
Monkeys, 215
Monks, etiquette toward, 398
Moon Publications, web site of, 47
Morocco, train travel, 350
Mosquitoes
    dengue fever, 230–231
    encephalitis, 237
    malaria, 238–243
    protection against, 209–210, 273
    yellow fever, 251
Motion sickness, 225–226
    treatment of, 225–226
Motoeuropa, 377
Mountain Travel/Sobek, 70, 80, 85, 89
    web site of, 48
Muggers, 320–322

MultiBank, 161
Multi–country trip, 20–21
Multiple–entry visa, 100

Nairobi, 24, 141–142, 267
Namibia, sights of, 458
National Alliance of Senior Citizens, 76
National Association of Retired Federal
    Employees, 76
National Geographic maps, 55
National Registration Center for Study
    Abroad, 336–337
National tourist offices, 25, 52
National Weather Service reports, 25
Nepal, sights of, 466
Newsletters, travel–related, 54–55
Newspapers, national airline specials ads, 136
News for Solo Travelers, 64
New Zealand
    sights of, 466
    train travel, 354
No frills carriers, 127, 128
Noise, and hotel, 272
Nord–West Express, 354
Northerner, 352
NTC Passport Books' Handbooks of the World,
    43

Office of Overseas Citizens Services, 420
Official Airline Guide, 36, 38
    online, 50, 53
Official Frequent Flyer Guidebook, The, 133
Official Tour Directory (OTD), 38, 76
Online services, 49–52
    America Online (AOL), 49–50
    CompuServe, 50
    Prodigy, 50–52
On the Loose series, 43
On Track, 145
Open jaw ticket, 127
Oral rehydration salts, 218
Orbit Global Travel, web site of, 48
Ost–West Express, 352
Outdoor Adventure Online, 49
Outdoor Adventure River Specialists, 85
Outdoor Vacations for Women over 40, 82
Outside Magazine, 54
    web site of, 48
Overbooked flights
    being bumped, 137
    overseas flights, 365–366
Overland tours, 83–84
Overseas Adventure Travel, 80, 83

Pacific Air Pass, 129
Package insurance, 109
Package tours, 74

Packing
    camping equipment, 199
    choosing clothing, 185–187
    clothing checklist, 188–192
    documents, 196–197
    guidelines for, 184–185
    jewelry, 200
    medical kit, 250–252
    miscellaneous gear, 193–196, 197–200
    toiletries, 192–193
    what not to take, 201
    See also Luggage
Pain, 245
Palace on Wheels, 356
Papua New Guinea, sights of, 468
Parasites, 226
    diseases caused by, 226
    schistosomiasis, 226, 244–245
    signs of, 226
Partners–in–Travel, 64
Partners for Travel, 64
Passport, 93–96
    expiration of, 95–96
    losing, 197, 325
    obtaining, guidelines for, 94
    passport agency offices, phone numbers, 94
    purpose of, 93–94
    renewal of, 94–95
    service for, 95
Passport Amendment/Validation Application (Form DSP–19), 95
Passport to Europe, 129
Pathfinder Travel, web site of, 48
PCTravel, 45, 48
Pearl's Travel Tips, 386
Peddlers, 413
Pennsylvania Travel, 38
People to People International, 81
Periodicals, travel–related, 54–55
Permits, 102–103
    purposes of, 102–103
    work permits, 103
Personal growth, and travel, 10
Personal property, insurance for, 106–107
Personal Travel Bulletin, 54–55
Peru
    sights of, 470
    train travel, 351–352
Photography, 439–452
    camera equipment, 442–444
    developing, 447
    of locals, 450–452
    photo taking tips, 440
    prohibitions, 308, 450–451
    showing photos/slides, 452
    See also Camera equipment

Physical fitness, and choosing destination, 21–23
Pickpockets, 317–319
    protection against, 318–319
Pioneer Railway, 355
Planning trip
    and changing world, 30–31
    choosing destination, 19–26
    with commercial tour operators, 52
    computer resources, 44–52
    cost factors, 28–30
    group travel, 59–60
    guidebooks, use of, 39–44
    information resources, local, 53–55
    itinerary, drafting of, 31–33
    with national tourist offices, 52
    solo travel, 57–58
    time factors, 26–28
    with travel agent, 33–39
    travel with partner, 58–65
Plowshares Institute, 80, 82
Polio, 243, 254
    prevention of, 242, 253
Political conditions
    avoiding political discussions, 306, 393
    disturbances, handling of, 311, 312
    safe versus risky destinations, 21
Political consciousness tours, 81–82
Polypass, 129
Post office, cautions about, 316
Powell's Travel Store, 55
Prambanan, 307
Preferred hotel rates, 140–141
Preview Vacations Online, 50
Prickly heat, 214–215
Privilege Card, 139
Prodigy, travel information, 50–52
Promotional discounts, hotel reservations, 141
Protecting Your Travel Dollar, 389
Provence, 343
PTT (Postal, Telephone & Telegraph) office, 419

Quark Expeditions, 89
Quinine, 241

Rabies, 243–244
    prevention of, 244, 254
Rail Europe, phone number, 145
Rail pass, 105, 359–360
    cost cutting methods, 145–146
    country/regional passes, 144
    Eurailpass, 143
    Europass, 144
    information sources on, 144
    VIA Canrailpass, 144

Rainbow Adventures, 83
Rajadani Express, 356
Rand McNally maps, 55
Rape, 330
Rarontonga, 136
Reality tours, 81–82
Rebaters, listing of, 38
Recommendations for Prevention of Malaria
    Among Travelers, 239
Red Cross, 210
Religion
    avoiding religious discussions, 306
    respecting customs, 400
Rembrandt, 354
Remus, 354
Reusch International, 159–160
Rick Steves' Best of..., 43
Romance, and travel, 12, 409–410
Room Exchange, 139
Rough Guides, The, 43
Rumtek Monastery, 348
Russia, train travel, 354
Russia Express, 354
Rwanda, 21, 142
    sights of, 463

Sacred valley of the Urubamba, 21
Safe Trip Abroad, A, 54, 155–156
Safety and security
    air travel, 361–362
    alcohol/drug related problems, 307–308
    bus travel, 348–349
    countries to avoid, 299–301
    disturbances, 311–312
    driving/car rental, 382–384
    encounters with law, 309–311
    firearms related, 308
    hitchhiking, 390–392
    hotel security, 322–324
    incidence of theft, 297–298
    information resources on risks, 299
    lost valuables, 325–327
    luggage, 303–306
    money belt, 301–302
    muggers, 320–322
    pickpockets, 317–319
    and political/religious discussions, 306
    prohibited photographs, 308–309
    reducing risk, 298
    scams, 312–317
    sneak thieves, 319–320
    train travel, 361–362
    wallet routines, 302–303
Sailing, serving as crew, 389
Salads, cautions about, 288–289
Sand flies, 215
Saverpass, 143

Saving money. See Cost cutting
Scams, 312–317
    common scams, 312–317, 380
Schistosomiasis, 226, 244–245
Self–esteem, and travel, 10–11
Sengiggi Beach Hotel, 61
Senior citizens
    airline ticket discounts, 137
    Elderhostels, 280
    Elderhostel web site, 47
    hotel reservations discounts, 140–141
    travel organizations for, 76
Servas, 88
Sexually transmitted disease, 245–248
    AIDS, 245–246
    gonorrhea, 247
    herpes, 247
    syphilis, 247
Shellfish, avoiding, 230, 234, 288
Shock, 248
Shoe removal customs, 397
Shoestring Traveler, 135
Shopping, 423–426
    authenticity, verification of, 426
    examining purchases, 425
    goods and services tax, 427–428
    preparation for, 424–425
    shipping purchases home, 427
    value–added tax, 427–428
Shopping with Your ATM Card, 158
Showers, in lodging, 270–271
Sierra Club, 80
Silver Fern, 354, 355
Single–Friendly Travel Directory, 64
Sleeping sickness, 248
Smallpox, 248
    prevention of, 248, 254
Smart Travelers Planning Kit, 76
Smart Traveller, The 38
Smoke detectors, lacking in hotels, 323
Snakes, 215
Sneak thieves, 319–320
    protection against, 319–320

Society for the Advancement of Travel for the
    Handicapped, 74
Society Expeditions, 89
Solo travel
    information sources for, 64
    reasons for, 57–58
    women, 329–333
Solo Travel International, 333
South Africa, train travel, 353
South America, climate zones, 24
South American Explorer, 54, 63
South American Handbook, 43
Southerner, 354

Soviet–American Homestays, 88
Specialty Travel Index, 36, 47
Sprint Express, 419
Sri Lanka, 21
Standard for Confident Travel, 77
Stand–Buys, Ltd., 128
Standby brokers, 128–129
Star Service, 36
State department
    crime/security conditions information, 299
    home contact in emergencies, 420
    State Department Citizens Emergency Center, 97, 299
    travel advisories, 48
    travel information, 52–54
Strains/sprains, 226
Student Ambassadors, 81
Student card. See International Student Identity Card
Subways, 372–373
    guidelines for use, 372–373
Sudameripass, 130
Sud–Express, 354
Summary of Health Information for International Travelers, 253
Sunburn, 226
Syphilis, 247

Tags, luggage, 183–184
Taj Express, 356
Taj Mahal, 53
Tambopata, 73
Tamil Nadu, 22, 25
Tanzania, sights of, 463
Taxis, 264–265, 370–371
Tea, 296
Teaching English Abroad, 104
Telephones, 417–420
    call–home services, 418–419
    cost cutting, 418–419
    tips for use of, 418–420
Temple of Karnak, 53
Ternate, 303
TerraQuest, 48
Tetanus, 249
    prevention of, 249, 254
Thailand
    sights of, 467
    train travel, 355
Thank–you gifts, 397
Theft
    credit cards, 156
    and mind–set of tourist, 298, 301, 312, 321
    traveler's checks, 152–153
    See also Safety and security

Third World
    bargaining, 169–174
    bus travel, 346–348
    officialdom of, 412
    tours to, 81–82
    transportation, 343–344
    travel considerations, 81
    use of term, 8
Thomas Cook European Timetable, 360
Thomas Cook's On the Rails Around Europe, 145
Thor 24, 140
Ticket brokers, 123
Ticks, 214–215
Time and culture, 397–398, 413
Time frame for trip, 26–28
Tipping, 402
Tips for..., 300
Tiruchirapalli, 274
Toilet paper, 272–273
    and left hand, 273, 397
    and train travel, 361
Toiletries, packing, 192–193
Toilets
    hotels, varieties of, 272–273
    public, 273
Toraja–land, 345
Tourist, use of term, 67–68
Tourist information, 265–266
Tourist quota, for train tickets, 358–359
Tourist seasons, and choosing destination, 25–26
Tourist visa, 99
Tours, 67–90
    advantages of, 68–70
    adventure tours, 73, 84–86
    affinity groups, 73
    Antarctic cruises, 88–90
    bicycling tours, 86
    consumer protection related to, 77
    disability groups, 74
    disadvantages of, 70–72
    ecological responsibility of, 79
    ecotourism, 79–80
    evaluation of, 77–79
    homestays, 87–88
    information sources on, 76
    lingo of tour operators, 76–77
    local guides, 75–76
    locally hosted tours, 73
    local tours, 74
    overland tours, 83–84
    package tours, 74
    political consciousness/reality tours, 81–82
    ratings of, 77
    standard tours, 73

Tours (*continued*)
 upscale tours, 73
 for women, 82–83
 working tours, 87
Train travel, 350–362
 in Australia, 353
 buying tickets, 358
 in Chile, 351
 in China, 355–356
 cost factors, 357
 in Europe, 354–355
 in India, 356
 in Kenya, 353
 meals, 361
 in Mexico, 352
 in Morocco, 352
 New Zealand, 354
 in Peru, 351–352
 rail pass, 359–360
 in Russia, 356–357
 seating, 359, 360–361
 security, 361–362
 in South Africa, 353
 in Thailand, 355
 tourist quota, 358
 in Zimbabwe, 353
Transitions Abroad, 54
Transit visa, 99
Transportation
 air travel, 362–369
 bicycles, 374
 bus travel, 344–350
 car rental, 374–384
 cruises, 388–389
 ferry/passenger ships, 386–387
 freighter travel, 385–386
 hitchhiking, 390–392
 minivans, 371–372
 sailing, 389
 subways, 372–373
 taxis, 370–371
 train travel, 350–362
Trauma, 249–250
Travel & Leisure, 54
Travel
 resistance to, 12–15
 returning home, 457–459
 rewards of, 3–5, 9–12
Travel agents, 33–38
 compensation of, 33–34
 consumer protection against, 35
 evaluation of agency, 35–36
 evaluation of agent, 36–37
 information sources of, 37–38
 itinerary drafting by, 32, 33
 rebaters, 38

Travel Agents Directory, web site of, 48
Travel Alert Bulletin, 54
Travel Avenue, 38
Travel Books, 49
Travel Brokers, 129
Travel Channel Online Network, 48
Travel.city, 48
Travel Companion Exchange, 63
Travel Connection, 45
Traveler, 54
Travelers checks, 150–153
 brands/denominations, 151–152
 disadvantages of, 151
 fee for, 151
 loss/theft, 151–152
Traveler's Corner, 49
Traveler's Emergency Network (TEN), 111
Traveler's Guide to Asian Customs and Manners, 43, 333
Travelers Health and Immunization Service, 205
Traveler's Pictorial Communication Guide, 337
Traveler's Tool Kit, web site of, 48, 51
Traveler, The CD–ROM, 55
TravelFest, 54
Travel Forums, 48, 49, 50
Travel Guard International, 107
Travel Handbook guides, 42
Travel Holiday, 54
Travel Info Exchange, 45
Traveling Europe's Trains, 145
Traveling Like Everybody Else: A Practical Guide for Disabled Travelers, 74
Travel InterLink, 140
Travelin' Women, 333
Traveller Information Service Master Index, 48
Travel Library, 48
Travel Links, 80
Travel Mates BBS, 45
Travel medicine clinics, 205
Travelogues, 20
Travel Online, 45
Travel partner, 58–65
 advantages of, 58–59
 avoiding getting lost, 64–65
 and costs, 59
 ideal partner, characteristics of, 60–63
 information sources/organizations for, 63–64
Travel Reimbursement Protection Insurance, 109
Travelshopper, 50
Travel Smart for Women, 333
Travel Sources forum, 52
Travel Tips for Older Americans, 54

Travel Unlimited, 48, 136
Travel Warning, 299
Travel Warnings and Consular Information
    Sheets, 53
TravelWeb, 48
Travel Weekly, 48
TravLtips, 380
Tripod, for camera, 443
Trip Planners, 43
True Rewards plan, 131
Tsetse flies, 215, 248
Tuberculosis, 250
Turtle Tours, 70, 85
Two–Thirds World, 8
    tours to, 81–82
Typhoid, 250
    prevention of, 250, 254
Typhus, 250–251

Underwater camera, 441
United Connection, 50
United States Information Service, 339
University of California, web site of, 49
Upscale tours, 73
Urinary tract infection, 228
USA Direct, 418
USA Today web site of, 48
U.S. State Department Travel Advisories and
    Background Notes, 49
U.S. Tour Operators Association, 77
U.S. and World Wide Travel Accommodations
    Guide, 280
UTELL International, 113

Vacationland, 139
Vacations to Go, 128
Vaginal yeast infections, 228
Value–added tax, 427–428
Varanasi, 343
Vatican Museum, 53
Venice–Simplon Orient Express, 354
VIA Canrailpass, 144
Video cameras, 453
Videos on travel, sources for, 44, 53
Vietnam Information, 48
Visas, 96–102
    application for, 100–101
    business visa, 99
    countries eliminating requirement, 97
    country requirements, information, 97
    sources on, 97
    expiration of, 102
    fees for, 101
    multiple–entry visa, 99
    necessity of, 96–97
    obtaining through service, 101–102

onward ticket requirement for entering at
    border, 97–98
tourist visa, 99
transit visa, 99
Visit Australia and New Zealand Airpass, 130
Visit Indonesia Decade Pass, 130
Visit Norway Pass, 130
Visit South America, 129
Visit Spain Airpass, 130
Vitamins, 208–209
Vouchers, hotel reservations, 141

Wallet, reducing theft risk, 302–303
Washing, to avoid disease, 209, 289
Water, 208, 289–296
    boiling to disinfect, 292
    bottled water, 291
    chlorine, 295
    dehydration, protection against, 290–291
    filtering to disinfect, 292–294
    ice as water, 291
    iodine to disinfect, 294
    parasites, 226
Weather
    and choosing destination, 24–25
    climate zones, 24
    information resources on, 25
Weather Channel Connection, phone
    number, 25
Weekends, airline ticket prices, 138
Western Union, 159
Whitewater rafting, 390
Wholesaler, of air–only tours, 123
Wide World of Maps, 55
Wilderness Travel, 85
Wildland Adventures, 80, 85
Wine, 296
Womanship, 83
Womantrek, 83
Women & Travel, 333
Women
    and Eurobus, 350
    guidelines for solo travel, 330–332
    harassment, high–risk countries, 329–
        330
    information sources for, 332–333
    rape, 330
    tours for, 82–83
Women Travel: Adventures, Advice and
    Experience, 332
Women in the Wilderness, 83
Woodswomen, 82
Work Abroad program, 104
Working abroad, 103–105
    directory for, 87
    information resources on, 104

Working abroad (*continued*)
  programs for, 104
Working tours, 87
Work permits, 103
Work Your Way Around the World, 104
World Alliance Directory, 280
World Immunization Chart, 206
World Learning, 87–88
World Malaria Risk Chart, 207, 239
WorldPhone, 419
Worldview TravelFacts, 52
Worldview Travel Updates, 52
Worldwide Adventures, 89
Worldwide Brochures electronic bulletin
  board, 45
Worldwide Discount Travel Club, 128
Worldwide Services Manual, 38
Worldwide Travel Facts, 50
Worldwide Uniques world map, 55
World Wide Web
  airline ticket auctions, 139
  travel information, listing of, 46–49

Yahoo, 48
Yellow card, 206
Yellow fever, 251
  prevention of, 251, 254
YMCA/YWCA
  information resource on, 280
  lodging, 280
Your Trip Abroad, 54, 96, 431
Youth Flexipass, 143
Youthpass, 143

Zanskar Valley, 22
Zanzibar, 26
Zegraham Expeditions, 88
Zimbabwe
  sights of, 462
  train travel, 353
Zoom lens, 442

Reader Survey

Your comments can make future editions of *Traveler's Tool Kit* more useful to other travelers, so please take a few moments to answer the following questions, or just send some of your thoughts and/or experiences to:

Traveler's Tool Kit Reader Survey
P.O. Box 43059
Bimingham, AL 35243

Name (optional): _____
Hometown:_____ State: _____
Your age:_____ Gender: M   F
Where did you travel: _____
Dates of your visit: _____

We'd also like your comments to these questions::
1. Comments about transportation?
2. Comments about lodging?
3. Comments about your luggage?
4. Comments about food or restaurants?
5. Was language a problem? How did you handle it?
6. Were you on a modest budget? moderate? no limit?
7. Was theft a problem?
8. Did you experience any threats to your safety?
9. If you took a tour, what were its good and bad points?
10. Did you travel solo or in a group? Would you change this next time?
11. Where have you most enjoyed traveling?
12. Can you recommend any great adventures?
13. What has been your most amusing experience
14. What surprised you the most while on the road?
15. How have your travels affected your "normal" life?
16. How was Traveler's Tool Kit most useful?
17. What could be included in Traveler's Tool Kit to make it more helpful?

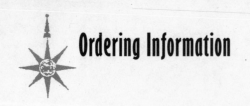

Ordering Information

I hope you'll consider making a gift of *Traveler's Tool Kit* to anyone who just needs some encouragement to get them on the road. If *Traveler's Tool Kit* is not available where you are—or if you would like to order several copies—write to:

Menasha Ridge Press
P.O. Box 43059
Birmingham, AL 35243

Phone: (800) 247-9437 or (205) 322-0439
Fax: (205) 326-1012

To communicate with the author, visit the *Traveler's Tool Kit* homepage site on the World Wide Web. The address is http://www.travelers-tool-kit.com

Future editions of this book will benefit immeasurably from your contributions. If you have an anecdote that supports a point, have spotted an error, or would like information on some area not covered, send a note to me via the publisher. I'd also love to hear how you've used information in the book.

Let the publisher know if you'd like a complete list of its books as well.